Second Edition

Women, Politics, and Public Policy

The Political Struggles of Canadian Women

Jacquetta Newman | **Linda A. White**

D1253528

OXFORD
UNIVERSITY PRESS

OXFORD
UNIVERSITY PRESS

Oxford University Press is a department of the University of Oxford.
It furthers the University's objective of excellence in research, scholarship,
and education by publishing worldwide. Oxford is a registered trade mark of
Oxford University Press in the UK and in certain other countries.

Published in Canada by
Oxford University Press
8 Sampson Mews, Suite 204,
Don Mills, Ontario M3C 0H5 Canada

www.oupcanada.com

Library and Archives Canada Cataloguing in Publication

Newman, Jacquetta A., 1964–
Women, politics, and public policy : the political struggles of
Canadian women / Jacquetta Newman, Linda A. White. — 2nd ed.

Includes bibliographical references and index.
ISBN 978-0-19-543249-7

1. Women—Government policy—Canada. 2. Feminism—Canada.
3. Women—Political activity—Canada. 4. Women's rights—Canada.
5. Women—Legal status, laws, etc. —Canada. I. White, Linda A. (Linda
Ann), 1967– II. Title.

HQ1236.5.C2N49 2012   305.420971   C2011-906913-X

Cover image: Seraficus/iStockphoto.com

Oxford University Press is committed to our environment.
This book is printed on Forest Stewardship Council® certified paper
and comes from responsible sources.

MIX
Paper from
responsible sources
FSC
www.fsc.org   FSC® C004071

Printed and bound in Canada

3 — 16

Contents

Preface

As we note in this second edition of *Women, Politics, and Public Policy*, it is worth taking the time to think critically about feminism in today's politics and, specifically, about how it relates to broader societal change. Some important questions to ask include: Have women in post-twentieth century Canada achieved equality? Is there still a need for a women's rights movement and a fight for gender equality in Canada? Does discrimination against women in the workplace and other public spheres still exist? Where should scholarly and activist focus lie, both in Canada and in developing countries?

This book, in tackling answers to these questions, continues to make the case that while it is important to celebrate how far Canadian women's lives have come in the past century, it is still critical to assess how far gender equality still has to go, both in our country and throughout the world. This text is a tool for examining and understanding the roots of this struggle and charting its progress. As instructors of upper-year courses on 'women and politics' and 'women and public policy in Canada', we have often felt frustrated by the sparse selection of textbooks encompassing the many aspects of women's political activity and its relationship to public policy and social change. The lack of a comprehensive and integrated core text, encompassing all aspects of women's political activity and public policy and accessible to first- and second-year students, was our impetus for writing the first edition of this text. In doing so, we kept the following goals in mind:

- to introduce students to women's politics in a broader sense;
- to illustrate that politics involves not only the institutions of government and representation but also social, cultural, economic, and legal structures;
- to introduce students to key concepts such as feminism, patriarchy, equality, and sameness and difference, and to describe how approaches to feminist theory have defined and problematized these concepts;
- to discuss the women's movement as a social movement and illustrate how it is not a unified edifice, and to demonstrate how debates over theory and strategy have worked to its advantage and disadvantage;
- to illustrate how debates over the goals of the women's movement are reflected in and inform both women's and government's actions regarding public policy in Canada;
- to provide useful information on government legislation, court decisions, and women's movement activity, as well as information on 'where are we now' so that the text will serve as a good reference source for students of women's studies, sociology, history, law, and social work in addition to political science;
- to illustrate the unique features of Canadian women's politics and policy advocacy so that scholars of women and politics outside the country can use the book to understand the peculiarly Canadian debates on the legal and political determination of women's equality.

In the four years since the first edition was published, there have been numerous developments and changes that come to bear directly on the study of women, politics, and public policy. Each chapter in the second edition has undergone comprehensive revision to reflect as many of these developments and changes as possible.

Highlights of the Second Edition

- New and expanded discussion of issues affecting Aboriginal women in Canada and the unique challenges they face
- Extensive new coverage on family, family law, and public policy, including changes in law regarding same-sex marriage and same-sex couples and child-rearing
- Inclusion of contemporary topics such as women in the post-industrial economy, Quebec feminism and nation-building within that province's unique society, third-wave feminism issues and representation of diversity, ever-changing definitions of 'family', women's role in the changing complexion of unions, 'lipstick feminism and raunch culture', human trafficking, child pornography, women and globalization
- Updated feature boxes covering such topics as Aboriginal feminism, abortion rights, women with disabilities, women and the global HIV/AIDS crisis
- Updated research and statistics throughout, including the 2007 Women's Political Participation Survey, the latest Canadian census, the most current Statistics Canada releases, recent reports from the Standing Committee on the Status of Women, and results and interpretation of recent Canadian polling data
- Questions for critical thought at the end of each chapter, encouraging the reader to draw connections between issues and apply concepts to situations and current events familiar in their everyday lives.

Acknowledgements

Our partners and children, who helped us survive the writing process during the first edition, were just as supportive through the reshaping of this second edition, and to them again we extend our enduring thanks and love.

We also offer special thanks to the plethora of research assistants, editors, friends, and colleagues who assisted on this project. Jointly we give great credit and thanks to everyone at Oxford University Press who saw us through the process of writing, revising, editing, and publication. Linda thanks Safiyyah Ally, Jim Farney, Kate Mulligan, and Susan Precious from long ago, all of whom did excellent work tracking data down, and Cheryl Auger, who did a fantastic job revising and updating the annotated bibliography. Linda also thanks the many students in the gender, politics, and family policy courses she has taught over the years for numerous stimulating class discussions. Those conversations really helped shape the final product. And most of all, she thanks her great female friends who set such outstanding examples of women living feminist lives.

Jacquie thanks the students who helped her collect research: Heather Marshall, Matt Harker, Melissa Kamphuis, and Cheryl Coordes. In addition, she especially thanks the researchers at Statistics Canada and the Library of Parliament, in particular Marie Drolet, Katherine Marshall, and Julie Cool. Without the consistently high-quality research and reports they put out to little acclaim, the work of academics would be much more difficult and we would know much less about the position of women and the nature of their lives in Canada.

CHAPTER 1

Introduction

In Episode 9, entitled 'The Beautiful Girls', in Season 4 of the hit television show *Mad Men*, Peggy Olson, the show's only female copywriter, debates Abe, a journalist she has previously met at a party, in a bar over drinks. He makes reference to the civil rights marches going on in the southern US at the time and chastises Peggy's ad firm for working with a corporate client that refuses to hire black workers in the South. Peggy defends herself by stating, 'I have to say, most of the things Negros [sic] can't do, I can't do either and nobody seems to care.... Half of the meetings take place over golf, tennis, and a bunch of clubs where I'm not allowed to be a member or even enter. The university club said the only way I could eat dinner there was if I arrived in a cake.' When Abe challenges Peggy's complaint by pointing out, 'There's no Negro copywriters, you know,' Peggy counters 'I'm sure they could fight their way in like I did.'

The ambivalent relationship of feminism to broader societal change has dominated the literature on feminism and social movements. As Luke de Smet writes about Peggy's character in *Slant Magazine* (21 September 2010), while many expect the character Peggy to be 'an agent of social change, and judge her arc based on its significance to the social upheaval of the 1960s, . . . Peggy is not some simple repository for our ideals; like everyone else, she is a self-interested character with her own goals, desires, and ambitions.'

In this second edition of *Women, Politics, and Public Policy*, it is worthwhile reflecting on the significance of feminism in early twenty-first century politics and its relationship to broader societal change. Have all the hard-fought battles of the twentieth century over equality been won in Canada? Is there still a place for a movement that focuses on women's rights and gender equality in the Canadian state? Has the need for a women's movement that focused on ending discrimination in the workplace and opening up places for women in the public sphere ended? Should our scholarly attention and activism focus more on life for women in developing countries and should we re-route our attention to global society rather than the Canadian state?

This book makes the case that, yes, there is a need for reflection, both on how far women's lives have improved over the past century in Canada, and on how far the gender equality project has to go, both within Canada and in the world. Currently, scholarly research raises the question of how the world's poor survive on two dollars per day (Collins, Morduch, Rutherford, and Ruthven, 2009); in Canada, we wonder how women continue to earn only 63 per cent of men's salaries (Morrow and Alphonso 2010, A1, A4). Gail Collins (2009, 3) begins her social history of the impact of feminism in the United States with a story of secretary Lois Rabinowitz's ejection from traffic court in New York City in 1960 because she was wearing pants. She then relates the story of how, in 2009, Lubna Hussein defied a Sudanese court ruling that convicted her of public indecency for wearing pants, a sentence that can carry with it 40 lashes (Osman and El Deeb, 2009, A3). Hussein chose to protest the law and demanded a public trial, which led the judge, in a show of leniency, to sentence Hussein to a $200 fine. She declined to pay it and instead opted for a month in prison in order to protest the continued existence of the public indecency law (ibid.). The gender justice and gender equality project, we argue, is in fact a continuing global, national, and sub-state project. The lessons we have learned and continue to learn in Canada may not always be replicable in other parts of the world, but they may be informative.

The purpose of this book is to examine women's position in Canada as political actors. We survey women's historical participation in and exclusion from public life and assess the effects of feminism and women's mobilization on Canadian public policies and politics. We also consider competing perspectives on women's struggle for equality. What does equality mean? What is the best way to achieve equality goals? How do women's perspectives differ when considering issues of race, ethnicity, and class? Our task is to examine from an analytical and critical perspective the intersection of feminist theory, the development of a movement, and how women act politically to change policy. Pedagogically, our goal is to open students' minds to the fact that 'women and politics' is a part of the mainstream discipline and a fascinating part of politics—and that there is much to learn about politics when the role of gender and the impact of feminism are taken seriously.

Feminism: What's in a Name?

What is a feminist? Lorraine Code (1993, 19) argues, 'Feminism is a theoretical project whose purposes are to understand the power structures, social practices, and institutions that disadvantage and marginalize women, and to devise innovative strategies of social transformation that will promote women's emancipation.' Cataldi (1995, 78) argues that feminist theory is about the study of sexism in a male-dominated society.

Most students would probably not offer such a sophisticated definition of feminism and would be more likely to define feminism according to their images of feminists. In a book on women, politics, and public policy, the question of what is a feminist becomes all the more significant because the answer must go beyond outlining the meaning of words such as feminist, feminism, patriarchy, difference, and politics. It speaks to the core question asked by Simone de Beauvoir: What is a woman? Women are defined by their position relative to men. They are not men, and this relationship gives rise to and justification for their oppression. The task for those fighting such oppression is to appropriate and deconstruct this definition—to take control of defining what a woman is, what is meant by the categories male and female, and who is a feminist.

Why study feminist politics and public policy?

Why is the subject of feminist politics and public policy so important, and why do we teach it? First, because not to do so would result in female students earning a three- or four-year degree in the social sciences based on studies predominantly focused on men. The course of our lives and our political well-being are determined by a world view that often reflects only the male perspective. It does not really speak to the more than 50 per cent of the population that is not male and, more often than not, white, middle-class, heterosexual, and able-bodied. This has consequences for a range of issues, from the fundamentals of access to employment, political power, security, and health care to seemingly more trivial matters, such as the need for adequate washroom facilities in public venues for both women and transgendered people. As Kathy Ferguson asserts, 'a political discourse generated from women's experiences of the world is different in significant ways from that created by men', and it 'is capable of transforming the male-ordered public world in important ways' (Ferguson 1987, 209). In other words, the way of thinking and speaking generated by a feminist or transgendered analysis is different from that generated by conventional analysis, and the public world is thus transformed by a gendered discourse.

Second, a lack of focus on gender leaves huge gaps in human knowledge. As Virginia Sapiro points out, the first big effect of introducing gender analysis to a discipline is to make women and sexual minorities visible by adding them to old problems and questions—that is, 'to take old research problems and strategies, and check to see whether the answer is different when we compare women and men, or look at women where we have been looking at men' (Sapiro 1991, 166). For example, Carol Gilligan (1980, 1982) in the early 1980s challenged theories such as Lawrence Kolberg's that women had a 'retarded' moral development compared to men because men are capable of developing an abstract sense of justice, based on rights and principles, and of separating self and other, whereas women tend to regard human lives as a network of social relations and prove less willing to take a moral stand and make adverse judgments of others. Rather than asking why women did not meet the male norm, Gilligan asked what was lacking in a theory that tended to find 50 per cent of the population anomalous or abnormal. She determined that theories of moral development had been constructed to measure only male methods of moral reasoning; they were thus deaf to the methods and moral 'voices' of women.

Similarly, literature on the welfare state has tended to focus on the labour practices, wages, employment/unemployment, pension policies, and so on, of the so-called Keynesian compromise (for example, Flora and Heidenheimer 1981; Ashford 1986; Ashford and Kelley 1986; Esping-Andersen 1990; Leibfried 2001). This focus on policies that benefit people in the workforce neglects a huge portion of the welfare state, which provides benefits for those—predominantly female—who remain outside the workforce. This scholarly neglect has only recently begun to be addressed comparatively by feminist social scientists studying European welfare states (for example, Bock and Thane 1991; Lewis 1993; Sainsbury 1994, 1999), as well as scholars in Canada (for example, Bakker 1996; Brodie 1996; Boyd 1997a; Evans and Wekerle 1997). Mainstream scholarship on the welfare state also neglects the historical efforts of women, particularly in progressive and socialist feminist organizations, to push for and develop early welfare protections for women and children not in the workforce. Often these services developed out of women's work as volunteers at the community level (for example, Andrew 1984; Skocpol 1992; Rowbotham 1992, 1999).

The contribution made by feminist scholarship is more than just 'adding women and stirring'. Feminist analysis and the inclusion of women's voices offer more than a mere critique of what traditional social science has left out. Rather, introducing gender and women to the study of politics has helped to clear up misunderstandings and false assumptions and conceptions in the literature, and has aided us in rethinking ideas and concepts that we take for granted. For example, women have been less active historically in formal politics, and even today women are significantly under-represented in legislatures around the world. This inactivity was traditionally attributed to women being less interested in politics than men and consequently less involved in political activities. When measured against men, women appeared to lack the same level of political engagement (for example, Schlozman, Burns, Verba, and Donahue 1995; Verba, Burns, and Schlozman 1997). However, women's lack of engagement in formal politics was considered unproblematic because women were generally viewed as apolitical and primarily oriented toward the private sphere—that is, the home—rather than the public sphere.

Feminist scholarship has challenged such views. Feminist scholars argue that the absence of women in politics is not because of a lack of interest but because of inequitable divisions and structures of power that present obstacles to women's engagement—obstacles that men typically do not face (for example, Vickers 1989; Bashevkin 1993). In addition, feminist scholarship has revealed that differences in observed political participation between men and women arise from differences in the nature of political activity rather than from a lack of political engagement or political ability. Traditional participation studies largely were and are confined to narrowly and conventionally defined politics. They centre on participation in formal, constitutional, government-oriented institutions or procedures, as though that were the only way to participate in public life. However, a full reflection of politics, as well as a comprehensive picture of women as participants, requires a broader definition of political participation, taking into account other kinds of activity that intentionally influence the making of public policy, such as community activism (for example, March and Taqqu 1986; Bookman and Morgan 1988; Naples 1998). Focusing on these other forms of political activity also helps to expand our notion of what the political is, revealing that grassroots politics and community activism are as much a part of politics as political activity at the national level.

Fourth, the study of women, politics, and public policy is about more than making women visible in the social sciences; it is also about making women and women's issues visible in real life, where policy decisions change people's lives. It connects political ideas to political action. For example, it may seem hard to believe now, but in the early 1980s Margaret Mitchell, a New Democratic Party (NDP) member of Parliament, faced ridicule when she stood up in the House of Commons and raised the issue of wife battering, saying that it was a public policy issue that merited federal government attention and demanding that sanctions against it be included in the federal Criminal Code. As Audrey McLaughlin, who would later become NDP leader, writes of the event in her autobiography, 'at least one MP made a joke of it, shouting, 'I don't beat my wife', and the House erupted in derisive laughter' (McLaughlin 1992, 28). Years of feminist scholarship and activism to raise awareness of these issues have made such a response from male MPs unthinkable today.

Similarly, the crimes of rape and rape within marriage were not considered serious problems until the last few decades of the twentieth century. As women activists and scholars made women's issues visible, other public policy issues such as pay equity, maternity and parental leave, child care, domestic violence, and sexual assault and sexual harassment suddenly became subjects of inquiry and public concern. They became political issues and entered the public discourse. Gendered analysis thus helps to expand the field of politics as well as areas of public activity. It exposed the fact that experiences considered normal and important are often limited to those of men and demands that experiences not shared by men must also be recognized as having social significance.

Fifth, introducing the concept of gender to the study of all human phenomena helps to expose androcentric biases and prejudices in traditional scholarship.[1] The idea of the 'universal male' has come under challenge in the scholarly community, with enormous implications for women's lives. Bringing a focus on women to research reveals that research rooted in men's experiences is not 'universal' experience at all and that lack of knowledge and bias in research is dangerous. Take, for example, the case of heart disease. Only recently has research determined that men and women present different symptoms when experiencing a heart attack. Men present with what is 'typically' described as crushing chest pain. Women who do not present with 'typical' (i.e., male) symptoms are often misdiagnosed. Because women's physiology (including heart size) leads women to experience pain lower down in the abdomen rather than in the chest, leading to nausea, they are treated as experiencing indigestion or 'anxiety'. The assumption that men are representative of all humans and that 'their experiences, diseases, proclivities, and interests can count as surrogates for the circumstances of all other adult members of the population' (Code 1995, 22) is simply inaccurate. The consequences, of course, are that when women present with non-typical, i.e., non-male, symptoms, they may be misdiagnosed and are thus placed at great medical risk or could die (Bains 2000, 33; Yelaja 2002).

Political and democratic theory have historically shown significant androcentric biases. For example, Jean-Jacques Rousseau is generally regarded as a democratic theorist and supporter of participatory democracy. However, Carole Pateman (1988) demonstrates in her critique of Rousseau's Social Contract that, given Rousseau's treatment of gender relations in *Emile*, he did not include women in his vision of the democratic social contract. When we talk about the 'democratic franchise', our picture of that democracy changes radically when we realize that until well into the twentieth century, 'democracy' applied only to propertied white males. Our understanding of what our practices are and have been, and what democratic theorists prescribe as democratic, changes when we consider the limitations of their thinking and their theories.

Sixth, feminist scholarship, by challenging us to ask different questions, can transform the practice of politics in the process. For example, politics as practised until recently has been characterized as masculine. Feminists regard war, power, conflict, corruption, and competition as masculine concepts and masculine actions. At the same time, some aspects of politics are traditionally considered feminine, such as social policy. International relations, to cite another example, was once focused almost exclusively on war, competition, and conflict; with the addition of feminist approaches it can now better encompass the study of phenomena such as 'human security', 'soft power', and peace studies.[2] Further, if the reason for women's historical exclusion from the military is valid—that military life is too cruel, dangerous, and violent—then why should men have to endure that sort of ordeal? Rather than asking whether women and men should have equal opportunities to serve in the military, why not ask whether we need a military at all (for example, Enloe 1990)?

Finally, feminist scholarship can introduce and integrate new methodologies that force us to question any universalizing categories and recognize not only that women are different from men but that women are different from one another. This recognition makes us cognizant of the importance of all women's voices. For example, if we do not hear the voices of women of colour, lower-income women, or differently abled women, we might assume that the experiences of white, relatively affluent, able-bodied women represent the experiences of all women. Thus, feminist scholarship contributes to a methodology that declares that there are no universal categories and that difference, including differences among women, must be incorporated into our studies. This raises the practical question of how differences can be recognized or defined without falling into further oppressions. How are biological, racial, and ethnic differences to be addressed? Should they be minimized or celebrated as the basis for political action? Should women demand the same treatment as men or focus their efforts on the recognition and protection of women's uniqueness? The different approaches to all these questions involve diverse and often contending interpretations of the interconnections of biology, the social construction of gender, the material conditions of women, and the consciousness of oppression and its causes. Feminist methodology, therefore, encourages a truly empirical commitment to understanding through engagement with the lived experiences of women via the recording of women's voices (Harding 1987; Vickers 1989).

Thus, adding a female dimension to the study and understanding of politics has been a necessary and transformative phenomenon. As subsequent chapters reveal, however, there is still a great deal of work to be done.

The new f-word? 'I'm not a feminist, but . . . I don't really know what it is'

Each year at the beginning of a course in women in politics, one of the authors conducts an unscientific and informal poll to determine how many of the students identify themselves as feminists. Since the course is predominantly female (a bit unusual in political science), covers feminist theory, and is cross-listed with the women's studies program, one would expect that most students would identify themselves as having a feminist orientation. Surprisingly though, the majority do not. Each year only 5 to 10 out of 20 to 30 students admit that they call themselves feminists.[3] The rest of the students express a great deal of sympathy for the goals of feminism and firmly believe that women are equal and should be treated as such; however, they are unwilling to call themselves feminists. They are more comfortable saying, 'I'm not a feminist, but . . .'.

The rejection of the term and therefore the identity attached to the word 'feminist' is a popular position. In the United States, studies conducted over the past few decades reveal only a small percentage of women (ranging from 11 to 27 per cent) are willing to identify as feminist (Ramsey et al. 2007, 611). Yet while many women are reluctant to identify as feminists, or rather to self-identify as 'post-feminists', they are sympathetic to efforts to achieve women's equality. As Ramsey (2007, 3) notes, 'research has consistently shown that the majority of women support feminism and the goals of the women's movement, yet they resist labeling themselves as feminists.' Their attitude is a quintessential reflection of the statement, 'I'm not a feminist, but … '.

Recent research conducted in Canada reveals an even stronger current of identification than previously thought. O'Neill, Gidengil and Young (2008) found, when analyzing the results of a 2007 Women's Political Participation Survey, that when asked 'do you consider yourself to be a strong feminist, not a very strong feminist or not a feminist at all', 7 in 10 women in English Canada stated that they identified themselves as feminists, either strong or soft, and 25 per cent identified as 'strong feminists'. They found that women between the ages of 41 and 60 were most willing to identify themselves as strong feminists—not surprisingly, as those women would have come of age during the second-wave feminist movement of the 1960s and 1970s. More surprisingly, 58 per cent of the women surveyed who were under the age of 30 were willing to self-identify as 'soft feminists', which O'Neill et al. (2008, 11) argues weakens the claim of feminism's demise. The plethora of websites and blogs that deal with third- and fourth-wave feminist issues, from Jessica Valenti's fourth-wave feminist blog (Solomon 2009, 24) Feministing.com, which bills itself as a blog devoted to 'young feminists blogging, organizing, kicking ass', to online magazines such as *Shameless* (http://www.shamelessmag.com, billed as 'for girls who get it'), *Bitch Magazine* (http://bitchmagazine.org, billed as 'a feminist response to pop culture'), and *Antigone* (http://antigonemagazine.wordpress.com/, which bills itself as covering women, politics, and the politics of being a woman), belies the death of concern over gender issues.

If the actual aims of feminism are not objectionable, then what is? The problem appears to be related to the term itself and the meaning it has taken on in a period of backlash against feminism in the mainstream culture and media. The idea of backlash rose to prominence with Susan Faludi's 1991 book, *Backlash*, in which she documented the rise of an anti-feminist message in the popular media, a message that suggested that women were miserable not because they were continually struggling against inequality but because feminists had rejected all that was intrinsic to women and had turned women into 'unwomen'. Feminism had become the new 'f-word'. Kamen (1991) summarized in this way the answers she received from college students in the United States when she asked them to describe feminists:

> bra-burning, hairy-legged, amazon, castrating, militant-almost-antifeminine, communist, Marxist, separatist, female skinheads, female supremacists, he-woman types, bunch-a-lesbians, you-know-dykes, man-haters, man-bashers, wanting-men's-jobs, want-to-dominate-men, want-to-be-men, wear-short-hair-to-look-unattractive, bizarre-chicks-running-around-doing-kooky-things, i-am-woman-hear-me-roar, uptight, angry, white-middle-class radicals.

This characterization is unfair on many levels, not least of which is the stereotypical and negative portrayal of lesbians. It also denies any possibility that, given the continuing social, political, and economic inequalities experienced by women, they might have every reason to be angry.

By association, any efforts with a feminist tinge are similarly suspect. All feminists are seen as 'male bashers'; the politics of feminism is about castrating and taking rights away from men; the purpose of women's studies courses and courses dealing with women as a specific category of study is to 'bash' men. These characterizations act to marginalize and delegitimize the efforts of women. As Sue Cataldi argues, to characterize feminism in this way turns the tables: it portrays women as aggressive in an unseemly way, diminishes what happens to them and blames the victim ('they get what they deserve'), and devalues the work women do and the struggles they undertake (Cataldi 1995). It is ultimately an attempt to censure, suppress, and erase expressions of anger. And, disturbingly, many women are willing to subscribe to this negative portrayal of feminists. Consequently, while the women's movement has been successful in making Canadians tolerant of efforts to secure equal rights and respect for women, it has lost control over its own identity. When women are asked to go beyond the critical stereotypes, they often respond, 'I don't really know what feminism is.'

So what is feminism? The term 'feminist' itself was coined by French socialist Charles Fourier in the early nineteenth century to refer to women committed to a socialist and community based utopia focusing on cooperative mutuality rather than capitalist competition. Today, when we look at the history of women's struggles in Canada, the common theme is the demand for rights and respect for women as persons autonomous from and equal to men. Feminists argue that the range of experiences open to women should not be limited by their sex or gender, and in turn that their experiences should be validated and respected as much as those of men. Feminism is also about women identifying themselves as systematically oppressed and recognizing that this oppression does not occur naturally because of differences between the sexes but rather because of the socially constructed inequalities and barriers to women's full participation in public life. Consequently, feminism is about defining oneself—about knowing who and what one is as a woman, identifying one's own oppression, and educating others about it.

Feminist politics is about developing a sense of political commitment and then undertaking to transform that oppression. As Cataldi (1995, 78) argues, it is a 'movement to end sexism—to end violence, oppression, exploitation, or unfair discrimination based on sex'. Its basic agenda is to give women choices in how they live their lives. It insists that women be free to define themselves instead of being defined by a patriarchal culture. Fundamentally, it is a struggle to keep choices open to women and ultimately to combat the oppression of all people.

Staking a claim for 'big tent' feminism

American feminist bell hooks (1981, 195) has suggested that feminism is 'to want for all people, female and male, liberation from sexist role patterns, domination, and oppression' and that 'feminism is for everybody' (2000). Paula Kamen (1991, 27) points out that the benefit of hooks's definition is that it 'makes feminism accessible to men in not naming women as the victims, leaves it to individuals to devise the strategy best for their own level of awareness and links it to other struggles against oppression'.

The representation of the women's movement as diverse and inclusive, however, is not without controversy and contention. The inclusion under the rubric of feminism of struggles such as class conflicts or community social activism that some may not explicitly identify as feminist raises the question of how strict a distinction exists between women's politics and feminist politics: can we define the women's movement as feminist, or does combining the two make the term 'feminist' somewhat meaningless? For the women's movement, this issue raises concerns about inclusiveness. Can the movement speak for all women, even those who do not consider themselves feminists? Should it speak for all women? Can the movement include men without losing its character as a 'women's movement'?

That the existing and constructed differences between men and women have been the rationale for the oppression of women makes the inclusion of men within the term feminism problematic. While men may experience oppression because of race, class, ability, sexual orientation, and so on, they cannot share the oppression experienced by women. Without that experience, the question emerges as to whether men can be feminists or whether it is better to label sympathetic men as pro-feminists and reserve the label 'feminist' exclusively for women and those who identify as women.[4]

The class nature of feminist politics has also proved problematic. The tendency to identify strongly as a feminist increases as women's income increases; that is, there is a positive relationship between rising income levels and self-identification as feminist. Women who are in postgraduate education, have graduated from university, or have some university education are far more likely to identify as feminists than those who have some high school education or are high school graduates (McGlen and O'Connor 1998, 12). This has led to accusations that feminism is only relevant to upper- and middle-class women and that the feminist movement only pursues changes that benefit an already privileged social group.

Generational differences have also been observed among those who identify themselves as feminist. Polls conducted in the United States, for example, have consistently found that age, education, and income level affect women's responses to feminism, with women aged 18 to 45 far more likely to consider themselves feminists than women aged 45 or older (McGlen and O'Connor 1998, 12). Conversely, some argue that 'second-wave' feminism does not speak to or represent the realities of 'third-wave' feminists. Generational differences within the movement have emerged as an issue of dispute, as young women respond to the 'hopeless antiquity and unhipness' of second-wave feminists and second-wave feminists chastise their daughters for lacking an appropriate consciousness and commitment to political action (Baumgardner and Richards 2000).

For some women, the perceived 'whiteness' and racial character of feminist politics has complicated their support for women's issues and feminist politics. Mansbridge and Tate (1992), in an interesting analysis of white and African-American responses to the Clarence Thomas Senate confirmation hearings, report that while black women in the United States were more likely to identify as feminist than white women (42 compared to 31 per cent), many more white women than black women reported believing Anita Hill's sexual harassment allegations about Clarence Thomas. Many feminist scholars have pointed out that white women, women of colour, Aboriginal women, francophone women, and lesbians often do not believe they have a lot in common on many issues, including 'core' feminist issues such as sexual assault and sexual violence (for example, Davis 1981; Backhouse and Flaherty 1992; Bannerji 1993; Carty 1993; Agnew 1996; Lahey 1999). Furthermore, feminist organizations themselves have often not been very welcoming of lesbians, gender-identifying females, and women of colour, partly because of implicit racism and homophobia and partly because these organizations usually ignore the unique aspects of their experiences (Backhouse and Flaherty 1992; Oulette 2002; Rebick 2005).

These divisions became evident at meetings of academic feminists and women who work in frontline agencies such as women's shelters, rape crisis centres, and centres for poor women, Aboriginal women, and women of colour; similar divisions emerged at larger gatherings such as the United Nations Forum on Women in Beijing in 1995. Arguments over priorities, strategies, appropriate action, and even appropriate consciousness abound. However, experience at these gatherings also illustrates the similarities and connections between women's and feminist struggles, based in particular on participants' shared identity as women and their struggles against power structures that are based on and perpetuate sexism.[5] These struggles share a vision of ending constructed hierarchies and structures of power that systematically disadvantage people based on characteristics of gender, class, race, age, and so on. That does not necessarily mean that black and white, privileged and unprivileged, old and young people have the same opinion on all issues. Indeed, these differences increase women's overall consciousness, not just gender consciousness.

The question then arises as to whether we exclude explicitly anti-feminist women from the movement, such as members of REAL Women of Canada (Realistic, Equal, Active for Life) or Phyllis Schlafly, leader of a US-based organization called the Eagle Forum and an anti-Equal Rights Amendment activist.[6] A case can be made for barring such women from the feminist tent but not because they argue that men and women are different (Schlafly 1986; the website of REAL Women: http://www.realwomenca.com/view.htm). As discussed above, Carol Gilligan argues that there are psychological differences between men and women, and few would accuse Gilligan of not being feminist. Rather, their anti-feminism arises not from recognizing difference but from not challenging and indeed endorsing discriminatory practices based on those differences. REAL Women's motto, for example, is 'Women's rights but not at the expense of human rights'. It opposes equal pay for work of equal value, permissive divorce legislation, and affirmative action and declares that the 'social and economic problems of women should be resolved by taking into consideration the effects on family life and society as a whole' (http://www.realwomenca.com).

We have argued that feminist thinking supports choice and promotes equality. Within this framework, it is possible that one may recognize some differences in skills between men and women, including different ways of leading or indeed different perspectives on controversial policy issues such as abortion, pornography, and prostitution, and still be a feminist. Where the feminist message gets lost, we argue, is in claims that women's difference should contribute to a particular ordering of power in which one type of skill or perspective is better than the other—in other words, a difference that promotes and sustains a hierarchy of men over women. We will use examples from American Phyllis Schlafly's (1986) writing because it epitomizes the anti-feminist position, even more than the perspective of REAL Women of Canada and right-wing politicians such as Reform Party MP Deborah Grey or Conservative MP Elsie Wayne.[7] For example, Schlafly argues that one of the defining differences between men and women is their sex drive. She contends that men's sex drive is much stronger than that of women and 'that is how the human race was designed in order that it might perpetuate itself' (Schlafly 1986, 158). Her argument is that women and girls should act in a certain way because of these expected roles; that is, they should control their sexual appetites in ways that are not required of men and boys. Feminists would argue, however, that it is wrong to demand that women and men act in certain ways simply because of societal expectations. Even if women's and men's biologies are different, why should that difference prevent individual men and women from trying new roles?

Schlafly similarly argues that women, not men, have a maternal instinct: 'the overriding psychological need of a woman is to love something alive.' She argues that that is why women have traditionally gone into teaching and nursing: 'they are doing what comes naturally to the female psyche.' She goes on to prescribe such societal roles to women.

Schlafly's vision of difference thus removes any notion of choice from both men and women. In her world, women cannot act as autonomous beings and men cannot act as nurturers; their actions are preordained by their natures. No challenges to traditional hierarchical structures of society can or should be made; as women's actions are preordained, so too is the dominance of men over women. Any efforts to 'eliminate the differences by social engineering or legislative or constitutional tinkering cannot succeed' (Schlafly 1986, 161).[8]

'Girls Wear Pink and Boys Wear Blue': Gender and the Social Construction of Women

The question we turn to now is why women's lives have been so profoundly affected by gender. Ann Oakley (1997, 33) writes, 'Women's oppression owes its particular nature to the ways in which society has built up layers of cultural expectation and prescription and has constructed material and political edifices to support these. Women, in the sense of women, are indeed cultural artefacts. Without gender, they are nothing.'

Why does such oppression arise? It emerges from the concept of gender and the process of gendering. 'Gender' was the term adopted by second-wave feminists to distinguish between the biological aspects of being female or male and the cultural expectations of femininity or masculinity. As the sex of a person is biologically determined, the gender of a person is culturally and socially constructed.

For example, in North America a social expectation is that parents will dress baby girls in pink and baby boys in blue. Myth has it that certain colours offer protection against evil spirits. Blue, possibly because of its association with the sky and heavenly spirits, was considered a particularly powerful colour. It therefore made sense for families to ensure the safety of their most valuable assets, male children, by dressing them in blue. Pink for girls was a later association, connected to European legends about the birth of girls inside pink roses (see 'Why baby colours' at http://www.unites.uqam.ca/zigzag/textes/babyR.html). The point is that there is nothing in nature that disposes one sex to one particular colour or another. The distinction between pink and blue separates girls and boys by adding social or culturally rooted associations to each sex based on the historical valuation of male children over females.

The process of gendering is thus not natural but rather social; it is socially constructed in the stories and myths that make up our culture. Women are gendered in a subordinate position relative to men based on the definition of their sex in opposition to the male: male/female, Adam/Eve, good/evil, mind/body, aggressive/nurturing, scientific/natural, rational/hysterical, centre/margin, normal/peculiar. That men are defined as normal and women as peculiar is significant because it denotes that men are the 'universal norm' or the 'subject'. Women are by definition not men; they are 'unmen'. They are the 'other' and thus outside the norm.

The idea of gender is controversial, even among feminists. First, questions can be raised about the relationship between gender and biological sex. Cultural expectations for women and men are not separable from observations about women and men's physical bodies. As the following box reveals, no absolute separation of gender and sex is possible. However, it can be argued that because the concept of gender is so closely associated with biological sex difference, it privileges sex in accounts of oppression and fails to address economic, racial, and ethnic differences and the subordination of women.

Furthermore, caution must be used in extending Western values and assumptions to non-Western situations. Vicky Randall (1987, 29) points out that despite cross-cultural variations, many feminist anthropologists maintain that it is sex roles rather than gender that show significant continuity—for example, women's primary responsibility for nurturing the family. In some societies, these roles are a source of power and widen women's political bases—for example, controlling food and information distribution and acting as links or mediators between birth families and marital families. As March and Taqqu (1986, 13–19) argue, Western culture created gender roles that became 'a supporting role without explicit recognition outside of the privatized household. It would be impossible to consider women in the industrialized West [and other cultures with a strict demarcation of the male public and female private] without looking at a triple foil of domestic privatization: physical marginalization, economic devaluation, and social depreciation.' Outside of Western cultures, this was not necessarily the case.

However, the language of gender is a way of undermining the seeming naturalness of the differences between men and women and the associated inferiority of women. Making this unnaturalness transparent means that the differences and inferiority can be challenged and dismantled.

Definitional Considerations: Sex, Gender, Sexuality, Gender Identity, and Gender Roles

Sex refers to the biological differences that distinguish men and women. It is a concept like age, ethnicity, and race, which describes the demographic composition of the population.

Gender refers to the cultural and social meaning of 'male' and 'female'—that is, the behavioural, cultural, or psychological traits typically associated with one sex.

Gender identity refers to the sense of belonging to a particular sex biologically, psychologically, and socially.

Gender roles refer to 'expectations or prescriptions about behaviour and characteristics of men and women, especially in relation to, or in comparison with, each other' (Stetson 1997, 10).

Sexuality refers both to sex drive and feelings about one's sex and one's gender.

Thus, when people talk about women's inability to serve in the armed forces, are they referring to sex or gender? Do some people think that women cannot fly an air force jet because of a sexual difference or because their gender (i.e., socialization or lack of experience) makes them unfit for combat roles?

Many people cite the importance of sex differences between women and men to justify differential attitudes toward and treatment of men and women, boys and girls. However, researchers such as Judith Lorber (1994) point out the problem with making rigid sex-based categorizations. For example, when a baby is born with ambiguous genitalia, does one declare its sex according to the observed genitalia or according to chromosomes? Or should parents wait until they can observe the child's gender characteristics?

This example reveals the limitations of binary categories such as male and female when we take into consideration the fact that people can be transvestites, transsexuals, or hermaphrodites. Furthermore, as Lorber (1994, 39) argues, 'menstruation, lactation, and gestation do not demarcate women from men. Only some women are pregnant and then only some of the time; some women do not have a uterus or ovaries. Some women have stopped menstruating temporarily, others have reached menopause, and some have had hysterectomies. Some women breast-feed some of the time, but some men lactate.' Thus, 'menstruation, lactation, and gestation are individual experiences of womanhood but not determinants of the social categories "female" or "woman"'. Similarly, not all men are sperm producers, and men who are transsexual women can still produce sperm. After puberty, 'boys will have more shoulder and arm strength and concentrated bursts of energy; girls will have more stamina, flexibility and lower-body strength.'

As many researchers now point out, 'training is the greatest contributor to strength and skill', and 'new studies in physiology show remarkable similarities between men's and women's strength, once the variables of height and weight are factored into the equation' (Dowling 2000, A19), in competitions such as wrestling and boxing. Differences in men's and women's athletic ability are being and may soon be completely overcome. For example, women did not run in marathons until the latter part of the twentieth century. During that brief period, women have reduced their finish times remarkably. Paula Radcliffe, the current world record holder, ran the marathon in 2003 in two hours 15 minutes and 25 seconds, compared to Carmem de Oliveira's run of two hours 27 minutes and 41 seconds in 1994 (http://www.iaaf.org/statistics/records/inout=o/discType=5/disc=MAR/detail.html). Granted, men's times are still faster than women's (the world record in the men's marathon was set by Haile Gebrselassie in 2008 with a finish time of two hours 3 minutes and 59 seconds). However, women are closing the gap. Female tennis players such as Venus Williams can serve balls as fast as the best male tennis players; women now compete in such Olympic events as pole-vaulting, once thought too difficult for the sex lacking upper body strength (Dowling 2000, A19).

The fact that women are excelling in these sports is even more impressive in that, as Lorber argues, 'speed, size and strength seem to be the essence of sports' so that women are 'naturally inferior at "sports" so conceived' (42).[9] Thus, does biological difference determine gender and consequently limit the degree to which inferiority can be eradicated by challenging culture, or does gender supersede sex, making biology meaningless?

Debates over the Meaning of Equality

Overwhelmingly, feminism to most people means support for the *equality* of men and women (Kamen 1991, 25). The problem that arises is what equality means. If one has equality as a goal, does that mean identical treatment? Different treatment? Or fair treatment? In fact, there is no one agreed-upon definition of equality, even within the women's movement. As women have struggled for changes in public policies and politics, they have often been asked to come up with a unified definition of equality, but that has proved very difficult. As we go through some of the specific policy areas in this text, students will see just how important this contestation over the meaning of equality is in understanding the politics of the women's movement.

Identical Treatment, Differential Treatment, and Fair Treatment

The question that we will pose throughout this text is: what does equality mean? That is, how do we measure whether equality has been achieved?

1. Some argue that equality should be defined as **identical treatment**. Identical treatment means that laws should be *gender-neutral*; that is, governments and society should not use sex at all as a justification for differential treatment. Those who adhere to this view generally believe that gender differences are wholly ir-relevant and that any distinctions made on the basis of sex should be regarded as suspect.

2. Some argue that equality should be defined as **similar but not the same or identical treatment**, which would allow for **differential treatment** as long as that differential treatment was not *arbitrary*. Differential treatment means that laws could treat men and women differently. They could take into account dif-ferences in men's and women's biology, for example, as long as there were good reasons for the differential treatment.

3. Some argue that equality should be defined as **fair treatment**. That is, gov-ernments should eliminate legislation based on stereotypes regarding gender and gender roles and should not deny to one sex a privilege that is enjoyed by the other without substantial justification. But governments should also help women to achieve equality by compensating them for past discrimination—as long as sex classifications are not used to perpetuate women's inferiority. That is, differential treatment could be allowed in order to level the playing field and promote, not hinder, women's equality.

To illustrate the differences between a fair treatment view of equality and the other views, Judith Lorber (1994, 52) discusses 'the bathroom problem'. As she points out, 'Most buildings that have gender-segregated bathrooms have an equal number for women and for men. When there are crowds, there are always long lines in front of women's bathrooms but rarely in front of men's bathrooms.' Thus, a strict same treatment policy of providing equal numbers of bathrooms for men and women disadvantages women. Lorber argues that if one takes into account the physiological, cultural, and demographic factors that affect bathroom use time in North America, one would see that true equality would mean levelling the playing field and 'providing more women's bathrooms or allow-ing women to use men's bathrooms for a certain amount of time'.

However, many advocates of this 'fair treatment' view of equality argue that it comes dangerously close to reinforcing sex-based legislation (i.e., differential treatment). Thus

they argue that what needs to change is androcentric thinking (see note 1 for definition). Instead of using men's bathroom needs as the norm in designing washrooms, use
women's needs. Same treatment would thus mean adding many more public washrooms overall (using women's needs to set the washroom quota) or to allow gender-
neutral washrooms. The latter would address the discomfort that transgendered men
and women or those undergoing sexual transition feel in using either male or female
washrooms.

The liberal feminist struggle from the first wave, much of the second, and into
the third wave of feminism focused on gaining equal power and access for women.
Efforts have been made to widen participation in the political world of those previously excluded and under-represented, particularly women but also racial and ethnic minorities. However, what constitutes equality and how it is achieved has proved
quite problematic for feminist theory and action. Equal treatment requires everyone
to be measured according to the same rules. That view of equality is based on an
understanding of universally shared characteristics, which minimizes the differences
between the sexes, between the privileged and underprivileged, and among women.
It makes all women the same, and then it makes them the same as men. Hence, some
have referred to it as a process of 'saming' (Irigaray 1993). It is particularly problematic
because equality as a condition is judged in relation to a universal position or referent—the white male.

Furthermore, as feminists of colour point out, the universal category of reference
is also white, making some women 'more equal' than others. Women with other social
and cultural experiences are marginalized and their experiences not fully validated
and recognized. This is not surprising because, as Iris Marion Young (1990, 131)
argues, 'where some groups are privileged and others oppressed, the formulation of
law, policy and the rules of private institutions tend to be biased in favor of the privileged groups, because their particular experience sets the norm'. Thus, we emphasize
that women's equality goals vary according to race, class, and sexual orientation and
that we should not understand women's quest for equality solely from mainstream
women's perspective.

The equality/difference debate raises a significant dilemma in the feminist movement. On the one hand, the universal principle of equality requires that differences
between men and women, whites and people of colour, privileged and underprivileged, able-bodied and disabled, cannot be recognized or given weight. On the other
hand, fairness and justice require that differences be recognized and given weight in
order to ameliorate existing disadvantages. Debates over maternity rights and protections, reproductive rights, and affirmative action illustrate this problem. Policies and
legal provisions in these areas are based on the recognition of difference and advantage
that specific groups possess at the expense or disadvantage of others. Issues around
maternity and childbirth are explicit in this regard because only women can get pregnant. Maternity leave provisions violate 'same treatment' equality principles because
they do not apply equally to men or to post-menopausal women. Similarly, affirmative
action programs require different treatment rather than same treatment. That different treatment, while addressing the needs of previously disadvantaged groups, can

disadvantage white males. Framed in the language of equality, these issues become problematic and create social tensions that can flare up in the language of backlash in which equality-seeking groups are accused of asking not for equality but for more than their fair or equal due.

Patricia Williams suggests that flexibility is needed, particularly when it comes to political and legal equality. She amusingly proposes that equality be addressed as a 'situational sausage':

> You have this thing called a sausage-making machine. You put pork and spices in at the top and crank it up, and because it is a sausage-making machine, what comes out the other end is a sausage. Over time, everyone knows that anything that comes out of the sausage-making machine is sausage. One day, we throw in a few small rodents of questionable pedigree and a teddy bear and a chicken. We crank the machine up and wait to see what comes out of the other end. (1) Do we prove the validity of the machine if we call the product a sausage? (2) Or do we enlarge and enhance the meaning of a 'sausage' if we call the product a sausage? (3) Or do we have any success in breaking out of the bind if we call it something different from 'sausage'? In fact, I'm not sure it makes any difference whether we call it sausage or if we scramble the letters of the alphabet over this thing that comes out, full of sawdust and tiny claws. What will make a difference, however, is a recognition of our shifting relation to the word 'sausage', by enlarging the authority of sausage makers and enhancing the cruel inevitability of the workings of sausage machines—that is, everything they touch turns to sausage or else it doesn't exist; or by expanding the definition of sausage itself to encompass a wealth or variation: chicken, rodent, or teddy-bear sausage; or, finally by challenging our own comprehension of what it is we really mean by sausage—that is, by making clear the consensual limits of sausage and reacquainting ourselves with the sources of its authority and legitimation. (Williams 1991, 107–10)

In working through the equality/difference coupling, the critics of the 'saming' nature of equality have asked feminism and feminists to re-examine their relationship with the concept of equality and recognize the damage equality based on a universal conception does to the experiences and lives of those who cannot conform to a referent that, far from being universal or neutral, reflects a privileged, able-bodied, white male position. In the third wave of the women's movement, there has been a shift from a monolithic and unified view of what women are to an understanding of the differences among women. For women's politics, the shift has meant a struggle to have this understanding of difference incorporated into the kind of political demands they make and want ultimately translated into public policy. This is far from an easy task.

The Debate over the Meaning of Public and Private

Much second-wave feminist analysis identified the family as the primary source of gender inequality. As Oakley (1997, 29) argues, 'the family "is" gender: mothers, fathers, and children may stand in a biological relationship to one another, but their behaviour is largely shaped by cultural factors.' And it is the family that stands at the

Case Study: Women as Prison Guards in Male Prisons

Later chapters will address specific debates over equality in a number of policy areas. However, to illustrate the complexity of the debate surrounding same treatment versus differential treatment, let us consider the issue of whether male guards should be allowed to work in female prisons since female guards may work in male prisons. This issue has been debated in both Canada and the United States. To understand the context of the debate, students should read a 1999 report by Amnesty International on the abuse of female inmates by male prison guards in the United States, accessible at http://www.amnesty.org/en/library/info/AMR51/053/1999/en.

Dr William F. Schulz, executive director of Amnesty International USA, and Geri Lynn Green, a San Francisco-based civil rights lawyer, were interviewed on National Public Radio's Diane Rehm show on 8 March 1999 (accessible via Real Live Audio at http://the dianerehmshow.org/shows/1999-03-08/women-us-prisons). In the interview, Dr Schulz reported that 70 per cent of the guards in US women's prisons are male, while about 90 per cent of the guards in Canadian women's prisons are female. Why? Because many men *and* women in the United States resist the idea of excluding men from direct contact with female prisoners on equality grounds, whereas there is less resistance in Canada. In the United States, the debate is framed as one of equality in employment. Under Title VII of the Civil Rights Act of 1964, which prohibits sex and other forms of discrimination in employment, women must be allowed to guard male prisoners. Thus, on the basis of equality, men should be allowed to guard women prisoners as well. Dr Schulz argues, however, that this view demonstrates a 'failure to recognize that there is a real difference' in the situation of male and female prisoners.

In Canada, in contrast, a 1993 Supreme Court decision held that male prisoners can be subject to cross-gender searches and surveillance, given that 'a substantially reduced level of privacy is present in prison', but that it is not discriminatory treatment for female prisoners not to be subject to the same cross-gender searches (*Weatherall v. Canada (Attorney General)* [1993] 2 S.C.R.). Similarly, a report by the Women's Legal Education and Action Fund (LEAF) on the question of cross-gender staffing in regional penitentiaries for women argues that 'the impact on federally sentenced women of cross-gender staffing will be severe. In particular, it will compound the existing power imbalance in gender relations in our society. This imbalance of power will be felt most acutely by those inmates who have suffered physical, sexual and/or psychological abuse at the hands of men' (LEAF n.d., 5). The Court in *Weatherall* reasoned that equality provisions under section 15 of the Canadian Charter of Rights and Freedoms '[do] not necessarily connote identical treatment; in fact, different treatment may be called for in certain cases to promote equality. ... Given the historical, biological and sociological differences between men and women, it is clear that the effect of cross-gender searching is different and more threatening for women than for men.' LEAF too argues that the section 7 rights of women (to security of the person) need to be balanced against men's equality rights in employment (section 15), but also that section 15 requires the state to 'treat federally sentenced women in a way that recognizes the reality of their lives and experiences'—that is, that they are disproportionately the victims of sexual and physical abuse by men (LEAF n.d., 24). The Supreme Court in *Weatherall* also argues that 'the important government objectives of inmate rehabilitation and security of the institution are promoted as a result of the humanizing effect of having women in these positions.' That is, 'women guards have an overall positive effect in institutions for men', whereas 'male guards have a negative effect on the female population' (LEAF n.d., 26).

What do you think?

centre of structures of patriarchy. Derived from the term *patriarch*, defined as the father and ruler of a family or tribe, patriarchy refers to social and cultural relations of power and control. Patriarchy means men's control over women's sexuality and fertility and encompasses the institutional structure of male domination (Rowbotham 1989, 72). It therefore describes the dominance of men over women and emphasizes the centrality of women's relationships to the family as a feature of their oppression.

The term also conveys a distinction between the male 'public' and the female 'private'. The 'public' refers to that part of society for whom and on whose behalf public decisions are taken and public policy made. This gives rise to the conception of 'public interest' or common welfare, which is essential to formal political action. Giving birth and child-rearing limited women's political and economic activity and focused their lives on the domestic world of the home and family. Men, without these commitments, could participate in the broader associations of society outside the home and in economic and political life. This separation fostered male dominance (1) by giving men greater ability to shape the public culture and thus maintain the subordinated, excluded position of the private women, and (2) by distancing the man from his family and making him the family representative in the public sphere, thereby giving him more authority in the private (Rosaldo 1974). Consequently, the public/private dimension of patriarchy results in a system of power based on sex in which men possess superior power and economic privilege (Eisenstein 1979, 17).

Not surprisingly, this division has significant political consequences as well. The distinction between public and private sets out certain assumptions regarding the political and the access of women to the political world. As Pierre Trudeau told Canadians in 1967, 'there is no place for the state in the bedrooms of the nation.' The private world of families and sexual relationships is off-limits to political interference. Women, intrinsically associated with reproduction, sexuality, and the private sphere, are consequently 'free of politics' or non-political.

However, to think of the private as something removed from politics, or to conceive of politics as immune from issues of sexuality and private concerns, is nonsense. (Just think of the impact a sex scandal can have on any politician.) The public and private clearly cannot be treated as separate worlds. Throughout history, not all women were exclusively of the 'private'. It could be argued that as the modern state developed, the division between public and private isolated upper-class and middle-class women. Yet lower-class women and women of colour continued to work. At the same time, relations in the public sphere, in the workplace, and in politics were moulded by the inequalities of 'private' sexual politics. In addition, as states and public policy regimes expanded, relations within the home and issues of sexuality were affected by public policy and regulation covering areas such as public morality, contraception, public health, housing, social security, and education.

Consequently, an important element of women's politics is to dissolve the boundaries between politics and women's lives, to subvert and make transparent the myth of the division between public and private, and to eliminate the fundamental structure of patriarchal systems. Once the public is conceived not as the self-contained domain of formal political institutions, and the private not as the self-contained domain of non-political family and sexuality, then politics will be seen as spanning both public and private spheres. In this way, it will be possible for women's experiences to be seen as political, and the recognition of experiences, needs, and access to public decision-making will be equal for all.

Is Feminism Relevant?

Students may ask, is there still a need for a women's movement in North America? Indeed, the popular press has run stories about 'the end of men' in their past domination of the workforce. Hanna Rosin's cover story in the July/August 2010 issue of *The Atlantic* notes that 'The postindustrial economy is indifferent to men's size and strength. The attributes that are most valuable today—social intelligence, open communication, the ability to sit still and focus—are, at a minimum, not predominantly male. In fact, the opposite may be true.' Women currently comprise four members of the Supreme Court of Canada, and the current Chief Justice, Beverley McLachlin, is a woman. Women made up 47 per cent of the workforce in 2006, up from 37 per cent in 1976, and 55 per cent of doctors and dentists and 26 per cent of senior managers (Almey 2006, 6, 9). So, should we be concerned about men's position in the workforce and higher education?

Perhaps this question can best be answered by considering some of the most important issues women must deal with in Canada today. The list might include combating violence against women; securing greater reproductive rights; achieving equal pay in the workplace and equal access to well-paying jobs; establishing public policies in areas such as child care that will make it easier to balance work and family life; securing greater funding for investigation into women's health concerns; fighting racism's effects on women; and achieving greater assistance for poor and single mothers. This list is not exhaustive, merely illustrative; nevertheless, these are issues that many women's groups, such as the National Action Committee on the Status of Women (NAC), the National Organization of Immigrant and Visible Minority Women of Canada (NOIVMW), and the Women's Legal Education and Action Fund (LEAF) address. Beyond these are broader issues affecting women, such as economic globalization, environmental degradation, and war. We need to address them as well and recognize the organizations of committed women who are active on these issues. Many of these activities and organizations will be explored in later chapters.

It should be clear at this point that there are no easy answers or compromises. Our hope is that as readers work their way through this text, they will gain a greater understanding and knowledge of the issues. In the next two chapters, we examine the theoretical positions that inform feminist struggles in Canada. We discuss a variety of these positions and their differing explanations for women's inequality and the relevance of differences among women, and their proposed solutions and strategies for changing women's lives. Chapter 4 explores the women's movement(s) in Canada, its history and component parts. It also examines the idea of social movements and the politics characteristic of such phenomena, making an argument for a conception of political participation that goes beyond mainstream conventional politics such as elections, parties, and parliaments (large-P politics) to include participation in 'unconventional' activities associated with civil society, interest groups, social movements, and voluntary agencies (small-p politics). In chapter 5, we examine women's participation in formal politics to assess how well women have succeeded in the traditionally male sphere of large-P politics and what barriers remain. In chapter 6, we discuss the practical realities of political change. Feminist theory aside, what matters is political change that betters the lives of Canadian women. Has the women's movement in Canada had an influence on policy outcomes that affect women? We argue that although measuring public policy influence is a complex task, we can plot the complex interaction between actors within the movement, actors within other movements, and state actors. Chapters 7 to 12 focus on substantive policy issues having to do with family, work and pay, and the body, including pornography, prostitution, reproduction, and new reproductive technologies. The final chapter discusses international aspects of the women's movement and the gendered nature of international politics.

CHAPTER 2

Modern Feminist Theory

In a textbook that takes as its focus the way that Canadian women have engaged in and are engaging in struggles against gender bias and oppression as political actors, some discussion of theory is necessary in order to understand the experiences of women and to devise solutions to the challenges in their lives. To grasp the role of feminist theory, let's begin with the following scenario:

> Jill is a 22-year-old undergraduate finishing a social science degree at a large university. She will be starting a Masters program in social work next fall. She is the single mother of Jack, a four-year-old boy who attends a subsidized cooperative daycare part-time on weekdays. Jill recently left her part-time job in a bookstore because a change in her hours would have required her to arrange additional child care. Jack's father moved out of town before the birth, and Jill has had no contact with him since then. At this point, Jill and Jack live with Jill's parents. Her mother has helped a lot with child care, but Jill worries that asking her to pick Jack up after school is too much of a burden. She is hoping that once she has obtained her master's degree in social work (MSW) she will be able to find a job and move into her own place. Jill does well in and enjoys all her classes but has found herself skipping her one evening class because she feels uncomfortable in the parking lot after dark.

The above description provides no explanation of why Jill's life is the way it is and why she acts the way she does. We do not understand why it is such a struggle for her to raise her child on her own while working, nor why she feels uncomfortable being on campus at night.

To understand Jill's life, we need to seek out those explanations, interpreting the descriptors of her life so as to make sense of her difficulties. Our interpretations are informed by the theories we hold regarding such things as the sources of oppression and empowerment that affect women's position in society and the economy, and the possibilities for change. Theories are generalizations about relationships between factors that help explain phenomena and organize, highlight, and give coherence to otherwise diverse events, processes, and institutions. They enable us to think more clearly about complicated events by putting many seemingly unrelated events into a larger context so that we can see the 'big picture' and gain perspective. Through theory we are able to explain, and possibly predict, what will happen in the future and devise ways to change that future.

'Sister, Can You Paradigm?': The Importance of Theory

Feminism involves theory that explains women's inequality in society. It seeks to explain how sexism and male domination of society arise and are maintained. Feminism identifies a problem and offers an explanation for the problem. However, feminist theory goes beyond mere explanation of women's oppression; it also seeks to prescribe ways to eradicate that oppression. It encourages us to move beyond beliefs and ideas to action, to move from feminist theory to a feminist political project. This is the point of Lorraine Code's (1993, 21) observation that 'theory—and consciousness-raising—are still fundamental to the movement . . . deriving ever more subtle analyses of the effects of patriarchy, defining and redefining the problems that have to be faced, and evaluating new strategies for change.' Consequently, feminist theory cannot be separated from the action of women and the women's movement.

This connection between theory and action can be referred to as *praxis*. Praxis is where understanding and action or, more technically, theory and agency intersect to inform each other. Humans come to understand and interpret their position in their surrounding environment (that is, in society). These understandings guide their action. Through informed action, experience leads to further understanding and interpretation, and ultimately action is understood and focused to remake their conditions. Praxis is, to put it crudely, the revelation that emerges from a sophisticated process of 'muddling through'. A theory guides our actions, and through the experience of action our theory is modified and transformed. This is not insignificant for an understanding of women's political activity. Feminist politics is about the continual creation and re-creation of the ideal of feminism and the ideals of society. It is about making change.

The relationship between feminist studies in universities and the activity of grass-roots feminists can be problematic. Part of the problem arises from the sometimes uncomfortable fit between theory and the movement. The focus on abstract theorizing by academic feminism can separate it from grassroots feminist practice. The esoteric theory produced by 'intellectuals' may not reflect and may be impractical for the day-to-day experience of women in general and grassroots activists in particular. The words are big, based on many presumptions of prior knowledge, and presented in ways that invite 'only argument, imply answers, or draw limits to women's involvement' (Greaves 1993, 151). The process is elitist and inaccessible to most women outside of small academic circles. The act of theorizing is also accused of being inherently male, replacing the empirical and emotional nature of women's lived experiences and consciousness-raising with the abstract and intellectualized world of the male academy.

Using the concept of praxis removes the idea of theory from its characterization as the esoteric and elitist purview of the ivory tower. Theory cannot be separated from the way lives are lived and political struggles are undertaken. To separate theory from action 'invokes a picture of human beings as headless chickens: the head, full of theory, lies inert and ineffective, while the headless body, empty of direction rushes around in mindless circles' (Evans 1997, 20).[1] The separation also dismisses the theorizing that occurs outside the academy in everyday life. For example, according to Barbara Christian (1997, 70–1), people of colour have a history of theorizing, not in the form of abstract logic associated with the academy, but in stories, proverbs, riddles, and the interplay of language. '[W]omen, at least the women I grew up around, continuously speculated about the nature of life through pithy language that unmasked the power relations of their world.'

As such, theory is a practical aspect of life and the efforts to bring about social change. It gives us something more than just a description of women's lives. It allows us to understand their situations, and it gives us visions of the possibilities of change. As such, the idea of praxis expresses potentialities, something between what simply *is* and what *ought* to be.

Theorizing about Women: A Modern Herstory

Since the starting point of feminist theory is the varied experiences of women and the situations in which they live and are disadvantaged, we cannot expect broad-based agreement on the sources of and solutions to those problems. What is common is the aim of feminist theory: to understand how the conditions of women have been determined by social, cultural, economic, and political structures and patterns. Beyond that, feminists differ on what they see as the primary aspects of women's oppression, and that leads them to focus on different questions and to develop different agendas for change. As we shall see in later chapters, these differences have resulted in differing approaches to and debates over appropriate strategies to address the issues that affect women, ranging from women's participation in politics and the labour market, to pornography, to surrogate parenthood. These different approaches involve diverse and often contending interpretations of the distinctions and interconnections between the biological determination and social construction of gender, the public and the private, and sameness and difference.

We follow the development of feminist thought chronologically, through 'modernity' to 'postmodernity', although we start in the 'pre-modern' period. In pursuing the discussion in this manner, we acknowledge that the duality explicit in the categories of modern and postmodern does present a limiting either/or typology. As discussed in the introduction, one of the goals of feminism is to break down the dualities that create a world divided into man/woman, subject/other, and so on. This is something that intersectionality, discussed at the end of chapter three, sees as required for a truly inclusive politics. In addition, unlike the presentation we will undertake in this and the next chapter, feminist thought is far from orderly, coherent, and chronological, since all the points overlap, contradict, agree with, and blur into one another. However, it is the nature of the task of telling a story that an order will be imposed on a series of events that are not necessarily orderly and chronological, creating a picture that appears cleaner and more organized than it really is. It is also the nature of the narrative that we cannot include all women but rather highlight as examples those with whom we are most familiar and those we feel help to illustrate the approach.

Pre-modern women writers: The importance of a good moral education

Chronologically, modernity is associated with the Age of Enlightenment and the emergence of scientific rationality, the idea of progress or teleology (the assumption of an inevitable progression along a path of development), freedom of the individual, and the secular political institutions of the modern European nation-state. Let's start our story, however, not with the first feminists (many strong women whom we would call feminists have existed throughout history) but with the earliest writings that have sometimes been characterized as feminist or proto-feminist.

Christine de Pizan (circa 1364–1430) and Mary Astell (1666–1731) are two such pre-modern women writers. Both were wedded to the notion of the divine right of the monarchy and the church and were explicitly concerned with women's relationship with God, religious morality, and Christian virtue. Both advocated educational opportunities for women, but education and religion converge in their work. The outstanding feature in their writing is the claim they make regarding women. Both argued that women were capable of reason and able to engage in intellectual work. What women lacked, they said, was an appropriate education. In *The Book of the City of Ladies* (1405/1982) and *The Book of Three Virtues* (1405/1997), de Pizan, responding to the literature of the time, which denigrated women as lascivious, fickle, and incompetent, demonstrated the heroic attributes of women through myth and history in three spheres—justice, rectitude, and reason. In creating a 'city of ladies', de Pizan devised a model for the development and recognition of feminine intellect and virtue. Mary Astell, 300 years later, made similar claims. In *A Serious Proposal to the Ladies* (1696/1970a), *An Essay in Defence of the Female Sex* (1697/1970b), and *Some Reflections on Marriage* (1694/1970c), she highlighted the contradiction inherent in men accusing women of being irrational on the one hand but on the other hand preventing them from learning. She also suggested that the belief in the inferiority of women might not hold if women were given greater educational opportunities. The two present a challenge to male control of learning and scholarship and the limitations placed on women to better their own intellects.

While both of these writers presaged the early 'modern feminists', such as Mary Wollstonecraft, Harriet Taylor, and John Stuart Mill, in their claims for women's reason and ability, they have an ambiguous relationship with the concept of feminism. In truth, it is not accurate to label either of them as feminist. Their educational vision for women assumed a private rather than public role for women. Both envisioned a feminine education for upper-class women that would enhance their abilities as wives and mothers within a conventional understanding of marriage. Neither advocated that women receive the same education as men. Despite her own thirst for knowledge, de Pizan did not recommend education for women generally. She argued that most women do not require an education to fulfill their social obligations (Delany 1997, 322). Women's educational experience would also be developed in a particularly private way. Both writers spoke of women entering separate cloistered communities to pursue their love of knowledge: de Pizan's city of ladies and Astell's Protestant convent.

Pre-modern Women Writers

Educated by her father, Christine de Pizan has been referred to as the first female professional writer. Widowed in her 20s, de Pizan cultivated her connections with the French nobility—her father and husband had both been attached to the court of King Charles V—as patrons for her writings. Her writing supported her children and her mother as well as herself. She was a prolific author, penning love poems, devotional texts, and political works. Once her children had grown, de Pizan retired to convent life.

Mary Astell, the daughter of a Newcastle coal merchant, was educated by a cleric uncle who encouraged her intellectual pursuits and interest in books. She did not marry and was supported throughout her life by wealthy, mainly female, friends and patrons. She wrote prodigiously on the topic of female moral education.

Neither was willing to radically challenge the social, political, and religious hierarchies of the time. For both, the preservation of hierarchies was necessary to guarantee social and political order. They believed that the social hierarchy and women's place within it was ordained by God and therefore carved in stone. This included women's subordination to their husbands and fathers. For example, while Astell (1970c) believed that relationships should not be founded on blind obedience, she also emphasized a rule-governed relationship between subjects and monarchs and husbands and wives. Similarly, de Pizan celebrated the superiority of women in their capacity for humility, gentleness, and other maternal qualities in the face of domestic tyranny (Gottlieb 1997, 288). A bad marriage was unfortunate but had to be endured. In other words, women's ability to 'lump it' was part of their moral strength; they would be rewarded in heaven.

While de Pizan and Astell were conservative in their positions even for their times, they are significant as women writers in their defence of women's intellectual abilities, a position that foreshadowed the demands of the early modern liberal feminists for equality for women through recognition of a universal human rationality and equal opportunities for education.

Liberal feminism: How do you define equality?

With the Enlightenment emerged solidly liberal principles upon which liberal feminism draws. Liberal feminism is the form of feminism most familiar to us. It draws its ideas and assumptions from familiar liberal principles outlined by political theorists such as John Stuart Mill. Many of us would define feminism as a belief that we should all have the same rights, or that women are equal to men and deserve the same respect, opportunities, rights, and pay, and that men and women should share roles. This is an outlook very much associated with 'modernity', which places high value on individual autonomy and self-fulfillment, and the idea that a 'just society' allows a person to exercise that autonomy and pursue self-betterment. Enlightenment belief in the reason of the individual and individual progress supports liberal claims for freedom to rationally pursue self-betterment, equality, and a collective polity of equals. High value is placed on human rights, civil liberty, and freedom from illegitimate hierarchies.

For women, the corollary of such principles is that there is no reason for them to be excluded from society. The early modern feminists claimed that society was made up of free and equally participating rational individuals, and this applied universally to both men and women. They rejected the idea that women's oppression was based in nature. Rather, women's oppression was the result of society's mistaken ideas about women's nature.

Consequently, liberal feminism focuses on overcoming attitudes and policies of exclusion. The emphasis is on equality of opportunity and transformation of the rules of society that exclude women. Women's struggles are for the equal rights, political inclusion, and full citizenship that will guarantee both men's and women's natural rights to pursue their interests and self-betterment. Gender justice, according to liberal feminists, 'requires us, first, to make the rules of the game fair and, second, to make certain none of the runners in the race for society's goods and services is systematically disadvantaged' (Tong 1998, 2). The idea of sameness, or the universality of human beings, infuses liberal feminism. As a result, liberal feminism has tended to be a reformist movement, advocating reform of existing social and political institutions rather than wholesale transformation.

The first demand for equality of rights and participation was enunciated by Olympe de Gouges in her *Declaration of the Rights of Woman and the Female Citizen* (1789/1989) during the French Revolution. However, the label of 'mother of liberal feminism' is generally applied to Mary Wollstonecraft (1759–1797) and her work *A Vindication of the Rights of Women* (1792). Wollstonecraft, responding to Jean-Jacques Rousseau's arguments in *Emile* (1762/1979) that women were far too irrational and manipulative to be allowed to participate in political society, pointed out that if women were incapable of reason they were then undistinguishable from 'brute animals'. As women were not 'animals', they had to be rational, and to deny them an education similar to that of men was to deny them the chance to develop their rational and moral capacities and so achieve full personhood. However, her work went far beyond merely advocating schooling for girls. She believed that individuals had natural rights to self-determination, which could not be usurped by authority based on arbitrary inherited title and divine right. This belief extended to the relationship between husband and wife, which should ideally be an equal partnership based on choice, not on hierarchical and hereditary rule.

One hundred years later, Harriet Taylor and John Stuart Mill made further claims for women's equality from a liberal philosophical perspective. Their arguments were based on acceptance of the 'rights of man' and the need for personal liberty. Like other liberal thinkers, they believed that given greater opportunities, individuals would correct all social inequalities. For women, this meant achieving the same political rights and economic and educational opportunities as men. In Mill and Taylor, not only is intellectual equality seen as a given, it is explicitly connected to political equality and the vote. Equality would result from women's suffrage (although applied only to a particular class of woman) because the vote would give women the power to change systems, structures, and attitudes.

Contemporary liberal feminism draws upon classical liberal visions of freedom and equality of opportunity. It has been characterized as a feminism of rights, which is liberal feminist Betty Friedan's point in seeing feminism as less a theory of women's oppression by patriarchy than a theory of human rights. Sex discrimination is unfair because it deprives women of their equal rights. Individual rights are an important part of a just society because they provide a framework within which individuals can follow their own paths, as long as the paths taken do not deprive others of the ability to be choosers as well. Social policy, or public policy in general, should therefore be structured to allow individuals to maximize their freedom without jeopardizing the community's welfare.

Liberal Feminists

Olympe de Gouges (1748–93) abandoned her family for a life in Paris where she made a name for herself as a playwright and pamphleteer. Semi-literate, she dictated her work, including the *Declaration of the Rights of Woman and the Female Citizen* (1789/1989), which called for the recognition of women as political, civil, and legal equals, with the same rights guaranteed to men in the French Revolution's *Declaration of the Rights of Man and the Citizen* (1789). During the revolution, she founded several women's organizations but ultimately became a victim of the Terror. She was guillotined in 1793 for being a feminist and rejecting the 'virtues inherent in her sex'.

Mary Wollstonecraft's (1759–97) place as a central figure in the struggle for women's rights was not recognized until the end of the nineteenth century because her love life and views on women's marital autonomy were considered too scandalous. Largely self-taught, her early unsuccessful attempt to establish a school for young women led to her first work, *Thoughts on the Education of a Daughter* (1787/1972). After surviving Paris during the French Revolution and responding to the misogyny of Rousseau's *Emile*, she wrote *A Vindication of the Rghts of Women* (1792/1970). She set aside her critique of marriage to marry fellow liberal radical William Godwin in 1797. However, the union was short-lived as she died giving birth to their daughter, Mary Wollstonecraft Godwin Shelley, the author of *Frankenstein*.

In political science, we are more familiar with John Stuart Mill (1806–73) and his work on liberalism. However, Mill maintained that after 1840 his work, including *On liberty*, was a joint effort with Harriet Taylor (1808–58). After meeting in 1840, Mill and the married Taylor established a deep and intense platonic friendship based on a shared philosophy and politics. They married in 1851 after the death of Taylor's husband. She is credited with an anonymous article on women's enfranchisement in the *Westminster Review* (1851); however, it is her work with Mill on *The Subjection of Women* for which she is best known. Although Mill wrote the book after her death, he said that it was her observations on women's experience and their joint discussions that had formed the book. After Taylor's death, Mill continued to advocate for women's rights and enfranchisement, both in his writing and as a member of the British House of Commons.

Betty Friedan (1921–2006) is one of the most influential North American women in the emergence of the second wave of feminism. Even today, her book, *The Feminine Mystique* (1963) is listed on right-wing websites as one of the 10 most damaging books of the past 200 years, along with *Mein Kampf* and *The Communist Manifesto* (http://www.humaneventsonline.com/article.php?id=7591). Friedan put her philosophical commitments into action by helping to found the US-based National Organization for Women (NOW), of which she held the presidency from 1966 to 1970. During the 1970s and 1980s, she helped to found other women's groups, such as the National Abortion Rights Action League (NARAL), and campaigned for the Equal Rights Amendment (ERA).

How these rights should be achieved, and how far the state should go in en-suring such rights, is open to debate. On the one hand, feminists adopting a more 'classical liberal' stance argue that all that can be expected is the formal removal of discriminatory policies and laws to enable women to compete equally with men. The state will ensure voting rights, freedom of speech, freedom of religion, and so on, to ensure that individuals retain their freedom. On the other hand, welfare liberal feminists advocate a much more proactive approach to achieving equality. Because not all individuals have an equal opportunity to pursue their desires, it is not enough to achieve formal equality; rather, the playing field needs to be made level first. Consequently, the state should promote economic justice as well as civil liberties. Society should not only compensate women for past injustices but also eliminate socio-economic as well as legal obstacles through temporary programs of preferential treatment, such as affirmative action and quotas.

Idealist liberals, materialist Marxists: Freedom and equality under Marxism

For liberal feminists, the exclusion of women from society, politics, economics, and so on is maintained by a set of formal and legal constraints that are rationalized by a belief that women are the 'weaker' sex. Therefore, women's subordination is not inevitable or determined by nature but is rather the result of mistaken beliefs and ideas in society. Thus, liberal feminism has an idealist as opposed to a materialist understanding of the roots of oppression. Marxist and socialist feminists, in turn, have taken this position to task, arguing that liberal feminism fails to recognize the material nature of women's oppression. That is, the social and economic circumstances of women shape their lives and their oppression. Consequently, equality of rights will have minimal impact if the material inequalities and the everyday experiences of women's lives remain unchanged. In other words, it is not a lack of rights and inclusion that is responsible for women's oppression but rather the social and political structure of capitalism.

Marxism has been important to the development of feminist politics because at the heart of the ideology it is a theory regarding the causes of oppression and because its ideals are aimed at inspiring political struggles directed toward the elimination of domination. The ideology attracted feminists in the 1960s and 1970s, who spoke of 'oppression' and 'liberation' rather than rights and equality. Marxist feminists such as Juliet Mitchell (1989, 297) suggest that 'we should ask the feminist questions, but try to come up with some Marxist answers.'

The materialism of the Marxist approach derives from its focus on relations of production. Rather than distinguishing between economics and politics, Marxism focuses on the way capitalism structures economic and power relations among classes. Through the contracting of labour to benefit the capitalist employer or the 'head of the household', capitalism alienates or separates workers from their labour and control of that labour. Labour becomes private property appropriated and controlled by someone other than the labouring person.

At Marxism's centre is an economic critique and an understanding that it is impossible to attain equality in a class-based society in which the wealth produced by the many is taken by the few. It calls not for equality rights but for the egalitarian ordering of productive and reproductive labour. Freedom and equality can only be achieved through the abolition of classes and the forced labour of capitalism. In this post-class society, individual talent will not be suppressed: rather, communism becomes the precondition for the full flowering of human individuality. Consequently, an underlying assumption in Marx's work is that the socialist revolution will provide the material basis for overcoming all forms of oppression, including the specific forms suffered by groups such as women.

Liberal political theory celebrated the individual rationality that was seen to be necessary for middle-class economic success and the rise of capitalism. In response, socialist political ideologies criticized the economic system from the perspective of workers, including women. For Marxist feminists, much of the focus of this work has been on women's economic independence and well-being and the intersection of their lives as workers and their position in the family. Consequently, Marxist feminism has made major contributions to feminist theories of work and employment, the labour market, and domestic labour. Specifically, it has focused on work-related concerns, the relationship between the institution of the family and capitalism, the trivialization of women's domestic work, and the relegation of women to certain types of work. It has sought an understanding of the sexual division of labour as a class division of labour.

The problem of the 'private woman'

Liberal feminism is quite ambivalent about the role of women in the public society balanced against their role in the home. For example, while both Wollstonecraft and Mill opposed the divine right of husbands over their wives, their writing contains an underlying understanding that women will continue to choose to be wives and play the central role in the family. This ambivalence about women's role in the public sphere arises because of the public/private division in liberal political thought. The idea of the public and the private is intrinsically associated with liberalism. The division was formulated to answer the question of what the legitimate extent of governmental authority should be. State authority should not extend to any intervention in the freedom of individuals to run their own lives beyond preventing people from harming one another. The belief that the state has no role in the private lives of individuals was bolstered by a view of the home as a 'haven from the heartless world'.

Consequently, an underlying theme in liberal feminism is that politics takes place only in the public sphere. For example, Betty Friedan in *The Feminine Mystique* (1963) identified the growing frustration that women experienced when trapped in the privatized gender roles of the supposed suburban domestic bliss as a women's 'malaise'. Her solution was for women to demand inclusion in the public sphere, thereby achieving 'full person-hood' and making their lives more meaningful. This view was attenuated in Friedan's later work, *The Second Stage* (1981), in which she adopted a more welfare liberal position, demanding the restructuring of both public and private institutions to ensure real equality for women and men. However, liberal feminists have tended to place less emphasis than other feminist approaches on the politics of daily life in the private sphere and the politics of sexual power and privilege.

The Marxist approach to women's oppression makes an attempt to address the private/public division, with Friedrich Engels's work giving the clearest arguments regarding the position of women. In *The Origins of Family, Private Property and the State* (1972), he argued that women's oppression originated in the introduction of private property and the collapse of the communal household. The family thus became a private service in which the woman acted as the head servant. This transformation

mirrored the broader development of a system of private ownership and an ensuing class system. Under capitalism, women face two forms of oppression: within the
labour force and in the private home. When women enter the labour force, they become alienated in the same ways as their male counterparts. Outside the workforce,
their role is to support the productive work of the male members of their families,
physically reproduce labour, and act as a 'reserve force of labour' to be called on as
a threat to keep those in the labour force in line. The division between male and female, and the notion of the family as private, complemented and supported capitalism.
Consequently, Marxism does not define the private realm as entirely separate from the
realm of politics.

As a first step towards emancipation, women must enter the sphere of public
production. Economic independence will free women from the need to sell themselves into the servitude of marriage, give them de facto equality with their husbands
and other male workers, and help them develop the appropriate worker consciousness to make common cause with their male counterparts in the struggle against
capitalism. This emphasis on bringing women into the public productive workforce
(or making socialized domestic work a public enterprise) reflects an assumption
that the private is less central politically than the public economic realm. That is
because Marxism's focus on economic relations rejects the possibility that the relations might be based on other forms of privilege, such as patriarchy. Marxism holds
that once oppression and class division are eradicated in the public sphere, then
emancipation in the private sphere will follow. The assumption that the private
sphere is less central to the politics of emancipation, and the rejection of other
explanations for women's oppression in the private sphere, gives rise to concerns
about sex-blindness in Marxist theory. The 'woman question' in Marxism is a question about women as workers, not as women or feminists. Although an important
site of women's oppression, the private is considered less significant than, indeed
marginal to, the main struggle.

'The "woman question" has never been a "feminist question"' (Hartmann 1981, 3)

Second-wave Marxist feminists such as Juliet Mitchell (1974) and Heidi Hartmann
(1981, 1982) widened the Marxist concept of production and reproduction to respond to the apparent sex-blind nature of Marxism and its difficulty in theorizing
the oppression of the private sphere. Hartmann (1981, 2–3) argues that a more
progressive union is required for the unhappy marriage of Marxism and feminism:
'[B]oth Marxist analysis, particularly its historical and materialist method, and feminist analysis, especially the identification of patriarchy as a social and historical
structure, must be drawn upon if we are to understand the development of western
capitalist societies and [the] predicament of women within them.' She argues that
gender creates another material axis in the division of labour, one that is governed by
patriarchal relations, which cross the bourgeois/proletariat class boundary, creating an
alliance of men subordinating women.

Mitchell (1974, 1984) introduces an approach referred to as 'dual systems',
which takes the capitalist mode of production as its starting point and explores patriarchal structuring of sexuality through culture and socialization as an intersecting
and complementary oppression. In the public sphere, capitalism dominates the relations of production, while in the private sphere patriarchy dominates the relations of

reproduction. Four key structures are relevant to the condition of women: production, reproduction, sexuality, and socialization of children. Three of these structures—reproduction, socialization of children, and sexuality—cannot be reduced to economics. Therefore, Mitchell rejects the single-cause Marxist feminist analysis and replaces it with a combination of a materialist account of capitalism and a non-materialist account of patriarchy.

It's both capitalism and patriarchy: Socialist feminism

The attempt to integrate capitalism and patriarchy brings us to socialist feminist approaches. As Tong (1998, 94) argues, 'although it is possible to distinguish between Marxist and Socialist feminist thought, it is quite difficult to do so. . . . [T]he differences between these two schools of thought are more a matter of emphasis than substance'.[2] This matter of emphasis is significant. Whereas Marxist feminists argue that women need to recognize their shared long-term interests with working-class men and should struggle on those grounds rather than just as and for women, socialist feminists argue that there is a need for autonomous women's action to combat patriarchy. In other words, socialist feminists admit to the existence of other types of oppression and the need to fight all oppressions in coalitions. However, when it comes to patriarchy, women have to engage in action as women.

Socialist feminists are unconvinced by either the liberal lack of understanding of the material nature of women's oppression or the Marxist privileging of material economic production. Economic revolution is not enough, but neither is the liberal approach of giving women more rights, because the non-material features of women's oppression are buried so deeply in human psychology and culture. Both approaches are doomed to failure and, come the revolution, women will still be tending the home fires, raising kids, feeding the revolutionary forces, and servicing the male revolutionaries physically. It is not inevitable that ending class oppression will result in an end to gender oppression. The fact that it is men, not classes, who dominate and oppress women must be recognized. Consequently, socialist feminism engages much more fully with the concept of patriarchy and presents a critique not only of the public world but also of the private world.

For example, Allison Jaggar (1983) focuses on the concept of alienation because of sex rather than the alienation of class. For Marx, the worker is alienated from her labour by capitalist structures. Jaggar argues that women experience alienation in a different way because they are also alienated by patriarchal structures. She explores gender-specific forms of alienation, such as the alienation of women from their own sexuality, reproductive capabilities, and bodies in patriarchal systems. Iris Marion Young's (1981) critique of dual systems theory argues that the focus should be on capitalist patriarchy rather than patriarchal capitalism. Analysis does not require one theory to explain capitalism and a second to explain gender-biased patriarchy; all that is needed is a theory that explains gender-biased capitalist patriarchy. Patriarchy is not a separate system of oppression within capitalism; rather, the two are intertwined. The division of labour, as opposed to class structure, constituted in capitalist patriarchy (or feudal patriarchy) dictates the position of women and the form of their subordination: the marginalization of women in the private sphere and as a secondary or reserve labour force.

Early Socialist Feminism

Generally, socialist feminism is recognized as a contemporary form of feminist theory and part of the second wave, emerging in the 1970s as a response to the perceived inadequacies of liberal, Marxist, and radical feminism. However, the same ideas and understandings can be found in some of the socialist and women's movements of the nineteenth and early twentieth centuries. The utopian socialists of the nineteenth century, such as Charles Fourier and Henri de Saint-Simon in France and the Owenites in Britain, experimented with communities that included alternative gender relations. Women's emancipation was linked to the idea of progressive social reform and historical change.

In the mid-nineteenth century, women such as Desirée Gay, Suzanne Voilquin, and Jeanne Deroin who were behind the French feminist journals *Voix des Femmes* and *La Politique des Femmes* of the 1830s and 1840s made connections between women's emancipation and cooperative socialism. In their view, these involved a struggle against the power of men in the family as well as both employers and male workers in production. In Britain, women were closely involved in the Chartist movement, which campaigned for universal male suffrage and in some instances for universal suffrage. According to Rowbotham (1992), many Chartist women had a strong sense of their rights as working-class women.

In the United States of the early twentieth century, the self-taught former factory worker and anarchist feminist Emma Goldman (1911/1969) argued that the oppression of women was bound up with sexuality and the lack of control women had over reproduction and their own bodies. A woman's right to control her own body was best defended by access to birth control and free motherhood. Goldman's anarchism could be characterized as a form of anarcho-syndicalism in which one's self-development is connected to developing a community of mutual sharing, and the liberation of women is intrinsic to this development. Her speeches on women's sexual emancipation, rebellion, and anarchism made her one of the best known, and possibly loved, anarchist agitators and speakers of her time (and even today); unfortunately, they also attracted the attention and ire of the US government, which deported her to Russia in 1919.

Throughout the twentieth century, the radical socialist critique inspired not only labour activists but also novelists such as Doris Lessing, theorists such as Simone de Beauvoir, and activist organizers and journalists such as Jessica Mitford. Many of the feminists at the forefront of the second wave when it emerged—even liberal feminists such as Betty Friedan—had their roots and training in the communist, labour, and leftist movements of the early twentieth century. Consequently, socialist feminism of the 1970s can be seen as the daughter of these earlier socialist and anarchist feminists as well as a response to liberal, Marxist, and radical feminism. The struggle was not just about ensuring equal rights or about ending legal oppression, class oppression, or sexual oppression, but all of these things and more.

Radical feminism: 'It's all about sex, baby'

As Roberta Hamilton (1996, 18) points out, second-wave feminism explored the way liberation required transformation of both the public and private spheres. However, these explorations 'were soon divided along political and theoretical lines into those calling themselves socialist feminists and those calling themselves radical feminists'. Both groups were fundamentally concerned with the issue of sexual oppression. However, while socialist feminism defined sexual oppression as confounded by issues of race and class, for radical feminism, sexual oppression was the most fundamental and the most universal oppression: it was all about patriarchy and sex.

In the public imagination, feminism is generally associated with the radical thought and politics of feminists of the 1970s and 1980s. Even those who consider themselves Marxist or socialist feminists acknowledge that it was the radical feminists who gave second-wave feminism of the late 1960s and 1970s its impetus and anger. The anger stemmed from experience in the 'liberation' movements of the 1960s—the new left, civil rights, student, and peace movements—when women found that they continued to be treated as second-class sex objects and girlfriends, their work and views unrecognized or met with male laughter and derision (Evans 1979). If women's oppression persisted in seemingly politically progressive movements, there had to be something much more fundamental in society that explained and maintained women's subordination. Radical feminists identified it as patriarchy.

Historically, culturally, and psychologically, theories of patriarchy argue that relations of dominance and subordination between the sexes are embedded in society. Sexual oppression, not class or formal legal subordination, is the fundamental oppression. Radical feminism is a theory and movement characterized by the insistence that sex is the fundamental division in society, a division to which all other differences, such as class, race, age, and ability are secondary. While the explanations for male dominance vary, the greatest weight is given to men's physical ability to control women. 'Sexism' is reflected in family arrangements, in gender stereotyping, and most perniciously, in the violence perpetuated against women in the form of pornography, wife and child abuse, and rape.

'The personal is political': Patriarchy and the private

The politics of radical feminism demonstrated the extent of violence against women in the home, the workplace, and the community. It was radical feminists who established the first rape crisis centres, women's shelters, and 'reclaim the night' marches. They were vociferous critics of pornography and the depiction of violence against women and children. Pornography was the theory, rape was the practice, claimed Robin Morgan (1980). They fought for women's control of sexuality and reproductive capabilities under the slogan 'our bodies ourselves'. In focusing on the aspects of women's lives that had been deemed to be part of the private sphere, they demonstrated that the 'personal was political' and how much of the activity that perpetuates women's oppression takes place within the home, a place protected from scrutiny by an ideology of privacy that maintains the invisibility of women's domestic labour and hides the abuse of women. Thus, there is a common thread in radical feminist thought: the primacy of sexual oppression in maintaining male dominance and patriarchy through the use of physical violence to control women's sexuality and reproduction. Beyond that, a broad range of views can be found in radical feminist thought.

Tong (1998) outlines three major debates between those she labels 'radical-libertarian' feminists and those she terms 'radical-cultural' feminists. First, there are debates over the need for a commitment to political lesbianism, which calls for women to separate themselves from the source of their oppression, namely sexual relations with men.

Second, there are disagreements over the nature of sex difference and whether socially structured genders can be overcome by a form of androgyny or by an essentially pro-women position that celebrates female sexuality and maternal abilities. Third, there are strategic arguments regarding the creation of a woman culture based on a separate sexuality and a pro-women orientation.

Essentialism versus social construction: Cultural radicalism and libertarian radicalism

In order to unpack the differences between libertarian and cultural-radical feminists, it is useful to look at the distinction between the biologically determined essential woman and the socially constructed gendered woman. The more libertarian radical feminists, not surprisingly, place more emphasis on sexual freedom, tending to focus on how patriarchy has constructed sexual and reproductive roles in a way that limits and oppresses women. Patriarchal society uses the physical facts, such as (1) men are generally bigger and stronger than women, and (2) it is women who give birth, as a basis for constructing the idea of the 'masculine' and the 'feminine'. Women's oppression is based on how patriarchy organizes and exaggerates these physical differences in terms of sexual and reproductive roles. The norms of patriarchal society control sexuality in a way that represses sexual desire, stigmatizes sexual minorities, disallows female pleasure and satisfaction, and takes the liberatory potential (and one assumes the fun) out of engaging in physical sexual activities. One way this is done is by associating physical sex with the male pleasure required to meet the reproductive imperative. Women are required to be passive, receptive, and vulnerable sex objects that men dominate, possess, and penetrate in order to keep the wheels of human procreation turning.

Consequently, women need to be liberated from their traditional sexual and reproductive roles. For example, Shulamith Firestone (1971) argues that women will never be entirely equal to men until they relinquish their childbearing function. That is, they need to be freed from their gender roles even at the level of biological reproduction. Kate Millett (1970) also argues that women need to be free to engage in any form of sex that they find pleasurable and satisfying. Firestone (1971) therefore calls for women to seize control of reproduction, including human fertility that would allow, for example, the creation of test-tube babies outside the womb. This view holds that only with the end of women's most radical difference from men can we envision the creation of a 'feminist revolution'. It would result in liberation from patriarchal structures and the creation of androgynous cultures unlimited by institutionalized and defined sex or reproductive roles. Hence, radical-libertarian feminism takes an optimistic view of all forms of sexual behaviour, an ambivalent if not forgiving position on pornography, and a view of natural reproduction as one of the causes (or, according to Firestone, the main feature) of women's oppression.

In contrast, Alcoff (1986, 298) argues, 'cultural feminism is the ideology of a female nature or female essence re-appropriated by feminists themselves in an effort to revalidate undervalued female attributes.' In exploring the ways in which patriarchy constructs women, this approach came to view patriarchy as removing or alienating women from their *female* nature by constructing and prescribing an unauthentic *feminine* nature. Why? Because the ability of women to give birth, create, and nurture life gives them power that men need to control. Thus, heterosexuality and romantic heterosexual love were created as institutions to enforce women's total emotional, erotic loyalty and subservience to men (Rich, 1997). Hence, radical-cultural feminism tends to take a pessimistic view of heterosexual sex, denounces any sexual practice that encourages male sexual violence, including pornography, and sees natural reproduction as a source of women's power and being.

The goal of radical-cultural feminism is to repossess the power and sense of true or essential womanhood in a gynocentric (women-centred) world. This would entail reclaiming control over women's reproduction and sexuality by creating new gynocentric values around which a women's society could be organized. Many of these values derive inspiration from women's spiritual or mystical experiences of their connection with non-human nature or with other women, with particular emphasis on the ability to give life (Daly 1979). Radical-cultural feminists distinguish between a feminine culture that is subordinated under patriarchy and *womanculture*, which is a culture of resistance consciously created by feminists. It is a political project intended to reclaim the identity of woman and to create *womanspace*, spaces built by women for women where they can connect and celebrate womanhood. One example is the women-only peace camp at Greenham Common in Great Britain, developed during the 1980s and 1990s to protest against nuclear weapons (Roseneil 1995). Women's experience and womanculture in personal life is to provide the inspiration and basis for a new vision of politics.

Sisterhood is powerful: Separation and political lesbianism

Radical-cultural feminism overlaps with the separatist thread found in radical feminism. If patriarchy is supported by compulsory heterosexuality that ensures women's sexual, economic, social, and psychological dependence, then heterosexuality is a form of cooptation. As Rita Mae Brown (2000, 398) observes, heterosexuality separates women from one another and ensures women's enslavement to men: 'You cannot build a women's movement if you don't commit yourselves to women, totally. Heterosexual women are committed to men.' To challenge this institution, women must withdraw and join other women in a form of 'political lesbianism'. By this expression, Adrienne Rich (1997, 322) means that the definition of lesbian must be expanded from a particular sexual experience to encompass 'the bonding against male tyranny, the giving and receiving of practical and political support . . . '. Lesbianism becomes an expression of solidarity based on 'more forms of primary intensity between and among women'. While sisterhood is powerful in this approach, therefore, it is also divisive as radical feminists dispute whether women's sexual conduct and choice of sex partner define them as a feminist or not.

Lesbian Feminism and the Backlash

Arguments regarding political lesbianism are often presented in very simplified forms that play well with the backlash definition of all feminism as male-bashing and all feminists as lesbians. However, political lesbianism is more complex and is itself a source of disagreement. Charlotte Bunch (1975) sees feminism as centred in lesbianism, in that lesbianism offers a critique of and challenge to the institutionalized heterosexuality that is the foundation of patriarchy. The rejection of given sex roles that results from expanding them to include lesbianism illustrates how the norms of heterosexuality are masculine and limit woman-centred understandings.

More radical lesbian feminists such as Adrienne Rich view lesbian feminism as the only pure feminism because it is essentially woman-centred. Political lesbianism, even as a practice of celibacy, illustrates the way the personal is political because one's private sexual preference becomes a form of prefiguring a womanculture and womanspace.

Within society, lesbians are doubly oppressed because of their gender and sexuality. The taboo surrounding lesbianism limits women's autonomy to determine their sexuality, making them available only for patriarchal heterosexual relationships. Today, the terms 'lesbian' and 'lesbian-feminist' are often used as an insult to separate and frighten women from making autonomous and uncoerced choices regarding sex. It may well be a weakness of the women's movement that it has not been as vociferous in condemning lesbian-bashing as it has been in pointing out that not all feminists are lesbians. This raises some interesting questions: Why does the accusation of lesbianism frighten women? Why does the association of lesbianism and feminism make some women uncomfortable with the term 'feminist'? Can a shared experience between lesbian and heterosexual feminists be found to build a common understanding of patriarchy and sexuality? Could radical lesbian feminists have a point regarding the compromised relationship between heterosexual women and men?

Motherhood issues: The essence of a woman

Locating women's power in their reproductive capabilities also speaks directly to issues regarding the nature of women. As Tong (1998, 76) points out, radical-cultural feminists 'claimed women's oppression was caused not by female biology in and of itself but rather by men's jealousy of women's reproductive abilities and subsequent desire to seize control of female biology'. To renounce natural reproduction in the way that Firestone suggests is to renounce that which makes women women. That women give birth and nurture gives them a different perspective on the world. The goal of creating womanculture is to select the best aspects of the female while rejecting the values and concepts that tend to favour the dominant patriarchal culture. As Sara Ruddick (1980, 355–9) argues, there is a value in maternal thinking—not its inauthentic fatalistic manifestation that trains daughters for powerlessness and sons for war and that encourages cheery denial and subordination—but in its transformative capacity, for example, to train 'children for strength and moral sensitivity'. From maternal practices emerge 'distinctive ways of conceptualizing, ordering, and valuing', and it is up to mothers to 'insist upon the inclusion of their values and experiences in the public world'. Ruddick's 'maternal thinking' is similar to Gilligan's observations that the capacity, if not the imperative, to consider others as well as the self and to understand the self's connectedness to other selves is associated with the practice of mothering and defines a woman's 'different voice'.

The question is whether this 'different voice' is created from the experience of mothering or from women's essential difference from men in terms of the ability to give birth and produce sustenance for a child. As Mary O'Brien (1989, 23) points out, birth is singularly a woman's act with a historical unity and continuity that has changed only twice, with its appropriation by patriarchy (to ensure paternity) and with the challenge presented by the availability of contraception. A second question is whether women's 'maternal thinking' is not only different from the prevailing instrumental-rationalist forms of patriarchal discourse intended to dominate but also superior to them. Some work seems to suggest that a women's perspective is more connected and egalitarian, peaceful as opposed to warlike, and oriented to the natural rather than to the technological—orientations evoked by feminists involved in the women-only peace camps and protests of the 1980s and 1990s and in ecofeminism. A further significant consideration is that while some women give birth and nurture, some choose not to or are unable to do so.

Ecofeminism

Ecofeminism represents a diversity of these positions—liberal feminist, cultural feminist, and socialist feminist—although the ideas associated with cultural feminism are most closely linked with ecofeminism. It celebrates the relationship between woman and nature through the revival of ancient rituals centred on goddess worship, the moon, animals, and the female reproductive system (Merchant 1992). Women's biology and nature are celebrated as sources of female power to resist male technology (Merchant 1992). Maria Mies and Vandana Shiva (1997, 498, 500) observe that there is a connection between patriarchy and the violence against women, other people, and nature. Women understand this connection because 'we have a deep and particular understanding of this both through our natures and our experience as women'. Women's liberation can only be achieved as part of a larger struggle for the preservation of life on this planet.

Conclusion: From Sameness to Difference, from Ideas to the Body

While modernity is a chronological designation, it also describes a 'state of mind . . . . a "form of life" rather than a "period of history"' (Jervis 1998, 1). In the 'modern' period, the ideas of the Enlightenment replaced understandings of the world based on religious knowledge and associated with fixed hierarchies of the community, substituting a belief based on science, reason, and the individual. In the Enlightenment view, the individual is the starting point for all knowledge and action, and it cannot be subjected to a higher authority than the individual's ability to reason. Rationality is universal to all human beings; it separates us from the animals. The natural and social condition of human beings can be improved by the application of scientific reason based on material facts and experimentation. Today, our understanding of our worl d often reflects these principles. For example, it seems second nature to us to believe that human beings are essentially equal, that scientific reason gives us the objective truth about our world, and that legitimate power is based on secular rational authority and our consent to that authority.

Feminism is of modern origin. The idea of a universal human rationality opened the door for women to demand recognition as equal to men. While the Enlightenment did not automatically result in an end to oppression (women were not necessarily considered part of the rational and free world of human beings), rationalist principles provided the basis and the language for a challenge to women's oppression. One of the interesting features of the development of feminist thinking in this period is how the contending interpretations of the interconnections of biology, gender, the material conditions of women, and their consciousness of oppression progress from a belief in the shared ideal of the rational woman and man to a celebration of women's difference centred in the female body itself.

Liberal political theory celebrated the individual rationality that was necessary for middle-class economic success and the rise of capitalism. It was about *ideas*. Liberal feminist claims to a shared rationality between men and women placed women on the political, legal, and civic map. To deny the similarity of men and women was to oppress women.

However, as other women viewed their experiences, many came to see their oppression as more than a denial of public rights and access to education. Marxist and socialist women criticized the economic system from the perspective of work and claimed the problem lay not with ideas but with the material nature of people's existence. For Marxists, the focus was on capitalist structures, while for socialist feminists the approach was more ambivalent, attempting to illuminate the relationship between capitalism and patriarchy. The general understanding was that the division of labour in both capitalism and patriarchy dictated the position of women, the forms of their subordination, and their marginalization in the private sphere. That is, there was something different in the material existence of women compared to that of men.

Radical feminists of the second wave adapted that understanding of the differences in existence between men and women, but they determined that the root of this difference was physical rather than based on social position. The personal became political because the female body was intrinsic to patriarchy. Women's oppression occurred because the only way men could control women's power—that is, their ability to reproduce and sustain life through nurture—was through physical domination. Hence, patriarchy was understood as a timeless, and indeed the first, form of domination. Rather than feminist politics being about the pursuit of universal ideas and shared citizenship, it was now about bodily difference and the celebration of the natural power that emerged from that body. Adrienne Rich (1976, 32) writes:

> The feminist vision has recoiled from human biology. . . . . It will, I believe, come to view our physicality as a resource rather than a destiny. In order to live a fully human life we require not only control of our bodies (though control is a prerequisite); we must touch the unity and resonance of our physicality, our bond with the natural order, the corporeal ground of our intelligence.

This celebration of the essential difference of women's bodies was problematic, however, as not all women are the same in their difference. As Audre Lorde (1983, 96) wrote in response to Mary Daly's celebration of womanhood, that celebration is based on an 'assumption that the herstory and myth of white women is the legitimate and sole herstory'. It also raised tricky and uncomfortable issues around whether women were defined by their bodily essence or by socialization. At the end of the second wave and in the last few decades of the twentieth century a third wave of feminism emerged and with it new philosophical approaches that would address questions not only as to what gave rise to women's oppression but also the very idea of what a woman is. It is to these philosophical approaches that we turn our attention in the next chapter.

Questions for Critical Thought

1. How do the different feminist understandings of the interconnection between material and ideal realities, biology and consciousness, explain gender and gender norms?
2. Can women's emancipation be based on an 'ethic of care' and a women's nature, or is it a feminist myth? What are the strategic consequences of a case for emancipation based on the assumption that women are different from men?
3. If historically the one thing all women have had in common is that they are women, how can an understanding of women's oppression not be based fundamentally on the female body?

CHAPTER 3

Contemporary Debates in Feminist Theory

As the previous chapter explains, the effect of radical feminism on contemporary feminism has been profound. In particular, radical feminism observed that science, or the modern epistemological understanding of the 'objective truth', was inherently vested in the interests of patriarchal society. This understanding was expanded to explore new forms of knowledge that recognized lived experience and did not prioritize one single 'objective truth' (Collins 1990). 'Vive la difference', the end point of radical-cultural feminism, is a celebration of female difference from the male. It is a unified and coherent understanding of woman that derives its commonality from the shared experience of physical biology.

What is the essential woman? The *Oxford English Dictionary* (OED 1985, 295) defines 'essential' as 'constituting, or forming part of the essence of anything; belonging to a thing by virtue of its essence'. An essence is necessarily implied in and indispensable to the composition of something. The essential qualities attributed to women are generally biological: women are defined by their sex, their biological difference from men. Such claims are problematic for feminist theory because biological reductionism often underlies anti-feminist attempts to rationalize women's subordination. It also does not fit well with the notion of the 'gendered' or socially constructed woman that is the hallmark of feminism's second wave. Women are not born but are made; they are fashioned in subordination and opposition to men by the social norms that set out expectations and prescriptions for what it means to be female. Consequently, rather than focusing on the historical divisions between liberal, socialist and radical feminism, much of the current debate in feminist theory centres on what is a woman and what defines womanhood, in other words, debates regarding feminist epistemology. According to Dietz (2003, 402), 'notwithstanding the constructivist turn and the proliferation of "gender studies", feminist theories today regularly, and often radically, disagree over the practical-normative significance of maintaining a conception of gender as, on the one hand, a binary configuration of masculine/feminine or male/female rooted in the idea of gender or sexual difference or, on the other hand, as a process or an effect of discourse that is constantly in production and therefore changeable and fluid'.

In addition, feminist epistemology must address the fact that women are not solely gendered. While a woman's life experiences will be defined on the basis of her gender, they are also defined by her position within race, class, ethnic, and colonial structures, etc.—oppression does not occur solely on the basis of gender. While it is worthwhile recognizing that our conception of 'womanhood' is socially constructed, not to recognize the diversity that exists within that category and the importance of race, class, ethnicity, sexual orientation, disability, and other forms of difference in the construction of one's oppression is itself oppressive.

This has significance for the action undertaken by women: do they claim the identity of 'woman' as a concrete reality shared by all women or reject it as a socially constructed subordinate within patriarchy? In what name and on whose behalf do women act? The result is a tension (possibly an irresolvable one) regarding the nature of 'womanhood'.

Dietz (2003) identifies three divergent oppositional perspectives on the conception of women: difference feminism, diversity feminism, and deconstruction feminism. In this chapter, we use this framework to explore the debates that emerged in feminist theory at the end of the second wave and explore the 'identity crisis' (Alcoff 1986 Dietz 2003) that was to emerge around the idea of what women are and for whom feminism speaks.

Difference Feminism

Fundamentally, difference feminism is based on a form of dualism, the assumption that the two sexes differ in significant ways and that the unique features of women are worthwhile and to be celebrated. According to Dietz (2003, 404) these approaches attempt 'to affirm a positive account of the female side of the gender binary or the female aspect of sexual difference. . . . [They] appeal, though with different emphases, to the female body, the maternal, or woman's universal oppression as unique means of access to ways of knowing the world or speaking/being within the patriarchal system'. The difference between approaches generally lies in how women are positioned: standpoint approaches focus on the material and psychological construction of women within and outside patriarchal social structures, while French post-structural feminism focuses on the 'psychical and symbolic' construction of women within and outside patriarchal discursive structures.

Standpoint Approaches

Presenting a critique to the dominant conventional epistemologies in social science and the policies derived from that science, standpoint theory privileges women's knowledge and experience. The writings of Carol Gilligan (1980, 1982), Mary Daly (1979), and Catherine MacKinnon (1983) are important particularly because of their re-examination of the position of women in the social sciences. Gilligan's reconceptualization of women's moral perspectives presented a critique of the role given to women within a philosophical and psychological tradition that made the experience of men the measure of all human experience. Mary Daly's *Gyn/Ecology* (1979) and *Wickedary* (1987) emphasized the creation of new words, terminology, and syntax for women to support a specifically women's based knowledge. Similarly, Catherine MacKinnon (1983, 255) emphasized consciousness-raising:

> As Marxist method is dialectical materialism, feminist method is consciousness raising: the collective reconstitution of the meaning of women's social

experience, as women live through it. . . . To the extent that materialism is scientific it posits and refers to a reality outside thought which it considers to have an objective [content]. . . . Consciousness raising by contrast inquires into intrinsically social situation, into that mixture of thought and materiality which is women's sexuality in the most generic sense (cited in Arneil, 1999, 103).

These approaches celebrate women's difference and argue that women's experiences and ways of knowing open up an understanding of the world and a knowledge previously hidden or unaccounted for in patriarchal ways of seeing. The production of feminist knowledge goes beyond just enunciating women's experiences within social science research. For Sandra Harding and other theorists such as Jane Flax (1990), Nancy Hartsock (1997) and Dorothy Smith (1987), the purpose of standpoint theory was to challenge the dominance of 'the Enlightenment vision captured by empiricism' (Harding 1989, 23) by providing a new approach to science and a fuller, more correct theory of labour and human activity. It is intended as a project of empowerment and social struggle to 'turn disadvantaged social position into powerful intellectual and political resources' (Harding and Norberg, 2005).

Starting from the Marxist argument that consciousness is derived from one's position in the structures of labour, standpoint theorists focus on the reproductive and emotional labour women undertake within patriarchal structures'. Women are to the proletariat as men are to the bourgeoisie and as patriarchy is to capitalism. Women's labour includes the 'mental, manual and emotional labor in women's work which provides women with a potentially more comprehensive understanding of nature and social life' (Harding 1989, 33). This understanding is unavailable in patriarchal science and life, because '[m]en's characteristic social experience, like that of the bourgeoisie, hides . . . the politically imposed nature of the social relations they see as natural' (Harding 1989, 25). As a consequence, value-free or unmediated knowledge is unachievable because patriarchy does not provide the intellectual and political resources to identify the oppressive features of its own beliefs and practices.

This is empowering and revolutionary because it recognizes and legitimates the subjugated knowledges of women (Harding 1989), and while the dominant paradigm of Enlightenment empiricism produces distorted and incomplete views of reality, the standpoints of the oppressed provide more complex, comprehensive, and correct understandings of the world. It is the preferred form of inquiry because, as Arneil (1999, 104) points out, 'the experience and perspective of woman as the excluded and exploited other is judged to be more inclusive and critically coherent than that of the masculine group'.

It is understood that other oppressions such as class and race also structure the individual's understanding of reality and produce different knowledge claims, but the privileged position of women tends to be maintained and thus undermines standpoint positions. Standpoint theory continues to posit the existence of a coherent feminist knowledge and, as such, a unified 'truth'. Harding (1989, 18–19) does speak for embracing instability in analytical categories and using 'these instabilities as a resource for our practice . . . [which] often has advanced understanding more effectively than restabilizations'. However, Mary Hawksworth (1989, 331) disagrees, arguing that the women's standpoint must be privileged if the 'perspective that emerges from women's oppression constitutes the core of a "successor science" that can replace the truncated projects of masculinist science'. As a result, in putting forward an approach to feminist theory and politics that privileges and celebrates women's ways of knowing based on their lived experiences and their bodies, standpoint theory appears to have a strong essentialist and possibly relativistic underpinning to its epistemology.

French Post-Structuralist Feminism

The ideas of female difference espoused by radical-cultural feminists and standpoint theorists can be seen in French post-structuralist feminism in which 'difference' is emphasized to question the concept of universal norms, including the category of woman. According to Dietz (2003, 406), while French feminism's view of sexual identity as a linguistically or discursively mediated phenomenon is shared by deconstruction feminism (to be discussed later), 'its commitment to the concept of irreducible sexual difference warrants its inclusion under the category of difference feminism'.

The work of French post-structuralist feminist theorists such as Julia Kristeva and Luce Irigaray grows out of the thinking of Simone de Beauvoir, focusing on women as the 'other'; the deconstruction project of Jacques Derrida, challenging the assumptions of identity and autonomy; and the post-structuralist psychology of Jacques Lacan, reinterpreting Freudian theory (Tong 1998, 194). They argue that because our understanding of reality is mediated by our systems of knowledge, in particular the words we give to things, our ways of knowing are not neutral but are constructed through a system of differences—'not this, therefore that'. Therefore, like standpoint theorists, Kristeva and Irigaray start from the specific position of the woman as the 'other' and the difference of women's bodies as central:

> . . . the female is determined socially, linguistically, and biologically by patriarchy, through entrance into the symbolic order and recognition of the primacy of the phallus. Thus female subjectivity is occasioned by the lack of the biological penis which gives her entry to the law of the father represented by the symbolic phallus. Woman is therefore positioned oppositionally within discourse, defined by her difference (Gamble 2001, 324).

Hence, women are the sex 'which is not one' (Irigaray 1985). Women's difference excludes them from the symbolic order, which is constructed by patriarchy. Both interpret the female body in its difference to the male, the lack of a penis, and the presence of a void.

According to Kristeva, this void or nothingness is fruitful (fecund) with possibilities because it is undefined, provisional, plural, diverse, and outside the norm. She argues that in the negative world of difference, feminine identity exists in a pre-regulative and anarchic world outside the symbolic order, which she terms the semiotic (Gamble 2001, 252). This allows the concept of the feminine to be fluid, amorphous, and provisional. She argues that the category of woman does not exist; 'she is in the process of becoming' (Tong 1998, 206). For example, think of the term 'mankind': it is intended to include all men and women, but it cannot really include women because they are not men; rather, they are 'unmen'. Therefore, women are outside the 'norm'; they are excluded outsiders. This may not be such a bad thing because if norms no longer apply to you, you can be anything you want—except a man. However, while the concept of woman has no essential meaning, it does have political meaning—it is politically useful. Kristeva writes:

> The belief that 'one is a woman' is almost as absurd and obscurantist as the belief that 'one is a man'. I say 'almost' because there are still many goals which woman can achieve: freedom of abortion and contraception, daycare centres for children, equality on the job, etc. Therefore, we must use 'we are women' as an advertisement or slogan for our demands. (cited in Tong 1998, 206)

For Kristeva, while the concept of 'woman' may be provisional, the category or label can be used in ways expedient to women's struggles and defined depending on experiences with other categories such as race, sexuality, age, socio-economic status, and so on.

Like Kristeva (1986), Irigaray (1985) focuses on women's difference and the links between language and sexuality, but she introduces a more essentialist vision, which Andemahr, Lovell, and Wolkowitz (2000, 81) refer to as 'corporeal feminism'. She goes further in valorizing female difference, particularly the 'radical otherness' of women's sexuality. She argues that historically, women have been forced to repress their sexuality within a model of masculine femininity. Women need to liberate themselves by finding and re-appropriating 'the feminine feminine'. This feminine feminine is plural, neither constrained nor defined by the 'scientific objectivity' of the masculine voice or the singular character of masculine sex. If this sexual difference were recognized, new horizons of plural and subjective knowledge would be possible—knowledge and understanding would be liberated (Arneil 1999, 196). In this way, the female body becomes a site of resistance to patriarchy. Tong (1998, 195) explains,

> The condition of otherness enables women to stand back and criticize the norms, values and practices that the dominant culture (patriarchy) seeks to impose on everyone, including those who live on its periphery.

What is common to both Kristeva and Irigaray is that they take the female body as their starting point; both 'tenaciously hold to sexual difference as a primary critical-analytical concept and a fundamental ontology of human existence' (Dietz 2003, 406). From this position they theorize how it has been produced and made meaningful in a subordinate way by language. Think of the concept of 'woman' not as a physical body but as a body of work, a body of culture, a body of text. The physical body is always present, but it is written on, interpreted, and represented by patriarchal society—and by women themselves. The body embodies the concept of woman. Thus, the concepts of difference and embodiment open up the possibility of plural subjectivities.

Taking the Risk of Essentialism

There are a number of similarities between standpoint theory and French post-structuralism, particularly the idea that women's 'outsider' or 'oppressed' position in patriarchy not only enables them to criticize the dominant culture, but also highlights their difference. Both approaches rest firmly on a dual perspective of the female body in difference and opposition to that of the male. However, in their celebration of women's difference, both remain committed to a universal, if not essential, conception of 'woman'. How can this be essentialist and socially constructed at the same time? As Diana Fuss (1989, 18) argues, the post-structuralist feminists take the 'risk of essentialism', and in doing so they point out the socially constructed nature of essentialism itself. On the one hand, constructionism cannot avoid essentialism in examining the production and organization of differences because there is continued reference to a common *a priori* category such as man/woman. On the other hand, essentialism has no essence in that 'essence *as* irreducible has been *constructed* to be irreducible'. It is 'a *sign*, and as such historically contingent and constantly subject to change and redefinition' (Fuss 1989, 18, emphasis in the original). In this view, essentialism has no one essence and is changeable in its forms. It cannot be avoided, but it is no longer a problem. The debate is repositioned; it is not about essentialism or social constructionism but about how and where various essentialisms can be used strategically. What categories are expedient for political action, resistance, or cultural action? This echoes Kristeva's view that while it may be provisional it can still be politically useful.

Dietz has problems with this, arguing that both approaches end with a coherent account of gender identity rooted in the difference between two sexes. Both approaches seek 'not to challenge the reality of this dyadic formulation or deny its logic [but] rather to explore its social, moral and political meaning and how it structures power'. Politically, even though diversity within women might be recognized, in privileging and celebrating the difference of women to men the assumption is that those differences will be overcome in the creation of a unified gender consciousness. Therefore, these approaches continue to be open to universalizing a category of women, and taking the risk of essentialism does not appear to pay off.

Identity Politics: The Politics of 'Who I Am and Who I Become'

Identity or diversity feminism is significant because it demands the rejection of a universal category of women and recognition of the diversity among women and their experiences. While female difference represented resistance to patriarchy and male privilege, it also represented a universal notion of the female. Women are defined not only by their gender but also by their race, ethnic grouping, class, ability, and sexuality. Diversity or identity feminism introduced the idea of plurality, heterogeneity, and multiplicity in theorizing about women. It emphasized the understanding that women are historically situated in unique relationships defined socio-culturally by ethnicity, religion, sexuality, class, colour, etc. In making claims to a number of often overlapping identities and differences among women, identity politics resists not only male privilege but also the privileging of the experience of white middle-class women.

Black feminists respond to radical feminism

At the end of the 1970s, black lesbian feminist Audre Lorde put this concern in writing in an open letter to Mary Daly:

> Mary, I ask that you be aware of how this serves the destructive forces of racism and separation between women—the assumption that the herstory

and myth of white women is the legitimate and sole herstory and myth of all women to call upon for power and background, and that non-white women and our herstories are noteworthy only as decoration, or examples of female victimization. I ask that you be aware of the effect that this dismissal has upon the community of black women, and how it devalues your own words (Lorde 1983, 96).

Lorde's message was that white women, in focusing on their oppression in patriarchal structures, were blind to the 'built-in privilege' of their whiteness. It was convenient to define women in terms of their own experience, leaving black and poor women as the 'other', because to conceive of difference within the category of woman was to run the risk of weakening the women's project of dismantling patriarchy. Black and minority feminists (for example, Davis 1981, 1989; hooks 1986) point out that it is possible to oppress people by denying or ignoring difference as well as by denying sameness.

Minority women face different limitations, as well as greater limitations, because of society's reaction to 'difference'. The history of slavery, colonial conquest, and other forms of oppression, such as sexual prejudice, has created a range of 'others' seen as different from white middle-class women. Stating that all women are the same, for example, ignores the enormous power differential in predominantly white societies between visible minority and white women or between rich and poor women. As bell hooks (1994) observes, the assumption that resisting patriarchal domination, rather than resisting racism and other forms of domination, is the true form of feminist politics, obscures the reality that women can and do participate in domination, as both perpetrators and victims.

In privileging the feminist cause over battling other forms of oppression, white feminists could not see the urgency for black women and other racially marginalized women to make alliances with the oppressed men of their own racial or ethnic groups and battle forms of oppression that for many of them were more acute (hooks 1981, 1989). Minority women thus called for a corrective in the movement, a broadening of the understanding of feminism, oppression, and equality, and a more inclusive understanding of the feminist project. In hooks's (1989, 2000) view, it is necessary to develop an inclusive process of bonding and dialogue that recognizes that patriarchal domination shares an ideological foundation with racism and other forms of group oppression. Like socialist feminists, hooks argues that all of these systems need to be eradicated. In recognizing the interconnectedness of sex, race, and class, she highlights the diversity of experience.

The idea of inclusion, recognition, and dialogue within diversity is thematic. The celebration of diversity is also a route to liberation in that it creates alternative ways of thinking, seeing, and knowing the world. Rather than seeing the dualistic world of male/female and subject/other, which Dietz (2003) argues standpoint and French poststructuralists could not overcome, the vision is of inclusivity and cross-pollination that could create consciousnesses that would break down the subject/object duality by living on and straddling 'borderlands'. Anzaldua (1990, 379) writes, 'the answer to the problem between the white race and coloured, between males and females, lies in healing the split that originates in the very foundation of our lives, our culture, our languages, our thoughts. A massive uprooting of dualistic thinking in the individual and collective consciousness.' In this vision of knowledge, each group speaks in a dialogue from its own standpoint, which is neither privileged nor marginalized, neither centred nor decentred. Through this, 'all people can learn to center in another experience, validate, and judge it by its own standards without need of comparison or need to adopt that framework as their own' (Elsa Barkley Brown, cited in Collins 1990, 236). Each group becomes better able to consider and understand the other standpoint: 'partiality and not universality is the condition of being heard' (ibid.).

Such an identity politics is empowering because through identity, oppression is identified and resistance to it is staged. It is liberatory in that identity is a political point of departure that enriches visions of change and joint struggles against oppression (Lorde 1984).

Post-colonial feminism: The voice of the subaltern

As a body of thought and writing, post-colonial feminism has much in common with the writing of black, Hispanic, and minority American feminism. However, the two emerged separately: black American feminism arose as a response to white middle-class radical feminism, while post-colonial feminism emerged out of French post-structuralism. Post-colonial feminism examines the multiple marginality and subordination of Third World women, oppressed not only by colonial Western imperialism but also by patriarchal structures of both the West and their own cultures and by Western feminism. In exploring this multi-dimensional and multi-levelled oppression, post-colonial feminism points to and illustrates the ambiguities and ambivalence of both identity and knowing an identity. As Gayatri Spivak (1988, 136) argues, 'in order to learn enough about Third World women and to develop a different readership, the immense heterogeneity of the field must be appreciated, the First World Feminist must learn to stop feeling privileged as a woman'. The approach must be heterogeneous because there is no one subaltern[1] identity or consciousness. She calls for recognition of a heterogeneous conception of women's experience and the relocating of non-Western discourses into new spaces where heterogeneity is the norm and a 'new worlding of the world' is created. Even post-colonialism is not immune from this ambivalence and ambiguity because there exists a complicity between post-colonial study and Western philosophical traditions, since post-colonial study is itself based on the post-structuralist and postmodernist thinking of the colonizing West.

The boundaries are blurry, and that is the point. Can a woman in a colonized country speak from her own culture? Not exactly, because that voice is defined by its position between (and not of either) the worlds of the colonizer and colonized, elite and non-elite, male and female, and so on. Consequently, the identity of the woman is defined by its plurality and its in-betweenness.

Like the borderlands evoked by feminists of colour (above), post-colonial theory introduces the concept of hybridity to suggest the shifting and multiple character of identities. Related to the concept of difference, hybridization refers to the combining of colonizer and colonized cultures that create a hybridized cultural identity that is neither one nor the other. (Facetiously, one can think of Taco Bell, where food is neither Mexican nor American but a combination of the two, intended to appeal to a wide range of tastes.) It is a 'third space' that can serve as a site of resistance by displacing and reinterpreting the history that created it (Sardar and Van Loon 1997, 120).

Hybridity unsettles notions of fixed identities. It can be seen particularly in the examination of migrant and immigrant identities, which do not fit comfortably in either the new society or the old one they have left behind, and the work of American non-white feminists negotiating the slipperiness of their own identities (for example, Trinh 1989; Mani 1998; Anzaldua 1990).

Aboriginal Feminism

In Canada the tensions between race and women's identities can be seen in the controversy regarding the status of Aboriginal women who marry non-Aboriginal men. Originally the Indian Act dictated that when a status Indian woman married a non-Indian man she would lose her Indian Status—her membership in the band and her rights to own property and live on reserve. This loss of status was permanent even if the marriage was to later break down. In contrast, the non-Aboriginal spouses of Aboriginal men could be accorded Indian status and associated band rights.

In 1973, in *Attorney General of Canada v. Lavell; Isaac v. Bédard*, the Supreme Court of Canada upheld this provision in the Indian Act in a ruling that 'defined equality before the law not to be a substantive requirement of the law itself, but a requirement of the way in which laws are administered' (Russell, et. al, 1989, 359). Aboriginal women could be treated differently in the administration of the Indian Act as long as all Aboriginal women were treated the same way. Changes were made in 1985 in light of the 1982 Charter of Rights and Freedoms. However, the issue was far from settled and in 1997 the Sawridge Band of Alberta challenged federal amendments to restore Indian status to women who had married out of the band. In *Sawridge Band v. Canada* (1997), the band argued that section 35 of the Constitution gave bands the right to govern themselves in a way that protects and supports their aboriginality. The 1985 changes violated the band's 'right to control its own membership by unilaterally imposing new members on the band' (cited in Dick, 2006, 98). These members, the band claimed, had compromised their indigenous identity by marrying non-Indian men and living away from the community. At issue was the question of what determines Aboriginal identity.

For some Aboriginal writers, feminism is unhelpful in understanding Aboriginal identity. For example, Mary Ellen Turpel (1993, 184) argues the *Report* of the Royal Commission on the Status of Women's objective of ensuring equality is an inappropriate starting point and irrelevant for her as a Cree woman. She explains that 'patriarchy' is not universal and that, traditionally, First Nations communities did not use the concept of 'equality' as an organizing principle prior to the colonization of North America: 'It is frequently seen by our Elders as a suspiciously selfish notion; as individualistic and alienating from others in the community' (180). Kate Rogers (1997, cited in Arneil 1999, 117) similarly points to cultural differences: '[A]boriginal women do not focus on the biological differences between men and women in the same terms as western feminists. [Rather, they] concentrate on the spiritual content of one's being' (Arneil, 1999, 117). Consequently, 'patriarchy' is a feature of white colonial culture and thus holds no meaning for relationships between Aboriginal women and men. As Turpel argues, 'to look only to an objective of equality with men is clearly insufficient for First Nations women's struggles and continued identities because this cannot encompass our aspirations as cultures' (1993, 183). To be relevant, feminism must recognize the cultural understandings and aspirations of those living different experiences.

On the other hand, writers such as Joyce Green (1993, 2001, 2007; see also Andrea Smith, 2007) argue that feminist theory is indeed relevant for Aboriginal women, as 'aboriginal feminists raise issues of colonialism, racism, sexism, and the unpleasant synergy between these three violations of human rights' (2007, 20–21). Aboriginal feminism is a requirement when confronting colonialism and patriarchy, since both 'phenomena exist in the context of colonial society, directed at Indigenous people, [and] have also been internalized by some Indigenous political cultures in ways that are oppressive to indigenous women' (22). While Aboriginal women do not experience patriarchal oppression the same way as white women, neither do they experience colonial oppression in the same way as Aboriginal men. Therefore, care must be taken when adopting the language of anti-colonization to highlight 'the gendered way in which colonial oppression and racism function for men and women, or to the inherent and adopted sexisms that some communities manifest' (Green, 2007, 23). Green argues that only by adopting a range of analysis of power relations, including both anti-colonial and feminist perspectives, will all the power relations and oppressions be made clear and addressed.

How does this relate to aboriginal identity and the idea of 'woman'? Is it too simplistic to say that it is a choice between oppressions, i.e., between patriarchy or colonization? Caroline Dick (2006, 108) recommends keeping in mind the differing experiences of the power relations at work at all levels. 'Aboriginal communities possess less power than the dominant society and the state that represents it; they have considerable influence over the lives of reacquired-rights women. The provision of group-specific rights leaves the weakest members of the community more vulnerable to discriminatory treatment by the group.' The reacquired-rights women are differently situated when compared to Canadian women, Aboriginal men, and even Aboriginal women who did not marry non-Indians, but is this difference enough to make them any less or more Canadian, women or Aboriginal? To put it crudely, it is not a situation of male/female, white/Aboriginal; it is a case of everything or nothing.

In defining gender, feminist theorist Donna Haraway (1999) warns against the universalizing tendency underlying the binary divisions of gender/sex and male/female.

> The evidence is building of a need for a theory of 'difference' whose geometries, paradigms and logics break out of binaries, dialectics, and nature/culture models of any kind. Otherwise threes will always reduce to two, which quickly become lonely ones in the vanguard. And no one learns to count to four. These things matter politically (77).

Defining gendered aboriginality highlights the complexities involved in identity and requires an understanding of 'woman' not just in opposition to the category of 'man' but also integrated with categories of race, ethnicity, class, etc. In addressing this complexity, Aboriginal women challenge feminist theory and the women's movement to learn to count to four and beyond.

'We're queer and we're here': The public, not private, world of queer theory

From the perspective of exploring and constructing sexual identities, queer theory pursues a similar rejection of strict categories based on the opposition of male versus female. As Hennessy (1993, 964) writes:

Queer theory calls into question obvious categories (man, woman, latina, jew, butch, femme), oppositions (man vs. woman, heterosexual vs. homosexual), or equations (gender = sex) upon which conventional notions of sexuality and identity rely. . . . [Q]ueer theory's post-modern conception of identity as an ensemble of unstable and multiple positions contests traditional formulations of sexuality as a personal issue.

For feminists, the introduction of the term 'queer theory' is attributed to Theresa de Lauretis in her introduction to a special issue of the journal *differences* in 1991, *Queer Theory: Lesbian and Gay Sexualities* (Code 2000; Hennessy 1993). The volume comprised a series of essays that explored the complex and often contradictory articulation of lesbian and gay sexualities and their negotiation with other differences that make up 'others'. With its focus on homosexualities, one of the features of this volume was 'to speak from and to the differences and silences that have been suppressed by the monolithic identities "lesbian" and "gay"' (Hennessy 1993, 966–7). It challenged the underlying heterosexuality, termed *heteronormativity*, within feminist theory, the women's movement, and in society, and rejected the earlier lesbian radical feminist position that sexuality should be determined by one's gender identity and that all feminists must be political lesbians.

Queer theory advocated a very public cultural politics that significantly contributed to debates about the public/private division of society. This was made possible and political, as de Lauretis identified, by the coalition of gay men and lesbians that emerged to respond to the AIDS crisis and the subsequent social backlash against homosexuals and lesbians (de Lauretis 1991, cited in Hennessy 1993). In this project, 'silence = death', and the personal was not only political but also very public. The most extreme political manifestation of this politics was the 'outing' of public figures and celebrities to illustrate that there is no true division between the public and the private.

For queer activists and queer theorists, sexuality is not a personal private matter but a public identity (Arneil 1999, 75). In the past, feminism and the women's movement had accommodated gay and lesbian identities by resorting to the language of rights that would protect one's right to a particular private sexual identity. Not surprisingly, however, this language of 'private identity' is problematic. It reduces sexuality solely to 'sexual behaviour' and confines it to 'specific personal relationships', leaving little room for a public identity that reflects one's sexuality. Consequently, queer theorists challenged not only the types of identity found in political theory but also the idea that a distinction should be and can be made between private sexuality and public citizenship.

Postmodern Feminism: Irony and Deconstruction

In *Feminism/Postmodernism*, Linda Nicholson (1990, 5) argues that there is a close affinity between feminism and postmodernism: '[P]ost-modernism is not only a natural ally but also provides a basis for avoiding the tendency to construct theory that generalizes from the experiences of Western, white, middle-class women.' The affinity lies in a shared critique of the principles that underlie modernity, such as the coherent essential individual, the revealing of objective truth through scientific reason and experience, the natural division of the public world from the private world, and so on. As a cultural, social, and political project, postmodernism sets out to illuminate those structures by disrupting and blurring their traditionally defined boundaries.

Dietz (2003) argues that the project of postmodern or deconstruction feminism is to dismantle the polarities of all categories because they are too restrictive, particularly that of man/woman, but also the 'preconstituted categories' of race, colour, class, sexual orientation, and gender. Everything is open to disruption and deconstruction.

Donna Haraway's (1985) essay 'A manifesto for cyborgs: Science, technology, and socialist feminism in the late twentieth century' is identified as an early example of this approach with its arguments regarding the malleability of identity (even at the level of the body) and the blurring distinction between the organic natural and the technological. As Kolmar and Bartkowski (2000, 360) put it, '[she] argues for epistemologies that resist such dualisms as nature/culture and is more interested in boundaries, partiality, and coalitions than in hierarchies, organic wholes and coherent identities'. Haraway (1990, 191) does this through her conception of the cyborg: '[A] cyborg is a cybernetic organism, a hybrid of machine and organism, a creature of social reality as well as a creature of fiction. . . . By the late twentieth century, our time, a mythic time, we are all chimeras, theorized and fabricated hybrids of machine and organism.' She intends the cyborg as an ironic symbol representing the contradictions in and presenting a challenge to mythic dualities and social constructions:

> The cyborg is resolutely committed to partiality, irony, intimacy and perversity. It is oppositional, utopian and completely without innocence. No longer structured by the polarity of the public and private, the cyborg defines a technological polis based partly on a revolution of social relations in the oikos, the household. Nature and culture are reworked; the one can no longer be the resource for appropriation or incorporation of the other. . . . So my cyborg myth is about transgressed boundaries, potent fusions and dangerous possibilities which progressive people might explore as part of needed political work (Haraway 1990, 192, 196).

The irony is very significant. The OED (1985, 484) defines irony as 'a figure of speech in which the intended meaning is the opposite of that expressed by the words used; usually taking the form of sarcasm or ridicule in which laudatory expressions are used to imply condemnation or contempt'. It is, as Haraway (1990, 190) points out, about holding necessary contradictions together through humour and serious play and '[i]t is also a rhetorical strategy and a political method'. Irony is significant because it presents an alternative narrative line or way of understanding that undermines the reality of the text or presentation. By doing so, it highlights the contradictions, makes transparent the social constructions, and undermines the coherence and the hierarchies.

For Haraway (1990, 216, 218), the image of the cyborg suggests ways out of the maze of dualism, questions the production of universal, totalizing theory, and deconstructs and reconstructs boundaries in connection and negotiation with others. The cyborg identity is dynamic, an unfixed and plural identity synthesized from overlapping and fusing outsider identities within complex and multi-layered contexts. It is also a hybrid that is considered monstrous, because it defines the limits of community

and acts as a form of blasphemy. As a result, the image of the cyborg violates the dominant distinctions that define society, 'subverting the structure and modes of reproduction of "Western" identity'. It is ironic and iconic.

Woman as cyborg is a difficult concept to accept. As Germaine Greer (1999, 418)
counters, '[i]f freedom is an out-of-body experience this feminist wants none of it.
. . . . It [the female body] is more wonderful in every way than any production of our
technology; women may well find that the liberation struggle becomes a struggle to
defend the female body, the source of all bodies, against the cyber-surgeons who will
inherit the hubris of those present day surgeons who think they make a better breast
than God.' Greer is reading the notion of the cyborg far too literally. Haraway is not
envisioning women's bodies as robotic creatures like Arnold Schwarzenegger in the
Terminator films; rather, her point is that we need to recognize that women's bodies
are already defined by their production in today's technological and natural sciences[2].
Women are already 'monstrous' because they are defined as the 'other'. The cyborg is a
metaphor, an invitation to appropriate the production of woman to create something
monstrous because it transgresses defined norms and opens up the ability to represent
and define oneself in resistance.

> The refusal to become or to remain a 'gendered' man or a woman, then, is an
> eminently political insistence on emerging from the nightmare of the all-too-
> real, imaginary narrative of sex and race. Finally and ironically, the political
> and explanatory power of the 'social' category of gender depends upon his-
> toricizing the categories of sex, flesh, body, biology, race, and nature in such
> a way that the binary, universalizing opposition that spawned the concept of
> the sex/gender system accountable, located, and consequential theories of
> embodiment, where nature is no longer imagined and enacted as resource to
> culture or sex to gender (Haraway 2007, 90).

In the work of Judith Butler, irony is taken further and the emphasis put on the
ironic performance of various categories of identity. Lorraine Code (2000, 69) describes Butler's work as follows:

> Butler is best known for her formulation of gender as performative, which
> articulates models of social life as a series of pre-scripted or ritual perfor-
> mances, with psychoanalytic description of femininity as 'masquerade' and
> philosophical accounts of linguistic performativity. . . . Compulsory gender
> performativity produces the naturalness of 'sex'. . . . [G]ay and lesbian paro-
> dies of gender, Butler argues, implicitly reveal the imitative structure of gen-
> der itself—as well as its contingency.

Butler's (1990, 16) interest is in identities and their instability. Generally, it is
believed that one's personal identity is derived from some innate quality, an internal
feature that 'establishes the continuity or self-identity'. However, she asks the question
'To what extent do regulatory practices of gender formation and division constitute the
identity, the internal subject, indeed the self-identical of the person?' In answer, she
argues that social and cultural understandings regarding the coherence, unity, and particularity of identities create that identity. In other words, one is given a label and lives

up to or becomes that label. There is no internal feature per se that defines gender; rather, the process of gendering—living up to or performing the accepted norm—creates gender.

It is the continued practice of dominant labels such as man/woman, male/female, feminine/masculine that maintains and regulates a system of compulsory heterosexuality. 'Intelligible genders' are those that behave within socially accepted and limited parameters. They set norms, become normal, and are thus 'natural' and stable.

So what about irony? To behave outside or to cross those norms, to engage in gender parody, undermines and highlights the contradictions. Butler (1990, 17) is interested in how gender performances, such as the gender parodies of drag queens and camp, undermine heteronormativity and the idea of 'woman':

> In as much as 'identity' is assured through the stabilizing concepts of sex, gender, and sexuality, the very notion of 'the person' is called into question by the cultural emergence of those 'incoherent' or discontinuous 'gendered beings' who appear to be persons but who fail to conform to the gendered norms of cultural intelligibility by which persons are defined.

The result of ironic presentation or (re)presentation is to highlight the instability and artificial character of identity. Ironic behaviour becomes a supremely political act, challenging the status quo and the social categorizations that include and exclude, and opening up the possibility of multiple identities. If the categories are artificial and unstable, they are open to change, and while categories may be limited to those that exist socially as norms, through performance new categories can be ironically created from old ones.

Deconstruction and postmodern feminism have come under criticism for their abstraction and inaccessibility to women outside 'academic' circles. The celebration of contingency gives few clues to a common feature around which a coherent and unified campaign may be organized. Further to this, critics have pointed out that the plurality, heterogeneity, hybridity, and instability emphasized by deconstruction and diversity feminisms are inherently fragmenting to the movement. As Bordo (1990, 149) puts it,

> Too relentless a focus on historical heterogeneity, for example, can obscure the transhistorical patterns of white, male privilege that have informed the creation of the Western intellectual tradition. More generally, the deconstruction of dual grids can obscure the dualistic, hierarchical nature of the actualities of power in Western culture. Contemporary feminism, like many social movements arising in the 1960s, developed out of the recognition that to live in our culture is not (despite powerful social mythology to the contrary) to participate equally in some free play of individual diversity. Rather, one always finds oneself located within structures of dominance and subordination—not the least important of which have been those organized around gender. Certainly the duality of male/female is a discursive formation, a social construction. So, too, is the racial duality of black/white. But as such each of these dualities has profound consequences for the construction of experience of those who live them.

Similarly, Dietz (2003, 417) making reference to Okin (1999, 23) identifies diversity approaches and the '"multiculturalism" they espouse in general as ignoring the rights of women and "inequalities between the sexes", even as they forward the rights of groups or cultures, thus reinscribing the very structures of domination that feminism resolutely opposes'. The argument is that feminist theory has been cast loose from its moorings because it has lost its grounding in the shared experiences of the material world (Benhabib 1990; Bordo 1990; Hennessy 1993; Code 2000). This gives rise to what some refer to as an 'identity crisis' (Alcoff 1986, Dietz 2003).

The plurality envisioned by today's feminism has significance for women's politics because the feminist movement is increasingly perceived as fragmented by a multi-plicity of identities. The priority for women subordinated because of race, ability, or sexual orientation may be to empower themselves as members of that subordinated group before tackling their subordination as women. Bordo (1990, 139) asks a telling question: '[J]ust how many axes can one include and still preserve analytic focus or argument?' The answer is troubling: either there are too many axes or categories to get a clear footing for action, or certain axes will be prioritized—for example, class over age, race over sexual orientation, or sexual orientation over ability. Where does differ-ence end, and which differences are being spoken for? Can a coherent feminist politics be undertaken in such a context?

Intersectionality: Finding Common Ground through a Geography of the Self

It is helpful to think of the various oppressions at work as intersecting one another, much like a meeting of roads that form the unique, whole, and coherent geographical space referred to as an intersection. The traffic intersection is a metaphor developed by Kimberlé Williams Crenshaw (1991) and used by Hankivsky (2005) which illus-trates that multiple oppressions are mutually constitutive and cannot be separated or prioritized.

> Race, class, gender and other forms of discrimination, such as sexual orienta-tion and ability, are the roads that structure social, economic, and political terrain. This metaphor captures the numerous systems of subordination that often overlap and cross and that create complex intersections. It allows us to avoid thinking of these dynamics as disjointed or simply parallel. It is within the intersections of these contexts that multiply burdened populations are located. They must negotiate the oncoming traffic and the injuries from the collisions of the various forms of inter-related and interlocking discrimina-tion, and decide whether these are pre-existing conditions or brought on by their particular acts and policies (Hankivsky, 2005, 993).

Intersectional thinking helps us understand that identity and the self are formed within the context of historical and social experience and as such are inherently re-lational. As Garcia Bedolla (2007, 239) argues, 'personal identity is a quintessentially individual experience, but the social, economic and political implications of the iden-tification are largely relationship. . . . [T]he role of intersectional social science is to accept the existence of the first and to focus its energies on disentangling and in-terrogating the second.' These relationships are constitutive and dynamic. Therefore, gender does not operate independently in politics but in a particular context and in connection with other aspects of individual and collective identity. The various identity categories are not predetermined or given, but, the 'dynamic production of individual and institutional factors' (Hancock 2007, 251). Identities and their intersections are the result of historical processes.

Therefore, as the introduction to a special issue of *Politics and Gender* (2007, 231) argues, 'intersectionality is a strategy for achieving liberation from oppression. If an intersectional perspective on political life helps us better understand the nature of oppression and inequality, then it will help us more effectively to dismantle the practices and institutions that sustain them.' Intersectionality provides potential for constructing a politics of liberation and helping us overcome some of the problems identified by Aboriginal feminists, discussed earlier in this chapter. Williams Crenshaw (1991, 1242, 1249), like the Aboriginal women critics of second-wave feminism, identifies the inherent destructiveness of prioritizing and singling out specific categories:

> The problem of identity is not that it fails to transcend differences as some critics charge but rather the opposite—that it frequently conflates or ignores intragroup differences. . . . Intersectional subordination need not be intentionally produced; in fact it is frequently the consequence of the imposition of one burden that interacts with preexisting vulnerabilities to create yet another dimension of empowerment.

However, in recognizing the mutually constituted, dynamic, multiple nature of identity, 'intersectionality can also more comprehensively answer questions of distributive justice, power and government function that are central to the discipline of political science and central to our world' (Hancock 2007, 249).

The Strategic Essentialism of Radha Jhappan

Canadian political scientist Radha Jhappan (1998, 2002) addresses the issue of intersectionality in the legal litigation of Canadian Charter of Rights and Freedoms cases. As discussed in chapter 1, the difficulty with equality-seeking through legal structures is the 'saming' that results from universal principles of equality. However, given the past success of the women's movement in making claims before the Supreme Court, it would be foolhardy to reject legal action as a means of bringing the concerns of women and minorities to the attention of state policy-makers and Canadian society more generally. The answer, Jhappan (1998) suggests, is to develop more flexible and fluid concepts of justice based on principles of fundamental justice.

Jhappan (1998, 65, 74) sees 'the essentialist definition of the "problem" of gender (race, sexual identity, or disability) as an equality/inequality problem [which] constrains the search for broader remedies to injustice'. This constraint is written into the Charter of Rights and Freedoms because section 15 of the Charter, for example, is structured in such a way as to require claimants to identify themselves by a characteristic that is implicitly contrasted to that of the dominant 'advantaged' group (such as race, national or ethnic origin, colour, religion, sex, age, or mental or physical disability). Equality means always having to say who you are equal to, always comparing one group against another, almost invariably on one axis, and, for this reason, it will not let claimants out of the similarly situated, likes alike, sameness/difference traps, regardless of the new language use. Sameness/difference is a function of essentialism and vice versa (ibid.).

Therefore, equality is impossible.

However, adopting Iris Marion Young's (1990) conception of difference and justice, Jhappan develops a more fluid and contextualized framework for pursuing remedies to the oppression of women and minorities. Rather than focusing on the equality provisions of section 15 of the Charter of Rights and Freedoms, which inevitably lead to essentialism and assimilation, Jhappan (1998, 81) is interested in sections 1 and 7, which speak to issues of fundamental justice: 'equality is but a sub-set of a much larger normative principle'—justice. Fundamental justice can be read in a more dynamic or provisional way because 'justice is a concept that is relative to specific cultures and pe-riods' (Jhappan 1998, 90). Therefore, justice provides a more fluid meaning of identity because it is a conception of dynamic ongoing domination and oppression, rather than an end-goal caught up in the equal/unequal dichotomy. Jhappan (1998, 96) writes, 'In contrast to the essentialist and assimilationist logic of equality claims and provisions, the justice approach switches the forces from the gender (or race, class and so on) *identity* of the claimant to the *relationship* in which they are oppressed' (emphasis in the original). The question then becomes what principles of fundamental justice are served by the exclusion of particular categories or identities? In this way the concept of justice is less totalizing, less given to universal similarities, and can be applied on a case-by-case basis.

Jhappan (1998, 105–6) is calling for an alternative and expanded reading of justice ap-propriate to the claims being made at the time, whether in the name of gender, class, race, ability, or sexual orientation. This creates a conceptual position from which to make claims but avoids the pitfalls of essentialist 'saming'. In so doing, she is suggesting that 'reclaiming justice from the traditional liberal, abstract universalist, rule- and process-oriented 'malestream' interpretations, which have dominated in theory and in law, will at the very least, enable women to fashion gendered but non-essentialist claims and so avoid some of the snares of the equality approach' (ibid.).

Conclusion: A Return to Praxis

One important lesson that can be taken from the current debates in feminist theory is the recognition that identities are multiple, socially constructed, provisional, and dynamic. If we conceive of identity politics as a process that is dynamic and ex-perimental rather than solid and unified, in which identities are constantly being defined and redefined, then politics is about deconstructing and reconstructing identities in order to confront, resist, and undermine the structures and processes that oppress. This politics is based on the material nature of our experiences, but is also based on ourselves as social beings and how our understandings and interpretations are socially constructed. These overlapping and shared identities, values, and issues are coalitional at both the individual and the collective level.

Politics therefore requires an emphasis on coalition and consensus-building (for example, Yuval Davis 1997; Mouffe 1992). Third-wave feminism is associated with the politics of coalitions. As Dietz (2003, 415) argues in her outline of current feminist theory, 'political theorists of the later type [Chantal Mouffe, Nancy Fraser, and Dietz herself] tend to understand identity not formally or philosophically, as prior, for example, to history, economy, culture, or society, but rather as interpretable only through this complex of elements and in relation to human practices and the effects of power'. The solution is to build coalitions around principles that will keep the pluralities together: for example, the dialogue and negotiation of transversal politics (Yuval Davis 1997); a radical plural democracy based on an articulating (bringing together) action of citizenship (Mouffe 1992); citizenship and equality based in difference, not sameness (Young 1990); or simply love and respect (hooks 1988). The principle of dialogue is particularly significant as a dialogue that respects differences and that recognizes that no community is homogeneous and that alliances and shared understandings can be achieved across broad divisions—but not for all and not all the time (Yuval Davis 1997). It speaks to a dynamic and ever-changing form of politics. Arneil (1999, 218) writes, 'Critical to this notion . . . is the idea that 'oppositional politics' must shift depending on the composition of the individuals and groups involved, on the nature and structure of forces which are being opposed and on the tactics and strategies of the local political struggle.' Such a politics is dynamic and requires pragmatism and openness, which allows actors to adapt in appropriate ways.

As we shall discuss in the next chapter, this form of politics evokes the idea of social movement and movement politics. It also brings us back to the concept of praxis and the phenomenon of a movement dealing with the visions generated by its various parts, sometimes in dispute and sometimes in collaboration, dealing with different strategies for action and, in some cases, differing goals and priorities concerning what really matters. Feminism should aspire to a radical citizenship based not on sameness but on difference—a coalition and consensus that is constantly negotiated and ever-changing and that speaks the language of intersections, networks, webs, tapestries, and interwoven and overlapping groups, identities, and individuals.

We should view feminist theory in much the same way. Rather than subscribing to or identifying rigidly with one or another approach, naming ourselves and squeezing ourselves into a particular box—I'm a liberal feminist, I'm a socialist feminist, I'm a radical feminist, I'm a postmodernist—we should be suspicious of strict categories and a single easy theoretical explanation. The approaches presented here did not appear in isolation; they overlap and inform one another, some in a complementary manner and some in conflict. In mapping feminist theory around a number of concepts, we find that as a whole, it is modern and postmodern, material and ideal, essential and socially constructed, sometimes reflecting the private, sometimes the public. It is this richness, complexity, and diversity that is compelling and speaks to the struggles, failures, and successes of women's politics.

Questions for Critical Thought

1. How significant is feminist theory to all struggles against inequality and oppression? Can the 'master's house' ever be effectively dismantled by using 'the master's tools'?

2. What is feminist politics without a coherent concept of 'woman'? Does feminism inevitably have to take the 'risk of essentialism'?

3. Donna Haraway (1999, 77) argues that

   > evidence is building of a need for a theory of 'difference' whose geometries, paradigms and logics break out of binaries, dialectics, and nature/culture models of any kind. Otherwise threes will always reduce to two, which quickly become lonely ones in the vanguard. And no one learns to count to four. These things matter politically.

   How do we learn to count to four? What sort of politics does this look like, and can it be anything but a very provisional politics of ambivalence?

CHAPTER 4

The Women's Movement in Canada

In the previous chapter, we frequently used the term 'women's movement'. In this chapter, we explore the women's movement as a social movement, look at the historical development of the Canadian women's movement, and discuss the importance of women's activity in the world of small-p politics as well as the mainstream large-P politics of political parties, elections, and governments.

Waves Eroding the Shores of Male Domination: Women's Struggles, Politics, and Movements

Alain Touraine (2000), the French sociologist and social theorist, argues that the women's movement is a true social movement in terms of the revolutionary changes it has brought to the political, economic, cultural, and social nature of society. However, the movement did not bring about these changes either in a coherent unified manner or necessarily under the banner of 'feminism'. As discussed in previous chapters, there have been and are multiple and continuing debates over what constitutes feminism and in which issues feminists should engage. This is significant not only for theory: it is also important because women's political struggles and activism and battles have not always been undertaken in the name of feminism. Indeed, they have not always taken place within a specific women's movement. Women have long been involved with men in radical politics and social movements, such as the pushes for democratization, unionization, and an end to slavery.

In the 'big tent' comprising the various struggles that together make up the women's movement, the common thread is an attempt to dismantle and reconstruct the structures and attitudes that oppress and subordinate women. The women's movement as a whole has demanded and struggled for political, economic, cultural, and social change and a redefinition of the place of women in society.

It was not until the late nineteenth century that a self-conscious women's movement with an explicitly feminist orientation appeared as a distinct entity in Britain and North America. This we identify as feminism's first wave.[1] Its most obvious feature was a demand for the right to vote, but it also involved more fundamental challenges to the denial of women's autonomy, including efforts to effect social change by campaigning for reproductive control and better working conditions in female trades. The second wave is associated with the emergence of the modern women's liberation movement at the end of the 1960s. It was a reaction to the perceived middle-class, institutionally focused liberalism of the first wave suffragists and to the inequality women experienced in the civil rights, student, and new left movements of the 1960s. It stressed a more 'personal' politics recognizing the structurally limited nature of women's lives, protesting inequality in the family, and claiming control over women's bodies through sexual emancipation. There was continuity between the two waves since, for many women, the struggle continued to involve demands for access to political decision-making and issues of workplace and economic rights. As with second-wave feminism, third-wave feminism presents a reaction to its precursor, in particular the monolithic and unrepresentative conception of womanhood or sisterhood. The third wave stresses the differing identities of women and recognition of the complex webs of oppression many women experience. It also requires recognition that many other women, not only Western, white, middle-class, educated women, and not all of them feminists, have been explicitly involved in actions to achieve an end to their oppression.

Why do we use the term 'waves'?

As Naomi Black (1988, 83–4) argues, the term wave aptly illustrates the activity of the women's movement over the past 100 years, 'reminding us that in social change, as in oceans, calmer patches are followed by new and stronger peaks of activity. The Second Wave also implies the image of a tide pouring in, each wave going further up the beach, with a continuity of organizational and individual efforts over time and a hope of progress.' Although Black evokes continuity in the analogy, others (for example, Vickers 1992; Dumont 1992) point out that the analogy is problematic because it marginalizes the important activity that occurs between the waves. However, use of the term wave does serve to highlight the periods when women mobilized en masse to work for change.

Alberto Melucci's (1989) distinction between mobilization surges and periods of latency is useful here. This conception acknowledges that a characteristic feature of social movements is a tendency to appear en masse for only limited periods. Outside of these periods, the movement is not inactive but working more 'quietly' in public and self-education, providing services in society, and sometimes cooperating with the state on policy. The public protest and confrontation characteristic of a mass mobilization is missing, but the movement is maintained, active, and creating the groundwork on which a mass mobilization and periods of surge can be based and made possible.

Each of the successive waves of the women's movement has thus drawn on and benefited from the legacy of preceding waves. There has been continuity to the movement, and each wave has elaborated strategies for survival, resistance, and change based both on past experiences and the need to confront new situations. The result is a movement that in many ways is institutionalized but is nonetheless made up of many diverse parts that express themselves in terms of different identities and concerns that are sometimes in dispute and other times collaborating. This is in keeping with its character as a social movement.

What is a social movement?

Social movements are expressions of collective action made up of heterogeneous political, social, and cultural networks engaged in a continual process of disputing, compromising, redefining, and adapting identities, strategies, and goals. They are not structurally specific and unified entities but rather networks of different groups and individuals working for a variety of aims and goals that fit within a broader demand for change (Newman and Tanguay 2001). In the case of the women's movement, this means that among the many identifications held by women, they see themselves as acting as and on behalf of women and espousing fundamental goals—an end to patriarchy and an end to women's oppression—that do not fit with the status quo. Social movements do not rely on formal organization for their emergence and maintenance since they often represent new forms of social or political identity, and they define success not simply in terms of influencing public policy—although that may be important—but also more generally in changing social attitudes and popularizing different understandings of politics and social norms.

These goals distinguish a social movement from an interest group: unlike interest groups, the movement's fundamental goals and forms of action are not negotiable within the existing arrangement of social power, in this case patriarchy. However, this distinction does not preclude women's organizations within the movement from adopting the form and activities of interest groups. As Della Porta and Diani (1999, 19) argue, organizations within a social movement may involve themselves in two types or systems of action, 'the party system and the social movement system'. Some organizations may, in fact, move from social movement characteristics to interest group characteristics and back again based on the political opportunities available to them—in other words, depending on the political and social context in which they find themselves. Therefore, it is useful to envision the women's movement spanning a continuum from interest group action to social movement action.

When we look at the women's movement, we see a diverse movement with a rich history, constructed on growing understandings of the experiences of women and the need for action to bring about social change. It is not especially cohesive, homogeneous, or given to espousing one specific goal but has developed as women have elaborated strategies to end women's oppression and make their lives better.

The Canadian Women's Movement

Functionally, the women's movement in Canada can be seen to be composed of four branches, although there can be some overlap and duplication among the branches. One branch consists of service providers: women's organizations whose primary purpose is to provide services to women, such as counselling, referral, birth control education, or shelters. A second branch consists of equal rights groups that campaign for equal opportunities in employment and politics. The third branch comprises groups espousing the social feminist goal of bringing women's private virtues into the public world. And the fourth branch comprises groups working for the 'self-determination' of a variety of identities and against racism. In addition to these branches, there is a fifth set of groups that some would place outside the women's movement and others would include (see our discussion in chapter 1), comprising organizations such as REAL Women that emerged as a response to feminist politics and that campaign for the maintenance of traditional social divisions between men and women.

We can also divide the movement in terms of who its participants claim to represent. Meg Luxton (2001, 66) identifies four distinct movements in this respect: a francophone movement based in Quebec, a predominantly anglophone movement in the rest of Canada, a movement of First Nations women, and a movement of immigrant women and women of colour challenging racism inside and outside the greater movement.

These divisions have posed obstacles to building a unified and coherent organizational network. Canada's geography also tends to fragment any coherent organizational structure. Not surprisingly, given Canada's large geographic area and relatively small, spread-out population, the primary focus has been on organizing at municipal and regional levels. Canadian federalism reinforces this tendency, with the division into federal and provincial jurisdictions and provincial governments' powers in many policy areas of concern to women. For example, the battle for suffrage, while won nationally in 1918 for all women 21 and over, also had to be fought provincially. In some provinces, women won the vote earlier than they did at the federal level (Manitoba, Alberta, and Saskatchewan in 1916, British Columbia and Ontario in 1917) but in others long afterwards (Prince Edward Island in 1922 and Quebec in 1940).

Because of these divisions, the women's movement in Canada, like other social movements such as the peace movement, has had to build coalitions of diverse groups when it acts nationally. As a result, it has tended to establish umbrella organizations at the national level that speak for a varied membership and work to find a common voice out of the tensions resulting from that diversity. This tendency is not out of keeping with the definition of social movement presented above, and as we shall see, it is a common theme in the history of the movement.

The first wave: political and civil rights

In *Canadian Women: A History*, Prentice, Bourne, Brandt, Light, Mitchinson, and Black (1988) make it clear that the lives of Canadian women have never been completely relegated to the private domestic sphere, separate from the public lives of men. From the earliest days, Canadian women have been involved in productive and remunerative work outside and inside the home. Widows and single women found ways of supporting themselves, ranging from teaching to domestic service to prostitution. For the majority of married women, domestic work such as farm work, weaving, sewing, taking in laundry, or looking after boarders was intrinsic to the family income. As Prentice et al. (1988, 84) make clear, 'If women were not supposed to engage in productive and remunerative work, they did not know it. Or if they thought that this was the case, they were soon disabused of the notion.' Only the wealthy had the luxury of the 'private woman' whose pursuits or hobbies were of an 'ornamental' nature.

However, practical realities are one thing but social norms another. While women had a stake in and worked hard in early Canada, traditional views of the division of the sexes and sexual inequality were maintained. Women were not seen as public persons in their own right in either the legal or political sphere. The assumption was that a husband had the right to control his wife's person and a father his daughter's until marriage. In rape cases, redress was not for the victim but for the father or husband because, to put it crudely, his goods had been spoiled (ibid.).

Women's activity in politics was limited to the influence they might have through well-positioned and powerful husbands. Although there are accounts of women participating in elections in Lower Canada and the Maritimes in the early nineteenth century (see Prentice et al. 1988, 98–9; Campbell 1989, 1990), Sharpe 1994, 63; by the middle of the nineteenth century women were excluded from the franchise by law.

While the lives of Canadian women in terms of their work remained intrinsic to the lives and livelihoods of their male counterparts, they were considered a 'world apart'. As the Canadian population grew in affluence and in numbers, 'in the upper middle class and affluent circles, . . . traditional class prejudice began to coexist with a new ideology of domesticity that, in theory at least, emphasized the difference between women and men more than those between the classes' (Prentice et al. 1988, 84). In urban areas, as industrialization took off, women found themselves more and more relegated to the private sphere as the industrial working world accentuated the division between work performed outside the home and that performed in the home. Increasingly, the male head of the household came to be viewed as the primary breadwinner.

With our early twenty-first century values, it is not surprising that we consider the first wave of the women's movement quite conservative, accepting as it did the position of women in the private sphere. This was the nature of the 'social' feminism or 'maternal' feminism characteristic of the first wave in Canada. The majority of the women activists who emerged in this period largely accepted the private/public division (Prentice et al. 1988; Valverde 1991, Brooks 2000;). In the last quarter of the nineteenth century, Canada was experiencing many social changes that affected Canadian families. Growing industrialization, immigration, urbanization, and imperial decline all had an effect on Canadian society. One result of the disruption, it was argued, was an increase in public drunkenness. Drunkenness became associated with a number of socially unacceptable behaviours—increased domestic violence, prostitution, desertion, and alcoholism—that threatened the family structure. Women's organizations focused their energies on the moral issues surrounding the family and the perceived threat to its maintenance. Underlying their arguments for a greater role in dealing with these issues was the belief that because of women's position in the private world, characterized by maternal graces and morality, they would bring virtue and morality to decisions made in the public sphere.

Charity was the significant feature of first-wave feminism in Canada. Women's organizations focusing on good works flourished, some associated with churches and others more secular. These associations, clubs, and groups functioned to bring together and create networks of women barred from public political and economic work. They also provided space for women to work for social reform, as many saw themselves as members of a reform movement committed to raising the standard as well as the quality of life in Canada. This reformist impulse in turn brought them to political action for suffrage and the right to political participation. As campaigns for social reform expanded, particularly those dealing with temperance and prostitution, women found that more political leverage was required to achieve action from national and provincial legislatures. An obvious way to create political pressure was the vote.

There is a significant upper-middle-class flavour to the social feminism discussed above. Not all women had the ability to pursue charity: some received charity themselves, and others could be considered victims of the zeal of charitable social reformers. Working women were suspicious of upper-middle-class women and their zeal for social reform, particularly prohibition, seeing their efforts as attempts at class domination (Prentice et al. 1988). Consequently, support for suffrage among working women emerged out of the belief that women should be on a more equal footing with men,[2] but

The Women's Christian Temperance Union in Canada

One of the new organizations that appeared in the late nineteenth century was the Women's Christian Temperance Union (WCTU). The primary goal of the WCTU was to change drinking habits, but it was also concerned with the promotion of family moral values through religious evangelism, voluntary social activism, and education programs. The WCTU became one of the largest non-denominational (although closely associated with evangelical Protestantism) women's organizations of the nineteenth century in Canada. At its peak in 1927, membership numbered over 13,000 people registered in all provinces. Ontario and Quebec had the highest membership, with 4,300 and 3,000 members respectively (WCTU 1927, 35).

The significance of the WCTU was that it provided 'a forum for middle-class women to become active participants in their own communities long before they were accorded the perquisites of full citizenship through the right to vote' (Sheehan, 1984, 103, 107). The desire for social reform quite naturally resulted in a desire for greater political influence, and the clearest route to this end was suffrage.

their primary concerns related to surviving in the working world and obtaining better wages and better work opportunities.

The obvious route for the collective organization of working women was through unionization. Some women did become involved and in a few cases formed their own women's unions and associations. While women have historically participated in union mobilizations supporting both male and female workers' demands, some union activities in the early twentieth century became more focused on women's issues and interests. For example, women were the predominant participants in the strike by Bell Telephone operators in 1907 and in the Eaton's factory strike of 1912 (Prentice et al. 1988, 130). However, women's union militancy was limited for a number of reasons: (1) it was difficult to organize women scattered among small shops or in home-based manufacturing; (2) unionization efforts tended to focus on organizing skilled male workers; (3) male unionists were often suspicious of and hostile toward women in the labour force, accusing them of taking men's jobs and keeping wages low; and (4) domestic obligations limited women's freedom to attend union meetings.

There was another, smaller group in the first-wave movement—women concerned with equal rights generally. This group demanded not only political rights but also political, economic, and social equality. Their push for suffrage and political rights was based on 'arguments of simple justice' and 'a viewpoint that stressed how much women resembled men, and how unjust it was that they should have fewer rights' (Prentice et al. 1988, 169). However, like working and union women, equity feminists were a marginal presence in a movement dominated by the more mainstream social-reforming social feminists.

By the first decades of the twentieth century, a number of groups of women were struggling for women's rights. An organization of interest to us in this period is the

National Council of Women (NCW). The NCW was a national network of women's organizations that formally advocated voting rights for women. It was formed in 1893
as a national umbrella organization with a membership made up of a diverse range of
women's organizations that chose to affiliate. It had a fairly broad focus, advocating
not only for suffrage and temperance through prohibition but also for better working
conditions for female domestic and factory employees, the rights of married women
to property, and measures related to public health (Burt 1994; Prentice et al. 1988).[3]
Although dominated by upper-middle-class urban social feminists, the NCW offered a
setting where social and equal rights views could coexist and cooperate. However, tensions existed in a number of areas. Arguments arose between social feminists and more
radical feminists regarding the militancy or lack of militancy of the suffrage campaigns.
Further tensions arose around class divisions. There were significant rural/urban differences between Western Canada and the East. And the movement remained white
and predominantly Anglo-Saxon.

However, the coalitional nature of the movement and the mix of feminisms reflected in it resulted in some interesting qualities that the movement would expand on
and develop once the surge of the early twentieth century ended. First, suffrage was
not the only focus of the Canadian movement; it was not the 'obsessive goal' that it
was in other countries. Second, while the NCW could act as a voice for many Canadian
women and did play an important role, the movement did not present a single unified
face. Its strength lay in its diversity. Third, unlike the British and, to a lesser extent, US
movements, the Canadian struggle for suffrage focused on the less militant and less
violent activities of petitioning, lobbying, public appeals and education, and leveraging
private connections with politicians (Prentice et al. 1988) This was a result of social
feminists dominating the movement. It remained for the most part non-violent and
less militant, shying away from hunger strikes and attacks on property and politicians. Consequently, even when the movement lost a unifying focus and much of its
surge when suffrage was achieved and when significant irreparable cracks appeared
in the coalition as a result of disagreements over World War I (1914–18),[4] it did not
disappear.

Social feminists moved on to a more restrained program of moderate social reform
(Burt 1994, 211). The campaign to have women considered persons under the law so
that they could hold Senate seats was not resolved until a 1929 ruling of the Judicial
Committee of the Privy Council in the UK,[5] and gaining parliamentary representation
continued to be a struggle.

Equity feminists continued to act on issues of labour, educational and social equality, and access to birth control. Indeed, equity feminism became a more dominant form
of feminism, particularly as women sought full inclusion in the professions, in the
business world, and at universities. Their efforts included establishing the Canadian
Teachers' Federation in 1920, the Federation of Business and Professional Women in
1930, and the Canadian Federation of University Women in 1919. At the same time,
women remained active in seeking better wages and working conditions and the self-
regulation of predominantly female trades such as nursing.

Equity feminists were much less inclined to work within the established political
system. After achieving formal political rights, women found that little had changed
because they remained marginalized within the political parties. This was not surprising, given that the dominant social norms regarding women had not changed

significantly. Because social feminism had earlier dominated the movement, women had not mounted a significant challenge to the gender roles of the day. The more radical equity feminists did put forward demands for greater equality, but their views and their unwillingness to compromise on issues they felt important to women, including birth control, did not find ready acceptance in society at large or in political parties in particular.

By the 1920s and 1930s, Canadian society was changing, and the lives of Canadian women were changing with it. Many had to work outside the home to help maintain the family income; they could no longer provide for their families by remaining in the home. Meanwhile, their efforts to live up to a conception of womanhood tied to motherhood and homemaking were becoming increasingly untenable. Within the home, many of women's traditional tasks were disappearing because of the pressures of urbanization and changes brought about by industrialization. But unfortunately, the social norms governing the position and appropriate behaviour of women were slow to catch up.

With World War II (1939–45), many of these social norms began to change more rapidly. Large numbers of women entered the labour force, answering the growing call for workers in industries supporting the war effort. Interestingly, Prentice et al. (1988, 299) point out that for Canadian women, 'an improved standard of living, not the call to loyalty and service, was their primary motivation'. The war-related labour shortage also led to the creation of women's paramilitary organizations and their admittance into the armed forces after 1942. Women's entry into public life en masse did not result in equality: women continued to be placed in subordinate positions, and traditional attitudes tended to prevail. However, women's public participation and their portrayal as public women (for example, the 'emancipated' Rosie the riveter) created a context that worked to undermine the traditional norms of the private housewife, mother, and daughter. As Sandra Burt (1994, 212) argues, 'women were increasingly viewed as a potential labour pool that could be pulled, as necessary, from their traditional jobs as wives and mothers (although they were expected to carry out these family functions as well). Both federal and provincial governments were driven by a new uncertainty about women's proper sphere.'

The second wave hits the beach: personal feminist politics

The second wave of the women's movement is often categorized as a 'new' social movement, one of the movements that emerged out of the political and social protests of the late 1960s. These movements were characterized as a new form of protest, which emphasized spontaneity and imagination in political action and an anti-bureaucratic and anti-institutional view of organization. The women's liberation stream of the second wave emerged as young women reacted to their experiences of being marginalized by male colleagues in the student, new left, and peace movements and the hippie counterculture, movements characterized by the progressive language of liberation and equality. These movements continued to be underpinned by traditional political structures and ideologies which these women rejected as inherently patriarchal.

The second-wave movement represented a new generation of women, and the analysis and aims expressed were much more secular and radical than the Christian morality of social feminism. It encompassed a wide variety of goals and groups, and while, as Sandra Burt (1994, 215) argues, the distinctions between them are not completely clear-cut, a number of visions can be identified. Equal rights feminism appeared dominant in English Canada, with a focus on attaining equal access for women to education, employment, and political representation. Socialist feminists were active, arguing for the overthrow of both class and gender divisions and working to build links between private and public production undertaken by women. Radical feminists also emerged, arguing that 'the personal is political' and that women were oppressed by a naturalized system of patriarchy perpetuated in the everyday practices of women's lives (Burt 1994). The second wave also saw the appearance of many small women's groups that voiced the concerns of specific women's identities. These groups represented Aboriginal women, Inuit women, black women, lesbians, farm women, immigrant and refugee women, and so on.

It is misleading, however, to categorize the second-wave movement as 'new'. As Jill Vickers (1992, 39) argues, 'many ideas about how to practise feminist politics were transmitted to the New Feminists from a generation of Old Feminists with whom they interacted in a number of sites of activity'. She points to organizations such as the Voice of Women (VOW) as a site of shared interaction and a bridge between the first and second waves. First and foremost, the Voice of Women was a peace organization, established in 1960 to work for an end to nuclear testing and Cold War politics. There was a social feminist element to VOW, as illustrated by its campaign for knitted clothing for Vietnamese children with the stipulation the clothing must be green or dark blue to camouflage children as protection from bombing or napalm attacks (Moffat 1982; Macpherson 1994). Protest against the Vietnam War and emerging second-wave feminist thinking had a significant impact on VOW, and by 1985 its philosophical position was more informed by these new feminist analyses, as illustrated in the statement: 'We reject a world based on domination, exploitation, patriarchy, racism, and sexism. We demand a new order based on justice and the equitable distribution of the world resources' (cited in Macpherson 1994, 144).

The transition from the first to the second wave was a response to the changing nature of Canadian society, to the developing views and understandings of women's oppression (based on and responding to those developed in the first wave), and to the women's movement's relationship to the protest movements of the 1960s. The organizational network of women's groups was much more developed in the second wave than it had been in the first, but the first wave and the inter-wave period had created the base on which the second could build and expand. And some women in the predominantly social feminist organizations of the first wave did in fact embrace tenets of liberal feminism.

According to Naomi Black (1988, 80), the surge in women's organizing in the 1960s was unexpected: 'In prosperous postwar Canada, women seemed to be doing well in both economic and political terms. Women were increasingly getting the education needed for better paying work, and public opinion supported the right to work and to get equal pay.' Politically, women had been elected to Parliament (between 1920 and 1970, 18 women were elected to the House of Commons) and had taken positions on municipal councils, even becoming mayors of major cities (for example, Charlotte Whitton was elected mayor of Ottawa in 1951), had been appointed to the Senate,[6] and had served as federal cabinet ministers.[7] However, the political record of women remained paltry compared to the optimistic outlook in the earlier part of the twentieth century. While by 1960 women had held the right to vote federally for over 30 years and even in Quebec for a generation, women were still not represented relative to their numbers in Canada. And the achievement of high political office by women continued to be the exception rather than the rule. Something more fundamental than lack of access to formal political rights appeared to perpetuate the subordination of women.

A growing number of women were employed outside the home and enrolled in post-secondary education, yet a double standard applied to these women, and the subordinate position forced on them was all too apparent. Young women who entered post-secondary education institutions[8] found that the concerns, experiences, and history of women were not represented in the curriculum. They found that their ability to achieve their ambitions was limited once they graduated compared to those of men. Not the least of their problems was a general assumption that they attended university to find good husbands—the infamous 'Mrs' degree. Although most of the women employed in wartime industry went back to the home at the end of the war, the number of women in the workforce, both single and married, soon began to rise steadily. By 1967 the total number of women at work equalled the number employed at the height of the war effort (Wilson 1991). Many of these women found that while work was available to them and federal legal guarantees for equal pay had been legislated in 1956, they were unlikely to advance in their careers as their male colleagues did, and as a whole they continued to be paid significantly less than men.

In short, the social norms governing the position and appropriate behaviour of women were vastly different from women's realities, and the gap between norm and reality made women's lives very difficult. This led to a growing disenchantment that found its way into the editorial pages of Canada's major women's magazine of the time, *Chatelaine*, and made Betty Friedan's *The Feminine Mystique* (published in 1963) a bestseller. Women came to recognize that the language of equality prevalent in the period of affluence following World War II did not really apply to them. While they had become legal 'persons' in 1929, they were not individual citizens. Their role in society was still defined by their position as mothers and wives based on their sex, not by their existence as equal public individuals, which would require them and their work to be equally valued.

Formal access to rights was clearly not enough to guarantee women's equality. Women's subordination was maintained throughout society, in political institutions, the workplace, schools, churches, clubs, and so on. Women's lives remained structurally and culturally limited, and the way to change this was to make the inequalities in both the public and the private spheres transparent. For women, there was no distinction between private and public: they had to overcome subordination in all spheres of their lives. Consequently, the personal became political, the private public, and old and new feminisms were brought together.

The result was a mobilization of women across the country to change their situation across a broad spectrum of political, economic, and cultural structures. Politically, women pressed for better representation at all levels of government and the bureaucracy and for greater sensitivity to women's needs in decision-making. In education, women pushed for curricula more appropriate for girls and women, equal opportunity in educational advancement, and the establishment of women's studies at the university level. In the workplace, women demanded equal pay for equal work, equality in career advancement, and an end to workplace sexual harassment. Both inside and outside mainstream politics, issues of sexuality, a women's right to control her own body, birth control, violence against women, domestic violence, pornography, and rape became lightning rods for women's activism. The focus was also on the cultural, as women sought to change the social norms around the naturalized subordinate place accorded to them in the media, in language, and in society in general.

Closely associated with this was the practice of consciousness-raising. Consciousness-raising brought small groups of women together to share their experiences of men, work, sex and sexuality, and so on. These sessions allowed participants to informally identify their oppression and better understand its roots. Consciousness-raising groups fostered a sense of shared experience, anger, and ultimately empowerment. Women came to understand that their personal grievances were political. As women transformed their anger into political action, consciousness-raising groups became a significant part of grassroots organizing. Informal consciousness-raising groups brought women to formal organizations. As Adamson, Briskin, and McPhail (1988, 205) argue, consciousness-raising was 'instrumental in actually mobilizing [women] as active participants in their own struggle for liberation'.

The importance of consciousness-raising groups in bringing women into the movement and in creating 'womanspace' should not be underestimated. As discussed in chapter 2, the creation of womanspace and 'womanculture' was a key feature of radical feminism's vision of a women's politics that reclaimed an identity connecting and celebrating womanhood. Throughout the second-wave period, women established women-centred services—rape crisis centres, health centres, abortion and contraception services, safe houses for battered and homeless women, centres for single mothers, women's studies programs, magazines, journals, art galleries, cultural centres, and publishing companies run for and by women. These vibrant grassroots efforts came to illustrate the second-wave's feminist character of 'women doing it for themselves'.[9]

As in the first wave, there were significant disputes and divisions within the second-wave movement. Radical, Marxist, and socialist feminists, and those who identified with the women's liberation movement, held anti-hierarchical and anti-institutional views, while liberal feminist groups maintained a 'commitment to the ordinary political process, a belief in the welfare state, a belief in the efficiency of state action in general to remedy injustices' (Vickers 1992, 40).

In addition, the relationship between English Canadian and French Canadian feminists was often tenuous. French Canadian feminism's association with Quebec nationalism, while both advantageous and disadvantageous for the Quebec movement, resulted in breaks in the relationship with English Canadian feminists, particularly during constitutional discussions regarding the position of Quebec in Canada. Disputes also emerged throughout the 1970s between the growing number of groups of minority women and the white middle class–dominated movement.

In 1966, 32 women's organizations in English Canada formed the Committee for the Equality of Women (CEW) to lobby the federal government to establish a royal commission on the status of women, while in Quebec the Fédération des femmes du Québec (FFQ) was formed. The two groups established a partnership in September 1966. These umbrella groups were able to accommodate a diverse range of views, but they tended to be dominated by liberal feminists, a situation that was compounded by the Royal Commission on the Status of Women, which in the late 1960s and early 1970s became a lightning rod for women's organizing.

Two Solitudes? The Women's Movement in Quebec

There are many reasons to consider the struggles of French Canadian women as distinct from those in English Canada. The first obvious difference is that Quebec women lagged behind women in other provinces in achieving political rights such as the right to vote provincially (1940) and civil rights within marriage (1964, compared to 1872 in English Canada) (Dumont 1992; Burt 1994; Tremblay 2002). The second is the difference in political culture. Historically, the conservative Catholic Church in Quebec promoted a tra-ditional role for women subordinated in the family and encouraged a view of women as the 'mothers' of Quebec, the guardians of agrarian francophone Catholic traditions within the family. These ideas were largely abandoned, however, during the Quiet Revolution of the 1960s, which associated women's aspirations for participation with the creation of a modern participatory Quebec polity and society. As a result, Quebec went from lagging behind English Canada to overtaking it in terms of the number of women elected to political office and social programs concerning child care and parental leave.

It would be misleading, however, to see Quebec women's struggles and feminist organiz-ing as solely a second-wave phenomenon of the 1960s and 1970s. Indeed, Quebec wom-en were as active as the suffragettes and first-wave feminists of English Canada at the time. Yolande Cohen (2000) divides the Quebec movement's history into three periods: a feminism of rights and demands for the vote (1890–1920), a period of social feminism advocating a second wave of women's enfranchisement (1920–60), and a feminism of political emancipation (1960–70). These periods correspond approximately to develop-ments in the rest of Canada. Cohen's contention is that Quebec women addressed the issues of femininity and feminism as their counterparts in other provinces did, the main distinction being the addition of nationalism to the mix (Cohen 2000).[10] Early women's organizing in Quebec centred on social feminist social reform in both anglophone and francophone communities. The Fédération nationale Saint-Jean-Baptiste, formed in 1907 as a forum for reform for French Canadian women, while tending to a more cautious and qualified feminism because of the church-centred French Canadian nationalist ideology, also displayed 'progressive aspects', and its 'questioning of the status quo severely weak-ened some of the most persistent prejudices concerning women' (Lavigne et al. 1979, 75). Les cercles des fermières, a secular forum for French Canadian women, was established by the Ministry of Agriculture in 1915 and organized French Canadian farm women. By 1945, its large membership, now able to cast ballots, worried the Church, which issued a directive for women to leave Les cercles and join a Catholic version, the Union catholique des fermières. As Dumont recounts, '[t]he reaction of women was revealing. Some 20 per cent complied . . . . while others, contrary to all expectations, resisted the various means of persuasion' (Dumont 1992, 79).

These efforts provided, as Dumont (1992, 86) argues, a 'process of changing mentalities . . . working slowly as much with the "ordinary" women in traditional women's associa-tions as with the more educated women aware of the impossible dead end that society offered to them'. Therefore, while second-wave feminism in Quebec arose at the same time as the Quiet Revolution and the emergence of Quebec nationalism, it was not cre-ated by the emergence of these movements. The foundation had been set in the early struggles against traditional private conceptions of womanhood.

However, in the progressive politics of the time, it is not surprising that many Quebec feminists would become allied with the emerging Quebec nationalist movement. As Tremblay (2002, 380) recounts, 'the writing of the Manifeste des Femmes Québécoises clearly echoes the manifesto of the Front de Libération du Québec', putting forth the cry of "No free women without women's liberation! No free women without Quebec's liberation"' (see also Dumont 1992). Quebec feminism found a home and a powerful ally in the nationalist movement, as both spoke the language of liberation and autonomy. The mainstream political manifestation of the movement, the Parti Québécois, was in the vanguard in terms of policies addressing the needs of women. However, just as English Canadian women found that their place in the progressive movements of the 1960s was not as equal as the language of those movements would suggest, by the end of the 1970s Quebec women were less sanguine about how closely allied their interests were with those of the Parti Québécois (Dumont 1992, 88).

The association between Quebec's women's struggles and the province's national-ist struggles has made the Quebec women's movement and the issues and strategies adopted by the movement distinct from those of the women's movement in the rest of Canada. It has also made the movement far more focused on provincial politics than on national politics. In 1981–2, while the Fédération des femmes du Québec (FFQ, estab-lished in 1966) supported proposed constitutional amendments, it had to deal with provincial sentiment that the government of Quebec was far more progressive than the federal government in looking after women's needs. The nationalist aspect of the Quebec women's movement and its association with the provincial 'state' has had an ongoing ef-fect on the relationship of Quebec's women's organizations with those of English Canada. For example, the membership of Quebec organizations in the National Action Committee on the Status of Women (NAC) can be characterized as 'on-again off-again' (Vickers, Rankin, and Appelle 1993). The conflict between federalist and separatist positions is not limited to national organizations such as NAC; it also creates divisions and tensions within the Quebec women's movement itself (Dobrowolsky 2000a, 58).

In summary, labelling the English and French elements of the Canadian movement as 'two solitudes' is a bit of dramatic hyperbole. This is not to downplay the distinctiveness of the Quebec movement, put so well by Dumont (1992, 89):

> The truth is that feminism in Quebec was stimulated and nurtured by the powerful nationalist movement which swept Quebec between 1963 and 1990. Whether opponents or partisans of sovereignty, the women of Quebec knew how to combine causes and, in this way, shaped feminism different from the rest of Canada.

As we shall see in later chapters, the close relationship between Québécois feminism and nation-building has had significant results in making Quebec unique within Canada. When policies regarding pay equity, employment equity, child care, and maternity leave are compared across the provinces, Quebec's social provision appears much more ad-vanced and progressive. Further to this, there appears to a greater acceptance of women in political roles within the province. As Tremblay (2009, 51–69) illustrates, Quebec is one of the few political jurisdictions where women do well in the first-past-the-post electoral system, winning a creditable number of seats in the mainstream parties and holding numerous key posts in provincial cabinets.

But there are also many similarities and shared concerns between the Quebec movement and its counterparts in the rest of Canada, as illustrated by Strong-Boag, Gleason, and Perry (2002, 376):

> For all that sets them apart, feminist politics in Quebec, as elsewhere, high-lights issues like employment equity, affordable daycare, and violence against women. December 6 is observed nationally as the anniversary of the massacre of 14 women by a gunman at the Université de Montréal.

The Royal Commission on the Status of Women and the National Action Committee (NAC)

In Canada, governments facing controversial issues often establish a royal commission or inquiry as a convenient way of appearing to address an issue without actually taking action through policy. Nonetheless, in the late 1960s it was difficult for women to obtain even this symbolic action. As Monique Bégin (1992, 26), secretary to the commission when it was finally established, observes, 'women did not represent . . . a constituency on the political agenda of the Canadian State'. Many events and women came together to force the establishment of the Royal Commission on the Status of Women. Canada had recently undergone a national evaluation of its identity with the Royal Commission on Bilingualism and Biculturalism, which tabled its reports in 1965 and 1967. In addition, English Canadian women's groups were impressed by the US Commission on the Status of Women (1961–3), headed by former First Lady Eleanor Roosevelt (Bégin 1992). The timing was also opportune because the Liberal government of the time was a minority government, with the New Democratic Party (NDP) holding the balance of power. However, even with pressure from the newly allied CEW and FFQ, women in the media, and female members of Parliament such as Liberal cabinet minister Judy LaMarsh and NDP member Grace MacInnis, it still took a threat of mobilizing large violent protests by two million women on Parliament Hill to compel the government to commit to a commission. As Dobrowolsky (2000a, 19) argues, 'straightforward lobbying was not enough: there had to be substantial collective coordination, strategic political allies, and a realizable potential for mass mobilization.' It also required the right timing.

On 16 February 1967, the government of Lester Pearson established the Royal Commission on the Status of Women (RCSW). Its mandate was wide-ranging: 'to inquire into and report upon the status of women in Canada, and to recommend what steps might be taken by the Federal Government to ensure for women equal opportunities with men in all aspects of Canadian society'. This included the 'laws and practices under federal jurisdiction concerning the political rights of women', the present and potential role of women in the labour force, marriage and divorce, taxation issues, and immigration and citizenship laws (RCSW 1970, ix).

The reaction of Canadian women was stunning. In response to brochures distributed in supermarkets and libraries, the commission received 468 briefs and '1000 letters of opinion' (RCSW 1970, ix). During hearings across Canada in 1968, some 890 witnesses appeared. In addition, 40 special studies were commissioned and published separately. The final report, released in September 1970, listed 167 recommendations and covered issues of economics, education, the law, reproductive control, child care, the needs of Aboriginal, Inuit, and minority women, and women's representation in public life. The report itself represented a lengthy analysis of the structural nature of women's inequality in Canada and a blueprint for its alleviation.

We spend time reviewing the RCSW because it was such a central event in Canadian second wave feminism. More than 40 years after its release, it remains an unfulfilled dream of what Canadian women need to ensure their equality. When it was released, it was, as one *Toronto Star* journalist described it, a ticking time bomb and a persuasive call to revolution (Bégin 1992, 22). Government action on the report was at best slow and in some areas—national child care and abortion most obviously—non-existent. However, for women's groups, the inquiry process illustrated what the mobilization of Canadian women could do, and the process of preparing briefs and making recommendations helped to spread feminist ideals among Canadian women's groups.

Significantly, it provided a target and a set of goals for women's organizing and confirmed that the personal grievances of many women were indeed political. The recommendations of the RCSW stood as a tangible list on which women's groups could focus their mobilizing efforts. They were also a set of criteria against which government action and inaction could be measured. One important feature was recommendation 155, which called on the federal government to fund women's groups and thus facilitate their access to public life (RCSW 1970, 49). Finally, the document outlined a relationship of Canadian women to the state framed in the logic that state action could remedy injustices through public policy choices based on a belief in social and political rights. As such, it fit comfortably with the language and activity of liberal feminists.

Monique Bégin (1997, 14), reflecting on the report 20 years later, sees this liberal feminist character as both a strength and weakness:

> The RCSW's report was inspired mainly by the idea of equal rights and equal opportunities and, to some extent, by a view of society based on the cultural feminism of Simone de Beauvoir. . . . This liberal feminist mindset explains why many of the report's recommendations were implemented—those involving reforms to laws, practices, or procedures, in particular. It also explains why there was lack of action on those recommendations which required radical change—that is, on those issues which Canadian society would consider too revolutionary, such as pay equity, day care, access to abortion, and economic rewards to homemakers. . . . The RCSW's focus on equal rights and opportunities also helps to explain the report's failure to examine such major contemporary issues as violence against women (sexual or physical) and its relative weakness on such topics as the participation of women in political life.

The RCSW marks a point at which many of the segments of the movement and streams of feminist thought came together around a common set of goals. This coalition was given an organizational identity in 1972 with the establishment of the National Action Committee on the Status of Women, which was intended to pressure government and ensure that the recommendations of the RCSW were implemented.[11] As Jill Vickers, Pauline Rankin, and Christine Appelle (1993) describe it, NAC was a 'parliament of women', bringing both 'reformist' liberal feminists and radical feminists into a coalition, even if tenuous.

For some, NAC was the voice of mainstream institutionalized liberal feminism (Adamson et al. 1988); others such as Bégin (1997) and Dobrowolsky (2000a) argue that the distinctions between these streams are not so clear-cut. Both liberal and radical feminists would influence one another. The more conventional liberal approaches generally recognized the need to act outside acceptable political avenues in some cases, while more radical approaches at times worked within the system, making use of government funding and support. While the coalition certainly experienced tension, the fact that NAC was able to manage the conflict and for the next 10 years function as the primary representative of women's pressure on the federal government was testimony to the strength of the alliance. At its inception, it had 30 member groups; nine years later the number had risen to 170. In 1984, nearly 300 groups claimed membership, and by the end of the 1980s there were more than 400 (Adamson et al. 1988, 71–2). Member groups included women operating local women's centres and shelters, minority and Aboriginal women, academic and business women, and women from the trade union movement. NAC's priorities in 2005 were wide-ranging, listing poverty; child care; violence against women; participation in governance and international institutions; protection of the rights of indigenous, immigrant, and refugee women; anti-racism; anti-homophobia; rights in health education, training, employment, and housing; reproductive autonomy; and environmental issues (http://www.nac-cca.ca/about/about_e.htm).

It can be argued that this diversity made NAC flexible in terms of the strategies and the issues it adopts. Initially, NAC focused on lobbying efforts and establishing a close working relationship with the state. This worked well, as the booming Canadian economy allowed the Liberal government of Pierre Trudeau to maintain a 'spirit of generosity and openness' (Bégin 1997, 17) and to increase spending in support of women's initiatives. However, circumstances changed in the latter half of the 1970s as the economy took a downturn. Faced with 'stagflation' in the economy and a significant increase in demands from a diversifying women's movement, governments became much more hostile. Ironically, Bégin (1997, 17) identifies 1975, the International Year of the Woman, as the start of the change: '[I]t was the last year in which women perceived a pro-active cooperation between women's groups and government.' While legal and legislative changes were achieved after this point,[12] such changes were commonly achieved in conflict with governments rather than in cooperation. Tellingly, many of these achievements were gained through the courts rather than through government.

Women and the Charter of Rights and Freedoms

The next focus of mass mobilization for the women's movement in Canada was the repatriation and reform of the Canadian constitution in the early 1980s. While women mobilized around the possibility of attaining constitutionally guaranteed equality rights, they were also motivated by the need to protect the rights of Aboriginal women, employment rights, economic rights, reproductive rights, and rights within the family. Across Canada, women closely followed, discussed, and researched the constitutional proposals and their position within them. This activity intensified when the federal government unilaterally brought forward its proposals, which included a Charter of Rights containing equality provisions that women's groups found too weak (Dobrowolsky 2000a). In parliamentary hearings on the proposal, women's groups such as NAC, the Canadian Advisory Committee on the Status of Women, the National Association of Women and the Law (NAWL), and the Canadian Abortion Rights Action League (CARAL) took similar stands regarding explicit mention of women's equality, but they also raised the broader issues of women's representation on the Supreme Court and in Parliament, education and reproductive rights, the status of Aboriginal women, and discrimination on the basis of marital status, sexual orientation, and political belief. There were some exceptions: the Fédération des femmes du Québec chose not to appear, and groups representing Aboriginal women, namely the Native Women's Association of Canada and Indian Rights for Indian Women, speaking from the position of being in both Canadian society and Aboriginal society, were much more critical of the broader constitutional proposals (Dobrowolsky 2000a). The response of the parliamentary committee was supportive of the positions outlined by women's groups because it fit with the government's interest in having emphasis placed on the Charter in its constitutional package. As a result, some of the women's movement's demands were met, particularly those around equality guarantees. Other demands, however, were left out. As Dobrowolsky (2000a, 50) puts it, 'women's groups were by no means the allies of the government at this point. The movement's diverse interests and commitments meant that demands exceeded what the federal government was prepared to concede.' And as events unfolded, it was not clear how sacrosanct even the equality provisions would be.

As negotiations proceeded, a federal-provincial proposal emerged to preserve the Westminster tradition of parliamentary sovereignty by allowing governments to override some of the provisions of the Charter, including the equality provisions. These provisions included section 28, which read: 'Notwithstanding anything in the Charter, the rights and freedoms referred to in it are guaranteed equally to male and female persons.' The women's movement responded by mobilizing a massive pressure campaign on MPs, members of provincial legislatures, and provincial premiers. Women across Canada phoned, wrote letters, sent telegrams, and protested in front of the legislatures, and eventually the premiers and federal government backed down, dropping the proposed ability to override the equality provisions of section 28.

The combined efforts of the movement had influenced the process of constitutional change, with most of the movement's demands for equality rights in section 15 met and the distinct gender equality provision of section 28 protected from override. Section 15(1) of the Constitution Act of 1982 (part 1 of which constitutes the Canadian Charter of Rights and Freedoms) sets out explicit equality rights, stating that 'every individual is equal before and under the law and has the right to the equal protection and equal benefit of the law without discrimination and, in particular, without discrimination based on race, national or ethnic origin, colour, religion, sex, age or mental or physical disability' (http://laws.justice.gc.ca/en/charter/). Section 15(2) protects the use of affirmative action programs by not precluding 'any law, program or activity that has as its object the amelioration of conditions of disadvantaged individuals or groups. . .' (ibid.). However, as Dobrowolsky (2000a, 62, 71) points out, the original vision of the movement had been 'much grander. . . . Ultimately, there was tremendous support for a single basic issue, women's equality, rather than a whole host of complex, equally fundamental feminist demands. . . . The "consensus" was more of a compromise and reflected the fact that a number of profound debates within the women's movement had to be glossed over, and that major demands were diluted, if not disregarded, given strategic decisions in response to deteriorating political developments.'

Constitutional guarantees of equal rights opened up a new avenue for pressing women's concerns. Women's groups started in earnest to press the courts to interpret the section 15 provisions to mean 'equality of result' as a means of ending systemic discrimination. Groups such as the National Association of Women and the Law and the Women's Legal Education and Action Fund became much more prominent in the movement.

Agreement on a liberal interpretation of equality rights was not unanimous, however. Many women remained committed to working on issues outside the courts, focusing less on the abstract language of constitutional rights and more on the reality of their everyday lives. NAC also played a part in this. As Meg Luxton (2001, 66) argues, one of the features that stimulated the participation of working-class women in the second wave of the movement was 'the organizational practices of the autonomous women's movement, especially as developed in the National Action Committee on the Status of Women'.

Within the labour force, issues of pay equity, discrimination in promotion, and the relegation of women to the badly paid pink ghetto of 'women's work' were significant. But concerns were not limited to pay and achieving a 'living wage' for women. They also included the culture of the workplace, such as sexualized dress codes for women workers such as secretaries, cashiers, nurses, and flight attendants, which often highlighted their sexuality to the detriment of comfort and job efficiency, and, even more disturbing, the acceptance of sexual harassment on the job. Outside of the labour force, women pressed for recognition of their unpaid work in the home. Some of these grievances could and would be pursued through legal channels, but others required concerted work by women through unions, informally in the workplace, and in grassroots networks of women.

The effort to change the culture regarding sexual harassment and domestic work was indicative of the movement's demand that the inequality and politics of the private sphere had to be recognized. This extended to battles regarding reproductive autonomy, the accessibility of contraception, and abortion. In local communities, they were addressed by organizations such as Planned Parenthood and women's health clinics. On the national front, reproductive autonomy and abortion became the focus of groups such as the Canadian Abortion Rights Action League (which closed in 2005 and was replaced by the Abortion Rights Coalition of Canada), the Pro-Choice Action Network, and Canadians for Choice. In the courts, abortion rights were pursued by the Legal Education and Action Fund (LEAF) and the National Association of Women and the Law (NAWAL), along with Dr Henry Morgentaler.

As we shall see in chapter 12, abortion is one of the most controversial issues pertaining to women's reproductive autonomy. In Canada, the battle over abortion was fought predominantly in the courts by Dr Henry Morgentaler along with various women's health organizations and women's legal campaigners. Since the 1960s, Dr Morgentaler had attempted to provide abortion services through free-standing clinics, mainly in Quebec but also in Manitoba and Ontario. The results of his efforts were several prosecutions followed by acquittals. In a final appeal to the Supreme Court in 1988, the law was stuck down and Canada was left with no law restricting or regulating access to abortion. In 1991, the federal Parliament's attempt to reinstate a new law was met with widespread protest from women's groups and was ultimately defeated in the Senate by one vote. Thirty-three further attempts to regulate abortion have also failed. However, this does not mean that access is without restrictions as regional variations in cost and in the existence of clinics or hospitals and doctors willing to provide abortion services means access is not equally available to all Canadian women. The abortion issue also became a flashpoint for an emerging counter-movement focused on women's traditional mothering roles and religious beliefs regarding when life starts.[13]

Choice in Canada

The Abortion Rights Coalition of Canada (ARCC) was formed in 2005, taking over from CARAL, as a nation-wide pro-choice group devoted to ensuring abortion rights and access for women. The ARCC's mandate is to undertake political and educational work on reproductive rights and health issues, specifically protecting and improving access to reproductive health services such as abortion and countering anti-choice campaigns. (see www.arcc-cdac.ca)

Formed in 2002, Canadians for Choice has as its mandate the prevention of unwanted pregnancies, the promotion of contraception, and the education of men, women, and children in the promotion of healthy, happy, wanted families. It is involved in education regarding reproductive health choices, researching and monitoring reproductive health policy, and acting as a resource centre for reproductive health information. (see www.canadiansforchoice.ca)

In the legal and legislative spheres, many of the struggles for women's autonomy were fought in terms of the body and as issues of freedom of choice, discrimination because of pregnancy, and the right to 'security of person'. This effort concerned the recognition and protection of women's autonomous control over their selves and, as a result, one of the major issues during this period was violence against women. The enormity of the problem was graphically and tragically illustrated for Canadians on December 6, 1989 when 14 young female engineering students were shot at the École Polytechnique de Montréal. Their murderer accused them of being, 'une gang des féministes'. This event was to become a rallying point for Canadian women and men to campaign for the eradication of violence against women and the creation of organizations such as the YWCA's Rose Campaign (www.rosecampaign.ca) and the White Ribbon Campaign (www.whiteribbon.ca), which focus on stopping violence against women. The federal government's response was to dedicate 6 December as a national day of remembrance for the 14 women in Montreal and for all those who have perished from violence against women and children. Further policy responses were pursued through efforts to institute stricter gun control, an approach that has not been without controversy. As recently as September 2010, the Conservative government narrowly lost a vote to kill the long-gun registry brought in by the previous Liberal government.

At the beginning of the twenty-first century, the idea that violence against women is unacceptable is a 'no-brainer'. However, that has not always been the case, and it can be argued that one of the successes of the second-wave movement was the change in public attitudes and norms regarding domestic violence. In demanding amendments to the Criminal Code and pursuing changes and protections through the courts, women's groups were able to change the structures governing violent behaviour. They also made changes by providing services for abused and assaulted women through networks of shelters and rape crisis centres. Slowly, general social attitudes changed regarding the acceptability of violence against women. However, the large number of cash-strapped and over-subscribed shelters and rape crisis centres testifies to the fact that such violence is far from eradicated.

The Rise of Neo-liberalism and the Changing Women's Movement

For NAC, the 1990s was a period of transition. It had always struggled to keep its coalition together since the various regional and ideological member groups did not always see eye-to-eye with the organization. As early as the 1980s, minority women's groups were emerging to pressure governments for funding, supportive policy, and recognition of their particular multiple oppressions. As noted above, the more critical women's voices in the constitutional hearings were those of Aboriginal women. However, Aboriginal, minority, refugee, lesbian, black, and poor women tended to be rendered invisible by the dominance of liberal equity feminism and a movement which still appeared very white, middle-class, educated, and professional. By the late 1980s it was clear that NAC also needed to speak for women marginalized because of race, ethnicity, ability, or age (Rebick 2005). By the mid-1990s, NAC had selected Sunera Thobani, a woman of colour, as its president. As NAC's own history says, this move was not without some pain. Molgat (n.d.) writes, 'Many white feminists, then as now, were forced to confront and challenge systemic racism as a part of the feminist movement. Thobani's presidency was peppered with much resistance and downright acrimony, which in many instances masked the progressive work that was being done in NAC.' This work included serving as the lead Canadian non-governmental organization at the World Conference on Women in Beijing and continuing campaigns concerning male violence against women and the effect of globalization on women. NAC worked to include minority women in its campaigns and struggled to keep its coalitions together. While some groups such as NWAC (Native Women's Association of Canada) and NOIVMW (National Organization of Immigrant and Visible Minority Women of Canada), while willing to work with NAC, chose not to affiliate, this period saw an increase in its member groups, as immigrant and refugee women's organizations, women of colour, and women in the labour movement affiliated with NAC (Molgat n.d.). Thobani was followed as President of NAC by another woman of colour, Joan Grant-Cummings, in 1996.

As Judy Rebick (2010), former President of NAC, points out

> Many people have blamed the anti-racist struggle in NAC for the decline of the organization. I reject these arguments. Instead, women of colour coming into leadership in NAC helped the organization remain vital long after it might have without the influx of new and more radical women challenging it on every level. Moreover, the women's movement remains the most diverse social

movement and pioneered the process of change that is now influencing many other social organizations.

She attributes the decline to the turn to the neo-liberal state and the associated cuts in funding to women's organizations such as NAC. The 1980s and 1990s saw the consolidation of a new-liberal economic agenda by both Conservative and Liberal governments. As we shall discuss in the following chapters, this was to have profound effects on social policies geared towards women and ultimately on the place of women in Canadian society. The language of politics became less focused on equality, replaced by an emphasis on individual opportunity, choice, and fairness. As a result the social, economic, and political needs of women became less and less salient.

This significantly altered the context in which the Canadian women's movement operated. As McKeen (2004, 74) points out, the mainstream movement represented by organizations such as NAC and the women's sections of the large unions came to focus not on specific 'women's issues' like child care, abortion, affirmative action, and pay equity, but on struggling against more general economic and labour changes that had resulted from government pushes for free trade, privatization, deregulation, and deficit and debt reduction. There appeared to be a growing diffusion in the focus of activities around women and work, while at the same time the growing number of minority women's groups demanded that the interrelations of racism, sexism, and classism, not only within work but in unequal experiences of poverty, be recognized and addressed.

Furthermore, the women's movement was encountering the resistance of an organized counter-movement. The demands that the women's movement had put forward required significant changes in society; but, it was not surprising that resistance and counter-movements would emerge. In 1984 a new women's group appeared on the scene, not an unusual happening since groups were popping up all across Canada. However, what set this group apart was its message. REAL Women—Realistic, Equal, Active, for Life—promoted an anti-feminist vision focused on preserving the 'traditional family' from the changing nature of Canadian society and the feminist agenda. Members saw their mandate as advocating for legislative and legal protection of the 'Judeo-Christian' understanding of marriage, the central role of women in the home, and the rights of the fetus. REAL Women and provincial organizations, such as the Alberta Federation of Women United for Families, claimed to represent a large silent majority of Canadians who were not feminists (MacIvor 1996). By the end of the 1980s, the group had found a willing ally in the Conservative government in Ottawa, which was generally hostile to the demands of women's and feminist groups.

As we discussed in the first chapter, Canadians came to reject the term 'feminist' and disparage organizations associated with feminists. Attitudes towards feminism became increasingly negative and feminists were consistently ranked below other identifiable groups, such as gays and lesbians, racial minorities, Aboriginal peoples, and big business. These changes marked the arrival of the backlash against feminism in Canada. The tide had turned against the second wave.

Backlash: The tide goes out on the second wave

What is remarkable is how successful both the government and the media were in redefining the image of Canadian feminism: the movement was no longer seen to be about women's social and political equality but as just one of many 'special in-terests' making unreasonable demands on the greater society. The image of feminist politics was transformed from that of equality-seeking to the seeking of greater advan-tage and superior treatment—in other words, inequality-seeking. This image made the movement vulnerable to accusations that it represented only a limited constituency of Canadian women. For governments facing difficult economic times, this transforma-tion made it that much easier to cut funding to women's programs and causes.

The cuts and vilification were felt across the movement, and the mainstream movement discovered that even legal opportunities could backfire. Those involved in the counter-movement against feminism, such as REAL Women, found that the Charter and its equality provisions could be used to oppose affirmative action, pregnancy leaves, the right of a pregnant woman to choose abortion without the father's consent, and similar policies, and could even be used to support the rights of those accused of sexual assault against those of the victim (Mandel 1992, 258).

It became very easy to blame the women's movement for its own problems. Divisions and disputes within the movement made it easy for the government and me-dia to characterize the movement as unreasonable and exclusive. During the debates over the Meech Lake and Charlottetown constitutional accords, NAC and the FFQ in Quebec took opposite positions, and when NAC took the 'No' position in the referen-dum on the Charlottetown Accord, the government of Brian Mulroney dubbed it the 'enemy of Canada' (Crow and Gotell 2000, 67). Even liberal feminists took a dim view of the movement in the late 1980s and 1990s. Bégin (1997, 20–1) writes:

> During the 1980s, feminists became widely seen as intolerant and dogmat-ic. Many women in positions of responsibility, who could have helped and who wanted to help, felt that they could never be feminist enough to meet the demands of the official constituency of feminists. A breach of trust and solidarity grew, accompanied by bitterness on both sides. At the same time, the issues presented to the government for action by the women's constitu-ency dealt increasingly with topics that were seen as marginal. The movement no longer seemed to represent the majority of women in Canada. Moreover, other political divisions crept in; it was only too easy for politicians to point to the fact that the Francophone element, reflecting Quebec's politics, was more and more absent from national women's groups and that Anglophone feminists were usually from Toronto, not from eastern or western Canada. The movement seemed to have little to say for, or to, significant subgroups in Canadian society—immigrant women, disabled women, domestics, farm women, poor women, or housewives.

It is testimony to the strength of the backlash view in society that even some femi-nists themselves put forward moderate interpretations of the backlash view. There was an underlying sense that the victim was to blame. However, it was never reasonable to expect organizational unity and a single voice from a movement that is by its nature a diverse and multi-faceted phenomenon. Just as there is an enormous range of per-spectives within feminism, the real world of women's organizations reflects diversity rather than a monolithic bloc. It is also unreasonable to expect cultural issues, such as patriarchal language and historical interpretation, to be presented in tidy political and policy packages. Consequently, it is easy to label such efforts at change as marginal and trivial. However, for many women, these issues were meaningful. As the Canadian state embraced neo-liberalism, Canadians became increasingly ambivalent about feminism, government funds and support were cut, and more and more women identified themselves as 'I'm not a feminist but . . . ', the movement became ever more frustrated and defensive.

It was in this context that Canada's first female Prime Minister, Kim Campbell, came to power in June 25, 1993, upon winning the Progressive Conservative Party leadership contest after Brian Mulroney's resignation. Although Campbell was a self-proclaimed feminist, her short tenure reflected the new relationship Canadians and the Canadian state had with women and feminists. Touted as a breakthrough for Canadian women in politics, Campbell found it hard to bring a feminist approach to government. As then President of NAC, Sunera Thobani, commented 'A female Prime Minister doesn't mean we've got women's equality in the country. . . . [T]he quality of life for Canadian women and their children is deteriorating' (Toughell 1993, A14). Thobani blamed the Tory neo-conservative agenda and saw little hope that Campbell would do anything differently. One way Campbell illustrated her commitment to the neo-conservative/neo-liberal turn was by significantly reorganizing the federal bureaucracy, cutting the number of departments and Cabinet Ministries from 35 to 23, and creating three 'superministries': public security, health, and Canadian heritage. As we shall discuss in chapter 6, this reorganization was to have a lasting impact on the place of women's issues within the bureaucracy and was a further step in the disappearance of women's issues and policy needs from the federal governing structures. Significantly for the women's movement, little was done to stop the cuts to women's programs and the funding of women's organizations.

I'll be a post-feminist in the post-patriarchy': The third wave?

As we discussed in the chapter on postmodern feminist theory, by the 1980s, philosophical currents were emerging that pointed to much more complex understandings of what defines womanhood. While many of these new writings were criticized as being too abstract and academic, they were not without influence in the movement. Faced with decreasing support from the state and greater society, feminism appeared to become much more self-reflexive and introspective and took on a much more cultural thrust.

By the 1990s, a cohort of women who had been defining their own feminist agenda and exploring the contradictions in their lived experience, not only as women but also with other identities, became visible. The result is a very personal and culturally defined feminism that expresses a great deal of frustration and 'in-your-face' unwillingness to conform not only to patriarchal standards but also to those set by second-wave feminism. As Shandi Miller (AWID 2001) describes

> There isn't a cohesive feminist movement of social activists working explicitly on definable 'women's' issues as there was in the 60s and 70s. It's obvious that the groundwork has been laid by these coalitions. Now people are trying to deal with the implications of this work on intellectual and personal levels, and to reformulate politics in terms of issues that are relevant now and in terms of many issues instead of those relevant to a particular few (AWID 2001).

Feminism had become increasingly concerned with working out the complexity and multiplicity of what 'woman' meant as an identity. Third-wave feminism emerged as Aboriginal women, women of colour, poor women, lesbians, and young women pointed out that their personal experiences were derived from intersecting and re-inforcing identities rather than from a homogeneous category of woman. They em-phasized the complexities and ambiguities of people's lives, illustrating the conflicts between equality and sameness. The third wave was built on concepts of difference rather than sameness and particularity rather than universality (Arneil 1999, 87). Consequently, much of the discourse regarding third-wave feminism is focused on is-sues of intersectionality, as discussed in chapter 3, and the understanding of complex individual subjectivities. Third-wave feminism became about gaining control and re-appropriating all possible identities available to women and celebrating all of those empowered selves. This project to appropriate and celebrate identities and challenge systemic oppression in the social norms made culture a significant sphere of conflict. Thus, while the political face of the movement appeared to decline, its activities could still be subsumed under the mantle of the movement.

The third wave brings together and highlights two sets of grievances, one based on women's similarity to men and the other on their differences, not only from men but also from other women. The traditional grievances are centred on the demand for equal rights and an end to discrimination and on the belief that women are similar enough to men that they should be given the same rights and privileges. This gives rise to the second set of grievances, since the equality sought seemed to suggest that women should behave like men. Consequently, the second set of grievances focuses on protecting and building women's individual identities and giving value to the quali-ties and roles associated with all forms of womanhood. The demand is that women be given equal status in society as diverse women. And as we discussed in the introduc-tion, a distinction is drawn between equality and equity.

NWAC and DAWN

NWAC: The Native Women's Association of Canada emerged out of an International Native Women's conference in Albuquerque, New Mexico, in 1971. While not originally a national organization, regional and local Native Women's groups formalized their annual meetings in 1972–73 as a national native women's committee. It was then mandated in 1974 to promote the well-being and equality of First Nation and Métis women politically, economically, and legally. During the 1970s through to the present, the NWAC tirelessly campaigned for the rescinding or significant remodeling of the Indian Act to ensure full equality for Aboriginal women within Act (see the chapter 3 discussion of Aboriginal feminism). In the past, NWAC has also worked to restructure the judicial and prison system to better meet the needs of Aboriginal women. The most recent campaign, a five-year initiative (2005-2010) called Sisters in Spirit, is intended to conduct research and raise awareness of the alarmingly high rates of violence against Aboriginal women and girls in Canada. (see www.nwac.ca/home)

DAWN: Founded in 1985, the DisAbled Women's Network (DAWN) is a national organization comprising and providing a voice for women who self-identify as women with disabilities. Responding to the levels of violence experienced by disabled women in Canada, DAWN sets as its goal the achievement of autonomous control of disabled women over their lives and the ending of discrimination against the disabled: 'to end the poverty, isolation, discrimination and violence experienced by women with disabilities. We are working to ensure we get the services and supports we need, have access to opportunities that non-disabled people take for granted, and have freedom of choice in all aspects of our lives.' (See www.dawncanada.net)

There are tensions within the third wave, particularly in the way it interacts with the second wave. One area of difference that can be identified is the shift in the interpretation of 'the personal as political'. 'Instead of being used to identify collective women's issues, feminists began to use it to explain how individual acts can empower women as a group' (Van Deven 2009, 29; also see Arneil 1999, 189–90). Third-wave feminists dismiss the second wave as old-fashioned and unrepresentative of their lives (Baumgardner and Richards 2000; AWID 2001; Rupp 2001). Second-wave feminists (and some non-feminists) accuse the third wave of being unfocused, self-obsessed, and not politically relevant.

However, Shandi Miller (AWID 2001) encapsulates the focus, diversity and enthusiasm of the Third Wave politics.

> I want to talk more about the linkages and contradictions of living in Canada in the new millennium, and working identity/pleasure/politics into issues of pop culture, youth activism, poverty, consumerism, anti-globalization movement, HIV/AIDS, immigration, technology and on and on (AWID 2001).

Within the movement, we can see these views reflected in the proliferation of groups that represent a variety of women. For example, when hearings were held in February 2007 by the House of Commons Standing Committee on the Status of Women on the potential impact of the change in mandate and funding cuts to Status of Women Canada, 27 groups appeared to speak against the cuts.[14] This committee itself was the result of concerted pressure on Liberal Prime Minister Paul Martin from women's groups, provincial and territorial women's advisory councils, and women MPs in 2004 and 2005. As reported in *Herizons* (Mitchell 2005, 2), this pressure included 'some good old-fashioned agitating' when St. John feminists Dorothy Inglis and Nancy Riche crashed a meeting of ministers responsible for the status of women with a list of five demands.

Many groups also make clear links between individual, national, and international issues, focusing on activities that are directed both locally and globally. Much of this is associated with the 1979 Convention on Elimination of All Forms of Discrimination against Women and the Fourth World Conference on Women in Beijing in 1995, which shall be further discussed in chapter 13. What these international agreements provide are benchmarks, goals, and commitments against which women's organizations can measure their own and other government's actions. In May 1999, the Canadian Feminist Alliance for International Action (FAFIA) was formed with the support of 35 Canadian women's groups to do just this. Quoting Lise Martin, executive director of the Canadian Research Institute for the Advancement of Women (CRIAW), one of the founding organizations, *Herizons* (1999, 10), reported,

> 'Its formation marks a new stage in Canadian women's political activism,' she said, noting the Alliance's focus on economic policies and their impact on women's equality. 'There is a determination to defend Canadian women's rights at the international level as well as at home.' Appearing before UN treaty, bodies bringing complaints to the United Nations when Canada is not complying and helping to negotiating agreements on women's human rights will be part of FAFIA's work.

With the formation of organizations and networks like FAFIA, there is also recognition that structures and events that influence women's lives and well-being are not solely domestic: women are as likely to be affected, and as significantly, by international events and decisions. As Shelagh Day (*Herizons*, 1999, 10) points out, 'women's economic inequality is affected not only by decisions taken in Canada, but by regional trade agreements, and by decisions taken by bodies such as the World Bank and the International Monetary Fund'.

Old Waves, New Waves, Mobilization and Latency

Leila Rupp (2001) asks an interesting question: is feminism the province of old (or middle-aged) women? She points to some suggestive patterns. First, the tension between waves is not new: similar tensions existed in the 1950s when newly mobilized young feminists viewed the earlier suffragettes as old-fashioned anachronisms. Second, women are 'more likely to experience dissatisfaction and develop a feminist consciousness later, rather than earlier in life' (Rupp 2001, 166). Third, the image of feminists as young and militant is associated with 'rare periods of "white-hot mobilization" as the 1910s and the 1960s/early 1970s, but even in those moments the age range of activists was wider than it might seem' (Rupp 2001, 165). Between mobilization periods, the job of maintaining activities tends to fall to the women who remained involved following the mobilization. As time goes on, this group naturally grows older. When a trigger for mobilization occurs, younger women become active in the movement, and during the 'white-hot mobilization' period, the media reporting on the protests find young angry women more appealing to viewers and readers than old angry women. Rupp's explanation fits with the tendency of the movement to experience moments of mobilization and latency, as we discussed at the beginning of this chapter.

We could argue that currently the Canadian women's movement is experiencing a period of latency. The white-hot period of mobilization has disappeared and along with it some of the groups that were the centre of the movement at the peak of its mobilization in the 1970s and 1980s. For example, NAC was hit particularly hard by the funding cuts made during the 1990s and was unable to adjust to the new political climate. By 2001 the organization was working to pay down a $200,000 debt and operating with a much smaller budget dependent on insecure project funding from Status of Women

Canada rather than the core funding which had been cut in 1998. By the end of 2003, significant layoffs had occurred; its President, Denise Campbell, had resigned; and the organization had been unable to hold an annual policy meeting for two years because of the financial difficulties. At the time of writing, NAC no longer has an active website or a presence on the Internet; a link from the Wikipedia entry leads to a page in the Internet archive 'way back machine' which lists its most recent site as June 15, 2008. Similarly, the National Association of Women and the Law had to lay off staff and temporarily close its doors in 2007. However, in 2008 a successful funding campaign enabled the organization to rehire staff and re-establish its presence.

This does not mean, however, that the women's movement has completely disappeared. A few of the organizations that emerged during the first wave, such as the National Council of Women, the Canadian Federation of University Women, and the Voice of Women, a peace organization, are still active and continue to advocate on behalf of Canadian women. Joining them are a number of second- and third-wave organizations such as LEAF, NAWAL, DAWN, the NWAC, MATCH[15], FAFIA, and the women's sections of the Canadian union movement. While some of these groups have had to scale back their activities (e.g., National Organization of Immigrant and Visible Minority Women of Canada [NOIVMW], the Canadian Research Institute for the Advancement of Women [CRIAW]), most were able to mobilize to address the cuts and policy changes made by the Harper Conservative government. For example, they did achieve a restoration of funds to Status of Women Canada after the drastic cuts made in 2007, albeit with new, much more restrictive funding guidelines for advocacy groups. Further to this, and making use of the political opportunities opened up at that international level, these groups have been able to bring some pressure for change and continue to highlight the significance of women's issues in Canadian society.

These groups and organizations can be characterized as abeyance structures. Abeyance refers to the holding process by which movements sustain themselves in unreceptive political contexts (Taylor 1987). They are significant because they provide political, cultural, social, and protest resources and an institutional history, much as the NCW, CFUW, and Voice of Women did in the period between first and second waves, that ensure the continuity and groundwork from which further mobilizations can be built (Taylor 1987; see also Morris 1984, 2000 and Whittier 1995). According to Verta Taylor (1987, 762), this is characteristic of mass movements that have succeeded in building a support base, achieved a measure of influence, but are confronted with a chilly political environment. They tend not to die, but rather to scale down, retrench, and adapt to changes in the political climate (Taylor 1987, 772). This certainly describes the Canadian women's movement at the beginning of the twenty-first century: with its membership numbers and funding contracted, it continues to devise strategies appropriate to the political context in which it finds itself, and maintains a voice for the women of Canada in the struggle for political, economic, cultural, and social change and a redefinition of the place of women in society.

Conclusion: Women and Social Movement Politics: The Power of Small-p Politics

Social movements provoke official action, especially by democratic governments. Whereas movement activists seek real change and permanent access to arenas of power, government actions may be symbolic or even cosmetic, a way of damping the fires of reform. Second-wave feminist movements in advanced industrial societies have generated an assortment of responses from their governments. The most striking consequence of over 25 years of women's movement activism has been the array of institutional arrangements inside democratic states devoted to women's policy questions (Stetson and Mazur 1995b, 1).

We shall be discussing the place of women's policy questions in more detail in later chapters. However, it is important at this point to note the success of the women's movement through the twentieth century in bringing the politics of women's existences into the open and making their oppression transparent. The movement has been most successful in achieving its demands for legal recognition of equality. It also has had success in influencing the policy decisions of the state, although as demonstrated during the 1980s and 1990s, the level of success in that regard depends on the broader economic and social context. Success in gaining equal access to formal political power has also been limited, as we shall discuss in the next chapter.

As a result, it is easy to pronounce either that the women's movement has met its goals or that it is dead, much as *Time* magazine announced in June 1998. However, such a view represents a belief that the activities that take place in social and cultural life are not fully political. Studies have largely been confined to a narrowly and conventionally defined idea of politics. Examinations of political activity and behaviour focus on participation in formal, constitutional, government-oriented institutions as if this were the only way to influence public policy. Citing the number of women in national party organizations, analyzing access to government on the part of the formal organizations of the movement and other such measures are misleading because much of women's politics occurs informally in community networks that focus on the day-to-day problems faced by women. As Naomi Black (1988, 97) argues, the tendency in social movements has been to emphasize the social, which has marginalized women's politics because they are discussed 'separately from what is regarded as normal politics'.

In the first wave, women's local organizing resulted in policy changes regarding regulation of alcohol and prostitution. While these policies and the vision of many social feminists were overly harsh towards particular classes of women, they did assert that women had a role in determining the public good. In the second wave, women's efforts to establish rape crisis centres, shelters for abused women, counselling groups, and contraceptive and family planning services were also driven by an understanding of the public good. All of these activities were connected to public policy—by making transparent the services women required, providing models for service provision, and often becoming the structures through which policy was applied by state funding. Even in a limited definition of politics, these activities are political when viewed this way.

Consequently, to obtain a full picture of women's political activities, we need to broaden our definition of politics to encompass all forms of activity that have as their goal the making of public politics and the public good. To do this, it is useful to think of two kinds of politics: a large-P politics associated with the affairs of state and the activities of parties and interest groups, and a small-p politics of grassroots, consensus-based community-building (Bellah et al. 1985). As we shall discuss in the next chapter, there are many reasons and explanations for why women tend to be badly represented in the world of large-P politics. However, in the world of small-p politics, women are often the backbone of local voluntary services and social movement organizations. The activities of women's politics fall along a continuum from radical women's protest groups that eschew any connection with the state to groups that work to create close partnerships with the state. The women's movement encapsulates this continuum.[16]

It should be clear that this continuum goes beyond the obvious activities in mainstream politics to include women's work in civil society. The history of the women's movement sheds light on the nature of the relationship between women as political actors and the state and the concept of citizenship. Unfortunately, until recently little attention was paid to such activity as political. Studies of civil society and social capital have illustrated the significance of women in small-p politics and, as a consequence, make significant and interesting observations regarding women's political activity (see Skocpol, 1992; Siim, 1994; Clemens, 1999; Lowndes 2000; Evans and Harell 2005; Gidengil and O'Neill, 2006; Newman, 2009a). While we must be careful not to put too much emphasis just on small-p politics as an answer for women's power (see Arneil 1999, and Newman 2009b), this approach is useful because 'it allows us to link informal community-based activity with broadly political phenomena, which helps us make visible significant forms of political power' (Newman 2009a). As we shift gears in the next chapter to examine women's representation in the world of big-P politics, it will be useful to keep in mind the issues discussed here.

At the beginning of the twenty-first century, we can look back and observe that the twentieth century was tumultuous for Canadian women, even revolutionary. Yet, as the wave metaphor reminds us, women have not experienced a steady progression forward. Instead, progress has come in a series of steps forward, and then back, like waves eroding a shoreline.

Questions for Critical Thought

1. Is there a future for the women's movement?
2. While the women's movement has been historically necessary to promote women's social status, is it needed today?
3. How useful is the wave analogy in describing the history and activities of the women's movement? Are periods of latency necessary for social movements like the women's movement?
4. Is the Third Wave significantly different from the Second Wave? What strengths and weaknesses did each wave bring to the struggles they undertook?
5. Should Canada undertake a Second Royal Commission on the Status of Women?

CHAPTER 5

Women's Participation in Formal Politics

In this chapter we examine women's participation in formal politics in Canada to assess how well they have succeeded in that traditionally male sphere and what barriers remain to impede their success. Women comprise over 50 per cent of the population in Canada, and the fact that they are not present in halls of government in proportion to their numbers raises the obvious question: why not? And is it fair? These are legitimate empirical and normative questions for all students of politics to ask, not just feminist scholars.

A further question to consider is why participation in formal politics is so important. Understanding the relationship between political inputs and policy outputs is crucial in connecting actions by the women's movement to policy outcomes. Some researchers argue, for example, that the quantity of representation will affect the quality of representation (Thomas 1994). If so, then it is important to know how many and what kinds of women hold political office. If the goal is to change public policy, then it is important for women activists to become involved in forums where public policy is decided. Thus, women's participation in formal politics is crucial.

In focusing on participation in formal politics, we do not mean to dismiss women's participation in other forms of politics. As outlined in the previous chapter, women's involvement in community groups, social movements, and interest-based politics is critical to advancing their equality concerns. But it is within governmental institutions that policies are determined, so women's presence there is important. We would argue, in fact, that it is important to do both—be involved in formal politics as well as in wider forums of political participation.

The question then becomes: what common barriers prevent the achievement of greater diversity in Parliament, and which barriers are more prevalent in Canada? What role do public opinion, political parties, news media, and political institutions such as electoral systems play in helping or hindering the achievement of greater representation, and what are the most important barriers facing women today? This chapter addresses these questions.

The Numbers: How Absent Are Women from Formal Politics?

Women's representation in public office compared to men is low throughout the world. The United Nations has identified gender equality in representation as a goal in both

Figure 5.1 | **Percentage of Parliamentary Seats Held by Women (Lower or Single House) in Selected Countries over Time**

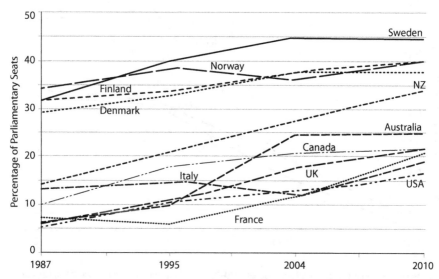

Sources: 1987 and 1995 figures from UN Statistics Division, The World's Women 2000: Trends and Statistics. Online. Available: http://unstats.un.org/unsd/demographic/ww2000/table6a.htm (accessed 2 April 2003); 2004 figures from UN Statistics Division, Statistics and Indicators on Women and Men. Online. Available: http://unstats.un.org/unsd/demographic/ww2000/table6a.htm (accessed 1 December 2010); 2010 figures from Inter-Parliamentary Union, Women in Parliaments: World Classification. Online. Available: http://www.ipu.org/wmn-e/classif.htm (accessed 2 December 2010).

the Convention on the Elimination of All Forms of Discrimination against Women (CEDAW) (Article 7) and the Beijing Platform for Action (Strategic Objective G. 182).

In its Beijing Platform the UN identified 30 per cent as the critical representation threshold to achieve in legislative institutions (Strategic Objective G. 182). The Geneva-based Inter-Parliamentary Union (IPU 2010) reports that as of October 2010, only 24 developed and developing countries' national parliaments had achieved that threshold, including Rwanda (56 per cent), Sweden (45 per cent), South Africa (44.5 per cent), Cuba (43 per cent), and Guyana (30 per cent). As of 2010, Canada ranked 50th out of 187 countries in terms of the percentage of women in the national elected legislature,[1] and ranked just above the worldwide average of about 19 per cent. Furthermore, Canada's position has slipped from the 21st place it held in 1997 because other countries' representation has improved. Canada's record is still higher than that of the United States, which tied with Turkmenistan at 72nd place in October 2010, with women comprising approximately 17 per cent in the House of Representatives and 15 per cent in the Senate.

As of 2010, women held approximately 22 per cent of the seats in Canada's House of Commons, 35 per cent of Senate seats, almost 24 per cent of the seats in provincial and territorial legislatures, and about 23 per cent of seats on municipal councils and mayoralties (see Figure 5.2), although that percentage varies widely by province and municipality. For example, in the 2003 provincial election in Quebec, women won

Figure 5.2 | Percentage of Women Elected or Appointed in Canada

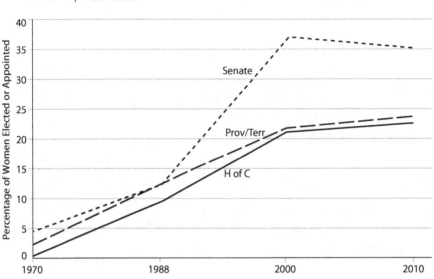

Sources: Federal and provincial/territorial figures 1970–2000 are from Trimble and Arscott (2003, 32); municipal figures from 2002, 2004, and 2009 are from the Federation of Canadian Municipalities (various); all 2010 current figures from Cool (2010, 1–2).

32 per cent of the seats in the National Assembly (MNAs), and in 2005, women comprised a majority of the leadership positions in the Parti Québécois (PQ) (Cool 2010, 2; Séguin 2005, A5). Yet by the 2007 election women's representation had slipped to 27 per cent of the seats.

Over the past few decades, women have made their greatest representational gains in the Senate, an appointed body. Prime Minister Jean Chrétien appointed 33 women senators during his terms in office, compared to Brian Mulroney's 12 and Pierre Trudeau's 12 (Parliament of Canada website: http://www.parl.gc.ca/information/about/people/Senate/WomenSenate.asp?lang=E&Hist=Y). Chrétien's appointments represented more than double the rate of appointment by each of his major predecessors. Trimble and Arscott (2000, 32) point out, however, that the women Chrétien appointed 'tended to be appointed later in life than men and to serve relatively short terms by longevity standards for that chamber'. Prime Minister Paul Martin appointed 6 women and 11 men as Senators in the course of a year; Stephen Harper appointed 11 women and 25 men as Senators in the 2006–10 period (Parliament of Canada website: http://www.parl.gc.ca/information/about/people/Senate/WomenSenate.asp?lang=E&Hist=Y).

Canada's record with regard to members of visible minorities and First Nations representation varies; neither group is represented proportionate to population. After the 2006 federal election, members of visible minority groups comprised about 8 per cent of the House of Commons (Black 2008b, 31). In 2006, visible minorities comprised about 16 per cent of the population (Black 2008b, 31). Thus, visible minorities were about halfway towards representation in proportion to their numbers in the population as of 2006 (see Table 5.1). Black (2008a, 247) notes that minority women in particular improved their representation as a proportion of women MPs and all MPs between 1993 and 2004 (see Table 5.2).

Table 5.1 | **Visible Minority MPs and Candidates, 1993–2006 in the House of Commons**

	1993	1997	2000	2004	2006
% of visible minorities in the population	9.4	11.2	13.4	14.9	16.2
MPs					
Number	13	19	17	22	24
Percentage	4.4	6.3	5.6	7.1	7.8
Ratio to population	0.47	0.56	0.42	0.48	0.48
Candidates					
Percentage	4.1	4.1	4.7	8.3	7.8
Ratio to Population	0.44	0.37	0.35	0.56	0.48

Source: Reproduced from Black (2008b, 31).

Table 5.2 | **Minority Women MPs Elected in the House of Commons 1993–2004**

	1993	1997	2000	2004
Total number of minority women compared to all MPs	11 (3.7%)	17 (5.6%)	19 (6.3%)	26 (8.4%)
Minority women as % of all women	20.8	27.4	30.6	40.0
Minority men as % of all men	24.8	24.3	22.6	22.0
Minority women as % of all minorities	15.5	22.7	26.0	32.9
Number of minority women by category				
Northern/Western European	–	1	2	3
Eastern, Southern European, and Jewish	8	12	13	14
Visible minority	2	4	4	8
Other	1	–	–	1

Source: Reproduced from Black (2008a, 247).

With regard to First Nations representation, as Ladner and McCrossan (2007, 11) point out, their historic lack of participation in formal politics stems in part from the fact that the Inuit were denied the right to vote until 1950 and that some Aboriginal people were not permitted the right to vote until 1960. Electoral participation among First Nations populations is generally lower than non-Aboriginal participation, although with huge variation by province. In the 2000 federal election, turnout ranged from a high of 67 per cent in PEI to a low of 35 per cent in Quebec and 37 per cent in Manitoba (Ladner and McCrossan 2007, 18). Furthermore, electoral participation varies on and off reserve. Ladner and McCrossan (2007, 15) note that in the 2004 federal election, the participation rate of First Nations on reserve was 52 per cent, and the rate for those living off reserve was 67 per cent.

The historic lack of electoral participation stemming from disenfranchisement and alienation from Canadian politics (Ladner and MCrossan, 2007) could also account for the rather small pool of Aboriginal men and women involved in formal politics. Tremblay (2003) notes that in the 1867–2003 period, only 17 self-declared members of First Nations have held seats in the House of Commons, only two of whom were women (Ethel Dorothy Blondin-Andrew, elected for the first time in 1988; and Nancy Karetak-Lindell, elected for the first time in 1997). One Métis woman has been appointed to the Senate—Thelma J. Chalifoux, in 1997. Black (2008a, 234) reports that 5 members of First Nations were elected to the House of Commons in 2004 (or 1.6 per cent of the House), whereas Aboriginal people comprise approximately 3.75 per cent of the Canadian population (Statistics Canada website: http://www12.statcan. ca/census-recensement/2006/dp-pd/tbt/Rp-eng.cfm?TABID=1&LANG=E&APATH= 3&DETAIL=0&DIM=0&FL=A&FREE=0&GC=0&GK=0&GRP=1&PID=89122&PR ID=0&PTYPE=88971,97154&S=0&SHOWALL=0&SUB=0&Temporal=2006&THE ME=73&VID=0&VNAMEE=&VNAMEF=).

One could say that there is a fairly low degree of income and occupational diversity in the House of Commons as well, given that the most common background professions among MPs is business and the law (see Table 5.3). Not surprisingly, few MPs have a background in occupations associated with women, such as nursing or clerical.

Quality versus Quantity: Trustee, Delegate, or Mirror Representative?

The next question to consider is whether mirror representation (that is, representation in proportion to population) is desirable. To answer this question, we have to understand the evolution that has occurred in democratic theories of representation. Traditional democratic theory emphasizes that once a candidate is elected to political office, she is there as an individual entrusted to represent the office because of her personal skills, intelligence, background, and so on. The representative is not an agent or delegate of voters but rather a wise mind entrusted by the public to make the 'best' decisions. Thus, the qualities of the representative matter, not necessarily the degree to which the representative reflects the views of the electors (Vickers 1997b).

To illustrate, we can quote Edmund Burke in a speech to the electors of Bristol in 1774: 'Your representative owes you, not his industry only, but his judgment; and he betrays, instead of serving you, if he sacrifices it to your opinion.' That quote reflects the view that elected officials should be required to exercise their judgment in the best interest of the collectivity they represent. The people choose leaders, not agents, and representatives should act as such.

This view of representation does not preclude the election of women, members of visible minorities, and so on, but it would be less supportive of mirror representation and indeed would tend to support the belief that focusing on a representative's demographic characteristics detracts from selecting representatives based on their expertise. This becomes particularly problematic in cultures that attribute 'rationality and wisdom' to masculine and not feminine natures.

Table 5.3 | A Comparison of Occupations and MPs' Previous Occupations, Late 1990s

	% of Canadian women employed in this occupation, 1999	% of women MPs employed in this occupation, occupation, 36th Parliament
Occupation WOMEN		
Senior management	0.4	17.9
Other management	6.9	4.5
Business and finance	3.1	4.5
Natural sciences/engineering/mathematics	2.7	1.5
Law, social sciences, education, government	9.0	46.3
Doctors/dentists/other health	1.1	3.0
Nursing/therapy/other health-related	7.9	3.0
Artistic/literary/recreational	3.4	6.0
Clerical and administrative	24.7	7.5
Sales and service	31.6	3.0
Primary industry	1.9	3.0
Trades, transport, and construction	1.9	0.0
Processing, manufacturing, and utilities	5.3	0.0
	% of Canadian men employed in this occupation, 1999	% of men MPs employed in this occupation, 36th Parliament
Occupation MEN		
Senior management	0.9	23.2
Other management	10.6	6.4
Business and finance	2.7	7.2
Natural sciences/engineering/mathematics	9.3	4.8
Law, social sciences, education, government	5.0	37.6
Doctors/dentists/other health	1.0	2.4
Nursing/therapy/other health-related	1.0	0.0
Artistic/literary/recreational	2.4	4.4
Clerical and administrative	6.9	2.4
Sales and service	18.8	2.4
Primary industry	5.9	8.0
Trades, transport, and construction	24.9	1.2
Processing, manufacturing, and utilities	10.6	0.0

Sources: Statistics Canada (2000, 128); Parliament of Canada, http://www.parl.gc.ca

Other democratic theorists focus less on the qualities of the representative and more on the act of representation. These theorists, such as John Stuart Mill, would argue that representatives are in office to act as agents or delegates of electors' interests. Those interests could be regional, business, environmental, or any area of concern. That is, we choose representatives based on how well we feel they will represent our concerns, and we attempt to ensure accountability by making the agent stand for elections. This does not necessarily mean that the candidate has to embody those interests to represent those interests. That is, one does not have to be a businessperson to represent business interests in office, or an environmentalist in order to represent environmental concerns. By logical extension, one does not have to be a woman to represent the concerns of women. The agent, in fact, may have little in common with the electors but must be able to channel what is in the electors' best interests. A more extreme view of interest representation is that representatives should only be delegates of constituency concerns. That is, they should translate the views of constituents directly, putting aside their individual judgment.

Mirror representation represents a third view. It holds that to be truly representative, a legislative body must reflect the groups it represents in the same proportion to their numbers in society. If women make up 50 per cent of the population, then women should make up 50 per cent of a legislature. If visible minorities comprise 10 per cent of the population, they should make up 10 per cent of a legislature. Hannah Pitkin (1967, 61) argues that mirror representation means being something rather than doing something. She is suspicious of this kind of representation, particularly the idea that the quality of representation is judged on the belief that being something is enough, which means that representatives do not necessarily have to be accountable for their actions to those they are representing. We assert, however, that attached to the idea of mirror representation is an assumption of acting for and not just standing for. That is, to represent means both to stand as an agent and to act as a trustee. Supporters of mirror representation argue that it is in fact the similarity in background that gives the representative an understanding of the needs of the constituents, making her a more reliable representative of constituent interests. They argue that mirror representation improves the quality of decision-making and that the similarity in background is therefore one of those personal characteristics, like expertise and occupational experience, that make a representative qualified for political office.

Arguments in favour of increasing women's representation

To improve the quality of the representative

Feminist researchers studying the idea of mirror representation point to the fact that women's views may be different from men's, and that the views of ethnic and racial minorities may be different from those of the majority. Why? Because as groups, women, racial and ethnic minorities, members of the working class, and so on, have different relationships with structures of power, they have different life experiences, and they have traditionally experienced exclusion from power. As a result, they have different demands, and different issues are important to them. Women, for example, may pay more attention to issues such as child care and education; visible minorities may pay greater attention to racial disparities. Thus, if a legislature does not have members of these groups in office, those issues can and likely will be ignored. As Mary Clancy,

Are Male Politicians out of Touch with Women?

To illustrate the perceived disjuncture between male politicians and the reality of women's lives, consider the following report by Jeff Sallot:

> NDP Leader Alexa McDonough warned women yesterday that the right to control their own bodies is threatened by the 'cowardly' and 'reprehensible' proposal of Alliance Leader Stockwell Day to allow a national referendum on abortion.
>
> In an appeal for feminist support, Ms McDonough also blasted Liberal Leader Jean Chrétien for 'incredible cuts to health care' that, she said, make it harder for women to get safe, legal abortions.

Sallot's article goes on to chronicle the breakfast at which McDonough spoke to a gathering of about 200 supporters during the lead-up to the federal election in November 2000. McDonough urged those in the crowd to consider carefully which candidates were attuned to the realities of women's lives.

Specifically, McDonough wondered if, rather than using jet-skiing and white-water rafting as part of their campaigns, the Liberal and Alliance leaders might instead try balancing work with caring for children, running a household, and keeping family appointments and commitments.

McDonough's speech was punctuated by a woman in the crowd calling out, 'I want them to live on $510 month.'

Source: Jeff Sallot. 2000. 'Chrétien, Day out of touch with women's lives, NDP leader says.' *The Globe and Mail* 4 November: A7.

former two-time Liberal MP for Halifax, stated in an interview recorded for the National Film Board video *Why Women Run*, it simply never occurred to her male colleagues that no woman had ever served on the House Finance Committee and that this situation should be addressed (Ralston 1999). Such issues are neglected largely because they are not part of the lived experience of members of the dominant groups in society. Thus, the quality of representation will improve when representation is more diverse.

To improve the quality of representation

Merely having more members of traditionally disadvantaged groups in office, however, will not necessarily ensure that those members will act on behalf of members of traditionally disadvantaged groups (Williams 1998). As Anne Phillips (1998, 234) argues, to support women's increased presence in representative institutions on the basis of interest-based arguments requires us to accept that 'women have a distinct and separate interest as women; that this interest cannot be adequately represented by men; and that the election of women ensures this representation.' A second argument in favour of increasing women's representation thus is to ensure accountability of those representatives to women. The idea is that representatives from disadvantaged groups will feel a degree of loyalty to their groups and will see themselves as 'fulfilling a mandate of difference'. In turn, members of those groups will have an expectation that their elected representatives will act in their interests—that female representatives, for example will 'work within the political system to open the political process to other women, serv[e] as points of access for women's groups, introduc[e] "private" issues onto the public agenda, and bring the multiplicity of women's perspectives into political debate' (L. Young 1997, 89–90). Because membership is the catalyst for accountability, it is believed that members of traditionally disadvantaged groups will be more willing to go out on a limb for their group than members of traditionally advantaged groups. Furthermore, Dovi (2002, 738) recommends that when selecting representatives, they should be chosen based on whether they possess strong mutual relationships with traditionally disadvantaged subgroups within the disadvantaged group so as to ensure an even broader understanding of the group's concerns and so that members of those subgroups can be brought into the process through their representatives' access. That is, there should be a sense of 'linked fate' between the representative and the represented.

This expectation to 'fulfill the mandate of difference' can be burdensome. In response to the question, 'Are you running as a woman?' US Congressional representative Patricia Schroeder in 1987 replied, 'Do I have an option?' (Witt et al. 1994, ix). But, some would argue, identification with the group is necessary. As Dovi (2002, 734) points out, representatives from traditionally disadvantaged groups who claim to represent only the 'common good' might be good representatives for other reasons, but they fail to meet the need for 'overlooked interests' to be represented in elected office.

Empirical research in Canada on the question of whether women representatives in fact fulfill the mandate of difference is mixed. While studies reveal that party affiliation is a major predictor of vote patterns among representatives (Gotell and Brodie 1996; Tremblay and Pelletier 2000), other research has uncovered evidence of cross-party cooperation on women's issues (L. Young 1997) and within-party gender differences (Erickson 1997; Tremblay 1998). Thus, both numbers and accountability appear to be necessary.

Justice and fairness

If the foregoing pragmatic reasons do not persuade, we should also consider justice or fairness arguments in support of increasing the representation of women and other traditionally disadvantaged groups. First, and most obviously, adequate mirror representation is important because, as Alexa McDonough argues, 'that is where power lies; that is where decisions are made' (in Ralston 1999). Since governments are powerful decision-making bodies, it is important to be where the action is.

Second, mirror representation is an important instrument of legitimacy. It demonstrates that members of traditionally disadvantaged and historically under-represented groups are as capable as older white men of serving in elected office (Sapiro 1981, 712). Furthermore, those elected to office can serve as examples to others, exercise leadership within their groups and communities, and make people feel that they are included in the political system (Phillips 1998, 228; Mansbridge 1999, 651).

Third, members of traditionally under-represented and historically disadvantaged groups are as entitled to the spoils of political office as white men. As Alexa

McDonough argues (in Ralston 1999), politics is a great job, with pay equity. Why should it not be an occupation open to everyone?

Finally, and perhaps most importantly, mirror representation upholds the notion of democratic self-government. That is, we believe it is wrong for the minority to rule the majority. Democratic self-government means that people should be able to make decisions about their community and about themselves by themselves. Thus, as Arscott and Trimble (1997, 4) argue, it might be true that men are quite capable of representing women's interests. But they 'cannot claim power for women and they cannot hold power in women's stead'. Democracy requires some level of participation in voting, in political parties, in elected office, and so on, for a community to be considered self-governing. As Stetson (2001) argues, a policy can be considered feminist not only if it has good effects for women (substantive considerations) but also if women are involved in making the policy (due process considerations). It is not good enough for men to make policy for women. Women must also be involved. Underrepresentation of communities is therefore problematic when decisions regarding those communities are being made.

Barriers to Women's Success in Achieving Elected Office

What, then, are the barriers preventing mirror representation? Researchers talk about 'political opportunity structures', that is, the 'forces, structures and ideas that characterize official political systems and that enhance or deter women's political participation' (Vickers 1997a, 200) and have identified a range of factors that affect women's opportunity structures. These can be grouped into three broad categories: ideational, social, and cultural; organizational; and institutional. Each of these factors can affect either supply or demand: they can deter women from running for elected office or they can prevent those who run from succeeding. In the balance of this chapter, we will assess which factors are currently the most important in preventing Canadian women from running for and succeeding in gaining elected office.

Ideational, social, and cultural barriers

Ideational, social, and cultural barriers can be summarized as the assumptions of systemic sexism manifested at the societal level that prevent women from succeeding when they run for elected office or discourage them from running in the first place. They include sex stereotyping, socialization to have little interest in politics, lack of preparation for political activity, lack of strong political networks, and the need to balance work and family. Many people assume that these factors are the primary reasons that women do not succeed in achieving elected office. Is that the case, however? Or are organizational and institutional barriers more significant?

Sex stereotyping

Researchers who focus on sex stereotyping investigate whether certain cultural attitudes towards women translate into voter resistance to women candidates. For example, studies have found that since women are seen as less assertive than men, they are expected to be less verbally aggressive in their electoral campaigns. Such feminine stereotypes raise questions about the ability of women to endure political contests and office, and as a result a certain percentage of the electorate will be pre-disposed not to vote for women candidates, particularly at the highest levels of po-litical office. As MacIvor (1996, 242) points out, formal politics is itself stereotyped as gladiatorial, competitive, and hierarchical, emphasizing winner-take-all rather than consensus and as such, it conveys the impression of being a very masculine domain that might be too challenging for women or that few women would want to participate in at all.

This is important because it not only affects the demand for female candidates but also the supply. Stereotypical beliefs can also affect how comfortable women feel about running, the platform they adopt, and the forms of politicking they practise. For example, as Kimberly Kahn (1996, 10) found, women may refrain from 'attack' adver-tising to show themselves in a better light, while aggressive advertising is an acceptable tactic for their male counterparts.

Surveys and research have allowed us to observe changes in Canadian attitudes regarding the acceptability of women candidates over time. In 1975, 9.8 per cent of women and 12.8 per cent of men surveyed reported that they would be less inclined to vote for a female party leader. However, by 1989, as Joanna Everitt (1998a, 754) found, 20.2 per cent of women were more inclined to vote for a female party leader, and 10.1 per cent of men said they too would be more inclined to vote for a female party leader. The vast majority of those surveyed—77.2 per cent of women and 84.4 per cent of men—said there would be no difference in their willingness to vote for a female as opposed to a male party leader. Only 2.6 per cent of women and 5.5 per cent of men said they would be less inclined to vote for a female party leader.

Some research has found that women can, in fact, be advantaged by sex stereo-types (for example, Iyengar, Valentino, Ansolabeher, and Simon 1997). As Black and Erikson (2003, 82) point out, 'Since women, as comparative newcomers to electoral politics, are less tainted by old style politics . . . and because voter stereotypes may characterize women politicians as being more honest or ethical than their male coun-terparts, women, on the whole, may attract more votes than men when placed in similarly competitive candidacies.' Women appear to do better when they campaign on 'women's' issues, such as social policy, and not as well when they campaign on 'men's' issues, such as the economy or defence, and men do not do as well as women when campaigning on women's issues. Consequently, women may be advised to 'run as women'. Other research reveals that voter support may vary depending on the lev-el of political office sought. Kathleen Dolan (1997, 32), for example, found that in the United States while women's support for women candidates remains fairly steady across local, state, and national offices (with a drop in support of just 16 points across offices), men's support for women candidates drops more precipitously (38 points) as the level of office increases.

The literature on stereotypes has not, however, provided definitive proof that women candidates are disadvantaged systematically when they run (Black and Erickson 2003). Results appear to depend on the data used, whether experimental or survey, and as Banducci, Everitt, and Gidengil (2002) found in their examination of the research literature as a whole, the differences really only appear in the application of stereotypi-cal traits and competencies.[2] That is, while female candidates are 'regularly subjected to "feminine" stereotypes, "masculine" stereotypes are not applied uniquely to male candidates except in campaigns for the highest political offices' (Banducci, Everitt, and

Gidengil 2002, 14). In fact, masculine personality traits, issue competencies, and beliefs similar to those of their male competitors were often attributed to women campaigning for office. Gidengil, Everitt and Banducci (2009, 186) found in a study of the 1993 Canadian and 1999 New Zealand election campaigns, which each had two female party leaders campaigning for office, that 'leaders' own personalities, campaigns, and parties mattered more to the traits respondents attributed to them than did their sex'.

Furthermore, Brenda O'Neill's (1998) research has uncovered a gender bias in favour of political parties that select women leaders. For example, in the 1993 Canadian election, the Progressive Conservative Party under the leadership of Kim Campbell managed to attract more female voters to their party than male voters, even though the party platform did not change significantly. Thus, while stereotypes are pervasive in the assessment of female candidates, they do not necessarily hurt these candidates.

Political socialization

Some argue that women are not involved in formal politics in high numbers because they are not socialized to take an interest in politics. Political socialization is the process by which society teaches its members the political values, traditions, norms, and duties that it deems desirable and acceptable. It is through political socialization that generally accepted ideas like deference to authority or the notion that 'politics is a man's world' can be passed on from generation to generation. Agents of political socialization may be the family, educational and religious institutions, the mass media, and the state itself.

How does political socialization affect women? It is argued that it can affect the supply of women candidates, turning them away from an interest in politics and cutting down on the eligibility pool, that is, those qualified for elected office. To illustrate this, let us look at one of Canada's great political men, Pierre Elliott Trudeau. At a symposium in 2000 honouring the life of the former prime minister, David Cameron, professor of political science at the University of Toronto, described Trudeau's socialization as the modern-day 'education of a prince': sent to the 'right' schools, world traveller, recipient of degrees from many countries, holding a legal degree. One could argue that Trudeau was socialized to become prime minister. How many women are similarly socialized to the idea, through their education, work experience, and so on, that politics is not only a vocation but also their vocation? How many young girls say, 'when I grow up I want to be prime minister', let alone a politician? An examination of socialization factors helps us to discover how the norms and values passed on regarding politics are different for girls and women and act to limit women's knowledge of and interest in politics.

Political socialization is a difficult factor to pin down, and it is controversial. As we argued in the preceding chapter, women have always engaged in political action but more in unconventional political activity than in formal politics. Thus, women's lack of involvement in formal politics could simply reflect a choice of how to fight inequality or it could reflect society's tendency to socialize girls to emphasize 'caring' and 'nurturing' in a private, voluntary capacity rather than in a public political campaign. That said, past studies in both Canada and the United States (for example, Kay, Lambert, Brown, and Curtis 1988; Owen and Dennis 1988) have uncovered gender differences in boys' and girls' and men's and women's orientations toward politics. Kay et al. (1988) found that women in Canada tend to be less likely to pay attention to

No Politics Here, Please

Consider the following story about the women's magazine *Glamour*:

> The Condé Nast magazine *Glamour* long prided itself on the fact that it was the only women's magazine that had a column about women in politics, written by contributors based in Washington. The column, 'Women in Washington: What Have They Done for Us Lately?' was one of the hallmarks of Ruth Whitney, *Glamour*'s editor of 31 years, who was replaced in September [1998] by Bonnie Fuller, the former editor of *Cosmopolitan*.
>
> Now Ms Fuller has decided the column should go. And Ms Fuller—who attracted readers by injecting an energetic sexuality into the pages of *Cosmopolitan*—has decided to add an astrology column, which will make its debut in the January issue. . . .
>
> Ms Fuller said that the idea for killing the column came from longtime *Glamour* editors. 'We want to have more impact with the coverage when we have news that's really important for readers,' she said. 'I think that what was happening—and this is what I heard from the editors who were working on it every month—was that there wasn't enough strong news every single month.' The astrology column, she said, was an idea that originated with readers and focus groups. 'They were clamoring for it. They all said they wanted horoscopes.'

Source: Alex Kuczynski. 1998. New editor of *Glamour* kills politics column. *The New York Times* 26 October: C7.

What does it say about women's political socialization when women's magazines generally do not have political columns, whereas men's magazines (even *Playboy*) do, and when the only political column in any women's magazine was cancelled? Does this reflect women's lack of interest in politics?

politics, to take an interest in an election, to claim a good knowledge of politics, to follow political news on television or in the newspapers, to discuss politics, or to try to convince others to vote a certain way. Recent studies confirm that women are less likely than men to be knowledgeable about politics in Canada—for example, women are less able to identify party leaders (Gidengil, Goodyear-Grant, Nevitte, Blais, and Nadeau 2003). They are also less likely than men to pay attention to election news or watch leaders' debates, to be members of political parties, or to contact a parliamentarian (Tremblay and Trimble 2003, 8). In addition, while voter turnout rates for women in the United States have been higher than men's since the 1980 presidential election, in Canada studies have revealed that women have a slightly lower turnout rate than men (Kay et al. 1988; Blais, Gidengil, Nadeau, and Nevitte 2002, 51). But data from the 1993 federal election reveal the same level of women's involvement in discussing politics (81 per cent) and only slightly lower levels of women's involvement in party work (8 per cent of men and 6 per cent of women). Earlier data from the 1988 federal election again reveal only slightly lower levels of involvement in signing petitions (69 versus 67 per cent), engaging in marches and rallies (26 versus 23 per cent), and taking part in sit-ins (9 versus 6 per cent) (Mishler and Clarke 1995, 137).

One spokeswoman interviewed by Meredith Ralston on the video *Why Women Run* (1999) reported that it is not hard to persuade women to get involved in politics, in campaign work, and so on. They like the backroom activity and find it fulfilling to help a candidate win. However, it is much more difficult to persuade them to run for office, either because they lack confidence or because it is not the way they picture spending their lives (due to not being socialized to think of politics as a vocation), or because it puts unacceptable demands on their time. However, Young and Cross (2003, 98), in a survey of political party members conducted in 2000, report very little difference in the activities men and women reported doing for their political parties. That is, women and men were fairly similarly involved in a range of partisan activities, including traditionally backroom activities such as attending riding association and nomination meetings and volunteering in election campaigns, as well as more visible activities such as fundraising, attending political conventions, and even seeking the party's nomination and holding elected office. The only task in which women were much less involved (an 8 per cent reported difference) was serving on a riding association executive. Thus, while the perception that women participate only in the backroom persists, women, like men, are actually quite involved in party politics.

When women do run for political office, it is often because they have been socialized toward an interest in and life in politics. Many female politicians report being born into political families with weak gender-role norms. Some women marry politically active men and become involved that way. Others are encouraged to enter politics by friends and colleagues. And some women become involved in voluntary organizations that politicize them. As we saw in chapter 3 with the first-wave suffragettes, it is a common political trajectory for women to become involved in local voluntary organizations, school boards, and so on, become more politicized and active on behalf of particular constituencies, and then jump from there into provincial or federal politics.

Lack of preparation for political activity

Related to political socialization is the issue of the extent to which women are socialized to pursue occupations compatible with a political career (for example, the legal profession, which can allow time off from practice to run for political office) or occupations that make them seem inherently 'fit' for political office (see Table 5.3). Only one MP during the period 1997 to 2005 had a clerical background, and only one MP had previously been a health care assistant. Yet the majority of employed women continue to work in traditional female occupations such as these. The importance of this occupational socialization has declined as women have entered traditionally male professions in greater numbers. Also, research in the US has found that women's career choices are no longer necessarily a liability in seeking elected office. For example, 40 nurses ran for various state offices in 1988, and all but seven were elected (McGlen and O'Connor 1998, 82). It is possible that women's careers and experiences in education, health, and social services may actually be a benefit, not a hindrance, depending on the nature of the office sought.

However, it is not only the occupation itself that is significant but also the benefits of professional involvement and political connections that accrue from certain occupations—for example, being a member of the Canadian Bar Association. MacIvor (1996,

240) labels these factors as social capital: the 'social knowledge, contacts, privileged access to culturally valued qualifications and social skills . . ... acquired through informal contacts with elite members, as well as by acquisition of elite skills and attitudes through formal channels (e.g., work in a law firm or a brokerage house)'. These are the 'old boy' networks of support that successful politicians rely on for connections, finances, and campaign help. Again, with women's increasing entry into traditionally male occupations, and the gaining of social capital, we should expect this factor to be of declining importance.

Balancing work and family

Because women bear a disproportionate burden of family responsibilities as a result of the continuing gendered division of labour in the home,[3] women with children are less likely to participate in the whole spectrum of politics 'from voting to political interest, from attending meetings to donating money' (MacIvor 1996, 237). It may also explain why women are generally less knowledgeable about current affairs: because of their work in the home, they have little time to keep track of the news. When participation rates of women without children are measured, they tend to be closer to that of men. Thus, women seem to be confronted with role conflict that affects their decision to seek political office. When faced with this conflict, they often remain childless, have fewer children, wait until their children are older to run for political office, remain single, or marry a supportive spouse—a Mr Thatcher, for example.

Women members of elected legislatures often report on the difficulty of juggling career, family, and political responsibilities. Holding office in Ottawa or in a provincial capital often means uprooting family or commuting long distances between the constituency and the capital on a regular basis. This can be a deterrent to women with young children and thus contributes to a lower number of women in the 'eligibility pool' for elected office.

For women who do seek political office, the tendency is to delay entrance. In 1992, for example, newly elected women in the US House of Representatives were an average of six years older than the men. In 1997, 26 per cent of men in the House were under 45 compared to only 14 per cent of the women (McGlen and O'Connor 1998, 83). In Canada, the age differences are not as great in the House of Commons but still significant. In the 37th (2000–4) Parliament, newly elected women were on average 4.3 years older than newly elected men, and the average age of female MPs was 1.2 years higher than the average age of male MPs (http://www.parl.gc.ca). Research has also found that women stay in elected office for shorter periods of time than men do (Docherty 2002b, 343). Male MPs tend to serve two terms in office on average while women serve one and a half terms. The argument, of course, is that women's delayed entrance into politics reduces the eligibility pool.

Some female politicians complain that society and the media place greater pressure on women to stay home with young children, and they can be punished at the polls or in the media for holding high-profile offices (Ralston 1999). In contrast, having young children at home is often just not an issue for men while they run for and hold political office. A study done by the US-based Center for the American Woman and Politics (CAWP) in 1984 found that women officeholders were more likely to state that the age of their children was a very important factor in their decision to run. 'Men, however, did not appear to hold reservations about running for or serving in public office while they had young children' (McGlen and O'Connor 1998, 83). In Canada's Parliament, among the MPs who have children, men have larger families (averaging 2.7 children) than women (2.3 children). Wendy Lill (in Ralston 1999), running for the first time as an NDP candidate in the 1997 federal election, stated that she tried to make her children look as old as possible and herself as young as possible when posing for the camera because of stereotypes: mothers are supposed to be nurturing, not going away to serve in political office.

Research also reveals that more women than men in elected office are not married. The pattern is striking at the federal level in Canada. In the 37th Parliament, from 2001 to 2004, approximately 46 per cent of women were married while 80 per cent of men were married (Canada. Parliament 2002). This is not a uniquely Canadian characteristic: in the US Congress in 1997, for example, only 15 per cent of men were unmarried whereas 36 per cent of women were unmarried (McGlen and O'Connor 1998, 84). It is also more common for women to be childless (nearly 37 per cent in the 37th Parliament compared to just under 27 per cent of men). However, single-parent MPs are more likely to be female than male (approximately 21 per cent compared to 7 per cent).

Another Barrier to Women's Electoral Success: Their Husbands! The Case of Elizabeth Dole

The following *New York Times* story is extremely enlightening, both because of the reporter's tone and because of the comments of Bob Dole on his wife Elizabeth's chances in her bid for the Republican presidential nomination in 1999. One has to wonder, 'what is wrong with this picture?'

> For all his devotion to Elizabeth Dole, and for all the blessings he offers her campaign for President, Bob Dole is nobody's compliant, stick-with-the-script, gaze-lovingly-at-your-mate political spouse.
>
> Three times she stood by his side as he ran for the Presidency and lost, and recalling her tireless campaigning he says, 'I'm her biggest fan and supporter and should do for her what she did for me.'
>
> But in his first extensive interview about the progress of his wife's campaign, Mr Dole said he wanted to give money to a rival candidate who was fighting for much of her support. He conceded that Mrs Dole's operation had had growing pains, was slow to raise money early and was only beginning to hit its stride. And while Mr Dole was hopeful, he allowed that he was by no means certain she would even stay in the race.
>
> 'She's getting there,' he said of her progress so far.
>
> Hedging his bets, perhaps, Mr Dole acknowledged that he wanted to contribute to the campaign of Senator John McCain, Republican of Arizona, a close friend who stuck by Mr Dole's side in the final, depressing weeks of his run against President Clinton in 1996.

Source: Richard L. Berke. 1999. As political spouse, Bob Dole is admirer, coach and critic. *The New York Times* 17 May: A1, A14.

Falling under the 'damned if you do, damned if you don't' category, being single can also be a handicap for women seeking elected office if they are seen as not capable of sustaining a relationship. Richard Gwyn, in a *Toronto Star* column in June 1993, writes with regard to Prime Minister Kim Campbell, 'the aspect of Campbell that may most distinctively mark her as different is that she is single.' Not that she was Canada's first woman prime minister, not that she accomplished some major changes in her brief tenure as prime minister, including major restructuring of the federal bureaucracy, not even that she was young—no, those factors pale in comparison to the fact that she was single and thus 'more isolated than [her] male equivalents', who included Pierre Trudeau (single until he had been prime minister for some three years, later a divorced single father) and lifelong bachelors William Lyon Mackenzie King and R.B. Bennett! Gwyn writes, 'Campbell has no cocoon to which she can retreat to escape from the brutal stresses of her job. She has no one she can count on always to be there for her, to talk her down from some crisis or disaster over a late-night scotch, or to offer advice untainted by career ambition, or to be the messenger of bad news that aides dare not pass along for fear they'll get shot. She has, that's to say, no Mila [referring to the wife of Brian Mulroney], and no Denis Thatcher' (Gwyn 1993, A19). Thus it would appear that the appropriate political role for women continues to be the private loving and supportive spouse rather than the public political figure, and as the story below illustrates, some men are not as good at playing the supportive role themselves.

Do ideational, social, and cultural barriers matter?

While these societal, cultural, and ideological factors can dissuade individual women from throwing their hats into the political ring, at the aggregate level over time we see more and more women willing to compete for elected office, although women's candidacies since 1993 have not achieved the zenith witnessed in the 1993 federal election when 476 women competed for office (see Figure 5.3). This willingness reflects a general societal trend toward accepting women in political office.[4] The problem does not appear to be a matter of supply but rather women's lack of success in achieving elected office in Canada. We therefore need to consider factors that may impede that success.

Organizational factors

Negative stereotypes of women in the media and bias in reportage

Researchers in Canada are beginning to explore the impact of the media on women's success in competing for elected office. The media's portrayal of campaigns and candidates can have a great deal of influence on public opinion. Kimberly Kahn (1996, 12) argues that the media have the power to affect people's information acquisition, to persuade, to set the agenda, and to encourage people to alter the criteria they use to evaluate public officials. Consequently, the media have a great deal of significance for women's electoral success. Coverage may affect the visibility of female candidates. It may influence the public to perceive a female candidate as less viable, particularly if she is running for a non-traditional post. The media may also be more focused on and critical of a woman's physical appearance and pay less attention to her actual platform and messages. Finally, the media may also influence key gatekeepers such as campaign donors and party leaders (Norris 1997, 150). The question is, then, are there negative

Figure 5.3 | **Women Candidates in Canadian Federal Elections, 1968–2008**

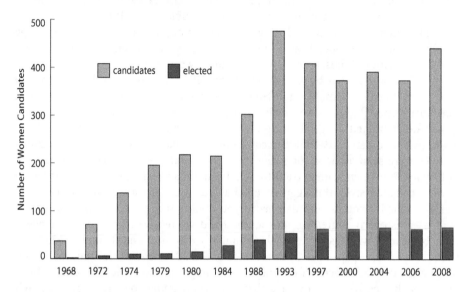

Source: Parliament of Canada http://www.parl.gc.ca

stereotypes of women in the media, or are there biases in reportage that could affect the viability of female candidates?

Kahn (1996) argues that just as voters use stereotypes in making electoral decisions, so do the media. Reliance on these stereotypes can create differences in the amount and substance of coverage given to male and female candidates. Women may be judged as less viable candidates and thus receive negative coverage or no coverage at all. Reporters may ask women candidates questions different from those asked of men and stress different issues when covering candidates. For example, coverage might emphasize a woman candidate's compassion and a male candidate's leadership abilities, or portray women candidates who exhibit traditionally male characteristics more negatively. Thus, analyzing the content of media coverage becomes very important in uncovering these 'frames'.

Pippa Norris (1997, 161), in a cross-national study of media coverage of 10 female leaders compared to that of their immediate predecessors (or, if retired, their immediate successors[5]) found that the male leaders were the subject of more news stories than the female leaders. Surprisingly, Prime Minister John Major of Britain received more daily coverage than the 'remarkable' Mrs Thatcher (158). There were some exceptions, such as Kim Campbell in Canada, but it is striking that women's visibility was lower, even when they held office at the highest level. Even more telling, Norris found evidence of some common media 'frames' in coverage of women leaders. First, women leaders were covered as 'firsts', as in 'the breakthrough this appointment signified for all women'. Second, women leaders were covered as 'outsiders', which tended to highlight their lack of conventional qualifications and prior political experience. Finally, women leaders were covered as 'agents of change', that is, leaders who would clean up corruption in politics. This media portrayal did change over time, and Norris (151) notes some improvements in coverage: 'The number of women referenced on newspaper front pages almost doubled from 1989 to 1995, going from 11 percent to 19 percent. During the same period, the proportion of front-page photos of women expanded from 24 percent to 39 percent, and on network television news, one-quarter of those interviewed as sources were women.'

In Canada, research by Everitt and Gidengil (2002; 2003) indicates that the media's treatment of female candidates is not overtly biased and sexist; however, like Norris, they find that the media use gendered images to cover candidates and gender-differentiated images that disadvantage women candidates. In federal leaders' debates, women party leaders received more media coverage when their actions or roles were seen as novel or when their behaviour was unexpected or atypical of females. If women leaders tried to be a bit more aggressive (that is, more male) in their debating style, this aggressive behaviour was emphasized in the media. It was a 'damned if you do and damned if you don't' situation in that they would be lambasted as overly aggressive on the one hand yet receive less media coverage if their behaviour was 'less noteworthy'. Similarly, Sampert and Trimble (2003), in their study of newspaper headline coverage of the 2000 federal election, found significant gender differences in coverage of the major parties. The NDP under Alexa McDonough received less coverage than the Tories under Joe Clark, even though both parties were underdogs in the campaign. The four male leaders received more coverage than their respective parties, but the NDP was featured in headlines more than McDonough herself. In a more recent study, Linda Trimble (2005) found more overtly sexist media framing in coverage of Belinda Stronach's run for the leadership of the Conservative Party in 2004. She found that much greater attention was paid to Stronach's looks, wardrobe, sexual availability, and personal background than to those of the male candidates.

Arguably, one of the most egregious examples of gendered media coverage was the press and especially the editorial cartoon coverage of Stronach's decision to cross the floor of the House of Commons and join the Liberal Party in 2005, just days before the Conservatives were set to vote non-confidence on a minority Liberal government budget bill. Cartoons portraying her 'whoring' herself to Prime Minister Paul Martin while betraying then-boyfriend and Conservative Party Deputy Leader Peter MacKay splashed across editorial pages, while stories spoke of her jilting 'poor' Mr Mackay (and not just the party). At a press conference soon afterwards, women members of the Liberal caucus complained that neither the press nor Conservative Party members reacted in the same gendered way when Conservative MP Scott Brison similarly crossed the floor in 2003 (Weber 2005).[6] Clearly, gender-differentiated media coverage remains a difficult problem for female candidates.

Political parties

Sylvia Bashevkin (1985), in her groundbreaking research on women and political parties in Canada, argues that two rules of thumb can be used to characterize political parties in Canada. One is 'the higher the fewer'. That is, as one moves from the lowest levels of party activity to the highest, one sees fewer and fewer women. Even at the local riding level, as Young and Cross (2003, 92) found, women traditionally perform the task of riding secretary and not the more 'responsible' tasks of riding treasurer or president. The second rule is 'the more competitive the fewer'. As positions become more sought after, they are more likely to be filled by men than by women. For example, women generally receive party nominations only when the party has little hope of winning, making potential male candidates less interested in running; in other words, the women candidates are sacrificial lambs. This lack of support for women could result from perceived societal stereotypes about the validity of women in politics. However, it could also be the result of self-interest on the part of male candidate party members reluctant to share power with women if it means diminishing their own status. As a result, women have been denied real power within the parties and, as the old adage goes, 'men make policy, women make coffee'.

The question is, do these patterns still hold true in Canada? To answer this question, we examine three areas for evidence of change: numbers of delegates to party conventions; numbers of women serving in leadership positions within the parties; and numbers of female candidates in riding nomination contests.

Bashevkin (1991, 66) notes that the number of female delegates to party conventions has increased. For example, at the 1967 national Progressive Conservative (PC) convention, 19 per cent of the delegates were female; by 1989, 46 per cent were female. At the 1968 federal Liberal convention, 18 per cent were female, but by 1990, 47 per cent were female. Thus, one can see that in these political parties, decision-making has opened up for female members. In fact, the federal Liberal Party passed a constitutional amendment in 1990 mandating that 50 per cent of all convention delegates be female, ensuring women's continued presence at national conventions. The Tories (Progressive Conservatives) adopted a similar measure, requiring that at least 33 per cent of constituency delegates be women, a figure the party had already surpassed (Young 2003, 84). One study (Stewart 2002) has found that the shift by some parties to allow all party members to vote for party leaders, rather having the leader selected by delegates at party conventions, has increased women's participation in leadership selection but their participation in traditional political conventions has gone down.

Another important trend is that the main political parties have opened up leadership positions to women. In 1983 women made up half of the NDP national executive and almost a quarter of the PC national executive. By 1990 women constituted 58 per cent of the NDP national executive and 43 per cent of the Tory executive. The number of women on the Liberal national executive, however, shrank during that same period from 43 per cent in 1983 to 38 per cent in 1990 (Bashevkin 1991, 67). The numbers have been good in the NDP for some time because 'in 1983 the party adopted new rules requiring that 50 per cent of executive members, as well as members of all critical party committees, be female' (MacIvor 1996, 260). Both the Liberal Party and the NDP have had women presidents, and Audrey McLaughlin was elected leader of the federal NDP in 1989, followed by Alexa McDonough in 1995. In 1993 Kim Campbell became the first female leader of the Conservatives.

The story is not as bright for the Reform Party, Canadian Alliance, and new Conservative Party. Young (2003, 87) notes that women have held very few of the more powerful positions within these parties, in line with the maxim, 'the higher the fewer'. Furthermore, these parties have not encouraged the recruitment of female candidates as other parties have (as described below). In 1993 women comprised 11.1 per cent of the candidates fielded by the Reform Party. In 1997 that figure dropped to

10.1 per cent, but rose under the Conservative Party, formed through the merger of the Canadian Alliance and Progressive Conservative parties. Women comprised 20.5 per cent of the candidates fielded in the 2008 federal election but only 16 per cent of the caucus, compared to approximately 25 per cent of the Liberal party caucus and 32 per cent of the NDP caucus (see Table 5.4). Granted, when the Bloc Québécois first competed for political office in 1993, women comprised only 13.3 per cent of its candidates. However, by the 1997 election, the percentage of female candidates had nearly doubled to 21.3 per cent (Young 2003, 83) and stood at nearly 27 per cent in the 2008 election (see Table 5.4). Women comprise nearly 31 per cent of the BQ caucus as of the 2008 federal election. Thus, we see divergent patterns in party support for female candidates in the major new parties.

Table 5.4 | **Number of Candidates and Winners by Political Affiliation and Sex, 2008 Federal Election**

	Candidates			Elected		
	Men	Women	% Women	Men	Women	% Women in Party Caucus
NDP	204	104	33.8	26	12	32.4
BQ	55	20	26.7	34	15	30.6
Liberal	194	113	36.8	58	19	24.7
Conservative	244	63	20.5	122	23	16.1
TOTAL (all parties including smaller parties)	1156	445		240	69	
			Success rate	20.8	15.5	

Sources: Elections Canada, http://www.elections.ca; Parliament of Canada, http://www.parl.gc.ca

The three main parties (that is, those that existed prior to 1993) did take proactive measures to recruit women candidates over the years. The boldest effort was made by the NDP, which in 1991 established an affirmative action program for candidates with the goal of sex parity. Unlike the rules requiring parity for executive and party committees, this program is not part of the party's constitution. However, it does require that riding associations search for female, visible-minority, and Aboriginal candidates, as well as candidates with disabilities, and ensure that someone from the targeted groups is on the ballot before the nomination is held (L. Young 1997, 88). Norm McCaskill (2000) points out that the provision really covers any groups recognized in the Charter of Rights that are under-represented in office—for example, gay and lesbian groups, youth (at the Ontario level), and francophones. It is against the NDP constitution to impose a candidate on a local riding, but the central party organization will parachute a nominee in to fulfill the requirement that there be a nominee from one or more of the targeted groups.

As for the Tories and Liberals, both have adopted formal recruitment efforts for potential candidates, such as mentorship programs. The National PC Women's Federation established a 'talent bank' to recruit female candidates for the 1993 election, while the Liberals established 'campaign colleges' for women candidates and their staff (Young

2002, 188). However, the Liberal Party's granting of special powers to the party leader in 1990 to appoint female candidates over the heads of local riding associations when the local association failed to nominate a woman has proved to be the most controversial measure. The Chrétien government used this power to parachute in a number of high-profile candidates, such as Elinor Caplan, a former Ontario MPP and health minister who won her riding of Thornhill in 1997 and went on to become a member of the Chrétien cabinet. For the Liberals, parachuting is a way of ensuring strong women candidates because parachuted candidates do not have to go through the nomination process in winnable and therefore often very competitive ridings. Controversy arises, however, because the practice removes the nomination from local party associations and appears anti-democratic. Feminists are divided on the issue: some see it as necessary to ensure equal numbers of women candidates in winnable ridings, while others criticize it as mere tokenism that does not contribute to real change.

Each of the three national political parties has attempted to address the obstacles women face in financing political campaigns. Before the passage of campaign finance legislation, the federal government imposed no limits on the amount of money that could be spent to win a nomination. This meant that contests for seats in winnable ridings could be nasty and expensive, disadvantaging women with few resources. The NDP responded voluntarily to these concerns by imposing a spending limit on nomination campaigns as well as an affirmative action requirement to search for women and minority candidates before holding a nomination vote, as mentioned above (Macqueen 1997, B2). In addition, in 1983 the NDP established the Agnes Macphail Fund, named for the first woman elected to the House of Commons, who ran for the Progressive Party in Ontario in 1921. Agnes Macphail funds are available to female candidates running for federal office. In a similar fashion, the Liberals established the Judy LaMarsh Fund in 1984, named for a cabinet minister in the Pearson government, and the Tories established the Ellen Fairclough Fund in 1986, named for the first woman appointed to cabinet (Bashevkin 1993, 107). The newer parties in the House of Commons, the Bloc Québécois and Reform Party/Canadian Alliance, did not establish similar funds (Macqueen 1997, B2).[7]

Another strategy that the Liberal government considered briefly and then dropped was to tie parties' post-election expense refunds to the number of women candidates they fielded (Leblanc 1999, A2). This idea was first proposed in the report of the Royal Commission on Electoral Reform and Party Financing.[8] At present, a registered party that wins a minimum percentage of the vote in a federal election and spends a certain amount of money in its campaign is entitled to partial reimbursement of its expenses. The plan was to increase the amount that would be reimbursed if a party fielded a certain percentage of women candidates.

At the same time, some political parties have responded to the perceived gender gap in voter support by enacting measures to attract women voters. The gender gap refers to observed differences in political orientations and/or behaviour based on sex (Gidengil 2007, 815). This electoral phenomenon has been observed and studied in the United States especially, where even a small margin can make a difference between a win and a loss in a two-candidate race. It was first noted in the 1980 US Presidential election when researchers found an 8 percentage point different in men's and women's votes for Ronald Reagan, with women less inclined to vote for Reagan (and Republicans in general).

In Canada, researchers have found some differences in political orientations and voting patterns between men and women. Gidengil's (2007, 815–16) survey of the research on gender gaps found that 'Canadian women are less likely than Canadian men to subscribe to some of the central tenets of liberal individualism, they are more reluctant than men to allow market forces to work unfettered and they are readier to support social programs to help those in need.' They also 'tend to be more "dovish" than men on military matters and they are more opposed to the death penalty. They are also more tolerant of new lifestyles and changing values, especially when it comes to same-sex marriage.' Gidengil (2007, 816) points out that these are statistical results: some women are more hawkish than men; are more supportive of tax cuts; and are less committed to social program spending. Thus, there is a danger in stereotyping all women in a certain way—and often in typically 'feminine' ways: more compassionate, more motivated by care ethics, and so on (Gidengil 2007, 816).

However, researchers have also observed that sex differences in political orientation do manifest in voting preferences as well. Over time we can observe that historically, women have moved more to the ideological Left (as reflected in support for the NDP), while men recently have moved more to the ideological Right (as reflected in support for the Reform Party in the 1990s) (Gidengil et al. 2006, 3); although again, this is not true of all women and all men (Gidengil 2007, 819). More interesting is the overall distribution in voting and how all parties make appeals to women and men, as well as youth, racial and ethnic minorities, specific regional populations, and so on. Some parties, such as the Conservative Party, have tried to broaden their appeal to women voters (Young 2003, 83) by trying to recruit more women candidates. As mentioned above, for example, the Progressive Conservative Party attracted more women voters in the 1993 federal election when Kim Campbell was party leader (O'Neill 1998). As Gidengil (2007, 821) points out, though, as a political strategy, parties need to consider many other aspects of voter identity that affect vote choice. For example, very large gaps emerge when one compares the level of political knowledge held by women with high incomes and those with low incomes, or that of visible minority women. Age also affects voter choice. In the 2008 federal election campaign a Strategic Counsel poll revealed that women over 50 were the most highly supportive of the Conservative party (46 per cent) while women under 50 were rather unsupportive (24 per cent of women under age 35 and 27 per cent of women ages 35–50) (http://www.thestrategiccounsel.com/our_news/polls/2008-10-10%20Ontario%20Poll%20%28re-porting%20October%207-9%29%20web.pdf).

The real test of the extent to which political parties accommodate women's involvement in formal politics is the number of women nominated and how many of them succeed in winning their ridings. This begs the question, how can one account for the huge gap between the number of women willing to throw their hats into the political ring and the number of women who win their ridings (see Figure 5.3)? Two factors appear to be of crucial importance: first, the parties for which women are most willing to run are not 'viable' parties; and second, the number of women running for viable parties remains low.

The importance of a party's viability—that is, its ability to win seats—has been confirmed in research by Pitre (2003) and Tremblay and Pelletier (2001). Both these studies also point to the importance of parties' willingness to do something about the lack of women candidates. That willingness varies by political party and depends upon the 'feminist consciousness' of party leaders (Tremblay and Pelletier 2001, 180). Among federal parties, the NDP nominates the most women candidates. As Table 5.4 reveals, 104 or 33.8 per cent of the candidates for the NDP in the 2008 federal election were women. Yet only 12 women were elected—a success rate of 11.5 per cent. In contrast, only 63 women competed on behalf of the Conservative Party but 23 were elected, marking a success rate of 36.5 per cent. In the 2004 federal election, which saw the Liberal Party take office as a minority government, 75 women competed on behalf of the Liberal Party and 34 were elected, marking a success rate of 45.3 per cent. The common denominator in both elections? Running with the most successful party. The success rate for women historically in the NDP was much lower than for the Liberals or Conservatives. In contrast, in Quebec, female candidates' success rate in competing for seats on behalf of the Bloc Québécois was 75 per cent in the 2008 federal election. Thus, one major means of increasing the number of women in the House of Commons would be to have competitive parties nominate more women. According to Equal Voice (2011), in the 2011 federal election, the NDP fielded the most female candidates by far of all the federal parties, with 125 female candidates or approximately 40 per cent of the candidate slate. The party that fielded the next largest slate of female candidates was the Green Party at approximately 32 per cent, then the Bloc Québécois, also at 32 per cent, the Liberals at 30 per cent, and the Conservatives at 22 per cent. Ironically, the NDP's breakthrough electoral success in the 2011 federal election yielded an electoral victory for female opposition MPs but not in the governing Conservative Party of Canada.

Research (for example, Erickson 1991, 1998) has also explored the phenomenon of the 'sacrificial lamb'. There is a perception that women are often nominated in ridings where the party has little, if any, hope of success and party workers have to 'twist people's arms' to run. Mary Clancy (in Ralston 1999), for example, mentioned that when she first ran for a federal seat, she was placed in a riding that the Liberals did not have a hope of winning. However, recent evidence at the provincial level indicates that the sacrificial lamb phenomenon is fading as women increasingly contest more winnable ridings (Studlar and Matland 1996). In the 2004 federal election, women were almost as successful as men in winning seats overall, although in the 2008 federal election, women were 5.5 points less successful in winning their ridings (see Table 5.4). MacIvor (2003, 31) notes that the margin of difference between the success rates of men and women candidates steadily narrowed from 8 per cent in 1984 to 3.3 per cent in 1993 and 0.3 per cent in 2000 (although it crept back up again to 3.2 per cent in the 2004 election and went down to 2.5 per cent in the 2006 election). Ironically again, the NDP's breakthrough victory in Quebec in the 2011 federal election yielded a number of victories for both female and male candidates who had not known, going into the election, that they were running in a 'winnable' riding.

Trimble and Arscott (2003, 49) attribute the diminishing significance of the sacrificial lamb phenomenon to 'more women with professional qualifications [being] . . . available to seek elected office'; 'strong, effective support within parties and by the women's movement [leading to] . . . increased representation by women'; 'financing prospects [that] have improved for women candidates'; and 'measures taken by some parties to boost the number of women candidates . . . influenc[ing] other parties to do the same (contagion effect)'. Tremblay and Pelletier (2001, 169) also found that male and female constituency party presidents evaluate candidates similarly and that during the selection process, 'it is the ungendered traits that women and men constituency

The Successful Sacrificial Lamb

Following the November 2000 federal election, journalist Daniel Leblanc chronicled the upset win by Liberal Julie Boulet in a riding that, at the time, was considered a Bloc Québécois stronghold impenetrable to a candidate serving Liberal leader Jean Chrétien.

Yet Boulet won with a 57-vote majority in the riding of Champlain, making her part of an unexpected resurgence for the Liberal party in Quebec in fall 2000, with the party increasing its seats in that province to 37 from 26.

> Ms Boulet said yesterday that she was assured Champlain was 'winnable' when she was asked to run. A senior Liberal said this amounted to routine assurance.
>
> 'When you're given a riding in a region like that, we're basically telling you, "Good luck!"' he said.
>
> During the campaign, Liberal strategists described the 41-year-old mother of two as the perfect candidate: a dynamic and charming pharmacist who had been the president of the popular Saint-Tite Western Festival.
>
> They added, however, that she didn't stand much of a chance—the Bloc won the riding by almost 8,000 votes in 1997.

Source: Daniel Leblanc. 2000. 'She had no chance but she won anyway: Upset Quebec victory reflects Liberal surge'. *The Globe and Mail* 29 November: A1, A4.

party presidents favour, not personality traits specifically associated with one gender or the other'.

This change in party attitudes can be attributed to pressure on political parties from women's groups, both inside and outside the parties. As Lisa Young (1997, 88) reports, 'since the early 1970s, women have formed several organizations with the purpose of increasing the number of women elected. These groups included Women for Political Action (1971–9), the Feminist Party of Canada (1979–81), the Committee for '94 (1984–94)[9] and Canadian Women for Political Representation (1986–8).' The National Action Committee on the Status of Women, the Canadian Advisory Council on the Status of Women, and the Fédération des femmes du Québec, among others, have also issued calls for the election of more women. All of these efforts have increased public awareness of the issue and placed pressure on parties to remedy the situation.

Do organizational factors matter?

While the lot of women in party organizations is improving, organizational factors—primarily the ability of the party to win elections and local party attitudes—remain crucial factors in accounting for the low number of women in the House of Commons. That more women candidates and party elites are found in the two parties least likely to form the federal government, the NDP and the BQ, is telling. The barriers are difficult to overcome because they not only require organizational change but also societal or cultural shifts. We will now turn to some political institutional factors that have been proposed to enhance women's electability.

Institutional factors

Incumbency

Incumbency is a barrier to any new candidate, male or female; however, for women it can pose a major obstacle. Incumbents have name recognition. For an already-sitting representative (an incumbent), the advantages of political advertising, news coverage of their activity, and the ability to 'claim credit' for policy decisions are significant. However, the biggest advantage held by incumbents is the prohibitive cost of electioneering, which gives a distinct advantage to the one already holding office and dissuades others from taking up the challenge (Docherty 2002a, 165). In the United States, incumbency is a significant feature of political campaigning, and it makes it very difficult for women and visible minority candidates to unseat the usually white male incumbents; on the other hand, incumbency also helps women and members of visible minority groups to retain their seats if they do manage to win.[10] In contrast, there is a high rate of turnover of seats in Canada's House of Commons and in provincial legislatures, which means that there are very few 'safe' seats and incumbency is less of a factor. Add to that the tendency of many MPs to retire after one or two terms in office, and one finds that incumbency 'does not create as much of a barrier to entry of new groups into the House as it would if the rate of turnover were lower' (Lisa Young 1997, 86). Furthermore, campaign spending limits prevent out-of-control election spending as one sees in the United States, where incumbents vastly outspend challengers. Instead, researchers point to nomination contests in competitive ridings as the major barrier for women to overcome, particularly since there are currently no spending limits on nomination contests.

Money

Campaigns cost money. One can say that 'the amount of money that different individuals and groups have to spend on politics influences who gets heard, what issues are debated, and how they are addressed' (Burrell 1998, 26). Furthermore, 'the ability of candidates to raise sizable amounts of money to finance a campaign helps to determine who gets elected'. For women, money is a significant issue, and there are stark monetary differences among male and female candidates' abilities to run for and compete successfully for elected office. As MacIvor (1996, 240) points out, 'Not only are women paid less than men on average, which limits their ability to fund their own political efforts, but their exclusion from elite networks denies them access to rich sources of political funds. It is much easier for a respected lawyer or financier to raise the thousands of dollars needed for a contested nomination than it is for a teacher or a nurse.' In addition, 'the risks of running for office are much greater for a woman, who may find herself deeply in debt after losing a nomination battle.' Since women on average earn about 70 cents for every dollar earned by a man, the money they will be able to draw on for nomination contests is also considerably less (Bashevkin 1991, 75). Women also have traditionally not been as involved in the financial and political circles that would allow them access to large contributors.

Finally, societal attitudes and perceptions that women cannot win mean that contributors may see them as a poor investment and therefore do not give money to women (Burrell 1994, 102–3).

Women are more fortunate in Canada than in the United States in that they do not have to raise as much money for their candidacies in general elections, mainly because of differences in campaign finance laws. In the United States, the federal government has rules in place as to the amount of money people can donate to a candidate or party but few rules as to how much can be spent on a campaign. In Canada, the opposite is the case: there are strict rules on what candidates can spend on a campaign but not so many rules on what people can donate.[11] The effect of these laws in the United States is to force candidates to raise large amounts of money to fund increasingly expensive campaigns. Interestingly, though, women in the United States have proved very capable at raising and spending money. Much of this can be attributed to a number of women's Political Action Committees (PACs), such as EMILY's List. These organizations collect money from members and contribute the funds to candidates' and parties' campaigns. In fact, Burrell (1998, 27) notes that in the 1988 and 1992 elections, women actually raised more money than men did, if one controls for incumbency.

As mentioned earlier, Canadian campaign finance laws help to level the playing field for men and women. Elections Canada fixes a ceiling on the amount of money that national parties and individual candidates can spend in an election, with spending monitored by a commission. Each party must file a detailed expenditure and revenue report each year as well as report contributions and income tax receipts to Revenue Canada. In return, candidates and registered parties receive generous reimbursement of their election expenses. As well, contributors to candidates and parties receive generous tax deductions. Lisa Young (1997, 87) thus argues, 'by preventing the excessive spending that characterizes American campaigns, broadening the contributor base, and reducing the personal financial risks assumed by candidates, these rules have made the financial barriers facing potential candidates less daunting.'

The 2004 amendments to the Canada Elections Act closed some of the loopholes that existed in federal campaign finance laws. Under Bill C-24, the federal government extended campaign finance regulations to nomination contests as well as leadership races. In the case of leadership races, the voluntary limits the parties had in place tended not to be rigorously upheld. For example, Jackson and Jackson (2001, 406) note that the Progressive Conservative executive stipulated a $900,000 spending limit per candidate, plus unlimited travel, during the 1993 leadership race. Kim Campbell reportedly spent at least four times that limit. And, as mentioned above regarding nomination contests, without spending limits, many of these races saw major spending on the part of some candidates, disadvantaging less wealthy or well-funded candidates.

The 2004 legislation also banned donations from corporations and unions to the national political parties and imposed limits on the amount of money individuals can donate to candidates. To make up for the lost revenue, political parties are now eligible for subsidies based on the level of the popular vote they received in the previous general election. Women politicians have tended to support these changes because they create a more level playing field in campaign financing (for more information, see http://www.elections.ca under 'election financing').

Electoral system

Finally, and perhaps most important, we need to consider the effects of the electoral system. Researchers have long noted the vagaries of the single member plurality (SMP) system.[12] The requirement for a simple plurality (<50+1) rather than a majority of votes (>50+1) cast in each riding in order to win a seat tends to advantage large brokerage parties such as the Liberals or regionally concentrated smaller parties such as the Reform Party/Canadian Alliance or Bloc Québécois. Small parties with diffuse support are disadvantaged because seats, not votes, determine representation in the elected assembly. A party may do very well and amass thousands of votes in each riding, but if it does not win the most votes in a riding, it will not hold that seat in the legislature. Effectively, if electoral support is not concentrated in specific ridings, it is difficult for the party to gain representation. This has two significant effects: first, the SMP system in the past has meant the political left has been weak in Canada. It also means that women's parties have little chance of success since it would be difficult to concentrate women's votes regionally. Second, SMP tends to encourage a high level of localism because parties need a local organization in every constituency where they run candidates. This grants a great deal of power to the local riding association and, as we discussed earlier, local riding associations may not be enthusiastic about running women and visible minority candidates.

Thus, many scholars (for example, Studlar 1999) advocate a proportional representation (PR) system in which seats are awarded based on the proportion of the popular vote a party receives in an election. Feminist researchers in particular tend to like PR because it removes the winner-take-all adversarial game that SMP establishes among the candidates. PR tends to support the creation of multi-member districts, and therefore voters' votes do not go to one candidate alone but rather to many candidates, which can include women and minorities. The zero-sum nature of voting is removed. PR also allows parties to practise an explicit affirmative action by placing women's names high on party lists. It improves women's representation in elected legislatures because it removes electoral barriers to smaller parties, which would win seats proportionate to their vote. For example, in Iceland a group of women decided to form the Icelandic Women's Party (Kvenna Althing). In the 1983 legislative elections, the party won three seats in parliament, and women's representation jumped from 5 to 15 per cent. By the early 1990s, that figure had reached nearly 25 per cent. Furthermore, not all of those seats are held by Women's Party members; rather, the presence of the party galvanized other parties into running women candidates who were successfully elected (Basden 1993). Consequently, PR is considered more conducive than SMP to the nomination and election of women to legislative office.

This view is borne out by comparative research, which reveals that countries with PR or even mixed PR/SMP systems elect more women than countries with SMP systems. Most researchers point to the near-parity rates of women in national legislatures in Sweden (45.03 per cent women as of 2010), Finland (40.0 per cent), Norway (39.6 per cent), and Denmark (38.0 per cent) (IPU, http://www.ipu.org/wmn-e/classif.htm). Richard Matland (1998), in a study of 24 developed and 16 developing democracies, found that the electoral system has a powerful, statistically significant effect in developed (but interestingly, not developing) democracies. Matland (1998, 115) predicts that were an industrialized democracy to switch from a majoritarian to a PR system, it would result in a 15.6 per cent jump in the female proportion of the national legislature. He notes, for example, the impact of switching from SMP to a mixed system in New Zealand in 1996: the proportion of women in the elected legislature rose from 21.2 per cent to 29.2 per cent after the first election under the new system.

There is a further benefit to the PR system in that it tends to change the nature of politics within legislatures. Rarely does one party win an overall majority, which means that parties have to negotiate and compromise to form effective governing coalitions. Therefore, the dynamic of legislatures shifts from adversarial to cooperative politics and policy-making, creating an environment, as some feminist researchers argue, in which women can do better.

However, we must be careful about placing too much faith in the PR system. Karen Beckwith (1992) argues that we should be cautious in stating categorically that PR systems advantage women running for elected office. She points out important exceptions to the PR rule: for example, in Italy under a PR system, women comprised only 8 per cent of the national legislature in 1992. The number of women elected to the French National Assembly did not vary much as a result of the switch from SMP to PR and back again in the post-World War II period. Other researchers (such as MacIvor 2003, 28) observe that in Israel, for example, women held only 18 of the 120 seats (9 per cent) in the national legislature as of 2003, even under a pure PR system in which the country comprises a single constituency of 120 members and in which there is pure proportionality between the percentage of popular vote received and the number of seats a party is awarded.

Obviously then, the type of electoral system alone is not the sole barrier to women's electoral success. Attitudes and culture continue to matter. As Beckwith (1992) argues, how well women do also depends on the party's attitudes towards women, not simply on the electoral system. Usually, the national or local party organization controls the list of party candidates. Women's names have to be placed high enough on the list to reflect the party's expected seat total if those candidates hope to be allocated seats in the legislature. In other words, women and other candidates from disadvantaged groups must depend on the willingness of their political parties to place them high enough on a party list based on the party's prediction of how electorally successful it will be so that those candidates are sure to be allocated seats. She also points out that in the Scandinavian countries in particular, women's electoral success could simply reflect the success of left-wing parties in those countries, not the type of electoral system per se. If the NDP were to be elected as the governing party in Canada federally, for example, we would likely see a huge jump in the number of women elected to office, as we did in Ontario in 1990 with election of the provincial NDP. There, the proportion of women elected jumped from about 15 per cent to nearly 22 per cent but declined to 15 per cent again in 1995 with the defeat of the NDP (Burt and Lorenzin 1997, 203).

Researchers have observed a similar phenomenon provincially in Quebec. Manon Tremblay, in a 2009 chapter cheekily entitled 'Women in the Quebec National Assembly: Why So Many?' observes that despite the SMP system in place provincially, in 2006, women comprised 32 per cent of the members of the National Assembly, just behind their comparators in Social Democratic countries. Tremblay (2009, 62) attributes women's electoral success in Quebec provincial politics to the lack of incumbency, and to the two main parties' willingness to run women candidates in competitive ridings.

Finally, Beckwith (1992, 23) argues that the presence of organized women's movements encouraging parties to nominate women can help. Tremblay (2009, 63) confirms that in the case of Quebec, because of the level of women's involvement in civil society and political parties, the main parties have seen women as an important constituency to woo. Societal changes such as an increase in women's labour force participation and higher levels of education for women, reinforced by changing societal attitudes, could all help to contribute to women's electoral success. Thus, women's success in gaining political office may reflect social, economic, and political change that allows and encourages them to participate more actively in public life.

Conclusion: The Problems of Supply and Demand

Institutional and organizational factors—the 'rules of the game', particularly the electoral system, money, and party attitudes—play by far the most pivotal roles in limiting the achievement of parity in Canada. Social and cultural factors are relevant because when they change, they push changes in the rules of the game. It is in fact a game of catch-up. Canadian society seems willing to give women a chance, if the organizational and institutional barriers are dismantled. Which organizational and institutional changes would be most effective, however, remains open to dispute.

As mentioned at the beginning of the chapter, women have had more success recently in obtaining appointed office rather than elected office at the federal level. The key to this success, however, appears dependent on having a sympathetic leader in power. For example, Prime Minister Jean Chrétien was often criticized for the number of women he appointed to the cabinet. In February 2003, after a high-profile cabinet shuffle that saw only one woman among 10 newly appointed members, the total number of women members of cabinet stood at 10 out of 38 ministers (including ministers, ministers of state, and secretaries of state). In response, backbench MP Carolyn Bennett, chair of the Liberal women's caucus, publicly complained about the lack of female appointments, especially given that all six new secretaries of state (junior positions) were men (Clark 2002, A1, A4). However, Bennett may have overstated the problem. Since 10 women of a total women's caucus of 39 sat in that cabinet,[13] approximately 26 per cent of women Liberal caucus members held cabinet office, which is better representation than women had overall in the House of Commons. In comparison, 28 of the 130 men in the Liberal caucus (approximately 22 per cent) sat in cabinet. Thus, the problem was, and still is, the scarcity of women legislators upon which to draw rather than unwillingness on the part of the prime minister to appoint women. Trimble and Arscott (2000, 36) report a correlation between the number of women in the House of Commons and the number appointed to prestigious positions such as cabinet office. The problem is one of supply, not demand, and the low number of women who succeed in winning seats for viable parties.

We do have to note that while a large percentage of the women who succeeded in entering the House were promoted by Chrétien, women did less well in Prime Minister Paul Martin's cabinet. Martin appointed 11 women to his 38-member first cabinet and nine women after a cabinet shuffle in July 2004. This demonstrates that an increase in the number of women cabinet members is not inevitable or constant, even under the same political party.

However, as Moncrief and Studlar (1996) found in their study of provincial-level cabinets, women have gradually been given increasingly important cabinet positions. This higher-level presence is important since research has demonstrated that women in elected office have made some difference in terms of policy outcomes and institutional change, but the changes are 'not as dramatic as the feminist progressive components might project nor as extensive as the women's movement had hoped' (Byrne 1997, 601). Byrne (1997) conducted interviews with 11 of the 13 women who served in the NDP cabinet under Ontario Premier Bob Rae between 1990 and 1995. These women identified themselves as substantive representatives of women's concerns and thus attuned to the demands of feminist movements in the province. The NDP's record in office demonstrates that the government did accomplish many progressive policy changes for women, including an extension of the provincial parental leave period, protection for home workers, and employment and pay equity. But both Byrne (1997) and Burt and Lorenzin (1997) report that it was difficult for the government to maintain its good relations with feminist and other advocacy groups and that within the caucus some female cabinet ministers found it difficult to speak out against collective decisions taken by cabinet. Thus, having women in positions of power in political office is important, but the ability to influence policy once there also matters. In the next chapter, we turn our attention to these practical realities and assess women's success in achieving policy change.

Questions for Critical Thought

1. Do you agree or disagree with the idea that women need to attain representation in formal political institutions in proportion to their numbers in the population?
2. What are the most important barriers to achieving gender equal representation in formal political institutions?
3. Does it help for women to 'run as women' when competing for elected office?

CHAPTER 6

The Practical Realities of Political Change

In this chapter, we connect the themes discussed in the first part of the book with the substantive policy discussions in the second part. Three major questions inform the discussion in this and subsequent chapters. First, what do women want and what are the goals of the women's movement? As previous chapters have demonstrated, this is a complex question. Feminist activists hope for political changes that better the lives of Canadian women. What 'better' means, however, is contested. We therefore have to talk about multiple and perhaps competing goals and women's movement(s) as opposed to a single women's movement, and we illustrate these debates as we examine each of the policy areas in the following chapters.

Second, does women's activism make a difference in terms of the achievement of policies that respond to the goals of the women's movement? And how does women's activism make a difference? One major purpose of this text is to illustrate how the goals of the women's movement are reflected in and inform both women's and governments' actions. We thus have to consider both processes and outcomes. In terms of means of political change, are the most effective avenues through women's movement activism, or by 'state feminist' agencies, or through litigation in the courts? Or is a combination of these efforts most effective? On the question of outcomes, is there necessarily a connection between women's activism and resultant policies? Or can we rely on governments acting 'for' women to yield beneficial policy results for women?

Dorothy Stetson (2001, 12), in conjunction with a number of other researchers, has worked out the following categories to judge the success of women's political mobilization for substantive policy change:

No response: women are not successful either at gaining access to decision-making or at affecting policy outcomes coinciding with movement demands.

Pre-emption: the state implements policies in accordance with women's demands but does not bring them into the decision-making process.

Co-optation: women penetrate the state decision-making apparatus but do not achieve the changes they desire.

Dual response: women penetrate the state decision-making apparatus and persuade the state to adopt policies that coincide with movement goals.

In other words, in Stetson's measures of policy success, women's political mobilization is deemed a success *only* if women manage to be involved in the process of decision-making as well as achieving their substantive policy goals.

The third question we examine is, then, does the participation of women in the policy process change the *process* of decision-making to make it more inclusive? Stetson (2001, 4) argues that one of the goals of the women's movement is to change the nature of policy debates so that they are conducted in feminist, or at least gender-aware, terms—for example, treating abortion as a women's issue rather than an issue of clarifying the legality of the procedure for doctors performing abortions. To what extent has women's action changed the process and not just the substance of decision-making?

In this chapter in particular, we explore the question of insider versus outsider strategies and how receptive governments have been in Canada to including women as policy actors, if not makers, in public policy development.[1] In subsequent chapters, we find that public policy change has been the result of a combination of elements, both conventional and unconventional, and a complex interaction between the actors within the movement, other movements, and state actors.

Question 1: What Do Women Want and What Avenues Exist to Express Demands?

As we discussed in chapter 4, it is misleading to refer to the women's movement as a coherent and unified entity: it is a social movement, heterogeneous, divided, unfocused, and coalitional in nature. Consequently, there is no single 'party line' regarding ideology and political strategy. In its politics and vision the women's movement is inherently diverse; indeed, one strength of the movement is that it can disperse, splinter, form, reform, and recreate itself. However, as Rowbotham (1989, 300) argues, that which is suitable for a movement finding sources of renewal is a challenge for a politics that must focus on concrete political campaigns. Translating diversity into focused, issue-specific political action can be problematic.

Diversity can work against women's effectiveness in the policy process. In Canada, the high point of the movement's inclusion in the policy process (during the 1970s) was characterized by the dominance of white, middle-class, educated feminists who established and worked through organizations such as NAC and the Canadian Federation of University Women. However, this period also saw the emergence and expansion of groups of much more marginalized women, those who emphasized the multiple oppressions of race, class, ability, and so on (Nadeau 2009). The result was the growth of diversity or, as some would argue, fragmentation, in the movement and debates over who spoke for women and which women were being spoken for. As Stephen Brooks (2000, 341) suggests, this has made it easier for governments 'to question as they now regularly do, whether NAC [and other women's organizations] truly represent the concerns and values of a majority of Canadian women'. It has become easy for the state to ignore or marginalize women's demands by accusing 'women' of, on the one hand, not knowing what they want and, on the other, asking for too much.

The Canadian women's movement, while successful in changing social attitudes regarding women's equality, has not fully 'solved the problem of how [the women's movement as a] social force can change the existing framework of political power' (Rowbotham 1989, 300). Efforts to effect policy change are pursued through agencies dedicated to women's issues, such as Status of Women Canada, as well as through political and education campaigns undertaken by women's organizations such as NAC and other groups, and the efforts of those groups to work through the legal and party systems. In other words, women activists 'have found themselves puzzling away between diffuse concepts of politics which have arisen in a social movement and the neater if more tired formulas, geared to goals, polls and campaigns' (ibid.). How are the visionary utopias of a social movement to be translated into workable political solutions?

The first overt political campaign to get the state to make significant changes on behalf of women was the effort of the suffragettes in the late nineteenth century and the early twentieth century to have the state recognize women as full citizens through the granting of the vote and the recognition of women as 'persons'. These campaigns emerged out of social feminists' efforts to 'transfer the values prevalent in the private world of the family to the public world of politics and labour' (Burt 1990, 191) and to have the state implement policies to protect the health, safety, and morality of families. The campaigns for temperance and eradication of prostitution had women not only as sponsors but also as the subjects of policy. As Marianna Valverde (1991) points out, at the turn of the twentieth century, the relationship of women to the state was a complex intersection of gender, class, and race, in which middle-class 'feminist' moral reformers demanded state action and regulation on issues of moral purity and sexuality that stood to drastically affect the lives of poor and working women, women of colour, and prostitutes. Similarly, state and middle-class women's concerns regarding population strength and 'racial purity' resulted in policies limiting the availability of contraception in order to encourage large families, as well as enforced sterilization for women who did not meet desired social norms (Prentice et al. 1988; Valverde 1991). Thus, women have not only been one of the most significant groups to consume and benefit from state policy, they have also been active in influencing that policy and in some cases have been victimized by policy.

Throughout Western industrial democracies, the relationship between women and public policy-making became stronger and much more intimate in the period following the Second World War, as widespread economic affluence combined with state commitment to social as well as political citizenship. This, along with increased female participation in the workforce, created expanded opportunities and needs for women to make public policy demands. By the 1960s, the emerging second wave of the women's movement sought wider changes, from 'equality-rights to a reshaping of the values informing all facets of social, economic and political life' (Burt 1990, 191). During the 1970s, feminists and women's organizations extracted real and valuable resources and power from policy-makers.

In Canada, after the successful push for the vote, Canadian women continued to work on welfare and labour issues. The changing nature of Canadian society and the Canadian economy increased women's opportunities and helped give rise to increased demands for the state to take action on women's equality, not only in politics but also in the labour force and the home.

Bringing women in from the margins of the policy process

In 1954 the federal government created the Women's Bureau in the federal Department of Labour. Its purpose was to investigate and provide information on the employment status of women. This focus reflected women's increasing participation in the work-force and the need of the booming post-war economy for more workers. While the bureau became a 'vehicle for bringing the positions taken by [women's] groups to the attention of policy-makers', its position within the Department of Labour was marginal and it lacked strength and resources (Burt 1990, 196).

Another significant vehicle in bringing women in from the margins of the policy process was the Royal Commission on the Status of Women, established in 1967 by the Liberal Government under Prime Minister Pearson. Monique Bégin, executive sec-retary of the commission and later a Liberal cabinet member (including being the first minister responsible for the status of women) argues that 'women did not represent, towards the end of the 1960s, a constituency in the political agenda or the Canadian state. . . . Anything that had to do with the "status of women" was channelled to the Women's Bureau' (Bégin 1992, 26–7). The royal commission, in contrast, put women's issues on the national agenda.

However, the story of the royal commission also illustrates the ambiguous and sometimes contradictory relationship between women's organizations and the state. While the commission set the groundwork for the relationship between women and the state for the 1970s, 40 years later significant recommendations such as national provision of child care, full pay equity, and access to abortion have yet to be imple-mented through state legislation. Bégin (1992, 36–7) laments that '[t]he state has dis-missed any attempts to fundamentally change the market rules or family arrangements' or otherwise to transform society. As Sandra Burt (2000) observes, while the state has tended to be sympathetic to claims that women should have equal access in politics and work, it has resisted the fundamental restructuring of relations between men and women in society as a whole. Nor has it provided the commensurate resources through gender-sensitive budget politics (Brodie and Bakker 2008).

One interpretation of the record of the royal commission is that it helped to take the teeth out of women's political action by offering piecemeal change and by giving some women's groups a special relationship with the state and a place within policy-making networks, thereby avoiding conflict and commitments to substantive change. Bégin (1992, 27) admits as much when she argues that, by creating the royal commis-sion and moving rapidly and positively on limited reforms, the government avoided bitter and constant confrontation with the women's movement. (The possibility of taming or co-optation will be taken up later in this chapter when we discuss women's public policy influence as insiders and as outsiders.)

However, we should not underestimate the effect of the royal commission in bringing women and women's groups into the policy-making process and developing a relationship between women's organizations and the state that would last through the 1970s. The commission played a significant role in mobilizing the women's move-ment in Canada, and its recommendations gave women a public policy focus in their demands that government act on implementing the recommendations.

The report of the royal commission (1970) recommended that the state make a commitment to giving women more influence in and access to the policy process. This was to involve a number of efforts, including expansion of the number of women within the offices of the state, creation of a cadre of 'femocrats' who would bring women's concerns to the fore in policy matters, and the creation of agencies within the government to focus on women's issues. As a result, in the early 1970s, the federal government created a number of women's agencies. The most powerful was Status of Women Canada, established in 1971 as an agency of the Privy Council Office, which assisted the minister responsible for the status of women. In 1973 the federal government allocated resources to a Women's Program in the Department of the Secretary of State to provide core and project funding for women's groups. In addition, in 1971 the federal government created the Canadian Advisory Council on the Status of Women (CACSW) as a council of women appointed by the prime minister to advise the government on the effects of policy on women.

In retrospect, this period represents the high point in the women's movement's relationship with the state and its influence on public policy. The context was opportune: the economic boom and the socio-cultural changes of the 1960s supported both the development of the women's movement and the state's approach to social policy. The Liberal government under Prime Minister Trudeau was sympathetic to the view that traditionally disadvantaged groups should have some role in the policy process, along with the typically powerful business and other interest groups, and that they could not do so without financial support (Timpson 2002/3, 43). The result, Sandra Burt (1990) argues, was that during the 1960s and 1970s the relationship between women's organizations and the state could be characterized as state-directed, as evidenced by the close relationship between women's groups and state agencies such as Status of Women Canada, the Women's Program, the Women's Bureau, and CACSW and in the funding made available to women's groups.

This relationship ended in the 1980s. Partly because of the success of state sponsorship, women's organizations had increased significantly in number and diversity of views, and the women's movement had become increasingly fragmented and divided. In addition, government willingness to associate closely with women's concerns and demands and to fund women's groups decreased as neo-liberal economic philosophies of government fiscal restraint became more prevalent. The Trudeau Liberal government was replaced by the more 'business-minded' Mulroney Conservative government, and the backlash against 'feminist' politics and demands became more pronounced (discussed further below). These developments led to a much more confrontational relationship between women's groups and the state. By the end of the twentieth century, the relationship of Canadian women to the state and their influence in the policy process had once more changed, requiring further changes in how women undertake politics and envision their relationship with the state. The movement became much more pluralist, competitive, and fluid, adopting strategies of working both 'with' and 'against' the state.

Question 2: How Do Women Go about Achieving Their Demands? Debates over Insider versus Outsider Strategies

Despite an important counter-current, the dominant mode of political discourse involves a commitment to the ordinary political process, a belief in the efficacy of state action, and a positive view of the state as a utility of value for women. This has focused women's movements on building co-operative political structures to interact with states and on retaining a tension between autonomy and integration. The movement's service orientation and willing-ness to depend on the state for financial support also moderates their stance. (Vickers 1992, 59–60)

The Canadian women's movement has adopted multiple strategies in dealing with the state and effecting policy change, including working both with and against the state. Operating inside the political system, women's organizations have worked to lobby government, engage with the bureaucratic structures that deal with issues of concern to women, and make presentations and representations to various access points such as public inquiries, task forces, royal commissions, and parliamentary committees, and have used the legal system to demand better policies and conditions for women.

Outside 'mainstream' politics, feminists have pursued less formal political action that has taken two forms: (1) extra-institutional forms of political expression, such as protest and public participation; and (2) the creation of women-centred services, such as shelters for battered women, rape crisis centres and hotlines, and support centres for oppressed women, that fill the void in available public services for women. These services have often come to rely on funding from both the state and the private sector, bringing them into the ambit of public policy and politics. The result has been the rise of significant doubts about insider versus outsider status, with government-funded centres finding themselves facing the problems experienced by traditional social ser-vice workers, such as a lack of resources and policy support (Hamilton 1996, 58). Many women, as a result, have become more politicized, and their relationship with the state has become more critical and tense.

The women's policy community

The relationship between Canadian women's organizations and the state has been characterized as a policy community or network. The concept of a policy community refers to a constellation of actors, both governmental and non-governmental, who share a common focus and language but not necessarily common positions and who, to varying degrees, shape policy outcomes over the long term. Networks develop as particular patterns of interrelationship within the community emerge; these networks have consequences for the development and delivery of policy (Coleman and Skogstad 1990; Pross 1990; Pal 1997). Communities and networks form and are activated when particular polices become salient political issues.

Burt (1990) divides the women's policy community into four branches. The first branch consists of service organizations whose primary purpose is to provide services to women, such as counselling, referral, education, or shelters. The second branch consists of equal rights groups that campaign for equal opportunities in employment and politics. The third branch Burt classifies as those holding social feminist goals (see chapter 4) and includes the National Council of Women, which was founded in 1893. The fourth branch consists of those groups that have emerged in response to feminist politics and campaign for the maintenance of the traditional social divisions between men and women, such as REAL Women of Canada. We can add to this list groups work-ing for the 'self-determination' of a variety of identities and against racism. The result is a complex, fluid, decentralized, and fragmented policy community and network.

The pluralism within the women's movement, and women's politics more generally, has a significant effect on the relationships and influence within the policy community. The policy community model works much more effectively if relationships are more centralized and structured. The ability of the group to speak coherently on behalf of an obviously powerful (either in terms of membership numbers or resources) constituency gives it influence. To be successful, non-governmental actors have to present themselves as relatively well-organized and institutionalized, with a regular membership base, a secure financial base, and policy expertise. It is also better to make demands around relatively narrow goals that can be accommodated within existing government policies or agendas (Smith 2000, 183). These features are not usually characteristic of social movements, which often find it difficult to combine the diffuse concepts of what matters in social movement politics and the neat, explicit goals found in mainstream institutionalized policies.

However, the policy community/network model of policy-making is not without merit. The general focus of the Canadian state has been to 'broaden out the policy development process to include more actors such as interest associations and various groups of experts' (Pal 1997, 192). In addition, the state has pushed for the creation of public/private partnerships and other alternative methods of program delivery, particularly by shifting social service responsibilities to private groups rather than public agencies (ibid.). These trends have significant ramifications for the section of the women's movement that is focused on providing women-centred services.

Influencing the state

Women's organizations in Canada have worked to influence state policy-making through a number of avenues, including lobbying parliament, using the media, making presentations to parliamentary committees, inquiries, and commissions, and working through the courts (MacIvor 1996, 336–8). However, as Dobrowolsky (2000a, 19) argues, the Canadian parliamentary system is not particularly hospitable to women's groups and demands: 'Beyond being constructed and dominated by males from relatively homogenous class, racial, ethnic, linguistic, and professional backgrounds, it is executive centred.' Many of the significant decisions affecting public policy are determined at the top, in the office of the prime minister and in the cabinet, both of which have been generally dominated by men.

However, the federal government is not the only access point for women's groups. They also work to influence policy at the provincial level, lobbying and working with provincial governments and even municipal governments. The Canadian constitution gives much of the authority over social and welfare programs to provincial governments, although the central government is not removed from the equation as it often has control over funding to the provinces and sometimes sets national standards, agendas, and strategies for policy. For women's groups, the result has been a balancing of focus between the two, sometimes three, levels of power. Federalism, some argue, is advantageous in that it creates multiple access points for groups trying to influence policy, with each province and territory having some kind of institutional apparatus, such as an advisory council or minister of state for women's policy (Brodie and Bakker 2008, 129-131). However, it can also create disadvantages, since it requires groups to divide their focus, thus diffusing their influence, and it can lead to fragmentation and growing regionalization of the groups within a movement. Dobrowolsky (2000a, 24) summarizes the dilemma of such an institutional structure: 'It can . . . contribute to both strained alliances and the siphoning of scarce resources. Yet one can also point to policy innovations that come as a result of federalism, and the potential safety mechanism of having more than one order of government to consider women's multiple interests and senses of identity.'

Presentations before parliamentary hearings, commissions, and inquiries are another popular avenue of influence. Some cynics suggest that the Canadian predilection for inquiries and commissions is a way for governments to defuse contentious political issues and put off action while appearing to be accomplishing something. But commissions and inquiries do not arise solely as a result of state initiative; rather, they are often a response to outside activism (Dobrowolsky 2000a, 20). As an access point in policy development, they help to provide a forum for the voices of women and women's groups. The Royal Commission on the Status of Women was a benchmark in terms of setting an agenda for women's public policy issues and in mobilizing women's groups. Other commissions and inquiries on issues ranging from the economy and Aboriginal affairs to reproductive technologies have also heard the concerns and demands of Canadian women.

A further strategy is to place women in positions of influence by getting feminists into political office (for an analysis of the success of that strategy, see chapter 5), encouraging feminist sympathizers in the bureaucracy, and cooperating with the various offices mandated to address women's issues. We thus should not underestimate the significance of the bureaucratic agencies to which women's groups can appeal.

State feminism

Recent research by people who study the success of women's groups in affecting policy change suggests that having advocates in the bureaucracy who act as insiders in the policy process is crucial to that success (Stetson 2001, 271). That is, women's policy agencies (institutional actors inside the state) play a crucial role in advancing the goals of women's movements in advanced industrial democracies (Stetson 2001, 1). These agencies have been labelled as 'state feminist', which refers to the 'institutionalization of feminism in public agencies promoting a women's policy agenda' or the institutionalization of feminist interests (Stetson and Mazur 1995b, 10). The women employed in these agencies and the women politicians who advocate feminist policies are sometimes called 'femocrats' (Stetson and Mazur 1995b, 10).

Women's policy agencies are important: first, because 'the establishment of women's policy machinery does allow some women to work full-time inside government, designing and implementing projects devoted to the improvement of women's status rather than being restricted to a part-time role outside as supplicants' (Stetson and Mazur 1995b, 5); second, because the existence of state feminist machinery has a potentially transformative effect on law and public policy. The traditional view is that bureaucracies are the very essence of inequality and therefore the policies of bureaucracies will not produce equitable results (for example, Ferguson 1984). However, the effect of these state feminist agencies may be to create 'feminism from above'.

As we discussed earlier, one of the outcomes of the Royal Commission on the Status of Women was to encourage the creation of a 'femocracy' of civil servants and agencies within the state bureaucracy that would bring women's concerns to the fore in matters of policy. The result was the creation of Advisory Councils on the Status of Women both at the federal level and in some provinces and territories. While their influence and autonomy have waxed and waned, Burt (1990, 195) argues that the 'Status of Women advisers sometimes have been important in affecting the impact of the women's lobby on policy formation. There is even evidence that they have performed an advocacy function within government when interest groups have been silent on an issue.' However, Burt (1990, 200) goes on to state that the agencies within government concerned with women's issues are marginalized: they 'have never enjoyed positions of autonomy within the bureaucracy'. Similarly, Sue Findlay (1987, 37) argues that women's presence in the bureaucracy was quickly institutionalized and consequently co-opted and de-radicalized.

There are two reasons why such co-optation or de-radicalization might happen: first, the filling of a position by a woman does not necessarily mean the position is filled by a feminist, and second, the self-interest of civil servants in terms of building a career and being promoted tends to attenuate any radicalism they may have. In fact, Stetson and Mazur (1995a) found that state feminism is generally more effective if the state feminist organization is separated out and located in a powerful ministry and if it is given adequate resources—that is, if it can scrutinize initiatives in a wide range of policy areas; if it is given a large staff, a minister, and even a cabinet committee; if it can provide funding to a wide range of women's organizations to aid in their development, without co-optation; and if it can bring in feminist activists or organizations to act as staff or advisors (see also Chappell 2002). Strong state feminist agencies tend to be created by left-wing governments that place gender equity on their agendas. State feminist agencies also tend to be strong if they are able to take both a centralized and a cross-sectoral approach to promoting gender equality in mainstream policy; that is, they should have a central coordinating office or be set up to coordinate women's equality policy in an authoritative manner. A statist political cultural tradition (a tendency for citizens to look to the state to solve policy problems) also helps. Finally, women's active participation in outside feminist organizations as well as in trade unions and political parties is an important complement to state feminist activities.

How important are these agencies in influencing public policy? In later studies, Stetson has found them to be crucial (Stetson 2001; see also Rankin and Vickers 2001). This is particularly the case if women's organizations are close to left-wing parties in power, as in Canada, where women's organizations tend to have closer relations with Liberal (centre) and NDP (left-of-centre) governments.

Even when a sympathetic political party is not in office, state feminist agencies play an important role in keeping issues on the policy agenda, particularly if those agencies are powerfully placed. Geller-Schwartz (1995, 48) argues that the agencies established in Canada in the 1970s have not faded away. They have been reorganized and their names and mandates modified, but while their autonomy and influence has waxed and waned, they have not disappeared. Dobrowolsky (2000a, 22) agrees. She states that 'Femocratic networks grew, were clipped, but then organizational offshoots emerged. This reflected the continuing tensions between state regulation and feminist resistance. Like hardy vines, feminists penetrated the walls, and when cracks were sealed, other entry points were pried open.'

The existence of the 'femocrats' is not enough, however. Stetson (2001, 295) also found that women's organizations have to be unified and place a particular issue high

on their own policy agenda for government to pay attention to the issue. Women's organizations can be successful in achieving their demands in the absence of strong state
feminist agencies but only if the policy process is relatively open. Even then, 'they are
likely to achieve only partial success by gaining access to policy arenas but not feminist
policy outcomes.' Thus, the lesson seems to be that coordinated outsider *and* insider
feminist activism is needed.

Dilemmas of insider and outsider status

Policy communities and state feminism place a premium on the achievement of insider
status to affect the policy process. Here we want to highlight some of the conundrums
of the 'insider' versus 'outsider' strategies for effecting policy change and the kinds of
compromises women's groups make in focusing their energies on political lobbying as
opposed to other strategies, such as political protest and consciousness-raising (education) activities.

The Dilemmas of Insider versus Outsider Strategies

The suffrage experience in the United States is exemplary of the debates among women's
groups about the 'best' strategy. While women's groups in many Western industrialized countries, including Canada, pressured governments to grant women the right to
vote, the debate over tactics was most stark in the United States. One organization, the
National American Woman Suffrage Association (NAWSA) focused a great deal of activity
on political lobbying. The Congressional Union for Woman Suffrage (CU), later named the
National Woman's Party (WP), which split from NAWSA, engaged in more radical tactics,
such as members picketing the White House during wartime and when arrested going
on hunger strikes and attacking the Democratic Party, which held power in Congress.
NAWSA members saw these tactics as alienating male politicians rather than bringing
them onside and continually chastised the CU for its tactics.

In the end, it is not clear whether the more pragmatic tactics of NAWSA or the more bold
tactics of the CU/WP won over congressional and state legislators. There are drawbacks
to both. As Schlozman (1990, 341–2) argues, the problem with protests is that they can
backfire: they 'may help win converts to the cause and generate sympathy within the
public and media, [but] they may alienate the policymakers who make the ultimate decisions'. In addition, political protests may result in an immediate but ultimately symbolic
policy response to defuse the pressing grievances: 'to realize and consolidate substantive
political benefits usually requires the kind of coordinated effort and sustained vigilance
and follow-through that are difficult to achieve in a decentralized political movement
relying on volunteer leadership and a rank and file whose enthusiasm may wane when
symbolic victories have been attained' (Schlozman 1990, 342).

While the struggle for suffrage in Canada was much more moderate, the choices between protest and cooperation were generally similar. Dobrowolsky (2000a, 19; 2000b)

argues that parliamentary cabinet government in Canada attenuates the 'straightforward interest group model of the American women's movement' and is less favourable to Canadian feminists. This has required the Canadian movement to adopt 'multipronged strategies . . . tailored to its particular political milieu'. The result, however, has been to keep a balance between protest and cooperation, much as in the United States. Thus, organized pressure groups have emerged to keep sustained pressure on Ottawa and Washington and on provincial and state governments.

From the perspective of both insiders and outsiders, the issue is one of political opportunity. The term 'political opportunity structure' is used to refer to the political context that either encourages or discourages activity. This includes specific configurations of resources, institutional arrangements, and historical precedents that facilitate the development of movements and their activities (Kitschelt 1986; Tarrow 1994). These structures enhance or limit the ability of actors to insert themselves into the political process through (1) determining the informational, financial, and ideological (in the form of grievances and issues) resources available; (2) setting the institutional rules of access, 'such as those reinforcing patterns of interaction between government and interest groups, and electoral laws' (Kitschelt 1986, 61); and (3) determining the success of other social movements, the influence of political parties, and the availability of influential allies. The political opportunity structures available at a given time determine a movement's decision to mobilize, the outcomes of collective action, and its institutional effects.

Focusing energy on gaining insider influence may lead to the 'embourgeoisement' of feminism (Schlozman 1990, 343). An example of the pitfalls of insider status is illustrated by the 1981 resignation of Doris Anderson as president of the Canadian Advisory Council on the Status of Women (CACSW). CACSW, a quasi-autonomous advisory council created by the state and made up of government appointees, was the epitome of an 'insider' agency. A crisis emerged when a conference organized by CACSW to discuss the place of women in the Constitution in light of the Trudeau government's proposed constitutional changes was cancelled at the request of the minister responsible for the status of women, Lloyd Axworthy. For Anderson, this was an example of undue government interference and political obstructionism. She accused CACSW of caving in to state directives and resigned as president. Whether or not CACSW was following orders from government officials or acting on its own, what matters is the perception that it had no autonomy and would push a women's agenda only as long as it did not conflict with that of its political masters.[2] Its insider status actually worked to delegitimize it as an advocate for women. The result was the mobilization of women who criticized the government's activities regarding CACSW and organized an alternative conference based on grassroots involvement. With CACSW in disarray, the 'outsiders' stepped in to fill the void. However, as Dobrowolsky (2000a) points out, this alternative conference was organized with a good deal of support from other 'insider' feminists.

As we saw in chapter 4, huge rifts existed between liberal and radical feminists in the second-wave feminist movement. Radical feminists took no interest in the state and were suspicious of all state involvement in their activities—for example, refusing government funding for women's shelters for fear of co-optation. Radical feminist groups often rejected involvement in organized politics because bureaucracies and other formal organizations that emphasize principles of impersonality and hierarchy are inherently antithetical to a feminism that emphasizes democracy and grassroots involvement in decision-making (Ferguson 1984; Tyyska 1998). Schlozman (1990, 339), in fact, describes pressure politics as 'a sphere of political activity characterized by reliance on the most traditional kind of old-boy political network, the unabashed pursuit of narrow self-interest, and, often, considerable scepticism about activity undertaken in the name of the public good'. Other women's groups chose to focus on other organizations with access to power, such as the trade union movement or professional associations, whose attentions are not exclusively directed to lobbying government (Burt 1995, 86).

But how well have those who accept the idea of involvement in the mainstream political system done in achieving equality for women? Looking at the experience of women's organizations in the United States, Schlozman (1990, 360) points out that there is very little difference overall between women's organizations and other representative groups in Washington. That is, in terms of the strategies they use, such as testifying at congressional hearings and contacting government officials on an official or unofficial basis, very few differences can be observed. Where differences can be seen is in the way women's groups are perceived by other organizations and the lawmakers they are trying to lobby. Schlozman (1990, 357–9) reports that women's organizations often felt that they were not taken seriously, that they were excluded from some of the 'old-boys networks', that men often felt threatened by the presence of women, that women's access often depended on the party in power, and finally, that women's groups often lacked the resources to which corporate-organized interests had access, such as money.

Schlozman's (1990) research raises the question, does pursuing influence through pressure politics sacrifice women's goals? Does being 'one of the boys' mean that women cannot pursue alternative tactics and still get results? Alternatively, in the absence of women's organizing, would governments be responsive to women? These are important questions to keep in mind as we explore substantive policy areas in subsequent chapters.

Debates over government financing of women's groups

One of the effects of the report of the Royal Commission on the Status of Women was the federal government's commitment during the 1970s to fund Canadian women's organizations. As Susan Phillips (1991) observes, one of the distinctive features of social movements in Canada is that many have developed closer relationships to the state than have their counterparts in other countries. Not only has the federal government allowed representatives of movements a place in consultation, but it also has provided substantial support to many organizations. This support, Phillips (1991, 197) argues, is based on the small-l liberal notion that 'government funding to . . . disadvantaged constituencies adds an element of fairness to the representation of the spectrum of interests in Canadian society.' It allows for the inclusion of voices from constituencies of citizens who—because of their location, lack of political and financial resources, or pursuit of 'unpopular' or socially challenging causes—are not perceived to be part of mainstream politics. However, it can make groups much more dependent on the state and consequently much more vulnerable to changes in the state.

This funding relationship has had significant implications for Canadian women's groups. Most government funding comes from the Women's Program of Status of Women Canada, the federal agency responsible for promoting women's equality in Canada (see http://www.swc-cfc.gc.ca/fun-fin/fp-pf/index-eng.html for a list of recently funded projects). Pal (1993, 221) reports that the budget for women's groups in the Secretary of State grew substantially in the 1970s and early 1980s, from $223,000 in 1973 to approximately $12.5 million in 1985. Starting with the federal Conservative Government under Prime Minister Brian Mulroney and continuing with the Liberal Government under Jean Chrétien, the federal government cut funding to the Women's Program so that monies for projects dropped to $8.25 million by 1999–2000 (Status of Women Canada 2000a). But as part of its Agenda for Gender Equality, adopted at the time of the Beijing +5 conference, the federal government directed more funds to the Women's Program (Standing Committee on the Status of Women 2005, 5). By the 2006–07 fiscal year, Women's Program grants increased to approximately $11.75 million (Standing Committee on the Status of Women 2007, 2). A change in government in January 2006 brought further shifts in the Women's Program budget. The government shifted about $5 million in monies spent on administration at Status of Women Canada into project funding, thus increasing the overall grants budget to $15.3 million by April 2007 (Standing Committee on the Status of Women 2007, 2). By fiscal year 2009–10, the grants budget had increased to approximately $25.5 million (Status of Women Canada Financial Statements, http://www.swc-cfc.gc.ca/account-resp/pr/fin/index-eng.html). The organizations and projects receiving funds varies from the Girl Guides of Canada's Girls for Safer Communities Project, to the Federation of Canadian Municipalities' National Women in Municipal Government Program, to a number of provincial and territorial-based initiatives (Status of Women Canada Funded Projects, http://www.swc-cfc.gc.ca/fun-fin/fp-pf/2009-2010/index-eng.html).

This funding is important to women's groups, Sandra Burt argues, because it gives 'women's groups a measure of legitimacy, guarantee[s] them a voice in the federal government's policy deliberations, and provide[s] the groups with the means to survive' (Burt 1995, 88). It thus provides a welcome and some would argue necessary basis for political action.

But what effect has this funding had on women's groups? One concern raised has to do with co-optation, a second concern with the vulnerability created by dependence on government funds. Regarding co-optation, some activists have worried that focusing on gaining and keeping government funding precludes other activities by women's groups and constrains their ability to oppose government actions. State largesse, after all, is not neutral; the state is careful about whom it chooses to fund. Funding will usually be given to those groups seen as 'relatively acquiescent . . . and which generally support government policies' (Phillips 1991, 198). Groups seen to be more radical or perceived to be outside the bounds of acceptability by the bulk of society are unlikely to receive funds. In addition, funds may be given with specific conditions and directions attached that result in a group having to tone down its demands and activities.

In her study in the early 1990s, Burt (1995, 88) found little evidence of co-optation of the women's movement. She found that the government exercised relatively little control over group activities and that 'government control over the spending of this money was restricted primarily to the establishment of guidelines for proposals

When It Comes to Government Funding, Are All Women's Groups Treated Equally?

Women's Program funding provides both core and project funding to 'promote the development, by women's groups, of projects and organizations designed (a) to increase their ability to participate in all aspects of society and (b) to assist women in bringing about political and institutional change related to the status of women' (Pal 1993, 216). Until 1989, Burt (1990, 199) argues, 'directors of the [Women's] program understood those guidelines to mean that only those groups which work to improve the status of women in Canada (that is, improve the potential for equal opportunity) are eligible for funding.' That meant such groups as the National Action Committee on the Status of Women (NAC), the Women's Legal Education and Action Fund (LEAF), and the Canadian Research Institute for the Advancement of Women (CRIAW). But it did *not* mean REAL Women, a socially conservative and some would argue anti-feminist organization. Soon after REAL Women formed in 1984, it asked the federal government for money to challenge the principles behind the government funding; it was refused. The Women's Program argued that the organization did not support the goal of gender equality as outlined in the government's funding criteria (MacIvor 1996, 335). In turn, REAL Women launched a media campaign to publicize the refusal.

The House of Commons Standing Committee on the Secretary of State subsequently reviewed the Women's Program's objectives and funding criteria. It reported in May 1987 and recommended that the objectives and criteria not be changed (save for additions such as a clause rendering ineligible any organizations, projects, and recipients whose primary purpose was to promote a view on sexual orientation), arguing that 'funding should be directed to women's groups whose main purpose is to improve the status of women in the home, the workplace, the community or the world at large [and whose] whole principles, objectives, and activities support the attainment of equality for women as stated in the Canadian Charter of Rights and Freedoms [and other legal documents]' (MacIvor 1996, 335). But under pressure from Conservative government backbenchers, the Women's Program did give REAL Women some money ($21,000) to hold a conference in 1989 (Pal 1993, 147).

In 1997 the federal government created narrower criteria more specifically targeted to groups whose program objectives are 'to increase women's equality' and whose focus is on 'women's economic status, systemic violence against women and girls, and social justice' (Status of Women Canada 1997). The Women's Program funding guidelines explicitly define equality with reference to documents such as the United Nations Convention on the Elimination of All Forms of Discrimination Against Women and the Canadian Charter of Rights and Freedoms and state that 'all applicant organizations must be able to demonstrate that they are committed to advancing equality for women' (Status of Women Canada, Women's Program 2002). Under these criteria, REAL Women would find it very difficult to receive government funding—with good reason, many in the women's movement would say, given its opposition to policies such as universal child care and pay equity (see www.realwomenca.com/index.html).

It should be noted that other groups also were barred from Women's Program grants, not just REAL Women. For example, in the late 1980s, program criteria explicitly forbade the granting of funds for projects 'whose primary purpose is to promote a view on sexual orientation', meaning lesbian groups, partly as a result of complaints from REAL Women (Ross 1988 35–6). In addition, groups that advocate more radical social change and on controversial political and moral issues such as greater access to abortion have found it difficult to access funds when they have tried.

for project or core funding.' Some members of women's organizations did fear, however, that their groups' goals and strategies were affected by the requirement that project grants conform to government guidelines, a fear that had intensified by the late 1990s.

As mentioned above, funding to non-governmental organizations declined significantly during the late 1980s and the 1990s. Thus, the second concern—the vulnerability caused by financial dependence—became more acute. Pal (1993, 8) reports that in the early 1990s, government funding accounted for between 50 and 80 per cent of women's organizations' budgets. By the mid-1990s, however, the level of government funding had fallen to $8.9 million (MacIvor 1996, 354) from $12.5 million in 1985. Women's Program spending for grants and technical assistance was projected at $10.8 million in fiscal year 2002–3 (Status of Women Canada 2002).

As a result, women's groups had to change their activities, focusing more on fundraising and less on political activity. They had to scale back their operations and cut back on paid staff to conserve their resources. Advocacy groups committed to achieving women's equality through political action have also found it difficult to obtain government funds under stricter guidelines. In a telephone interview on 21 August 2002, Kripa Sekhar, then vice-president of NAC, noted that the change in federal funding criteria introduced in 1997 shifted focus away from supporting advocacy and lobbying work and more toward research projects and service provision. That limited many organizations' ability to have a base budget from which to run advocacy campaigns.

A report by the Standing Committee on the Status of Women in 2005 documents many of the concerns the Committee heard during consultations with organizations in May 2005. It notes that 'core' funding refers to 'financial support that covers basic "core" organizational and administrative costs' whereas program funding 'tends to focus exclusively on project costs' (Standing Committee on the Status of Women 2005, 2). Funding for core activities allows an organization 'a degree of independence in selecting and implementing program and organizational objectives. Within a project-based funding model, the control of the content generally lies with the funder' (ibid.). Furthermore, '[c]ore funding tends to be of longer duration, and is considered a more predictable form of funding. Project funding is invariably short-term' (ibid.).

The changes in funding criteria, along with the cuts to core funding, have had a devastating effect on all women's advocacy organizations but most visibly on the National Action Committee. At the height of its influence in the early 1990s, NAC was the most visible and powerful women's advocacy organization in Canada, weighing in on the Meech Lake and Charlottetown accords, for example, and receiving strong attention from government. Throughout the 1990s, NAC broadened its policy concerns significantly, grappling with issues affecting Aboriginal women and women of colour, as well as poverty and other social justice issues. It attempted to become a visibly more inclusive organization, electing Sunera Thobani as the first woman of colour to serve as NAC president in 1995. By the early 2000s, however, NAC was in financial trouble, accumulating over $250,000 in debt by 2001 (NAC 2003), which forced it to lay off its staff. It has not held annual meetings or had an executive director since then (Carmichael 2004, A10). Past reliance on government funding weakened the ability of the organization to survive independent of government support.

Since the election of the Harper Government, further changes have been made to Women's Program funding. The Harper Government was under a great deal of pressure from socially conservative groups such as REAL Women of Canada to abolish Status of Women Canada out of continuing concerns that it funds 'anti-family' and 'anti-life' groups (National Association of Women and the Law 2006). Surprising, then, was the federal government's decision to increase project funding by early 2007 by redirecting funds spent on administration. In late 2006 the government announced it would close 12 of 16 regional offices and cancel the Policy Research Fund, which funded independent policy research (Standing Committee on the Status of Women 2007, 2–3). The Conservative Government changed the terms and conditions of the Women's Program as well, most notably eliminating the goal of seeking to 'advance equality for women'. The mandate now is 'to facilitate women's participation in Canadian society by addressing their economic, social and cultural situation through Canadian organizations' (ibid.). The criteria regarding eligible organizations changed as well, from 'Women's organizations in Canada whose objectives are to promote equality for women in Canadian society' to 'Incorporated not-for-profit and for-profit Canadian organizations whose mandates are consistent with the objectives of the Women's Program' (ibid., 4). The new criteria also limit funding for advocacy activities (ibid., 11). It is rather astonishing, to say the least, that the Women's Program is no longer mandated to promote women's equality!

Question 3: Do Women's Actions Succeed? Changing the Substance of Public Policy

MacIvor (1996, 338–48) lists a variety of factors that can determine women's effectiveness in influencing public policy. Both long-range factors, such as the political, social, and economic climate, and short-range factors, such as the ideology of the government in office, have significant effect. Institutional factors, such as the division of powers in the Constitution, which often requires the involvement of both the federal and provincial governments in policy decision-making, and the Charter of Rights and Freedoms and its rights-based discourse, play a role. In addition, agency factors, such as the characteristics of the organized groups themselves and the characteristics of the policy pursued, can facilitate or hinder policy change.

At the beginning of the twenty-first century, neither the long-range nor short-range factors have been propitious for women's groups. As Dobrowolsky (2000a, 20) observes, 'while the women's movement flourished under opportune conditions, it was challenged by state structures and directives especially when the economic climate turned colder.' And, we might add, when the cultural climate turned colder. We can identify at least three related reasons for the decline in substantive influence. First, the economic downturn of the 1980s spawned an attitude of fiscal conservatism on the part of both levels of government, leading to cuts in many social programs that directly affected women's lives. Second, this fiscal conservatism also led to reductions in state funding for non-governmental organizations, accompanied by a growing antipathy towards 'pressure politics' and a decline in state tolerance and space for social movement politics in general (Phillips 1991, 1994). Finally, the general backlash against feminist demands that emerged in the 1980s made governments less inclined to cooperate with the women's movement.

Consequently, women pressing for policy change have found it harder to get a hearing. Access to policy development forums is not as open as it was in the 1970s and early 1980s, and the claims and demands made are not perceived to be as legitimate as they were earlier. For insiders, there is pressure to 'keep their heads down' rather than to be seen associated with unpopular views or demands. This is compounded by the marginalization of women's agencies within the government.

In the 1990s, a major structural reorganization of federal departments initiated, ironically, by the first female prime minister, Kim Campbell, and retained in large part by the Chrétien government, broke up the Secretary of State programs. The programs for women and people with disabilities were transferred to the new Human Resources Development Canada where, as in the old Women's Bureau, they are likely to be overshadowed by employment programs. Governments have been more inclined to support an agenda based on equal legal rights than to deal with the systemic social and economic differences between women and men in Canadian society. In practice, this has meant a focus on equality of opportunity and formal legal equality, such as removing discriminatory provisions from existing laws, rather than on substantive equality that may involve major redistributive programs such as child care or addressing the economic disadvantages that women face (Burt 1997, 255–6).

Annis May Timpson (2001, 5) illustrates this division in the preface to her study of women's employment equality and child care:

> In the course of . . . two fascinating interviews, I learned that while the bureaucrats in the Workplace Equity Program had strong links with the Canadian Human Rights Commission, those working on the 'kids' file' in HRDC were in frequent contact with their counterparts on the Child Health Program in Health Canada. As our conversations proceeded, I realized that the bureaucrats in the Workplace Equity Program and the Children's Task Team—working just two floors apart in HRDC—hardly knew each other. To me this verified how, by the late 1990s, questions about women's employment equality and child care in federal policy had been driven apart.

Other examples of this fragmentation include the federal government policy on women's employment equality, which is seen as an issue of sex discrimination and equal opportunity; child care, in contrast, is seen as a child development issue or related to social assistance.

In 2000 (323–4) Burt gave a rather pessimistic assessment of the future of women's voices being reflected in Canadian public policy development:

Ironically, as feminists have become clearer about the need to gender Canadian politics, governments have been moving away from even counting women in numerically. In spite of the federal government's apparent commitment in 1995 to a gender-less strategy of policy development, women today are counted in less and less often when governments are making policy choices. . . . [I]t is due fundamentally to the ever-increasing commitment of Canadian governments to economic citizenship and to the associated values of individual initiative and self-reliance. Within the context of this neoliberal social order, Canadian women are moving into a new century within a policy agenda that makes it increasingly unlikely that their governments will want to take their interests into account.

Even more depressing is Brodie and Bakker's (2008), Hankivsky's (2009), and others' pessimistic analysis of Canadian governments' commitment to gender-based analysis in policy-making. Canada, as a participant in the Beijing Conference in 1995, committed to 'an active and visible policy of mainstreaming a gender perspective in all policies and programs so that before decisions are taken, an analysis is made of the effects on women and men respectively' (United Nations 1995, paragraph 79). As Hankivsky (2009, 116) documents, the Canadian government has declared in a number of documents its commitment to providing gender based analysis in policy-making. Yet, Hankivsky (2009, 116) concludes, gender mainstreaming 'has not brought about radical changes in the realm of policy'. Bakker and Brodie (2008, 7) argue that fiscal pressures experienced by governments in Canada have led to policy-making that has profoundly affected labour markets and social programs, and 'the progressive disappearance of the gendered subject, both in discourse and practice' in pursuit of the bottom line. We document these pressures in subsequent chapters.

Conclusion: Has Women's Activism Made a Difference?

At the beginning of this chapter, we outlined two measures by which to evaluate women's policy success. Women's political mobilization is deemed a success only if (a) women manage to become involved in the process of decision-making and (b) women manage to achieve their substantive policy goals.

Regarding the question of whether Canadian women's movements have changed the process of politics and in turn have been best served by insider or outsider tactics, the literature displays some ambivalence. Tyyska (1998) argues that women have been better served by insider tactics on the child care issue, crediting women in the Liberal caucus, for example, for alerting the policy community to the Mulroney child care initiative in the late 1980s that would have expanded child care funding but watered down regulations regarding that funding. Dr Henry Morgentaler, in his convocation address to University of Western Ontario graduates in June 2005 on the conferral of his honorary doctorate, argued that one need no longer engage in civil disobedience to achieve political change in Canada. Reflecting on his own experiences in the abortion movement, including his own acts of civil disobedience to have abortion laws changed, he concluded that one need no longer adopt such outsider tactics and can work effectively within the existing political process to effect change (Alphonso 2005, A3).

In contrast, Byrne (1997) argues that while the strong presence of women in cabinet in the Ontario NDP government (1990–5) correlated with some progressive policy outcomes for women, including employment equity, the legalization of midwives, and same-sex spousal benefits for government employees, the changes were not as dramatic or as permanent as feminists had hoped, and it is not clear that the policy process itself changed much. For example, the government did not maintain links with the feminist community despite a strong culture of consultation with community groups, and the policy agenda was taken over by concerns with fiscal restraint in the latter part of the government's term, making it difficult for the government to fulfill its promises (for example, regarding expanded child care funding). Thus, it is not clear to what extent the presence of 11 women in a cabinet of 26 transformed the process of policy-making.

From the movement's perspective, Montpetit, Scala, and Fortier (2004) argue in a very interesting study of NAC's involvement in policy deliberations over assisted reproductive technologies that while engaging in policy discussions with government officials did not hinder NAC's ability to be critical and to voice those criticisms to the government, it was hampered by its decision to consult with its diverse membership for policy advice. Doing so produced so many different opinions and such conflicting advice that it was very difficult for NAC to provide clear advice to policy-makers, which caused it to lose policy influence.

Canadian researchers have also given ambivalent responses to the question of the linkages between women's mobilization and substantive policy success. The answer often depends on the policy area studied. Vappu Tyyska (1998), for example, credits the women's movement in Canada for raising awareness of the need for child care services for working families, though federal and provincial governments have been slow to deliver substantially increased funding for these services, and supply has not increased particularly significantly in Canada outside of Quebec. Feminist organizations were also successful in blocking policy action on the part of the federal Conservative government in the late 1980s to provide some expansion of child care funding, which they deemed inadequate and which had attached to it insufficient regulations (Tyyska 1998). Lorna Marsden (1980) credits NAC with helping to improve federal pay equity laws in Canada, particularly in promoting the idea of equal pay 'for work of equal value'.

Cheryl Collier (2005), however, argues that it is difficult to establish a direct link between movement activism and substantive policy outcomes. In her study of social movement activism in Ontario from the 1970s to the present in the areas of child care and anti-violence policy, she found that strong social movements can positively impact government policy agendas and, conversely, weak social movements can facilitate negative government responses (Collier 2005, 21). However, it is difficult to establish a direct causal link between movement strength and progressive policy results without considering the impact of other factors, such as partisan composition of the government, government openness to women's movement concerns, and consensus on the legitimacy of the issue.

What lessons to draw from these experiences continues to be debated within the feminist community. Feminist representation within and mobilization outside of government appears crucial, yet even with such representation and mobilization, the ability to affect the policy process still seems limited. How representation and mobilization play out in the specific areas of family, work and pay, and the politics of the body will be the subject of subsequent chapters.

Questions for Critical Thinking

1. Is it problematic to achieve policy outcomes that are 'good' for women even if women are not included in the processes of policy-making?

2. What are the advantages of having a specific department or bureau dedicated to advancing gender equality within government, versus having each unit in government with representative 'femocrats'?

3. 'A strong civil society is dependent upon government funding of civil society organizations.' Discuss, with reference to the history of women's organizations in Canada.

CHAPTER 7

What Is a Family?

If, as discussed in previous chapters, the division of society into public and private spheres has overwhelming significance for the majority of women's lives, then the institution of the family is integral to women's lived experiences. What, then, is a family? At first glance, the answer seems obvious, but it can be ideologically charged and politically polarizing, as the debate over the legalization of same-sex marriage in Canada demonstrates. Is the family a 'natural, prepolitical, hierarchical, indissoluble, and private association made up of a heterosexual couple and their biological children' (Minow and Shanley 1996, 5)? Or is it a socially constructed, positive agent of nurturance and care that encompasses all possible unions of people?

How one answers the question as to what a family is has important implications for women's equality. It leads to further questions about the role of the state in defining the family. Should the state have the power to define what constitutes a family? Should the state see its role as sustaining viable and vibrant families and thus provide policies and programs for families, such as early childhood education and care, maternity and parental leave, family allowances, and other benefits? Or are these programs and services best regarded as private (that is, familial or market) responsibilities, or lower down in the rankings of government priorities? We find that there is very little consensus on these issues, even within the feminist community.

States and Families: Debates in Feminist and Political Theory[1]

Minow and Shanley (1996) argue that three major legal and philosophical approaches to understanding the family, as well as the degree of appropriate state intervention in the family, currently exist: contract-based theories, rights-based theories, and community-based theories. These theories can be placed on a continuum from the most intervention (community-based theories) to the least intervention (contract-based theories). Each of these theories prescribes different roles for the state and different solutions to questions of marriage, the dissolution of marriage, and other arrangements, such as surrogacy contracts. Each has different implications for gender and gender relations.

Advocates of **contract-based theories,** in Canada most notably Will Kymlicka (1991), argue that families should be regarded as any other contractual association. For example, the partners to a marriage contract should be allowed to set their own terms for their relationship. The state could require certain minimum standards regarding the care, education, and well-being of any children in the family, but otherwise, individuals would be limited only by their self-assumed obligations. Couples could decide on the rules governing their marriage or cohabitation and, in the case of marital breakdown, their separation or divorce. Contracts would dictate the division of assets and financial support without involvement by the state. A contractual view of families would not preclude any individuals from entering into a marital agreement, including those of the same sex. Contracts could also facilitate bringing children into a family, including children born through contract pregnancies (that is, surrogate mother arrangements), and regulate adoption arrangements.

This view of the family allows individuals to decide for themselves, privately, the division of labour within the relationship, financial issues, what happens if the marriage dissolves, and so on (see, for example, Weisbrod 1994, 811). It also allows very little role for the state in determining who can enter into such contracts. In other words, the parties to the contract could be any two (or perhaps more) people. The state's interest would lie in enforcing the contracts and scrutinizing their content to ensure that they are fair.

Some feminists[2] have embraced contract-based theories as more liberating than theories that suggest a 'natural' ordering within the family and prescribed gender roles. This view of the family is seen as a radical means of undermining traditional perceptions of the role of women within the institution of the family. With regard to contract pregnancies, for example, it holds 'that childbearing and child rearing are quite distinct human functions and that child rearing need not be and should not be assigned exclusively to the woman who bears the child' (Minow and Shanley 1996, 10).

Marriage Contracts

The case of Hartshorne v. Hartshorne, 2002[3], decided in the British Columbia Court of Appeal, illustrates the controversy over marriage contracts:

Robert Hartshorne, a lawyer, and Kathleen Baldwin, another lawyer, were married in 1989 after cohabiting for four years and after the birth of their first child in 1987. On the day of the wedding, Ms Baldwin signed a marriage contract drafted by Mr Hartshorne, which stated that she agreed to an 80/20 division of the family assets in favour of Mr Hartshorne should they divorce instead of the usual 50/50 division of assets as outlined in the BC Family Relations Act. The couple did divorce in July 1999, and Ms Baldwin subsequently challenged the marriage contract, arguing that the agreed division of assets was unfair.

While the BC Family Relations Act contains a provision allowing couples to enter into marriage agreements, it also contains a provision that allows a court to order a different division of assets if that division is deemed unfair with regard to:

(a) the duration of the marriage,
(b) the duration of the period during which the spouses have lived separate and apart,
(c) the date when property was acquired or disposed of,
(d) the extent to which property was acquired by one spouse through inheritance or gift,

(e)   the needs of each spouse to become or remain economically independent and self-sufficient, or

(f)   any other circumstances relating to the acquisition, preservation, maintenance, improvement, or use of property or the capacity or liabilities of a spouse.

In the majority opinion, Justices Anne Rowles and Carol Huddart argued that while couples were entitled to enter into such contracts, and courts should respect these private agreements, it should be acknowledged that '[w]hat the parties view as fair at the time of executing the agreement may become unfair as the relationship evolves and as circumstances change'. The two justices noted that Ms Baldwin had stayed at home since 1987 to raise the couple's two children (one of whom has special needs). It was only in 2001, after the breakdown of the marriage (and after a court ordered Mr Hartshorne to help pay her fees for reinstatement as a member of the Law Society of BC) that Ms Baldwin resumed her law career at an annual salary of $52,000. Mr Hartshorne, in contrast, had continued to work and earned an annual salary of $267,000 in 2000. They noted that 'the agreed division did not consider sufficiently either the respondent's [Ms Baldwin's] need to become or remain economically independent and self-sufficient or the contribution she made to the appellant's [Mr Hartshorne's] career by her sacrifice of career development to homemaking and child care responsibilities' or the length of the relationship. They thus ordered a 54/46 division of assets.

In a dissenting opinion, Justice Allan Thackray deemed that the marriage contract was entered into by 'two highly educated, mature adults' who had 'negotiated an agreement with legal advice' and who understood the agreement into which they had entered. He argued that '[c]ontracts, whether arising out of personal relationships or commercial endeavours, are, apart from legislative directive, subject to the same law of contract. In the case at bar the circumstances come perilously close to making the marriage agreement a commercial contract'. Courts should not ignore the expressed intent of the contract, and the agreements should not be regarded as any less binding. He agreed, however, that the 80/20 division of assets was unfair, given subsequent developments in the marriage, but suggested a 63/37 split instead.

You can read the full decision online at http://www.courts.gov.bc.ca/jdb-txt/ca/02/05/2002bcca0587.htm

In many ways, families are already governed by contract. Marriage and divorce laws, for example, establish contractual obligations between parties. Some feminist critics, including Minow and Shanley (1996), have critiqued this as a general approach to family law, however, pointing out, first, that it assumes equal power relations between contracting parties when often that is not the case. As Minow and Shanley (1996, 11) state, 'the assumption that bargains will be freely struck masks configurations of social power that provide the backdrop to any contracts'. One party could enter a contract with less bargaining power than another, and it would be difficult for either party to challenge the terms of a contract that the courts and the state would assume was freely entered into. For example, in the case of surrogacy contracts, a woman might agree to provide surrogate services because of her own poverty. In the absence of such poverty, she might not agree to perform the service. Thus, can one say that she has full free choice to enter into the contract? As Minow and Shanley (1996, 11) argue, 'to depict a woman who agrees to bear a child because it is the only way to bring her household income above the poverty line as exercising her "freedom" ignores the restraints or compulsions of economic necessity.' This is a feature of the family relationship identified by Marxist and socialist feminists as a uniquely female form of oppression. It causes the objectification of women's bodies and reproductive labour.

The second set of criticisms raised by some feminist theorists is that contract theories do not accurately or adequately describe the nature of familial relations (Iris Marion Young 1997, 108). In particular, the notion of the autonomous individual denies the importance of community and the importance of communal ties in forming familial relations. To see familial relationships as only governed by contract denies the dependencies that arise between, for example, a husband and wife and a surrogate mother and the child she has agreed to bear. Those ties cannot be anticipated and, some would say, should not be negated by a contract. Very specific or narrow contracts also do not allow for flexibility that may be required if the nature of a relationship changes.

As one might guess, contract-based theories of the family hold a negative view of the state, in many instances with good reason. State power has been used in the past to uphold laws that forbid same-sex couples from entering into a marriage contract, and that disadvantage women within a marital contract, such as taking away wives' right to property or to take out loans without their husbands' consent (Morrison 2001, 341). However, arguing that familial relationships should only be governed by contracts denies any public involvement or any public interest in those arrangements. It raises such questions as whether the state should enforce child support responsibilities as a matter of public interest, even if the parties do not agree with the idea of child support. Should the state be required to enforce a prenuptial agreement, even if it deems the agreement to be unfair? And should the state have no say over who should be allowed to marry, including polygamous marriages, child marriages, group marriages, and so on?

Rights-based theorists are much more supportive of state intervention, but only if that intervention is in the interest of protecting vulnerable individuals within familial relationships. In this view, the state should not conceive of rights as belonging to families existing as a harmonious whole but rather to individuals within those families and perhaps even in opposition to the family. Rights-based theorists demand a public articulation of individual rights as the basis of familial relations and state responsibility to uphold those individual rights (Minow and Shanley 1996, 20). Thus, for example, rather than seeing the family home as the private sphere, the state should 'step across the threshold' in order to protect family members from domestic violence. One has a right to be free from abuse; therefore, the state has a responsibility to protect individuals from abuse.

Why is state intervention seen as so necessary? According to rights-based theorists, it is necessary because the family can be oppressive, especially toward women and toward non-traditional and non-heterosexual couples (Iris Marion Young 1997, ch. 4). Susan Moller Okin (1989, 135–6) argues that marriage and the family, as currently practised in our society, are unjust institutions that 'constitute the pivot of a societal system of gender that renders women vulnerable to dependency, exploitation, and abuse'.[4] Marriage and child-rearing create asymmetrical vulnerabilities for women and men. The traditional division of labour within marriage, with the wife staying home to take care of children and the husband in the paid labour force, 'makes wives far more likely than husbands to be exploited both within the marital relationship and in the world of work outside the home' (Okin 1989, 138). Society expects (and biology in the earliest months requires) women to be primarily responsible for caring for children. This expectation leads women to structure their work lives so that they can perform that caregiving function and give priority to their husband's paid work life. Married women often tend to work fewer hours than men or choose careers that will be compatible with raising children. Because of this, women earn less money than men. The irony is that a woman's power in the family is at its lowest when the woman is contributing the most to the family as a housewife raising preschool children. And 'the only resources that affect marital power [in a positive way] are those—such as income, success, and prestige—that are valued in the world *outside* the marriage' (Okin 1989, 157, emphasis in original). Thus, a married woman's status largely depends on her husband's, which would be lost to her if she were to exit the marriage.

Okin (1989) thus argues that there is something *structural* about the traditional heterosexual (and generally white, middle- or upper-class) family form that creates unequal power relations—which would be replicated if men were the primary caregivers and women the primary breadwinners. This asymmetrical vulnerability, she argues, disappears when one moves away from the heterosexual family form and one person is not assigned the role of homemaker (Okin 1989, 140), or when the family comprises an unmarried couple that does not pool their assets or assume that one person will be the primary caregiver.

Therefore, the state must protect the vulnerable in these power imbalances, such as women who have subordinated their careers to perform unpaid labour for the family. The state, for example, should ensure equitable division of property and other assets if the marriage dissolves and ensure that both parties have access to earnings in the household.

Further, equality must be established within the family, ending the rigid designation of roles. That is, there should be an 'equal sharing of paid and unpaid work between men and women', such as equal responsibility for child-rearing and for participating in the labour market (Okin 1989, 169). However, it is important that these rights rest with the individual, not the family unit as a whole, because that allows women to make individual choices without interference from their spouses over such matters as the continuation of a pregnancy or the use of birth control.

This view of the family addresses head-on the power imbalances that can be perpetuated when the family is regarded as a private institution subject to very little state interference. It allows for some 'public articulation of the kinds of freedoms that deserve protection and the qualities of human dignity that warrant societal support' (Minow and Shanley 1996, 20). But some dangers in this view should be noted as well.

For example, there may be a danger in demanding 'protection' for women when so much of women's efforts are focused on rectifying differential treatment that is discriminatory. There is an aura of paternalism in the notion that married women are a vulnerable group in need of protection, which makes it difficult to assert women's equality claims and demands for 'same treatment'. Liberal feminist legal analysts, for example, have applauded the courts' moves toward equalization of assets in the event of divorce rather than continuing spousal support for women, which was common in the past.

The level of state involvement can vary according to an individual's income/class and ethnic/racial background. The state has proved much more likely to intervene in poor families, in those who receive social assistance, or in those whose members are visible minorities or immigrants. For example, in order to ensure women's 'protection', some US state governments require women to reveal paternity in order to establish eligibility for social assistance and so that the state can pursue child support on the supporting parent's behalf.

Another danger lies in whether the state will strike the appropriate balance between rights and responsibilities. Some advocates of joint custody arrangements, for example, point out that it is problematic to require men to contribute more in terms of child support, to address earnings differentials between spouses, and at the same time to privilege women's caregiver role and award children predominantly to mothers in the case of marital breakdown. Demanding greater equality in familial relations can lead to the erosion of some of women's privileges within marriage. In other words, if we wish to encourage both parents to participate in the raising and financial support of a child, should that mean that men have greater say than they do currently under law over whether a woman should have a child or whether men should have to pay child support?

The third problem with a rights-based view of the family is the question of whose rights should receive priority. Feminist rights-based theorists may say, 'that's easy: the rights of women'—that is, the vulnerable or traditionally disadvantaged group. In the case of surrogacy arrangements, however, whose rights should the state protect? The right of a childless woman to purchase gestational services from another? Or the rights of a surrogate mother to void a contract if she so desires? This suggests that we need to think about the proper ordering of values in society if we choose to demand a greater role for the state in the family, action that makes many feminists nervous.

Community-based theorists have stepped into the fray to offer their ordering of values. They acknowledge the pivotal place of the state in promoting particular family forms by regarding families not as private associations but rather as crucial institutions that help to order civil society and the polity. Thus, they argue, the state should have a role in outlining the realm of the good and what forms of human existence should be preserved and promoted.

While the voices of social conservative thinkers in Canada have been strong in the media and popular culture—for example, Danielle Crittenden (1996; 1999) and her husband David Frum (1996), organized women's groups such as REAL Women (http://www.realwomenca.com), and political parties (most notably the Reform Party/ Canadian Alliance/Conservative Party of Canada)—communitarian thinkers who present more nuanced arguments relating to the problems and solutions facing 'the family' have been less vocal in Canada than in the United States.[5]

Community-based theorists such as Elshtain (1982), Galston (1995), and Glendon (1987) have a positive view of both the family and the state and a negative view of untempered individualism (that is, selfishness) and market values, both of which undermine the possibility of a 'shared life of civic virtue' (Elshtain 1982, 445). The family is beneficial to society in taming 'untrammelled self-interest' because it requires that people act for the larger good. Elshtain (1982, 442) criticizes liberal contract-based views of the family, arguing that 'there is no way to create real communities out of an aggregate of "freely" choosing adults.' At the same time, she disputes rights-based claims that the family is an oppressive institution. Rather, the family is an essential institution for the support and nurturance of 'vulnerable human life' (Elshtain 1982, 447). Families are inherently social, not individual, tying parents and children to schools, neighbourhoods, and the larger community. What exists in families are 'relationships of moral connection' and dependency (Minow and Shanley 1996, 19), which both a rights-based and contract-based discourse fail to highlight.

Because the family is so central to society, community-based theorists feel it is imperative for the state to protect and sustain the family unit in a preferred form. The state should decide which intimate relationships should be supported publicly and which should not be (Galston 1995, 139). Questions as who should be allowed to marry are 'questions for the community to decide, based on tradition, normative theories of the good, or other collective judgments' (Minow and Shanley 1996, 15).

The problem is that there is little agreement among community-based theorists as to what 'the good' is. Many communitarians, for example, oppose same-sex marriage because they believe the institution of the family is designed to support the reproduction and raising of children (for example, Elshtain 1991). Others support same-sex marriage in the name of protecting the social institution of marriage and in order to preserve and promote the idea of stable, long-term, committed relationships (for example, Sandel 1989). But they are in agreement that such issues should not be left solely up to the couples themselves or be considered matters of 'rights' alone.

Accompanying this reverence for the family unit is fear on the part of both community-based theorists and social conservatives that the traditional two-parent family is declining or weakening. Both argue that the decline of the 'intact two-parent family' is of tremendous concern for social policy-makers because such decline is responsible for our most pressing social problems (for example, Whitehead 1993). Elshtain et al. (1993, 34) write, 'The most important single indicator of childhood problems—from poor health to poverty to behavioral problems to school dropout to criminality—is whether or not a child grows up in a stable, functioning family.'

Communitarians and social conservatives offer different explanations for the weakening of the two-parent family. Social conservatives, such as one-time US Vice-President Dan Quayle, argue that challenges put forward by the feminist movement are eroding the notion of the traditional two-parent family.[6] Most communitarians take a more nuanced position, pointing to a host of social causes, including 'not fostering a family-friendly environment', 'economic pressures on parents, especially mothers', 'making the raising of children an ever more challenging task', and declining family incomes even in two-parent households, making it difficult for families to maintain an adequate standard of living (Elshtain et al. 1993, 25–7).

Yet communitarians are not averse to emphasizing cultural factors that they feel lead to the decay of the family, such as excessive individualism that encourages people to abandon their family responsibilities (Struening 1996, 136, 138–9). For example, some parents work long hours not simply because of economic pressure but because of 'excessive careerism or acquisitiveness'. The decline of the two-parent family is also seen as a result of rising divorce rates because of a 'widespread culture of divorce' (Elshtain et al. 1993, 27–30).

Community-based theorists do not advocate that we return to an era of strict gender roles—that is, the male breadwinner and the female caregiver (Elshtain et al. 1993, 31, 33; Galston 1995, 143). Family stability should be the goal, and the state and employers must 'enable parents to be parents' by providing such advantages as flexible work hours, opportunities for parents to work at home, more generous paid maternity/parental leaves, and cash allowances to all families rather than just tax exemptions to working families (Elshtain et al. 1993; Etzioni 1995). At the same time, the state should make it harder for parents to divorce by introducing 'braking' mechanisms 'that require parents contemplating divorce to pause for reflection' (Galston 1995, 146). In the case of marital breakdown, the state should ensure adequate child support for the custodial parent (Elshtain et al. 1993, 31). Also, the state should discourage births outside of marriage and establish paternity for all children at the time of birth 'to ensure that fathers do not avoid their parental responsibilities' (Elshtain et al. 1993, 29–30). It should engage in public campaigns against out-of-wedlock birth and teen pregnancy.

Karen Struening (1996, 149), in a response to these social conservative and community-based arguments, argues that family stability is important but must be balanced with other goods, including women's equality. While social conservatives and communitarians may contend that the best cure for childhood poverty is a two-parent family, they ignore the structural impediments that cause women to be economically disadvantaged in the first place. They also do not address the reasons for family breakdown, one of which might be violence in the home. Iris Marion Young (1997, ch. 5) goes further and disputes the empirical evidence that community-based theorists cite to back up their claims that children from single-parent families are worse off than children in 'intact' two-parent families. Both advocate public policy shifts that would give women greater support and more choices in life, not merely a choice between poverty and marriage.

Other-Mothering: Race, Culture, and the 'Preferred' Family Form

Some feminist scholars (for example, Collins 1990) have unveiled the racism behind arguments about the demise of the two-parent family, as well as the limitations of theories that do not acknowledge other structures of caregiving. They argue that there has been a conflation of causes and effects: in the United States, many single-parent families are headed by women of colour. Many of those women happen to be poor; thus, there is an association between being of colour, being poor, and being in a dysfunctional family. The image of the black 'welfare queen' is particularly pernicious in the United States. In Canada, stereotypes tend to focus on Aboriginal women, women of colour, and those of lower incomes.

Collins (1990) also points out that the notion of the nuclear family is particular to the white, middle-class modern family in which one person (the mother) is invested with full responsibility for mothering her children. However, in African-American communities, it is very common to have 'other-mothers'—women in the extended family or community who assist blood-mothers by sharing the mothering responsibilities. The women in the other-mother role receive recognition for the socially rewarding activity they perform (Collins 1990, 120).

In Canada, many immigrant communities also practise other-mothering in which grand-parents in particular provide a great deal of caregiving for grandchildren. Researchers studying immigration and settlement patterns in Canada have found that when couples with children relocate to Canada, they often send their young children back to their home country to be cared for by extended family members until the children are old enough to attend school and the family does not have to bear the costs of child care (Bernhard, Landolt, and Goldring 2005).

Similarly, the practice of other-mothering and a woman-centred family unit emerged out of necessity in African-American communities in the United States because of the severe disruption to families under slavery when children were orphaned by the sale or death of their parents or were conceived through rape. It has continued because of the absence of fathers and husbands as a result of the high rate of incarceration of black men and in families in which the mother may be very young or an addict. This is a model of truly com-munal rather than individual caregiving, and it is, as bell hooks writes, 'revolutionary in this society because it takes place in opposition to the idea that parents, especially mothers, should be the only childrearers' (as quoted in Collins 1990, 122). It challenges the notion of children as the 'property' of their biological parents. And it suggests a different way of conceiving the responsibility for child-rearing beyond that of the nuclear household.

Some of the revolutionary aspects of other-mothering include less emphasis on gender role differentiation. Both boys and girls learn to care for other children in the extended household. Also, even though the caregiving may be woman-centred, the family struc-ture as a whole may include the physical presence of men with culturally significant roles. That is, the centrality of mothers is not predicated on male powerlessness. Furthermore, it does not prescribe particular gender roles when it comes to labour market participation. African-American women, for example, have long integrated the notion of economic self-reliance with mothering. It is only in the white middle-class households of the past few generations that the notion of a stay-at-home mother flourished.

The benefits to society are myriad as well. Other-mothering emphasizes community values and provides one basis for women's political activism and power. As Collins (1990, 129) writes of her own community, '[n]urturing children in Black extended family networks stimulates a more generalized ethic of caring and personal accountability among African-American women who often feel accountable to all the Black community's children.'

Despite all of these benefits, the practice of other-mothering must be qualified. The danger in promoting the notion of the 'super-strong black mother' is the idea that 'moth-ers should live lives of sacrifice has come to be seen as the norm' (Collins 1990, 116). It is difficult to raise children, and encouraging women to be strong and self-sacrificing makes it harder to escape to a positive gender role. Furthermore, the view of the strong black mother can shut men out of a caregiver role. Still, other-mothering offers a power-ful contrasting view of the family that incorporates many of the concerns of community-based theorists but at the same time protects and promotes the notion of gender justice important to rights-based theorists.

Iris Marion Young (1997, 129–30) concludes that there is nothing wrong with public policy to promote particular ends. Children do need attentive love, nurturance, stability, and so on. But social conservatives and communitarians are wrong to assert that a particular kind of family best embodies these values for children when they can be realized in many different family forms: single-parent families, blended families, extended families, and so on. Thus, public policy should promote and encourage particular ends and purposes for families, not one specific form of 'family' to attain those ends. Young (1997, 130) writes, 'For the sake of protecting children and other household members, the state can properly intervene in or punish particular actions or inactions within families, especially violence and serious wilful neglect, but this is quite different from punishing or favouring families based on their composition alone.' Such biased preferences for the heterosexual two-parent family put burdens and stresses on the many families that do not adhere to that form, which can make it difficult for them to raise children well. However, the view of the family as a natural, pre-political, and private institution comprised of a heterosexual couple and their biological children still finds some adherents, even though much of the common and civil law and much philosophical thinking and societal opinion have departed from this view.[7]

The Evolution and Structure of the Family in Canada

Families in Canada have evolved quite radically over the past half century from the so-called 'traditional' family form consisting of a heterosexual couple and their biological children, although scholars such as Stephanie Coontz (1992) points out that the family form venerated in popular culture in the 1950s did not exist through most of human history. The traditional view of the family was that of a natural, organic, hierarchical, and indissoluble private association (Minow and Shanley 1996, 5) comprising certain (for example, heterosexual, non-blood-related) members of society. Later on, it was seen as the only legitimate environment for procreation and for raising children, but traditionally, the focus of marriage was the relationship between husband and wife. In fact, the ability to consummate a marriage, not the ability to procreate, remains one of the requirements of a valid marriage (Payne and Payne 2001).

Common law principles upheld the authority structure consisting of the man as head of the household and familial representative in the public sphere. In this conception of the family, women were seen 'naturally' as mothers, biologically destined to reproduce and care for children. Husbands were the head of the household and responsible for protecting their wives. Under the common law doctrine of 'coverture', men and women became one in marriage; a woman's individuality disappeared as she came under the legal responsibility and protection of her husband (Morrison 2001, 339). Married women were therefore not allowed to act as their own agents at law, meaning that they could not enter into contracts, for example, or have property rights, unlike under civil law in which husbands and wives were considered two distinct persons (Morrison 2001, 341). Additionally, children were under the control of the husband, who was the legal guardian of (legitimate) children. The marriage of husband and wife conferred legitimacy to any offspring and duties to the father for their maintenance, protection, and education (Morrison 2001, 343). Thus, children born outside of marriage, widows, single women, and abandoned wives and children all fell outside these legal norms (Minow and Shanley 1996, 7).

From the middle of the nineteenth century, this common law regime came under pressure, with attempts to grant married women some legal rights, for example, as well as to extend the vote to women (a clear activity of the public, not private, sphere). As more women participated in the labour market, the idea of a strict hierarchy within the household, with the husband as head, diminished. It was not until the second wave of feminism that women's rights advocates challenged the last vestiges of the patriarchal family head-on and more egalitarian familial relations emerged in terms of both the husband-wife relationship and the parent-child relationship.[8] Neil Nevitte and Mebs Kanji (2002, 66) report that Canadians now rank first among those surveyed in 12 advanced industrial societies for their attitudes on egalitarianism in spousal relations.

From the statistical evidence, we know that people in Canada are marrying and having children later in life, but that most choose to have children within the institution of marriage. It is still much more common to be in a marital relationship, with or without children (68.6 per cent in the 2006 census), than in a common-law relationship (15.5 per cent), although the number of common-law families has continued to increase over the past few decades and, since 2001 has done so much more rapidly than the number of married couple families (Statistics Canada 2007a). Marriage rates have dropped from 7.8 for every 1,000 people in Canada in 1980 to 4.7 in 2003 (Statistics Canada 2000, 40; Statistics Canada 2007b). The average age at first marriage has risen for women from 22 in 1971 to 26 in 1990 and 28.5 in 2003. Men's average age at first marriage has increased from 24.4 in 1971 to 27.9 in 1990 and 30.6 in 2003 (Statistics Canada 2000, 40; Statistics Canada 2007b). Women are also waiting longer to have children and are having fewer of them. The average age at which women had their first child was about 29.7 in 2004, compared to 26 in the late 1960s (Statistics Canada 2000, 35; Statistics Canada 2006). The fertility rate in Canada as of 2003 was 1.53 children per woman (Statistics Canada 2006).

The number of families headed by a single parent has stabilized over the past decade. Members of lone-parent families comprised 15.9 per cent of the population in 2006, up slightly from 15.7 per cent in 2001 (Statistics Canada 2007a, 13). Of those, the vast majority (80.1 per cent in 2006) were headed by women (Statistics Canada 2007a, 13), although Statistics Canada (2007, 15) points out that the number of lone-parent families headed by men has increased substantially in the 2001–06 period because fewer women are being granted sole custody after divorce. In 1980, over three quarters of women were granted sole custody after divorce; by 2003, only 48 per cent of divorces resulted in women being granted sole custody. Also, the divorce rate has declined from a high of 362.3 per 100,000 population in 1987 to 223.7 in 2003 (Statistics Canada 2000, 42; Statistics Canada 2005).[9]

Statistics Canada collected data on same-sex couples in both the 2001 and 2006 censuses. While the proportion of married (0.1 per cent of all couples) and common law couples (0.5 per cent) that are same sex is quite small compared to heterosexual couples, the number of same-sex couples grew 32.6 per cent between 2001 and 2006, in large part reflecting the legalization of same-sex marriage in Canada in 2005 (Statistics Canada 2007a, 12).

Policy and Law: Who Can Be a Family in Canada?

How do the families reflected in the statistics presented above relate to a Canadian state that has significant power over how they are recognized in law and public policy? As Minow and Shanley (1996, 5) argue, 'while loving and committed relationships might presumably exist without the state, there are in fact no family or family-like relationships that are not shaped by social practices and state action'. The state intrudes, regardless of whether one thinks of that involvement as a good or a bad thing. Conversely, the state also confers a degree of autonomy upon the contracting individuals to regulate themselves.

The Canadian Family: A Federal or Provincial Issue?

As with most public policy discussions in Canada, jurisdictional issues come into play. While most family law falls within provincial jurisdiction, responsibility for family law and policy is in fact divided between the federal and provincial governments. The Constitution Act, 1867, for example, under section 91 (26), grants the federal Parliament exclusive power to make laws with regard to 'marriage and divorce'. Provincial legislatures, however, under section 92 (12), are granted exclusive power over the 'solemnization of marriage in the province' as well as 'property and civil rights in the province' under section 92 (13). Indeed, a great deal of family law falls under the provincial property and civil rights provision because it encompasses such matters as matrimonial property, spousal and child support, adoption, custody, and so on (Hogg 1997, sec. 26–2). In fact, all family law matters in Quebec apart from divorce fall under the Quebec Civil Code (Payne and Payne 2001, 9).

In practice, this jurisdictional division leads to some complexity in family law. For example, the Divorce Act is a federal statute, but the regulations on obtaining a divorce are provincial and thus vary by province (Kronby 2001, xviii). Matters of support and custody that arise during divorce proceedings are governed by the federal statute, but if those matters arise independently of divorce, they are governed by provincial and territorial legislation (Payne and Payne 2001, 20). Therefore, both federal and provincial courts can be involved in resolving family disputes.

With regard to marriage, the federal Parliament makes laws regarding the essential validity of a marriage, that is, the rules regarding the legal capacity of people to marry, including rules regarding recognition of foreign marriages (Bailey 1999, 33), although many of these rules also developed through common law. Provincial and territorial legislatures make laws regarding the formal validity of marriage, such as the ceremonial requirements for recognition of a marriage, who can perform marriages (solemnization), the issuing of marriage licences, and so on (Payne and Payne 2001, 33).

Canadian legislators have taken it upon themselves to enact a variety of laws governing who can marry. Thus, the question of who can form a family becomes in some sense who *the state says* can marry. Payne and Payne (2001, 1, 10) argue that much of family law in Canada deals less with what comprises a family than with family breakdown and dissolution, and less with the rights of families than with the rights of individuals within families. Current laws cover three main relationships: marriage (both formation and dissolution); parenthood; and non-marital family relationships such as shared households. Family law is complicated because many of the laws vary by province. As well, because most of Canada (except Quebec) is governed by a common law system, not civil law, which is therefore not codified, the rules can be modified by court decisions and be subject to judicial precedent. Regulations in Canada cover issues of consent (marriages must be entered into freely, without coercion), mental capacity of the contracting parties, the ability of the parties to consummate their marriage, consanguinity (the degree of blood relationship between the parties), minimum age limits, marriage to more than one person, and marriage between partners of the same sex (Payne and Payne 2001). Behind these regulations lie important issues of equality and access to marriage.

Miscegenation

Historically, there have been fewer bans on marriage in Canada than in the United States, where 'anti-miscegenation' laws (bans against interracial marriage) existed until the Supreme Court declared them unconstitutional in 1967. Canada's laws regarding interracial marriage were more hidden. In 2004, Velma Demerson published a memoir of her experience of being arrested and sentenced to a reformatory in 1939 for 'incorrigible behaviour'. Her crime was dating or, more specifically, being engaged to a Chinese man, Harry Yip, with whom she was to have a child. She was sentenced to a year in Toronto's Mercer Reformatory for Females for her behaviour, giving birth in detention, and her child was kept from her until her release 10 months later. In Ontario until 1964, the Female Refuges Act gave great powers to police and judicial officials to regulate women's morality (Sangster 2001).[10] A judge or magistrate only needed someone to provide a sworn statement about a woman's incorrigibility and the hearings were held in private (Sangster 1996, 240). Incorrigible behaviour included promiscuity, pregnancy out of wedlock, public drunkenness, and interracial relations. The rules were in effect anti-miscegenation (anti-race mixing) laws in disguise. In later decades, the law was used in Ontario to target Aboriginal women in particular (Sangster 1996, 259).[11] Other indirect anti-miscegenation laws were on the books in British Columbia. For example, to prevent Chinese men from marrying white women and thus staying permanently in Canada, the BC government passed laws forbidding white women from working in Chinese restaurants (Albanese 1996, 128).

Multiple marriages

Laws regarding polygamous relationships vary across the country. Sections 290, 291, and 293 of the federal Criminal Code prohibit the practice of bigamy and polygamy and make it an indictable criminal offence with punishment of imprisonment for up to five years (http://laws.justice.gc.ca/en/C-46/39219.html). Yet section 1(2) of the Ontario Family Law Act recognizes 'a marriage that is actually or potentially polygamous, if it was celebrated in a jurisdiction whose system of law recognizes it as valid' for the purposes of the Family Law Act itself. This means that spouses in polygamous marriages entered into in another country have the same rights and responsibilities as spouses in monogamous marriages—for example, with regard to the division of property, spousal and child support, and so on upon separation or death (http://192.75.156.68/DBLaws/Statutes/English/90f03_e.htm). Similarly, courts in British Columbia have determined that the wording of the BC Family Relations Act, which defines a spouse as someone who has 'lived with another person in a marriage-like relationship for a period of at least 2 years' also covers polygamous relationships for the purposes of the Act (n.a. 1991, 4). Thus, the Criminal Code ban on polygamous marriages seems to contradict provincial law and evolving common law. In fact, in 2002 *The Globe and Mail* revealed that in 1994 the federal government knowingly granted permission to a BC polygamist's three wives to stay in Canada permanently, despite the fact that polygamy is illegal in Canada and polygamous marriages are not recognized as legitimate under federal immigration rules (Matas 2002, A1, A4). Over the years, the BC Government has faced pressure to prosecute members of the fundamentalist Mormon sect in Bountiful, BC which practises polygamy. In 2009, the BC Government charged two members of the sect but the charges were stayed on a technicality. Rather than appeal the decision, the BC Government referred the question of the constitutionally of the Criminal Code provisions to the BC Supreme Court. The court began its inquiry in November 2010 (Stueck 2010).

The issue of polygamy in Canada has become intertwined with issues of multicultural diversity. Some Muslims have wanted the ban on polygamy lifted on the grounds of respect for their cultural autonomy and integrity (Parekh 1996, 273). They see Western society's ban on polygamy as 'dishonest, hypocritical, and racist', since people in the West do not practise monogamy in a strict sense because that implies sexual intercourse with only one person and only within marriage (Parekh 1996, 274). In the West, monogamy is defined as sexual fidelity to one's partner in marriage, which rules out having simultaneous partners. Yet many in society turn a blind eye to extramarital affairs, and children of those affairs receive less legal protection than children of the marriage.

From a feminist perspective, polygamy is a very difficult issue with multiple implications for women's equality. The kind of polygamy usually practised involves men having multiple wives (polygyny), not the other way around (polyandry) (Parekh 1996, 273). And women in polygamous relationships are in relationships of dependency. Thus, some (e.g., Campbell 2005, 36) argue that recognition of the marriage is important so that women have recourse to the law—for example, to have support agreements upheld in the case of marital breakdown or to be allowed to immigrate if their husbands decide to move.

Same-sex relationships

Perhaps most controversial has been the question of whether the state should allow same-sex marriage in Canada. To understand court rulings and government legislation in this area, we have to look at the evolution of the law in five areas: anti-discrimination on the basis of sexual orientation; recognition of same-sex relationships as equivalent in law to common-law relationships; adoption rights; child custody rights; and most recently, same-sex marriage rights. The laws in these areas have evolved as a result of court rulings, changing societal norms, and advocacy group activity.

Anti-discrimination laws

The federal government decriminalized homosexual activity as part of amendments to the Criminal Code in 1969, and over the years the federal Parliament and provincial legislatures, save for the province of Alberta, voluntarily amended their human rights acts to prohibit discrimination on the basis of sexual orientation. Some of the legislative changes preceded and others followed some significant court rulings, including *Egan*, 1995, in which the Court ruled unanimously that discrimination on the basis of sexual orientation is barred by the Charter of Rights and Freedoms, and *Vriend*, 1998, in which the Supreme Court ruled that the Alberta government had to 'read in' sexual orientation on the list of prohibited grounds of discrimination in its provincial human rights legislation.[12]

Recognition of same-sex relationships in law

Recognizing same-sex *relationships* in law as equivalent to married or at least common-law has been a more challenging endeavour in Canada, meeting greater resistance. Some of the resistance has been monetary: extending benefits to same-sex partners costs governments and private employers money.[13] Thus, many governments and private employers resisted expansion of benefits until pushed by court rulings and decisions of human rights tribunals, while others changed their laws and policies in anticipation of losses in court.

Same-sex partners have gained access to 'pension benefits, welfare assistance, workers' compensation, life, health and disability insurance, and tax advantages' (Payne and Payne 2001, 53) and even the right to conjugal visits with their partners in prison (Laghi 2000, A4). Along with these rights come responsibilities. Since the 2001 tax year, the federal government has required all common-law couples, including same-sex couples, to file their income taxes jointly, which gives them the benefits (as well as the burdens) of joint filing. That means, for example, that one partner in a same-sex relationship can claim the other partner or a child as a dependent and deduct child care expenses (Laghi 2000, A4). In 2002 the federal government also formalized the practice of allowing gay men and lesbians to sponsor their foreign same-sex partners as immigrants and for one partner to be considered a dependent when they apply for immigration together (Hurley 2005, 27). And in 1999 the Supreme Court issued a definitive ruling in *M v. H.*, 1999,[14] in which the Court declared that the opposite-sex definition of 'spouse' in the Ontario Family Law Act was unconstitutional under section 15 of the Charter. Thus, it was no longer constitutional to exclude same-sex couples from employment and other benefits such as spousal support. Effectively, the ruling required all governments—federal, provincial, municipal—to allow same-sex couples the same access to spousal benefits as heterosexual (common-law) couples.

Some of the resistance to these advances, however, has been moral, with critics arguing that treating same-sex couples as equivalent to opposite-sex couples legitimizes those same-sex relationships and therefore condones those sexual practices. These attitudes have proved difficult to change. And access to the benefits and obligations of common-law partners still does not provide the same rights as those of married couples, as will be seen below.

Adoption rights

In Canada there were, until recently, no adoption procedures permitting a gay or lesbian partner of a biological or adoptive parent to adopt the partner's child and become the child's second legal parent. That means that if the biological parent were to die, the partner, even if he or she were the primary caregiver, would not automatically get custody of the child because he or she would not be recognized as a family member. The child would not automatically be entitled to the non-biological parent's property and other assets. A child with two legal parents, on the other hand, has two sources of support and inheritance rights, as well as access to an array of benefits provided by the parents' employers, such as health insurance. Moreover, if the parents' relationship were to end, both would be entitled to seek custody or visitation and both would be responsible for the child's support.

Adoption laws have typically evolved to allow individuals, not just couples, to adopt, which means that over time gay men and lesbians have won the ability to adopt or foster a child as individuals. Thus, in some same-sex couples, one partner would file an adoption application to be considered a child's legal parent. But that does not resolve the problem of custody for the second parent. Consequently, gay and lesbian couples with children have pushed for legislative changes that would allow dual parentage to be acknowledged immediately upon birth registration or adoption so that the second partner does not have to go through the process of adoption in order to have custody rights acknowledged under law. The more challenging issue has been, therefore, whether a gay or lesbian couple may *jointly* adopt a *non-biologically related* child, or jointly register as parents when one partner in a lesbian relationship gives birth to a child or one partner has a child from a previous relationship. All of these scenarios require the state to acknowledge the two partners as a couple, akin to a heterosexual couple.

When the NDP government in Ontario first attempted to deal with this issue in 1994, public outcry and objection from within government as well as opposition party ranks defeated legislation that would have granted same-sex couples all the rights and benefits of opposite-sex common-law couples, including adoption rights. In an effort to save the legislation from defeat, then attorney general Marion Boyd announced that the government would remove the provision allowing same-sex couples to apply for child adoption, to no avail, as the legislation was defeated (McInnes 1994, A1). A number of court rulings[15] since then, however, have prompted provincial legislatures to amend their legislation and allow same-sex couples to jointly adopt a child (see Lawlor 2001, A8 for BC; Panetta 2001, A4 and Philp 2001, A3 for Alberta). Indeed, three years after the NDP's attempt in Ontario, the BC government managed to pass similar legislation, including adoption and custody rights, without fervent opposition as in Ontario (Rayside 2008, ch. 4). In fact, only nine of the 75 MLAs voted against the legislation; one provincial Reform Party member supported the legislation (McInnes 1997, A3). The 2005 federal legislation permitting same-sex couples to marry should remove the last vestiges of discrimination in law in the area of adoption, giving same-sex married couples the same privileges as opposite-sex married couples in that regard. Although marriage per se does not clear up issues of parental rights in all cases, as discussed in chapter 8.

Child custody rights

Courts have had a mixed record in awarding custody to parents who are gay or lesbian (Rayside 2008, ch. 7). In some earlier cases, custody was denied to the homosexual parent (for example, *Case v. Case*, 1974, and *Bernhardt v. Bernhardt*, 1979).[16] More often, judges tend to award custody on the basis of the best interests of the child and consider homosexuality to be a factor only if there is some established link between the parent's homosexuality and harm to the child. However, judges can be biased in terms of how they interpret 'best interests'. Gay or lesbian parents have fared better, for example, if they can convince judges that they are discreet about their lifestyle and that they will not try to 'recruit' the child into that lifestyle (for example, *K. v. K.*, 1975, in Alberta; *D. v. D.*, 1978, in Ontario).[17]

Same-sex marriage

By the early 2000s, a number of court challenges to the common law definition of marriage as that between one man and one woman worked their way through the courts, culminating in the Supreme Court reference decision in December 2004, and the subsequent passage of the federal Bill C-38, the Civil Marriage Act, that legalized same-sex marriage in Canada. Some may ask why the conferral of same-sex marriage rights is so important, especially since the Supreme Court of Canada in 1995 ruled that discrimination on the basis of marital status is a violation of the equality provisions of the Charter of Rights and Freedoms. One answer is that there are still certain rights in Canada unavailable to couples who are not married. The Supreme Court ruled in December 2002, for example, that unmarried couples are not entitled to the same 50/50 division of property that married couples are.[18] Instead, the status of common-law couples' benefits depends on a province's legislation. Legislation in the Northwest Territories, Nunavut, Saskatchewan, and Manitoba automatically includes unmarried couples in matrimonial property laws. British Columbia, Nova Scotia, and Quebec 'allow cohabiting couples to register their unions and include a plan for property division in the event of collapse', but in all other provinces and territories matrimonial property laws apply only to married couples (although federal and provincial benefits plans do apply to unmarried couples) (CP 2002 re Manitoba; Tibbetts 2002).

Ironically, the Supreme Court's decision not to extend the same property rights to cohabiting couples strengthened the justice claims of same-sex couples, who argued that not being able to marry places same-sex couples at a disadvantage (Makin 2002b, A13). Gay rights activists regarded the denial of marriage rights as serious not only because it meant discrimination in law but also because it delegitimized same-sex relationships. In religious terms, marriage is the marker between moral sex and immoral sex, between the 'licit' and 'illicit', as Iris Marion Young (1997, 103) argues, and reinforces this distinction by 'granting privileges to those who fall on one side of the line and stigmatizing those who fall on the other side'. If one is barred from marrying, one's sex practices are automatically deemed to fall on the illicit or immoral side.

The explicit barriers to same-sex marriage, however, were not clearly stated until the early 2000s and instead rested on common law principles. There was no federal Marriage Act declaring that 'thou shalt' or 'shalt not' marry equivalent to the 1986 Divorce Act in Canada.[19] Instead, the federal definition of marriage as the 'lawful union of one man and one woman to the exclusion of all others' was outlined in the Modernization of Benefits and Obligations Act, 2000 (Bill C-23), an omnibus bill that amended 68 federal laws that discriminated against same-sex couples with regard to eligibility for social and tax benefits. Section 1 (1) of the Act, however, stated explicitly, 'For greater certainty, the amendments made by this Act do not affect the meaning of the word 'marriage', that is, the lawful union of one man and one woman to the exclusion of all others' (http://laws.justice.gc.ca/en/m-8.6/82266.html). That section was added on the urging of Canadian Alliance and some Liberal MPs (CP 2000).

A number of provincial appeal court decisions, however, pressured the federal government to amend that definition of marriage. In May 2003, the BC Court of Appeal unanimously ruled that the prohibition on same-sex marriage was unconstitutional but suspended the decision until July 2004 to give governments time to amend their legislation.[20] The Ontario Court of Appeal followed with a similar ruling in June 2003 but declared it to have immediate effect, allowing same-sex couples the right to wed immediately.[21] Similar court rulings followed in Quebec, the Yukon, Manitoba, Nova Scotia, Saskatchewan, and Newfoundland and Labrador in 2004. At the end of June 2005, only three provinces and two territories refused to issue marriage licences to same-sex couples.

One week after the Ontario Court of Appeal ruling, the federal government declared that it would not appeal the provincial appeal court rulings but would introduce new legislation to legally recognize same-sex marriages (Lunman 2003, A1, A8). However, the justice minister at the time, Martin Cauchon, announced that certain aspects of the new legislation would be referred to the Supreme Court of Canada.

The Supreme Court issued its reference decision regarding same-sex marriage on 9 December 2004.[22] It determined that legislation defining who has the legal capacity to marry falls under the jurisdiction of the federal Parliament. However, matters of solemnization fall under provincial jurisdiction. Thus, the federal Parliament does not have the authority to legislate exemptions to existing provincial solemnization requirements. The Court also ruled that the equality provisions of the Charter include marriage of persons of the same sex but that the Charter's provisions regarding freedom of religion also protect religious officials from being compelled to perform a marriage contrary to their religious beliefs.

The Court declined to rule on whether the opposite-sex definition of marriage is constitutional. It did rule that since the federal government was going ahead with the proposed legislation, regardless of the reference outcome, and had accepted the rulings of the lower courts, then a ruling on the constitutionality of an opposite-sex requirement for marriage served no legal purpose. Furthermore, the Court reasoned, the same-sex couples who had initiated the constitutional challenges relied on the finality of the court rulings and had acquired the right to marry, and the Court was hesitant to put those rights in jeopardy. Thus, the Court did not feel it appropriate to answer a reference question for a matter that had already been ruled on at the lower court level and which the federal government chose not to appeal. In other words, if a government wanted an answer to the question, it should appeal the lower court rulings to the Supreme Court. Finally, the Court was aware that the federal government wished to achieve a uniformity of laws across the country and an answer to the question would have put that in jeopardy.

In February 2005, shortly after the Supreme Court's reference ruling, the Liberal minority government under Prime Minister Paul Martin introduced Bill C-38 in the federal House of Commons to define in statute that marriage can legally occur between any two persons to the exclusion of all others.[23] That legislation passed in the House of Commons in late June and was proclaimed into law in July 2005, making Canada the fourth country to legalize same-sex marriages, following the Netherlands (2001), Belgium (2003), and Spain (a month earlier) (Hogg 2006, 712).

Gay and Lesbian Activism Regarding Family Rights

As Rayside (2008, ch. 3) points out, most gay and lesbian groups in the late 1960s and early 1970s were decidedly against the institution of the traditional family, including monogamy. The AIDS epidemic beginning in the 1980s, however, brought home to partners in same-sex relationships the serious impact that lack of recognition of their relationships had. Same-sex partners were routinely denied the privileges of hetero-sexual couples when it came to such issues as hospital visitation, medical decision-making, funeral arrangements, inheritance rights, and custody rights if the ill partner had a child. As well, Rayside (2008) points out that as more gays and lesbians were willing to come out of the closet and challenge their exclusion from the workplace and institutions such as the church, there were more potential challengers to exclusionary laws in all issue areas.

Lined up on one side of the issue were gay and lesbian activist groups and others such as trade unions, facing off against social and religious conservatives, who see same-sex relationship issues, and particularly same-sex marriage, as a huge threat to the tradi-tional institution of the family. Rayside (2008) notes groups such as the Lesbian Mothers' Defence Fund, formed in Toronto in 1978 to support lesbians engaged in custody battles and the LGBT Parenting Network, formed in the early 2000s to support same-sex parents. The decision to deal with relationship issues was hugely divisive even in the 1980s and 1990s, as activist groups pushed for adoption rights, unsuccessfully in Ontario and suc-cessfully in British Columbia. EGALE (Equality for Gays and Lesbians Everywhere) did focus on relationship issues in the 1990s but worked more on having sexual orientation added to the Canadian Human Rights Act and gay-bashing recognized as a hate crime. But as gay and lesbian groups succeeded in challenging other forms of discrimination, same-sex marriage became the next logical challenge.

Relationship equality? A post-mortem

In a 2002 article written prior to the legalization of same-sex marriage in Canada, Brenda Cossman documents some of the ambivalence gay activists felt about be-coming members of the marriage 'club', an institution, as outlined above, that is criticized for its heteronormativity, that creates dominant and subordinate subjects, and that has not been transformed simply because the couple is same sex. Instead, relationships between individuals of the same sex are being transformed: de-politi-cized, de-eroticized, and privatized—in other words, 'normalized' just like straight folk (Cossman 2002, 484). The struggle to obtain formal equality in law has come 'at the expense of transgression and subversion' (Cossman, 2002, 486). Marriage as an institution has not been undermined; just the membership roster has been ex-panded. All the critiques feminists have raised about marriage still hold (Young and Boyd, 2006).

Furthermore, not all the issues surrounding relationship recognition have been ironed out. The laws in some countries, most notably the United States, have not caught up to those in Canada, raising questions about the validity of marriages performed in one state or country but not recognized in a state or country where a couple resides. Cossman (2008, 158) reports that courts in some states have recognized marriages performed elsewhere in order to allow couples to get divorced; other courts have not, leaving these couples in legal limbo. The struggle to obtain legal dissolution of a marriage can be viewed on the one hand as an attempt by litigants to have their relationships acknowledged in the first place (Cossman 2008, 163). On the other hand, these couples are seeking the ability to sue each other in court for the privilege of relying on each other for financial support, including child support. Cossman (2005; 2008) points out that it is a pyrrhic victory to privatize support for dependent relationships in this way.

Conclusion

This chapter reveals that families exist in a social context. Families are not wholly private organizations, even though both political theory and public policy have treated the family as the paragon of the private sphere. We have highlighted just how complicated the law can be when the state tries to define who can be a family and what the family is, yet the definition is crucially important in terms of the benefits it allows to some but withholds from others. While the law has become increasingly open to a variety of family forms, Canadian public opinion still sits uncomfortably between beliefs about equality and fair treatment on the one hand and well-entrenched, religion-based views about sexuality, reproduction, and the family on the other.

   While cultural and religious views are often difficult to change, they can be shaped by changes in law and policy. Nicholas Bala (2005), a family law scholar at Queen's University, has observed that two changes to the way we regard marriage in law have made it easier to legalize common-law and same-sex marriages. First, marriage as a religious institution and then a legal institution was rooted in differential treatment on the basis of sex (for example, a woman was subsumed under her husband's authority upon marriage). Second, the principal focus of marriage was on procreative legitimacy. Over the past few decades, the law in Canada has become less gender discriminatory, treating both parties equally—most laws refer simply to 'spouses', for example, not husbands and wives. It is also now possible to have a child outside of marriage without many legal ramifications—for example, in terms of inheriting property. These two changes in law in turn weakened the arguments for excluding common-law and same-sex relationships (see also Okin 1996). Critics fear the next frontier in relationship recognition is polygamy (Cossman 2008), as the reference case regarding the validity of the Criminal Code provisions forbidding polygamy reveals. The BC Crown attorneys are resting their arguments on claims that polygamous relationships lead to 'physical and sexual abuse, the subjugation of women, and familial conflict' (Keller 2010). But, as one psychologist testified at trial, how is that different from harms in monogamous marriages (ibid.)? While the outcome of this trial remains uncertain at time of publication, we can be sure that issues of legitimate and illegitimate relations will continue to be debated in both law and culture.

Questions for Critical Thought

1. Debates between contract-based theories, rights-based theories, and community-based theories rest on different views of the family and the appropriate degree of state intervention in the family. Which of these theories do you think guide current family law and policy in Canada? Which should guide legislators and policy-makers?
2. How far should the state go in recognizing a diversity of family forms?
3. The concept of 'other-mothering' challenges at a fundamental level the notion of familial responsibility and suggests care of others is a community responsibility. Do you agree or disagree with this notion of community responsibility for care?

CHAPTER 8

The Family, Law, and Public Policy

In this chapter we examine three areas of contention in current law and policy governing family relations: (1) divorce, spousal support, and child support; (2) child custody after divorce or separation; and (3) family violence. Susan Boyd, in her 2003 book, *Child Custody, Law, and Women's Work*, laments how 'completely, shockingly, gender neutral' recent efforts in family law reform have been, and she 'tries to show why this approach is deeply flawed and tragically wrong'. In the cases we examine, we deal precisely with that dilemma within the feminist movement. Should gender neutrality be the order of the day regarding such issues as child custody and spousal support? Are mothers' and fathers' roles symmetrical or asymmetrical in terms of their familial roles and responsibilities? If they are asymmetrical, what are the implications of adopting a norm of symmetry in determining what should happen in the event of family breakdown? In others words, how much should governments and the courts take into account women's differential position in the family in making law and public policy?

Case 1: Divorce, Spousal Support, and Child Support

Divorce rates in Canada are nearly half that in the United States (2.2 per 1,000 population in 2008, compared to 3.7 per 1,000 population) and are lower compared to a number of other countries in the world, including Belgium (3.3 per 1,000 population), Denmark (2.7), the United Kingdom (2.4), Germany, Sweden, Australia, and New Zealand (2.3) (OECD Family Database SF 3.1 http://www.oecd.org/document/4/0 ,3343,en_2649_34819_37836996_1_1_1_1,00.html). Currently, about one in every four marriages break up in Canada and, as of 2004, the divorce rate was approximately 21.8 per 10,000 population, declining from a peak of 36.4 per 10,000 population in 1987 (Vanier Institute of the Family 2010, 44).

The conditions for obtaining a divorce in Canada prior to the 1968 divorce law reforms were very onerous. Kronby (2001, xviii) reports that if one lived in either Quebec or Newfoundland, one could not obtain a divorce under provincial law. Instead, one had to petition the federal Senate to pass a statute dissolving the marriage. In other provinces, the only ground for divorce was adultery, save in Nova Scotia, which allowed for divorce on the grounds of matrimonial cruelty as well (Payne and Payne 2001, 10). In 1968, with the passage of the first national Divorce Act, the federal government made divorces easier to obtain by adding new grounds, including cruelty and marital breakdown (with a minimum three-year separation), which, along with adultery, covered the vast majority of cases that came to court (Kronby 2001, xviii).

In 1985 the federal government amended the Divorce Act to a fully 'no-fault' system so that the only ground for divorce now is marital breakdown, whether as a result of adultery, cruelty, or separation for one year. 'No-fault' does not mean that no fault is involved in the breakdown of a marriage but rather that the rules regarding divorce no longer require litigation over issues of fault (Glendon 1987, 65). Prior to no-fault laws, in order to obtain a divorce one had to demonstrate before a court that the partner had committed some act that prevented the marriage from continuing, such as cruelty, adultery, desertion, and so on.

Spousal support

The move toward a no-fault system of divorce has not been without controversy among feminists. Some, such as Glendon (1987), argue that the fault-based system gave considerable bargaining advantage to a legally innocent spouse whose partner was impatient to get a divorce. It also ensured protection for women who spent part or all of the marriage as a housewife and caregiver (Glendon 1987; Mason 1988). Under a no-fault system, the principle is to ensure that each partner achieves independence.

Prior to the 1968 Divorce Act, the finding of fault usually obliged the guilty party to support the wronged party. The 1968 Act removed that obligation and instead established equality of support rights and obligations and made financial need and spousal ability to pay the criteria for awarding support (Payne and Payne 2001, 10–1). As well, courts no longer interpreted marriage breakdown as requiring lifelong financial support for a dependent spouse but rather support until the dependent spouse became financially self-sufficient. Any maintenance awarded was thought to be temporary.

Current divorce laws also encourage the equal division of assets after marriage. However, when it comes to their financial situations both within marriage and after marital breakdown, men and women are not similarly situated. Thus, some feminists have argued instead for the principle of 'equitable' division that takes into account the differing economic positions of the spouses. While section 14(6d) of the Divorce Act states that spousal support orders should 'promote the economic self-sufficiency of each spouse within a reasonable period of time', sections 15(7) and 17(7) of the Act explicitly state that in determining the amount of a support order or any variation to a support order, the courts should '(a) recognize any economic advantages or disadvantages to the spouses arising from the marriage or its breakdown; (b) apportion between the spouses any financial consequences arising from the care of any child of the marriage over and above any obligation for the support of any child of the marriage; and (c) relieve any economic hardship of the spouses arising from the breakdown of the marriage'.

Both feminist arguments and these sections of the Divorce Act have been reflected in Canadian Supreme Court rulings in recent years. For example, in *Moge v. Moge*, 1992,[1] the Supreme Court ruled unanimously that determinations of spousal support should take into consideration the 'general economic impact of divorce on women'. The Court found it was unreasonable to expect Mrs Moge, who had played the role of homemaker throughout her marriage and then raised three children on minimum wage working as a maid in a Winnipeg hotel, to be economically self-sufficient even 16 years after her separation from her husband. Had she not had to take care of her children and support herself, with a supplement of $150 per month in spousal support from her ex-husband, she might have had the time and financial resources to enrol in classes and train for a better-paying job. Yet she managed to send all three of her children to university.

Justice L'Heureux-Dubé, in her reasons for judgment, recognized that traditional marriages, in which husbands play the role of breadwinner and wives remain outside the paid labour market and act as homemakers and caregivers to children, can leave wives economically disadvantaged on the dissolution of the marriage. Quoting Justice Rosalie Abella, then on the Ontario bench, Justice L'Heureux-Dubé stated that it is 'hard to be an independent equal when one is not equally able to become independent'. The justices in this decision seemed to acknowledge that the barriers to equality that women face are structural and come as a result of past adherence to traditional gender norms. The achievement of substantive equality thus might require differential treatment.

By the early 2000s, the federal government developed uniform national guidelines for courts and lawyers to refer to in negotiating and ruling on spousal support awards. These guidelines (not enforceable as child support guidelines are) emphasize the idea of income-sharing and narrowing the disparities in income after divorce rather than simply considering the budgetary demands of each party. The guidelines offer a range of calculations based on such variables as duration of the marriage and the presence of and number of dependent children (Crosariol 2004, B11).

Child support and enforcement

According to Statistics Canada (2010b, 20), the vast majority of court-ordered awards in 2009–10 were for child support only (anywhere from approximately 70 per cent of support awards in Alberta to 93 per cent in BC) rather than for spousal support or spousal and child support. In a large majority of support awards, the recipient was female (on behalf of her children)—95 per cent or more in the provinces surveyed in 2009–10 by Statistics Canada (2010b, 21).[2]

Courts have increasingly acknowledged that children should be entitled to a lifestyle that reflects the higher income earner's wealth in cases when parents are divorced and one parent earns over $150,000 per year. In the 1999 Supreme Court ruling *Francis v. Baker*,[3] the Court awarded Monica Francis $10,034 per month in child support payments from Thomas Baker, whose personal worth was estimated at $78 million. Mr Baker left his wife when his two daughters were 20 months and five days old. She was forced to return to a teaching job within three months and for years lived a very modest lifestyle with her two daughters. Mr Baker in turn lavished his two daughters with expensive vacations and gifts but refused to provide any financial support from which his wife might benefit.

The Supreme Court rejected the idea that the federal child support guidelines placed a cap on child support for wealthy families and determined that it was up to the paying parent to demonstrate to the court that the child support payment was too high. Furthermore, 'child support undeniably involves some form of wealth transfer to the children, and will often produce an indirect benefit to the custodial parent' (Makin 1999b, A1). A few years later, the Ontario Court of Appeal ruled that an Ontario salesman who earned an annual income of $4.1 million should pay $36,000 per month in child support for his four children, a record amount in child support that allowed for such things as a cottage and expenses associated with skiing and golf (Makin 2002a, A1, A9).[4]

Child Support: A Taxable Benefit?

Until 1997, parents who received child support payments were taxed on those payments, while the parents paying the awards received a tax credit. Suzanne Thibaudeau, a divorced mother of two, challenged this tax on child support, arguing her case all the way to the Supreme Court of Canada (and losing).[5] She asserted that the law discriminated against women because most custodial parents are women and are therefore as a group unfairly burdened with the tax. The case garnered a great deal of media attention. Consequently, even though Ms Thibaudeau lost in the Supreme Court, the federal government agreed to amend that section of the Divorce Act in any case so that the recipient of child support no longer has to pay taxes and the payer no longer receives a tax deduction.

Rates of compliance with court-mandated support orders vary significantly throughout the country. Statistics Canada (2010b, 24-27) measures compliance rates based on regularity of payment and fullness of payment. With this measure, it found compliance rates varied from 63 per cent of cases in PEI to 91 per cent of cases in Quebec in 2009–10.

It should be pointed out that women ordered to pay support do not have a good record of compliance either. Stetson (1997, 205) reports that in the United States (statistics from Canada are difficult to find) in the early 1990s, only 43 per cent of fathers awarded child support received the full amount (compared to 52 per cent of mothers) and only 20 per cent of fathers received a partial amount (compared to 24 per cent of mothers), which means that 37 per cent of fathers and 24 per cent of mothers received no payment. At the same time, it should be noted that in both Canada and the United States fathers constitute the vast majority of parents who renege on child support payments.

Parents who fail to pay child support are increasingly vilified, referred to in the media and vernacular as 'deadbeats', and often face quite harsh punishments. In both Canada and the United States, governments and courts have engaged in wide-ranging efforts to enforce support agreements. While enforcement of child support is a popular measure, it is very difficult to do. Many parents have no visible means of support, and many will disappear into the underground economy if the state tries to take such measures as garnisheeing wages. When support orders are not enforced, however, the recipients often have to rely on social assistance, thus motivating governments to enforce the agreements. During the 1980s and 1990s, every province and territory in Canada created a maintenance enforcement program of some kind to help recipients collect child and spousal support (Statistics Canada 2010b, 6). In addition, all of Canada's provinces and territories have reciprocal support enforcement arrangements that authorize the enforcement of support orders made in other Canadian jurisdictions (Department of Justice Canada http://www.justice.gc.ca/eng/pi/fcy-fea/sup-pen/

enf-exe/index.html). However, many of these programs are criticized as ineffective. For example, the Office of the Ontario Auditor General (2010, 97) reports that outstanding arrears in child and spousal support stands at $1.6 billion as of 31 December 2009.

As one example of how provincial governments are grappling with this issue, the Ontario government has implemented a number of changes to help people granted support orders to obtain the money. Since 1987, the Ontario government has had a Family Responsibility Office to ensure that support payments flow from the people who make support payments (payers) to people who receive them.[6] The office has information about every support order issued by courts in Ontario and acts to enforce those orders, along with private agreements that have been filed with the courts, using a number of enforcement mechanisms. It arranges for support payments to be deducted automatically from the payer's paycheque or pension cheque or, alternatively, payers can send cheques directly to the office (although some payers manage to convince their employers to pay them 'under the table' and avoid the wage garnishee [Mallan 2004, A1]). The office also has the power to garnishee federal income tax refunds and other federal sources of income, such as employment insurance benefits, a power granted under the authority of the Family Orders and Agreements Enforcement Assistance Act (1987), and the Garnishment, Attachment and Pension Diversion Act (1983) (Statistics Canada 2005, 8). In 1996, the Ontario Government passed the Family Responsibility and Support Arrears Enforcement Act, which instituted a number of other changes that expanded the definition of income from which the Office could deduct support. Currently, the FRO can report the payer to the credit bureau, seize the payer's bank account or assets, suspend the payer's passport, seize lottery winnings, suspend the payer's driver's licence, or take the payer to court.

Such enforcement mechanisms, however, require staff to track down 'deadbeat' parents, which is a very difficult task. The Liberal government in Ontario made a number of changes to the FRO soon after its election in 2003, committing $40 million over four years in its first budget to develop a computer system of case management. It announced that special teams of workers would be created to track down deadbeat parents. Then in June 2005, the provincial legislature adopted a number of measures to toughen the Family Responsibility and Support Arrears Enforcement Act, 1996, including increasing the maximum jail term for failure to comply with court orders from 90 days to 180 days and suspending defaulting payers' hunting and fishing licences (it already allowed for the suspension of driver's licences). The legislation also gave the office the authority to post identifying information about defaulting payers on a public website (FRO 2004a). Such a 'most wanted' website had already been established in Alberta to identify parents who fail to pay child support, giving their names, ages, and last known employer (Mahoney 2004, A7). Despite these changes, the 2010 Ontario Auditor General's report (95) found that the FRO 'is not yet successful in effectively achieving its mandate of collecting unpaid child and spousal support payments'. The Auditor General found that the delay in initiating enforcements was at least five months; payers and recipients do not have access to their assigned case workers and have to rely on call centres but call volume is so high that nearly 80 per cent of calls do not go through; no one is assigned to proactively oversee a case; for cases that go into arrears months go by before enforcement action is taken; and the office reviews and works on only about 25 per cent of its total cases. Thus, the maintenance regime does not work well for families dependent on that support.

The Price of Support

The increasing attention paid to child support has raised issues having to do with child custody. A 2005 case decided by the Canadian Supreme Court involved a dispute between Joanne Leonelli-Contino and her ex-husband Joseph Contino over how much child support Mr Contino should pay for his son Christopher in a shared custody arrangement (Schmitz 2005a, A7).[7] Christopher lived primarily with his mother from the age of three and spent every other weekend and Thursday nights with his father. In 2000, when the child was 14 years old, Ms Leonelli-Contino enrolled in a night course and agreed to let Christopher stay with his father Tuesday nights as well. Because the child was now with him more than 40 per cent of the time, a provincial court judge in 2001 ordered a reduction in monthly child support payments from $563 to $100. Ms Leonelli-Contino appealed that decision to divisional court in 2002, arguing that she had in effect hired a very expensive babysitter since her agreement to let her ex-husband take care of the child an extra four nights per month (an 11 per cent increase) resulted in an 85 per cent reduction in her child support. The divisional court agreed and boosted the monthly amount to the full $688 required under 1997 federal child support guidelines establishing pre-set amounts that a non-custodial parent must pay (Mr Contino's annual income was $87,315).[8] The divisional court awarded the full amount even though the boy was living with his father nearly 50 per cent of the time. Mr Contino then appealed to the Ontario Court of Appeal, which ruled that the divisional court was wrong and ordered the support payments reduced from $688 to $400 per month. Both parents were unhappy with the result—hence the appeal to the Supreme Court of Canada. Mr Contino believed his support obligation should be $250 per month.

The justices ruled (with one dissent) that the spouse paying child support cannot automatically expect to have support payments reduced because he or she is spending more time with the child. Each case must be decided individually; however, the justices articulated the view that increased time spent with a parent does not necessarily translate into extra expenses. The Court set Mr Contino's support payments at $500 per month.

Case 2: Child Custody

The vast majority of couples in Canada work out their custody arrangements by agreement. In some cases, one parent does not want custody at all, but in others a judge may need to intervene to decide custody according to particular standards or criteria laid out in law. Until the nineteenth century, because children were regarded as their fathers' property and fathers were granted sole rights to children under common law, fathers were automatically entitled to custody of their legitimate children (a common law norm of paternal right) (Millar and Goldenberg 1998, 209). By the mid-nineteenth century, British law allowed mothers the right to petition for custody of young children, provided they had not committed adultery. Paternal preference, however, was still the legal norm until the beginning of the twentieth century, when the legal norm shifted from paternal to maternal preference. Under that norm, courts assumed that children, particularly young children of 'tender years' were better off with their mothers after marital breakdown, based on gendered assumptions of women's innate capacity to nurture and care for their children (Mucalov 2001, 21; Boyd 2003a, ch. 2). As Boyd (2000a, 163) argues, however, the 'tender years' doctrine 'never represented a firm presumption in favour of mothers. The presumption was highly contingent on "good behaviour" and on strict expectations of mothers'. Women who 'served prison terms, First Nations mothers, poor mothers, and even "uppity" or feminist mothers' could find their fitness challenged. And because women tend to be poorer on average than men, they may not have access to as many resources as men do to fight for custody.

The 'Fit' Mother

Societal beliefs about what a good mother is can affect women's treatment under the law. The 'cult' of motherhood can work against women or, perversely, in their favour as well. Scholars such as Lorraine Greaves et al. (2002), Molly Ladd-Taylor and Lauri Umansky (1998), and Karen Swift (1995) have documented societal views and media portrayals of 'bad' mothers: those who deviate from the norm of self-sacrificing, other-directed, caring, and nurturing parents. Society may view deviance from idealized views of motherhood as worse than normal crimes. The media give far more coverage to stories about mothers who murder their own children than about fathers who do the same. At the same time, fathers generally receive far stiffer sentences when convicted of murdering their own children than mothers who do the same (Anderssen 2002a, F4; Saunders 2002, A1, A2).

However, the law can be much more punitive when it comes to women's failure as mothers. For example, juries in a number of states in the United States have held women accountable for failure to protect their children from an abusive spouse or partner, declaring that they knew or should have known that their children were in danger. Fathers, in contrast, have rarely been convicted for 'failure to protect' their children from mothers' abuse (Anderssen 2002b, F7). The most notorious case may be that of Russell Yates, who remained unpunished for his failure to protect his children after his wife, Andrea Yates, was convicted of murder and received a sentence of life imprisonment for drowning their five children. He left the children in his wife's care even though she had been hospitalized for psychosis and had tried to kill herself (Mallick 2002, A15). Holding one spouse responsible for failure to protect children from harm appears even more punitive if the spouse is also an abuse victim and is thus in a situation in which it is difficult to escape from harm. Pualani Enos (1996, 264) argues that in those cases, courts should 'evaluate the behavior of the battered woman in the context of her violent situation and should give weight to the acts of violence and continued intimidation'.

Strong challenges to the maternal preference norm began to arise in the 1970s when fathers' rights advocates argued that fathers were no longer simply providers and disciplinarians but also participants in childbirth and in the nurturance and physical care of children. They therefore should be allowed to play a role in parenting even if the marriage breaks down. These advocates asserted that women were given unfair advantage in custody determinations because the gender-based stereotypes favoured them as parents. Liberal feminists also scorned these gender-based stereotypes and endorsed the application of the gender-neutral principle of 'best interests of the child' (Boyd 2003a, 8).

By the 1970s, the Supreme Court of Canada had rejected the doctrine of maternal preference. Instead, courts attempted to make gender-neutral custody determinations based on the doctrine of 'best interest of the child', with no automatic preference for one parent or the other. This principle was enshrined in the 1986 amendments to the federal Divorce Act (section 16(8)). Under the 'best interests of the child' doctrine, courts are to determine each parent's parenting skills and compare the environments each parent can provide. While the federal Divorce Act currently does not, many provincial statutes outline specific criteria that the courts must take into consideration when determining the best interests of the child, including which parent has taken greater responsibility for parenting on a daily basis, which parent can best fulfill the child's needs, and so on (Payne and Payne 2001, 260).[9] But as Cohen and Gershbain (2001, 123) point out, the legislation does not rank the criteria or suggest what to do if they are in conflict. How judges weigh the value of the role as primary caregiver versus who can better provide the necessities of life can vary depending on the judge. The criterion of 'best interests of the child' thus gives judges enormous discretion and 'requires that judges rely on personal assessments, biases, and values' (Mucalov 2001, 12; see also Guggenheim 1994).

The fathers' rights lobby

Since the 1980s, courts have made major moves to award joint or shared custody. Joint custody can mean either joint legal custody, in which both parents are given authority over major decisions affecting the child, or joint physical custody, in which the child lives part-time with one parent and part-time with the other, or both (Payne and Payne 2001, 255). Statistics Canada (2002a) notes that the number of sole custody decisions in divorce and custody cases handled by the courts has declined over time. In 1988 approximately 76 per cent of cases were settled in favour of the wife alone. In 2000 that figure fell to approximately 54 per cent. By 2004, the latest available data reveal that the figure is 45 per cent (Statistics Canada 2010a). In 1986, just after major amendments to the Divorce Act, 15 per cent of cases were settled in favour of the husband alone; by 2000 that figure had declined to 9 per cent. By 2004 the figure was 8 per cent. In 2000 37 per cent of dependents were awarded jointly to husbands and wives, compared to 10 per cent in 1986 (Brean 2002). By 2004, joint custody was awarded in nearly 47 per cent of applications for divorce (Statistics Canada 2010a).[10]

Even in the absence of a joint custody award, the federal Divorce Act sections 16(10) and 17(9) stipulate that children should have as much access to the non-custodial parent as is 'consistent with the best interests of the child'. As a result of this principle of maximum contact, non-custodial parents tend to be granted much greater access privileges to children than was the case 20 years ago, when the typical access arrangement allowed a non-custodial parent to 'spend a few hours with the child at the weekend and a few days with the child during school holidays' (Payne and Payne 2001, 253). Today, non-custodial parents are typically awarded access privileges one weekday evening, alternate weekends, and four to six weeks during the summer, with shared access on a rotational basis for other holidays. Mucalov (2001, 21) reports that some custody arrangements even have children living with each parent during alternate weeks. The legislation also creates an incentive toward maximum contact because if access arrangements include contact time of more than 40 per cent, child support for the non-custodial parent is reduced.

Fathers' rights advocacy groups[11] now argue that judges' consciousness of gender discrimination has been heightened to such an extent that they might now be biased in favour of women (Kaminer 2000, 62), even with so-called gender-neutral principles in place.[12] Payne and Payne (2001, 259) argue that in determining best interests of the child, courts tend to favour: (1) preservation of the status quo if a child is already in a stable home environment; (2) granting custody to the mother if she was the primary caregiver during the marriage; and (3) keeping siblings together. Statistics show, however, that when men do fight for custody in the courts, they win about 50 per cent of the time and their success rate has not varied much over time (Mason and Quirk 1997, 235, reporting data from their US study).

Fathers' rights advocates argue that child support laws increasingly require men to shoulder a greater share of the financial burden without increasing their say in how children are raised. They also argue that mothers have an incentive to limit fathers' access to children so that their time with their children does not exceed 40 per cent, which would entitle them to a reduction in child support. Moreover, provinces have very stringent maintenance enforcement laws and programs in place but no programs to enforce access to children except in cases of flagrant violation of access orders (Laing 1999, 248). Fathers' rights advocates cite research indicating that maximum contact with both parents is better psychologically for children.[13] Women's rights advocates, in turn, point to other studies that claim that the best arrangements are those that are the least conflictual (Landsberg 2003, A2).

Many scholars note that fathers' rights groups have become increasingly influential (Bala 1999; Laing 1999; Boyd 2000a). For example, as Cohen and Gershbain (2001, 127) observe of the 1998 final report of the Special Joint Committee of the House of Commons and Senate on Custody and Access, *For the Sake of the Children*, 'although the suggested language of the preamble is neutral, both the tone of the Hearings and the content of the *Report* suggest the Committee sought to correct a perceived bias against fathers'. Among other things, the report recommended: that in determining the best interests of the child, judges should consider 'the importance and benefit to the child of shared parenting' (#16) and maximum contact; that divorcing parents be encouraged to develop parenting plans 'setting out details about each parent's responsibilities' (#11); that divorcing parents be encouraged to attend at least one mediation session (#14) (Canada 1998a, 1998b); and that there be 'coercive sanctions targeted against the "non-cooperative" parent and criminal sanctions against women who make "false allegations"' (NAWL 2002).[14] The idea behind 'shared parenting', which can be distinguished from joint custody, is that 'both parents would be presumed equal under the law when raising their children', unless the court found one parent to be unfit (Tibbetts 2003, A9). This means that even in the absence of joint physical or even legal custody, both parents would be involved in and have equal say over decision-making with regard to the children.

The feminist response

One would think that women's rights activists would support the trend to joint custody and increased visitation because it reinforces what women's rights advocates have argued all along: that there is no biological basis to parenting and men should be more involved in the tasks of parenting. Increasing fathers' access to children and involving them in decision-making could be a means of ensuring an ongoing and meaningful role for fathers in their children's lives. One might expect as well that fathers who are more involved in child-rearing would be more committed and more likely to pay child support.[15] Shared parenting could also lead to gender-neutral parenting—that is, equal sharing of parenting responsibilities.

The problem, feminists argue, is that in reality men's parenting roles are changing very little (for example, Boyd 2003a). Women remain the primary caregivers both in marriage and after marital breakdown, yet the laws are being framed as though all men were equal participants in the parenting relationship. As in the case of spousal support, to assume that women and men are similarly situated in custody situations is a mistake. Boyd (2000b) argues that mothers continue to obtain custody in the majority of divorces and continue to play the role of primary caregiver even in shared custody arrangements. In the latter case, women are more likely to take care of their children during the week, be responsible for getting them to school, and manage their after-school activities, medical appointments, and so on. Shared parenting arrangements that allow for joint legal custody of children have been described as a means of giving fathers greater say over their children's education, health care, and religious training, without them having to assume primary physical care (Delorey 1989; Boyd 2000a). The onus of caregiving responsibility still tends to fall on mothers, including the responsibility to ensure that children remain in contact with the non-residential parent. In other words, a gendered division of labour is reinforced even after marital breakdown (Delorey 1989; Boyd 2001).

The requirements of joint parenting can place enormous restrictions on the custodial parent's life (Boyd, 2010). Their ability to relocate is limited, and relocation could be considered a material change of circumstances under section 17 of the federal Divorce Act, which would allow a court to consider variation in custody or access (*Gordon v. Goertz*, [1996] 2 s.c.r. 27). In a recent BC Court of Appeal ruling, the court denied outright permission to a mother with sole custody to move from Vancouver to Houston after her company closed the Vancouver office and asked her to relocate (Boyd, 2010, 138).

Many advocates for battered women also oppose the idea of joint legal and physical custody and maximum contact because, in cases of domestic abuse, it forces the mother into continued contact with her abuser. Maximum contact provisions make it difficult for women to prevent visitation of some kind since a close relationship with both parents is presumed to be in the best interests of the child (Kelly 2009, 333-334). The norm of shared parenting and even mediation and parenting plans 'require ongoing contact between abuser and non-abusing members of the family and provides opportunity for continuation of abuse and control. The caregiving parent may be rendered powerless to provide for the needs of the children . . . without the abuser's consent and this consent may be withheld by the abuser to demonstrate ongoing control' (Laing 1999, 244). The principle of maximum contact, feminists argue, should therefore not be privileged over other considerations so as to permit abusive spouses to have control over their ex-spouses through mandated contact with their children. Negotiation, parenting plans, and mediation all assume 'competing but equal interests and power' which is likely not the case in instances of domestic abuse (Laing 1999, 244).

Some fathers' rights advocates respond by claiming that 'mothers falsely allege spousal and child abuse in order to win custody of their children' and that 'lawyers, police officers, therapists, and shelter staff are complicit in these "false allegations" (the so-called "weapon of choice" in custody cases)' (Laing 1999, 248, quoting fathers' rights advocates' presentations at the 1998 Special Joint Committee hearings). Many fathers' rights advocates point out that not all family violence is directed at women and that men can suffer abuse as well.[16] However, as we shall see in the next case study, women are more likely to be severely beaten or killed by their husbands than men by their wives, so the allegations made by fathers' rights groups ring false among most feminists.

Possible Implications of Mandated Contact Post-marital Breakdown

As researchers have pointed out, women who are victims of domestic abuse may still be required to facilitate the ex-spouse's access to their children in order to be seen as a 'friendly parent'. According to section 16(10) of the Divorce Act, the court 'shall take into consideration the willingness of the person for whom custody is sought to facilitate such contact'. If a judge determines that continued contact is in the child's best interest, such women may be in danger of losing their children to the abusive ex-partner if they fail to facilitate the contact, even though maintaining contact can continue the abuse or even endanger their lives.

To understand the implications of such a dilemma, consider the case of Valerie Lucas. In December 1999, Ms Lucas, a mother of three children, was shot and killed by her ex-husband in a parking lot in Oshawa, Ontario, in front of two of her children, aged two and nine months. She had gone to the parking lot of the Oshawa Holiday Inn to meet her former husband, Robert Bateman, with whom she shared custody of the two children. She and her ex-husband would meet every other weekend so that he could take the children. A month before her murder, Ms Lucas had requested that a justice of the peace issue a peace bond to prevent Mr Bateman from coming near her, but her request was denied despite the fact that he had threatened and harassed her so much that she had written a letter to police asking for protection when she met Mr Bateman to drop off her children. Ms Lucas was right to fear for her life. Mr Bateman pleaded guilty to second-degree murder in November 2001 and was sentenced to life in prison with no chance of parole for 21 years (n.a. 1999, 4A; Huffman 2001, 4).

Statistics Canada (2009, 49) reports that while the spousal homicide rate has declined since data collection began in 1974, 51 women in Canada were killed by their spouse or ex-spouse in 2007, while 14 men were killed. Furthermore, in the vast majority of cases, police were aware of a history of family violence between the accused and victim prior to the spousal homicide (Statistics Canada 2005, 50). This suggests that courts should take past history of family violence much more seriously and not award joint custody when there is a proven record of violence by one spouse toward the other.

The impact of feminist mobilization on Bill C-22

In response to the 1998 report of the Special Joint Committee of the House of Commons and Senate on Custody and Access, the federal Liberal government in December 2002 introduced amendments to the federal Divorce Act and other Acts (Bill C-22) that moved away from the concept of shared parenting and instead adopted the language of parenting responsibilities.[17] The federal Divorce Act currently uses the words 'custody' and 'access' and defines custody broadly to include 'care, upbringing and any other incident of custody'. The English wording in the Act does not explicitly define access, but section 16(5) states that '[u]nless the court orders otherwise, a spouse who is granted access to a child of the marriage has the right to make inquiries and to be given information as to the health, education and welfare of the child'. Bill C-22 proposed to remove the terms 'access' and 'custody' from the Act so as 'to do away with the connotations of winning and losing custody of children and access rights to them' (Lunman 2002, A1, A5). It proposed to replace the words with 'parenting orders' in order to imply shared parental responsibility.

Martin Cauchon, the justice minister at the time, in introducing the legislation, stated that the proposed changes were designed to recognize parental responsibilities, not parental 'rights' and that neither parent should presume a 'right' to care (Tibbetts 2003, A9). Furthermore, the legislation would not mandate shared parenting, despite the strong lobbying of fathers' rights groups and Canadian Alliance members in the House of Commons (Mulgrew 2003, B4). Instead, courts would be directed to take into consideration the parents' history of care for the child when determining best interests and to consider the child's need for stability. The legislation also moved away from the principle of maximum contact as a starting point, particularly in cases of domestic abuse (Boyd 2003b, 3).

The rationale for such legislation may have been influenced by studies that reported the impact of automatic shared parenting laws in countries such as the United Kingdom and Australia, where instead of resolving disputes over custody and access, 'litigation [had] actually *increased* over the meaning of parental responsibility and the extent of parental rights' (Boyd 2003b, 1, emphasis in original; see also Rhoades 2002). It appears that the justice minister was also responding to women's rights organizations, such as the National Association of Women and the Law, the Ontario Women's Justice Network, and the Ontario Women's Network on Child Custody and Access, which lobbied the minister and provincial ministers of justice extensively in the consultation process initiated after the release of the Special Joint Committee report in 1998 (Côté, Cross, Curtis, and Morrow 2001; NAWL 2002).[18]

Beyond gender neutrality and maternal preference: The 'primary caregiver' test

Feminist legal scholars such as Boyd (2001, 2003a) propose that the 'best interests of the child' test 'should be interpreted in a way that recognizes equality interests and gendered caregiving patterns that are relevant to the well-being of children' (NAWL 1998). The National Association of Women and the Law, in its brief to the Special Joint Committee on Child Custody and Access, argued that legislation should 'articulate a presumption that custody of children should be with the primary caregiver', that 'future promises regarding caring for children should not be given the same weight as a history of caring for the child', 'that the person who is the primary caregiver should also be the person who has the primary decision-making authority', and that 'any definition of primary caregiver [should] take into consideration the diversity of people's lives'.

Furthermore, courts should also recognize that a child's best interests and that of the custodial parent are intertwined. Custodial parents are more restricted in terms of employment—having to live near a school, unable to work late, and having to take time off work when a child is sick. Therefore, courts should be more willing to defer to the decisions of the custodial parent—for example, to relocate (Boyd 2000b; Boyd 2010).

The primary caregiver concept is controversial because it requires that courts recognize arguments of difference, not gender neutrality, when it comes to custody and access (Boyd 2000b). The primary caregiver presumption means 'the parent who was the primary caregiver of children while a relationship was intact . . . would be presumed to be the parent who should receive custody, unless shown to be unfit' (Boyd 2003a, 17). The outcome of the primary caregiver doctrine may not be much different from that of the 'maternal preference' or 'tender years' doctrine, although it springs from a different rationale. It is not a biological argument, rooted in gendered assumptions about women's natural abilities to care for children, but rather is rooted in awareness of the economic and social reality that women continue to shoulder the bulk of child-rearing responsibilities and are economically disadvantaged. It can thus be applied in a gender-neutral fashion (unlike 'maternal preference') and allows courts to recognize and value 'the often undervalued female work of nurturing and organization of childcare' regardless of who does it (Boyd 2003a, 18).

In a more recent article, Boyd (2010, 154) goes further in articulating the factors that judges should take into consideration when resolving parenting disputes:

> past patterns of care and responsibility, including primary caregiving; the type of relationship each parent has with a child; whether there have been patterns of domination, or worse, a climate of coercion and fear between the adults or between the adult(s) and children; whether the parents have elected a shared arrangement; degree of geographical proximity between parental residences; ability of the parents to get along well and communicate; confidence in the other parent's parenting competence; and the impact of proposed arrangements on a caregiver's ability to be emotionally available and attentive to a child and the child's views and needs.

But Boyd (2010, 155) concedes that it is difficult to create space for considerations of parental asymmetry in an age of 'rising fathers' rights and gender convergence'.

The pitfalls of the seemingly gender-neutral but still gendered primary caregiver test

The problem with taking into account women's differential position in society is that it opens the door for courts and lawmakers to fall back on gender-based stereotypes particularly when dealing with women and men who fall outside the 'typical'. Men who really do participate equally in their children's lives and want to continue to be part of their lives after a marital breakdown may find it difficult to convince judges of their commitment. Conversely, women who engage in paid employment outside the home could be penalized for the time they spend away from their children.

Two cases highlight the problem. BC MLA Judy Tyabji lost custody of her children in 1993 because a judge determined that as a member of the BC legislature, she had a 'more "aggressive" career-oriented lifestyle than the father, Kim Sandana, who lived in the rural outskirts of Kelowna and worked in a grocery store' (Boyd 1997b, 253). This case reveals some of the pitfalls that women who step outside typical parental patterns may face. If a woman pursues a career, for example, this could be used as grounds to deny that she is the primary caregiver. Some may argue that the ruling was progressive because it signalled the judge's willingness to value the male-at-home caregiver. But if judges do not view men's and women's choices in the same light, women can be disadvantaged in the courtroom.

In a second case, 19-year-old Jennifer Ireland lost custody of her three-year-old daughter after enrolling at the University of Michigan and placing her child in a child care centre. The biological father, Steven Smith, who had been ordered to pay child support when Ms Ireland began attending school, contested custody even though he and Ms Ireland had never been married and he rarely visited his daughter. He lived at home with his parents and worked as a part-time maintenance worker at a local park, and he planned to have his mother take care of the child while he was at work. A lower court judge awarded custody to Mr Smith, ruling that a blood relative was a more appropriate caregiver than a child care centre. The ruling was overturned on appeal (Eyer 1996, 13), but the case reveals some interesting gender biases among some judges about what constitutes a good caregiver. For a woman, it is being at home, not working. For a man, it is being a good breadwinner. In some judges' view, women have to prove they are caregivers by actually providing the care, whereas men are not required to do the same. In fact, if a man can offer up a 'surrogate' mother 'in the form of a new wife or paternal grandmother who will be at home during the day, his chances of obtaining custody are enhanced' (Boyd 2003a, 15).

'Single mothers by choice' and biological fathers' rights and responsibilities

In recent years in Canada, a number of cases have raised the question of how much authority a biological father should have over the life of a child when the child is born outside of marriage. This question becomes especially pertinent as the state increasingly presumes that a biological father is responsible for the financial support of his children, even if the father and mother never married. For example, a Supreme Court judge in British Columbia awarded a retroactive payment of $641,842 in child support to Suzanne Clayton from a man with whom she had had an affair and a son. While the father, Douglas Gordon, had nothing to do with his son's life, he had agreed to pay $500 per month to their son while he was growing up. Years later, Ms Clayton learned that Mr Gordon was very wealthy, earning an average income of more than $1.4 million annually even at the time he agreed to the $500 per month payment in 1985. The judge ordered additional support payments of $4,599 per month until the child reached age 18 (Matas 2003, A1, A7).

A divisional court judge in Ontario pushed the idea of paternal responsibility even further. Judge Hugh O'Connell ordered a man to pay $2,355 in support to a woman even though they never lived together and only dated for about nine months, during which time she became pregnant. The support award was intended to cover her prenatal expenses, such as the purchase of maternity clothes and prenatal classes. The man, Mark Tatoff, claimed that he always intended to pay child support after the baby was born, but the judge felt that the woman, Andrea Danovitch, was entitled to support for her prenatal expenses as well (Makin 1999a, A1, A9).

Further problems arise when an unwed mother decides to have nothing to do with the birth father, perhaps because he was violent, or because their relationship was not a long-term one, or she has 'concerns about his ability to be a constructive parent', or she 'plans to parent with a same sex partner', or because she may wish to 'parent autonomously or without a partner' (Boyd, 2010, 144). If a father offers some form of financial or emotional support for the child, even if the mother rejects the assistance, it is possible that the father will be seen to have done enough to establish parental rights, including access rights, even if it is against the wishes of the mother (Kelly 2009, 335–6). As Kelly (2009, 336) documents, some judges have deemed children's relationship to a father as in their best interest and that children 'do better with the influence of both parents' (quoting expert testimony in the case *Johnson-Steeves v. Lee*).

This issue of father's rights becomes particularly complex in the case of a mother's wish to give her child up for adoption. Drakich (1989) documents a Canadian case in 1988 in which the Saskatchewan Court of Appeal awarded child custody to a 21-year-old father over the objections of the mother who wanted to place the child in an adoptive home that could offer financial stability. Drakich (1989, 81) notes that '[i]n awarding custody to the father, the judge stated that the natural father should not be deprived of the custody of his child:

> "[M]erely because his youth and immaturity and his inability to provide a home and resources the equivalent of those offered through adoption . . . the father is not to be deprived of the right to demonstrate his ability to give loving care to his son except where the prospect is so unrealistic as to place an unacceptable risk on the welfare of the child."'

In light of such decisions, some feminists have argued that, given the biological mother's responsibilities in gestation and birth, mothers should have sole authority in matters of adoption, without interference from the father.

Another issue regarding biological fathers' rights is the question of abortion. Given the considerable financial responsibility that the state now expects fathers to assume, some have argued that they should have a say in whether or not the woman has the baby. Courts in Canada effectively and in the United States explicitly have barred spouses or ex-partners from having any such power.[19] The idea that a man should have the power to force a woman to have an abortion is extreme. Some have suggested instead that men should have an opportunity to terminate their parental rights and responsibilities during a limited period.[20]

A case in the United States highlights these issues as well as the consequences for men of even casual sexual encounters. The Illinois Appeals Court ruled in February 2005 that a man could sue his former lover for emotional distress after she saved sperm from a sexual encounter six years before and then used it to get pregnant. The man, Dr Richard Phillips, did not know about the child until two years later when the woman, Dr Sharon Irons, filed a paternity lawsuit and demanded monthly child support payments. Dr Irons was awarded payments in the amount of $800 per month after a DNA test proved that Dr Phillips was the father. Dr Phillips then sued Dr Irons for emotional distress, fraud, and theft (of sperm). Dr Phillips claimed that he had trouble eating and sleeping and was haunted by feelings of being trapped in a nightmare (AP 2005). At the lower court level, the judge dismissed the claims of distress and theft, but the appeals court found that Dr Irons's actions were deceitful and unorthodox and had led to extreme consequences, so allowed the emotional distress suit to proceed at the lower court level, although it dismissed the theft claim. In this case, Dr Phillips was not consulted about whether he wanted to have a child but was expected to pay child support for the child that was subsequently produced. This case highlights that every sexual encounter can lead to life-changing consequences for men just as it can for women.

Same-sex couples, gamete donors, and parental rights

Even more controversial is the issue of how to assign parentage in the case of children born into lesbian and gay families. As we discussed in chapter 7, the law's assignment of parentage confers important benefits, including the right to make decisions about a child's upbringing and, should the couple's relationship dissolve, access and visitation rights.[21] Parentage also confers important responsibilities, such as financial support. Same-sex couples have in the past resolved second parentage acknowledgment in law mainly through the second parent's application to adopt any children in the family, which is now permitted through common law rulings or legislation in all provinces and territories save Prince Edward Island and Nunavut (Kelly 2008–9, 191 at n. 19). Second-parent same-sex adoptions can only occur, though, with the consent of the biological mother and biological father, if known, they 'involve a waiting period, usually require hiring a lawyer, and cost several thousand dollars to complete' (Kelly 2008–9, 192).

As same-sex marriage has been legalized, and more and more same-sex couples are seeking out assisted reproductive technologies in order to have children, more and more children are being born into an existing relationship of two same-sex parents who seek the right to list themselves as co-parents on birth registration documents. Kelly (2008–9, 192 at n. 21) notes that two same-sex parents can now appear on a child's birth certificate in Alberta, BC, Manitoba, New Brunswick, Ontario, and Quebec, but that that alone does not ensure legal recognition of parentage. Complications have ensued when gamete donors have asserted parental rights as well, based on their biological ties. Indeed, same-sex two-parent listings are not possible in British Columbia and Ontario if the sperm donor is known (Kelly 2008–9, 192), demonstrating a strong preference in law toward biological as opposed to social parentage.

Two perspectives have emerged within the gay and lesbian community on how courts should deal with the issue of whether to grant parental rights to sperm or egg donors/surrogates (Kelly 2004–5, 160–161). One perspective is that courts and legislative reforms should protect the 'homo-nuclear family', meaning the law should recognize two parents only upon birth or adoption, regardless of whether those two parents are homosexual or heterosexual. Indeed, federal and provincial legislation in Canada presumes that any child conceived via assisted reproductive technologies in a heterosexual context is the child of the two parties to that relationship (Kelly 2004–5, 163; Kelly 2009, 340). Those who support the 'homo-nuclear family' view argue this presumption of two parents should be extended to same-sex couples so as to prevent sperm or egg donors from asserting parental rights, and especially to prevent judges from inserting a 'father' into the life of a child or children of a lesbian couple who have chosen not to have a father figure in their child or children's lives. If the law follows this perspective it would grant parental rights automatically to the second parent in the same-sex couple, and it would sever any legal rights of sperm or egg donors/surrogates as it does in the case of heterosexual couples.

Another perspective argues that courts and legislative reforms should be quite fluid in the definition of family and acknowledge multiple parents, so as to accurately take into account the diversity of family forms that currently exist. Supporters of this perspective are concerned that the law does not simply award parental rights to those couples who mirror most closely heterosexual two-parent couples. Some same-sex couples who have children through the assistance of sperm or egg donors/surrogates want the children to have a relationship with the donor. As Kelly (2004–5, 169) points out, absent the legal option to declare multiple parents, any action by a second parent in a same-sex couple to adopt a child would sever the legal relationship of the child with one biological parent. In some families, this severing of ties is not desired.

The concern raised regarding the multiple parent perspective is that judges some-times go out of their way to 'find fathers' and will insert a biological father into a family unit out of a belief that children need fathers (Kelly 2009, 340). By implication, then, a family comprising two mothers is 'incomplete'. Kelly (2009, 340) notes that while judges have 'found fathers' in a few Canadian and comparative judicial decisions,[22] she knows of no cases 'in Canada or elsewhere in which a court has reconfigured a gay family in order to find a 'mother'. Kelly (2008–9, 191 at n. 18) argues, therefore, that same-sex mothers still struggle to be recognized in law as parents: 'being in a common-law or marriage relationship with the biological mother does not create an automatic presumption in favour of maternity . . . and no amount of caregiving will guarantee that the court will support a non-biological mother's claim'. The one exception is the province of Quebec.

The first decision in Canada to recognize multiple parents is *AA v. BB*.[23] In this case, B.B. the sperm donor, had been listed on a child's birth certificate along with the biological mother, C.C. A.A., the same-sex partner of C.C., then applied to be added to the birth certificate as a third parent. Kelly (2009, 348) notes at the time that it was not possible in Ontario to list two mothers on a child's birth certificate. The two women were the primary caregivers to the child and the donor played little role in the child's life, but they did not want to sever the sperm donor's parental status. The Ontario Court of Appeal accepted this argument as in the child's best interest. Kelly (2009, 349) argues that this case reveals the court's willingness to accept non-nuclear families, but emphasizes that it does not challenge the notion of the need for a father in a family.

Case 3: Family Violence, Domestic Violence, Violence Against Women

We name this section 'family violence' to reflect the federal government's own naming of the issue (Statistics Canada 2003b) as well as that of the national organization set up to distribute information on the issue (National Clearinghouse on Family Violence, or NCFV). The term 'family violence', as opposed to 'wife battering', signals that violence in the home can be experienced by all family members, including male partners and children. Recent Statistics Canada surveys show that men are as likely as women to face abuse from their partner (Philp 2000, A3; Foss 2002, A8). However, it should be empha-sized that women experience the consequences of family violence more acutely (Eliasson and Lundy 1999, 283). Women are more likely to experience more severe forms of vio-lence, such as choking, beating, and sexual assault, more likely to require medical atten-tion or hospitalization, and more likely to fear for their lives (Statistics Canada 2003b). More women die at the hands of their spouses (51, or 5.7 per million couples, in 2007) than men (14, or 1.6 per million couples) (Statistics Canada 2009, 54).

The term 'domestic violence' seems less appropriate in that it suggests that vio-lence against women only happens in the home and is not part of a broader set of experiences that includes rape, sexual assault, sexual harassment, and so on. Some feminists and women's groups in fact argue that violence against women in the home is 'part of a broad-scale system of domination that affects women as a class', and that is 'structural in the social inequality between women and men' (MacKinnon 1992, 186). Furthermore, it intersects with such factors as race, immigrant status, poverty, lack of job skills, and child care responsibilities. Thus, merely portraying such violence in gender-neutral terms is not helpful to understanding the issues (Crenshaw 1993, 1241; Weldon 2004). While we use the term family violence, we recognize these mul-tiple layerings of the issue and try, as much as possible, to convey the gender-specific aspects of the phenomenon.

The evolution of legal rules regarding family violence

As mentioned in the previous chapter, under the common law doctrine of coverture, men and women became one on marriage; a woman's individuality disappeared as she came under the legal responsibility and protection of her husband. Since her husband was responsible for her, older common law principles permitted a husband to 'restrain' her and 'correct' her behaviour, 'as he is allowed to correct his apprentices or children' (Morrison 2001, 341). What developed in the common law courts, then, was the 'rule of thumb': that is, 'a husband's legitimate authority to use violence to control his wife, children, and other family members was limited to the use of a stick no larger than his thumb' (Stetson 1997, 355). Because a husband had to answer for a wife's misbehav-iour, the law thought it reasonable to give him power to restrain her. Family violence was a legitimate form of punishment for misbehaviour and police and courts were un-able and unwilling to prevent or punish domestic assaults.

The overt condoning of violence against women disappeared along with the idea that wives are the property of their husbands; however, it was not until 1982 that the Canadian government included marital rape under expanded sexual assault provi-sions of the Criminal Code (Gotell 1998, 78; Weldon 2004, 6). Until then, the law precluded a woman from claiming rape within a marriage. Section 143 of the Criminal Code stated that '[a] male person commits rape when he has sexual intercourse with a female person who is not his wife'.

The criminalization of marital rape occurred at the same time that other laws de ing with violence against women were expanded. For years, feminists had strugg¹ have rape redefined as a crime of assault rather than one of passion out of cor' as violence rather than sex (MacKinnon 1992; Gotell 2010). The introduc' term 'sexual assault' in the Criminal Code, replacing 'rape', served to comʳ sexual violence is violence and could happen to anybody.

By the late 1980s and early 1990s, the Canadian government had not only rec-ognized the importance of the issue of violence against women but had also begun to frame the issue in language that feminist advocates had been pushing for years (Gotell 1998). The 1983 reforms to the Criminal Code ended the rape provisions and instead developed a three-tier structure of sexual assault offences with charges determined based on degrees of violence (Gotell 2010, 210). The reforms also criminalized acts such as non-consensual sexual touching and sexual acts that do not involve penetra-tion. The reforms also removed the requirement for the victim's complaint to be cor-roborated and for the complaints to be 'recent'. The reforms restricted the ability of the defendant to cross-examine victims on their sexual history and banned the publication of victims' names. Additionally, the reforms criminalized sexual assault within mar-riage (Gotell 2010, 210). In later reforms to the Criminal Code, the federal government went even further in specifying what consent means and what it means for the accused to 'take reasonable steps to ensure consent' (Gotell, 2010). In other words, an accused cannot just reasonably believe consent exists but also must take reasonable steps to ensure consent (Gotell 2010).

Rape Shield Laws and Drunkenness as a Defence

The federal government has demonstrated willingness to recognize gender arguments regarding assault in its responses to Supreme Court of Canada rulings. The 1983 Criminal Code amendments to sexual assault laws included restrictions on the extent to which a complainant could be questioned on her past sexual history during a trial—a legal 'rape shield'. The idea behind rape shield laws is that a woman's sexual history is irrelevant to her sexual assault; just as in other crimes, the victim's past is not an issue in determining the guilt and punishment of the accused (for example, a police officer does not ask a man whether he has been mugged before). In 1991, however, the Supreme Court struck down the Criminal Code provision that protected victims of sexual violence from being cross-examined on their prior sexual behaviour.[24] The Court ruled 7 to 2 that all relevant information must be admitted at trial. Because this provision did not allow any scope for judicial discretion, relevant evidence could be excluded (Gotell, 2010).

The federal government, under Justice Minister Kim Campbell, responded to the ruling im-mediately, meeting with women's groups to draft new legislation (Stuart and Delisle 2001, 683). Based on those consultations, the government drafted a new rape shield law that protects victims of sexual assault from being cross-examined unless a judge decides such questions should be permitted. Judges thus can decide whether the evidence is relevant to the defence, rather than allowing defence lawyers merely to go on a 'fishing expedition' during cross-examination. The revised provisions also, Gotell (2010) argues, narrow the range of evidence permitted to be deemed relevant because the law defines what is meant by 'consent' and lists a number of situations in which consent is automatically presumed not to exist, for example, when the complainant is deemed incapable of consenting.

Similarly, in the case of Henri Daviault,[25] the federal government responded swiftly with new legislation after the Supreme Court ruled that the 72-year-old Mr Daviault was so drunk when he committed sexual assault against a 65-year-old woman that he had reached a state akin to insanity or automatism, such that he was incapable of forming *mens rea* (intent). Mr Daviault never denied the sexual assault against the complainant, who was partially paralyzed and confined to a wheelchair. But he said that after consuming seven or eight beers and almost a full 40-ounce bottle of brandy, he was too drunk to know what he was doing. Six of the Supreme Court judges agreed that he was incapable of passing the legal test of having a 'guilty mind' and thus accepted the *mens rea* defence. Intent to commit a crime must be established in crimes of specific intent such as first-degree murder. In this ruling, the justices specified that in crimes of general intent, such as assault and sexual assault, drunkenness could only be used as a defence in very rare circumstances.

However, soon after the Supreme Court decision, quite a number of cases emerged in which the defence claimed the accused was too drunk to form intent. On the urging of women's groups, the federal government introduced legislation making it impossible for people accused of assault or sexual assault to use drunkenness as a defence. The view was that there should be a standard of conduct that can be reasonably expected of people in crimes of general intent even when they are intoxicated. In other words, if one wanted to prevent oneself from committing assault, one should not drink so much! In drafting the bill, the federal government was very careful to explain the purpose of the legislation in order to protect against potential Charter challenges; indeed, the preamble of the law states explicitly that Parliament had clear concerns about the impact of violence against women and children and about the link between intoxication and violence.

Finally, in 1997, the federal government responded to the 1995 Supreme Court decision in *R. v. O'Connor*[26] by adding sec. 278 to the federal Criminal Code to clarify legislatively the common law test established by the Court regarding disclosure of victims' records (Gotell, 2002, 255). Those provisions were subsequently upheld in *R. v. Mills*.[27]

Also, in the early 1980s, the federal government established the Family Violence Prevention Unit in the Department of Health and Welfare to provide education and coordination of federal activities on family violence. It also established the National Clearinghouse on Family Violence to provide information on family violence and, in the late 1980s, the Family Violence Initiative, which coordinates action on family violence, including funding for shelters, policy research, public education and training, and support for community groups. The Family Violence Initiative was discontinued in 1994 but was restarted in 1997 (Weldon 2004, 6, 13, 14).

Debates within feminism over the issue of family violence

Combating family violence is clearly a feminist issue but, as with most issues, opinions vary on how to deal with it. Nancy Hirschmann (1997, 1997) points out some of the dilemmas facing policy-makers and police in deciding how best to help women and children in situations of family violence. Policy-makers and society in general used to hold the view that the home was inviolable and what went on behind closed doors domestically was not the business of the outside world. If violence occurred outside the home, it was a public matter. But the state could not cross the threshold of the home without good reason.

Feminist organizations have made great efforts to convince the state that it has an interest in crossing the threshold of the home to help vulnerable members in the family (Okin 1989). However, state intervention presents a Catch-22 to feminists because privacy and autonomy are very important factors in a host of matters, such as contraception and consensual sexual relations. As Hirschmann (1997, 194) points out, 'freedom from patriarchal restrictions to choose lies at the heart of contemporary feminist struggles . . . [but] [d]omestic violence presents a fundamental challenge to existing liberty discourse because it raises questions about the construction of choice. . . . The example of a battered woman who remains with her abuser strikingly reveals the inadequacy of existing freedom theory from a feminist perspective'.

In the case of family violence, one can see a number of barriers, both external and internal, that could prevent a woman from leaving a relationship in which she suffers abuse. The physical abuse itself, as well as the fear of the abuse, act as both external and internal constraints. Economic dependence and the inability to earn enough money to become financially independent are external constraints, as is having nowhere to go. Women may also experience internal, psychic constraints against leaving an abusive relationship: the internalization of a belief that violence is normal, for example, or feelings of love for the partner, depression, low self-esteem, or religious convictions (Hirschmann 1997, 197).

The result is, according to Hirschmann (1997, 200), 'complex emotional *and structural* factors that take away many of a woman's choices, that make her *feel* as if she has no choice'. For many women, leaving the relationship is not a complete solution because they may lack resources to cope on their own when they leave a shelter. In such situations, they may see returning home as a choice, as an autonomous act of agency, as coping (Hirschmann 1997, 202, 204). We can even understand 'battered woman syndrome' (abuse to the point that a woman loses the power to save herself) as an act of agency, of survival. It does not mean that women want to be beaten but rather that internal and external barriers interact to prevent the exercise of other options. Women thus need to be empowered so that they can see their options realistically and struggle to increase and maximize those options. In terms of policy, the solution would then be to reduce the external and internal constraints that prevent the victim from making free choices.

Some jurisdictions have laws in place requiring mandatory arrests for family violence, which means that even if the victim does not want to press charges, police are obliged to make an arrest if they see evidence of abuse. About half of the US states have such laws in place. In Canada, a 1982 parliamentary report encouraged the provinces to adopt mandatory arrest policies in cases of suspected spousal abuse; those measures were eventually implemented (Gotell 1998, 47). Hirschmann (1997, 199) argues, however, that 'the feminist distaste for such a response should be obvious. . . . [S]uch approaches deny that a battered woman can even know what she wants. . . . [I]t denies the agency of the woman and fails to respect her capacity to make choices and act on them'.

Racism also plays a role in shaping responses to family violence. As Crenshaw (1993, 1242, 1244) points out, women's experience of abuse and sexual violence can vary depending on their race or ethnicity. Racism may prevent police and prosecutors from taking abuse in visible minority or First Nations communities as seriously as they do in white communities or to hand out as severe convictions when the victim is a member of a minority community or is a First Nations member (Dylan, Regehr and Alaggia 2008; Razack, 2000). The most notorious case in recent history is that of Robert Pickton, charged with murdering 26 women and convicted in 2007 of murdering six

Battered Woman Syndrome and Self-Defence

Some women facing extreme violence in the home feel they have no option other than killing their abuser in order to protect themselves or their children. At trial, they have offered up the plea of self-defence on the grounds that they felt they had to kill their partner in order to save their own lives.

In *R. v. Lavallee*, 1989,[28] the Supreme Court of Canada heard a case in which a 22-year-old woman in a common-law relationship, Lyn Lavallee, shot her partner of three or four years, Kevin Rust, in the back of the head and killed him. Ms Lavallee claimed that the shooting was an act of self-defence that occurred after an argument during which she had been beaten and after multiple instances of abuse. During previous years, she had made frequent trips to the hospital for treatment of 'severe bruises, a fractured nose, multiple contusions, and a black eye' but did not tell hospital staff the truth about how she sustained her injuries. In her statement to police, she claimed that she feared for her life that night after her partner loaded some guns and told her either to kill him or he would 'get her' after other guests at a party in their home had left. She fired once through a window screen, then he turned away from her and she shot him.

At trial, a psychiatrist offered testimony that Ms Lavallee was a victim of battered woman syndrome in support of her claim of self-defence. The psychiatrist testified that her 'ongoing terror, her inability to escape the relationship despite the violence and the continuing pattern of abuse which put her life in danger' all accounted for Ms Lavallee's decision to shoot her partner that night.

A jury acquitted Ms Lavallee, but that verdict was overturned by the Manitoba Court of Appeal. At issue in the Supreme Court of Canada was whether the evidence of the psychiatrist should have been allowed at trial. The Supreme Court ruled that indeed it should be allowed in order to assist the jury in determining whether Ms Lavallee 'had a reasonable apprehension of death or grievous bodily harm and believed on reasonable grounds that she had no alternative but to shoot'. The justices agreed that in order to determine whether Ms Lavallee's use of force was reasonable, a jury had to understand what she had been going through and the fear she felt. In other words, the timeline of the events leading up to the action should be extended further into the past. The Court thus broadened the standard of defence by instructing judges and juries to take into account the experiences, background, and circumstances of the accused when determining whether she believed she was at risk of serious bodily harm or death and thus had to use force to save herself.

Typically, in order to prove self-defence, a defendant has to demonstrate that there is 'reason to believe that [s]he is in imminent danger of death or serious bodily harm at the time of the killing, and [s]he used force proportionate to that directed at h[er]' (Stetson 1997, 360). In other words, the defendant has to demonstrate three things: proportional force, reasonable belief of necessity, and imminent danger (Hartline 1997, 160). Feminist advocates of a gendered notion of self-defence argue that the existing standard is that of a 'reasonable man' who is facing danger, not a 'reasonable woman', which makes it very difficult for women to plead self-defence successfully. The rules governing self-defence are really designed to deal with single moments that may arise, such as the case of two men involved in a bar fight when one pulls out a knife, not the case of a woman caught

in a continuously violent relationship with a stronger man (Hartline 1997). It is often difficult, for example, to demonstrate an immediate and direct threat, given that the time
of the killing and the times of violence might not be immediately linked. It may also be
difficult to demonstrate proportionate use of force because the killing often occurs when
the abuser is unarmed and vulnerable—for example, when he is asleep.

Feminist lawyers and researchers have advocated the development of a 'reasonable
woman' standard in cases of homicide when the assailant claims repeated abuse, something that the Supreme Court of Canada acknowledged in *R. v. Lavallee*. Hartline (1997,
166) argues in favour of a standard of 'preemptive self-defence': first, the justice system
should 'abolish the imminence requirement in cases where individuals are repeatedly
and seriously assaulted by the same person' because 'if a battered woman waits until a
threat of death or severe bodily harm is imminent, it is too late for her'; second, it should
reinterpret the requirement of reasonable belief to one of a reasonable woman, not
reasonable person that would take into consideration any long-term victimization that
the person has experienced; and third, 'the requirement of proportionality [should] be
retained, although certain assumptions made under traditional self-defence would be rejected'. For example, one could open up the time frame under which a person could use
deadly force and remove the requirement that one can only use a weapon if the assailant
bears a weapon.

The idea behind this defence is not that a woman has killed to protect herself from
being killed at that very moment but rather is protecting herself from slow but certain
destruction. Furthermore, it recognizes the physical and emotional power imbalance in
such relationships and that there may be external impediments restricting a woman's exit
options 'so that in many cases, killing their abusers is the only feasible way they have of
severing the relationship and preserving their own lives' (Hartline 1997, 168).

Critics of this approach have argued that such a defence removes responsibility from
women to exercise their exit options and could open up the possibility of women using
this defence when they have not in fact faced battering or taking action against their
abuser too early. The challenge for policy-makers, police, and feminist advocacy groups,
of course, is to ensure that measures are in place so that women do not have to contem-
plate such action as an option.

women (Cameron 2010). Those women had disappeared from Vancouver's Downtown
Eastside from the late 1990s to early 2000s. Many of the women were prostitutes and/
or drug users and many of the women were members of First Nations, leading First
Nations groups to demand a role in the public inquiry into police conduct in the investigation of the disappearances (Assembly of First Nations 2010).

In the case of familial abuse, some women from minority communities may be
unwilling to report abuse to the police because of an underlying suspicion of police
authority (Crenshaw, 1993). Consequently, they may be reluctant to call the police or
press charges because they do not wish to get involved in the criminal justice system
themselves or subject their abuser to it as well. Identifying one's own abuse may lead
to ostracism from the community. Language barriers and illiteracy make it difficult for
some immigrant women to find out about and take advantage of resources available to
them. Women who are illegal immigrants may feel trapped into staying in a marriage

rather than risk deportation. They may feel wholly dependent on their husbands, rely-ing on them for information and not knowing their rights (Crenshaw 1993).

Policy responses

Canadian law and policy has responded in a number of ways to the problem of fam-ily violence. The first set of responses has been to restrain the abuser's violence and increase the victim's options to secure her safety (Statistics Canada 2003b, 54). Many governments have amended their assault laws to increase the power of police to re-move an abuser from the victim's home, such as introducing warrantless arrests as well as cooling-off periods, restraining orders, special protection orders, and anti-stalking laws that make it a crime to threaten, follow, or harass a person (Stetson 1997, 357). Governments also provide special training for police officers so that they better under-stand the dynamics of domestic violence, the legal issues involved, and what interven-tion programs are available (Statistics Canada 2003b, 53).

More recently, several jurisdictions in Canada have developed more comprehen-sive family violence programs to encourage earlier intervention and greater account-ability for their behaviour on the part of abusers (Statistics Canada 2003b, 52). Early intervention programs are used in cases of first-time offenders when no weapons were used and the victim did not suffer significant harm. If eligible for the program, an ac-cused can opt to plead guilty and then be ordered to attend a partner assault counsel-ling and education program while out on bail. The victim is usually protected during this period by a no-contact, no-communication order and is consulted throughout the process. After the accused has completed the program, the court receives a progress re-port that can be taken into consideration in sentencing (Statistics Canada 2003b, 58).

The advantage of such programs is that they encourage rehabilitation—the model used in cases of child abuse—rather than merely punishing the offender. Early inter-vention recognizes that incarcerating the offender can hurt the entire family by depriv-ing them of a breadwinner, for example. The program frames family violence as a social problem that can be overcome through education and rehabilitation.

The debate between rehabilitative and punitive solutions is especially strong with-in First Nations communities in Canada. In recent years, these communities have cre-ated First Nations-based justice systems that many argue better take into account the needs and traditions of Aboriginal peoples. Indigenous methods of dispute resolution focus not on punishment but rather on restitution and atonement and on reintegra-tive community-based solutions. Thus, a major question in the Aboriginal community is whether First Nations men charged with family violence or other related offences should be diverted from the criminal justice system into a more Aboriginal-based jus-tice system (McGillivray and Comaskey, 1999).

Anne McGillivray and Brenda Comaskey (1999) found in their interviews of 26 First Nations women that 'respondents valued jail terms for reasons of punishment, denunciation, and their own personal safety'. But they also valued treatment in order to 'ensure future safety for themselves or for other partners of their offender' (125). At the same time, they 'doubted the effectiveness of treatment without jail' (ibid.). McGillivray and Comaskey (1999) found that their interviewees tended to view diver-sion programs (counselling and healing in the community rather than going through the justice system) as the 'easy way out' (127), and 'unless diversion could guarantee treatment and victims' safety, and be immune to manipulation by abusers, they would not support it' (133).

Regarding increased support for victims, the federal government has introduced a number of measures to facilitate the participation and protection of victims and witnesses in criminal justice proceedings. For example, judges are now required to take the safety of victims into account in any bail decisions, and family members can now seek restitution from the offender for expenses they incur if they have to flee the family home to protect themselves from harm. Judges may also impose publication bans to protect the identity of victims or witnesses. In 1993 the federal government introduced anti-stalking legislation (criminal harassment under the Criminal Code) and strengthened these provisions in 1997 (Department of Justice Canada 2005b, 6). In Ontario, courts now provide interpreters to assist victims who do not speak English or French to communicate with police, Crown prosecutors, and victim support staff. The courts also offer victim/witness assistance program staff who are trained to give information and support to victims and the courts select certain Crown attorneys for training in the prosecution of family violence cases (Statistics Canada 2003b, 52–3).

Another set of reforms focuses on providing women with exit options. In the past, the only option open to women was divorce or separation on grounds of physical cruelty if they could prove it in court. During the second wave, feminist activists set up special shelters for battered women. The first federal funding for rape crisis centres and battered women's shelters came in 1972 under the Women's Program of the Secretary of State (Gotell in Tremblay and Andrew 1998, 76). The Canada Mortgage and Housing Corporation (CMHC) provides part of the capital funding assistance for these shelters, which also receive provincial and local dollars as well as community program support. Between 1992 and 2008, the number of shelters grew from 376 to 569 (Statistics Canada 2003b, 46; Statistics Canada 2009, 5). The number of women and children admitted to shelters in 2001–2 reached close to 56,000 women and 45,000 children (Statistics Canada 2003b, 49). By 2007–8, that number had increased to 62,000 women and 38,000 children) (Statistics Canada 2009, 8).

Feminist scholars of family violence argue that women should be able to make their own choices while recognizing that those choices are 'deeply, fundamentally and complexly constructed for women' (Hirschmann 1997, 200). Thus, laws and public policies should be set up to give women more discretion in deciding whether to prosecute (Hirschmann 1997). Also, courts should not grant child custody or give generous visitation rights to fathers if that compromises women's safety and prevents them from moving out of the province or community. Gotell (1998, 45) argues that any adequate response to family violence must 'encompass a broad range of interventions, including: expanded social welfare and child care programmes to provide women with economic independence; increased funding for social housing, second-stage housing, and job-training; increased and stable funding for shelters and crisis centres; funding for counselling, follow-up, and outreach programmes; culturally appropriate services for Aboriginal and immigrant women; services addressing the situations of women with disabilities; public education; and gender sensitivity training for police and court officials'. However, the problem that Hirschmann (1997) and others raise is that even if these resources are in place, some women will not feel powerful enough to use them. And certainly there are cases of women being murdered even though they have employed all the available strategies to protect themselves, such as getting a divorce, relocating, establishing a new identity, and prosecuting the offender for criminal harassment.

Conclusion

In each of the three policy areas covered in this chapter—divorce and support, child custody, and family violence—there is a wide variety of opinions on how governments and courts should deal with the issues as well as a great deal of policy action in response. Most strikingly, in each of the policy areas, a number of feminists have advocated differential treatment as a policy solution that recognizes that women and men are not similarly situated in the institution of the family. These voices and perspectives are not hegemonic; for different reasons, liberal feminists as well as men's groups have challenged such differential treatment arguments. However, they have been quite successful in setting the agenda for a number of policy changes over recent decades.

The recognition of difference in law and public policy is not without consequence: while it can benefit women who are disadvantaged by traditional family structures and power dynamics, it can also punish women who live 'unorthodox' lifestyles. Women's rights advocates therefore need to spend a great deal of time reflecting on what is the best course of policy action, particularly in light of women's position in the family, society, and the economy. Given that women's advocacy has had some success with policy-makers, an appropriate motto for the movement would be 'be careful what you wish for; you might get it'.

Questions for Critical Thought

1. Should laws and public policies regarding the family uphold strict gender neutrality or should the state acknowledge gender differences in caregiving for the purposes of awarding parental rights and responsibilities?
2. Should the state take any and all measures to assign parentage to fathers for the purposes of financial and other support?
3. How should the state respond to domestic violence in cases where victims refuse to lay charges?

CHAPTER 9

Pin Money, McJobs, and Glass Ceilings

> [A]ll human work is *gendered*; both paid and unpaid work is structured by a system of gender relations, which is in turn embedded in all other social institutions (Benoit 2000, 3).

The purpose of this and the next chapter is to explore issues faced by women working in both paid and unpaid labour. In this chapter we look at the evolution of women's work in the public sphere, while in the following chapter we discuss state public policy responses to the inequalities in women's employment and incomes. Three main issues must be highlighted with respect to women's work and economic well-being. First, most of the work in the home is women's responsibility and it is generally unpaid. Second, women are disadvantaged in the paid labour force: statistics consistently show that women are paid less on average than their male counterparts for the same or similar jobs, and their chances for promotion and advancement in many areas are limited because of their gender. Third, women's equality in the labour market is interrelated with issues of child care, child and family poverty in single-parent families, and social trends, including the increased number of woman-led single-parent families. While Canadian women in the twenty-first century have a wealth of opportunities, they still face pronounced obstacles that do not exist for men.

The Story of Women's Work in Canada

Women have always been involved in the public labour force. When Sojourner Truth, the black feminist and abolitionist of the nineteenth century, asked the question, 'Am I not a woman?' she was pointing out that for certain classes of women, hard labour in the public sphere was a given. The economics of slavery, farming, and industrial work demanded that women work in the fields and factories. As Phillips and Phillips (1983) point out, most of human history was not characterized by a wage economy. People did not work for wages but rather collected, hunted, and grew products for trade and for their own sustenance. The family was the primary unit of economic production, and women were indispensable. In the fur trade, trapping provided the family with meat, and the family worked to prepare the furs for sale; in early agriculture, the entire family was involved in the work required to produce crops for sale. All members of the family were intrinsic to the family economy, and all members had to fulfill their particular roles if the family was to survive. Women's work included the added dimension of birthing and mothering the children, but in such a productive system this role could not be separated from other productive roles; there was no separation of the public economy and private life.

Industrialization and concurrent urbanization broke up the family as a productive unit. While the process would occur later in Canada than in Europe, by the mid-nineteenth century industrial labour dominated the economies of Central Canada along the St. Lawrence River. It would take longer in the West where the farming economy prevailed, but urbanization and technological change eventually had an impact, changing the nature of the work performed and bringing to an end the small family farm by the end of the twentieth century. On the East Coast, women were introduced to factory labour early. The dominance of the fishery industry created a labour market in which men fished and women worked in processing plants, dressing and readying fish for market in early production lines.

In the wage economy, the family became increasingly separated from the economy. The male wage-earner became the primary provider, and the assumption was that the head of the household would receive a wage to support the family. The wife would tend to the private needs of the family and not participate in the 'productive' economy. As Wilson (1991) points out, housework seriously curtailed the ability of women to work outside the home, and even by 1931 only about 10 per cent of employed women were married. In addition, the separation of the family from production and wage-income meant that home labour was not considered part of the productive process and was therefore invisible.[1] This becomes significant when one considers that women often brought extra work and income into the home by keeping boarders, sewing, teaching, doing laundry, and working as 'cleaning ladies' in other homes.

At the same time, some women were employed in factories. Early textile industry employers 'advertised for families even in rural areas, offering the inducement that children would remain under the family's supervision while allowing the mother to earn an income, although this was really designed to get a family of workers for the price of one living wage' (Phillips and Phillips 1983, 8). Even if married women did not work in factories, the rest of the family did. Children and unmarried women would go out to work to bring in further income. Phillips and Phillips (1983, 7) note that 'in 1871 women and children made up 42 per cent of the industrial workforce in Montreal and 34 per cent in Toronto'. In the case of married women working in the paid labour force, child care and housework duties fell to younger daughters, who were then forced to leave school.

More attractive to women with families was piecework—that is, manufacturing jobs, primarily in the textile trade, that could be done at home. In this sub-contracting system, a middleman would collect work completed at home by women and sell it to a larger manufacturer. The work appealed to women because it allowed them to look after their children and in some cases have the children help with the labour. It was certainly attractive to employers because it let them pay next to nothing for each piece completed, reduced their capital investments, limited the ability of the women to organize, and enabled them to sidestep any regulation of factory conditions. Piecework persists today even in pockets of the industrialized world because of continuing access to cheap labour, more often than not provided by women. The work of last recourse for women, of course, was prostitution, a trade to which many working-class women turned because of their family's destitution or abandonment by their husbands.

By the turn of the twentieth century, the growth in technology and consumption created new opportunities for some women. Expanding businesses required administrators and clerical services, and new shops needed cashiers and salesgirls. As office bureaucracies grew, the work was broken up into menial and repetitive tasks, and the large number of women attending commercial colleges provided a supply of workers for clerical jobs. The male clerk/personal assistant was replaced by the female secretary-typist (the males being promoted to managerial positions). Phone companies provided another area of employment for women as operators.

The expansion of the state also opened up opportunities for women. As the state took responsibility for and expanded education and health care, women found work as teachers and nurses. When working in hospitals, nurses tended to be considered a form of cheap labour, particularly since their hospital work was considered part of their training. Consequently, hospital jobs were difficult to find, and many trained nurses had to work privately in situations much like those of domestic servants, with low pay and little job security. Educated middle-class women were more likely to go into teaching. Since public school teaching had previously only been open to men, women faced some resistance when they tried to enter the public system. However, the demand for teachers created by the expansion of the school system and public support for compulsory education required compromise. Women were therefore deemed fit to teach the lower elementary grades, while secondary schooling remained the domain of men. According to Phillips and Phillips (1983, 15) women were seen as a good fit with the lower grades because of their ability to mother. However, the primary determinant was cost: women would accept less pay than men.

That women could be paid less than men was a significant element in the expansion of employment opportunities for women. For example, as Copp (1974, 32) found of working-class Montreal in 1911, the average weekly income for an adult male worker was $10.55, while women and children received on average $6 and $4 respectively. Phillips and Phillips (1983, 10) cite an 1889 royal commission finding that while Eaton's paid male salespeople $10 to $12 per week, it paid a first-class female salesperson only $6 to $8 a week. Furthermore, 'In the Kingston Cotton Company, women received 57 per cent of the average male wage . . . [and] in 1910 the average wage for a woman employed in manufacturing was only $5.44 per week, which was at or below minimum subsistence levels for a single person' (ibid.).

The problem was not just low wages but also the number of hours of work required: women commonly worked longer hours than men. Shop girls might put in 15- or 16-hour days, and work in the dress trades could last 10 hours daily, with an extra five to six hours added during high season. Piecework was completely unregulated regarding time spent on the job, and the practice of paying by piece (more pieces equalling more money) encouraged extended hours of work. Employers were more than happy to pay less and require longer hours. They could also use the threat of women's employment to pressure male employees into accepting lower wages and longer hours.

Between a Rock and a Hard Place: The Reserve Labour Force

Historian Terry Copp (1974, 44) describes the dilemma faced by working-class families in Montreal at the turn of the century:

> Working class families were . . . caught in a classic bind. Since the head of the household normally did not make enough to support his family, his children had to contribute to the family's income through their own labour. Yet the availability on the labour market of large numbers of children and young women helped keep men's wages at the subsistence level.

This is a classic description of how the 'reserve labour force' can be used to keep wages low. Very rarely is there full employment in capitalist economies; rather, there is always a pool of unemployed or partially employed workers. The cycle works as follows: when employment opportunities expand and the market reaches close to full employment, employers find it difficult to find people to fill jobs. The labour market becomes a seller's market, and consequently, wage rates rise as prospective employees can demand higher wages. As wages go up and profits go down, employers start to rationalize their production to limit the required investment in wages by introducing mechanization and/or by letting employees go. Unemployment then goes up, and employers are able to dictate the level of wages. The labour market is now a buyer's market. For employers, it is best to have a large pool of unemployed persons available because they can then threaten to fire employees and replace them with people willing to accept less money just to get a job. Employees have to decide whether it is better to take lower wages and have a job or to have no job at all.

Historically, as more and more women entered the labour market, it was understood that they would be paid less than men, and because they had little choice, women were willing to accept work for lower wages. Moreover, employers could use the threat of hiring women to force male employees to accept lower wages. That is why unions were traditionally hostile to working women, considering them interlopers who took work away from men and let employers keep wages low by accepting low wages (Prentice et al. 1988).

Women are not the only workers in the reserve labour force. In today's economy, developing countries provide such labour reserves, and corporations can threaten to move jobs to countries where people are willing to work for lower wages. However, women were and continue to be an obvious part of the reserve labour force because they are not fully integrated into the industrial economy and are willing to work if the family situation demands it. Employers can use women to fill places if necessary, then force them out of the workforce when they are no longer needed.

Working conditions in the factories did prompt cries for state regulation of factory life. However, the push for labour reform focused more on the lot of working children than it did on that of working women. Limits were placed on the number of hours children and women could work in factories: in 1911 the limit was set at 60 hours per week, then dropped to 58, and in 1915 textile workers were limited to 55 hours per week (Copp 1974, 45). Boys could not start working until age 12, girls until age 14. The thrust of this campaign was to get children away from work and into school, but while it did lead to some children leaving work, it added stress to working-class families trying to make a living wage. As a result, mothers and older unmarried daughters were forced to work to make up the lost income. When governments did pass legislation to regulate women's working conditions, they did it out of concern over the effect of factory conditions on women's reproductive and mothering roles. Consequently, women were almost entirely restricted to light manufacturing such as the textile trades, which were among the most poorly paid and regulated, or to work in the unregulated service industries.

Why was there so little concern about the poor wages, working conditions, and long hours of working women? Essentially because women were not considered a serious part of the labour force: men were the primary breadwinners, while married women worked for supplementary income, or 'pin money', and unmarried women worked for the experience and the freedom the money afforded them. The idea that a woman might be the main breadwinner and have to support herself and a family was not part of the employment equation. Not only did women's housework remain invisible, but their public work and its conditions received little recognition as well. The exception was prostitution, which was vilified by many of the reformers of the early twentieth century as a social scourge. However, the campaigns to eradicate prostitution did not focus on the economic plight of these women but rather on their so-called moral impurity and the threat they posed to public health.

The glamour of Rosie the Riveter

The effect of the First and Second World Wars on women's employment situation is more complex than the common portrayal of empowered women smiling in munitions assembly plants. As Benoit (2000, 152) argues, 'the feminization of the work force during the two world wars indicated that women in Canada and the US were quite capable and more than willing to work for pay. This applied equally to married women and even those with small children, provided subsidized day-care facilities were available.' However, as Phillips and Phillips (1983, 31) argue, 'despite the experience of women in the labour market during both wars, there is little evidence that it comprised much more than a temporary, war-induced aberration'. In neither war was the recruitment of women immediate. Both wars were preceded by economic depressions, and women were recruited only after the pool of unemployed males had been depleted. In addition, as soon as the wars ended, women were dismissed from their positions and were expected to return to their housework. However, the periods of prosperity following both wars did see an expansion of opportunity for women in clerical fields and merchandising. Thus, in the 1920s, '[c]lerical and sales work began to overtake domestic service or manufacturing as the most suitable jobs for women. By 1931, half of all employed women worked in service or clerical jobs' (Wilson 1991, 70).

The Great Depression reversed the expansion in women's work opportunities, and social pressure on them as a result of rising male unemployment dissuaded many women from working. However, some employers were happy to let men go and hire women for much lower wages, and as family incomes declined both in urban areas and in drought-stricken farming communities, women had little choice but to look for work.

The Second World War had more of an impact on women's employment patterns than the first. Wilson (1991, 80) notes that '[m]ore women were gainfully employed, more employed women were married, and more women worked in non-traditional jobs'. The real significance of the wartime expansion of opportunities was the effect it had on attitudes towards working women. Rowbotham (1997) identifies a new confidence in themselves as workers among women in Britain and North America. The war clearly showed that women were not only capable of working but also wanted to work. Wartime recruitment propaganda framed the issue of women working in terms of their civic duty. Governments and employers made clear to them that their efforts were intrinsic to the national war effort. It was therefore not surprising that women expected they would be treated as full national citizens at the end of the war.

As Timpson (2001, 16) recounts, this sense of empowerment did not go unnoticed by the federal government, which established a subcommittee of the Advisory Committee on Reconstruction to examine the effect of the transformation from wartime to peacetime on women. The report concluded that while the call to home and family would lead women out of the workforce, some women would prefer to remain employed and this desire should be respected and supported by entitlement to the same 'work and . . . remuneration, working conditions and opportunities for advancement' as men. However, this would not be the case: at the end of the war, women's employment dried up, and many were let go to open up jobs for the returning men. Timpson (2001, 16) notes,

> In the immediate post-war period, 80,000 women were laid off from the war industries in order to open up jobs for men who were returning to the civilian labour market in search of work. . . . Moreover, married women who had been employed by the federal government during the war found it difficult to maintain their posts when marriage bars were re-introduced and not completely removed until 1955.

An end to government-sponsored child care further limited the ability of married women to work, while popular culture also encouraged them to leave work and return to the home. Advertising, magazines, and new television programs extolled the virtues of the good wife and mother; now women's civic duty was to look after the boys in the home. Consequently, at the end of the war, the participation of women in the workforce seemed much as it was at the beginning of the war: those who did participate were young, unmarried, and concentrated in jobs considered to be 'women's work'.

It was not until the middle of the twentieth century that the number of women in paid employment began to climb significantly. According to Wilson's (1991, 86–7) study of historical statistics, Canadian census data show a gradual increase in female labour force participation 'from 14.4 per cent in 1901 to 29.3 per cent in 1961'. The wars represent time-limited blips in this increase. For example, one-quarter of Canadian women were employed in 1939, but by 1945 one-third were in paid employment (Timpson 2001, 13). This proportion fell substantially after the war, and it was not until 1961 that slightly more than one-quarter of Canadian women would once again be in paid employment (Wilson 1991, 83). When married women returned to the workforce in the 1960s, however, significant increases occurred.

The reason for the increase in the 1960s was the economic boom experienced by Western industrial economies at that time. Employers needed more employees, and the expanding service sector opened up more jobs for women. Although many married women worked because of need, there was also growth in the number of married women who worked to supplement the family income and to be able to buy the modern conveniences that were now available. Other changes made it easier for married women to enter the labour market—for example, lower birth rates lessened the burden of childcare. Once the immediate post-war baby boom ended, family size began to drop, and by the mid to late 1960s the boom generation was old enough for their mothers to be able to return to work. Technological advances, such as automatic washing machines, dryers, microwave and convection ovens, automobiles, supermarkets, and fast food, reduced the time required for housework, allowing more time for work outside the home. In addition, the expansion of the welfare state opened up jobs for women as the government looked for employees suited for the 'caring' professions.

Several first-wave women's organizations played a significant role in bringing women into professional work and organizing them once they were there. These organizations included the Canadian Teachers' Federation, formed in 1920 to organize women within the teaching profession; the Federation of Business and Professional Women (1930) which worked to support women in business; and the Canadian Federation of University Women, which had been active since 1919 in getting women admitted to universities and into both academic and professional programs.

Of course, women still had to balance work inside and outside the home. Women themselves as well as employers who needed more workers had to adapt to the time women had to spend in the home. One solution was part-time work. In 1953 Statistics Canada reported that 3.8 per cent of the labour force was employed in part-time work. By 1989 one in seven workers (14 per cent) was employed in part-time work, many of whom were women (Duffy and Pupo 1992, 44). In November 2009, 19 per cent of employed Canadians older than 15 were in part-time work. Of the part-time employees 25 years and older, women comprised 71 per cent and men 29 per cent (Statistics Canada 2009a). The concentration in part-time work means that while the number of women in paid employment rose, as did their wages, women's pay overall declined in relation to men's pay.

It was also during the 1960s that women emerged as a significant segment of the union movement. Historically, the relationship between women and unions was uncertain. Some unions would speak up on women's work concerns, while others were suspicious of and reluctant to support workers they saw as stealing men's jobs. Until the 1960s, the union movement was 'overwhelmingly male'—women comprising only 16.4 per cent of all union members—and tended to espouse the general societal norms around women's position in society (Luxton 2001, 68–9). The increasing number of women in work by the 1960s was combined with a new wave of unionization in the public sector. The growing militancy of public sector workers resulted in the expansion of the union movement into the state-funded public clerical, teaching, social service, and other sectors that employed large numbers of women. As Adamson, Briskin, and McPhail (1988, 77–8) point out, 'in the early 1970s women had become increasingly active in their trade union and in organizing. By the end of the twentieth century and into the twenty-first century the face of Canada's unions seems increasingly female. In 2004, 32 per cent of female employees belonged to a union, an increase that appears to offset the eight per cent decline in male union membership over the last forty years. By the mid-2000s, there was almost gender parity in Canadian union membership (Statistics Canada 2006, p. 112). The question of how to go about taking feminism into the union movement generated a debate among feminist and union activists: should that struggle involve non-unionized women as well as women already in trade unions?' The coalition of feminist and trade union organizations would continue to sort out its relationship and goals from the 1960s and 1970s to the present (for example, Rebick 2005, ch. 7).

The increase in the number of women in the workforce was becoming a political concern. In 1954 the federal government established a Women's Bureau within the Department of Labour to gather information regarding women's employment for government use in determining labour policy. However, it was the report of the Royal Commission on the Status of Women in Canada (1970) that would most comprehensively address the position of women in the Canadian economy. Among the four principles adopted by the royal commission, women's employment came first: '*women should be free to choose whether or not to take employment outside their homes.* The circumstances which impeded this free choice have been of specific interest to our inquiry. Where we have made recommendations to improve opportunities for women in the work world, our goal has not been to force married women to work for pay outside of the home but rather to eliminate the practical obstacles that prevent them from exercising this right' (RCSW 1970, xii; emphasis in original). In its list of recommendations, numbers five through to 68 directly address issues of women's employment equality and opportunity.

However, as discussed in previous chapters, the RCSW had its most significant influence in presenting an agenda for change to newly formed women's groups and anti-poverty organizations. As Wendy McKeen (2004, 44–5) observes, the demand was now for an ongoing discussion of national social policy, and groups such as 'Seekers of Security Welfare Rights, Winnipeg Welfare Rights Movement, Mothers on Social Allowance, the Unemployed Citizens' Welfare Improvement Council, and the Single Parent's Association along with the NAC and other women's groups established campaigns to address women's poverty and workplace discrimination.' The Trudeau government's positive response to the work of the commission created new opportunities for this coalition, particularly the women's groups within it. The government created agencies mandated to address the report's recommendations and the needs of Canadian women (see chapter 6).

However, by the 1980s, the shift in the government's focus towards rolling back the reach of government policy and the push for North American free trade and an integrated continental market significantly altered the opportunities for the women's movement. The mainstream movement, such as NAC, and the union-oriented movement, according to McKeen (2004, 74), shifted its focus 'away from traditional "women's issues" (e.g., daycare, abortion, affirmative action, and pay equity) to broader economic and labour issues such as free trade, privatization, deregulation, and trade policy'. There appeared to be a growing diffusion in the focus of activities around women and work, while at the same time the growing number of minority women's groups demanded that the interrelations of racism, sexism, and classism not only within work but in the unequal experiences of poverty be recognized and addressed.

While all this was occurring, the number of women joining the workforce continued to climb. Women aged 15 and over accounted for almost three quarters (72 per cent) of the rise in employment between 1975 and 1991. During that period, the total number of working women increased by 65 per cent, from 3.4 million to 5.6 million. By 2005, Canadian women had one of the highest labour force participation rates in the world (Marshall 2006, 7). In November 2009, 63 per cent of Canadian women were in the labour force accounting for 46 per cent of Canadian employees. Male employment had continued to fall to 73 per cent of Canada's male population and 53 per cent of the total workforce. Unemployment statistics were also harder on men in November 2009, with the male unemployment rate at 8.1 per cent of those still participating in the Canadian labour force against 6.2 per cent unemployment among women workers (Statistics Canada 2009a).[2] However, the picture is not as bright when one examines the nature of women's jobs: the work was more often than not part-time and in the service sector. However, women's employment did expand in administrative positions. In 1991, 40 per cent of those working in jobs categorized as administrative were women, up from 27 per cent in 1981. This rate of growth does need to be qualified in that it could be 'attributable to changes in occupational definitions, such as some clerical jobs being reclassified into the management/administrative category' (Zukewich Ghalem 1994, 143). Women were no longer 'secretaries'; they were 'personal assistants' and 'administrative assistants'. Women continued to be severely under-represented in manufacturing, construction, and materials handling jobs, 'ranging from 22 per cent in the primary industries to only 2 per cent in construction' (ibid. 144), although by 2001, they had doubled their participation in agricultural and manufacturing occupations (Cooke-Reynolds and Zukewich 2004). At the end of the first decade of the twenty-first century, 56 per cent of women were still employed in two occupational categories characterized as 'women's work': sales and services and clerical and administrative occupations (Statistics Canada 2007).

The Grounds of Economic Inequality

The double nature of women's work: One person, two shifts

As the participation of women in the public world of paid employment grew, it did not mean that they were excused from their duties in the private sphere. Many women work a 'double shift', one outside the home and a second in the home that includes domestic duties such as cooking, cleaning, and child care. The Statistics Canada General Social Survey of 1992, which included time use surveys, found that Canadians spent 25 billion hours on unpaid work, as much time as they spent on paid work (Jackson 2000, 89). Women performed most of this work, 78 per cent more time than men (1,482 hours compared to 831 hours per year). The bulk of this unpaid work (95 per cent) included such tasks as meal preparation, cleaning, clothing care, shopping, and providing transportation for family members. The remainder (5 per cent) included volunteer work and helping friends, neighbours, and relatives—again, work women often perform.

According to the 2006 census, between 1996 and 2006, the rate of women engaged in unpaid housework has remained fairly constant at 92.6 per cent. The share of men participating in unpaid housework did increase by 3.5 percentage points from 84.4 per cent in 1996 to 87.9 per cent in 2006. About 19.8 per cent of women spent 30 unpaid hours or more a week performing housework in 2006, down 4.8 per cent points from 24.6 per cent in 1996, a reflection, according to the 2006 census, of a decline in the number of adults in private households with children. The overall participation of women in unpaid child care activities fell between 1996 and 2006 from 42.3 per cent to 40.7 per cent. However, a smaller proportion of women were devoting long hours to unpaid housework than was the case 10 years earlier. At the same time, the proportion of men who spent any unpaid time caring for children rose from 77.1 per cent to 79.5 per cent but, like their female counterparts, they were putting in more time. 'Just over one-fifth (21.8 per cent) spent 30 hours or more each week in 2006 caring for children compared with only 16.9 per cent in 1996' (Statistics Canada 2009b). This double burden is more than just an issue of fairness; it also has significant consequences for women's health, their levels of political engagement, and the economics of the state. First, the need to balance work and domestic responsibilities results in stress. In the early 1980s, a group of American human resources specialists (Greenhaus and Beutill 1985, 78) found that work/family conflict is positively related to the number of hours worked per week, to the amount and frequency of overtime, and to the presence and irregularity of shift work. It was a finding that would not surprise women who work both inside and outside the home (and it probably would not surprise women who work entirely within the home either). These conflicts have an effect on a woman's mental health and make women 'tend to be more depressed and less satisfied' (Tiedge et al. 1990, 70). Such stress can have serious repercussions on the family and on work; it was considered enough of a social problem that Statistics Canada addressed it in a report on the Canadian Census and General Social Survey of the 1990s (Fast and Frederick 2000, 151–3).

In a report for the Vanier Institute for the Family reviewing numerous studies done on the work/family balance, Jacques Barrette (2009, 3–4) found,

> . . . work/family conflicts have progressively worsened in the last 10 years. The percentage of parents who have a hard time juggling work and family has steadily risen since 1996 and now sits between 46 per cent and 61 per cent. Some studies suggest that this situation will likely continue to deteriorate. These trends are cause for alarm. The research clearly shows that the worse the work/family conflict becomes, the weaker the outcomes on various physical and psychological health indicators among parents and their children. . . . Perhaps not surprisingly, more mothers claim that their work hinders them from performing their parental role.

Frederick and Fast (2001, 8) address the decline in satisfaction levels for both paid and unpaid work. The effort to juggle the two types of work and growing stress 'is a concern for employees and employers alike since it may lead to burnout, poor health, dissatisfaction with life at home or on the job, lower productivity and employee turnover'. The people who experienced the most time stress were, not surprisingly, working mothers.[3] 'Women generally tend to feel more time-stressed than men, regardless of length of workday or presence of children. . . . ' (Marshall 2006, 25). Again, this has consequences not only for employees but also for employers in terms of absenteeism and workforce turnover.

Second, the time-consuming unpaid work undertaken by women has serious consequences in terms of their ability to engage in activities in the public sphere outside of the workplace and the home. As we discussed in chapter 5, women are often too busy or too tired to become politically active. Some may find that working with small community groups close to home and with family-related organizations, such as parent-teacher associations, is reasonably easy to undertake; however, this volunteerism is not traditionally considered 'political'. As a result, women are considered to be less interested in political affairs and less willing to engage in them. The United Nations Development Programme (2000, 23) highlights the obstacles to political participation that women around the world face: 'women in particular play multiple roles. In most countries they are perceived as having "primary" responsibilities as wives and mothers for which they receive no overt remuneration. They may also enter the labour market, formal or informal, beyond the immediate household economy. A political career usually emerges as a second or third job.'

Third, work performed in the home is not recognized as productive, even though it would be difficult for the economy to function without it. As Marilyn Waring (1996, 50) makes clear, the work that women perform in the home is invisible because it does not directly produce profit. When the productive capacity of a state is measured, it includes 'all goods and services that actually enter the market'. For example, 'cooking, according to the UNSNA [United Nations System of National Accounts], is active labour when cooked food is sold and economically inactive labour when it is not'. Consequently, while a maid would be considered an active worker, a housewife would not. Money must change hands and be accounted for by the state, most often through the payment of taxes.[4]

The Value of a Stay-at-Home Mother

It can be difficult to assess the value of the unpaid work largely undertaken by women. Jackson (2000) suggests two approaches, 'opportunity cost' and 'replacement cost'. The opportunity cost approach bases the value on what the woman would earn if she was working for pay in the job for which she trained. However, this approach is problematic because, for example, a sales clerk who chooses to remain at home would give up a smaller wage than a university professor would. The replacement cost approach is based on the pay received by people who do similar work. This is further divided into a generalist assessment, using the wage rate for domestic employees, or the specialist approach, which breaks down the tasks and assesses each one according to the rates charged by specialists who do such work (for example, cooking with cooks, cleaning with cleaning services, child care with babysitting services). The problem is the approach's assumption that a woman performing these tasks in her home would be as efficient as a 'professional' uninterrupted by other tasks, which requires multi-tasking in housework.

Yet these approaches do give some sense of the value of the unpaid work. Using the generalist approach, Jackson (2000) calculated the value at $235 billion in 1992, equal to one-third of Canada's gross national product (GNP). Jackson's work included both men and women, with the understanding that women undertook two-thirds of the work.

We use the specialist approach to look at the value of the unpaid work provided by a stay-at-home mother. What might she expect to earn for the year if she lived in London, Ontario, in 2004?

Table 9.1 | The Value of a Stay-At-Home Mother

Service/Provider	Frequency	Average Market Rate	Annual Expense
Child care	50 hours/week	$221.50/week (for a preschool toilet-trained child)[5]	$11,075 (for 50 weeks)
Transportation/errands	5 round trips/week of approximately 8 km	$120/week[6]	$6,000 (for 50 weeks)
Domestic cleaning	1 cleaning/week	$150/week (3 hours @ $50/ hr)[7]	$7,500 (for 50 weeks)
Laundry	4 hours/week	$41.00/week @ $10.25/hr (Ontario minimum wage as of March 31, 2010)[8]	$2,050 (for 50 weeks)
Meal preparation, planning, cleanup	12 hours/week	$123/week @ $10.25/hr	$6,150 (for 50 weeks)
Grocery shopping	3 hours/week	$30.75/week @ $10.25/hr	$1,537.50 (for 50 weeks)
Financial/paying bills	1 hour/week	$10.25/week	$512.50 (for 50 weeks)
Miscellaneous	7 hours/week	$71.75/week	$3,587.50 (for 50 weeks)
		Total	$38,412.50 per annum

Based on table by Barbara Wylan Sefton (1998, 28–9)

This categorization of productive work is significant because national GDP (gross domestic product) and GNP (gross national product) figures and economic accounting influence the decisions made by lending institutions, international policy-makers, and governments. According to Waring (1996, 49), GDP and GNP figures are used to quantify 'areas of what are considered the national economy so that resource allocations can be made accordingly. Governments project public service investment and revenue requirements for the nation, and plan new construction, training and other programmes necessary to meet those needs, all by using their national accounts.' In this accounting system, there is no recognition that the unpaid work undertaken in the home is truly work, that women who work in the home are working, and that the work is necessary to support public productive work in the economy (see also Crittenden 2001).

As discussed in chapter 2, Marxist feminists have identified the value of this domestic work. They argue that while the public and private were separated in the culture, patriarchy fit like the hand in the glove of capitalism. Women could not be fully integrated into the economy of paid labour because capitalism was built on and supported by women's unpaid labour in the home. It was women who fed and clothed the labourers and physically reproduced new workers. The economic system could not survive without the unpaid work carried out in the home, and the lack of recognition given to this work meant that those who profit from the economic system also profit from the unpaid work. If we were to compensate women for their unpaid work in the home, which has been suggested in campaigns for a guaranteed annual income and for a true reflection of the productive capacity of a state, money would have to be found to cover close to one-third of the production of Canada (Jackson 2000).

The family wage: 'Women care for families, they don't pay for them'

The term 'living wage' is a bit of a misnomer. For most of the nineteenth and twentieth centuries, a living wage was thought of as a wage large enough to provide a living for a male family head and his dependants, including his wife. The reality through much of this period, however, was that employers did not pay a true 'living family wage', and the result was much working-class poverty and the continued participation of many women in the workforce. However, the assumption persisted that a woman's wage represented 'supplementary' income. As Lahey (1999, 231) argues, when women demanded equal pay, the result was a movement for '"the family wage", conceived as a way to meet women's demands for apparent wage equality while continuing to pay men more, not on the basis of their sex but on the grounds that they had a social obligation to support themselves as well as their wives and children on their earnings' (Lahey 1999, 231).

We may shake our heads at the quaintness of the notion of a family wage, and for the most part, as more women have entered the labour force and the economy has changed in the late twentieth–early twenty-first century causing labour market adaptation, it has become less significant. According to Katherine Marshall (2006) at Statistics Canada, the expanding role of women in the Canadian labour force has 'been the main impetus for eroding the cultural idea that men should be primarily responsible for paid work while women look after unpaid household and family duties'.

However, this does not mean that the continuing differentials in overall wages earned by men and women, and the reluctance to fully institute pay equity (particularly in light of the increasing number of woman-led single-parent families), have disappeared. Marshall (2006) goes on to argue that while there has been convergence in labour market roles and to some extent in private domestic roles this does not mean that wages and work-life stresses have improved for women. In fact, it would appear that the stress of achieving a 'family wage' and a reasonable work-life balance has worsened for both sexes.

Employers may be well over the idea that women's earnings are simply pin money for the family, but accepting that men's work schedules are increasingly affected by home responsibilities such as picking up children from daycare, staying home with a sick child, or taking parental leave, is relatively new. Changing workplace practices, such as on-site daycare and flexible work arrangements, as well as labour legislation such as parental, maternity, and compassionate care leave, confirm that 'WLB (work-life balance) has emerged as a critical public policy issue in Canada' (HRSDC 2005). The increasing number of dual-earner families and a heavier overall workload make balancing a job and home life that much more difficult (Marshall, 2006, 5).

Access to child care

According to Statistics Canada (Zhang 2009) if you are a woman with children you will earn less than a woman without. 'Age-earnings profiles of Canadian mothers and women without children show that women without children systematically earned more than women with children' (Zhang 2009, 6). On average the earnings of women with children were 12 per cent less than those of women without (ibid., 11). This situation, referred to as the 'family gap', 'child penalty', or 'motherhood earnings gap', has a great deal of significance not only for women, but for Canadian society generally. As Zhang (2009, 5) observes,

> . . . studying the earnings gap between women with and without children helps to better understand issues related to parents' decisions about family size. As in other developed countries, the fertility rate in Canada has declined and stayed below the replacement level for many years. One reason for the low fertility rate may be the high costs associated with childrearing and child care.

For working women, child care may be the most significant issue influencing access to employment. If you are a single mother of small children, you are less likely than a woman in a two-parent family to be employed. In the past, female lone parents with children under the age of 16 participated in the labour market to a greater extent than women with partners. In 1976, for example, female lone parents' participation rates were 10 per cent higher than those of women with partners. By 1983, however, the roles had reversed. Now it is much more common for women without partners not to participate in the labour market until their youngest child enters grade school. In 2004, 46 per cent of female lone parents whose youngest child was under age three were employed, as were 63 per cent of those whose youngest child was between three and five, and 75 per cent of those whose youngest child was between six and 15 (Statistics Canada 2006, 107). Women with partners are more involved in the paid labour market, even when their children are young. Their corresponding paid labour market participation rates were 65, 70, and 77 per cent in 2004. Female lone parents' relative lack of labour market participation speaks to the difficulties of balancing work and family responsibilities, particularly finding adequate and affordable child care on a single salary (White 2001b). In contrast, the number of two-parent families in which one parent stays home full-time has dropped from approximately one-half of families in 1976 to approximately one in five (22 per cent) in 1997, although it should be noted that the number of stay-at-home fathers has nearly doubled since 1976, from 41,000 to 77,000 (Statistics Canada 2000, 110). Of those parents who took a leave for a birth or adoptions between 2001 and 2006, approximately 23 per cent chose not to return to work. According to Statistics Canada (Beaupré and Cloutier 2006, 16),

[F]or a majority of parents who stayed at home, their decision was motivated by a desire to raise their child themselves (54 per cent). Many parents
also report staying at home due to a subsequent or intended pregnancy. . . .
[N]early 24 per cent of parents did not return to work for financial reasons,
with child care services being too expensive. . . . Professional reasons were
cited by 8 per cent of parents who were unable to return to their job, because
their employer had not offered the position they were seeking or they lost
their job.

Finding adequate child care is not just an issue for single mothers; it is an issue for
all mothers. According to Benoit (2000, 92), 'women are more likely to absent themselves from paid work during the early year(s) of a child's life, to exit from employment in
times of sickness of an older child or other dependants, to be the main care giver to children in the aftermath of separation and in general to organize their employment schedule
around the needs of others'. These absences can be confirmed statistically: of the women
who were out of the workforce for more than six months, 62 per cent said they did so
for family reasons (Fast and Du Pont 2000, 81). These absences were over and above
day-to-day absenteeism because of a child's needs, professional development days at
school, and ill or vacationing child care providers. Thus, as Drolet (2003, 20) found, 'in
1998, women with children spent less time working full-year, full-time (68 per cent of
their years of potential work experience) than women without children (87 per cent of
their years of potential work experience). At the same time, the average hourly wages of
mothers were 2 per cent less, overall, than those of women who did not have children.'
    While it can be argued that balancing work and family life and access to child care
as a key component of that balance is an issue for both parents, the presence of children has far more significance for women's absentee rates than for those of men. Using
data from the Statistics Canada Workplace and Employee Survey (WES) for 1999 and
2001, Zhang (2007, 17) found that 'women with young children took about two days
of unpaid absence more than women without young children'. While it was found that
the presence of young children in a family did not have much effect on the absenteeism of men, 'it does seem to increase the days of unpaid absence for women' (ibid.).
In 2005, a Statistics Canada Fact Sheet (Statistics Canada 2005c) on work absences attributed the rising trend in work absences to 'the aging workforce, the growing share of
women in the workforce, especially mothers with young children; high stress among
workers, and the increasing prevalence of generous sick and family-related leave at the
workplace'. In 1997, women in full-time employment with preschool children lost 4.2
days per year, while men lost an average of 1.8 days. It should be noted that by 2004,
the gap was closing, with women and men with young families losing a comparable
amount of time for family reasons (Statistics Canada 2005c). In addition, women were
more likely to choose part-time work because of child care. While a large number of
both men and women indicated their part-time status was a personal preference or
because of schooling, a much larger percentage of women (14.3 per cent) than men
(0.9 per cent) reported in 2004 that their reason for working part-time was to care for
children. When this is broken down by age, the numbers are even more telling: 33.7
per cent of women aged 25 to 44 listed child care as the primary reason for taking
part-time employment, compared to 32.6 per cent for other reasons, 18.6 per cent for
personal preference, and 6.7 per cent for schooling. For men aged 25 to 44, 3.2 per

cent listed child care as their reason for working part-time (Statistics Canada 2006, 26). (Part-time employment is further discussed later in this chapter; see McJobs, part 2: Part-time concentration.)

Why are women more likely to absent themselves for family reasons? Out of the many reasons, two appear most significant. First, in working couple arrangements it is the spouse with the lowest income who is most likely to take time off because the loss of income will be less. Given the continuing pay differentials between men and women, it is often the woman who has the lower income and therefore takes the time off. The idea that the lower-earning spouse has greater responsibility for child care is also reflected in tax policy in that deductions for child care are claimed by the lower-income earner. The message is that the lower income is a secondary income and that it is the employment situation of the lower-income earner that necessitates the child care rather than that of the primary 'family wage' earner (Skrypnek and Fast 1996, 803). Zhang (2007, 17) makes a similar observation in looking at sick-day use: 'women generally take unpaid absences for childcare purposes and couples may attempt to minimize the costs of childcaring since women's wage rates are generally lower than that of men's'.

The second reason that women absent themselves from the labour market more frequently than men is culturally based. Societal expectations that women are the family caregivers create a great deal of tension for working mothers. Society continues to be ambivalent about mothers working, particularly when the children are of preschool age. In fact, public opinion on gender roles and the 'correct' familial structure remains somewhat inconsistent. An Angus Reid Group (1999) poll of 2,499 Canadians found that 57 per cent agreed (22 per cent strongly and 35 per cent somewhat) that 'the state of the family is a national crisis and the government must take steps to alleviate that crisis', and a large majority (78 per cent: 32 per cent strongly and 46 per cent somewhat) agreed that 'parents today are not strict enough with their children'. Many were not supportive of government 'doing everything possible to encourage one parent to stay home' (23 per cent not supportive and 17 per cent not very supportive at all). Instead, a large majority (73 per cent: 31 per cent strongly and 42 per cent somewhat) agreed that 'both the man and the woman should contribute to the household income', and a majority (20 per cent strongly and 36 per cent somewhat) agreed that 'having a job is the best way for a woman to be an independent person'. Yet, a majority (55 per cent: 21 per cent strongly and 34 per cent somewhat) also agreed that 'a pre-school child is likely to suffer if both parents are employed'. At the same time, a strong majority (69 per cent: 26 per cent strongly and 43 per cent somewhat) agreed that 'an employed mother can establish just as warm and secure a relationship with her children as a mother who does not work for pay', and two-thirds (18 per cent strongly and 50 per cent somewhat) agreed that 'day care is good for children'. Thus, Canadian public opinion and policy prescriptions regarding the family reflect profound ambivalence. This ambivalence has been bolstered by the backlash of the 1980s and 1990s, which blamed a wide range of social problems, such as youth delinquency and falling educational achievement, on women who chose to go to work (see chapter 7).

Griffen (2002, 7) points to a very serious flaw in assumptions that working women would leave paid employment if changes were made to the tax policy:

There are more than 2 million mothers with children under the age of six and more than 60 per cent of them are in the paid labour force. . . . If you combine the loss of tax revenue with the amount of money needed to actually provide enough in tax incentives so that they could all afford to stay home, a rough calculation would have the remaining taxpayers coughing up an additional $37.5 billion annually.

While such particularly glaring faults of logic can be pointed out, the problem remains that norms about stay-at-home mothers continue to have a hold in Canadian society and affect what kind of public policies governments adopt.

McJobs, part 1: The pink collar ghetto

In 2006, 67 per cent of employed women were working in teaching, nursing, or a related health occupation, in clerical or administrative jobs, or in sales or service positions (Statistics Canada 2008, 376). When current employment patterns are broken down by occupation, we find that 56 per cent of Canadian women are employed in two occupational categories, sales and service and clerical and administration.

> Just over 2.3 million women were employed in sales and service occupations in 2007, accounting for 29.3 per cent of all working women over the age of 15. About one-third of these women worked as retail salespeople, sales clerks, cashiers or retail supervisors. An additional 2.2 million women (27 per cent) worked in business, finance and administrative occupations. A smaller but still significant number of women also worked in occupations related to social science, education, government service, and religion (985,000 or 12.3 per cent of women), and there were also 813,000 (10.2 per cent) employed in health occupations. Overall, relatively few women were found in occupations in a primary industry (only 115,000 in farming, forestry, mining, or fishing) or in trades, transport, and equipment operation (173,000) in 2007 (Statistics Canada 2007, 52).

This area of the economy and labour market is considered 'women's work': the 'pink collar ghetto'. Historically, when women moved from the farm, they were drawn into occupations that fit with the duties they undertook in the home. Phillips and Phillips (1983, 9) note that '[r]ather than cooking and baking and preserving for their families, women were working in biscuit factories. . . . Instead of sewing their children's clothing, women bought clothing from the companies they worked for.' It was not a huge jump to move from teaching children in the home to teaching a class or from tending sick family members to nursing on a ward. In the case of teaching and nursing, additional training was necessary, but the fundamental skill was the ability to nurture. These skills, along with corresponding interpersonal skills, would also be sought after in sales and clerical work.

Benoit (2000, 11) makes a distinction between male and female employment as hard (hierarchical and power-based) jobs and soft (emotional and nurturing) jobs:

> [S]oft (emotional) service jobs (such as flight attendants) tend to be assigned to women, while men frequently are appointed service jobs located at the heel of capitalism; 'male' jobs (e.g., bill collectors) are based on the 'hard'

approach, involving duties such as deflating customers' egos and causing them to feel guilt or fear to pay their outstanding debts.

It is assumed that women's so-called natural and socialized tendencies to nurture make them ideal for soft jobs such as sales clerk and secretary. Concomitantly, because of their hard masculine requirements, it is assumed that male jobs should be accorded higher prestige and hence higher wages.

To see how this distinction characterizes various occupations, we can examine the transformation of the secretarial position during the twentieth century. In the nineteenth century, secretarial work was undertaken by men, bright young business apprentices who kept accounts, correspondence, and records. For example, in Charles Dickens's classic, *A Christmas Carol*, Bob Cratchit is secretary to Ebenezer Scrooge. While the story hinges on the poor treatment of Bob Cratchit, secretarial work at the time was a well-respected middle-class profession that afforded opportunity to advance into a business position. Indeed, during Scrooge's visit with the Ghost of Christmas Past, we see how he himself got his start as a secretary to Mr Fezziwig.

As the twentieth century progressed, both business and state bureaucracies expanded and, with the technological innovations that produced the typewriter, photocopiers, and calculators, secretarial work became more menial and less reliant on handwriting and mathematical skills. Women were seen as an obvious group to draw on to meet the expanding need for typists and other office support staff. As a result, secretaries were no longer considered junior business partners or apprentices; they were more like domestic servants or wives at work, undertaking repetitive tasks such as typing, organizing the boss's day, taking his calls, and bringing him his coffee. As the secretarial field became dominated by women, its prestige collapsed, and few men would apply for such positions.[9] With further technological change, particularly the introduction of computers, the secretarial position is once again changing and in some cases disappearing. As the boss becomes adept at composing his own letters on the computer, sending e-mail, and keeping track of his appointments on pocket computers such as the iPad or Blackberry Playbook, his need for a stenographer diminishes, and his secretary becomes an administrative assistant or has been let go.[10]

In an environment of occupational segregation that constructs the pink collar ghetto as a sort of public domestic service, not only is women's work gendered as nurturing, it is also sexualized. This sexualization is implicit in assumptions about the way women should dress at work, either in formal or informal uniforms. In the restaurant industry, the most egregious case of a required sexualized appearance on the job is Hooters. The name quite obviously suggests that the criteria for employment are a good push-up bra and a willingness to wear a tight-fitting T-shirt. More subtle forms of sexualization can be found in bars where young women's uniforms include short skirts or in offices where receptionists are expected to look both appropriately 'professional' and 'inviting'. One has to ask whether the serving of drinks, the answering of phones, and the greeting of people require a specific dress code. It does—if the provider of the service is expected to project a sense of caring servitude, including the possibility of sexual service.

During the 1960s and 1970s, flight attendants were particularly beset by this problem. Their dress code required them to be highly made up and to wear tight skirts and high-heeled shoes. (Can one imagine less appropriate footwear for evacuating an airplane?) Along with the uniform came a host of myths around the work of airline 'host-esses', expressed in phrases such as 'coffee, tea, or me?', 'the mile-high club', and 'fly me'.

Without belabouring the uniform issue, our point is that occupational segregation, along with emphasis on the nurturing nature of women, tends to focus attention on the sexual nature of women. There is little separation of the sexualized female body from the body that is the female employee. Such sexualization can easily lead to workplace sexual harassment. And, while it does not explain all workplace harassment, which at its root is based on the unequal power relations between employer and employee, it does help to explain the long-lasting societal and political acceptance of workplace harassment. It has taken the concerted effort of women's groups and women's sections of unions, and many years of lobbying and action through the courts, to have the issue of workplace sexual harassment addressed.

Legislating and Litigating Sexual Harassment

Workplace-based sexual harassment is considered a discriminatory practice under the federal Canadian Human Rights Act (since 1983; see MacIvor 1996, 385) as well as under provincial and territorial human rights acts. Sexual harassment is considered an issue of equal employment opportunity that prevents individuals from working and living without being hindered by discriminatory practices (Department of Justice Canada 2004b). Sexual harassment is also covered under the Canada Labour Code and provincial and territorial labour codes. Division 15.1 part 247.1 of the Canada Labour Code, for example, which covers all persons who perform a function or duty on behalf of the government of Canada, as well as federally regulated businesses such as banks and telecommunications companies, defines sexual harassment as 'any conduct, comment, gesture or contact of a sexual nature: (a) that is likely to cause offence or humiliation to any employee; or (b) that might, on reasonable grounds, be perceived by that employee as placing a condition of a sexual nature on employment or on any opportunity for training or promotion' (Department of Justice Canada 2004a).

Courts and human rights commissions in Canada have tended to be quite sensitive to at least the principle that women face certain problems on the job that men tend not to. Employers, however, have been quite resistant to the concept of sexual harassment and especially that they are responsible for creating a workplace free of harassment. Employers' arguments tended to fall along the lines that any sexual relationship between employees is a private manner, not an employment matter; that sexual relations were undertaken voluntarily by women or at least were not unwelcome; and that even if adverse employment decisions resulted from such relationships, it was not because of the sex of the victims but because of individuals' refusal to accede to sexual demands.

The landmark Supreme Court of Canada decision on sexual harassment was *Janzen v. Platy Enterprises Ltd.*, 1989.[11] This case marks the Court's definitive recognition of sexual harassment as a form of sex discrimination, following a number of human rights tribunal and lower court rulings. The Court affirmed a broad definition of sexual harassment as 'unwelcome conduct of a sexual nature that detrimentally affects the work environment or leads to adverse job-related consequences for the victims of the harassment' and affirmed that sexual harassment involves an abuse of power.

This definition and approach to sexual harassment differs from trends in US courts, where the law tends to divide harassment rigidly into two categories: the first is known as quid pro quo harassment and refers to 'an exchange of sexual favors for job advantages' (Stetson 1997, 328, n. 8). Such sexual advances are connected to rewards or punishments for the employee (such as a university professor offering a student an 'A for a lay'). While common in the past, such overt forms of harassment tend to be less frequent, or at least less overt, in the workplace today. The second form of harassment is known as hostile or poisoned environment harassment, which refers to 'more generalized unwelcome sexual advances' (Stetson 1997, 328, n. 8) that an employee is required to endure as a condition of work.

The Canadian Supreme Court's definition encompasses both these forms of harassment. Further, the Court noted that not all women present in the workplace had to be subject to the same treatment in order to demonstrate that sexual harassment occurred.

Litigation following *Janzen v. Platy* has been centred on such issues as what 'unwelcome conduct' actually means, how one must demonstrate adverse consequences, who is responsible for the behaviour, and what remedies should be available to victims of sexual harassment. It is these issues that continue to bedevil women's organizations such as LEAF and make this area of law particularly challenging for women's equality.

McJobs, part 2: Part-time concentration

As mentioned above, women are much more likely to work part-time than men are, and many do so because of family responsibilities. According to the Statistics Canada Labour Force Survey of November 2009, of the 2,095,400 Canadians over the age of 24 employed part-time, 1,494,000, or about 71 per cent, were women. The number of men 25 years or older working part-time was recorded as 601,300 (Statistics Canada 2009a, 3). When asked why they worked part-time, nearly 34 per cent of the women aged 25 to 44 year responded that it was because of childcare responsibilities, compared to 3.2 per cent per cent of men (Statistics Canada 2006, 109). Vosko, Zukewich, and Cranford (2003, 16) refer to part-time work along with other alternative work arrangements as 'non-standard employment' or 'precarious work'. The term non-standard employment was adopted to respond to the increase in work that does not fit within the model of traditional stable full-time work, in which an employee 'has one employer, works full year, full time on the employer's premises, enjoys extensive statutory benefits and entitlements, and expects to be employed indefinitely' (ibid.). It includes not only part-time work but also temporary work ('temping'), contract and seasonal work, multiple job holding, and self-employment as a single individual (without employees). Job security (really insecurity) is central to the characterization of non-standard employment and is linked to the growing casualization of work and the end of social expectations that an employee will remain with the same employer from the end of schooling to retirement.

The rise of non-standard employment in the early 1990s was fuelled by increases in self-employment and full-time and part-time temporary work, positions that were much more likely to be filled by women. For example, in 2006, 11 per cent (nearly 900,000) of employed women in Canada were self employed (Statistics Canada 2008,

376). As Vosko, Zukewich, and Cranford (2003, 18) found, 'women made up the majority of casual temporary employees, most of whom work part time while men dominated seasonal forms of temporary paid work, most of which is full time. Women are also more likely to take employment with a pre-determined end date.' Whether casualization occurred because of the influx of women into the workforce or the influx of women into the workforce was a response to the casualization of work is a chicken-and-egg argument. However, as Vosko, Zukewich, and Cranford (2003) argue, when we adopt a gender analysis of the labour market, it becomes clear that many workers, predominantly women, are not employed 40 hours a week for 50 weeks of the year. Employers like part-timers because for the most part, they do not have to pay them as much as full-timers and they are not required to provide benefits.

As a result, women are generally in a much more vulnerable position as employees, with less job security, fewer benefits, and lower wages overall. When we look at minimum wages in Canada, it is women who are most likely to be receiving the minimum wage (Sussman and Tabi 2004, 7). The record in other types of non-standard employment is not much better. Vosko, Zukewich, and Cranford (2003, 18) point out that 'the wage growth for temporary work has not kept up with that for permanent work.' Furthermore, 'the "solo" self-employed generally work fewer hours and earn less money than those who employ others' (Cooke-Reynolds and Zukewich 2004, 17).

A great deal of occupational segregation by gender also occurs in non-standard work. Men are much more likely to be employed in seasonal full-time work (landscaping, road maintenance, and some building trades). While both men and women are self-employed in business services, the largest proportion of women self-employed employers work in 'consumer services . . . such as laundry, hair care and esthetic services' (Vosko, Zukewich, Cranford 2003, 23). Fewer hours and segregation into service industries have very real consequences since it is much harder to attain the number of hours required for employment insurance benefits, including maternity and parental leave benefits, and it is difficult to achieve full benefits once workers reach retirement age.

Occupational segregation and glass ceilings

Segregation does not occur solely between occupations; it also characterizes the position of women in the work hierarchies within occupations. Pat Armstrong (2000, 188) gives this illustration of the division of men and women in the highest and lowest levels of work:

> [I]f we look at the ten lowest and ten highest paid occupations, women account for only 20 per cent of those in the ten highest paid occupations, but made up over 70 per cent of those in the ten lowest paid occupations. While nearly 5 per cent of employed males were in the ten highest paid occupations, this is the case for just under 2 per cent of employed women.

When we compare these statistics to the fact that in the second half of the twentieth century, women's educational achievement had caught up to and in some cases surpassed that of men, we have to ask why women remain concentrated on the lowest career rungs. In the early twenty-first century women made up the majority of undergraduate students and numbered close to 50 per cent of students in many master's programs. In November 2009, women made up 56 per cent of the undergraduate body at the University of Western Ontario and 55 per cent of the Master's Degree students (University of Western Ontario 2009a). Generally, the higher a woman's level of education achievement the higher her wages will be (in 2003, an average of $53,400 for those with university degrees), but the amount continues to fall below that of her male counterparts. 'In fact, with the exception of the relatively small group of those with only some postsecondary education, the earnings of women employed on a full-time, full-year basis in 2003 were only about 70 per cent of those of their male colleagues at all levels of education' (Statistics Canada 2006, 139).

Why do the educational investments women make not pay off as they do for men? One reason is educational segregation. Female students tend to gravitate towards arts and social science programs at university, rather than science and engineering. Within the social sciences, women are much more likely to be found in psychology, sociology, administration and commercial studies, and history, than they are in political science, economics, and business. Take, for example, the University of Western Ontario, where in the 2008–09 year, women made up 56 per cent of the undergraduate body, outnumbering male students 11,271 to 8,785. However, when the numbers are broken down, we see a pronounced gap in some faculties: women made up 73 per cent of Western's arts undergraduates, 73 per cent in the education program, 74 per cent in health sciences, 62 per cent in music, and 72 per cent in information and media studies. Men constituted 60 per cent of students in the business faculty and 80 per cent in engineering. The faculties with the most even gender balance were law, medicine, natural sciences, and social sciences. The only department that had seen a significant change in its gender balance from 2003, was dentistry where women accounted for 52 per cent of the students, up from 44 per cent (University of Western Ontario 2009a).[12]

As with political life, within the academy there is an effect of 'the higher, the fewer'. At the University of Western Ontario women make up 55 per cent of the Master's degree enrolments, but at the PhD level the balance shifts to 42 per cent women to 58 per cent male (ibid.). At the professional level, women account for only 30 per cent of the University of Western Ontario's full-time faculty. In only one faculty were there more women than men—health sciences (62 per cent women)—and only the education faculty approached gender parity, with 48 per cent women and 52 per cent men (University of Western Ontario 2009b).

Even for graduates of faculties with a gender balance, a gendering of occupations occurs post-graduation. In medicine, for example, women tend to be drawn into more 'female' and 'caring' fields such as psychiatry, pediatrics, and family medicine. Men are more concentrated in specialist fields such as orthopedic surgery and high-technology medicine (Quadrio 2000). In the legal profession, women are more likely to work for the state than for private firms. Within private practice, they are more likely to be salaried than partners and to focus on areas such as family and real estate law (ibid.).

One explanation for the under-representation of women in certain segments and levels of the medical and legal professions is that the educational requirements for further specialization conflict with women's domestic and family responsibilities, particularly since the need for additional education generally occurs when women are most likely to start families. This results in a vicious circle: when women leave their profession to start and raise families, it tends to reinforce assumptions that the promotion of women is a bad investment because at some point they will resign as a result of family and marital responsibilities.

. While women have increased their presence in many professions, they continue to find obstacles to advancement beyond a certain level in corporate and administrative hierarchies because of educational and occupational segregation. The barrier they encounter in trying to break into the top echelons of their occupations is referred to as the 'glass ceiling', an invisible form of job discrimination that prevents the promotion of large numbers of women to higher-paying and more prestigious jobs traditionally held by men. The occasional token woman does achieve advancement, but more widespread promotion does not occur, resulting in a continued under-representation of women in the higher levels of business, bureaucratic, and political structures. The process is similar to the one discussed earlier regarding the under-representation of women in political leadership roles: it is a form of gate-keeping by which women are selectively excluded from positions of power. As a result, the members of an advantaged group continue to establish and maintain a virtual monopoly over power and elite positions.

Under-representation perpetuates itself. One reason for this is that the availability of good female role models affects the way junior women starting their careers interpret their work and opportunities. In studying women in the legal profession, Robin Ely (cited in Murrell 2001) found that junior women in firms that are well sex-integrated would view female senior partners as good role models. In male-dominated firms, junior women were likely to view the few senior women as owning their positions for reasons other than merit or to believe that they had rejected their femininity in favour of more masculine attributes. In addition, the junior women in these firms had much more pessimistic views about their chances for promotion because of their gender.

Explaining Gender Roles and the Wage Gap: It's Not Rocket Science, It's Social Science

Growing convergence: gender work roles

As we discussed earlier, Canadian women have one of the highest labour force participation rates in the word and, as more and more women have entered into employment, the gender roles have tended to converge. 'While the difference in labour force participation rates for men and women aged 25 to 54 was 24 percentage points in 1986 (94 per cent for men versus 70 per cent for women), in 2005 it stood at 10 points (91 per cent versus 81 per cent)' (Marshall 2006, 7). Since women are as likely to be in paid employment as are men, the corresponding differences in work roles and the division of labour are starting to disappear.

> Since 1986, of the total time spent on paid and unpaid work, women aged 25 to 54 have proportionally increased their average daily time at a job (4.4 hours of 8.8 in 2005), while men have increased their time on housework (1.4 of 8.8 hours in 2005). As women's job attachment has increased, so too has men's involvement in housework and childcare. Women's increasing hours in paid labour (and thus income), combined with 'normative changes in the direction of equality and sharing' (Beaujot 2006, 24) is likely to further reduce gender differences in the division of labour in the future (Marshall 2006, 16).

Can this be attributed to the movement of women into the labour force? The short answer is yes, but the underlying impetus brings us back to the idea of the 'family wage'. As we discussed earlier, traditionally a living wage was thought of as a wage large enough to provide a living for a male family head and his dependants, including his wife. We could therefore conceive of a family wage as a household income that would allow a family to live 'comfortably' in the context of their times. This seems rather vague, but because it is so dependent on contextual values there is not a great deal of work establishing a specific 'family wage'. Rather the focus is on the determination of average incomes, household incomes, low income cut-offs, poverty rates, etc. However, one thing that appears abundantly clear in today's context is that, for most Canadians to make a 'family wage', both adults in a household must work outside the home.

This is borne out in analysis of the Canadians' income and employment patterns. As early as 1992, the National Action Committee on the Status of Women (cited in Brodie 1995, 20) identified that family incomes were dropping and more hours at work were required to support the household. In 2006, 'the proportion of dual-earners among husband-and-wife families with children under 16 at home rose from 36 per cent in 1976, to 58 per cent in 1992, to 69 per cent in 2005' (Marshall 2006, 12). In 2005, 69 per cent of Canadian families reported as dual-earners while only 21 per cent were single-earner families (ibid.). (Of those single-earner families, 89 per cent had stay-at-home moms, while 11 per cent had stay-at-home dads, up from 9 per cent in 1992). There were no longer significant differences in the rates of employment between married and unmarried women. The days of the stay-at-home wife appeared to have ended.

The changing nature of the Canadian economy also helps explain some of the convergence between men and women that has emerged in the Canadian labour market. Today's economy in Canada is characterized as being much more oriented towards resource-based and service-based industries than it is to manufacturing industries. Traditionally, economic development in Canada has tended to focus more on the development and export of resources, with some manufacturing development and supporting service-based development, but by the end of the twentieth and the beginning of the twenty-first centuries the pattern has clearly been one of decline in manufacturing jobs and growth in service-industry jobs. We need only look at the Labour Force statistics (Statistics Canada 2009a, 2) for an illustration of this:

> [T]he Service sector showed substantial employment gains (+73,000) in November, with the largest increase in education (+38,000) and small gains in the number of other industries. Employment has little changed in the goods-producing sector in November. Between October 2008 and March 2009 employment fell in almost all industries, especially manufacturing and construction. Since March 2009, employment has slowed its decline in manufacturing, while it has picked up in construction and in a number of service industries.

While this really is a snapshot of the Canadian labour market at a specific time—a period in which the economy was said to be starting its climb out of the recessionary period of 2008–09—it is also characteristic of the twenty-first century western industrial economy based on the flexible-specialization of predominantly financial, management, knowledge, and service industries. It is an economy in which the growth in employment is ironically in those areas generally associated with women's part-time and service work. It is not surprising, then, to see that the unemployment rates recorded in the November 2009 Labour Force Report (Statistics Canada 2009a, 3) found men more likely to be unemployed than women. Men had an unemployment rate of 8.1 per cent (participating in the labour force either by actively looking for work or collecting EI), compared to 6.2 per cent for women. (Youth between 15 and 24 were the hardest hit, with 15.4 per cent listed as unemployed.)

Observers such as Janine Brodie (1995, 76) argue that this is indicative of the feminization of the work force, as 'stable full-time, high paying jobs are rapidly replaced by part time—and precarious—employment, the kind of work that marked the gendered division of labour and political power in the post war years.' It also points to further convergence of gender roles in the labour market, as more and more men are displaced from high-paying, full-year, full-time manufacturing jobs into full-time and part-time service jobs (most often without union support). As Elizabeth Wilson (1988) and Donna Haraway (1991) (cited in Brodie 1995, 76) point out, it is here that the labour interests of women and men converge over commonly shared low pay and long hours.

Marshall (2006, 12), in her research on role convergence, points to the sharing of long work hours both outside and inside the home.

> Not only has the number of dual-earners increased since 1992, so too has the average daily amount of time these couples spend on paid work and housework combined (up to 0.5 hours per day, a result of 0.7 hours more paid work but 0.2 hours less housework). The net change within couples was due to an increase in husbands' paid work and housework (0.3 hours and 0.1 hours respectively), and an increase in wives' paid work and decrease in housework (0.4 hours and -0.2 hours respectively).[13]

This does not appear to be a particularly satisfactory situation for any member of the family and, as we saw earlier in this chapter, there is a growing body of research that outlines the physical and psychological effects of the work-life balance. However, this is only a convergence in roles; it is not parity. While domestic work rates have risen for men, they have risen much more slowly than women's workplace participation. 'In both 1992 and 2005, each partner in dual-earner couples did 50 per cent of the combined paid work and housework each day. However, wives did 45 per cent of total paid work but 65 per cent of housework in 1992. By 2005, these proportions stood at 46 per cent and 62 per cent' (Marshall 2006, 12).

It also asks us to address some fundamental issues about our economic system, our understanding of what is a family, our expectations of individual and family care, and what we mean by equality: Do we mean economic equality or something greater? Are we as citizens focused on our economic needs or on our social needs? How do we manage the work-life balance in a way that lets us live comfortably and fully not only as workers but as citizens? Some of these questions we will address in the next chapter, others will have to be worked out as the changes in economy and our social constructions of family become clearer. However, in this convergence between gender roles in work we see these as not only significant questions for women, but also for men.

Continuing Divergence: The Wage Gap

Although we can point to convergence in gender work roles, there continues to be persistent difference in the average wage of men and women. Canadian women overall continue to make less money than Canadian men do. In 1976 women made 59 per cent as much as men, and by the turn of the century, women employed full time earned just 72 per cent as much (Cooke-Reynolds and Zukewich 2004, 27). However, the percentage does change depending how one looks at the differences. Marie Drolet (2008), looking at gender wage differentials in three different ways, found that in 2008 among all workers, women earned 64.7 cents for every dollar earned by men, among all full-time, full-year workers it was 71.9 cents, and based on hourly wage rates for a specific job it was 83 cents.

Drolet's argument is that, on the one hand, measurement matters because gender wage inequality is complex and changes in the role of women in the labour market have resulted in improvements and a narrowing of the gap. However, on the other hand, as she found in 2001 (2001, 10), when wage differentials are measured and the numbers change, gender wage differences are 'remarkably persistent' and very slow to change.

Something other than pure cost-benefit rationalization must be at work. Since women make substantially less on average, it actually makes good economic sense to hire only women because an employer would get the same work done at less cost. Then, as more women are hired, the pressure to increase their wages should grow as employers compete for an increasingly scarce female workforce. However, this is not the case.

The lack of wage equalization involves complex factors. In 2001, Drolet argued that one of the differences between men and women that affects their earnings is work experience. As a group, women are far more likely to withdraw from the labour market during their working lifetimes. Career interruptions have repercussions for earnings because they affect job seniority and promotion, which directly relate to the size of one's paycheque. The longer one is absent from the workforce, the more likely that one's job skills will become outdated; therefore, a person returning to work will require retraining or else they may be unable to return to the same job—which often means starting again at the bottom of the pay scale. Women, who are most likely to experience planned periods of work withdrawal, are more likely to seek and accept employment in low-wage jobs and 'precarious employment' because it is often easier to exit and re-enter such jobs.

Finally, job training and the on-the-job learning experience generally take place during early career-building and as such often coincide with the time when women start building families. Drolet (2001, 7) therefore argues that 'the timing of labour force withdrawals may have important long-term implications for future earning patterns'.

The field of education chosen and ensuing employment segregation also partly explain the gender wage gap. Because wages among occupations differ and some occupations are more predominantly male or female, it is not surprising that occupational segregation is related to the male-female wage gap. As Drolet (2001, 9) points out, '[a]bout 15 per cent can be explained because men are more likely to graduate from engineering and applied sciences programs. . . . However, the prevalence of women graduating from health science and education programs . . . reduces the explained component by 5 per cent to 9 per cent.'

Thus, while Drolet's (2001, 9–10) primary concern is establishing an appropriate method to account for the gap between men and women's wages,[14] she does find that 'a substantial portion of the wage gap cannot be explained':

Differences between men and women in the labour market may reflect genu- ine differences in preferences, pre-labour market experiences, expectations, or opportunities. It is therefore difficult to distinguish between choice-based decision and differential treatment based on sex. . . . Employers are constantly making decisions regarding hiring and promotion and may use sex to predict future work commitment. Some firms may hesitate to hire women because women have, on average, more career interruptions and more absences for family reasons than men.

In other words, the difference between men's and women's earnings may only be explained when we factor in more systemic elements, such as social norms and cul- tural understandings regarding the differences between men and women.

Changes in the Canadian labour market have ameliorated some of the factors that are attributed to creating the wage gap. As Drolet argued in 2008, 'it's not my mother's labour market'. In 2008, when factors such as experience, education, and occupational concentration were controlled for, women made 93 cents for every male dollar (ibid.). The gap has narrowed, the result of improvements in real hourly wages, which have increased 12.6 per cent for women compared to 2.2 per cent for men; the more stable employment rates experienced by women; increased job stability for women with little gender difference found in short-term retention rates; absenteeism and quit rates (see also Zhang 2007); improved education, which has translated into higher wages and shifts into higher-paying occupations; and, finally the decline in the wages of men re- sulting from de-unionization and the economic shift away from high-paying manufac- turing/productive industries (Drolet 2008). There is also the factor of generational and cultural change as younger employers are more accepting of women in the workforce and less likely to discriminate on the basis of gender, which has resulted in a decline in differential treatment by employers.

It is good news, but as we found in examining the convergence in gender work roles, we cannot be too sanguine about the gains made by women. At the end of the day, women still fall behind men and a wage gap continues to persist. Overall women still make less.

This has ramifications for the state of women's lives in Canada. Canadian women are more likely to be poor than are Canadian men. In 2003, women accounted for 53 per cent of all Canadians on low incomes. That meant that 12 per cent of Canadian women lived in low-income situations, compared to 11 per cent of the male popu- lation (Statistics Canada 2006, 143). Women heading single-parent families, senior women, and visible minority women were even more likely to be poor. While there had been a drop in low-income rates in senior women (9 per cent in 2003 compared to over 25 per cent in the 1980s), the rates were twice that of senior men (ibid. 143). Thirty-eight per cent of Canada's female-headed single-parent families fell below the low-income cut-off (ibid. 144).[15] In 2001, 14 per cent of the total female population of Canada identified themselves as a visible minority, a 25 per cent increase from 1996 (Statistics Canada 2006, 24). With variations among the various minority groups, visible minority women are nearly twice as likely as non-visible minority women to have low incomes. In 2000, 29 per cent of visible minority women fell below the low-income cut-off, double the number of non-visible minority women but about the same rate as visible minority men (28 per cent) (Statistics Canada 2006, 254). Visible minority women are more likely to experience unemployment and more likely to experience workplace discrimination (ibid. 246 and 254).

Aboriginal women in Canada tend to suffer even more from unemployment and lower incomes, as well as lower life expectancy, greater health problems, and domestic violence (Statistics Canada 2006). In 2001, Aboriginal women's unemployment rate (17 per cent) was twice that for non-Aboriginal women, although the rate was lower than that of Aboriginal men. Further to this, when employed, Aboriginal women tend to be heavily concentrated in low-paying occupations and earning among the lowest incomes in Canada. In 2001, the median income was $12,300 (falling to $11,000 for those living on reserves), about $5000 less than the median for non-Aboriginal women. As a result, 36 per cent of all Aboriginal females lived in households with incomes that fell below the low-income cut-off for 2001 (Statistics Canada 2006, 199–200).

As a result of all these disparities and the state's effort or lack of effort to alleviate them, women are significantly affected by public policy choices regarding employment equity, employment access, employment benefits, child care, and welfare provision. In the next chapter, we examine these public policy choices and discuss what federal and provincial governments have done to address issues of employment and income equality.

Questions for Critical Thought

1. Work and family conflicts have progressively worsened in the last 10 years (Barette 2009). How can public-private workloads be made fairer? How do we manage the work-life balance in a way that lets both women and men live comfortably and fully not only as workers but as citizens?

2. In the fight for labour equality, should women work with the state, with unions, or by themselves?

3. Much of the productive work in our society is invisible. Is it necessary to change what we consider to be and how we measure economic productivity? Should we go further and measure well-being rather than productivity (i.e., Gross National Well-being rather than Gross National Product)?

4. Does the changing nature of industrial economies in the early twenty-first century advantage women? Is the narrowing of the wage gap between men and women a sign of women's progress or of increasing shared instability in employment and economic well-being?

CHAPTER 10

Challenging Market Rules and Balancing Work and Family Life

From a social standpoint, women deserve equal treatment in the labour market. From a legal standpoint, it is important that women achieve a level of economic equality that reflects the equality granted through the constitution and legislation. Economic equality is equally important for all Canadians, however, not just women, since women's labour is necessary for the continued growth of the Canadian economy.

Discussions of equality that focus on concepts of individual rights can be difficult, as we have seen. While there may be social acceptance of the idea that women should have equal rights as individuals and citizens, the understandings of what equal rights means are contentious. Many would agree that equal rights for women means having access to the same opportunities as men in the workforce, but the distinctive needs that exist because of sex and gender—for example, maternity leave and child care—require a much more complex analysis of what is meant by equality.

After the Second World War, the rise of the welfare state—that is, increased state commitment to both social and political citizenship—opened up opportunities for women but also required increased policy attention and action. During this period, women's dependence on men in interpersonal relationships lessened, as evidenced by increasing divorce rates. Dependence did not disappear; rather, it was largely transferred to state institutions and social programs. Currently women receive a larger portion of their total incomes than men do from government transfer payments. In 2003, 17 per cent of women's total income in Canada came from transfer payments, double the figure for men (9 per cent) (Standing Committee on the Status of Women 2007, 11 & 22). According to the Report of the Standing Committee on the Status of Women on women's economic security (2007, 23), 'Old Age Security and Guaranteed Income supplements make up the single largest component of government transfer benefits received by women, 4 per cent of women's income came from the Canadian and Quebec Pension plans, 3 per cent from Child Tax benefits, 2 per cent from social assistance benefits, and another 2 per cent from employment insurance payouts (23).

As we discussed in chapter 6, women have been intrinsically tied to the state and public policy-making. This relationship has seen women not only as consumers and clients of state programs but also as active advocates working to influence policy. As Brush (2002) points out, the social policy and the welfare state provide an avenue to build lives free from husbands and families through better, jobs, equal pay, support for homemaking, and better childcare provision. 'That is, just as social provision can give workers leverage against the forces that compel them into the labour market, it potentially provides women [with] leverage against the forces that relegate care work, childbearing, household formation, and sexuality to normative femininity in the context of marriage' (Brush, 2002, 164). Many of the efforts of the women's movement to address the problems women encountered at work and in balancing work and family life put them in a direct relationship with the state and positioned them as particular types of citizens, based on their gender, race, and class, etc. For this reason among others, as Nancy Fraser (1994) warns, we must not be too sanguine about the possibility of state policy bringing about women's economic equality.

For example, a citizen-worker model, which aims to ensure workplace employment equity through women's access to the same jobs as men, requires women to have the same standards and goals as men (Fraser 1994, 604). Equality 'saming' cannot accord full respect to work outside the citizen-worker model, such as unpaid private work in the home. As a result, such an approach works only for 'women whose lives most closely resemble the male half of the old family-wage ideal couple. It is especially good for childless women and for women without other major domestic responsibilities that cannot easily be shifted to social services. But for those women, as well as for others, it falls short of full gender equity' (Fraser 1994, 605).

Policies that support and recognize women's private labour—in other words, caregiver parity models—also have disadvantages. Giving financial remuneration for childbearing, child-raising, housework, and other forms of socially necessary domestic labour recognizes the significance of such labour to society's economic well-being and the unique role of women in providing that labour. However, it does so by reinforcing the belief that this labour is private and 'women's work', and it encourages the continuation of a gendered division of labour. It 'sets up a double standard to accommodate gender difference while institutionalizing policies that fail to assure equivalent respect for feminine activities and life patterns' (Fraser 1994, 610; see also Brush 2002).

In Fraser's (1994) view, neither model addresses the gendered division of labour and the social norms that support this division. When one adds the fact that the 'postwar welfare state was designed for the male breadwinner family model' and that these institutional arrangements have become fixed (Myles and Quadagno 2000, 57–8), then major change cannot start from a blank slate but must work instead with existing arrangements.

Throughout this chapter, we examine the various means by which feminist organizations and actors have attempted to achieve economic equality for women. We reveal some of the paradoxes of these policies and in the conclusion reflect on how to resolve the dilemmas raised by both the citizen-worker and caregiver parity models that have been so dominant in Canadian policy discourse.

A History of Workplace-Based Policy Change

In 1956 the federal government passed equal pay laws that established equal pay for women and men performing the same jobs. The law was not perfect. For example, Burt (1994, 213) notes that the 'complaint procedure was unwieldy and rarely used'. But as she points out, the legislation was important 'for the recognition of the principle that women and men could find themselves similarly situated in the public sphere'. In 1967 the federal government amended the Public Service Employment Act to deal with sex discrimination (Findlay 1987, 35). However, it was the report of the Royal Commission on the Status of Women in Canada (RCSW) that most comprehensively addressed the position of women in the Canadian economy. As mentioned in the previous chapter, of the four principles adopted by the commission, the employment of women came first, with the commission stating that 'women should be free to choose whether or not to take employment outside their homes'. In addition, the remaining principles were also intimately related to the ability of women to enter paid employment: '[T]he care of children is a responsibility to be shared by the mother, the father and society. . . . [S]ociety has a responsibility for women because of pregnancy and child-birth, and special treatment related to maternity will always be necessary. . . . [W]omen will for an interim period require special treatment to overcome the adverse effects of discriminatory practices' (RCSW 1970, xiii).

Clearly, women's paid employment was of significant interest to the RCSW. As Timpson (2001, 27) argues, the commission recognized 'how women's demands for gender equality in the sphere of employment were intrinsically linked to their demands for recognition of the different responsibilities men and women had for childcare . . . [and] placed the concept of equal employment opportunity for men and women squarely on the federal policy agenda'. The commission went beyond the concept of simple employment equity to address the complexities that emerged from women's mothering roles.

The goals of the royal commission's recommendations and cabinet acceptance of the report in principle were one thing; the reality of implementation was quite another. The government's acceptance of the report did not translate into concerted action regarding women's employment (see chapter 9). Monique Bégin (1992, 36–7) argues, 'What the state failed to do was set in motion the radical changes requiring the transformation of society. . . . The state . . . dismissed any attempts to fundamentally change the market rules or family arrangements'. Instead, governments, both federal and provincial, focused on employment-based 'equity rights' rather than on the more complex equality issues. The thrust was toward equal opportunities in public sector hiring, encouragement of women's participation in government training programs, and efforts addressing sex discrimination in federally regulated workplaces. Sandra Burt (2000) observes that the state's tendency is to be sympathetic to claims that women should have the same opportunities as men in politics and work but to resist the fundamental restructuring of relations between men and women in society as a whole. Consequently, success has been far greater in policy areas that involve public 'equality rights' claims than in areas that require redress of the gendered division of labour. Progress can be observed on issues framed in terms of anti-discrimination, but there has been less progress on issues concerning private and domestic work.

Success has also hinged on the willingness of the state to remain committed to the development of equality through social policy and intervention in the political economic structures. In the past two decades, the focus has been less on the development of social citizenship and a return to more responsibility-based understandings of political citizenship combined with a much less interventionist state. As Brodie and Bakker (2007, 1) point out, 'pressures to reform Canada's social policy regime, which took shape in the postwar years and matured in the 1960s and 1970s, have been linked to the ascendance of neo-liberal thinking, both in partisan politics and within policy-making circles, and to broader shifts in the Canadian economy, labour markets

and social structures'. Whether these changes are referred to as the institutionalization of a neo-liberal political economy (Brodie 1996; Philipps 2000; Brodie & Bakker
2007) or its modification as the 'social investment state' (Dobrowolsky & Jenson 2004,
Dobrowolsky and Lister 2008, Dobrowolsky 2009), the result is that the state no longer focuses on equality-making through social policy, but rather takes legitimizing and
enforcing market outcomes as its role. Lisa Philipps (2000, 1) illustrates this in her
examination of Canadian tax policy.

> Canadian tax policy increasingly discourages people from relying upon gov-
> ernment programs or services to meet their basic welfare needs, but en-
> courages them to rely instead upon private resources obtained through the
> market, or if necessary from family or charity. I argue that by promoting
> personal responsibility in this manner the tax code is contributing to an ero-
> sion of the ideal of social citizenship and replacing it with a new model of
> market citizenship.

Bakker and Brodie (2007) refer to this as the fiscalization of social policy, in which
the goals of social provision are pursued through tax credits and eligibility for state aid
is determined by taxable income. In terms of social investment, the purpose of the state
is to support the building of 'human capital', increasing the capacity of everyone to engage in paid work through the expansion of 'opportunities' (Dobrowolsky 2009, 11).[1]
The language is no longer about equality but about opportunity, choice, and fairness.

To return to our earlier point, this entrenches the tendency of the state to pursue
policy that works to provide equal access but does not address fundamental inequalities. It continues to strongly emphasize the ideal society as comprising 'citizen workers'. The political economic needs and claims of women, along with many women
themselves, are rendered invisible and absent from policy decisions.

Anti-discrimination, Equity, and Equality: Pay and Employment Equity Policies

As discussed in the previous chapter, the labour market has proved inadequate, without state intervention, to bring about workplace equality and remove discrimination
in the job market. The first step in addressing pay discrimination came when government recognized in law that women should be paid the same for doing the same
work as men.

Legislation to ensure that women receive equal pay dates back to Ontario's 1951
Female Employees Fair Remuneration Act. The federal government made its first administrative arrangements for women's equal pay in 1956 when the Female Employees
Equal Pay Act guaranteed the same pay for women and men engaged in the same or
essentially similar work. This legislation did not apply to all female federal employees,
however, and combined with other provincial equal pay regulations to create a patchwork of federal and provincial legislation that covered some women but not others.

The federal government rescinded its legislation in 1966 and transferred equal
pay provisions to the Canada Labour Code. In 1975, the Quebec government enacted
the first provincial human rights legislation containing provisions for equal pay for
equivalent work in the same workplace. In 1970 the federal government had ratified

the International Convention on the Elimination of All Forms of Racial Discrimination, which included a statement on the right to equal pay for equal work (Department of Justice Canada 2005a). What 'same' or 'equivalent' work meant, however, remained ambiguous and narrow in scope. While addressing the plight of women in essentially the same work situations as male colleagues, the concept of equal pay for the same work was very limited. Equal pay for same work complaints could only be made if the jobs being compared were considered essentially the same. In fact, it was fairly easy for employers to re-categorize jobs and be able to claim that they were not the same. The wording of the laws, the requirement that individuals had to initiate complaints, and so on, led many to complain that these laws were ineffective.

Furthermore, equal pay laws did little to address the fact that women and men did not and still in some ways do not do the same work and that many occupations are undervalued simply because women do the work. When women did not perform the same work as men, employers could legitimately continue to pay women lower wages than men.

Feminist activists therefore had two options: (1) encourage women into traditionally male and higher-paying occupations through education, workplace recruitment, and so on; or (2) work to have women paid more for the jobs they do perform. However, as mentioned in the previous chapter, breaking through the 'glass ceiling' of the highest professions has proved difficult for women, visible minorities, and people with disabilities. Furthermore, as many feminists have pointed out, demanding that women strive to succeed in a man's world undermines the value of the work that women do in many of the caring and service professions, and continuing poor remuneration in those jobs will not encourage men to enter them, thus reinforcing job segregation. A great deal of feminist activism has therefore been devoted to increasing wages for work that women do.

From equal pay to pay equity

A 1970 Ontario court decision helped a little to broaden the concept of equal work to 'substantially the same work' when the court ruled that female nurses' aides and male hospital orderlies, while not doing exactly the same jobs, were performing substantially the same work within the meaning of the Ontario statute (McDermott 1996, 92). The report of the Royal Commission on the Status of Women also included 10 pages specifically on equal pay ending a final recommendation calling for pay equity rather than equal pay for identical work.

Pay equity establishes that people who work for the same organization in jobs that are different but of equal value to their employers should be paid the same wages. It requires that jobs should be paid according to their worth: that is, the skill, effort, responsibility, and working conditions required to perform the job. It is different from the concept of 'equal pay for equal work', which states that people doing the same job for the same organization should be paid the same wages. Pay equity policies are designed to address the persistent wage gap found as a result of job segregation, question the traditional valuing of jobs, and reveal the gendered assumptions behind market rates. The classic question is, why is a truck driver paid more than a child care worker? In practice, however, pay equity laws in Canada generally require a narrower reassessment of jobs than the example of child care workers and truck drivers.

The 1977 federal Human Rights Act adopted the language of equal pay for work of equal value, and one year later the Canadian Human Rights Commission issued guidelines for the factors to be taken into consideration when assessing value (Department of Justice Canada 2005a). At the provincial level, by the end of the 1980s, Manitoba (1985), Ontario (1987), Nova Scotia (1988), Prince Edward Island (1988), and New Brunswick (1989) had adopted pay equity legislation, most of which applied only to public sector employees. However, the 1987 Ontario Pay Equity Act applied to both public and private sector employers with 10 or more employees (Fudge 1996, 74). The Act also applied to part-time as well as full-time workers, and it allowed for an independent tribunal, the Pay Equity Commission, to oversee the implementation of the Act.

The key for women workers, of course, was to find an appropriate male comparator—that is, 'a male job class with the same or less value that receives higher wages' (Fudge 1996, 74). But in government agencies where the workforce is overwhelmingly female, finding a male comparator is difficult, if not impossible. Soon after its establishment, the Pay Equity Commission did a study of some female-dominated job sectors and concluded that the best way to deal with gender wage discrimination in those agencies was to allow for consideration of wage rates in 'proxy' establishments.

In 1993 the Ontario NDP government expanded the 1987 legislation. Significantly, the 1993 Act included proxy comparison as a method of determining the value of work performed. Proxy comparison meant that women in sectors of the economy where there were no obviously comparable male occupations could be compared with employees in other establishments. After 1993, with proxy pay equity amendments, child care workers in non-profit community-based programs were able to compare themselves to child care workers in municipal programs, where pay equity had already been successfully implemented (Ontario Coalition For Better Child Care 2005, 3).

When the Conservative Party under Mike Harris defeated the NDP in 1995, one of its first moves was to pass the omnibus Bill 26, which removed the proxy method from the Pay Equity Act and capped pay equity increases for workers already covered by proxy. Unions in Ontario, particularly those representing large numbers of women, immediately challenged these moves. In September 1997, an Ontario divisional court judge ruled the Harris government's actions unconstitutional. The government had violated section 15 of the Ontario Human Rights Charter by discriminating against women in proxy sector workplaces because it capped pay raises for those women but not in workplaces using other pay equity methods. This and a second ruling in 2003 restored equity raises for approximately 100,000 public sector workers (Rusk 1997, A1, A6, and Ontario Coalition for Better Child Care 2005, 3).

While the Ontario court battles can be viewed as successes, the issue of pay equity is far from settled nationally. For example, even the federal government balked at a 1998 Canadian Human Rights Commission decision requiring it pay up to $5 billion in back pay to 200,000 past and present public workers until a federal court judge upheld the ruling (Wallace and Fisher 1999). Some provinces, such as BC in 2001, have repealed pay equity legislation and amended provincial human rights codes. Newfoundland throughout the 1990s refused to fulfill pay equity promises in the name of fiscal restraint.

Support in the courts for pay equity can be troublesome and particularly time consuming. For example, in 1993, the Public Service Alliance of Canada (PSAC) filed

a complaint against Canada Post. In 2005, the Canadian Human Rights Tribunal upheld the complaint which was then appealed by Canada Post to the Federal Court.
Three years later the Federal Court ruled in favour of Canada Post, arguing the Human
Rights Tribunal had not completed all the steps in making a comparison between the
female-dominated 'clerical and regulatory' working group and the male-dominated
'postal operations group'. The resulting appeal by PSAC to the Federal Court of Appeal
was dismissed in February 11, 2010 on the grounds that the case was not about pay
equity and employer liability, but rather that the original tribunal had made a review
error regarding an appropriate proxy (see *Public Service Alliance of Canada v. Canada
Post Corporation*, February 22, 2010, 2010 FCA 56). It was a 27-year process, resulting in a ruling that highlighted the legal complexity of determining comparisons and
comparator groups.

In 2004 the Supreme Court upheld the Newfoundland Supreme Court's dismissal
of union grievances against non-payment of pay equity wage adjustments, concluding
that while the Newfoundland government's actions amounted to gender discrimination, the 'Newfoundland and Labrador women workers' rights to equal pay did not
outweigh the importance of preserving the fiscal health of a provincial government
through a temporary but serious financial crisis' (Moorcroft 2005, 6).[2]

Pay equity policies have in fact not proved to be a panacea for addressing gender
wage disparities. As Pat Armstrong (1997) and Julie White (1993) observe, while the
system in Ontario resulted in some gains for women it also had significant failings. It
did not cover the contingent and temporary work force (Fudge 1996, 77). More generally, Armstrong (1997) notes that evaluations of worth continue to be based on a male
conception of valued work where '[r]esponsibility for money is more highly valued
than caring for people[,] [g]arbage removal is considered more onerous than cleaning
dirty diapers, police work more dangerous than dressing the wounds of patients with
contagious diseases' (Armstrong 1997, 135). Society has not resolved the question of
whether caring for people is more important than caring for people's investment portfolios (Magid 1997, 332), How does one avoid typical class prejudices in the assessment
of skills, responsibility, and so on? Are blue-collar jobs worth more than white-collar
jobs, for example? Julie White (1993, 70) points to another important drawback. While
pay equity laws resulted in some gains for women, '[t]he technicalities of the procedure
cast the false impression that the result is scientific and objective, accurately determining fair wages for women, and therefore the final word on the issue'. Any wage disparities are thus solvable, when in practice that has not been the case.

So much depends on the support of governments for equity policies and the economic context in which pay equity and employment equity claims are made. Can
public sector agencies, already under financial constraint, afford to make the necessary wage adjustments? In the current political economic climate, the support for
pay equity does not appear to be there. In 2007, federal government hearings on
the economic security of women heard evidence of the need for the federal government to implement the recommendations from the 2004 Pay Equity Task Force report,
which, according to NDP members of the Standing Committee on the Status of Women
Committee, were 'conspicuously absent from the final study' (Standing Committee on
the Status of Women 2007, 73).

In 2007, Mary Cornish, chair of the Equal Pay Coalition, made a fairly disheart-
ening assessment regarding Ontario's program: 'Ontario's persistent wage gap shows

many women never received the benefit of the province's legislation and others lost the gains they initially made for various reasons' (Cornish 2008, 22). The province's need to maintain fiscal stability outweighed the requirements of pay equity with the result that, in the 20 years after the law's passing, the budget of the Pay Equity Commission and Hearings Tribunal was cut in half and the pay equity legal clinic eliminated (ibid.).

Canada's pay equity system has come under criticism internationally. In 2003 the United Nations Committee on the Elimination of Discrimination against Women urged Canada to undertake measures to speed up the implementation of pay equity. Pay equity was enshrined as an international principle in 1951 with the Convention on Equal Remuneration (no. 100) by the International Labour Organization (ILO). In 2006, an ILO report set out the factors required to achieve pay equity which included clear standards, mechanisms of enforcement, and the creation of a commission to enforce the standards (Côté and Lassonde 2007, 10). In Canada, the 2004 Pay Equity Task force established to investigate pay equity in Canada after the UN criticism reached similar conclusions and found the federal system was ineffective and needed to be made proactive.

In 1997 Quebec did institute a proactive pay equity program which, in a 2006 ILO report, compared favourably with five other jurisdictions (Sweden, the UK, Netherlands, France, and Switzerland). As a proactive program, in Quebec, the responsibility for implementing pay equity lies with the employer, who is obligated to demonstrate that there is no wage inequity for predominantly female classes. (Côté and Lassonde 2007, 8, citing Chicha[3] 2006).

Bill C-10: Pay equity in a recessionary age

The Canadian federal government response to demands for a more proactive approach was introduced by Stephen Harper's Conservative government as the Public Sector Equitable Compensation Act (PSECA) within the omnibus Budget Implementation Act (Bill C-10) of 2009. That the Act was included within a much broader piece of budget legislation certainly raised suspicion among women's groups and unions and it became clear that PSECA represented a controversial approach to and redefinition of pay equity in the federal public service. In March 2009, Bill C-10, the Budget Implementation Act and the Public Sector Equitable Compensation Act became law.

The federal government and Treasury Board argue that PSECA is a significant step forward in achieving pay equity in the federal public service because it sets out a proactive, rather than complaints-based, approach that 'makes employers and bargaining agents jointly accountable for ensuring that wages are fair for all employees through the collective bargaining process...'(Treasury Board of Canada Secretariat 2009, 1). By including pay equity within collective bargaining processes, disputes will be resolved in a more timely manner. In addition, accountability and collaboration will be enhanced because both employer and union/bargaining agent would be 'jointly accountable for ensuring equitable compensation' (ibid., 4).

However, streamlining the process by integrating implementation into collective bargaining challenges the principle of pay equity as a human right. Critics of PSECA (such as the Public Service Alliance of Canada, NWAL, LEAF, Canadian Federation of University Women, the Canadian Feminist Alliance for International Action, and the Canadian Labour Congress) argue that while the previous approach was obviously broken, the current program will not help achieve pay equity.

> Their main concerns were that the legislation contravened the Charter as well as Canada's international human rights obligations; that pay equity must remain a human rights issue and not form part of a collective bargaining scheme, as set out in the new legislation; that the PSECA compels women to file complaints alone, without the support of their union; and that the PSECA will restrict the substance and application of pay equity to the public sector (Standing Committee on the Status of Women 2009, 5).

The concern is that pay equity becomes a bargaining chip that is open to negotiation. In cases where bargaining fails to achieve pay equity, workers must file complaints as individuals (the Act penalizes unions who assist members in filing complaints) and consequently face the legal costs and stresses of pursuing their claims. In addition, by placing pay equity within the bargaining process, PSECA removes it from the purview of the Canadian Human Rights Commission and 'prohibits public sector workers from filing complaints for pay equity violations with the Canadian Human Rights Commission' (Canadian Feminist Alliance for International Action and Canadian Labour Congress 2010, 24).

PSECA only covers employees in the federal public sector which, according to the Treasury Board Secretariat, includes over 400,000 workers (Treasury Board Secretariat 2009, 4). Most workplaces in Canada are regulated by legislation at the provincial level. However, the adoption of PSECA by the federal government does establish a model and an agenda for provinces looking to amend their existing programs to introduce more proactive approaches that fit well with the changing economic climate. By tying pay equity to bargaining and making it more of an employment issue than a human rights issue makes it easier to manipulate definitions of equity to fit with the economic climate and the vagaries of the market.

Employment equity

Another major initiative on the part of women's groups, as well as visible minority groups and others traditionally disadvantaged in the labour market, is employment equity (as it is known in Canada) and affirmative action (as it is known in the United States). White (1993, 76) argues that 'the purpose of employment equity is to enable women and other disadvantaged workers to take an equal place in the labour force'. The goal of such policies is to ensure that those who have been traditionally kept from positions of power be given access to those positions. Merely ceasing a discriminatory hiring or promotion practice, however, may not be enough to overcome racist or sexist attitudes due to the lingering effects of previous discrimination. Thus, employers may need to take some kind of proactive initiative, either voluntary or under legal compulsion, to ensure access for traditionally excluded groups.

Employment equity occurs when an organization goes out of its way to make sure that there is no discrimination against women, minorities, or people with disabilities. Strategies are put in place to remove institutional barriers created by discrimination and prejudice with the goal of creating access to positions historically closed to these disadvantaged groups. This can take the form of establishing quotas for hiring members of these groups, or providing training or retraining to help them achieve promotion. Magid (1997, 141, n. 8) argues that there are at least two different methods of achieving the purposes of affirmative action: (1) to redistribute people in occupations based on their group's proportion in the population, or (2) to intervene in ongoing systemic discrimination in order to create real conditions of equality of opportunity but with no fixed goals as to what proportion of the population one succeeds in hiring. The first goal suggests some kind of quota system as a remedy; the second suggests redistributive hiring and promotion policies but not explicit quotas.

These policies, even more than pay equity policies, tend to be controversial because it is commonly believed that race and gender should be considered irrelevant to employment and admissions decisions, which is certainly what feminists and other equal rights activists have argued all along. But affirmative action/employment equity makes gender and/or race a consideration in hiring and admissions decisions, and opponents charge that affirmative action represents reverse discrimination.

In Canada, the first official articulation of the concept of employment equity came in the RCSW recommendation that the federal government take special steps to increase the number of women in male-dominated jobs within the public sector. Later on, human rights agencies established by the federal and provincial governments played an important role in pushing for the remedial action inherent in employment equity programs. For example, in the 1980s the Canadian Human Rights Commission adopted a strong position advocating employment equity programs in the face of what it determined was systemic discrimination against women and minorities, and it mandated the federal government to adopt such a program in the federal public service (Timpson 2001, 75–6).

In 1983 the Royal Commission on Equality in Employment was established by the federal Liberal government under Prime Minister Trudeau and headed by Rosalie Abella, now a Supreme Court Justice. Its mandate was to inquire into the opportunities for employment of women, native peoples, disabled persons, and visible minorities in certain corporations owned by the government of Canada and to report on the most efficient, effective, and equitable means of promoting employment opportunities, eliminating systemic discrimination, and assisting all individuals to compete for employment opportunities on an equal basis (Timpson 2001, 95). Abella, in fact, broadened the understanding of work equality not only to address issues of equity but also to link issues of employment equality with those of child care (Timpson, 2001, 96). The commission's focus was on equal pay, affirmative action, and child care.

The term employment equity 'was created by Abella as a Canadian variant of the American concept of affirmative action' (ibid. 118) whereby 'all federally regulated employers [had] to develop and maintain employment practices designed to eliminate discriminatory barriers in the workplace and improve, where necessary, the participation, occupational distribution, and income levels of the target groups'.

The federal Conservative government under Brian Mulroney adopted some of the recommendations of the Abella Report in its 1986 Employment Equity Act. The Act covered all federal employees as well as those in federally regulated industries with 100 or more employees. Employers were to collect workforce data on four designated groups—women, visible minorities, Aboriginal peoples, and people with disabilities—each year and file it with the federal government, outlining numbers of employees in those designated groups as well as salaries, hirings, promotions, and terminations of designated group members (Armstrong and Cornish 1997, 72). This was expanded in 1986, under the federal contractors' program, to include all federal contractors with 100 or more employees and with contracts of $200,000 or more.[4]

While the Act appeared to have some teeth, and certainly daunting documentation requirements, employers in fact had the power to determine their own goals and targets, and few penalties and fewer sanctions were actually imposed. Each employer was accountable only for demonstrating 'good faith' efforts to achieve the goals, not for actually achieving them. For example, there is no sanction for failure to improve the representation of a designated group if the required report is submitted and a plausible reason given for the lack of progress (Agocs and Osborne 2009). Nor did governments effectively enforce contract compliance rules (Armstrong and Cornish 1997, 72). In the face of these criticisms, the federal government revised and strengthened its employment equity legislation in the fall of 1995. The Act extended coverage to the federal public service and required employers to make 'reasonable progress towards achieving a representative workforce by designing and implementing employment equity plans in consultation with employees and any bargaining agent' (Armstrong and Cornish 1997, 72). The Minister of Labour was responsible for advising employers, analyzing employers' reports, and reporting to Parliament on progress in meeting employment equity goals (Human Resources and Skills Development Canada 2001, 4). This responsibility was moved to the Department of Human Resources and Skills Development when the Department of Labour was reorganized. In 2010 it was the Minister in charge of the Treasury Board who reported to Parliament. The Act also mandated a review of the legislation every five years by a committee of the House of Commons.

The federal government managed to strengthen its employment equity legislation without the controversy that the NDP government in Ontario had experienced a few years before. Under the Ontario Employment Equity Act of 1993, the province became the first jurisdiction to extend employment equity to provincially regulated private sector employers with 50 or more employees, as well as covering the entire public sector, including schools, hospitals, universities, and colleges. In all, it covered 17,000 Ontario employers. As with the later federal amendments, it required employers to establish numerical goals regarding the accommodation of designated groups in the workplace, and to set timetables for the achievement of a representative workforce. It gave unions the right to negotiate plans with the employer. It also gave an independent Employment Equity Tribunal the power to 'review and assess the results of the employment equity plan and to order action if employers had not taken the appropriate steps for ensuring a more representative workforce' (Armstrong and Cornish 1997, 72).

One of the first acts of the incoming Conservative government in 1995 was to repeal the Ontario legislation through Bill 8, An Act to Repeal Job Quotas and to Restore Merit-Based Employment Practices in Ontario. The title accurately sums up the Conservative critique of the previous legislation, even though it in fact contained nothing about quotas or about neglecting merit in hiring and promotion decisions (Armstrong and Cornish 1997, 77). Since the Act had been in force for such a short time—just two years—it is difficult to assess whether it had any effect on improving hiring and promotion practices. However, even after the 1995 repeal, Ontario unions continued to bargain for equality-promoting provisions in collective agreements and to use anti-discrimination provisions to further the rights of disadvantaged employees (Cornish and Faraday 2009, 19). All was not lost as employment equity obligations for provincially regulated employers continue to be sustained by a number of different laws, according to Cornish and Faraday, (2009, 12), such as the Human Rights Code, the Labour Relations Act (LRA), the Pay Equity Act (PEA), anti-discrimination collective agreement provisions and the Charter of Rights and Freedoms.

In other provinces, equity policies and programs are highly variable and uneven. In 2001, Quebec adopted an act respecting equal access to employment in public bodies and amending the Charter of Human Rights and Freedoms, which applied to all public bodies with 100 or more employees in the municipal sector and in the education, health, and social service systems. It also applies to other organizations, such as Crown corporations, and the Sûreté du Québec with regard to its police force. Enforcing the Quebec legislation is the responsibility of the Commission des droits de la personne et des droits de la jeunesse, which consults with employers and reviews employer programs and results. Conflicts that occur between an employer and the Commission are resolved by the Tribunal des droits de la personne. The remaining provinces with some form of employment equity policy include British Columbia, Manitoba, Ontario, Saskatchewan, Nova Scotia, New Brunswick and Prince Edward Island; however, these programs apply only to the provincial public service. In Newfoundland and Alberta, while debate over employment equity has occurred, no equity legislation or policies exist (Human Resources and Skills Development Canada 2001, 5–6).

Consequently, according to Agocs and Osborne's (2009) comparison of employment equity policy in Canada and Northern Ireland, the division of power between federal and provincial levels has significantly limited the success of employment equity in Canada: '[L]ess than 5 percent of the workforce falls within the federal sector covered by the Act; most employees [who] work within the provincial jurisdiction are not covered by federal employment equity legislations. The provinces have chosen not to adopt employment equity policy frameworks similar to the federal model.'

Evaluating the success of pay and employment equity policies

The pursuit of anti-discriminatory labour practices through pay and employment equity policies fit well with a model of achieving equality through litigation and legislation. Early successes in achieving commitments to employment and pay equity were soon compromised, however, by diminishing support on the part of both society and the state for such equality-seeking initiatives. As Agocs and Osborne (2009, 257) point out, '"political will" is code for mobilization of political support within a structure of power relations'. Employment equity programs quickly became the bogeyman in the backlash against feminism and women's rights in the 1980s and 1990s. Employment equity was branded as making women and minorities 'more equal' than others. Programs were challenged as disadvantaging and discriminating against men. Opponents even took to delegitimizing and belittling women and minorities hired into jobs, accusing them of having acquired their jobs 'only because they were women or minorities' rather than on their merit.

This backlash complemented the ascendance of neo-liberal political economy and policy-making in Canada under both Liberal and Conservative governments. For example, for many Ontarians, the Harris government's repeal of proactive strong employment equity in 1995 was the first shot across the bow of government-supported equity policies. It presaged the changing focus from policy provision for social equality to policy provision towards legitimizing and enforcing market outcomes. (It should also be noted that a number of former members of the Harris government and associated political strategists at the time of writing are part of or associated with the Harper Conservative government in Ottawa.) Subsequently, public policy has come much more into line with the interests of corporations and the responsibility for employment equity implementation, as with pay equity, was given to employers to set or in the case where unions were active, to be negotiated between employers and unions. The result was a clear limitation of the number of workers who come under employment equity programs and the emergence of compliance falling to the voluntary acceptance by the employer and the voluntary responsibility of employees and union members to push complaints. As Agocs and Osborne (2009, 246; quoting Abu-Laban and Gabriel 2002) observe, 'one result is that mandatory employment equity designated to address systemic discrimination has given way to individualized and voluntary "diversity management" approaches favoured in the current business climate'.

As Agocs and Osborne argue (2009, 248), 'the big picture is that since the origins of employment equity policy there have been some gains for women and visible minorities, but very little improvement for persons with disabilities and Aboriginal people'. Women, Aboriginal people, and persons with disabilities remain underrepresented in firms covered by the Act, relative to their availability in the labour force. The 2008–09 Federal Employment Equity report to Parliament (Treasury Board Secretariat 2010, 28) reported the following findings: women, Aboriginal peoples, and persons with disabilities were well represented relative to the work force availability (WFA), with women making up 54.7 percent of employees in the core public administration with a 52.3 WFA; Aboriginal peoples 4.5 percent of employers with a WFA of 3.0 percent; and persons with disabilities 5.9 percent with a WFA of 4.0. However, while exceeding their WFA, women continued to make up a disproportionate share of the employees in the Administrative Support category, the number of Aboriginals had remained unchanged, and the percentage of women with disabilities had declined (ibid.). The representation of visible minority groups in the core public administration had declined relative to their WFA (ibid.).

Further to this, as noted above with regard to pay equity, employment equity policies could not fully address the inequalities in the labour market because, as Timpson (2001, 84) argues, they are predicated on a conception of gender equality, or sameness, rather than on gender difference, and of achieving equality through individual redress. Consequently, the obstacles that many women face in attempting to enter or gain promotion in full-time full-year employment, such as child care and family duties, are not factored into such programs. Furthermore, these policies can do nothing to stop employers from restructuring the workforce with consequent massive layoffs (McDermott 1996). Finally, while some of the most pernicious forms of discrimination can occur in small business settings, contract work, and home-based work, legislative exemptions for small firms and the exclusion of many of these contingent forms of work from the legislation means that many employees are not covered by its provisions.

These criticisms have led Carol Lee Bacchi (1999) and others to call for a focus on wage solidarity as a solution to pay and employment inequities. That is, we should focus on ways of raising the wages of those at the bottom of the wage hierarchy through such policies as higher minimum wages, flattening of job hierarchies, and decreasing the differentials between high- and low-paid workers (Bacchi 1999, 88). It is well known that the wage differentials between the highest- and lowest-paid workers in North America are great compared to those in many European countries. Defining the problem as one of class-based discrimination collectivizes both the problem and the solution, and focuses attention on universal solutions rather than on individual capacities and workplace contributions.

Balancing Work and Family Life: Child Care and Other Family Responsibilities

The Commission adopted four principles: first, that **women should be free to choose whether or not to take employment outside their homes**. The circumstances which impede this free choice have been of specific interest to our inquiry. . . . The second is **that care of children is a responsibility to be shared by the mother, the father and society**. Unless this shared responsibility is acknowledged and assumed, women cannot be accorded true equality. The third principle specifically recognizes the child-bearing function of women. It is apparent **that society has a responsibility for women because of pregnancy and child-birth, and special treatment related to maternity will always be necessary** (RCSW 1970, xii, emphasis in the original).

Employment and pay equity programs, while constituting a step forward for some women, do not address the problem presented by women's roles as caregivers in the private sphere. This is not to say that the Canadian women's movement has neglected the issue. In fact, unlike its sister organizations in the United States, women's groups in Canada have paid a great deal of attention to issues of child care (compare Rebick 2005 with Barakso 2004).

By the 1960s, as more women entered the workforce, working women, feminist activists, and 'femocrats' within the civil service were actively trying to put child care on the public policy agenda. The Women's Bureau in the federal Department of Labour pushed to have the government address the concerns of working women with family responsibilities. However, as Timpson (2001, 19) observes of the period, while the Women's Bureau was successful in getting an agenda on discrimination at work adopted, it viewed the issue of child care as lying outside its jurisdiction. As a result, the issue was left to the Family and Child Welfare Division, which meant that child care would be viewed as a welfare issue rather than as an employment issue.

One policy success for working mothers was the establishment of paid and job-protected maternity leave. Although British Columbia adopted a Maternity Protection Act in 1921 and New Brunswick passed similar legislation in 1964, it was not until 1970 that maternity leave provisions were written into the Canada Labour Code, stipulating that governments should provide protection for employees who take time off for childbearing (Skrypnek and Fast 1996, 798–800). In 1971 the federal government authorized women to apply for income replacement under what was then called the unemployment insurance (now employment insurance) program. These provisions were extended to fathers in 1990.

It should be noted that federal employment insurance (EI) does not provide full income replacement but rather income amounting to 55 per cent of the employee's salary up to a cap (currently $457 per week). Quebec's separate provincial maternity and parental leave program replaces up to 75 per cent. The result is that for most households maternity and parental leave will result in a decline in household income. Some employers provide salary 'top-ups' based on negotiated benefit packages and collective agreements. In a Statistics Canada examination of trends in the proportion of mothers with a paid job who received a maternity or parental leave benefit top-up, Katherine Marshall (2010, 5) found that only 20 per cent of new parents received an employer top-up.

Of all the new mothers in 2008, 327,000 (85 per cent) were employed before giving birth. Of this group 262,000 (80 per cent) reported receiving paid maternity and/or parental leave benefits (EI/QPIP), and 51,000 received an employer top-up to these benefits—representing one in five EI/QPIP beneficiaries [under the program one must receive EI/QPIP benefits to receive the top-up].

This means that a vast number of women receive little salary beyond federal employment insurance benefits, and thus a maternity leave of a full year (as permitted under current EI rules) may not be affordable for many of them. Even for those who receive top-ups, Marshall (2010) found that most (80 per cent in 2008) received top-ups for less than 6 months of their leaves (the average period being 19 weeks). Therefore, for many women the top-up will not cover the full maternity leave. As a result, 'the reality is that relatively few mothers are on paid leave with full earnings replacement—EI/QPIP plus an employer top-up—for the duration of their time off (ibid. 8).

Furthermore, not all parents participating in the workforce are eligible for maternity and parental benefits. That is because the federal program applies only to salaried workers, such as doctors or real estate agents, not the self-employed, and eligibility for benefits requires that one work a certain number of hours during the previous year. Marshall (2003, 11) reports that approximately 39 per cent of mothers with newborns in 2001 did not have access to parental leave benefits because they were self-employed, were not previously employed, had not worked sufficient hours to qualify for benefits, or did not apply for them.[5] In 2008, there were 386,900 mothers with infants less than 13 months of age. Of these, 85 per cent had worked in the past 18 months, while 15 per cent had not and were therefore not eligible for benefits. Of the 85 per cent with a year and a half of work, 20 per cent were ineligible for benefits while the remaining 80 per cent (262,400) received benefits (Marshall 2010, 6). Therefore, just 68 per cent of women with children under 13 months of age were eligible for maternity benefits. In 2007, 32 per cent of mothers with newborns either did not qualify or did not apply for maternity benefits. Women who do temporary, contract, or part-time work are less likely to be eligible for the benefits than women who work full-time; the current requirement is for 600 hours of insured work to have been undertaken in the previous 52 weeks. (In fact, given the pattern of women's labour market participation in the childbearing years, men are more likely to be eligible for benefits than women are!)

As with other programs geared toward women and children, parental leave provisions are much more expansive in Quebec. In 2006, the régime québecois d'assurance parental (RQAP) was brought in to ensure benefits that cover maternity, paternity, parental, and adoption leaves for eligible workers, either salaried or self-employed. Two options are given: a longer period with lower benefits or a shorter leave period with higher benefits. In addition, the program eliminates the two-week qualifying period required by national EI, increases the maximum insurable income, and considers workers with low insurable earnings (as little as $2000) to be eligible (Bakker and Brodie 2007, 14).

Once any maternity or parental leave benefits are exhausted, parents must decide whether to return to the paid workforce or not. If they choose to return, they face a number of hurdles. Finding quality child care is very difficult and remains a significant public policy challenge. The Royal Commission on the Status of Women recognized the importance of the issue for women's workplace equality in the early 1970s. Recommendations 115–20 of the commission's final report all dealt with the provision of and access to child care, including instituting sliding-scale fees based on parental income and building more child care centres. The report, in fact, recommended the establishment of a national daycare program, the costs of which would be shared by the federal and provincial governments.

The federal government had already established childcare subsidies in the 1966 Canada Assistance Plan (CAP) for parents receiving social assistance (Timpson 2001, 9). However, this was child care envisioned as a welfare provision rather than as an entitlement to facilitate women's employment participation. As Timpson (2001) argues, this distinction between welfare provision and work entitlement was the policy pattern that would prevail for decades.

Second-wave feminist groups, such as NAC and unions in advocacy group/labour coalitions, took up the fight for a 'universally accessible', 'publicly funded', 'not-for-profit', and 'non-compulsory' daycare system (Colley 1983). By the 1980s, those pressing for child care policy also included child care advocates and various groups of for-profit and non-profit daycare providers. According to Dobrowolsky and Jenson (2004), the political opportunities of the late 1960s and 1970s, particularly with the inroads made by the RCSW into the public policy arena, created 'space [for women] to voice their premise that childcare was indispensable to equality of opportunity between women and men'.

However, in keeping with the coalitional nature of social movements and the diversity among feminist and other political and social visions, views on the connection between women's equality and childcare varied even during this period. As Dobrowolsky and Jenson (2004, 160) argue, feminists were in the midst of debates over equating womanhood with motherhood and 'the notion that "all mothers" needed, wanted, or preferred the same child care service, was a point of contention. The result was that not all feminists were willing to be advocates for child care.' And while advocates for child care were supportive of the link between women's rights and child care, 'their *primary concern* was not to lobby for childcare in order to promote gender equality in the workplace but rather to pressure governments to develop a *universal public service for children*, with decent employment conditions for childcare workers' (Timpson 2001, 90, emphases in original). Added to this was debate within the child care community over for-profit versus not-for-profit delivery. As Dobrowolsky and Jenson (2004, 162) recount, as government policy focus shifted in the 1980s to cost-cutting and attention shifted from child care to child poverty, 'child care advocates were folded into a larger movement focussed on children and poverty; in it, increasingly, the women's movement was sidelined.' The coalition was fragile indeed.

While regulated child care spaces did increase during the 1970s and 1980s from 83,500 to 243,543, according to Duffy and Pupo (1992, 30), this only covered 13 per cent of children who needed care. Between 2001 and 2004 the number of spaces grew by 152,493, an average growth of 50,831 spaces a year. Growth tapered off after 2004, between 2004 and 2006 spaces increased by 32,688 in each year, and between 2006 and 2007 growth decreased to 26,661, 'the smallest increase in regulated childcare in some years (Childcare Resource and Research Unit 2007, 1). In 2008, the number of regulated child care spaces was 867,197 (a 29,791 increase over 2007) which covered 18.6 per cent of all children aged 0 to 12 and 20.3 per cent of children under five (ibid.). While many of these services were licensed and regulated, many were not. In 2008, only 15 per cent of total child care spaces were in regulated family child care centres (Childcare Resource and Research Unit 2009). Skrypnek and Fast (1996, 796) note as well that '[q]uality of regulated childcare as reflected in staff qualifications, staff ratios, maximum group size, and programming, also varies. In many provinces, requirements fall short of recommendations of early childhood experts. And, in some provinces, out of school centres, family day homes, nursery schools, and drop in centres are not licensed or regulated'.

In the early 1980s, the Liberal government in Ottawa began establishing a policy for national child care, but this effort was derailed by their election defeat in 1984. The Mulroney Conservative government was left to 'pick up the torch' and, in response to public pressure, the Abella Report (1983), and the Cooke Task Force on Childcare (1986), it introduced the 1987 National Childcare Strategy. The biggest component of the strategy was a promise to commit $3 billion over seven years, or $429 million per year, to develop child care where needed and to change the federal/provincial cost-sharing arrangements by removing child care from the Canada Assistance Plan.

On the one hand, separating child care funding from CAP would have removed the stigma of child care as a welfare service. However, doing so also would have effectively terminated the open-ended funding then available under CAP (which provided one federal dollar for every provincial dollar spent). The government also proposed to loosen requirements that existed under CAP that limited funding to not-for-profit centres' operating costs. Instead, Bill C-144[6] would have allowed funding of the operating costs of commercial daycare centres as well. And the Bill would not have imposed national standards on the provinces in return for receiving federal child care funds.

Many child care advocacy and other groups mobilized immediately against the government's National Childcare Strategy.[7] Since the advocates' ideal was universally accessible, publicly funded, comprehensive, not-for-profit, and high-quality daycare, they saw the changes as a huge step backward in their fight for a national daycare system. Other, more conservative groups such as REAL Women opposed the legislation as well because they opposed the federal government encouraging non-parental forms of childcare and the participation of women in the labour market (Phillips 1989, 172). REAL Women instead argued that governments should be providing more support to those who chose to stay at home with their children.

The federal government went ahead with part of its proposed child care strategy and introduced Bill C-144, the Canada Childcare Act, in the House of Commons in July 1988. The legislation gave the provinces the option of either retaining the exist- ing funding under CAP or moving to block funding. Once provinces moved to block funding, however, they could not go back (White 2001c). Then Parliament dissolved in anticipation of the November 1988 election, killing the legislation. Although the Mulroney government vowed to reintroduce the legislation if re-elected, it did not do so in its second term. Instead, it engaged in what in retrospect were quite mod- est cost-cutting measures, overshadowed by the massive spending cuts initiated by the Liberal government under Prime Minister Chrétien, elected in 1993. While the federal Liberal Party had campaigned on increasing child care spending if elected— specifically, to spend $720 million on child care over three years and create up to 50,000 new regulated spaces per year for three years—once in office, the Liberals did not fulfill their promise, citing fiscal constraints and an economic downturn.

The compromise was to address child care through the tax system with the cre- ation of the Childcare Tax Credit in 1993. In the 1997 federal budget this was changed to the Canadian Child Tax Benefit (CCTB) and the National Child Benefit Supplement (NCBS) was introduced, which allowed for additional support for low-income families with children. These benefits replaced the old family allowance and child tax credit, the former implemented in 1944 and the latter in 1978. It is composed of two com- ponents: the base benefit and the national child benefit (NCB) supplement, which provides tax-free, income-tested monthly payments for children under 18. Currently, this program represents the largest single expenditure by the federal government on child care.

In making child care part of the tax system, the federal government has effectively limited the number of Canadians able to claim child care support. Eligibility is deter- mined by family income as reported on income tax returns. Once past certain family income thresholds, monies must be returned to the government. As Brodie and Bakker (2007, 11, quoting Paterson, Levasseur and Teplova 2004, 132) point out, 'in July 2003, for example, CCTB of $1,169 was claimed back at [a threshold of] $33,487 and the NCB of $1,463 was claimed back at $21,529'.

For most Canadian parents, government support for child care comes by means of federal tax deductions through the child care expense deduction (CCED). This tax pro- gram compensates parents who participate in the labour market for their child care ex- penses by allowing the lower-earning parent (usually female) to deduct those expenses from her income. Currently, the maximum amount that can be claimed is $7,000 for each child under age seven and older children with severe disabilities, and $4,000 for each child aged seven to 14 and children over 14 with moderate disabilities. While the maximum deduction is high, many parents are unable to claim the CCED because they must provide receipts. Many caregivers refuse to issue receipts so that they can avoid paying income taxes. For this reason, and also because the amount of benefit depends on income level, the most well-off, who can afford to pay for formal care, benefit most from the system.

In the late 1990s, efforts were undertaken to develop shared programs between the federal government and the provinces as illustrated in the National Children's Agenda included in the Social Union Framework of 1999. This gathered momentum in 2000 when the federal government reached two agreements with nine of the provinces (all except Quebec) and the territories. One was the Federal/Provincial/Territorial Early Childhood Development Agreement, reached in September 2000, under which provincial and territorial governments agreed to use federal funding to improve and expand services in four priority areas: pregnancy, birth and infancy; parenting and family support; early childhood development, learning, and care; and community supports. The second was the Multilateral Framework on Early Learning and Childcare, reached in March 2003, under which the federal government agreed to provide $900 million over five years to support provincial and territorial government investments explicitly in early learning and child care (White 2004). However, further comprehensive early learning and care initiatives under the leadership of Prime Minister Paul Martin would come to nothing as the Liberals were defeated in the January 2006 election.

Interestingly, child care was a prominent issue in the 2005–6 election campaign (Newman 2008). The Liberals proposed a national program of early learning and child care through continuation of their efforts to draw up bilateral agreements with the provinces, while the opposition Conservative Party proposed a policy that would leave child care decisions to parents through the provision of a direct payment of $100 per month for each child under six (Liberal Party of Canada 2006; Conservative Party of Canada 2006). While the significance of child care for voters in the January 2006 poll is open for question, what can be said is that the Conservative Party's election to minority government status brought to an end the defeated Liberal government's push to build a national plan. On assuming power, the Harper Conservatives announced that the already established bilateral agreements would be honoured for only one year and the program ended in March 2007.

As a replacement, the 2006 Speech from the Throne promised the establishment of the program put forward by the Conservatives during the election, the Choice in Child Care Allowance, later renamed the Universal Child Care Benefit, which provides $1200 per annum for each child under six. This was accompanied by the Community Child Care Investment Program (Child Care Spaces Initiative) which provides tax credits for employers who create new child care spaces for employees and the wider community (Cool 2007, 11). Further to this, the Minister of Human Resources set up a ministerial committee on the Government of Canada's Childcare Initiative to advise on programs to increase child care access. In 2007, the committee returned with a series of recommendations which were hardly new: increase the supply of child care spaces, expand parental leave under Employment Insurance in order to decrease the demand for child care, increase parents' ability to pay for high-quality child care, increase awareness and understanding of child care needs, and address child care staffing challenges (ibid. 11). The government's response was the redirection of $250 million from the Community Child Care Investment Programs to the provincial and territorial governments to build child care spaces. It also announced the Child Care Spaces Initiative, a 25 per cent tax credit for businesses that created licensed child care spaces in the workplace (ibid.).

While the $100 per month is touted as a universal program, the amount is taxable with the result that expenditures are means tested through the tax system. Brodie and Bakker (2007, 14) outline a serious criticism of the program:

> [I]t has been criticized for favouring two-parent families that can afford a stay-at-home parent to attend to childcare needs. Because the benefit is taxable off the income of the lowest-paid spouse, families with one spouse, either unat-tached or minimally attached to the labour forces, will realize larger financial gains from the program than two working parents, or single parents in the work force. In other words, this program effective[ly] subsidizes a particular family form—the male breadwinner model.

Further to this, as the following table illustrates, the cost of monthly child care (when spaces are available) far outstrips $100 per month. The amount promised can only come close to covering costs if parents choose informal and unregulated care ar-rangements. Consequently, the policy facilitates a continuing privatization of child care that falls to predominantly female care givers (Newman 2008).

More than 30 years after the Royal Commission on the Status of Women tabled its recommendations, affordable, regulated, and accessible child care is still a press-ing issue for many Canadian working mothers. A 2004 Organization of Economic Cooperation and Development report (OECD 2004) described Canada's child care sys-tem as 'a patchwork of dismal programs that offers basic babysitting but not much more' (CBC 2004). The OECD found Canada's system to be 'chronically under-funded and found subsidies inequitably distributed to a small number of the poorest families.' This was set against findings that 'Canada has among the highest percentage of work-ing mothers of young children, yet it invests less than half of what other developed nations in Europe devote on average to early-childhood education' (ibid.).

One of the explanations for this dismal assessment of Canada's child care policy is that while child care policy in Canada has been developed as a federal/provincial cost-sharing program, substantive jurisdiction is constitutionally granted to the prov-inces. Achieving a national child care program requires agreement with the provinces, something that has so far proved elusive (White 2001a). In its absence, child care ex-ists as a particularly fragmented program that varies from province to province to ter-ritory. Child care costs vary by province and territory. Some provincial and territorial governments provide assistance directly to families and/or subsidize some spaces for low-income parents; others provide subsidies to child care facilities.

As the history of child care policy in Canada shows, there is no guarantee that funds distributed to the provinces will actually be directed to child care. As Cool (2007, 7) argues, 'the degree of flexibility given to the provinces and territories in allocating these funds has led to variances in service and programs. Although some jurisdictions have chosen to increase or improve childcare services, others have not invested in childcare at all. In fact, some provinces have witnessed a decrease in avail-ability and affordability of childcare since 2001.' Further to this, since the 1990s, cuts to the funds allocated to the provinces through the Canada Health and Social Transfer (CHST), combined with provincial government welfare cutbacks, mean that the entire program has been chronically underfunded.

Table 10.1 | Child Care in Canada by Province

Provinces	Average monthly cost for child care in regulated daycare centres*	Percentage not-for-profit 2008	Number of regulated child care spaces 2008	Percentage of Children 0-12 who have access to regulated child care spaces 2008	Children receiving fee subsidies 2008
Alberta	Not available	49	73,981	13.7	10,616
British Columbia	$618.75 After school $250.	56	87,538	15.4	14,922
Manitoba	$437.33 School age $244.	95	27,189	15.5	9,600
New Brunswick	$520 School age $274.	33 (est)	15,506	16.2	5,424
Newfoundland and Labrador	$975 School age not available	30	5,972	9.2	2,078
Northwest Territories	$600 School age not available	100	1,768	20.5	Information not available
Nova Scotia	$503 School age $330.	50	13,711	11.6	2,863
Nunavut	$577.50 School age $315	100	1,013	11.2	Information not available (est. 193)
Ontario	Not available	76	256,748	13.6	126,097
Prince Edward Island	$613 School age not available	42	4,424	22.2	1,786
Quebec	Not available	86	368,909	36.1	All spaces are subsidized
Saskatchewan	$497 School age $301	100	9,173	6.3	3,718
Yukon	$563 School age $275	64	1,262	27.9	502

* average of costs for infant, toddler, and preschool full-time (5 days per week, 8 hours per day) care.

Data source: Jane Beach, Martha Friendly, Carolyn Ferns, Nina Prabhu, Barry Forer. 2009. 'Early Childhood education and care in Canada 2008'. Childcare Resource and Research Unit, 15 September 2009, Childcarecanada. org, http://www.childcarecanada.org/ECEC2008/index.html, Accessed June 10, 2010.

Once again, Quebec proves to be the exception in the provision of child care, and it is often the Quebec program to which child care advocates point as a model for a national program. Quebec has made a clear effort to develop a province-wide system of regulated child care and early childhood learning spaces for all parents, working or not. Parents are required to contribute a flat fee of $7.00 per day, which was raised from $5.00 per day in 2003. The program recognizes three types of day-care provision: child care centres, daycare centres, and home child care providers. All three are subsidized, although home child care provision appears to receive less subsidy (Lefebvre 2004). As a result, the highest number of Canadian children in some form of care is found in Quebec, with 67 per cent of children aged 6 months to 5 years in care. Much of this is institutional, with 52 per cent of Quebec's children attending some form of daycare centre. However, the program is not uncontroversial; it is argued that it is too expensive (in 2004 the child care cost the provinces nearly 2.96 billion dollars) (Lefebvre 2004, 53); it is a 'one size fits all' program that cannot accommodate parents working shifts outside of a 9-to-5, Monday to Friday workweek; it penalizes low-income families claiming their federal child tax benefits; it is the cause of increased behavioural difficulties in Quebec's children; and it does a poor job of ensuring quality care (Lefebvre 2004; Baker et al. 2007; Kozhaya 2007, A14). Child care advocates counter these arguments. In 2003, the program was re-formed by Jean Charest's Liberal government, which raised the cost to $7.00 per day and expanded the role of for-profit daycare centres in the program. The area upon which both critics and supporters agree is that access is not perfect and demand for spaces still outstrips the spaces available. However, compared to the other provinces, working and nonworking parents now have much greater access to and support in finding child care.

Thus, with the exception of Quebec, government support for child care is currently quite minimal. Most federal child care spending in Canada currently comes in the form of tax benefits (income) rather than direct service support/provision. With the promised continued expansion of the child tax benefit, and with comprehensive federal-provincial-territorial programs proving more difficult to negotiate, more monies continue to go towards tax benefits for families rather than towards program development.

Child care in the 2000s: From child care to early learning and care

It is interesting to observe a parallel trend emerging in the United States and Canada during recent years that involves the uniting of child care and early childhood education policy streams (White 2004). Actors, including government actors, no longer talk only about 'daycare' or even 'childcare' but also child care's explicit connection to early childhood development or early childhood education. The Liberal Party under Paul Martin made a pledge during the June 2004 election campaign that, if victorious, the Liberal government would provide $5 billion in additional federal money to the provinces and territories, which would be devoted to early learning and child care programs (contingent, of course, on provincial and territorial approval).

This change in rhetorical and policy focus from women to children, as Dobrowolsky and Jenson (2004) argue, has significant consequences for women. The policy focus on child care as only early childhood education or early childhood development raises concerns about the ability of child care programs to respond to the needs of working

parents and support parents' labour market participation. Many early childhood education programs, such as preschool and kindergarten programs, are half-day programs,
which makes them problematic for working parents. Child care programs, in contrast,
have typically been structured around a full workday (though many parents and advocates complain that more programs are needed to support parents who work on shifts
or weekends). Dobrowolsky and Jenson (2004) warn of the danger of government
attention being directed exclusively to children and children's programs. As these authors point out, refashioning the social rights and citizenship regime in Canada from
poor adults to poor children and then to children will likely downplay the issue of
women's equality.

Others, such as Myles and Quadagno (2000), point out that child-centred policies do not necessarily preclude a policy focus on women's equality. After all, it is in
the economic interest of the state to encourage and support women's labour market
participation along with guaranteeing a healthy and educated future workforce. State
support for child care meets both these goals. As White (2004) argues, politicians seem
more and more willing to accept that something must be done to improve the settings
in which the vast majority of young children find themselves for at least part of the day.
However, as Dobrowolsky and Jenson (2004, 172) warn, policy-makers 'do not always
make the distinction between childcare and "quality" childcare'. Ultimately, we should
not lose sight of the simple fact that the economic well-being of children is intrinsically
linked to the economic well-being of women.

The major challenge that remains for working women is how to balance work and
family life. As Timpson (2001, 69) argues, '[i]n short, although the 1970s witnessed
significant improvements in the development of federal policies to promote women's
employment opportunities and reduce employment discrimination against them, the
issue of how women were supposed to enjoy these opportunities while maintaining
responsibility for the care of their children was deflected away from the federal agenda
in the early stages of the Trudeau government'—and, one could argue, has remained
there ever since.

Conclusion: What Is to Be Done?

In Canada, while provincial and federal governments have been willing to work on addressing the issues of equality of work and opportunity, they have been much less willing to address the complexity of opportunity when women's differences are involved,
particularly when it comes to recognizing and supporting the private work of child and
elder care predominantly provided by women. As a consequence, Benoit (2000, 97)
argues, Canadian programs to support women in work and alleviate their poverty have
been 'sporadic', 'short-term', and 'do not provide essential social benefits, including
transportation and childcare'.

At the beginning of this chapter, we discussed the citizen-worker and caregiver parity models of gender equality. The first endorses adherence to male norms of
workplace participation and recommends the commodification of many of the tasks
that many women currently perform as unpaid labour (such as child care, house-
cleaning, and so on); the second calls for greater rewards and status to those who
perform traditionally female tasks on their own (that is, without purchasing those
services on the market).[8]

Nancy Fraser (1994) is pessimistic about the capacity of either model to bring about true economic equality. State public policy will continue to uphold underlying patriarchal gender norms, whether that policy is predicated on a vision of the universal breadwinner, in which opportunity for full employment equal to that of men is provided for women, or on caregiver parity, in which women's private work in the home is recognized and accorded proper financial value. Fraser (1994) argues that true gender equity is based not only on equal respect for women and men but also on more substantive and tangible factors, such as equality of resources or equality of capabilities. Unfortunately, the resources and capabilities that women bring to society are not valued as highly as those contributed by men. For Fraser (1994, 595), gender equity demands that society develop assumptions that require 'not only parity of participation in socially valued activities, but also the decentering of androcentric measures of social value'. The current approaches to women's economic equality do not fully meet this vision of equality because they do not advocate or envision making fundamental changes to market rules and family arrangements.

A third perspective, therefore, argues that the best route to gender equality is through a true acknowledgment on the part of society that social reproduction should be valued and that shared responsibility on the part of both men and women for parenting and employment should be the norm. Laws, public policies, and societal norms should encourage both men and women to participate equally in the employment world and shoulder domestic tasks together. This represents a significant change in law and social practice that would require major workplace adjustments. Employers would have to provide more flexible work hours for all parents, allow men in particular to scale back their work without penalty, and provide other 'family-friendly' policies, such as longer maternity and parental leave programs with better compensation, pension credits for family caregivers, and part-time work with the same employee benefits as full-time work. Such a shift would probably require some state support and involvement as well, not only to enforce employer obligations but also to ensure that small businesses, for example, are able to provide the same family-friendly benefits as large firms.

The advantages of such a change are clear. As Benoit (2000, 3) points out, 'in some capitalist societies where the right to care has been institutionalized . . . relations between men and women are relatively egalitarian compared to those countries where caring work remains invisible and under-valued'. In other words, not only does society benefit from ensuring that the tasks of social reproduction are being performed but women stand a better chance of achieving equality.

What needs to be done is complicated, and many would argue that the goal of shared parenting and work responsibilities is utopian. Yet obvious first steps include significant alleviation of the poverty and workplace discrimination experienced by women through state intervention. We cannot lose sight, as Benoit (2000, 5) reminds us, that no matter how problematic state policy may be, state social and labour policies do make some difference to women's lives; they 'make the difference between a solo mother living in poor or moderate circumstances; between caring work made visible and valued or its opposite; and between relative equality between the sexes and pronounced inequality'. However, in the long term, a complete restructuring of the social norms around the feminine/masculine division and the conception of public and private labour is required. Men and women must recognize and be sensitive to their shared responsibility for both public and private work. That would erase the social norms around the distinction between public and private, between earning and caring.

A Not-So-Utopian Shared Parenting and Housework Model: Spain

A recent story in The Guardian reveals that legislative encouragement of shared parenting and housework is not so difficult to achieve:

> Spanish men will have to learn to change nappies and don washing-up gloves under the terms of a new law designed to strike a blow at centuries of Latin machismo.
>
> The law, due to be passed this month, is likely to provoke a revolution in family affairs in a country where 40 per cent of men reportedly do no housework at all. It will oblige men to 'share domestic responsibilities and the care and attention' of children and elderly family members, according to the draft approved by the Spanish parliament's justice commission.
>
> This will become part of the marriage contract at civil wedding ceremonies later this year.
>
> 'The idea of equality within marriage always stumbles over the problem of work in the house and caring for dependent people,' said Margarita Uría, of the Basque Nationalist party, who was behind what is an amendment to a new divorce law.
>
> 'This will be a good way of reminding people what their duties are. It is something feminists have been wanting for a long time.'
>
> Failure to meet the obligations will be taken into consideration by judges when determining the terms of divorces. Men who refuse to do their part may be given less frequent contact with their children. . . .
>
> The change to the Spanish legal code will see domestic obligations added to a list of marital duties that currently includes fidelity, living together, and helping one another.

Could such legislation become a reality in Canada?

Source: Giles Tremlett. 2005. 'Blow to machismo as Spain forces men to do housework.' The Guardian 8 April http://www.guardian.co.uk/gender/story/0,11812,1454803,00.html.

What does all this mean for women's economic, social, and political action? In summarizing the story of women's work in Canada, their economic situation at the beginning of the twenty-first century, and their struggles for recognition, compensation, respect, safety, support, access to untraditional occupations, and time off from the two or three shifts required of them, we leave the last word to Nancy Fraser (1994, 612–13):

> This means building movements whose demands for equity cannot be satisfied within the present gender order. . . . This approach would not only deconstruct the opposition between breadwinning and caregiving; it would also deconstruct the associated opposition between bureaucratized public institutional settings and intimate private domestic settings. . . . The trick is to imagine a social world in which citizens' lives integrate wage earning, caregiving, community activism, political participation, and involvement in the associational life of civil society—while also leaving time for some fun.

Questions for Critical Thought

1. What features of Quebec politics explain the province's progressive policies toward the balancing of work and family life?
2. How has the shift from Keynesian political economy to neo-liberalism changed the model of citizenship for Canadian women (and men)?
3. Is it likely that the recommendations made by the RCSW regarding women's employment will ever be met?

CHAPTER 11

Regulation and Control of Women's Bodies

Feminism is, in large part, a movement to give women the right to control their own bodies, not just in terms of reproduction but also in terms of what to do with those bodies and what to put on those bodies. Feminist attention to matters of the body has focused on understanding who possesses and controls the female body as well as reasserting women's control over their own bodies. How best to achieve that control, however, remains controversial, as will be illustrated in each of the areas discussed below: beauty images, prostitution, and pornography.

As with issues examined in previous chapters, we need to understand the various feminist perspectives on each of these issues, and how those perspectives are reflected or not reflected in legislation, jurisprudence, and public policy in Canada. Indeed, within the feminist community, there is enormous disagreement on what the nature and scope of law and public policy should be.

Beauty and the Body

Carla Rice (1994, 44) writes, 'Everyday, everywhere, millions of women are engaged in chaotic, controlled, ritualized and routine acts of self-harm. We are quietly depriving ourselves, starving ourselves, bingeing, purging, and exercising excessively, equating emotional well-being with meeting an unattainable ideal. We are also numbing ourselves with drugs or alcohol, cutting, bruising and burning ourselves, or dissociating, in an attempt to survive by escaping our bodies entirely.'

The 1990 publication of Naomi Wolf's *The Beauty Myth* marked the launch in popular culture of feminist critiques of societal standards of female beauty. However, feminists had already been working for decades to dispel the deeply entrenched idea that women must live up to some feminine ideal (Brownmiller 1984). The issue of bodily control was present even in the earliest decades of the movement. As Bordo (1993, 18) points out, at the first feminist mass meeting in the United States in 1914, feminist political demands included the 'right to ignore fashion' as well as the right not to have to wear makeup.

Second-wave feminists were very conscious of the politics of the body. A number of the pioneers of the second-wave movement, such as Susan Brownmiller (1984), specifically studied the construction of femininity. Books such as Susie Orbach's (1978) *Fat Is A Feminist Issue* exposed the issue of dieting. In *Hunger Strike*, Orbach (1986) tackled the problem of anorexia. As Bordo (1993, 19) points out, the 'very first public act of second-wave feminist protest was the "No More Miss America" demonstration in August 1968' in the United States. At that pageant, feminists earned the label 'bra burners'. Although not a bra was burned, bras, 'girdles, curlers, false eyelashes, wigs', and copies of women's magazines of the time such as *Ladies' Home Journal* and *Cosmopolitan* were thrown into a 'Freedom Trash Can'.

Growing intolerance of the most blatant sexism has meant that overtly degrading images of women now receive quick commentary, if not challenge. As one example, Canada's Terra Footwear Ltd. was forced to pull an advertising campaign in October 2003 after a major union mobilization in opposition to what was seen as sexist advertising. The company had embarked on a billboard ad campaign featuring female models in sexually suggestive poses, dressed in lingerie and work boots. About 600 billboards went up across Canada (CP 2003c, A9). The company website showed a video commercial for the boots, featuring topless dancers. Union officials, along with the operating engineers in Manitoba, spoke out against the ads, declaring them offensive and sexually discriminatory. The union was part of the 95,000-member Manitoba Federation of Labour, which then threatened a product boycott when the company refused to pull the ads. The 250,000-member Canadian Auto Workers followed suit, calling on the Canadian government to cancel contracts with Terra for military boots (cbc.ca, 2003). While the company defended the ads, calling them funny (the line on the billboard was 'You probably can't keep your eyes off the bootlaces') (Dabitch 2003), it ultimately pulled them.

Despite gains such as these, efforts to transform the (mostly) female body have reached new heights (or lows). For example, reality television shows such as *Extreme Makeover* (2002–5), which subject people to extreme physical transformations, proliferate on network television. In *The Swan* which ran on the Fox TV network in 2004, 17 contestants received major reconstructive surgery: 'all received tooth veneers, 16 had liposuction, 15 had forehead lifts, 13 had nose jobs, 13 had lip augmentations and 11 had breast augmentations' (Kuczynski 2004), and then competed in a beauty contest. In 2005, the program was cancelled because of falling ratings. In 2007, *Extreme Makeover* was also cancelled, its popularity eclipsed by its spinoff *Extreme Makeover: Home Edition*. However, this has not detracted from the popularity of less physically invasive make-over programs such as *What Not To Wear*, which runs British and American versions, and which helps nominated participants conform (willingly and unwillingly) to current fashion trends and norms.

If one is not sure what the ideal feminine image is, the media provides an overwhelming number of examples in shows such as *America's Next Top Model* and *Sports Illustrated Swimsuit Model Search*, which promote the idea that beauty is a women's primary commodity (Rice 1994, 48). This commodity is often an Anglo-American ideal, which has both class and race implications. There is a certain expressed truth to the adage that 'you can not be too rich or too thin', particularly in the popular media. According to Michael Sandal in *The Case Against Perfection* (2007), the focus on appearance reflects and reinforces class privilege: 'in a culture where appearance is too often linked to status and self-esteem, low income individuals pay a substantial price when they cannot afford to meet conventional standards' (cited, in Rhode 2010, 96). Cosmetic surgery is becoming increasingly popular in Latin America and especially in Asia (n.a. 2003a), where women tend to seek out cosmetic surgery to remove more 'Asian' features. For African-Americans the desire is for narrow noses and lips. As

Rhode (2010, 43) points out, 'although minorities are significantly underrepresented among groups with substantial discretionary income in the United States, they have similar rates of cosmetic surgery . . . much of it oriented towards obtaining a more Anglo-European appearance'. At the same time, the beauty products industry is expanding greatly in China, Russia, South Korea, India, and Brazil.

The monetary impact of the pursuit of this feminine ideal is enormous. The 'beauty enhancing' industry is a giant among industries. In 2003, *The Economist* (n.a. 2003b) estimated the worth of the industry on a global scale at $160 billion annually, a figure that includes all products, cosmetic surgery, health clubs, and diet aids. In 2009, market analysis of the industry put sales of beauty products at $191 billion worldwide with Western Europe representing 29 per cent of the market and North America and developed Asia both accounting for 20 per cent (Solca and Wing 2009, 139). This does not include spending on diet-related products, an industry that in 2009 was worth $59.7 billion in the United States alone (Rao 2010), or cosmetic surgery. In 2008, the global market for cosmetic surgery services was $31.7 billion, a market that was expected to climb to $40.1 billion by 2013 (Elder 2009). In the United States alone, according to the 2008 report of the American Society of Plastic Surgeons, 12.1 million cosmetic procedures were performed. This was an increase of only 3 per cent over 2007, and it was reported that total spending, at $10.3 billion, was down 9 per cent from the previous year (Miller and Washington 2009, 213). This decline was attributed to the economic recession of 2008–9 (ibid. 213.) as consumers opted for cheaper, more minor aesthetic improvements. Also of note was the growing popularity of cosmetic surgery among male baby boomers who accounted 'for nearly 10 per cent of all procedures' (ibid. 214).

In addition, books on weight loss and diet products have proliferated as obesity levels rise, leading some to suggest that the diet industry actually contributes to obesity (Cummings 2003). Rice (1994, 45) writes, 'We have been raised in a culture where body size is of paramount importance, where thinness is equated with health, attractiveness, morality, sexuality' and where 'a woman's essential value is based on her ability to attain a thin body size'. As a result, she argues, the vast majority of women express dislike for their body while continually dieting, which has been found to lead to weight gain.

What is generally underplayed is how painful the pursuit of beauty can be. In the 1980s, one plastic surgery technique involved the use of lasers to burn off top layers of skin in order to reveal the flesh underneath, a procedure that required weeks of recovery and 'also had nasty effects on non-white skin, often leaving Asian patients with dark spots' (n.a. 2003a). Lifestyle columnist Leah McLaren, writing in *The Globe and Mail* in 2000, described the excruciating pain of a 'Brazilian' (a.k.a. 'porn star' or 'Barbie') bikini wax. She notes that plush towels are often 'placed between the jaws of a client to prevent her from grinding the teeth out of her skull while receiving a bikini wax' (McLaren 2000, R3). Post-surgery recovery from breast augmentation has been described by one client as 'more painful than childbirth' (Graydon 2005, F7), and the long-term health risks of such surgery are still being investigated. However, health concerns have not decreased the popularity of surgical procedures. In 1992, a moratorium on the use of silicone breast implants came into force as a response to incidents of rupturing implants; however, this did little to dampen the popularity of augmentation surgery and in 2004 the moratorium was lifted. The number of breast augmentations undergone by North American women rose during the moratorium from 33,000 in 1992 to 237,000 in 2002 (Graydon 2005, F7). Between 2000 and 2008, the market for breast augmentation grew by 45 per cent, and in 2008, even accounting for the small decline in the industry, 307,000 breast augmentations were performed in the United States (Miller and Washington 2009, 213). Popular culture seems to glorify the pursuit of beauty as entailing necessary pain and suffering, ignoring the significant effects on health that can arise as a result.

The question is, why are so many women willing to subject themselves to such treatments? Can we claim that patriarchy requires women to live up to these ideals? Are women victims of the idealized body image or free choosers? Feminists' answers to these questions reflect a great deal of ambivalence.

Some feminist writers, when confronted with the fact that many women choose to submit to such procedures, assume that they 'are somehow mistaken or misguided. They have had the ideological wool pulled over their eyes' (Davis 1991, 29). Others focus less on women's 'false consciousness' and more on relentless societal norms that force women's compliance. Carla Rice (1994) describes this relentless onslaught of media and other images as a war over defining what is female in which the conflict is 'waged on the landscape of our bodies. . . . The effects of such struggle on our bodies, minds, and spirits are similar to the effects of violence on the landscape of any other war—suffering, chaos, starvation, mutilation, devastation, and even death' (44).

Starvation is a particular concern as the media trend has been to represent women as increasingly thinner than the average. According to the Media Awareness Network (www.media-awareness.ca 2010), 'twenty years ago, the average model weighed 8 per cent less than the average woman, but today's models weigh 23 percent less'. While it is not clear that this is explained by models getting smaller or by the increasing size of women generally (if we take the concern raised regarding an epidemic of obesity seriously) (Wang and Beydoun 2007; Slater et al. 2009); what cannot be denied is that the media does a poor job of portraying the bodily reality of most women. In addition, in 2007, the *New York Times* reported that not only were models getting thinner, they were getting younger. 'Despite American industries proposing that models under 16 [years of age] be banned from runways . . . in Australia recently, the naming of 12 year-old Maddison Gabriel as the face of Gold Coast Fashion prompted that country's Prime Minister to decry the loss of innocence. . . But people want the "littlies," [children] and they want them thin' (Trebay 2007). For many feminists and commentators, the result of this media presentation of unattainable models of feminine beauty is the increasing number of diagnosed eating disorders, the generalized dissatisfaction of women and girls regarding their appearances, and the multi-billion dollar diet, beauty, and cosmetic surgery industries.

The American Psychological Association's Task Force on the Sexualization of Girls (APA 2007) summarized a number of studies that measured the effects of objectification on adult college-aged women and high school-aged girls. They reported that exposure to and endorsement of sexually objectifying images (often described merely as 'narrow beauty ideals' although such ideals are often objectifying) can affect self-esteem and body image and can lead to depression and eating disorders or to self-objectification which in turn leads to depressive symptoms, cognitive impairment, and lower self-esteem (Lamb 2010, 297).[1]

This gets to the heart of the 'beauty system' (Code 2000, 39) which feminists have shown is integral to the production and regulation of appropriate forms of femininity and to asymmetrical relations of power both between the sexes and among women. In her, 1975 essay, 'Visual Pleasure and Narrative Cinema,' Laura Mulvey introduced the concept of the Male Gaze to examine the power relations involved in the act of viewing, looking, and being an audience. The argument is that cultural products such as media representations presuppose a 'neutral and naturalized' masculine viewpoint. Therefore, women are always positioned as and accustomed to being the object of male viewing. This relationship is unbalanced because women do not return the gaze, and as a result 'man is reluctant to gaze'. For a woman to assume the role of 'gazer' or looker, she does not do so as a woman but by taking on a masculine role. In this relationship, women are always positioned as the object of desire and it is the attention of the male gaze that is sought. As such, the male gaze can be seen to produce and maintain gendered and heteronormative positions.

As Deborah L. Rhode (2010) points out in *The Beauty Bias: The Injustice of Appearance in Life and Law*, the way in which one's appearance is perceived and judged has both policy and legal implications. 'Injustices related to appearance fall along a spectrum, and involve everything from debilitating discrimination and social stigma, to the costs of conformity in time, expense and physical risk' (3). Numerous studies show that in our society, judgments regarding others are often made on the basis of appearance, including decisions regarding hiring and firing. As we discussed in chapter 9, it is more often than not the work undertaken by women that requires particular idealized and gendered forms of appearance. While most democracies prohibit discrimination on the basis of sex, race, and ethnicity, 'personal appearance' can be an allowable bias when it is not defined within these parameters. As such, employer requests for particular appearances and dress styles may at worst hide discrimination based on race, ethnicity, gender, class, age, and size, and, at best, limit an employee's privacy, dignity, and personal self-expression. Further to this, such concerns do not account for the reality of the financial and time burdens involved in meeting set standards of personal grooming which fall predominantly on women.

Naomi Wolf (1990, 10) goes further, suggesting that the beauty system and the associated concept of the male gaze are deliberate methods of psychological control of women on the part of those in power who wish to prevent women from succeeding in the public sphere. Wolf (1990, 10) argues that as more and more women breach the power structure, 'the more strictly and heavily and cruelly images of female beauty have come to weigh upon us. We are in the midst of a violent backlash against feminism that uses images of female beauty as a political weapon against women's advancement: the beauty myth.' Patriarchy enforces these impossible standards to exhaust and dispirit women, forcing them to obsess about their appearance and ultimately exercising social control over them: '[T]he ideology of beauty is the last one remaining of the old feminine ideologies that still has the power to control' (Wolf 1990, 16). Rice (1994, 45) notes that, ironically, as women have moved more and more into the public sphere, their fixation on body size makes it seem as though they are literally trying to take up less physical space.

Botox as a feminist issue?

In December 2009, *New York Times* columnist Judith Warner reported that Terry O'Neill, president of the National Organization for Women, had issued a statement protesting a proposed levy of 5 per cent on cosmetic surgery procedures being discussed as part of the US Senate's comprehensive health care reform legislation. O'Neill, Warner wrote, saw access to cosmetic procedures as a women's issue, as it allows older women to compete for jobs against younger men and women. The Botox issue exemplifies the women's movement's adjustment to 'the realities of life in our culture, where many of its basic goals . . . have stalled or are even backsliding'. Warner writes, 'This is what happens when equal pay stalls, abortion rights wither, and attempts to improve child care and workplace flexibility die on the legislative vine year after year. Women's empowerment becomes a matter of a tight face and flat belly. You control what you can control.'

Other feminists fundamentally disagree. For example, Elizabeth Grosz (1994) and Luce Irigaray (1985) criticize Mulvey's conception of the male gaze as 'being overly monolithic' and its denial of the pleasure women might find in being objects and subjects of desire (cited in Code 2000, 219). Mary Anne Doane (1987) suggests that femininity itself can be performed in a way that undermines and disrupts the dichotomy of male/female and subject/object. In recent years, the use of constructivist, postmodern, and post-structuralist perspectives that view beauty, femininity, and sexuality (which underlies discourses of female representation) as cultural discourses has opened up possibilities for beauty practices not only as sites of oppression, but also of creativity, subversion, and empowerment (Code 2000, 39). In this way, body alteration is argued to be a means of taking control of one's body and the way others see one's body.

In other words, instead of women being victims of prevailing beauty norms, they are turning them to their own advantage (Davis 1991, 22). Davis (1991, 23) points out that one has to try to understand why women would choose to engage in such dangerous and painful procedures, and argues that such procedures may really be 'about being ordinary, taking one's life in one's own hands, and determining how much suffering is fair'. The reaction of contestants in reality television shows such as *Extreme Makeover* attests to this theory: the women invariably weep with delight at the transformation, as do their families and friends. Similarly, Meredith McGhan's (2000) essay on how she became a topless dancer describes how participating in the sex industry gave her confidence and helped her overcome a negative self-image. She found it an empowering, not disempowering, experience to be considered beautiful by men—although she confesses that her body image, while bolstered, was dependent on the 'outside forces' that defined what beauty means (McGhan 2000, 175).

Lipstick Feminism and Raunch Culture

For many women, there are no easy answers, and there is a great deal of ambivalence regarding the female body and issues of appearance. It is certainly interesting how something so seemingly superficial gives rise to debates between women, feminists, and in the courts, but when 'the personal is political', how one conceives of and expresses oneself will unavoidably be political. The questions and ambivalence come from determining whether self-expression is an act of resistance or the result of oppression.

In her 2005 book, *Female Chauvinist Pigs: Women and the Rise of Raunch Culture*, Ariel Levy identified the emergence of a form of feminism, in tandem with the increasing 'pornographication' of Western industrial societies, that argues the expression of female sexuality and desire, whether heterosexual, lesbian, or bisexual, as a form of empowerment. The terms 'Do Me', 'babe', 'lipstick', and 'Girlie feminism' had already appeared in the popular press. These referred to emerging themes in third-wave feminism that advocated expressions of femininity and female sexuality as a challenge to objectification and defied any restriction, whether patriarchal or feminist, that controlled and defined what girls and women could wear, say, or do (see Baumgardner and Richards 2010 and Edut 2003). In terms of personal aesthetics and sexuality, the expression of this approach to feminism was to do what felt good and gave one pleasure. Through this, girls and women become empowered as they freely chose what and who they are. The third-wave girl is positioned as 'a new robust young woman with agency and a strong sense of self. . . . While Third-Wavers welcome multiple imaginings of sexual encounters, partners, sexualities, and ways of being, they also welcome the choice to empower themselves by ironically taking on stereotypically feminine roles and performing them with panache' (Lamb 2010, 300). The autonomous choice to wear makeup, strip, pole-dance, buy sex toys, and engage in girl-on-girl exhibitionism can be a feminist position and young women need not automatically be positioned as victims.

The Lipstick and Girlie feminists of the third wave picked up on the celebration of the female body and sexuality as a way to erase the differences and double standards in moral judgments made regarding female sexual expression and male sexual expression, i.e., the pejorative difference between 'slut' (female) and 'ladies' man' or 'player' (male). It also was a response, on the one hand, to the backlash characterization of feminists as ugly, unshaven, unfashionable, and anti-sex, and, on the other, to the limiting and oppressive aspects identified with second-wave feminism. Using popular culture, sometimes along with feminist language, these activists see themselves as transforming 'negative images of women and unhealthy messages about personal relationships or political roles into more open, diverse, and accepting portrayals of women and the many ways women can act in society' (Scholz 2010, 123).

This is not limited to the clothing and activities of pornography-inspired 'raunch culture'. In looking at the role of both the hijab (Islamic headscarf) and 'porno-chic' in Europe, Linda Duits and Liesbet van Zoonen (2006), argue that 'public discourse construes controversial sartorial choices of girls as a locus of necessary regulation. . .' (104). This is illustrated in the policy discussions, most often at the school level, but not unheard of at the level of the state, on setting rules that ban certain types of clothing in the schools and other public institutions. The headscarf has become a flash point of a contemporary social dilemma around multiculturalism, while the thong and skimpy belly t-shirt are flashpoints for contemporary social debates regarding morality and the decline of society. As Duits and van Zoonen point out, male clothing choices have not met with a similar form of politicization. Consequently, in the matter of personal choice of what to wear and what not to wear, women may act as agents of resistance to modern western ambivalence regarding Islamic identity in the case of donning the hijab, or as agents of resistance to narrow views of female sexuality in patriarchal society in the case of thongs and belly t-shirts. The hijab and the thong both become symbols of political agency and resistance to objectification.

However, the following question must be asked: what does empowerment mean? Zoë D. Peterson, (2010, 307), in exploring answers to this question, explains that feminists 'struggle with whether sexual empowerment should be conceptualized as a subjective internal feeling of power and agency or an objective measure of power and control'. The concern is that equating feelings of agency with cultural institutional power may be a mistake because, as Lamb (2010b, 308) points out, 'it over-invests in a model of free-will and choice in a marketplace of ideas and images that seek to define and construct girls' [and women's] sexuality'. Feeling emboldened sexually is not necessarily the same thing as empowerment. As Whitehead and Kurz (2009) found in a study of recreational pole-dancers,

> As an individual activity, [pole dancing] can be constructed as empowering through the extent to which it affords women the opportunity to exercise a form of 'choice' and 'control'. It may also provide a vehicle for women to resist hegemonic notions of femininity as passive and modest. However, . . . one must consider that activities experienced as liberating on an individual level may often secure societal-level oppression in covert ways. Thus, pole dancing may reinforce societal notions of both masculine and feminine sexuality as a result of encouraging women to construct themselves as erotic objects (241).

In many cases, this bodily and sexual empowerment is ironically very similar to that of the sexualized porn-star female in popular culture and the market, to the simplistic, plastic stereotypes of female sexuality constantly reiterated throughout our culture (Levy 2005, 197). While subjective empowerment might validate a woman's own experiences and action, it will most likely not get her into a university program, an executive position, or elected political office. We have yet to see a pole-dancing marathon to raise awareness of and funds for feminist political representatives. Further to this, the focus remains pointedly on the female body as the focus of a gaze whether objective or subjective, thus supporting a view that women and girls are only their bodies and that satisfaction with one's body defines one's own happiness.

Prostitution

Feminism is also ambivalent about women who engage in the sex trade. The traditional arguments either hold that prostitutes are immoral women whom society should marginalize and prosecute because of their work or take the economic liberal line that sex is like any other commercial product that should be ownable and saleable (Posner 2003; n.a. 2004; Auger 2010). According to Sylvia Law (1999–2000, 532–3), feminists, in contrast, agree on three main points: 'First, they condemn the current legal policy enforcing criminal sanctions against women who offer sex in exchange for money. Second, they agree that authentic consent is the *sine qua non* of legitimate sex, whether in commercial or non-commercial form. Third, all feminists recognize that commercial sex workers are subject to economic coercion and are often victims of violence, and that too little is done to address these problems.' Beyond that, Stetson (1997, 298–9) and Brock (2000) identify three main feminist views on this issue.

First, the **sex work** perspective (Davidson 2002) holds that prostitution is a form of legitimate work that women, faced with a range of bad jobs, may choose. Women should therefore have the right to be sex workers without fear of prosecution. Governments should repeal laws that make voluntary sex work a crime, including laws against solicitation and brothels. Instead, governments should regulate the work using business and commercial codes. Decriminalization would also make sex work much less dangerous and allow governments to prosecute those who hurt prostitutes (see also n.a. 2004).

Second, the **abolitionist** perspective holds that governments should strive to eliminate prostitution because it inherently involves the sexual use and abuse of women by men. Most women do not choose prostitution voluntarily but become trapped into performing sex work because of homelessness and economic deprivation, drug addiction, or coercion. Prostitution is not a 'service' or 'work' but rather the selling of the body, indeed the self, to men for sexual use. Radical feminists such as Kate Millett (1970) argue that the problem with the term 'sex worker' is that the work is not about selling sex but about men's sexual pleasure. Sex workers are also at risk of assault, rape, robbery, and sexually transmitted diseases. MacKinnon (1993) argues that prostitution is not an activity that uncoerced women would choose to do. Advocacy should therefore involve setting up social programs to help prostitutes find alternatives to selling sex as well as prosecuting and punishing the customers rather than the women who engage in the work.

However, neither the sex work nor the abolitionist perspective helps us in grappling with cases in which a 'nice, young, middle-class girl' becomes a call girl to pay for university (Schmidt 2000, R7) or a woman table dances to feel in control of her sexuality (McGhan 2000). These are not marginalized women but young women who have agency, who have choices, and who choose to participate in the sex trade. Deborah Brock (2000, 79) labels this third perspective on prostitution as **outlaw**: viewing sex work as a stepping stone to a better career or as an expression of sexual freedom. Prosecution of prostitution, therefore, merely reflects society's oppression of sexual behaviour deemed outside the norm rather than oppression of gender (Brock 2000, 92).

There is strong evidence of support for all of these perspectives in Canadian law and advocacy, with the traditional view of sex workers as immoral holding sway for the longest period. Brock (2000, 91) argues that sex for money has generally been one of the most stigmatized forms of sexual expression, along with sex aided by pornography or sex toys, homosexuality, and promiscuity. The most privileged (acceptable) forms of sexuality are 'heterosexual, married, monogamous, and procreative'. As Cheryl Auger (2010) argues, Canadian Criminal law and municipal by-laws that prohibit prostitution and regulate other forms of work associated with the sex trade, (e.g., escort services, body-rubbing and stripping, sex workers) present a discourse of public respectability and morality, constructing sex workers 'as unnatural and abnormal . . . threatening sexual deviants'. This helps to justify the exclusion of sex workers from 'full community membership and all its rights and protections, including the right to bodily integrity and police protection from violence' (Auger 2010, 2).

Thus, according to Julie Cool (2004, 7) prostitution 'is one of the most dangerous occupations in Canada'. The Canadian Centre for Justice Statistics notes that, between

1991 and 2001, 73 prostitutes were killed while working. These numbers under-represent the actual figure, as they include only those cases in which the police were able to determine that the death occurred in the course of engaging in prostitution-related activities (cited in Cool 2004, 7). In 2007, police reported that 15 prostitutes were killed as a direct result of their profession, up from an average of 7 per year for the previous decade (Li 2008, 11). In Alberta, the RCMP, responding to the 'large numbers of unidentifiable bodies of prostitutes disposed in remote rural areas in Alberta', have established a registry of persons considered to be at risk of becoming homicide victims (Cool 2004, 7). In a similar move, the police forces of Halifax and Edmonton have started collecting DNA samples from local prostitutes. The danger was highlighted in 2007 by the charging and subsequent conviction of Robert Pickton for the murders of six prostitutes from Vancouver's Downtown Eastside and the revelation during the trial that he had admitted to slaying another 43.

As with the violence, (see Valverde 1991; Auger 2010), the impact of regulations against sex work—whether these be vagrancy laws, solicitation laws, or even public health protection and community cleanliness laws—falls largely on the female sex workers rather than the purchasers of the services. Most studies (75 to 80 per cent) suggest the majority of persons who work as prostitutes are women, while almost all the clients are men. (Cool 2004, 6). On the streets, Aboriginal women and women trafficked into Canada, are over-represented. A study of prostitution in Quebec noted that minority and Aboriginal women were over-represented in prostitution in Montreal, and that these women were likely to face greater violence from clients. In the western provinces, Aboriginal women also tend to be over-represented on the streets (Cool 2004, 6).

Historically street walkers were charged as vagrants and under section 164.1 of the federal Criminal Code.[2] However, in 1970, the Royal Commission on the Status of Women argued that the vagrancy statute was discriminatory since 'in addition to being gender-specific, it exhibited moral condemnation of women while restricting their activities in the public sphere, permitted the use of arbitrary police powers, and stigmatized women through the acquisition of a criminal record' (Brock 2000, 83–4). In 1972 the federal Liberal government repealed all vagrancy laws and made prostitution itself legal, but it outlawed street solicitation by any person for the purpose of prostitution (section 195.1 of the federal Criminal Code). Such a law, of course, makes it very difficult actually to engage in prostitution-related activity (Jeffrey 2004, 83). While the law is formally gender-neutral, in practice the majority of those prosecuted are women.

In 1978 the Supreme Court of Canada, in response to a challenge of the solicitation law, ruled that the police could no longer arrest someone for a single proposition of sex but rather the solicitation had to be pressing and persistent.[3] Furthermore, the interior of a car could no longer be considered a public space, which meant that if a solicitation occurred there, it would not be illegal. After strong criticism from urban community groups, some mayors, police associations, and others that these rules made it very difficult to arrest anyone for prostitution, the federal government established a Special Committee on Prostitution and Pornography (the Fraser Committee) to review various options. The committee was also mandated to review the issue of pornography, an issue, Brock (2000) argues, that had garnered more of the women's movement's attention than prostitution.

In its report, the Fraser Committee recognized the feminist argument that social and economic factors explain why women engage in sex work and therefore
they should not be prosecuted criminally for it. The committee also recommended
partial decriminalization of prostitution in brothels in order to address the issue of
unsafe working conditions. However, in 1985, the Conservative government under
Brian Mulroney, instead of following the committee's recommendations, toughened
the criminal law to make it easier to prosecute by outlawing solicitation on the part of
either worker or client. It also explicitly stated in section 195.1 that a motor vehicle
located in a public place or open to public view is a public place. The problem of street
prostitution was framed as one of 'nuisance' and public order in the legislation (Jeffrey
2004, 86, 91); that is, prostitution produced noise, littering, and traffic congestion, as
well as lowering property values and making non-prostitutes fearful about walking the
streets themselves (Brock 2000, 85–7). Further efforts at decriminalization have met
continued resistance from community residents' groups, who manage to persuade officials that street work is a property crime.

Currently it is not illegal to exchange sex for money. What are illegal are the
practices involved in making such an exchange. It is illegal to communicate for the
purposes of prostitution in a public place (section 213, Criminal Code of Canada). The
definition of public place can be interpreted quite broadly to include not only a public
street, but cars or large windows open to public view. This does not mean that prostitution can be undertaken in private spaces, either. Section 210 of the Criminal Code
makes it illegal to keep a 'common bawdy house', a location kept or occupied for the
purpose of prostitution. It is also illegal to be an 'inmate of a common bawdy house'
and to be found in a common bawdy house without a lawful excuse. Any place habitually used for prostitution such as a house, apartment, or parking lot can be considered
a bawdy house. Those who aid the exchange by transporting or directing another to
a bawdy house are considered complicit and liable to criminal sanction. Section 212
prohibits procuring and living on the avails of prostitution, with consideration of who
is a 'pimp' being quite expansive: 'evidence that a person lives with or is habitually in
the company of a prostitute or lives in a common-bawdy house or in a house of as-
signation is, in the absence of evidence to the contrary, proof that the person lives on
the avails of prostitution . . . '. This can include roommates, spouses, adult children,
and anyone that a sex worker has hired to help manage the business (receptionists, ac-
countants etc.) or provide security (bodyguards and bouncers) (section 212 [3] of the
Criminal Code, cited in Auger 2010, 4).

Further to this, municipal licensing laws introduce another level not only of regulation but confusion. As Cheryl Auger (2010) points out 'most of the practices associated
with prostitution are criminalized yet municipalities across Canada are quietly collecting licensing fees from businesses [escort services, erotic massage parlours, strip-clubs,
etc.,] that exist on the margins of federal law' (2). On the one hand, these municipal
regulations add a further layer of surveillance and policing of sex workers, but on the
other, the licensing systems suggest that sex is a semi-legitimate business and, when
licenses are dutifully paid, a possibly lucrative revenue source for municipalities.

The Economist (n.a. 2004) notes that the trend in the 1980s, in Europe in particular, was to loosen criminal sanctions on prostitution and devise ways of managing the
trade—essentially adopting a liberal perspective. For example, the Netherlands legalized the use of brothels in 2000 with the intention of controlling and regulating the

industry to protect against human trafficking and abuse of prostitutes, both minors and adults. The results have been both positive and negative: while the industry has shown itself to be quite lucrative and oversight of voluntary prostitution services has raised working standards, alarm has been sounded regarding issues of human trafficking and the use of illegal immigrants in underground 'involuntary' and unregulated sex services. While these criminal enterprises are more harshly penalized, in the context of combating the exploitation of involuntary prostitution the fact that the number of prostitutes with pimps does not seem to have decreased is a cause for concern' (Daalder 2007, 13). Sweden has taken a different route. In 1999, it decriminalized the act of selling sex, but became the first country to criminalize the act of buying sex (Malarek 2009, 238). Therefore, the onus of culpability has been removed from women and put on the predominantly male clientele. However, critics such as Petra Ostergen (cited in Malarek 2009) point out, this has unduly affected the economic livelihoods of those women who have voluntarily chosen the profession. The new laws have made it harder for them to find clients and the increased need for secrecy on the part of the purchaser has made it harder to deal with difficult or 'perverted' clients (Malarek 2009, 244).

Modern Slavery: Human Trafficking and Sexual Exploitation

The preparations for the 2010 Winter Olympic Games in Vancouver highlighted a dark side of such international celebrations and, as we shall discuss in the final chapter, the significance of women's bodies and their ability to control those bodies in both domestic and international politics. The issue is human trafficking and in examining its mechanisms we see the blurring of distinctions between the public and private and the local and the global. The concerns raised regarding the Vancouver Olympics was that the event would create an increased demand for prostitution and also give an easy cover-story for victims to be presented as 'visitors' by traffickers (Future Group 2007, also see *Vancouver Sun* November 2, 2007).

Human trafficking is defined in the United Nations Protocol to Prevent, Suppress and Punish Trafficking in Persons, especially Women and Children (2000), as

> [t]he recruitment, transportation, transfer, harboring or receipt of persons, by means of the threat or use of force or other forms of coercion, of abduction, of fraud, of deception, of the abuse of power or of a position of vulnerability or of the giving or receiving of payments or benefits to achieve the consent of a person having control over another person, for the purpose of exploitation. Exploitation shall include, at a minimum, the exploitation of the prostitution of others or other forms of sexual exploitation, forced labor or services, slavery or practices similar to slavery, servitude or the removal of organs. The consent of a victim of trafficking in persons to the intended exploitation set forth [above] shall be irrelevant where any of the means set forth [above] have been used.

While this can include a number of forms of forced labour and slavery, according to evidence presented to the Parliamentary Standing Committee on the Status of Women (2007, 1), '92 per cent of victims are trafficked for the purpose of sexual exploitation'. Neither does it apply solely to those who are trafficked across borders: trafficking for the purpose of prostitution occurs both internationally and nationally. In fact, according to the RCMP, recent convictions in Canada have mostly involved victims who are citizens and/or permanent residents of Canada (RCMP, 2010). The most vulnerable are Aboriginal girls and women. 'Aboriginal women and girls are driven into [trafficking] by poverty and conditions on the reserve, sometimes by conditions of abuse. They are then sold throughout Canada. Basically their handlers start them in Vancouver. They work for them there for awhile, then they're sold to someone in Winnipeg and then to someone in Toronto . . .' (Chantal Tie, National Association of Women and the Law, cited in Standing Committee on the Status of Women 2007, 10). In her testimony to the Committee, Erin Wolski, from the Native Association of Canada, noted that in some of the numerous cases of missing Aboriginal women, trafficking should be considered a 'possible source for information' (ibid. 9).

While Canada is a signatory to the United Nations Protocol, Canada's track record in dealing with the offence has not been great. Canada has been identified as a transit and destination country for human smuggling. NGOs estimate that 2,000 persons are trafficked into the country annually, while the RCMP puts the numbers at 600 to 800 persons, with an additional 1,500 to 2,200 passing through on route to the US (RCMP 2010, and US State Department 2009). In its 2006 report on Human Trafficking, *Falling Short of the Mark: An International Study on the Treatment of Human Trafficking Victims*, the Future Group, an NGO advocating Canada take a much more active stance against human trafficking, gave Canada the lowest score (F), compared to the United States as the highest (B+) in terms of best practices and providing support for victims of trafficking.

In 2005, the Criminal Code was updated to specifically prohibit human trafficking; however, trafficking was not specifically defined. The 2005 amendments established that recruitment, transporting, transferring, receipt, holding, concealment, harbouring, and exercising control over a victim were indictable offences. Further provision was made to remove the possibility of a victim giving consent undermining any indictment. Further to this, since 2002 the Immigration and Refugee Protection Act has prohibited human trafficking *into* Canada which, while providing for cross-border trafficking to Canada, does little to aid victims trafficked within and from Canada.

A primary concern is the difficulty of getting victims to come forward and of providing support for them once they have. As the Future Group (2006, 13) reported, 'Canada has ignored calls for reform and continues to re-traumatize trafficking victims, with few exceptions, by subjecting them to routine deportation and fails to provide even basic support services'. Victims find that it is impossible to access support in Canada without risking deportation. And, as the Standing Committee on the Status of Women heard, gender inequities in Canada's general immigration policy encourage trafficking by making it a last-resort option for migration.

> [M]any women don't qualify under the skilled worker point system, particularly if they come from countries where women are significantly disadvantaged. They are not going to have the higher education; they are not going to have

the skills to qualify (Chantal Tie, National Association of Women and the Law, Standing Committee on the Status of Women, 2007, 19)

[W]e have a promotion of illegal migration, and as a result, we have a promotion of trafficking, because without illegal migration, you don't have a place for trafficking. So we have to close the circle by looking at these issues together. This is why it is important to focus on trafficking from the perspective of labour markets, migration, and immigration laws, legal and illegal—legal immigration laws and illegal migration practices (Armand Pereira, International Labor Organization, Standing Committee on the Status of Women 2007, 19).

In 2007, the Standing Committee on the Status of Women presented its report, *Turning Outrage into Action to Address Trafficking for the Purpose of Sexual Exploitation in Canada*, along with 33 recommendations to Parliament. In 2007, Conservative MP Joy Smith was successful in having Parliament unanimously pass a motion urging the development of a national plan to combat human trafficking. In February 2010, the 21st Winter Olympics were held in Vancouver to generally positive reviews. While the issue of human trafficking did gain some attention, little had changed in terms of policy. In June 2010, amendments were made to the Criminal Code, a result of a successful private member's bill sponsored by Conservative MP Joy Smith. An Act to Amend the Criminal Code (minimum sentences for offences involving trafficking of persons under the age of 18) introduced a new human trafficking offence and mandatory sentences for offenders, but only in relation to the trafficking of children under the age of 18. As Smith commented at the Bill's passing, 'Canada also needs a comprehensive national action plan to combat human trafficking that addresses the multifaceted aspects of this crime. We need to have a federal strategy in coordination with provincial and territorial governments that focuses on prevention initiatives [and] greater protection (Smith 2010)'

For more information on human trafficking see:
Benjamin Perrin. 2010. *Invisible Chains: Underground World of Human Trafficking*, Toronto: Viking Canada.
United States State Department. 2010. Trafficking in Persons Report 2010. Available at: http://www.state.gov/g/tip/rls/tiprpt/2010/

The trend in Canada during the past few years has been to crack down on prostitution, primarily because globalization of the sex trade has enhanced the most exploitative aspects of the business, including trafficking in women and children for prostitution and links to organized crime (Shenon 2000, A5; see also Ehrenreich 2002; Thorbek and Pattanaik 2002). This fits with the position taken by mainstream feminists in Canada; as Brock (2000, 79) argues, the view of prostitutes (especially young prostitutes) as victims of patriarchal oppression has the strongest currency and decriminalization is not a popular option. This has resulted in prostitutes in Canada feeling somewhat rejected by the Canadian women's movement. Brock (2000) charges that mainstream feminists have often ignored sex workers' rights arguments and Overall (1992b, 705) argues that 'women who work in the sex trade industry often feel condemned and rejected by many feminist women'.[4]

Some sex trade workers have mobilized into organizations that work to protect their rights. The first such organization was founded in San Francisco in 1973 and in 1985 the International Committee for Prostitutes' Rights formed. In Canada, Sex Professionals of Canada (SPOC) is the new name for the Canadian Organization for the Rights of Prostitutes, which was formed in 1983 with the goal of decriminalizing prostitution in Canada.

On 28 September 2010, organized prostitutes in Canada achieved a measure of success when in a case brought by three sex-workers (*Bedford v. Canada*), Ontario Court Judge Susan Himel ruled that the restrictions on the operation of a bawdy house, living off the profits of prostituting and soliciting for the purpose of purchasing sex are unconstitutional because they violate the right to 'life, liberty and security of the person'. The ruling in *Bedford v. Canada* was intended to allow prostitutes the ability to conduct business inside without fear of arrest, fully communicate with and scan clients, and to hire private security. Himel wrote in the ruling that she 'found that the law as it stands is currently contributing to the danger faced by prostitutes'. Further to this, she made reference to the rejected 1985 Fraser Report, pointing to the recommendation 'that the adult prostitute be given leeway to conduct his or her business in privacy and dignity, by moving indoors in small number in order to protect safety. . . . [and] adults engaging in prostitution could and should be counted on to be responsible for themselves, and therefore should be entitled to give their earnings to whomever they wish provided no coercion or threats were present' (DiManno 2010).

The response was vociferous with both the Federal and Ontario governments supporting an appeal of the decision. In her ruling, Himel had made provision for a 30-day stay motion, later extended to 60 days to allow for a period of transition in the law or for an appeal. On 2 December 2010 the stay was further extended by Ontario Appeal Judge Marc Rosenberg until 29 April 2011. At this time, Federal Minister of Justice Rob Nicholson stated, 'it is the position of the government that these provisions [the original sections of the Criminal Code] are constitutionally sound . . . and deter the most harmful and public effects of prostitution' (Department of Justice Canada 2010a). Organized sex workers attempted to placate concerns regarding an explosion of solicitation and pimping. Nikki Thomas, a spokeswoman for Sex Professionals of Canada, stated, 'this is about human rights and our ability to look after ourselves, our partners and our children. You won't see a huge explosion of sex workers in the streets' (Makin 2010). At the time of writing the case of *Bedford v. Canada* is awaiting appeal.

Pornography

While the mainstream Canadian women's movement has been more focused on pornography than on prostitution, as with other issues having to do with the body there is no consensus about what pornography is and what, if anything, should be done about it. As Lise Gotell (1996, 279) argues, '[t]he very definition of pornography, the nature of pornography's relation to sexual domination, as well as the wisdom of state censorship, remain deeply contested issues within Canadian feminism'. Alisa Carse (1997) identifies no less than five positions on pornography, some feminist and some not: (1) offence-based restrictionists, usually religious and moral conservatives; (2) absolute protectionists of free speech; (3) harm-based restrictionists such as MacKinnon (1987; Mackinnon and Dworkin 1997) and Dworkin (1981); (4) qualified protectionists of free speech (who question the 'harm' argument); and (5) special exception protectionists (defenders of gay and lesbian pornography).

We devote a great deal of attention to the harm-based restrictionist view because it has been enormously influential on Canadian law and on the public's conception of pornography (Cossman, Bell, Gotell, and Ross 1997). Catharine MacKinnon's (1987, 262, n. 1) definition of pornography is commonly cited though constantly debated. She writes:

Pornography is the graphic sexually explicit subordination of women, whether in pictures or in words, that also includes one or more of the following: (i) women are presented dehumanized as sexual objects, things, or commodities; or (ii) women are presented as sexual objects who enjoy pain or humiliation; or (iii) women are presented as sexual objects who experience sexual pleasure in being raped; or (iv) women are presented as sexual objects tied up or cut up or mutilated or bruised or physically hurt; or (v) women are presented in postures of sexual submission, servility, or display; or (vi) women's body parts—including but not limited to vaginas, breasts and buttocks—are exhibited, such that women are reduced to those parts; or (vii) women are presented as whores by nature; or (viii) women are presented being penetrated by objects or animals; or (ix) women are presented in scenarios of degradation, injury, torture, shown as filthy or inferior, bleeding, bruised, or hurt in a context that makes these conditions sexual. Pornography also includes 'the use of men, children, or transsexuals in the place of women'.

Carse (1997, 236) adds to this definition the statement that behaviours that degrade and subordinate are pornographic if they are portrayed in such a way as to endorse those behaviours. In other words, if the images do not glorify, they are not pornographic.

Scholars such as MacKinnon (1987, 1997), Dworkin (1981), and Brownmiller (1975) clearly fall into the harm-based restrictionist camp. Pornography is dangerous, they argue, first and most controversially because depictions of violence against women lead to acts of violence against women. As Robin Morgan (1980, 139) famously wrote, '[p]ornography is the theory, and rape the practice'. A report by the Federal/Provincial/Territorial Working Group of Attorneys General (1992) also made that claim, not without opposition and a disclaimer from the federal justice minister at the time. Second, depictions of women that degrade and dehumanize are problematic because they affect society's attitudes towards women. Pornography depicts the view that women enjoy forced sex and forced pain. It '"works insidiously to damage the standing and power of women within the community" and hence injures their equality' (Carse 1997, 248, n. 23, quoting Ronald Dworkin). Pornography teaches 'ways of seeing and ways of being; it shapes and fosters attitudes, expectations, patterns of desire, of sexual arousal and response, and other overt behaviors that can result in harm to women—not only physical violence and forcible sex but also disdainful and dismissive treatment, incompatible with our status as equals' (Carse 1997, 238). Third, the pornography industry abuses and exploits women in the making of its products. Women are often coerced into participating in pornography by boyfriends or husbands. The most widely publicized case was that of Linda Marchiano (a.k.a. Linda Lovelace) who, years after making the film *Deep Throat,* condemned the industry and her captor, Charles Traynor (Lovelace and McGrady 1980; MacKinnon and Dworkin 1997, 60–8).

However, MacKinnon and others differ from offence-based restrictionists, who aim at banning the depiction of all nudity or sexually explicit materials. MacKinnon (1987) argues that pornography is different from *Obscenity*. Obscenity law is concerned with a community's morality, defined by men, and thus 'prohibits what it sees as immoral, which from a feminist standpoint tends to be relatively harmless, while protecting what it sees as moral, which from a feminist standpoint is often that which is damaging to women' (152). Pornography, she argues, 'causes attitudes and behaviors of violence and discrimination that define the treatment and status of half the population' (147). Thus, it should be treated entirely differently from obscenity. 'Pornography' she continues 'is not bad manners or poor choice of audience; obscenity is' (154). Why, then, is the eroticization of male dominance and female powerlessness seen as harmless whereas prurient images are seen as harmful?

MacKinnon (1987) also distinguishes between *Erotica* (that is, sexually explicit materials depicting relations between consenting adults) and *Pornography*, which is designed to degrade and dehumanize. Many feminists, in fact, have called for the loosening of rules against obscenity because these rules are often used to control or suppress human sexuality and sexual freedom.[5] Thus, MacKinnon (1987, 149) argues that bringing a feminist lens to these issues changes how we view them: a feminist analysis moves us away from discussing pornography as 'obscenity' and the control of morality to saying that pornography is about power over and control of one sex by the other based on the assertion of certain gender roles. Pornography is about the control of women's sexuality and defining the limits and boundaries of that sexuality through the portrayal of women as subordinate, as man-pleasers, as sexual objects, and so on.

For all these reasons, pornography causes harm—not just to individuals but to women as a group—and thus the state should act, not to censor it but rather to treat pornography as discrimination on the basis of sex and make it a civil rights violation (MacKinnon 1987, 146). That is, make pornography an exception to First Amendment (i.e., free speech) protection in the United States and make the production, sale, display, and distribution of pornographic materials civilly actionable. Such a law would allow those harmed by pornography to sue the producers and sellers of pornography for damages. Use of a civil injunction could also stop the future sale of a piece of material demonstrated to be harmful. Furthermore, the threat of civil liability could serve as a powerful economic disincentive to those who traffic in pornography (Carse 1997, 239).

In the 1980s, MacKinnon and Dworkin successfully lobbied two US city councils—Minneapolis in 1983 and Indianapolis in 1984—to pass laws declaring pornography a form of sex discrimination and allowing women to sue for civil damages. Both laws were struck down. Instead, MacKinnon and others were much more persuasive with the harm-based argument in the Canadian Supreme Court.[6]

R. v. Butler, 1992[7]

In August 1987, police entered Donald Butler's store in Winnipeg, Manitoba, and seized his inventory. The police charged Butler with numerous counts pursuant to section 163 (then section 159) of the federal Criminal Code, including possession of obscene materials for the purposes of distribution and sale and selling and exposing obscene materials to public view. At trial, he was convicted on a small number of charges, but most of the material was deemed protected expression under the Charter. Thus, Butler was acquitted on those charges. The Crown appealed the acquittal and Butler cross-appealed the convictions. At the appeal court level, the court upheld the Crown's appeal and dismissed Butler's appeal of his conviction. Butler then appealed to the Supreme Court of Canada, arguing that section 163(8) of the federal Criminal Code, which defined obscenity as 'any publication a dominant characteristic of which is the undue exploitation of sex, or of sex and any one or more of the following subjects, namely, crime, horror, cruelty and violence', violated section 2(b) of the Charter, the fundamental freedom of thought, belief, opinion, and expression, including freedom of the press and other media of communication. Butler lost the appeal in a 9–0 ruling that declared section 163(8) of the Criminal Code constitutional.

However, the Court issued a narrower interpretation of what can be deemed to be obscene under section 163(8).[8] The Supreme Court noted that a variety of tests have been established to determine what is obscene. First, the *Community Standards of Tolerance* test emphasizes that what is obscene is not a matter of personal taste, nor is it a standard of tolerance of a particular local community; rather, it reflects the standards of the community as a whole (that is, the nation). As Justice John Sopinka wrote, 'the community standards test is concerned not with what Canadians would not tolerate being exposed to themselves, but what they would not tolerate other Canadians being exposed to . . .'. Second, the test of *Undue Exploitation of Sex* asks *Whether Sex Is Depicted as Degrading and Dehumanizing*. Justice Sopinka stated that 'degrading and dehumanizing materials place women (and sometimes men) in positions of subordination, servile submission or humiliation'.[9] It was these depictions of sex that the Court found problematic, since the justices accepted the argument that images that are degrading and dehumanizing cause harm. Furthermore, they were persuaded that such images are antithetical to equality values because they violate principles of equality between men and women as well as the inherent dignity of all human beings.

The Court did not wish to restrict all forms of sexual expression on their face but rather required an examination of the context within which materials were created. The Court thus discussed the third test, *Artistic Defence or Internal Necessities*. That is, even material that offends community standards may not be considered undue 'if it is required for the serious treatment of a theme. . . . To determine whether a dominant characteristic of the film is the undue exploitation of sex, the courts must have regard to various things—the author's artistic purpose, the manner in which he or she has portrayed and developed the story, the depiction and interplay of character and the creation of visual effect through skilful camera techniques. . .'.

Despite the variety of tests available, the Court had not specified the relationship between the tests. Justice Sopinka thus articulated another test by which he divided pornographic material into three categories:

(1) explicit sex with violence (violence meaning actual physical violence and threats of physical violence);
(2) explicit sex without violence;
(3) explicit sex without violence that neither degrades nor dehumanizes subjects.

In the ruling, Sopinka argued that number one definitely falls under section 163(8) because it is expressly mentioned in the Criminal Code. Number two may be covered. But number three would definitely not fall under section 163(8). Sopinka stated, 'The portrayal of sex coupled with violence will almost always constitute the undue exploitation of sex. . . . Explicit sex which is degrading or dehumanizing may be undue if the risk of harm is substantial. Finally, explicit sex that is not violent and neither degrading nor dehumanizing is generally tolerated in our society and will not qualify as the undue exploitation of sex unless it employs children in its production.'

The justices then argued that the reason why the community does not tolerate such depictions is that it does not tolerate harm. What, then, was the meaning of harm? Here the influence of LEAF, MacKinnon, and others can be seen.[10] Harm, said Justice Sopinka, 'predisposes persons to act in an anti-social manner as, for example, the physical or mental mistreatment of women by men, or, what is perhaps debatable, the reverse'. Depictions of sex with violence can be prohibited because 'this type of material would, apparently, fail the community standards test not because it offends against morals but because it is perceived by public opinion to be harmful to society, particularly to women'. In *Butler*, even though the Court did not find any proven cause-effect relationship between viewing pornography and harm to women, it accepted that it was reasonable of Parliament, based on the evidence, to draw the conclusion that sexually explicit materials are harmful to society, specifically to women and to children. The Court accepted that, while restrictions on such expression violated section 2(b) of the Charter, such violation was reasonable because Parliament had as its goal the prevention of harm to a specific social group. That is, a government can reasonably step in when one group seems to be prospering at another's expense. Women and children are viewed as vulnerable groups that need to be protected.

While the Court's opinion was unanimous, Justice Gonthier, with Justice L'Heureux-Dubé, went further in a concurring opinion, stating that even explicit sex without violence could also be seen as harmful. A depiction of sex without violence in a film or magazine probably has little potential to harm, but if it appears on a poster or billboard, then it could rightly be regarded as undue exploitation of sex that the community would not tolerate. Furthermore, the Court seemed to accept that pornography is not equivalent to political expression when it stated that this form of expression does not stand on an equal footing with other kinds of expression that directly engage the core freedom of expression values, such as pursuit of truth and promotion of democracy. The Supreme Court could thus assign the lowest value imaginable to pornographic expression, especially if it accepted the broad societal harm argument.

Many individuals and groups hailed the ruling because, at least in the majority opinion, it broadened the constitutional protection of sexual expression that is merely erotic. As Sopinka wrote, 'Some segments of society would consider that all three categories of pornography cause harm to society because they tend to undermine its moral fiber. Others would contend that none of the categories cause harm'. That is why the community as a whole should serve as an arbiter in determining what amounts to an undue exploitation of sex. Women's groups such as LEAF lauded the decision as a victory for women's equality because it acknowledged that women are treated differently in society and thus need special protections in order to have equal opportunities.

Arguments against pornography's regulation

Immediately after the *Butler* decision, many individuals and organizations decried the rationale that the justices had used to defend the legislation, as well as LEAF's position (for example, Busby 1994). We can identify three perspectives critical of the ruling: those advocating absolute protection of free speech, those advocating qualified protection, and those advocating special exceptions.

Absolute free speech protectionists

This argument has two versions: first, pornography is simply speech, and the state should not regulate sexually oriented expression at all; and second, any arguments in support of regulation are dangerous because they can backfire. Originally obscenity was equated with the depiction of sexual acts in general, including contraceptive devices and information. Thus, many contemporary feminists are wary about any law that smacks of censorship. As Marilyn Fitterman, a founding member of Feminists for Free Expression (http://www.ffeusa.org), states 'What censorship censors first is always women. Then come gays, sex education and art. Freedom, first of all, means free speech'.[10]

Qualified protectionists

Qualified protectionists argue 'restrictions on speech are appropriate when the speech is harmful, but only if the harm prevented through the restrictions is greater than the harm introduced by the restrictions' (Carse 1997, 227). They point out that a definitive connection between pornography and direct physical harm has not been demonstrated; the evidence is not clear that one is the direct result of the other. Many people view pornography, but not all become rapists

Some, such as Lise Gotell (1996, 1997) and Cossman and Bell (1997), criticize the anti-pornography feminists for assuming that all women see sexuality as the 'unremitting, unequaled victimization of women' by male heterosexuality. Anti-pornography laws, as well as anti-violence initiatives, 'promote an image of women as silent and passive victims and idealize the state as protector' (Gotell 1996, 304). Yet women can be agents who make their own decisions and act on them and who may wish to use or view some forms of pornography. As we discussed in the section on the body, pornography can be experienced as pleasurable by women, help them explore their own sexuality, and as a result be a tool for empowerment.

This is certainly the view of sex-positive feminists of the second and third waves, who produce women-positive and diverse forms of pornography, for example, Playgirl TV, and feminist sex-activists, and adult film producers Candida Royalle, Susi Bright and Annie Sprinkle (Tisdale 1992; Dominus 2004, AR1, 6; Levy 2005). The problem then has been that until now the sex industry has reflected the heterosexual male perspective. Given that it is difficult to eradicate pornography, one solution might be for the sex industry to broaden depictions of sex (for example, see the grrl magazines *Bitch: Feminists Respond to Popular Culture* and *Bust*).

Special exceptionists

Some feminists have spoken out against the *Butler* decision for a different reason: the law has historically played a role in repressing gay sexuality, and obscenity laws in particular have been used to silence gay sexual expression. A major effect of the *Butler* decision was that 'Straight, mainstream pornography appears to be flourishing. But any representations that hint at alternative sexualities continue to be subject to intense scrutiny' (Cossman and Bell 1997, 4)

Gay and lesbian materials in particular became the target of Canada Customs in the wake of the decision. Within two months of the Supreme Court ruling of 27 February 1992, Toronto police made their first arrest using the *Butler* decision. They charged the manager of Glad Day Books with obscenity for selling a magazine called *Bad Attitude,* which contained depictions of bondage aimed at lesbians.[11] Carse (1997 251, n. 43) notes that 'On July 16, 1992, Judge Frank Hayes, of Ontario Court Regional Division, invoked Butler in reviewing gay magazines seized at the border, declaring anonymous homosexual encounters "harmful" to the community, and describing the sexual activity depicted in the magazines as "subhuman" and "degrading . . . without any human dimension"'. In a 2000 ruling on a constitutional challenge of the Customs Act and the Criminal Code obscenity provisions, the Supreme Court of Canada agreed that Canada Customs had carried out a harassment campaign against a Vancouver bookseller, Little Sisters Book and Art Emporium, by repeatedly seizing books and videos the customs officials deemed obscene, but would be considered legal if they originated in Canada.[12]

Gotell (1996, 310) argues, however, that the test established under the *Butler* decision to distinguish what is degrading and dehumanizing from that which is merely erotic remains a profoundly conservative test. Even under the standard of a national community, a court could rule that images of gay and lesbian sex are more offensive to community standards than are heterosexual materials. In that case, the test could be used to justify declaring the images obscene, without questioning whether the community's view of obscenity was fair or just (Gotell 1996, 298). Some special exceptionists, therefore, are not 'exceptionists' at all. Given the potential for discrimination on the part of state officials when determining what is obscene, they would argue that any law that upholds any views or any judgments of sexual morality should be abolished.

Finding a Balance between Rights: LEAF and Little Sisters

In 1990 the owners of Little Sisters Book and Art Emporium launched a lawsuit against Canada Customs over its practices and challenging the obscenity provisions in the Criminal Code that Customs officials were using to deem the material obscene.

In its efforts to find a balance between using the obscenity law to protect women and supporting the equality rights of gays and lesbians, LEAF presented a very complex argument.[13] LEAF argued that Canada Customs had violated the equality and expressive rights of lesbian women and gay men because it failed to protect against discriminatory treatment on the part of its officials. However, LEAF did not reject the harm-based test of obscenity that it supported and the Supreme Court upheld in *Butler.* What was required was a more contextualized use of the obscenity law because 'simple extrapolations about harm concerning heterosexual materials' may not be appropriate when applied to materials by and for the gay and lesbian community. That does not mean that all gay and lesbian materials should be subject to a general 'exemption, the test should be whether the materials cause real harm, an increased propensity to violence or serving to foster the unequal position in society of those groups protected by the *Charter's* equality guarantee'.

Not all feminist groups agreed with LEAF's perspective on the issue. An international women's group, Equality Now (http://www.equalitynow.org), also intervened in the case arguing that pornography is distinct from erotica and gay and lesbian pornography can be a threat to sexual equality. As Janine Benedet (2001, 189–90), counsel for Equality Now, wrote in a 2001 article some of the materials Little Sisters sold did meet the definition of pornography as sex-based harm because 'It eroticizes dominance for both the abuser and the abused. Where gay men identify with the abuser, it contributes to the normalization of rape. Where they identify with the abused, it promotes self-hate'.

R. v. Sharpe, 2001[14]

Soon after the *Little Sisters* case, the Supreme Court ruled on a constitutional challenge to another section of the Criminal Code, enacted in 1993, that provides a broad definition of child pornography and prohibits the possession of child pornography.[15] Even the most ardent civil libertarians agree that there is nothing wrong with Parliament criminalizing the possession of child pornography that involves the sexual exploitation of children or youth in its production. The BC Civil Liberties Association (BCCLA 2000), in its factum to the Supreme Court in the case of *R. v. Sharpe*, states that 'The making of such pictures involves the commission of a criminal offence, and their possession and distribution represents a continuing, serious violation of the dignity of children or youth employed in its production'. Thus the issue is one of how far legislation can go in criminalizing the possession of images that do not involve the actual exploitation of children.

In this particular case, John Robin Sharpe was charged with two counts of possession of child pornography under section 163(4) of the federal Criminal Code (other sections of the Criminal Code criminalize the making and distribution of child pornography). He challenged the constitutionality of the prohibition of mere possession of child pornography as a violation of freedom of expression provisions in the Charter. A British Columbia trial court judge agreed with Sharpe and struck down the Criminal Code provision, and the majority of the BC Court of Appeal concurred. The Supreme Court in a January 2001 decision reversed these lower court rulings and upheld the Criminal Code provision, with the majority again acknowledging that the possession of child pornography can harm children because it can encourage pedophiles and distort their view of children.[16] The Court qualified its 9–0 ruling by allowing narrow exceptions to protect private fictional works, such as a personal diary not intended for distribution, as well as drawings or photographic depictions of oneself engaged in lawful sexual activity. The Court left room for the defence of artistic merit as well. However, the ruling left some questions unanswered, such as whether merely viewing child pornography on the Internet without downloading or printing it is a violation of the law (Makin 2001, A1).

The Supreme Court ordered a new trial for John Robin Sharpe, and in March 2002 a BC Supreme Court judge ruled that Mr Sharpe's collection of personal stories of acts of child pornography had some artistic merit and thus did not fall under the definition of child pornography (Armstrong 2002, A1, A4). In response to this ruling, the federal government introduced new legislation in December 2002 to remove the defence of artistic merit and substitute a defence of 'public good'. That is, anyone claiming a defence of artist merit 'would have to show any risk it poses is outweighed by the public good it serves'. It also proposed to broaden the definition of child pornography to include materials that 'predominantly feature descriptions of prohibited sex acts with children' (Bailey 2002, A12). The proposed legislation died, however, when the federal Liberals called an election in 2004.

The Liberals were successful in putting through the amendments to the Criminal Code regarding the use of the Internet to sexually exploit children. Coming into force in 2002, Bill C-15A, dealt specifically with the use of the Internet to lure children for criminal purposes. It is now illegal to transmit child pornography from one person to another, to post or link with child pornography on a website, to export child pornography, or to possess child pornography for the purpose of exporting, transmitting, or making it available (sections 163 and 164). It is also illegal to use the Internet to communicate with a child for the purposes of committing a sexual act (section 172).

The Internet has also been the focus of the Harper Conservative government's approach to child protection. At the time of writing, two bills—C-22, *An Act Respecting The Mandatory Reporting of Internet Child Pornography by Persons Who Provide an Internet Service* and Bill C-54, *An Act to Amend the Criminal Code (Sexual Offences Against Children,)* or the Protection from Sexual Predators Act—were wending their way through the Parliamentary process.[17] Both bills deal with the use of the Internet to sexually exploit children. Bill C-22 requires Internet service providers to report all suspected material and safeguard evidence if they believe a child pornography offence has been committed on their service. There are penalties for non-compliance. The broader C-54 sets mandatory sentences for sexual offences involving child victims, but also creates two new offences, making it illegal for anyone to provide sexually explicit material to a child for the purpose of facilitating the commission of a sexual offence against a child, and to use telecommunications including the Internet to communicate with another person to agree or make arrangements to commit a sexual offence against a child (see Library of Parliament Legisinfo, openparliament.com, and Department of Justice Canada 2010b and 2010c).

It is not surprising that the Internet has become a focus for controlling and regulating pornography. The terrain of debate over pornography, prostitution, and female images has radically changed with the proliferation of pornography on the Internet. The proliferation of both the medium and the messages has left many wondering what regulation is possible now that pornography is ubiquitous. From video on demand, available through cable television, to webcams that allow viewers all over the world to watch sex acts on the Internet in real time, to online strip shows that allow customers to email instructions to performers, the proliferation of 'cyberporn' is astonishing. A conservative estimate places Internet pornography as a $2.5 billion per year industry in the United States alone (Evans 2004, A3). Most recently, 'e-porn' has expanded into wireless devices such as BlackBerries, with the wireless pornography industry expected to grow to $90 million within four years (Evans 2004, A3). It is also estimated that in 2000, 5.5 million North Americans each spent more than 11 hours per week on porn sites, which meets the definition of addiction (Cheney 2000, F4). To quote one psychologist who treats people with pornography addictions, 'Once it was possible to control pornography. . . . But that time is past. Now, we have to deal with it' (Cheney 2000, F4). Cross-national efforts continue to be made, however, to staunch the proliferation of child pornography (e.g., Davidson and Gottschalk 2011).

Conclusion: Lessons from the Body Wars

This chapter brings to mind a number of lessons for feminist lawmakers and advocates of policy change. First, advocates and lawmakers should not assume a homogeneous perspective on any of these issues. We cannot assume that 'well, naturally, because she is a woman, she thinks "x"'. In the crafting of any feminist policy strategy, the voices of as many women as possible need to be listened to and heard. Second, we are reminded that laws may be written in a general way, but they are often selectively enforced, most often against those deemed most marginalized or most 'deviant' from the norm. Therefore, in developing a feminist policy on body politics, consideration of the effects of legislation and policy on the most marginal should be paramount. Finally, lessons from the past reveal that feminist voices can make a difference in the body politic. While some feminists may disagree with the outcome, feminist organizations have been influential in shaping law and policy in a number of instances. Such power should be acknowledged and wielded wisely.

Questions for Critical Thought

1. In a patriarchal society, can a 'politics of the body' be undertaken without being corrupted or undermined? What would this politics look like?
2. In terms of prostitution, which holds the greater promise of making women's lives better, the sex worker or abolitionist approach? Can a balance be achieved between the perspectives of prostitution as a business and prostitution as a form of abuse? How would this be expressed in policy?
3. Is there a way to develop law and policy regarding pornography that does not define women as victims? How can laws against *pornography* be enforced without the personal views of *obscenity* on the part of individual state actors coming into play? What kinds of policy responses can/should emerge in Canada, given the ubiquity of electronic forms of pornography?

CHAPTER 12

Reproductive Rights and Technology

No issue generates as much conflict as the issue of policies having to do with reproduction and reproductive rights. From confrontations between pro-life and pro-choice activists outside abortion clinics, to the shooting of doctors who perform abortions, to clinic bombings (Rodgers 2002, 341), the level of violence surrounding the issue sets it apart from any other women's rights issue. Each actor and organization involved believes that the stakes are high. From the religious right's perspective, the issue boils down to protecting the life of the fetus. From feminists' perspective, it concerns women's power and control over the decision to bring life into the world. Because the issue affects everyone involved so profoundly and raises questions about how we define humanity, it tends to harden perspectives and makes people unwilling to compromise (Luker 1984; Tribe 1990).

This chapter surveys the range of issues that fall under reproductive rights. It begins with a brief history of the legislation and public policy affecting women's reproductive rights, including contraception, sterilization, and abortion. It then documents the debates over and battles to change legislation in these areas. Finally, it explores some contemporary issues, including fetal protection laws, infertility and assisted reproductive technologies, surrogacy, and sex selection, all of which challenge conventional feminist thinking on these issues.

Government Regulation of Reproduction

Until recently, women's access to contraception, including voluntary sterilization as well as abortion, was very limited. Both the United States and Canada were early adopters of legislation to prohibit abortion and contraception information and use at a relatively early stage compared to European countries, with many European countries following suit only in the 1920s and 1930s (Gauthier 1996, 31). Regarding contraception, section 179 of the 1892 Canadian Criminal Code made it an indictable offence to 'offer to sell, advertise, publish an advertisement of or have for sale or disposal any medicine, drug or article intended or represented as a means of preventing conception or causing abortion' (Childbirth By Choice Trust 1998, 13–14).

Soon after Confederation, the Canadian government consolidated the various vagrancy laws (used to arrest prostitutes) and passed the Postal Service Act in 1875 and the Customs Act in 1879 to prevent people from using the mail to transmit materials deemed obscene either within Canada or across the border. It then passed the first Criminal Code provisions in 1892 to outlaw the sale or exposure of any material deemed obscene (Cossman and Bell 1997, 13).

It is important to understand the connection legislators made between obscenity and abortion and contraception. Victorian morality did not separate reproduction from sexuality. Contraception was seen as an intimate sexual issue or, worse, as an encouragement of premarital and extramarital sex. Thus, contraception was seen 'along with rape, prostitution, and pornography as part of the general moral corruption and decay of society' even for married couples (Stetson 1997, 98).

Contraception remained illegal in both Canada and the United States until the 1960s, although law enforcement officials increasingly declined to prosecute alleged offenders before the laws were struck from the books.[1] In Canada, after Justice Minister Pierre Trudeau's famous declaration in 1967 that 'the state has no business in the bedrooms of the nation', the federal Liberal government in 1969 decriminalized a great deal of behaviour having to do with reproduction and sexuality, including removing the law that made illegal the distribution of birth control devices. At the same time, it decriminalized same-sex sexual relations and reformed divorce law, as well as decriminalized abortion in some instances.

Abortion was the most controversial issue addressed. As Stetson (1997, ch. 4) points out, governments have approached restrictions on abortion in two ways, one that considers the phase of pregnancy and the other the reason for abortion. Both of these approaches involve determining when the state can interfere to prohibit abortion.

English common law used to deem abortion a criminal act only after 'quickening'—that is, the point when the woman first feels the fetus move, usually around the end of the fourth month (but well beyond the first trimester) (Stetson 1997, 133, n. 6). The Catholic Church in the past had its own rule, known as 'ensoulment', which it determined occurred in a male fetus at 40 days' gestation and females at 80 days' gestation (Stetson 1997, 133, n. 6).

Section 272 of the 1892 Canadian Criminal Code stated that '[e]veryone is guilty of an indictable offence and liable to imprisonment for life who, with intent to procure the miscarriage of any woman, whether she is or is not with child, unlawfully administers to her or causes to be taken by her any drug or other noxious thing, or unlawfully uses any instrument or other means whatsoever with the like intent'. Section 273 of the Criminal Code specified that any woman who attempts an abortion on her own fetus was liable to seven years' imprisonment. McLaren (1993, 797) notes, however, that doctors were not liable if they induced a miscarriage because they believed the life of the mother was at risk.[2] In practice, doctors would often perform abortions for other reasons, even though they risked prosecution and the loss of their medical licence.[3]

Laws criminalizing abortion gave enormous power to doctors to determine whether a woman should have an abortion. The law reflected the growing power of doctors over women's lives, at the expense of midwives, who were overwhelmingly female, and other lay practitioners, who used to provide the bulk of health care services. From about the mid-1800s in North America, regular doctors made a concerted effort to take over the delivery of obstetric and gynecological services. McLaren (1993, 803) argues that doctors in the nineteenth century were among the strongest supporters of the criminalization of abortion, in part to 'eliminate the competition of midwives and irregular practitioners'. Many doctors also opposed the procedure for moral reasons.

Women's Abortion Experiences in Canada before Decriminalization

The Childbirth By Choice Trust (1998) edited collection records the experiences of more than 60 women who volunteered to tell anonymously their stories of how they obtained an illegal abortion in the decades before its decriminalization. What becomes clear from these reports is that women from all classes, races, ages, occupational and personal backgrounds, and religious backgrounds experienced illegal abortions. Many of the women had been married at the time they sought the abortion, although more and more unmarried women sought the procedure by the 1960s because their access to birth control remained restricted even as contraception, though still illegal, became increasingly available to married couples. As one woman stated in her account, 'Anyone who is against abortion should have four children in five years and then see how they feel about it' (31).[4] All were determined to end their pregnancy despite the law and even though it was often difficult to find someone to assist them and the fees abortion providers charged were exorbitant. Many abortion providers had no medical qualifications, thus risking the lives of the pregnant women. As the Childbirth By Choice Trust (1998, 27) collection states, 'an illegal abortion story from the 1960s describes the same primitive procedure as a story from the 1920s. . . . [B]y the 1960s heart transplants were being performed in Canada, while abortions, being clandestine, remained such remarkably crude and dangerous operations'. The techniques women used to expel their own fetuses were brutally damaging, involving the consumption of poisonous liquids, deliberate falls, and the insertion of sharp objects to damage the uterus. Many women died in their attempt to abort, often leaving other children behind. For many women active in the pro-choice movement, it is the fear of returning to these dangerous times that motivates them to fight to keep abortion legal.

By the 1960s, however, doctors were increasingly demanding that governments decriminalize abortion, fearing that they could be arrested for performing abortion services in violation of the Criminal Code.[5] The Criminal Code amendments passed in 1969 clarified the rules for doctors regarding when abortions could legally be performed, but a number of people raised concerns about the restrictions the rules imposed on access to abortion. The law required that hospitals willing to perform abortions had to create a therapeutic abortion committee (TAC) composed of at least three medical practitioners (none of whom would actually perform the abortion) who would decide whether an individual could have an abortion. The committee would determine whether the life or health of the pregnant woman was endangered before granting permission, thus giving the power to decide to physicians, not to women themselves. Physicians convicted of performing abortions without TAC approval could be sentenced to life imprisonment, and pregnant women risked two years' imprisonment for attempting a self-induced abortion (Haussman 2001, 68).

The 1969 decriminalization of abortion for 'medically necessary' reasons thus went some way towards protecting women's liberty, but critics argued that the change in law was really intended to protect doctors from prosecution. It would still be up to a doctor to decide whether a woman's life or health was threatened by the continuation of a pregnancy. Doctors themselves were also still subject to regulation, since abortions could only be performed in approved hospitals and after approval by a therapeutic abortion committee. The 1969 legislation was based largely on the recommendations of the Canadian Medical Association (Childbirth By Choice Trust 1998, 131).

Feminist Challenges to Restrictions on Reproductive Rights

While the 1969 amendments met some of the demands made by women's groups and other organizations (for example, the Canadian Bar Association, the Canadian Labour Congress, social welfare agencies, and even some churches) some abortion activists, such as the Canadian Alliance for the Repeal of the Abortion Law (CARAL) (formed in 1974; later known as the Canadian Abortion Rights Action League), agitated for the law to go further and allow abortion on demand, giving control over the decision to have an abortion to women themselves. These groups engaged in a variety of tactics, including lobbying for repeal of abortion laws and litigation to have the law overturned. They also established independent abortion clinics in defiance of the law and engaged in social action, such as organizing the 1970 Abortion Caravan, which traveled from Vancouver to Ottawa to publicize feminists' demand that abortion should be removed from the Criminal Code (Brodie, Gavigan, and Jenson 1992, 44).

At the same time, the pro-life movement mobilized in the 1970s and 1980s, although not to the same extent as in the United States since abortion remained illegal in Canada except in exceptional circumstances, unlike the US situation. Over time, the pro-life movement has grown stronger and has engaged in more militant tactics, such as fire-bombing the Toronto Morgentaler clinic (Jenson 1997) and shooting abortion providers.

One year after the 1969 Criminal Code amendments, Dr Henry Morgentaler was arrested in Montreal for performing abortions in a clinic that operated outside a hospital and, of course, did not have a therapeutic abortion committee. In fact, Dr Morgentaler was arrested twice and faced three jury trials before the Supreme Court struck down the Criminal Code provisions in 1988. In all three jury trials preceding the 1988 decision, juries refused to convict him, demonstrating that the abortion law was becoming unenforceable in many parts of Canada. In 1983 Dr Morgentaler decided to open abortion clinics in Winnipeg and Toronto, again to challenge the Criminal Code provisions that forbade free-standing abortion clinics. He was arrested, and the charge against him for opening the Toronto clinic became subject to Supreme Court review in *R. v. Morgentaler*, 1988.

The *Morgentaler* decision was considered a progressive but incomplete victory for the pro-choice movement. While it removed all regulations regarding abortion from the Criminal Code, the Court did not declare that women have the right to choose an abortion. Furthermore, because the majority's reasons did not declare a right to abortion but merely scrutinized the existing law in terms of its protection of security of the person, the ruling in *Morgentaler* did not preclude government from passing new legislation that would remedy the most glaring defects of the process for procuring a legal abortion and declare all other abortions illegal.

The Mulroney government attempted to do just that soon after the Supreme Court ruling. In May 1988, the government announced that it would allow a free vote in

The Morgentaler Decision

In a five to two decision, the justices on the Canadian Supreme Court found section 251 of the Criminal Code unconstitutional. In striking down the law, the majority of the Court did not declare a constitutional right to abortion but rather that the regulations the Canadian government imposed on those trying to procure an abortion violated section 7 of the Canadian Charter of Rights and Freedoms. The constitutional violation was thus found to rest on the issue of substantive due process.

Section 7 of the Charter states that '[e]veryone has the right to life, liberty and security of the person and the right not to be deprived thereof except in accordance with the principles of fundamental justice'. Chief Justice Dickson, supported by Justice Lamer, and Justice Beetz, supported by Justice Estey, ruled that the procedural difficulties put in place by the law were so onerous that they violated principles of fundamental justice and could not be justified in a free and democratic society. The problem was not that the government restricted women from having abortions but rather that the procedural requirements established under the law prevented women from having a procedure that the law deemed legal. For example, the requirement that a TAC be composed of three doctors, not including doctors who performed abortions, meant that many hospitals did not have enough doctors to comply with the law. The law required that abortions be performed in accredited hospitals or in those approved by provincial governments, but the law did not require provincial governments to approve. Many small hospitals could not attain accreditation because they were too small. Other, religious-based hospitals had no desire to set up TACs. The Badgley Report, commissioned in 1997, stated that less than half of all hospitals in Canada were eligible to perform abortions and only half of those eligible actually set up TACs. In certain regions of Canada, therefore, it was very difficult to obtain an abortion. Thus, the law interfered with a woman's ability to receive timely medical treatment, and the delay had significant impact on the woman's security of person.

When the majority of justices considered whether the restrictions on women's rights were reasonable in a free and democratic society (the section 1 test of the Charter), they did not state that women had an unqualified right to abortion in which all restrictions would be unreasonable. In fact, Justices Beetz and Estey accepted that it was reasonable for a government to balance the rights of the unborn with the rights of women by impos- ing certain restrictions on obtaining an abortion. But if a government felt it reasonable to deprive women of their liberty to decide for themselves whether to have an abortion, then those restrictions should be procedurally just. Furthermore, if the legislation al- lowed a woman to procure an abortion when her life or health was at risk, the procedures themselves should not put the woman at risk.

Justice Wilson's reasons for the decision, however, offered a more substantive interpreta- tion of what 'principles of fundamental justice' mean in section 7. Justice Wilson at the time was the only woman on the Supreme Court, and she was the only one to argue that the justices should consider whether the substantive restrictions, not just the procedural restrictions, on women's section 7 rights comported with principles of fundamental justice. Justice Wilson began with the premise that the Charter 'erects around each individual, metaphorically speaking, an invisible fence over which the state will not be allowed to trespass'. The right to individual liberty is tied to the concept of human dignity. Respect for human dignity means allowing people to make their own personal decisions regarding, for example, marriage, child-rearing, contraception, and so on. Section 251 involves denial of the dignity of women because it takes away their choice to determine for themselves whether to have an abortion: under the law, Wilson argues, '[s]he is the passive recipient of a decision made by others as to whether her body is to be used to nurture a new life. Can there be anything that comports less with human dignity and self-respect?' Not only were women's section 7 rights violated by the Criminal Code provisions, so too were their section 2 rights. Section 2 states that everyone has fundamental freedom of conscience and religion in Canada, which includes the decision on whether or not to have an abortion. In forbidding abortion, Wilson argued, the law imposed one conscientiously held view at the expense of another.

In addressing the more substantive questions of liberty of choice and freedom of conscience, therefore, Wilson approached the question of the constitutionality of the Criminal Code provisions in a much different way from that of her male colleagues.[6] She also dealt with the question of reasonable limits (section 1 analysis) in a much different way. She stated that the primary objective of the legislation was to protect the fetus, which, she agreed, was a perfectly valid legislative objective. The question, then, was how to design legislation to protect the fetus so that the law violated a woman's liberty as little as possible. Wilson prescribed essentially the trimester model developed by the US Supreme Court in *Roe v. Wade*. That is, fetal rights become stronger as time goes on in the pregnancy. Wilson stated in her opinion that '[t]he precise point in the development of the foetus at which the state's interest in its protection becomes "compelling" I leave to the informed judgment of the legislature which is in a position to receive guidance on the subject from all relevant disciplines. It seems to me, however, that it might fall somewhere in the second trimester'. The problem with section 251 of the Criminal Code was that it took away the decision of the woman at all stages of the pregnancy. It did not simply limit a woman's right to choose but completely denied it and therefore could not be supported under section 1 of the Charter.[7]

the House of Commons on a 'menu' of three principles to choose from, ranging from strongly anti-abortion to strongly pro-choice, with the stages of pregnancy/trimester approach as the middle ground (Brodie, Gavigan, and Jenson 1992, 67–8). However, the opposition parties refused to allow the government to introduce its motion. The government then withdrew the motion and in July 1988 put forward a new motion with a single set of principles, adopting the stages of pregnancy approach, and invited MPs to introduce their own amendments. In all, 21 amendments to the government motion were introduced, each of which was defeated, as was the government's main resolution (Studlar and Tatalovich 1996, 80).

After the 1988 federal election, the re-elected Conservative government introduced Bill C-43, which revived the 1969 legislation, criminalizing the procedure (with a prison term of two years) except in cases in which the medical practitioner felt the health or life of the woman would be threatened in the absence of the procedure. The legislation eliminated the therapeutic abortion committee requirement and allowed the decision to be made by one physician as to whether a woman's health (physical, mental, or psychological) or life would be threatened were her pregnancy to be carried to term (Studlar and Tatalovich 1996, 80). The bill passed in the House of Commons by a vote of 140–131 in May 1990. The Childbirth By Choice Trust (1998, 154) reports that as soon as Bill C-43 was introduced in the House of Commons, at least 60 doctors stopped performing abortions and many obstetricians and gynecologists reported that they would stop performing abortions if the bill became law. Soon after, Toronto-area newspapers reported two abortion incidents: one woman was injured by an abortion provider and another died from a self-induced abortion using a coat hanger.

In January 1991, the Senate voted down Bill C-43 on a tied vote of 43–43, the first time in 30 years that the Senate had defeated a piece of government legislation. Haussman (2001, 82) attributes the defeat largely to intense lobbying by pro-choice groups on pro-choice Senators.[8] Ironically, all of the female Conservative Party House members voted in favour of Bill C-43 (Haussman 2001, 81), but in the Senate, among those who voted against the legislation was Pat Carney, a former cabinet minister in the Conservative government who was also pro-choice. No federal government since then has attempted to reintroduce legislation criminalizing abortion, although numerous private members' bills have been introduced but not passed in the Canadian House of Commons that range from efforts to recriminalize abortion, to declaring an embryo and fetus as human and therefore to define abortion as homicide, to criminalizing abortions after 20 weeks' gestation, to punishing a third party who murders a pregnant women with an additional Criminal Code offence (Richer 2008, 20–23; Abortion Rights Coalition of Canada, 2010).

Canadian public opinion seems to back the government's decision not to reintroduce abortion legislation. Canadians' support for abortion has remained fairly steady: a 1965 Gallup survey found that nearly 75 per cent of Canadians supported abortion in cases when a woman's health was in danger (Tatalovich 1997, 109), while a 2002 Gallup survey revealed that a majority of Canadians (57 per cent) believed that abortion is morally acceptable, compared to 40 per cent who believed it is morally wrong (Mazzuca 2002). A 2010 EKOS Politics poll found that 52 per cent of Canadians polled described themselves as 'pro-choice' while 27 per cent described themselves as 'pro-life', 10 per cent described themselves as 'neither', and 11 per cent stated 'don't know' or offered no response.[9]

New Challenges for Pro-choice Feminists

Access to abortion

While the legal restrictions on abortion disappeared in wake of the *Morgentaler* decision, access to abortion services has not necessarily increased. Although abortions are supposed to be funded along with every other medically necessary service in order to receive federal funding under the federal spending power (Richer 2008, 6–7), many provincial governments have fought to limit the funding[10] and/or performance of abortions in their province. Few hospitals across Canada—only 15.9 per cent as of 2006 (Shaw 2006, 1), down from the 17.8 per cent the Canadian Abortion Rights Action League (2003, 13) reports in 2000-2001—actually perform abortions, forcing women to rely on private clinics; yet two-thirds of abortion procedures are still performed in hospitals (Childbirth By Choice Trust 2005). Those hospitals are disproportionately situated in urban areas close to the US border and wait times for the procedure can be up to six weeks (Shaw 2006, 1). In Prince Edward Island no hospitals perform abortions.[11] Women using private clinics often face pro-life picketers when entering and exiting the clinics. Furthermore, while Ontario, BC, Alberta, and Newfoundland fully fund abortions performed in private clinics, some provinces and territories, such as Nova Scotia and Quebec, only partially fund such abortions, while New Brunswick and PEI do not fund abortions performed in private clinics (Erdman 2004, 1, 3; Shaw 2006, 21).[12]

The situation in the Maritimes illustrates the access difficulties many women experience. The PEI government will only fund *medically necessary* abortions performed in hospitals outside the province, which means that women from PEI cannot get an abortion in any hospital in Atlantic Canada unless it involves a medical emergency (Erdman 2004, 2). In the wake of the 1988 *Morgentaler* decision, the New Brunswick government decided to allow only abortions performed in hospitals, not in private clinics, only up to 12 weeks' gestation, and only by a gynaecologist, and to require the prior approval of two doctors (Richer 2008, 12). In the early 1990s, only three hospitals in New Brunswick were accredited to perform abortions (CP 1994, A4), and by 2005 only one performed abortions (MacAfee 2005, A5). But the province refuses to provide reciprocal billing arrangements to cover the costs of having an abortion out of province (Richer 2008, 12). Dr Morgentaler continues to battle New Brunswick for full funding of the operation, arguing that their refusal violates the Canada Health Act (Richer 2008, 10–11). The Nova Scotia government banned all free-standing abortion clinics in the wake of the *Morgentaler* decision, an action that the Supreme Court struck down as provincial intrusion into federal criminal law jurisdiction.[13] Dr Henry Morgentaler then opened an abortion clinic in Halifax in 1989, which he closed 14 years later.[14] That means that women who wish or need to use a private clinic in the Maritime provinces have to travel to Fredericton.

Finally, because abortion is a medical procedure, it is regulated in the same way as any other medical procedure, meaning that doctors themselves determine the regulations that govern their actions. Thus, the Canadian Medical Association defines abortion as the 'active termination of pregnancy up to 20 weeks' gestation' (Childbirth By Choice Trust 2005). In general in Canada, doctors do not perform abortions after 20 weeks unless they are deemed medically necessary. For example, the College of Physicians and Surgeons of Alberta (2000) regulations state that the decision to terminate a pregnancy prior to 20 weeks' gestation can be made between a patient and her doctor. Between 20 and 23 weeks, if a patient has been informed that her fetus is likely to have a serious genetic or other disorder, she can choose to request termination of the pregnancy, in consultation with a 'perinatal centre team'. Then, '[a]fter 23 weeks/0 days a pregnancy may be terminated in a public hospital in Alberta [sic] if prenatal assessment identifies a fetal condition which is confidently predicted to be inherently lethal during early neonatal weeks of life'. With these regulations in place, more than 90 per cent of all abortions in Canada are performed in the first trimester of pregnancy, and third-trimester abortions are very rare (Childbirth By Choice Trust 2005). The Canadian Abortion Rights Action League (2003, 9) notes that some doctors refuse to provide referrals for abortions and others will stall patients in order to prevent a woman from procuring an abortion within these gestational limits.

Kaposy (2010, 21) notes that all of these restrictions on access affect women differently. Those women who have the means to pay for services, who live in urban areas,

and who are not intimidated by the process will find their access to this medically necessary procedure is little impeded. However, '[w]omen who are poor, geographically
isolated, especially young, addicted, abused, disabled, or otherwise vulnerable will be
less able to overcome barriers to access'. For these women, little has improved in terms
of access to services despite legalization (see also Shaw 2006, 39–46).

Fetal right to life: *Borowski v. Canada* (Attorney General), 1989[15]

One problem that abortion rights activists have encountered in using the language
of rights is that it prompts challenges from those who claim competing rights. In the
Morgentaler decision, the Supreme Court did not resolve the question of what 'life'
means under section 7 of the Charter and in particular whether fetuses have a right
to life. Joseph Borowski launched just such a judicial campaign in 1978 to have the
courts declare that the Bill of Rights (subsequently the Charter of Rights, specifically
section 7) should be interpreted to include the right to life of the unborn (LEAF 1996,
51). That is, the unborn should be considered 'persons' under the law.

Borowski first had to convince the Supreme Court that he had 'standing', meaning that he was eligible to 'stand' in proceedings on behalf of the unborn. In 1982 the
Court ruled that he did have standing, broadening the eligibility of people to take
constitutional cases to the Supreme Court under the Charter. However, by the time
Borowski returned to the Supreme Court to plead his substantive case, the Criminal
Code abortion provisions had already been struck down. The Supreme Court thus
decided that the case was moot. Since Borowski's complaint was technically about
the abortion law and since the Court had struck down the abortion law, the Court
was able to argue that the matter about which Borowski went to court no longer existed. Lawyers for the pro-life cause argued that even so, the Court should clarify the
meaning of section 7 of the Charter and declare that it included the right to life of the
unborn. The Court ruled unanimously, however, that that would have amounted to a
private reference and only governments can pose hypothetical questions to the Court.
Thus Borowski's case was rejected.[16]

Fathers' rights: *Tremblay v. Daigle*, 1989[17]

Since the *Borowski* decision, anti-abortion forces have mounted other challenges to
the law. They found a champion in Jean-Guy Tremblay, who in 1989 challenged the
right of his former girlfriend, Chantal Daigle, to have an abortion without his consent.
Tremblay asked the court for an injunction against her having an abortion, claiming
he had a paternal right to protect the fetus. While he admitted to physically abusing
Ms Daigle and said that he had little interest in raising the child, both the trial judge
and the Quebec Court of Appeal sided with Tremblay, agreeing that the fetus had a
right to life under the Quebec Charter of Rights.[18] Chantal Daigle then appealed to
the Supreme Court of Canada. She was already ineligible for an abortion in Quebec
since she was by then 22 weeks pregnant (LEAF 1996, 103). In the midst of presenting
arguments to the Court, Daigle's lawyer announced that she had already obtained an
abortion. While this act made the case moot, the judges felt that they really should give
a more definitive answer on the issue than had been given in *Morgentaler* and *Borowski*
and hear from numerous organizations with intervener status.[19]

The Court ruled in Daigle's favour, but once again the ruling steered clear of fetal rights. The Court held that the fetus had no right to life under the Quebec Charter of Rights, the Quebec Civil Code, or common law. Since no government action or legislation existed declaring a right that would allow someone to interfere with a woman obtaining an abortion, she could not be prevented from doing so. Again, the Court did not have to deal with the substantive issue of whether fetuses have rights under the Canadian Charter (McCourt 1991, 917).

Women's rights versus fetal rights

All of these cases leave unanswered the question of what the rights of the fetus are, although the Canadian Supreme Court has clarified the point at which the law recognizes the fetus as an independent person. In R. v. Sullivan, 1988,[20] the Court was presented with a case in which two midwives were accused of causing the death of a fetus/infant in the birth canal during a home birth. Mary Sullivan and Gloria Lemay, who had received no formal training as midwives (Shaffer 1991, 1370), were charged under two sections of the Canadian Criminal Code, criminal negligence causing death (section 203) and criminal negligence causing bodily harm (section 204). In a BC court, both were convicted on the charge of criminal negligence causing death because the trial judge felt that since section 203 of the Criminal Code refers to causing the death of another 'person', rather than 'human being', as defined in section 206 of the Criminal Code,[21] the law could be interpreted as recognizing a fetus in the process of being born as a 'person' and thus alive (Shaffer 1991, 1373). On appeal, however, the BC Court of Appeal reduced the charge to criminal negligence causing bodily harm. The appeal court's reasoning, unlike that of the BC Supreme Court judge, was that the fetus at the time was still in the birth canal and still part of the mother. It thus was not yet a human being and not yet a person. The Crown then appealed that appeal court ruling to the Canadian Supreme Court, but the Court dismissed the Crown's appeal.

Similarly, in an Ontario lower court ruling, R. v. Drummond, 1996,[22] a judge dismissed a charge of attempted murder against Brenda Drummond, who shot her fetus in utero with a pellet gun in a claimed suicide bid two days before his birth. He was subsequently born alive, and surgeons successfully removed the pellet from the child's brain. The Court held that a charge of attempted murder could not be supported since the fetus was not a person for the purposes of the Criminal Code of Canada. Ms Drummond subsequently pleaded guilty to failing to provide the necessities of life to her infant son (CP 1997a, A6).

The issue of the moral and legal obligations of pregnant women to their unborn children is extremely complex and divisive. On one side of the debate are those who argue that a mother owes a duty of care to the fetus during pregnancy because her actions and behaviour can affect fetal development. Others would go further and argue that a woman's right to control her body could be restricted to protect the fetus (Condit 1995, 43). On one side of the debate are those who argue that judicial or legislative interference in maternal autonomy subordinates 'women's rights to control their bodies and pregnancies and treat them as nothing more than fetal containers' (Condit 1995, 44).

Whereas the feminist movement in the past paid a great deal of attention to reproductive issues that fall broadly into the category of inhibiting the development of new life (birth control, sterilization, and abortion), society in general now pays significant attention to medical advances that can monitor new life, such as ultrasound, amnio-centesis, and fetal surgery (Achilles 1993, 488). As Daniels (1993) and Condit (1995) point out, with technological advances that have allowed people to see inside the womb, the fetus has gained visibility and status as an 'individual' with medical interests distinct from those of the pregnant woman. Technological advances have also moved back the point of 'viability' when the fetus can survive on its own outside the womb. These developments have led to the idea that the fetus might have 'gestational rights' and that physicians might have separate obligations to the fetus as a 'second patient' (Condit 1995, 34–5).

Condit (1995) cautions, however, that the more one sees a fetus as an indepen-dent entity, with rights, the fewer rights pregnant women may be granted to make decisions that affect the fetus. It is important to keep in mind that fetuses, unlike children, cannot exist without the woman, so it may be dangerous to regard fetuses as independent. Many of the cases discussed above require the state to 'reach through' the woman to get to the fetus. Such a sacrifice of personal liberty is not required of men, or of anyone in any other circumstance, even to save the life of another.

For example, the law prohibits the state from compelling one family member to give up an organ in order to save another family member's life (Nelson and Milliken 1988, 1065). Organs cannot be removed from a cadaver without the consent of the next of kin. As Nelson and Milliken (1988, 1065) write, 'We see no good reason why pregnant women should be treated with less respect than corpses'.

Feminists also raise the 'slippery slope' argument. Acceptance of fetal rights might not only lead to laws banning abortion,[23] it could also impose even greater controls on pregnant women and even on potential mothers. State prohibitions might include bans on illegal activities (women could be required not to use amphetamines or illegal drugs while pregnant, for example), but they could also apply to legal activities, such as drinking alcoholic beverages, using hot tubs, smoking, eating junk food, gaining more than 20 pounds, or having sex. Courts might also compel women to quit their jobs or remain in bed because of perceived risks to the fetus.

One might even foresee the control of women's behaviour before pregnancy at the pre-conception stage. In the past, the state and employers enacted 'protective labour legislation', which regulated the hours women worked to ensure that they would re-main healthy childbearers and mothers.[24] Daniels (1997) points out that many activi-ties men engage in, such as drug and alcohol use and generally unhealthy habits, affect sperm but society does not impose on men the same duty to care. Instead, from warn-ing labels on tobacco and alcohol products to signs in women's washrooms warning of the dangers of drinking while pregnant, the message is that only women can cause harm to their fetuses (Daniels 1997, 587).

Feminists also warn about the dangers of 'fetal viability' as a test of the time when doctors can intervene in a pregnancy and treat the fetus medically. Such interventions could come earlier and earlier in the pregnancy as technological advances push back the time in the pregnancy when fetuses are deemed viable (Kolder, Gallagher, and Parsons 1987, 1195). If intervention becomes a common practice, would doctors be obliged to perform surgery or risk negligence and/or murder charges should the fetus die without the intervention? Drawing a clear line between what is a fetus and what is a human being is therefore crucial for women's rights and for legal certainty for all the actors involved.

Maternal duty to care

At the lower court level in Canada, some rulings have challenged the idea of parent-child immunity—that is, that a pregnant woman cannot be held accountable for injuries inflicted on the fetus—although again this challenge has not been successful at the Supreme Court level in Canada. In *Dobson v. Dobson*, 1997,[25] a New Brunswick lower court judge ruled that a child could seek damages from its mother for disabilities suffered in a car accident when still in the uterus (CP 1997b, A6).[26] Typically, courts in Canada have recognized that people who inflict damage on a fetus can be held responsible, but only if the fetus is born alive. The New Brunswick judge in this case, however, ruled that a mother should be treated no differently from any other party. On appeal to the Supreme Court of Canada in 1999,[27] with the Canadian Abortion Rights Action League intervening, the Court ruled that in fact the relationship of the fetus to the mother is different from that of any other party and one cannot apply existing tort rules regarding duty of care (though Parliament would be free to do so if it so desired, as long as it adhered to the Charter). Furthermore, to recognize such a duty of care would constitute a severe intrusion into the lives of pregnant women and thus violate liberty and equality interests of pregnant women. The majority decision, written by Chief Justice Lamer, stated that '[i]n light of the very demanding biological reality that only women can become pregnant and bear children, the courts should be hesitant to impose additional burdens upon pregnant women . . . . The imposition of tort liability in this context would have profound effects upon every pregnant woman and upon Canadian society in general. . . . The best course, therefore, is to allow the duty of a mother to her foetus to remain a moral obligation which, for the vast majority of women, is already freely recognized and respected without compulsion by law'.

The lower court ruling in *Dobson v. Dobson* was handed down before the Supreme Court ruled on a similar issue in *Winnipeg Child and Family Services (Northwest Area) v. G. (D.F.)*, 1997.[28] In this case, a lower court judge in Winnipeg ordered a pregnant woman to be confined to an addiction treatment centre because of a concern that her solvent abuse would produce brain damage in her child. The Manitoba Court of Appeal overturned that ruling, arguing that fetuses have no rights under Canadian law and courts therefore have no legal basis to order a mentally competent person to undergo treatment or medical intervention that he or she does not want. The Supreme Court, which heard from a host of interveners on both sides, including the Canadian Civil Liberties Association, the Canadian Abortion Rights Action League, LEAF, some government agencies, and the Evangelical Fellowship of Canada, agreed with the Manitoba Court of Appeal ruling. Both the Manitoba Court of Appeal and Canadian Supreme Court ruled that pregnant women have the moral responsibility to care for unborn children but that there is no legal obligation that would allow the state to compel a pregnant woman to do something she did not want to do. In other words, a pregnant woman's *ethical* obligation to care for her fetus could not be *legally* enforced. Furthermore, criminalization, forced detention, and after-the-fact punishment of pregnant women could deter women from seeking treatment when it is really needed.

From Rights to Reproductive Freedom

The difficulties that arise from absolutist and purely individual rights-based arguments regarding abortion rights is the reason why many feminist advocates urge a switch from the language of abortion rights to 'reproductive freedom' or 'reproductive rights' or 'reproductive justice', concepts that capture an entire spectrum of reproductive issues. As many US feminists (for example, Brown 1983) have observed, legalization through the US Supreme Court's acceptance of abortion as a privacy right creates other problems for the pro-choice movement: it articulates abortion as a 'negative' liberty—that is, a right created by the recognition that there is a sphere of privacy into which the state may not intrude. It does not, however, compel the state to ensure that abortion services are provided as a medically necessary service (Brown 1983). Therefore, 'choice', Stetson (1996, 213) argues, 'if all it requires is that the government not limit abortion, has turned out to be a narrow foundation for policy' because it leaves a woman's pregnancy, financial situation, and everything else up to her alone.

Some feminists thus urge a move away from the language of 'choice' to the language of 'equality' when advocating for abortion rights. Some abortion rights advocates argue that society should pay more attention to eradicating the underlying inequalities that make abortion a necessity for so many women: poverty, racism, and so on. Groups such as the Ontario Coalition for Abortion Clinics and unions affiliated with the Canadian Labour Congress have emphasized that for women to have real reproductive freedom, the enabling conditions such as clinics and funding must be in place (Haussman 2001, 64). Women often do not control the conditions under which they become pregnant, and they also do not have much control over the conditions under which they rear children. 'Women's reproductive capacity is thus an integral part of women's "equality problem", along a spectrum of situations' (LEAF 1996, 61), including economic and cultural equality.

Furthermore, access to abortion and contraception alone do not liberate women because '[w]hen a woman seeks an abortion, she is already pregnant; the important question is how she became pregnant' (Stetson 1996, 214) and whether she had the power to say no to sex in the first place. Individual rights, after all, mean little if a woman 'is part of a social structure that limits her alternatives severely or lacks resources to break out of these constraints' (Stetson 1996, 215). Wendy Brown (1983, 323) argues that abortion should not be seen as a 'positive good' but as an 'unhappy necessity' for women's freedom. Stetson (1996, 216) points out that the language of reproductive 'freedom' can be more powerful than the language of reproductive rights: it can apply both to individuals and to women as a group; it does not require that a woman be left alone in her zone of privacy but rather that her needs should be considered so that she can achieve freedom. And the focus on reproduction, rather than just on abortion, brings to the table the need for the good prenatal care, child care, housing, and so on that are necessary to that freedom.

This idea of reproductive freedom reflects a generational shift in the movement. 'Third-wave' reproductive rights advocates such as the Third Wave Foundation and Choice USA in the United States advocate a broader agenda than abortion rights alone, including 'comprehensive sex education, emergency contraception, affordable prenatal care for low-income women and, for immigrants, improved access to reproductive health care by providers who speak their patients' native language' (Clemetson 2004, A10). More established abortion rights organizations in the United States, such as NARAL Pro-Choice America (formerly the National Abortion and Reproductive Rights Action League) argue that it is still important to work to uphold *Roe v. Wade* and maintain focus on that battle (Clemetson 2004, A10). The younger generation of feminists appear to have greater ease in accepting the abortion issue as complex and nuanced and in agreeing that restrictions such as a 24-hour waiting period, requiring parental consent for minors, and even informing and consulting with men when wives and girlfriends get pregnant may be appropriate (Stepp 2004, C4).

Technology has shifted feminists' perspectives. For example, technologies that reveal the sex of a fetus make sex-selective abortions possible. Thus, many no longer advocate an absolute right to abortion on demand if that means aborting fetuses for any reason whatsoever, such as a disability or 'wrong' sex (Stetson 1996, 216).

Medication Abortion as an Alternative to Surgical Abortion

In a *New York Times Magazine* article entitled 'The little white bombshell', Margaret Talbot (1999) documented how the introduction of combination drugs that induce abortion, such as mifepristone (otherwise known as RU-486) and misoprostol, could (potentially) radically alter the terrain of the abortion wars.[29] The use of drugs to encourage the body to expel the fetus without surgery can be used in the early weeks of pregnancy before the embryo becomes a fetus, decreasing ethical concerns about abortions (which typically are not performed until about the eighth week of pregnancy). The procedure is much more discreet because any doctor may prescribe the medication and women can self-administer the drug in the comfort of their own homes. Doctors reluctant to perform surgical abortions out of fear of anti-abortion violence can prescribe the drug with a degree of anonymity, even in rural areas. Abortion can thus be more easily folded into regular medical practice' (Talbot 1999, 41).

Pro-life groups opposed to any form of abortion such as Operation Rescue in the United States attempted to block the availability of these drugs but failed when the Food and Drug Administration approved the drug's use in 2000 'for the termination of early pregnancy, defined as 49 days or less, counting from the beginning of the last menstrual period' (Food and Drug Administration, 'Mifeprex [Mifepristone] Information' http://www.fda.gov/cder/drug/infopage/mifepristone/default.htm). In fact, mifepristone has been approved for use in 46 countries as of 2010, including a number of more conservative religious countries in Europe (Gynuity Health Projects 2010).

It is thus rather shocking to note that Canada has not approved mifepristone for use as an abortifacient. Another drug, methotrexate, is approved for use but it does not work as well as mifepristone; indeed, the mifepristone/misoprostol combination is the only one that the World Health Organization approves and indeed lists amongst its Model List of Essential Medicines (Erdman, Grenon, and Harrison-Wilson 2008, 1766–7). As a result, only 1 to 2 per cent of abortions in Canada are pharmaceutically induced, which means women rely almost exclusively on surgical abortion, a technique that is more invasive and more public (Erdman, Grenon, and Harrison-Wilson 2008, 1766). Given that 25 per cent of abortions are performed within the first nine weeks of pregnancy, and medication abortion can be safely administered up to nine weeks, a lot more abortions could be performed with medication rather than surgery (Erdman, Grenon, and Harrison-Wilson

2008, 1766). In fact, Erdman, Grenon and Harrison-Wilson (2008, 1766) note that '[i]n France, Scotland and Sweden, more than half of eligible abortions are pharmaceutically induced with mifepristone'.

Erdman, Grenon, and Harrison-Wilson (2008, 1765) point out the problem of relying almost exclusively on surgical abortion in Canada. As discussed above, only certain hospitals perform the surgery, only some provinces and geographic locations have private clinics, and only certain doctors are trained to perform the procedure. Given the absence of facilities, the wait time for those services is high—up to six weeks in some areas.

One thus has to conclude that lack of mifepristone approval is a restriction on women's access to health care. Access to medication abortion, of course, does depend on a doctor's willingness to tell the patient about the drug and a pharmacist's willingness to dispense it. Consequently, anti-abortion groups are working to prevent the communication of information about the procedure and to have laws in place allowing pharmacists to refuse to dispense medicine about which they have ethical objections. So far, the College of Pharmacists in various provinces and nationally have issued codes of ethics that favour patient autonomy and thus medication accessibility. For example, the National Association of Pharmacy Regulatory Authorities has developed a Model Statement Regarding Physicians' Refusal to Provide Products or Services for Moral or Religious Reasons. That statement 'mandates that objections be conveyed to the pharmacy manager, not to the patient, and that referrals be made while 'minimizing inconvenience or suffering to the patient or patient's agent' (Alarcon 2009, 749).

Various provincial professional bodies, such as the British Columbia College of Pharmacists, have also issued statements that prohibit depriving patients of access to legal pharmaceutical services because of religious beliefs or personal convictions (Alarcon 2009, 749). If a pharmacist has a problem with dispensing a legal medication, he or she must refer patients to another pharmacist (Wynn et al. 2007, 259). In BC, if no one else is available to dispense the medication, then the objecting pharmacist must do so (Alarcon 2009, 749). In Saskatchewan, the policy warns explicitly against 'preaching' and states that it would be 'improper and unethical conduct if the pharmacist used the opportunity to promote his/her moral or religious convictions, or engage in any actions, which demean the patient' (Alarcon 2009, 749). Yet, Saskatchewan, along with Alberta, Manitoba, and Nova Scotia, does not enforce the mandatory dispensing of products or referral that are contrary to the pharmacist's moral conscience (Alarcon 2009, 750). Indeed, an Alberta pharmacist was reinstated to her position after she sued for the right to refuse to dispense abortifacient drugs and contraceptives (Alarcon 2009, 751). Medication abortion is thus not a perfect solution to the problem of abortion access, but policy-makers should at least have to justify in public the foot-dragging on legal approval.

Assisted Reproductive Technologies (ARTs)

Feminists now increasingly pay attention to new technologies that help in the creation of new life, not just technologies that inhibit the creation. As Rona Achilles (1993, 488) points out, 'reproductive technologies can empower or disempower women, depending on how they are used and on the social context in which they are used'. On the one hand, these reproductive technologies give hope to infertile parents. But in the application of reproductive and genetic technologies, conflicts arise as to the rights of the many parties involved (Blank and Merrick 1995, 99). Some of the concerns feminists raise include: the commercialization of procreation (as in the sale of eggs and sperm) and the commodification of women's bodies (as in surrogacy contracts); the role that third parties play in the reproductive process and the rights they have, whether that party be a surrogate mother, a fertility clinic, or some other party; the further medicalization of the reproductive experience; and the potential eugenic uses of these technologies, such as genetic testing (Achilles 1993, 503).

Policy-makers have paid greater attention to these issues in recent years as demand for assisted reproduction has grown. Health Canada (2004) estimates that up to one in eight couples in Canada experiences infertility. In Canada a couple is generally classified as infertile if they have been unsuccessful in conceiving after one year. Infertility and the rise in infertility can be attributed to a variety of factors, including environmental and occupational health hazards, the use of specific drugs or devices such as IUDs, and the decision on the part of many people to postpone childbearing until their 30s or 40s (Achilles 1993, 512, n. 9).

The increase in the number of same-sex couples has also led to increased demand for a variety of services including gamete donation and surrogacy (Kelly 2008–9). As discussed in chapter 8, the use of ARTs raise important questions of legal parentage related to child custody (and child support in the case of family breakdown) (see, e.g., Campbell 2007). At issue as well is same-sex couples' access to ARTs in the first place (e.g., Cameron 2008).

Artificial or assisted insemination (AI)

The most widely used and least complicated means of assisted reproduction is artificial or assisted insemination (AI). This technique simply involves inserting a syringe full of sperm when a woman is ovulating, with or without concurrent hormonal treatments. Assisted insemination replaces sexual intercourse; fertilization of the egg by the sperm occurs within the body. While the technique is relatively straightforward, the issues surrounding the use of it are not.

First, Angela Cameron (2008, 111–12) points out that this technique is governed by regulations in the Assisted Human Reproduction Act. The Act prohibits assisted insemination occurring outside of a fertility clinic—in other words, self-insemination is illegal, yet this may be the preferred method for lesbian parents who use sperm donors. Another regulation, the Processing and Distribution of Semen for Assisted Conception, bars men who have had any male sexual partners since 1977 from donating sperm, without first getting special permission from the government (Cameron 2008, 110). Since 2000, if a gay man wants to donate sperm, it must be to a willing person with 'special application by their doctor, a medical screen, and dispensation from the Minister of Health'. These regulations have the effect of barring gay men from fertility clinics and thus lesbian couples from legally obtaining the sperm of a gay man.

Sperm and egg preservation do increase options for people who might wish to conceive children in the future, such as those undergoing radiation for treatment of cancer or those who decide to undergo sterilization but might worry that they will change their minds at a later date. However, there are numerous ethical questions surrounding genetic material preservation. First, given that men can donate multiple semen samples and those samples can be used in many AI procedures, it is possible that a single donor could produce many genetically related children. This raises health issues should those children have relationships and offspring with each other—technically, incest. Further, as Blank and Merrick (1995, 88) observe, the '[c]ryopreservation of eggs and embryos, as well as of sperm, permits the combination of germ cell materials from persons of different generations . . .[which] may allow identical twins to be born years or even generations apart'.

The ability to harvest semen or eggs from the body also raises concerns about bodily integrity. For example, in 1999 the New York Times reported that a woman had given birth to a child using sperm she had retrieved from her dead husband (AP 1999, A11). This case raised the ethical question of whether a person must give consent to become a parent.[30] In coming years, the issue of egg donation could easily become messily entangled with that of abortion. Scientists recently reported that they could extract eggs from female fetuses aborted in late term, grow the tissue for a few weeks in a lab, and insert the eggs into an infertile woman. Opponents of abortion and some ethicists decry such a procedure. As one spokesperson was quoted as saying, '[i]magine having to tell the child born of this procedure, "Your mother was a dead baby"' (Galloway 2003, A10).

Artificial Insemination also raises questions about parentage and parental rights and responsibilities. Cases have arisen in which sperm donors have claimed parental rights after finding out they have contributed genetic material in the creation of a child, even if that parental claim violates the wishes of the mother, the heterosexual couple, or the same-sex couple. A number of scholars have raised concerns about the impact of courts and legislatures automatically assigning parenting rights to sperm donors (e.g., Boyd 2007; Campbell 2007; Kelly 2008–9; Kelly 2009). Indeed, courts and governments have taken a variety of positions, sometimes rooted in biology, sometimes in the sperm donor's relationship to the child's mother, and sometimes rooted in the sperm donor's social relationship with the child (Kelly 2009, 316). The concern in these cases is the extent to which courts and governments feel it is necessary to 'find a father' for children of same-sex parents.

Children conceived through a sperm donor have sought the identity of the donor, not only to learn more about their genetic parent for medical and other reasons but also, in rare cases, to demand financial support (Kondro 2000, R3). Policy-makers and courts have yet to sort out the knotty issues surrounding anonymity and genetic parenting. British Columbia became the first province in Canada to prevent anonymity of sperm after Olivia Pratten, a woman conceived via anonymous sperm donation from a Vancouver clinic, challenged the law that denied her access to the donor's information. Under BC law, children of adoption can get access to donor information once they reach adulthood. A Provincial Supreme Court judge ruled in May 2011 that the different treatment of adopted children and children born of sperm donation was discriminatory (Dhillon 2011).

The case was complicated by the outcome of a 2010 Supreme Court of Canada decision on the constitutionality of the federal Assisted Human Reproduction Act. The Court ruled in December 2010 that parts of that Act are outside the regulatory authority of the federal government.[31] The BC Government had claimed that regulations regarding fertility clinics fell under federal jurisdiction and thus the plaintiff, Olivia Pratten, could not demand action on the part of the BC Government. Since the Supreme Court ruled that regulatory authority falls under provincial jurisdiction, the BC Court went ahead with its ruling on the validity of Pratten's Charter claim to equality discrimination. At the time of writing, the BC Attorney General is deciding whether to appeal the ruling, which protects sperm donors whose genetic material was already used, but removes anonymity for future donors (Dhillon 2011).

Assisted reproductive technology (ART)

Three major techniques fall under the category of ART. The most widely known is in vitro fertilization (IVF), which involves the removal of eggs from a woman's body after which they are fertilized, encouraged to begin cell replication, and then transferred back into the woman's uterus. Gamete intrafallopian transfer (GIFT) involves a slightly different procedure. Eggs and sperm are both guided into the woman's fallopian tube so that fertilization can occur naturally there. Zygote intrafallopian transfer (ZIFT) involves the fertilization of eggs outside the body, as with in vitro fertilization, but then the eggs are transferred into the woman's fallopian tubes.

The use of ART has raised multiple issues and concerns. The procedure usually involves hormone therapy in advance of egg retrieval in order to stimulate the woman's body to produce as many eggs as possible for retrieval and fertilization. Given that the chances of success are fairly low on each individual attempt, and given that the procedure is very expensive, more than one embryo is often implanted to increase the chances of success. This often results in multiple births and/or premature babies, which can add financial and psychological stress to the family. As a result, the use of ART is often paired with the selective termination of some of the fetuses (Overall 1992a, 243). Aborting some of the pregnancies reduces the risk to the mother and the surviving fetuses, but it is a procedure that has been attacked by abortion opponents.

A number of cases have arisen since the early 1990s, all of which involve trying to grapple with what to do with the estimated thousands of extra embryos created in the ART process.[32] Many couples are uneasy about destroying the embryos. Canada recently allowed the establishment of a not-for-profit embryo adoption program that allows couples to donate their embryos to others who are having difficulty conceiving (Priest 2002a, A1, A4). The development of ART has created the possibility that women having trouble conceiving because of their age or for some other reason may use donor eggs. In other words, a fertilized egg can be implanted into a woman other than the one who supplied the egg. In fact, three different mothers are possible: the egg donor, the uterine mother (that is, the one who incubates the child in utero), and the social mother. Two different fathers are possible as well: the sperm donor and the social father (Achilles 1993, 505). ART may even make it possible to transfer an embryo into a man's abdominal cavity, possibly resulting in male pregnancy!

Given the possibility that at least five parents could be involved in a child's birth, major battles have arisen over the issue of who the parent is under law. Before it became possible to fertilize, freeze, and store human embryos (or sperm for that matter), there was no question as to who the 'owner' of the embryo was: it was the gestational mother because the egg was hers and the embryo was part of the woman throughout the entire pregnancy. Now it is often left up to the courts to decide who the mother is. In Britain in 2002, for example, a case arose in which a white woman gave birth to twin babies after she and her husband, who was also white, used a fertility clinic. It was clear at the birth that the twins were not the couple's genetic children because they were black. Soon afterwards, it was discovered that sperm from another man had been used to fertilize the woman's eggs. The white couple wished to keep the twins, but the genetic father wanted the court to rule on his parental rights. The court ruled that while the man whose sperm was used was the legal father, the twins would be allowed to stay with the couple and the man in the couple could apply to adopt the children (n.a. 2003c).

Many feminists worry that the costs involved in ART and the commercialization of human reproductive parts require government intervention to prevent exploitation. Most clinics in Canada charge between $5,000 and $10,000 for a single ART treatment cycle, which gives a couple on average only a one-in-three to one-in-four chance of giving birth to a baby (Hughes 2000, A15). The total costs sometimes run much higher, given travel costs to the treatment centre, lodging, time off work, and so on. Therefore, in Canada ART is currently available only to those with resources. Researchers have also tracked the increase in 'reproductive tourism' which involves travel to jurisdictions with fewer regulations or lower fees, such as India, in order to secure treatments or procure the services of a surrogate (e.g., Ikemoto 2009).

Commercialization raises other problems. In Canada we have always paid men for sperm donation: Achilles (1993, 507) reports payment of $15 to $75 for each ejaculate. But a market in human eggs is emerging as well. While women are often paid much more for their eggs because of the hormone treatments and surgery required to retrieve them, some fear that the sums paid could lead to the exploitation of vulnerable and often desperate donors and consumers. For example, a *New York Times* story reported that a person in the United States was willing to pay up to $50,000 to an egg donor if she was at least 5 feet 10 inches tall, athletic, and smart, with a score of at least 1400 on her Scholastic Achievement Test, and no major family medical problems (Kolata 1999, A10). As we shall discuss later, federal regulations introduced in Canada in 2004 deal directly with these issues.

Surrogate motherhood

The practice of 'surrogacy' (a misnomer since the actual surrogate mother is the one who does *not* carry the child to term and deliver it [Achilles 1993]) also causes deep divisions in society and within the feminist movement (Shanley 1993). In surrogate or gestational parenthood arrangements, infertile couples or individuals sign pre-conception contracts with a woman who agrees to carry a child to term for them. On the surface, surrogacy seems an ideal solution for an infertile couple who would like a child genetically related to at least one of them. It raises a host of questions, however, including whether parties have a right to enter into such contractual arrangements and whether the state should uphold the contract if agreement breaks down.

Most babies are turned over to the contracting parents, but a famous custody dispute between a gestational and biological mother, Mary Beth Whitehead, and a contracting biological father, William Stern, arose in the United States in 1988 over Baby M.[33] Elizabeth Stern believed that she could not carry a child to term because she had an undiagnosed form of multiple sclerosis, although there was some speculation by Ms Whitehead that Mrs Stern was simply avoiding the inconvenience of pregnancy (Achilles 1993, 512, n. 8).

The Sterns contracted with Ms Whitehead in February 1985. In that contract, she agreed not to smoke, drink alcoholic beverages, use illegal drugs, or take medication without written consent from her physician. She would submit to prenatal testing, and if it were determined that the fetus had defects, she would have an abortion if the Sterns demanded it. She would also assume all risks, including the risk of death and postpartum complications. She and her husband agreed to terminate all parental rights after birth. Ms Whitehead was paid a $10,000 fee for her services (which is quite low, given the labour involved: it amounts to a wage of about $1.57 per hour). If she miscarried before the fifth month, there would be no payment. If she miscarried later or the child was stillborn, she would be paid $1,000. If she conceived an 'abnormal' child and aborted, she would receive $1,000. If she refused to abort, the Sterns' obligation to her would cease (Achilles 1993, 499).

Ms Whitehead changed her mind about turning over the baby after she gave birth. The result was a lengthy court battle in which a New Jersey trial judge upheld the surrogacy contract as enforceable. Furthermore, the judge found, because of her actions after the birth of the child (she and her husband kidnapped the child and were on the run for three months), it was in the best interest of the child to be with the Sterns. The New Jersey Supreme Court overturned that decision on appeal, ruling that the contract was unenforceable because it involved baby-selling, a monetary inducement for adoption, and a pre-birth adoption agreement, all of which are illegal. Ms Whitehead was deemed to be the legal mother,[34] but custody was awarded to the Sterns, with visitation rights for Ms Whitehead, since the court found her to be unstable.

Another key US case that has framed the policy discussion around surrogacy is that of *Johnson v. Calvert*, 1993.[35] Here the legal outcome was quite different. The case dealt with the issue of gestational surrogacy in which the child is genetically related to both the contracting mother and father. In this case, the surrogate provided the gestational womb for the contracting couple but not the genetic material. The case was particularly complicated because two women met the legal definition of mother: the one who provided the egg and the one who nurtured the child in the womb and gave birth to it. Adding to the complications were race factors: the surrogate mother, Anna Johnson, was black, Native American, and Irish. Mark Calvert, the contracting father, was Caucasian and his wife Crispina was from the Philippines (Achilles 1993, 501), leading the superior court judge to rule that Johnson was a genetic stranger to the child (Place 1994, 908). Unlike the New Jersey Supreme Court in the Baby M decision, the Supreme Court of California upheld the surrogacy contract, ruling that without the contracting parents' actions, the child would not exist. Whoever *intended* to procreate the child was the natural mother (Place 1994, 908). While the couple agreed to pay Johnson $10,000 in instalments and purchase a life insurance policy of $200,000, the court ruled that the monetary payments were not a sale of parental rights but rather simply compensation for services.

Feminist positions on pre-conception contracts

Some feminists argue that women have a right to enter a contractual arrangement to bear a child and moreover to receive money for their services. Prohibitions on surrogacy and judicial refusal to uphold pregnancy contracts infringe on women's autonomy and freedom of choice (Shalev 1989). To prevent women from engaging in such services suggests that women are not competent to make these choices or to be paid for their labour. Why should we expect women to perform such labour for nothing when men are paid just for donating sperm? Surrogacy is also useful in severing the notion that 'biology is destiny' in the case of child-rearing. That is, the child-rearing tasks should not necessarily be assigned to the woman who bears the child (Shanley 1993, 619). It means that women who cannot physically bear children can still care for them, but with more of a genetic connection than in adoption or foster parenthood. And a man who commissions a pregnancy generally undertakes fatherhood quite consciously and thus would be more involved in caring for the child.

Others argue that the problem with pre-conception contracts is the contract. First, a woman might not enter a contract as a free chooser but rather because of economic circumstances. For example, in the Baby M case, the Sterns fit the typical profile of contracting parents: white, married, well-educated, wealthy, and in their late 30s or early 40s. William Stern was a biochemist and his wife was a pediatrician. Ms Whitehead fit the typical surrogate profile: she was a young mother who had dropped out of high school as a teenager, married, and had two children. Her husband was a sanitation worker (Achilles 1993, 498).

As mentioned earlier, some pre-conception contracts are quite strict in controlling women's behaviour while pregnant. What might happen to the surrogate mother if she refuses to follow the dietary regimen outlined in a contract, for example? Could she be sued for breach of contract, or could a contracting couple obtain a court order to enforce the contract? A number of contracts require the woman to deliver a physically 'perfect' baby or a particular number of children. If a couple 'orders' one baby but the gestational mother carries two or more, who is the responsible 'parent' of the other child or children? The contracting parents may claim, 'We only ordered one!' or 'We only ordered one free of physical defects and diseases!' That would leave the gestational mother responsible for children she might not have the resources to raise on her own. Framing such arrangements as contracts creates the impression that parents are purchasing 'products', not 'people' (Guichon 2001, A13). Thinking of women as gestational incubators also denies the bond that develops between the mother and the fetus.

Currently, Canada prohibits baby-selling and charging adoption fees. Parents cannot buy and sell custody rights during a divorce, and we prohibit the sale of human organs. Why then would we allow surrogacy contracts? Mary Lyndon Shanley (1993) therefore suggests that women should be allowed to gestate fetuses for other families, but those gestational services should be seen as 'gifts', with compensation for medical and living expenses the only payment allowed. Furthermore, pregnancy contracts should certainly not be enforceable.

Assisted Reproductive Technologies: Feminist Policy Prescriptions

Medical advances and technological innovations in reproduction and genetics have complicated the issues regarding birth and the female body for both feminists and governments. Feminist responses as to how these issues should be dealt with in public policy can be placed on a continuum (although with no clear consensus on the issues).

Some feminists conceive of the issue as a right to reproduce and to be able to do so with as little government interference as possible. Others would go further, arguing that the right to reproduce entails having access to all the available technologies to assist in that reproduction, and that factors such as wealth, marital status, sexual orientation, and the jurisdiction in which one lives should not impinge on the right to equal access to those techniques (Overall 1992a, 247). At the other end of the continuum are those who would argue for an outright ban on the use of ARTs. The Catholic Church, for example, still declares that assisted insemination with donor sperm is adulterous (Achilles 1993, 493).

The feminist community is deeply divided on these issues, as illustrated by the multiple perspectives heard at the public hearings of the Royal Commission on New Reproductive Technologies (Baird Commission) in 1990 (for example, McCormack 1996). The Baird Commission had in fact been set up in response to a request by NAC and a number of other women's organizations for a public inquiry on the issue of reproductive technologies (Scala, Montpetit, and Fortier 2005). During the hearings, NAC called for a complete ban on all reproductive technologies, seeing them as 'fertile ground for the continuing exploitation of women, especially economically disadvantaged women' (ibid.). Some of NAC's member organizations did emphasize the need for reproductive choice, and NAWAL recommended against criminal law as a form of regulation. Other women's groups and individual presentations strongly disagreed with NAC's perspective. For example, '[l]esbian and single women argued that societal norms regarding the traditional heterosexual marriage have effectively limited their opportunities to have children. . . . Appealing to 'family values' sentiments, lesbian and single women argued that access to reproductive technologies would permit individuals outside the heterosexual relationship the opportunity to be parents' (Scala, Montpetit, and Fortier 2005).

Many feminists are uncomfortable with the 'strong rights' argument for reproductive rights. Overall (1992a, 248) argues that recognizing a strong right to reproduce

> would shift the burden of proof on those who have moral doubts about the morality of technologies such as IVF and practices such as contract motherhood. For it suggests that a child is somehow owed to each of us, as individuals or as members of a couple, and that it is indefensible for society to fail to provide all possible means for obtaining one. Thus it might be used . . . to imply an entitlement to hire contract mothers, to obtain other women's eggs . . . all in order to maximize the chances of reproducing. In other words, recognition of the right to reproduce in the strong sense would create an active right to access to women's bodies and, in particular, to our reproductive labour and products.

Instead of framing the discussion as an individual rights issue, Overall (1992a, 250) argues, we should 'critically examine the artificial barriers, such as marital status, sexual orientation, and ability to pay, that hinder women's fair access to reproductive technologies'.

Others raise the concern that with the advent of these technologies and medical interventions, there is a danger of seeing procreation and birth as an 'industrial' production process. That is, these reproductive technologies involve the further medicalization of women's reproductive experience, similar to what happened when doctors took over from midwives and other lay practitioners. And their existence will exert strong pressure on women to attempt to have children of their own genes rather than adopt or take in foster children.

Genetic Testing and Sex Selection

Some critics worry that with medical advances making it possible to detect genetic and other abnormalities in fetuses, parents will be increasingly compelled to think about their duties to society. Blank and Merrick (1995, 98) argue that prospective parents who carry genetic diseases may be seen as having a duty to refrain from contributing their own eggs or sperm in a fertility treatment and instead use others' eggs and sperm. *The Globe and Mail* reported a case in 2002 in which a woman carrying a gene that can trigger early-onset Alzheimer's disease underwent an ART procedure that involved screening her lab-made embryos for the disease before they were implanted. In this case, the woman who underwent the procedure will probably not be able to care for her child in a few years' time because she is affected by the disease herself (Abraham 2002, A1, A9).

Genetic screening was a common practice in the past. Blood tests to identify couples at risk of giving birth to a baby with Tay-Sachs disease or sickle cell anemia, for example, are routinely performed. As Paul (1997, 104) points out, 'some genes are unreservedly bad. Those that produce Tay-Sachs disease, muscular dystrophy, Huntington's Chorea, and other serious conditions bring only misery to their bearers and unnecessary expense to society.' She argues, however, that '[t]he struggle to eliminate disease genes must be sharply demarcated from past [eugenic] policies that targeted ethnic and religious minorities and the poor'. Others question the use of tests for diseases like cystic fibrosis or even Down's syndrome since parents may feel pressure to abort those supposedly 'defective' fetuses. At issue, therefore, is whether all children should have a chance at life, regardless of their disability, or whether society has a responsibility to ensure that children who are born are those 'with a sound physical and mental constitution, based on a sound genotype' (Paul 1997, 100). Do parents have the right to choose to give birth to a child with a physical disability that will invariably require more public resources for his/ her care? Further, prenatal technology such as ultrasound or amniocentesis can also be used to discover the sex of the child, thus opening up the possibility of parents selec- tively aborting on the basis of sex (Achilles 1993, 508).

The Royal Commission on New Reproductive Technologies did not counsel a total ban on prenatal diagnosis for congenital anomalies and genetic disease, and indeed prenatal screening for women aged 35 and over is increasingly common in Canada. Feminists have raised strong objections to the practice of sex-selective abortions but not to disability-selective abortion. Indeed, many support procedures such as amniocentesis on the grounds of reproductive freedom (Shakespeare 1998).

Adrienne Asch, an ethicist at the Boston-based Hastings Center Project on Prenatal Testing for Genetic Disability, argues that '[a]borting a fetus because physical or men- tal disabilities are detected is no more acceptable than using genetic testing for sex selection or to weed out those with a particular sexual orientation' (Picard 1999, A9).

Furthermore, Paul (1997, 111) makes a significant observation regarding class and ethnic differences among women regarding the decision to abort a fetus with disabilities: 'nonwhites and the less wealthy and educated are more tolerant of handicaps'. If one opposes sex-selective abortion, however, should one not also oppose disability-selective abortion? If we do not oppose such practices, are we on the slippery slope to eugenics/genetics-based births and the 'population improvement' ideas that reigned in the late nineteenth and early twentieth centuries?

Assisted Reproductive Technologies: The Government's Response

Between 1993 and 2004, the Canadian federal government worked very hard to come up with regulations that would address all these reproductive issues, including one not covered above: human cloning. The 1993 royal commission final report recommended a ban on some practices, such as human cloning, and regulation of other practices. Health Canada first introduced a voluntary moratorium on nine problematic ARTs in 1995 in order to give the federal government time to draft legislation (Scala, Montpetit, and Fortier 2005), but it was not until March 2004 that Bill C-47, An Act Respecting Assisted Human Reproduction and Related Research, received royal assent, after interest groups such as the Canadian Medical Association and the Canadian Bar Association criticized the original drafts of the legislation as too punitive (Scala, Montpetit, and Fortier 2005).[36]

While NAC and other organizations were successful in persuading the federal government that some practices should be outlawed, they were not successful in having all procedures outlawed. The legislation outlaws human cloning (including human-animal hybrids); sex-selective techniques; commercial surrogacy (including payment for acting as an intermediary in a surrogacy arrangement); surrogacy by anyone under 21 years of age; the sale of human eggs, sperm, embryos, or human cells with the intention of creating a human being; the posthumous use of human reproductive material unless the donor consented to such use before death; and the use of donor eggs, sperm, and so on, from anyone under 18 years of age. Furthermore, surrogate mothers cannot receive any compensation unless a qualified medical practitioner confirms that she is unable to continue working while pregnant without risking her own health or that of the fetus.

The Act is also intended to protect the health and safety of those who use ART procedures by regulating activities in a number of areas, including the storage and handling of embryos and the disclosure of information to people who wish to know if they are genetically related as a result of an ART procedure. This protection is extended to ensure that all research in the area is regulated as well. The Act also allows for limited use of leftover human embryos in stem cell research, a controversial decision opposed by pro-life groups, and establishes the agency Assisted Human Reproduction Canada (AHRC), which is responsible for licensing, inspecting, and enforcing activities controlled under the Act (Health Canada 2004). The agency monitors fertility clinics to ensure the health and safety of those using them and will begin to collect data.

While the Assisted Human Reproduction Act goes a long way in ironing out what is prohibited and what is allowed in the area of new reproductive technologies, the

Act remains controversial. Media reports and scholarly research highlight the diffi-culties that lesbians encounter in obtaining sperm for artificial insemination (Makin 2005, A9; Cameron 2008). As mentioned above, in the mid-1990s, the federal gov-ernment developed new regulations regarding the donation of sperm in response to the tainted blood scandal, which saw thousands of people unknowingly infected with HIV. The new regulations require that any sperm samples taken from anyone who is not a spouse or sex partner of the recipient must be screened for illness and genetic defects and be quarantined for several months before being used in fertility treatment in a clinic. The law also prohibits sperm donation from gay men or men over 40. Since lesbian couples are completely dependent on donor sperm from non-partners, they are all subject to these regulations.

In the early 2000s, a lesbian couple wanted to use the sperm of a gay friend who in fact was the father of the women's child. The couple thus wanted to use his sperm again but was forbidden by the new regulations because the donor was over the age of 40, and was uncomfortable going through the regulatory process to have his sperm 'approved' through a sperm bank because he did not want others to have access to his sperm. They thus launched a challenge to these regulations, arguing that they were a violation of section 15 equality rights under the Charter as well as section 7 'security of the person' provisions, since under these rules, no lesbian would automatically be en-titled to artificial insemination, as heterosexual women are if they are using the sperm of their male partners. In 2007, the couple lost their challenge at the Ontario Court of Appeal (see also Cameron 2008).[37]

Conclusion

As we have seen, technological advances are changing the nature of the discussion on reproductive rights and choice. No longer do many feminists advocate an absolute right to abortion in all cases. Many feminists are wary, for example, about sex-selective abortions that new technologies make possible. At the same time, new pharmaceutical products make it possible for women to abort at home, removing the need for state consent or a great deal of medical involvement. Reproductive technologies raise new issues and dilemmas regarding fertility. All of these issues require feminists to rethink the politics of the body and the appropriate degree of state intervention and state support.

Recent developments in the United States, with passage of numerous restrictions on abortion at the state level and the always-present possibility that US Supreme Court judges could overturn *Roe v. Wade*, mean that the abortion wars could intensify again. If pro-life groups are successful in achieving further restrictions on abortion, or if the US Supreme Court does reverse the principle of reproductive rights as articulated in the *Roe v. Wade* decision, such actions could escalate the abortion battle and trig-ger ripple effects both in Canada and in the developing world. Indeed, the Canadian government's initiative to prioritize maternal and child health in developing coun-tries (undertaken at the June 2010 G8/G20 summit in Muskoka/Toronto), but to omit abortion and contraception from its maternal health plan (Government of Canada 2010), exposes the ironies of contemporary public policies related to women's equal-ity: underpinning many areas of law and public policy is a moral regulation of sexual-ity and reproduction that prevents the full realization of women's equality. The lack of commitment to abortion and family planning in the Harper government's special initiative demonstrates that there are morally acceptable and morally unacceptable aspects of maternal health in the developing world in the minds of Canadian government officials. It is also clear from our own experience with doctor shootings, the protest over recognition of Dr Henry Morgentaler at the University of Western Ontario Convocation ceremonies in 2005, and the continuing need for women to go to hospitals and private clinics for abortions—sites of much protest—that Canada is not isolated from the larger public debate on abortion, particularly the one taking place south of the border. Women's movement activism remains critical to shaping that debate.

Questions for Critical Thought

1. 'Twenty-first century feminists should focus less on abortion rights and more on reproductive freedom in general.' Do you agree or disagree? Why?
2. In Canada, would you say the courts or policy-makers have been the most facilitative of reproductive rights over the past two decades?
3. What do you think about the concept of 'maternal duty of care' when it comes to the developing fetus?
4. Assisted reproductive technologies have opened the door to a number of practices unheard of even a few decades ago. What do you think is the appropriate feminist response to the use of these techniques?

CHAPTER 13

Global Women's Politics

In this final chapter, we turn our attention to the situation of women outside of Canada and examine women in the international context. While the discussion will be less focused on public policy than many of the previous chapters, it will highlight many themes regarding women's struggles for policy influence and political change that we have addressed so far in the book. In addition, as discussed in chapter 4, much of the focus of Gen-X feminism is on broader issues that affect the entire planet. A new generation links their feminism to issues of social, economic, and environmental justice, in solidarity with other women around the world. This may very well be where the future of feminism lies, along with its relevance to a new generation of women.

The focus of international relations has traditionally been influenced by stereotypical male norms and values. To illustrate this, think of some traditional international issues: war and security, national independence, and state-to-state diplomacy. These issues are considered 'high politics' in which the primary focus is on state actors, government officials, and international and non-governmental organizations in relationships of power. They traditionally encompass military issues, the security of the state as opposed to people, and the pursuit of national interests vis-à-vis other states. Theoretical debates in the field deal with issues such as what level of analysis (individual, state/society, and international system) best explains state behaviour, the role of anarchy in international relations, and the like.

The 'low politics' of international development, culture, democratization, and environmental problems have until very recently been treated as peripheral both in news coverage and in the study of international affairs. Today, 'low politics' has become more important because of the growing realization that environmental degradation and global poverty are important sources of insecurity and, some have argued, could lead to what Robert Kaplan (1994) has called the 'coming global anarchy'. Kaplan's understanding of anarchy is not the traditional realist understanding of anarchy as simply a lack of authority over states, but rather the insecurity, chaos, violence, and absence of authority that might spread in societies around a world that is unable to address poverty, environmental degradation, and other social and economic problems with a global dimension. Even though attention to 'low politics' issues has led the media to report more frequently on topics of disease, malnutrition, human rights, and environmental devastation, for the most part, women remain largely invisible in these reports.

As Cynthia Enloe (1990, 12; see also Enloe 1993) argues, international relations is a bastion of masculinity seemingly unaffected by women's or feminist ideas because 'making women invisible hides the workings of both femininity and masculinity in international politics'. She (1993, 51) argues that foreign policy and international relations are largely constructed as masculine by 'self-consciously honed public policy'. Without this culture of masculinity, state power predicated on a monopoly of the use of force (militarism) looks rather shaky:

> Feminist theorizing has demonstrated that both capitalist-centered and state-centered theories may have dramatically underestimated the power it requires to militarize any society. Decisions about whether men and women should be trained together, policies designed to identify homosexuals, memos about men's access to prostitutes, meetings to hammer out a policy that defines the carrying of umbrellas as 'unmanly' for army officers, official debates over whether to turn a blind eye toward rape during wartime or soldiers' wife battering in peace time—all are exercises of public power intended to construct gender in such a way as to ensure that militarization stays firmly on the rails.

The language of masculinity is conflated with the culture of militarism and high politics and becomes a manly pursuit characterized by male bonding, not only in the army and on the field of battle but also between policy-makers privy to state secrets and responsible for the affairs of state. Women need not apply.

Gendering International Relations

Even today, a perusal of many first-year international relations texts will find women's issues and gender perspectives lacking or absent altogether. Within the academic discipline (and in many foreign policy and international bureaucracies), the dominant paradigm is 'realism', which fits nicely with the focus on high politics. Realists start from the assumption that conflict is endemic in international relations. The closest disciplinary challenger, liberalism, counters that conflict is neither inevitable nor the natural order but rather attenuated by the needs of international trade and the ability of actors to cooperate, often through the creation and functioning of international institutions. However, in neither paradigm are issues of gender visible. As Stienstra (2000, 236) points out, it is 'see no evil, read no evil, teach no evil'. While other ideological positions, such as Marxism, receive mention, particularly in connection with international political economy, gender is not seen as relevant to the study undertaken in the discipline. To quote Peterson and Sisson Runyan (1993, 9), '[g]ender is not a traditional category of analysis in IR [international relations], either in terms of "what" we study or "how" we study it. Nor has gender been raised very often as an issue in IR policy-making'.

One way of including women in international relations is to 'add women and stir'. In this approach, examples applying specifically to women are included in discussions, along with a nod to 'gendered international relations' perspectives as an alternative approach to studying global relationships. However, gender has never been fully integrated into conventional positions, realist or liberal. Instead, women are appended to the discussion as a discrete and separate phenomenon (Stienstra 2000, 258).

Credit for bringing feminist perspectives to international relations study is often given to Cynthia Enloe's (1990) *Bananas, Beaches and Bases*[1] in which she explains that international relations is constructed as a masculine discourse. The concepts of sovereignty and territoriality, for example, emphasize difference and competition. A more feminist discourse, however, would view the world as more connected and interdependent. And by focusing so much attention on the state, IR theory neglects other important actors, including international organizations, transnational actors, and, importantly, women. While women are invisible in the global system, they are a requirement for it to function. 'Gender makes the world go round' and recognition of the roles undertaken by women in supporting global political, economic, and social systems is necessary to fully understand international relations.

Feminist international scholarship thus argues that international politics needs to focus less on ideas that divide the world into us/them, international/domestic, and public/private and more on interdependence, the mutual benefits of cooperation, and broader definitions of security to include not just security from armed attack but also from environmental degradation, structural violence, and so on. Robin Morgan's (1984) *Sisterhood is Global* was also influential in emphasizing that women represent the world's proletariat responsible for much of the world's productive capacity, which is invisible, part-time, and poorly paid. Globally, women are linked by this shared oppression.

Women's actions outside academia—organizing around the world, linking concerns, and making transparent the global position of women—are equally if not more responsible for bringing gender to the fore in global politics. Much credit can be given to the United Nations Decade for Women (1976–85) for establishing a convergence of women's issues and movements around the world. During this period, world attention was brought to the global plight of women through data collection focused on gender issues and consolidating the discourses on women's rights and development (Peterson and Sisson Runyan 1993; Berkovitch 1999). The result, according to Berkovitch (1999, 119) was that the 'framing [of] women's issues in the context of development brought about qualitative and quantitative changes on both national and international fronts'. It also highlighted the diversity of women around the world and their issues and concerns.

Taking the third-wave feminist vision of the fragmented and 'non-essential' nature of the category of woman, Tong (1998, 212) argues that 'global feminism' addresses the differing experiences of women's oppression based on their position in the global system—whether she 'is a citizen of a First World or a Third World nation, an advanced industrial or a developing nation, a nation that is colonialist or colonized'. While there are debates within this approach, particularly regarding the relationship of First World women to Third World women and who speaks for 'women', the emphasis is on blurring the distinction between the global and the local and making it clear that local actions have effects at the global level and in different localities. An illustration of this connection is the movement during the 1970s to encourage breastfeeding over the use of infant formula in First World countries that ultimately resulted in baby formula manufacturers altering their campaigns to sell formula to developing countries. Those campaigns had weakened breastfeeding traditions in developing countries and increased infant mortality from contaminated water used to mix the formula. A gendered approach thus 'begins with the assumption that International Relations is not only what states practice but the day-to-day activities of people who are shaped by and in turn shape what happens at the global level' (Stienstra 2000, 240).

Global feminism advocates understanding and action in terms of 'thinking globally and acting locally', but also 'acting globally, while thinking locally'. Such advocacy represents a challenge to conventional international relations approaches because the emphasis is not on state actors but on the experiences and perceptions of people embedded in different positions within global structures and processes. Therefore, as Peterson and Sisson Runyan (1993) argue, adopting a gendered lens requires highlighting and confronting the underlying inequalities in an international hierarchy in which power and resources are distributed at great cost to groups marginalized because of gender, race, class, age, sexual orientation, and ability as well as geography. It also requires a model of the world not composed solely of conflicting and competitive interests but rather comprising a network of complex social interactions that are sometimes in conflict but at other times cooperating. A feminist view of international relations illustrates that women are everywhere in international relations, and they may be positioned both as oppressed and oppressor.

Gender Makes the World Go Around

As noted earlier regarding women's participation within the domestic political elite, a system of gate-keeping, institutions, and processes at the international level limits the number of women in the international relations elite. This is obvious at meetings of organizations such as the G8 and NATO and even at the United Nations where the majority of individuals holding power are men. Most heads of state or government are men; most legislators are men; most diplomats are men; virtually all senior military officers in armed forces the world over are men; and virtually all combat troops are men. When women do appear, they often have been socialized and trained in a way that fits within the masculine character of male leaders and other elites. For example, former prime minister Margaret Thatcher, who led Britain through the Falklands War in the early 1980s, was referred to in the popular press as the 'Iron Lady' or 'Winston Churchill in a dress'. The appeal was not to her femininity but to her masculine-like resolve and steadfastness. Similarly, Condoleezza Rice, former national security advisor to George W. Bush and US Secretary of State from 2005 to 2009, is characterized not in terms of her gender but in spite of it. For example, CNN (2004) says of her, 'Condoleezza Rice's name is derived from an Italian musical term that means "with sweetness", but when it comes to protecting the United States and its interests there is nothing sugary about her. Four months into the US-led war on terror, the poker-faced national security adviser is still not mincing words—or showing any signs of weakness.' Her replacement in 2009, Democratic Senator and former First Lady Hillary Clinton, has experienced this masculinization and defeminization on an even more acute level throughout her political career, portrayed in the media as a 'radical feminist, emasculator and difficult wife' (for example, see Templin 1999 and Burrell 2000). However, despite outward appearances, many women are present. If we look at the day-to-day practices of state foreign policy, we see that the work of its male representatives is based on the work of their female secretaries or diplomatic wives. It may seem rather trivial to mention diplomatic wives, but as Enloe (1990, 452) points out, 'thousands of women today tailor their marriages to fit the peculiar demands of states operating in a trust-starved international system'. In fact, in the secret world of diplomatic and military politics, the very guarantee of trustworthiness is linked to the employee being in a 'stable' and 'supportive' marriage.

The reliance on secretarial support also puts women squarely in the 'trenches' of international relations. The state agencies that undertake foreign and military policy and the corporations tied into international activity are often large bureaucratic enterprises. These organizations require clerical workers, cleaning staff, coffee and tea providers, and so on. As women dominate clerical, cleaning, and food provision occupations, it is not surprising that women fill many of these invisible positions. As Enloe observes (1990, 451–2), 'even in small states without the huge bureaucratic machines, the public agencies rely on women for their smooth running. If secretaries went out on strike, foreign affairs might grind to a standstill.'

The Women's Movement and International Relations

Women have a long of history of advocating for women's rights and influence in international relations. For over a century, an international network of women has struggled to address the issues and work on behalf of women around the world. As we discussed in the history of the Canadian women's movement, the scholarly tendency is to view women's movement activity in waves, a view that often overshadows the continuity of the movement by emphasizing distinct evolutionary stages in its development (for example, Rowbotham 1992; Pierson 1995; Rupp 1997). Furthermore, the 'wave' analysis has shortcomings in that it focuses too heavily on women's issues and the movement's activities in Europe and the Americas. Eurocentrism has been present throughout much of the international women's movement, something that has been recognized and addressed in recent decades.

However, while we cannot claim complete universality for an international women's movement and its objectives, we can identify one idea that has informed its activities: the political and economic marginalization of women both within states and globally works to the detriment of all of humankind. The international women's movement can be characterized as one of the original transnational movements. It is remarkable how much activity occurred across continents and oceans long before women were granted the right to vote within their own countries. Without access to the decision-making institutions of their home states, women made efforts to organize across borders as early as the 1850s. Women cleverly used international solidarity and mobilization to complement the struggles being fought at local levels (Keck and Sikkink 1998; Berkovitch 1999). The movement's origins lie in the anti-slavery campaigns of the early 1800s and later campaigns for women's suffrage, primarily in the countries of Europe and North America. Women missionaries were also involved in campaigns to address women's situations in some colonial holdings—for example, against foot-binding in China in the late 1800s and against female circumcision in Kenya during the 1920s and 1930s (Keck and Sikkink 1998, 59–72).

The most visible first-wave face of women's international activism appeared on the suffrage issue. As Keck and Sikkink (1998, 52) observe, historical research 'stresses the mutual influence and international cooperation among women suffrage movements around the world'. As women were granted suffrage in more and more countries, international organizing efforts increased because women given the right to vote in one country were freed both to support other national struggles for suffrage and to champion other international causes. Suffrage was one issue among many, and national and international women's organizing did not occur in a vacuum: Sinha, Guy, and Woollacott (1999, 7) observe that 'it has been widely recognized that just as international feminist networks themselves developed out of initiatives of various national feminist organizations, the development of international networks in turn helped stimulate feminist organizing at the local, national and regional levels'. First World women came into contact with Third World women whose activities emerged out of the nationalist movements of decolonization.

Among the largest international organizations of the period were the International Council of Women, the International Alliance of Women, and the Women's International League for Peace and Freedom, which advocated for international peace. The creation of the League of Nations gave support to these organizations 'and opened up a new arena for women's mobilization by offering a central world focal point' (Berkovitch 1999, 109). That focal point excluded much of the southern part of the world, but it nonetheless created an environment that allowed for the proliferation of international organizations and activities aimed at improving the lives of women. It also closely associated the international women's movement with emerging structures of international law and international governmental organizations (IGOs).[2]

That emerging relationship would be carried on by the United Nations after 1945 and recognized in the UN's founding charter, 'the first international instrument containing a wide-ranging sex-equality provision' (Berkovitch 1999, 118). As Keck and Sikkink (1998, 168) point out, the history of the international women's movement in the second half of the twentieth century is 'a litany of UN meetings: Mexico, Copenhagen, Nairobi, Vienna, Cairo, Beijing'. Women's groups and activists who had hoped to have more influence on the UN process—and then found that 'when the delegations took their seats at the [UN's] founding conference, only a few included women' (Rupp 1997, 222)—continued to mount a challenge internationally, which would bring women's issues to the front and centre of the UN's agenda 30 years later.[3]

It is difficult to overestimate the impact of the United Nations Decade for Women (1976–85) on women individually and on the women's movement worldwide. Pierson (1995, 362) argues that '[e]ven the most jaundiced . . . had to concede that declaring 1975 International Women's Year had succeeded in educating public opinion and women, in particular, to a wide range of women's accomplishments, grievances, and just demands and in legitimating women's place on the social agenda'.

A conference in Mexico City in 1975, the first of three that would span the decade, helped to bring together a global agenda for women and an international network of women's organizations and activists. The growth of the international women's network can be measured in the growth in conference attendance since then. Six thousand people registered for the NGO forum in 1975, while 114 NGOs were invited to the official meetings. Ten years later in Nairobi, registration for the NGO forum had more than doubled to 13,500 people, with 163 NGOs given access to the formal conference (Clark, Friedman, and Hochstetler 1998, 9). As Keck and Sikkink (1998, 169) argue these

> international conferences did not create women's networks, but they legiti-
> mized the issues and brought together unprecedented numbers of women
> from around the world. Such face-to-face encounters generate trust, infor-
> mation sharing, and discovery of common concerns that gives impetus to
> include new groups. . . . Lucille Mair of Jamaica, secretary general of the
> Copenhagen conference, said of the Mexico City conference: 'Mexico City
> focussed on some fundamental issues . . . but it did something that, while

less tangible, may be in some ways more important than anything else: It established a network.'

The Mexico City conference was not without rancour since the interests and demands espoused indicated a significant divide between those from the North, who emphasized equality and anti-discrimination, and those from the South, who emphasized their more pressing issues of male and female poverty and development. Similarly, the Copenhagen conference of 1980 also experienced divisions during debates over racism and Zionism. Particularly telling were the disagreements regarding female genital mutilation/circumcision in which delegates from the South accused those from the North of a Western imperialist crusade to save the Third World from its backward cultural practices (Stienstra 2000, 234). Unfortunately, these divisions and debates overshadowed the areas held in common by the participants.

However, by bringing women and groups together, these conferences facilitated the exchange of concerns, arguments, and ongoing and expanding dialogue. According to Clark, Friedman, and Hochstetler (1998, 10–11), 'by the time of the Nairobi conference [in 1985], the increased representativeness among the participants—and the shared conference history—allowed for more expanded and integrated dialogue in the hundreds of workshops and meetings held'. The network could be characterized as truly international, and by the end of the UN Decade for Women there was a real sense of a coherent and focused international women's movement. The Nairobi World Conference on Women took place in the midst of the crisis of Third World indebtedness and the implementation of austerity policies policed by the World Bank and the IMF (International Monetary Fund) and reflected a widespread recognition that the issues of development, equality, peace, and human rights were integrally connected to women.

As S. Laurel Weldon (2006) argues, the conferences and meetings not only illustrated how the international women's movements were increasingly divided along lines of race, sexuality, ethnicity and class, but they also facilitated the recognition of those differences. Through continued meetings and conferences, particularly on the topic of violence against women, networks of trust and 'norms of inclusivity' were developed that allowed a transnational movement to mobilize people 'not only across differences of race, class and sexuality but also across differences of language, national context, level of development, and the like' (55).

The conferences also provided training for international women's activists who developed organizational structures and strategies that would make the international network far more effective. Clark, Friedman, and Hochstetler (1998, 13–16) identify two features that help explain the success of the international women's network. First, meeting at conferences facilitated the building of coalitions through caucusing. For example, the Women's Environmental and Development Organization coordinated a 'linkage caucus', which circulated documents that provided a base of information for NGO advocacy. During the conference, numerous caucuses met daily to discuss issues and strategies. Second, the NGOs and activists worked the media, providing background information and NGO positions and putting the media in touch with supportive delegations.

The Beijing conference in 1995, the Fourth World Conference on Women, was huge in comparison to the previous three conferences. More than 300,000 people participated in the NGO forum, with an unprecedented 3,000 accredited NGOs. NGO representatives delivered one-third of the plenary speeches. While NGOs did not have access to the more sensitive inter-state negotiations, they did, according to Clark, Friedman, and Hochstetler (1998, 15) 'make Beijing a "Conference of Commitments"'. While governments refused to accept responsibility for upholding the promises made at the conference, NGOs pushed for accountability by publicizing every promise made by an official delegate.

Within the UN system, these meetings, which brought together women grassroots activists and women development specialists, helped bring women's concerns into development policy. The understanding that women did not necessarily benefit from and in fact could be negatively affected by 'gender neutral' economic development arose out of the early meetings in the 1970s. The result was the introduction of a women-in-development (WID) approach with projects that attempted to bring women's concerns into development and the UN structure (Henderson and Jeydel 2010, 223). After the Mexico City conference in 1975, the UN created the UN Voluntary Fund for Women, now UNIFEM, and the International Research and Training Institute for the Advancement of Women (INSTRAW) to address the issue of women in development. However, women NGO activists were quick to point out that, while an important step, WID ultimately did not recognize the unique features of women's experiences (Henderson and Jeydel 2010, 225). It was an approach that just added women and stirred and lacked a deeper analysis of systemic gender power imbalances and women lives.

The final declaration of the Fourth World Conference on Women, the Beijing Declaration, was a clarion call for the recognition of the rights of women around the world but also for recognition that while the world's women are diverse, they experience poverty and disempowerment because of their gender and that 'women's rights are human rights'. The declaration also sets out a series of benchmarks against which the actions of the UN and its associated organizations, women's groups and NGOs, the private sector, and, most important, the signatory governments, could be measured. One of the commitments made at the Beijing conference was to the development of an approach that would fully integrate women in development programming and bring a gender lens to all policy. Gender would be mainstreamed.

Gender mainstreaming as a strategy sought to avoid the segregation of women into a 'gender project' by integrating gender into all development projects, such as increased literacy, better access to health care, or improved public services. As the United Nations argued, 'gender mainstreaming entails bringing the perceptions, experience, knowledge and interests of women as well as men to bear on policy-making, planning and decision-making'. For example, a program sponsored by the United National Development Fund for Women (UNIFEM) works with governments to design gender-responsive budgets that take into account women's concerns across all expenditures (health, pensions, public utilities, tariffs) rather than segregating funding for women's issues solely into one office or department (which can often marginalize women's concerns) (Henderson and Jeydel 2010, 226).

The *Review And Appraisal Of The Beijing Platform For Action*, published in 2001, sees some achievements in terms of the implementation of gender perspectives in macro-economic policy-making. There are also indications of efforts to include gender in policies associated with sustainable human development and employment and to increase women's participation in all levels of political and economic decision-making. However, many signatory states argue that inadequate financial and national resources have limited their efforts to meet their Beijing commitments (United Nations 2001, 17–33). The UN Development Programme (UNDP), which has defined its gender mainstreaming tasks as expanding the capabilities, opportunities, and choices that allow women 'to claim their rights and move into full substantive equality with men', and 'support[ing] national capacities to respond positively to women's interests and concerns', is straightforward regarding its inability to meet its commitments regarding gender mainstreaming.

> Despite good intentions and some real progress, the development community, UNDP included, is still falling short in delivering on its promises. Many of the problem areas were identified in the UN Secretary General's Review and Appraisal of the Implementation of the Beijing Platform for Action. These areas include the development of accountability mechanisms, allocation of sufficient resources, attention to gender equality, the targeting not just of soft areas for gender mainstreaming (such as health and education) but also of supposedly 'gender-neutral' areas such as infrastructure development and economic policies, and strong political commitment and will (UNDP, 2010).

As we look around the world today, women's equality and empowerment has still not been achieved. It is apparent that much still has to be done to meet the commitments made at Beijing over 10 years ago.

For the international women's network, the struggle continues, but this is cause for optimism. As Waring (2004) observed in an address to women in London, Ontario, in 2004, '[w]omen have learned that powerlessness can be countered by community'. The international movement of women represents such a community.

Women's Issues in Global Politics

Representation: Women in political office

> At its 39th session in New York in 1995, the UN Commission on the status of women addressed the issue as a first priority in its 'Critical Areas of Concern'. Key passages in the report of the secretary general read: '[T]he advancement of women in other areas will be jeopardized if equality in political participation and decision making is not achieved.' Reference was also made to the close reciprocal relationship between general advancement of women and the participation of women in politics. . . . [T]herefore, the advancement of women should be considered a priority in terms of national decision making, and women should participate as full partners in all these decisions (cited in Waring 1996, 129).

Without political representation, women's ability to effect change is limited. Looking at world averages, women make up only 15.6 per cent of the world's democratically elected assemblies. This proportion varies quite radically among regions: women make up 42 per cent of the assemblies in Nordic countries but only 9.6 per cent of the legislative assemblies in Arab countries (see Table 13.1).

The world average represents an increase during the post-World War II period in both the proportion of women and the number of democratically elected legislative assemblies, from 3 per cent in 26 assemblies to 18.7 per cent in 187 countries in 2009 (IPU 2009). Formal limitations continue to exist in countries such as Kuwait and the United Arab Emirates, where women are not granted full suffrage and access to electoral politics. According to UNIFEM (2008, 21), the past decade has seen a significant increase in the proportion of women in national assemblies from 11.6 per cent in 1995 to 18.4 per cent in May 2009. The previous 20 years (1975 to 1995) had seen an increase of less than 1 per cent. However, even at the accelerated rate of the past decade gender parity, where neither sex holds more than 60 per cent of the seats, will not be achieved by developing countries until 2047 (ibid.). While women have increased their numbers in assemblies, the adage of 'the higher, the fewer' appears to apply worldwide, much as it does in Canada. Women are still under-represented in positions of decision-making authority such as cabinet posts. The United Nations (2000a, 165) observes, 'In 1998, there were 45 countries in which women held no ministerial positions. . . . [W]omen held neither ministerial nor sub-ministerial positions in 13 countries.' Not surprisingly, it is in the Nordic countries that women are more likely to be found as ministers. It is also interesting that women are more likely to hold 'social ministries and law and justice ministries, than [they are] economic and political ministries' (United Nations 2000a, 166). This had not changed in 2008: '[W]omen in public office tend overwhelmingly to be clustered in "social" policy-making positions' (UNIFEM, 2008, 26).

Table 13.1 | Women in National Parliaments: Regional Averages

	Single or Lower House (%)	Upper House or Senate (%)	Both Houses (%)
Nordic countries	42.0	—	—
Europe (including Nordic countries)	21.8	19.6	21.4
Europe (excluding Nordic countries)	16.9	16.9	16.9
Americas	22.4	19.9	22.0
Asia	18.7	16.6	18.5
Sub-Saharan Africa	17.7	20.4	18.0
Pacific countries	13.2	23.6	15.3
Arab states	10.1	7.6	9.6

Source: Inter-Parliamentary Union. *Women in National Parliaments.* 31 December 2009: http://www.ipu.org/wmn-e/world.htm.

This lack of representation has consequences for women as citizens. As Waring (1996, 163) states, 'We are, universally, half of humankind. We are guaranteed equal rights to participate in political and civil life. Nowhere do we experience this equality in reality.' Article 7 of the Convention on the Elimination of All Forms of Discrimination against Women calls upon the signatories 'to take all appropriate measures to eliminate discrimination against women in political and public life of the country'. Article 8 calls for states to ensure that 'women, on equal terms with men and without discrimination, [have] the opportunity to represent Governments at the international level and to participate in the work of international organizations'. The Beijing Declaration also affirms the equal right to participate in governance and to contribute to the defining of political priorities, and so on. However, in a world of sovereign states, it is hard, if not impossible, to achieve compliance with international law (particularly when it comes to women). For example, the United States has yet to fully ratify the Convention on the Elimination of All Forms of Discrimination against Women. What these declarations do is help to reinforce international connections among those working to achieve increased political representation for women.

The recent trend in democratization around the world has opened up some opportunities for women. According to Jane Jaquette (1997), the efforts of an international network to heighten women's awareness of their political potential, women's responses in protesting against economic hardship brought about by globalization, and increased access to education are building a critical mass for women's political power through representation. However, she qualifies this observation, saying that 'radical change is unlikely'. Women have not historically voted as a bloc because they represent a diverse number of interests and all parts of the ideological spectrum. Therefore, a critical mass in women's representation is unlikely to result in a critical mass for 'women's interests'. In other words, representation is not the 'be all and end all' for ensuring women's political influence.

Violence against women: Women's rights are (hu)man rights

> Significant numbers of the world's population are routinely subject to torture, starvation, terrorism, humiliation, mutilation and even murder simply because they are female. Crimes such as these against any group other than women would be recognized as a civil and political emergency as well as a gross violation of the victim's humanity. (Bunch 1990, 486)

The preceding quote from Charlotte Bunch's (1990) article, 'Women's rights as human rights', makes a significant connection regarding the violence perpetrated against women because of their gender: this violence must be recognized as a violation of human rights.

Viewed this way, it is clear that violence against women is one of the most common violations of human rights around the world. According to UNIFEM Canada (2009) globally 'six out of every ten women experience physical and/or sexual violence in their lifetime. . . . For women and girls 16–44 years old, violence is a major cause of death and disability. In 1994, a World Bank study on ten selected risk factors facing girls and women in this age group, found rape and domestic violence more dangerous than cancer, motor vehicle accidents, war and malaria'.

In the past, the link between violence against women and human rights violations was not as clear as we understand it to be today. Simply put, in the realm of (hu)man rights, women were invisible because their suffering is not 'universal'; they are not men. These are not human rights because they are not universally experienced. As both Waring (1996) and Bunch (1990) point out, there are a number of rationalizations for this: (1) the abuses perpetrated against women are private rather than public; if they were public they would then be open to the scrutiny of the state; (2) the state is not an active agent in the victimization, which is a requirement for human rights abuse. Human rights abuse is 'solely a matter of state violation of civil and political liberties'. As a result, such conceptions of human rights do not accord women full citizenship or even access to the term 'hu(man)', and women's suffering is rendered invisible.

However, states are fully implicated, able to act, and sometimes do act when human rights violations occur in the private. As Bunch (1990, 491) notes, '[h]uman rights activists pressure states to prevent slavery or racial discrimination and segregation even when these are conducted by nongovernmental force in private or proclaimed as cultural traditions'. States are also implicated because 'if a state facilitates conditions, accommodates, tolerates, justifies, or excuses private denial of women's rights, the state will bear responsibility. The state will be responsible not directly for the private acts, but for its own lack of diligence to prevent, control, correct, or discipline such private acts' (Rebecca Cook, cited in Waring 1996, 119). The state must be seen to be acting with due diligence.

Waring (1996, 119) provides the example of a Fijian woman applying for refugee status on the grounds that she was fleeing continuing domestic abuse. Appropriate complaints and reports had been made to state authorities, along with numerous further complaints regarding the non-enforcement of a non-molestation order by the police. She notes, 'In such a case, the state is in complicity with the battery, since the state has tolerated and excused private acts that have been subject to judicial procedure, and has not prevented or controlled them when recourse to state agents were sought.' Other examples include state support for female circumcision through provision of the procedure in state-run hospitals. This indicates a passive tolerance that can be construed as a form of persecution for women who have fled rather than have the procedure performed. Many forms of discrimination are codified in customary and religious practices and consequently are tacitly supported by state law. Thus codified, these practices are also implicitly political, Bunch (1990, 491) argues, because they are the result of the structures of power, domination, and privilege in a society.

Fundamentally, according to Bunch (1990, 491), this form of discrimination kills, and it kills solely on the basis of gender. Women's rights as human rights are thus connected to the issue of violence against women.

Therefore, it can be seen as testimony to the work and activism of an international women's movement that, by the end of the 1990s even mainstream human rights groups and the conventions and agreements that make up international law 'had made violence against women a priority area. More than 170 governments had signed a declaration against violence against women, and women in more than 20 countries had won the right to seek redress for human rights violations in the international community (through the Optional Protocol to CEDAW)' (Weldon, 2006, 64). Early resolutions on women's issues in the United Nations systems had been focused on ensuring women's access to basic political economic and social rights. In the 1970s that focus shifted to women as mothers, but mid-way through the 1970s 'the term "violence against women" began to be heard in international meetings such as the First World Conference on Women in Mexico City in 1975 (ibid. 59). According to

Weldon, (2006, 59), '[i]n spite of this growing awareness among activists, however, governments were silent on the issue of violence against women. [A]ctivists at these early meetings were divided over what the most important women's issues were, how to define these issues, how and whether activists ought to pursue policy change, and how discussions ought to be organized in international meetings'. In 1979, the United Nations adopted the Convention on the Elimination of All Forms of Discrimination against Women (CEDAW) and, while the Convention did not address violence against women as a violation of their human rights, it provided a platform from which an international campaign could be built.

It may seem rather odd, after our discussions in earlier chapters about other feminist philosophies challenging liberal feminism and its focus on 'sameness' and 'essentialism', that we should come back to a discussion of rights. A passage by Latin American activist Susanna Chiarotti, cited in Keck and Sikkink (1998, 165–6) illustrates the importance of this dialogue on rights:

> We began to make the connection between violence and human rights when a 'companera' from Buenos Aires brought us the article by Charlotte Bunch on 'Women's rights,' which she got at a meeting in California on Leading the Way Out. I was the only one in my group that read English and when I read it, I said to myself, 'Hmmm . . . a new approach to human rights. This we have not seen before. And a new approach to violence as well.' So I told the other women in my group, 'It seems to me that this would be the key to end our isolation.' Women's groups are not isolated from each other, but society's reception of us is 'there are the women again with their stuff'. 'This new approach,' I said, 'would be very interesting, because we could recruit a lot of people who are not going to be able to say no.' So I translated the article for them during our meetings. See how powerful theory is? I am an activist, but this theoretical piece made a great difference in our work. Later, we learned about the petition campaign calling for UN recognition of women's rights as human rights. We thought the petition was a useful tool because it was so well crafted. Its language is irrefutable; you would have to cover yourself with shame if you didn't accept it. This began a new conceptualization of the violence theme, and we started to bother people from human rights organizations to broaden their vision. . . . I think that for us it is a strategic lesson, in the sense that it tells us, 'Let's look for more allies. And to find them, let's look for languages that cannot be rejected.'

The emphasis on violence against women provided a point around which the concerns and experiences of women around the world could converge. As Keck and Sikkink (1998, 171) state, it 'appeared to offer clearer avenues for activism'. A focus on violence against women seemed much easier to pursue than more generalized issues of women and development. As Charlotte Bunch observed in an interview with Keck and Sikkink (1998, 171), 'there are everyday things you can do about it, from wherever you are'. The focus on violence against women represented one coherent and focused way to address the roots of women's subordinate status, a first step in attacking the systemic reasons for women's inequality.

For example,

When women from every region of the world spoke of their own experiences of violence, as they did at the Tribunal organized by NGOs at Vienna [1993], governments had a more difficult time denying that violence was a widespread problem. Northern governments could not maintain that violence was a problem only in so-called 'less civilized' countries, and Southern and Eastern countries had greater difficulty arguing that concern with violence was an issue cooked up by ethnocentric Western feminists. When these issues were raised at regional preparatory meeting entirely comprised of Southern representatives, they could not be dismissed so easily (Weldon 2006, 61).

The focus on women's rights, according to Dorothy Hodgson (2002, 4), 'enabled activist women to adopt new languages and strategies to circumvent and reframe enduring debates over women's empowerment mired in the potent, contradictory terms of "culture", "tradition", and "modernity"'. As Susana Chiarotti, the activist in Buenos Aires, argued, the conception of women's rights as human rights opened up a form of praxis that allowed her group to focus on action suited to their context and find further allies in the human rights advocacy community to help in their struggle. For S. Laurel Weldon (2006) these experiences allowed the movement to develop a set of shared norms or 'standards of behavior, ranging from standards of mere appropriateness to standards delineating rights and obligations' (Weldon 2006, 57). This allowed the originally divided global movement of women to come together to form a strong and unified transnational movement.

As a result of the campaigns to recognize women's rights as human rights, we can point to a number of examples of success. In 1993, the World Conference on Human Rights in Vienna in its statement outlined fundamental principles, including that 'the human rights of women and the girl-child are an inalienable, integral, and indivisible part of universal human rights'. The result was the *Declaration on the Elimination of Violence against Women*.

Gender-based violence and all forms of sexual harassment and exploitation, including those resulting from cultural prejudice and international trafficking, are incompatible with the dignity and worth of the human person, and must be eliminated.

In 1995, at the Beijing conference, governments agreed to include violence against women as a crucial area of concern and since 1997, UNIFEM has help to fund anti-violence initiatives in more than 70 countries. Significantly, in 1999, an Optional Protocol was added to CEDAW with the purpose of giving the Convention more power of enforcement and permitting complaints to be made on behalf of individuals. 'The Protocol contains two procedures: (1) A communications procedure allows individual women, or groups of women, to submit claims of violations of rights protected under the Convention to the Committee. The Protocol establishes that in order for individual communications to be admitted for consideration by the Committee, a number of criteria must be met, including those domestic remedies must have been exhausted. (2) The Protocol also creates an inquiry procedure enabling the Committee to initiate inquiries into situations of grave or systematic violations of women's rights' (Division for the Advancement of Women 2000–9).

In Canada in 1993, a Saudi Arabian woman was granted refugee status on the grounds of her sex. She had shown that she faced prosecution in her own state because she refused to wear a veil, traveled unaccompanied by male relatives, and sought a university education. In 1994 Canada granted refugee status to a Somali woman who fled Somalia with her daughter because the daughter was to undergo female circumcision. The Refugee Board agreed that the home state could not be counted on to protect the girl from the procedure (Waring 1996, 102) This protection for women refugee claimants fearing gender-related persecution was codified in Canadian law in 1993 (Mowani 1999).

It should be noted that Canada has been both a leader and a laggard on women's rights issues. Shelagh Day (2003, 126–35) argues that 'there are instances in which Canada is out front. . . . For example, Canada has been a leader in bringing forward issues of violence against women, and in recognizing gender violence in the context of war as a crime against humanity.' While the Canadian state has been willing to get behind statements in principle with no legal force, it has been slow in its support for enforceable pieces of international law. Day (2003, 132) concludes, 'Canada is sometimes a leader on women's human rights and sometimes is not, depending on its assessment of its own vulnerability to liability or embarrassment'.

Women's rights require more than just a focus on violence against women. Even Bunch (1990, 497–8) qualifies her rights focus: 'The danger in pursuing only this approach is the tendency to become isolated from and competitive with other human rights. . . . [T]he creative task is to look for ways to connect these approaches, and to see how we can go beyond exclusive views of what people need in their lives.' In fact, international human rights treaties cover a range of rights—civil, political, economic, social, and cultural. According to Day (2003, 129) 'each of these treaties contains specific commitments to the equality of women'. As we have seen in our discussion of women's politics in Canada, it is hard to have economic, social, and cultural rights recognized as 'real' rights in the courts. And as discussed above, it is difficult to change the state's perspective on its responsibility regarding rights—that is, having the state adopt a role that 'posit[s] the state not as a violator of rights, but as the potential implementer of them' (ibid.). In the case of the Optional Protocol to CEDAW, while it is a breakthrough in the recognition of women's rights, it is also *Optional* : 'States must be party to the Convention and the Protocol. The Protocol includes an "opt-out clause", allowing States upon ratification or accession to declare that they do not accept the inquiry procedure' (Division for the Advancement of Women 2000–9).

Migration: Women on the move

Women move, and they do so for many reasons, including economic need and personal security or because they are forced to do so. According to the United Nations (UNHCR 2001, 25), international migration has become a great concern. One of the most significant trends has been the increased number of migrant women in streams that had heretofore been primarily male. In 2000 there were 175 million migrants, an increase of nearly 100 million from 1960 (79 million). Roughly half of these were women and, among the reasons for their migration were the unique problems they faced because of their gender. This included both international migrants, who move to other countries, as well as internal migrants, who relocate in other parts of their own countries. While many women accompanied or joined family members, increasing numbers migrated on their own to obtain work, as the principal wage earners for themselves and their families (Forbes Martin 2004, 4).

Most women move voluntarily, but a significant number are forced migrants who have fled conflict, persecution, environmental degradation, natural disasters, and other situations that affect their habitat and livelihood (ibid.). According to the United Nations High Commission for Refugees (UNHCR), women constituted approximately half of the 6.1 million refugees in 2009. In 2008, women and girls represented on average 49 percent of the persons of concern for the UNHCR, 47 per cent of the refugees and asylum seekers and 50 per cent of all Internally Displaced Persons (IDPs) and returnees (UNHCR 2009, 2). For the UNHCR, the number of female refugees is significant because it recognizes that as a result of 'women's roles[s] in caring for and protecting children in crisis situations, strategies to assist and empower them require a more differentiated approach' (UNHCR 2001, 3).

According to Baines (2003, 168), 'advocates for refugee women working within and outside the Canadian state have achieved remarkable things in the past decade'. These achievements include Canada adopting a position that makes it possible for women refugees to apply if they are escaping from situations of domestic violence, rape, or the oppressive social norms of their home countries. However, Baines (2003, 155–70) notes that while there have been some successes for refugee women, continuing assumptions regarding gender still make it harder for women in the asylum process to enter Canada:

> [A] number of factors belie Canadian efforts to extend protection to refugee women. First, the Canadian government has responded to the escalating worldwide refugee crisis by invoking new policies and practices to restrict access to the Canadian asylum system. . . . Second, while specific measures such as the Guidelines and the Women at Risk program seek to manoeuvre individual women through a gender-biased system, the number of women gaining access is minimal. . . . Third, while the Guidelines challenge the division between public and private, . . . they ignore the similarities in the experiences of violence that lead to persecution [within the Canadian state].

In other words, the Canadian state judges the actions of other states without recognizing that it needs to put its own house in order regarding violence perpetrated against women.

Much of the surge in modern-day migration is a result of the globalizing economy. People move within regions and around the world for employment opportunities and this has profound socio-economic, political, and demographic repercussions. Areas of migrant inflow face challenges in terms of integrating migrants into society and providing appropriate living accommodation, primarily within the fast-growing urban centres. Areas of outflow are left with aging populations and woman-headed families to maintain domestic and agricultural economies. Women may spend considerable periods of time without their male partners, spouses, sons, and fathers, which means they must maintain families and farms, often with only small amounts of financial support in the form of remittances. Women in particular are increasingly migrating for work. According to the International Labour Office (ILO), half of the estimated 200 million migrants worldwide are women. Women and girl domestic workers make up a large portion of these numbers, with Asia as the primary source of migrant domestic workers; for example in Saudi Arabia approximately 1.5 million domestic workers from Indonesia, Philippines, and Sri Lanka are employed. In Latin America, women domestic workers make up 60 per cent of internal and cross-border migrants and in France more than 50 per cent of migrant women are employed in domestic labour (WIEGO 2009).[4]

In addition, many women migrants find themselves working in the 'entertainment' industry, which often involves prostitution (for example, Thorbek and Pattanaik 2002; Outshoorn 2004). It is not uncommon for young girls to be sold by their impoverished rural families to traffickers who sell them to brothels, primarily in South and Southeast Asia. Worldwide, young women and girls are lured overseas with stories of legitimate jobs and then find themselves trapped in the sex trade, working to pay off the cost of their immigration and amass enough money to start a new life or fund a way home. These female populations are particularly vulnerable. In 1999, the United Nations (2000b, 2) identified trafficking of women and girls as one of the criminal activities that had increased with globalization. This was borne out by the UN Report on Trafficking in Persons in 2009, which found the most common form of human trafficking, accounting for 79 per cent, was for sexual exploitation; the next highest was forced labour or slavery at 18 per cent (CNN 2009). It was also noted that the global financial crisis of 2009 had made the situation more acute, particularly in Cambodia (UNIAP 2009) where women responding to layoffs and indebtedness were turning to sex work.

It is this population that is at greatest risk for contracting HIV/AIDS, and it is in the sex trades that the most rapid increase in infection rates is found. For example, while the HIV/AIDS epidemic started later in Asia, in Vietnam HIV prevalence among female sex workers increased five-fold between 1994 and 1998 (United Nations 2000a, 67). Closely related to trafficking in women and girls is violence and abuse. Vulnerability to violence and abuse is more generally found and would appear to be much more prevalent in the female migrant community (United Nations 2003).

According to Keeble and Ralston (2003, 136–54), the international community has undertaken efforts to establish agreements outlawing trafficking in and sexual exploitation of women, and Canada supports these efforts as part of its 'human security' agenda. They conclude, however, that while 'the rhetoric is very convincing and the words are extremely clear, the Canadian government is committed to a rights-based approach on its anti-trafficking efforts'. This commitment is qualified in its implementation. '[T]he many departments (DFAIT, Justice, Employment and Immigration, Status of Women, HRDC, and CIDA) sometimes work at cross-purposes or, indeed, not at all to alleviate, if not eliminate, the victimization of these women, particularly for the purpose of prostitution' (Keeble and Ralston 2003, 152). At the international level, work is ongoing between the International Labour Office, unions such as the IUF (International Union of Food Workers) and NGOs like WIEGO (Women in Informal Employment Globalizing and Organizing) and IDWN (International Domestic Workers Network) to establish an international convention on domestic work which would bring about fairer wages and protect against abuse for those women who migrate to work as domestic servants and nannies.

Work: Women and the economics of globalization

'Women perform 66 per cent of the world's work, produce 50 per cent of the food, but earn 10 per cent of the income and own 1 per cent of the property' (UNIFEM 2008).

Women now account for at least one-third of the world's labour force and their numbers continue to increase. The United Nations (2000a, 110) notes that '[b]etween 1980 and 1987, women's economic activity rates increased in all regions, except in Southern Africa, Central Asia, Eastern Europe, and Oceania'. This increase is the result of a number of factors. In many countries, women have achieved more control over their fertility and reproductive cycles, which expands their employment opportunities; attitudes toward working women have changed in the face of their increasing numbers; and public policy regarding child care, maternity leave, and part-time work has made it easier for women to seek work. In the South, development policies encouraging small community-level enterprises, including credit programs specifically for women, have enhanced women's entrepreneurship and employment opportunities. Worldwide, the expansion of the service sector and light manufacturing associated with economic globalization has led to the employment of large numbers of women.

However, as we discussed in the chapters on women and work in Canada, this expansion has not occurred without serious problems and drawbacks for women. While we can see that self-employment as well as part-time and home-based work have expanded opportunities for women's participation, these forms of employment are subject to a lack of job and income security, lack of benefits, and low income. Women are more likely to experience greater unemployment than men and for longer periods (United Nations 2000a). Women are also more likely to experience underemployment, spending more time than men do on work in the home and less time in the workplace. While more women are in the labour force, they still retain their domestic responsibilities. As a result, women may remain unemployed while carrying a large burden of unpaid work and, because that work is unpaid, they are not seen as contributing to economic development or national production. Women worldwide tend to be grouped in the lower end of a gender-segregated labour market, concentrated in service or light manufacturing industries where they seldom hold positions of authority. Their income levels and career advancement persistently lag behind those of men with similar skills.

Consequently, in its 2005 assessment of the world's women the United Nations reported:

Today's global world is one of widening income inequality and for many, increasing economic insecurity. Informal employment, far from disappearing, is persistent and widespread. In many places, economic growth has depended on capital-intensive production in a few sectors rather than on increasing employment opportunities, pushing more and more people into the informal economy. In others, many of the jobs generated by economic growth are not covered by legal or social protection, as labour markets are de-regulated, labour standards are relaxed and employers cut costs. . . . As a result, a growing share of the workforce in both developed and developing countries is not covered by employment-based social and legal protection (United Nations 2005).

Economic globalization and the transition to free-market neo-liberalism has had a significant impact on the working lives and economic well-being of women. Greater economic liberalization and integration within the world economy has meant that labour markets have become more flexible, increasingly based on short and part-time work, which is the type of work dominated by women. Therefore, a feminization of the world economy in the wake of globalization has occurred as a result of the increase in 'irregular forms of work, casual forms of employment, such as outworking, informal subcontracting, part-time labour, homework, informal activities and other forms of labour that are unprotected by standard labour regulations' (United Nations 2001, 286).

The reliance on a flexible informal workforce is problematic. Increasingly, rather than the formalization of informal employment, the trend has been to the transition of formal employment to informal. This may represent a growth in work opportunities for women, but the fact remains that average earnings are higher in formal employment than in informal employment.

> Women workers are not only concentrated in the informal economy, they are in the more precarious forms of informal and women tend to be concentrated in 'the more precarious forms of informal employment where earnings are the most unreliable and the most meagre. While in some instances, their income can be important in helping families move out of poverty, this is only true if there is more than one earner (United Nations 2005, 6).

Therefore it is not surprising that some estimates put women at 70 per cent of the world's poor (UNIFEM Canada, 2009), and concerns have been raised regarding the state of women's poverty in light of the global financial crisis of 2009. 'The International Labour Organization estimates that the economic downturn could lead to 22 million more unemployed women in 2009, jeopardizing the gains made in the last few decades in women's empowerment and economic security' (ibid.; see also UNIFEM, no date).

This exploitation is compounded by the declining power of the state in the face of economic globalization. Along with the changing nature of work, there has been a decline in the enforcement of labour standards. The United Nations (2001, 288) notes that exploitation goes beyond the inability or unwillingness of states to enforce or implement labour standards. In many instances, governments adopt policies to lighten the regulation of industry, lower public spending, and privatize state-owned enterprises in an attempt to free financial flows and open up trade. Such policies have profound consequences for the well-being of women since states rarely introduce complementary mechanisms to ensure social welfare and provide for the needs of the people. The responsibility for social services falls to families, particularly the female members. In addition, such state policy has weakened the labour union movement, which in the past provided many women with a mechanism for pursuing their claims for equality.

As Macdonald (2003, 40–54) points out, 'trade does indeed have a female face. The gender division of labour within the family and the wider society thus means that women are affected differently than men by changes in the global economy. These efforts are not straightforward, however, but depend also on race, ethnicity, location, nationality, age, sector, and other factors.' As we discussed in chapters 9 and 10, while Canadian women are among some of the most economically fortunate in the world, significant gender inequalities in income and employment persist. These inequalities are supported, in some cases, by the Canadian state's unwillingness to thoroughly transform the gender norms that govern so much of its behaviour. A similar attitude is reflected in the Canadian state's efforts to address the economic inequalities experienced by women outside of Canada, predominantly in the developing world. As Rebecca Tiessen (2003, 108–23) argues, the Department of Foreign Affairs and International Trade, the Canadian ministry charged with implementing Canadian development objectives, itself has a gendered institutional culture, which limits its ability to develop programs for sustainable development that do not continue to 'reinforce the status quo, preventing any real opportunities to address gender inequality'.

Health: Global HIV/AIDS

The explicit recognition and reaffirmation of the right of all women to control all aspects of their health, in particular their own fertility, is basic to their empowerment (Beijing Declaration, 1995).

One area requiring increased attention is the gender dimensions of human immunodeficiency virus/acquired immunodeficiency syndrome (HIV/AIDS). The increasing toll of the disease among women has become an issue of global importance. Female controlled methods of prevention need to be developed. The fact that care-giving responsibilities are required of women worldwide needs to be taken into account in the development of policies and strategies (United Nations 2001, 34).

At the beginning of the twenty-first century, one of the most pressing problems is the spread of HIV/AIDS. This is a women's issue. According to the World Health Organization, globally HIV/AIDS is the leading cause of death for women in their reproductive years (15–44). While unsafe sex is the main risk factor in developing countries, the WHO also points to biological factors, lack of access to information and health services, economic vulnerability, and unequal power in sexual relations as contributing to the high rate of exposure among young women (WHO 2009). UNAIDS (the Joint United Nations Programme on HIV/AIDS 5) reports that in 2008, 33.4 million people lived with HIV/AIDS; 2.1 million of these were children under 15. Of the adults with the disease, women comprised 50.02 per cent or 15.7 million. The situation is most dire in sub-Saharan Africa, where the rate of infection is higher among women (accounting for 60 per cent of estimated infections) than among men. The situation is most acute among young women aged 15 to 24, where the 'prevalence . . . [is] on average about three times higher than among men of the same age' (Gouws et al. 2008 cited in UNAIDS 2009, 22). As the UN report on the world's women (2000a, 67) observes, 'women are bearing an increasingly large burden of the disease—a burden made even greater by the fact that women are also more likely than men to care for children who suffer from the disease'. Biologically, a woman's risk of contracting HIV/AIDS as a result of unprotected sex is greater than it is for men. Again, the UN report on the world's women (2000a, 68) notes that '[w]omen have a larger surface area exposed to their partners' sexual secretions than do men and there is higher concentration of the virus in men's semen than in women's secretions'. However, as the UNAIDS Update for 2009 reports, this vulnerability is further increased as a result of social and cultural factors. For example, 'women's vulnerability to HIV in sub-Saharan Africa stems not only from their greater physiological susceptibility to heterosexual transmission, but also to the severe social, legal and economic disadvantages they confront' (UNAIDS 2009, 22). Some cultures deny or severely limit women's access to public health services, educational opportunities, and, most important, to reproductive health information. This denial is extremely problematic because studies show that access to education and information reduces infection rates for women, along with alleviating other reproductive issues. According to the United Nations (2000a, 69), 'sex education encourages young people to postpone their first intercourse, thus helping to protect young people not only from early pregnancy, but also from becoming infected with HIV and other STI [sexually transmitted infections]'. In addition, programs to educate sex workers on the practice of safe sex also cut infection rates (ibid. 70). UNAIDS studies in sub-Saharan Africa bear this out: '[W]hile studies prior to 1996 generally found either no association between educational status and HIV risk or found that the highest risk was among the most educated, data collected after 1996 have tended to find a lower risk among the most-educated people' (Hargreaves et al. 2008 cited in UNAIDS 2009). This connection between higher education and lower infection rates is found across all global regions (UNAIDS 2009). However, the power imbalance between men and women limits the success of such programs. The threat of physical abuse or need for money creates an acute vulnerability, making women unable to exercise their rights and autonomy. Women will often not require their partners to wear a condom, fearing abandonment, retribution, or violence. This often happens in the sex trades: even when women are aware of the risks, they lack the power to make their partners wear protection.

The HIV/AIDS crisis represents an overwhelming challenge to achieving the rights of all women to control all aspects of their health. It becomes a significant issue within the rubric of women's rights as human rights. For the international community, the immediate task is to ensure that 'all methods of prevention including female controlled methods . . . [are] secured as well as access to treatment for those infected. HIV transmission from mother to child, including the dilemma centred around breastfeeding, deserves greater attention and ethically sound strategies' (United Nations 2001, 88). However, to succeed in accomplishing the tasks, the international community will have to confront cultural and religious beliefs and conceptions surrounding the female body and the female as reproductive agent. Further to this, it will have to confront the structural issues of economic globalization and free trade that result in the push towards privatization of health and social services.

The right to control all aspects of one's health and body and the HIV/AIDS issue combine as a clear illustration of two slogans popularized by the women's movement: 'the personal is political' and 'thinking globally, acting locally'. We certainly see the blurring of distinctions between private/personal and public, local, and global, because the individual female body becomes a global political issue. Seen from this vantage point, women are very much embedded in international relations.

Continuing Struggles for Inclusion and Recognition

Can we eradicate sexism? Can equality of women be achieved? Through the 'acronym soup' of the United Nations, the proclamations of the World Conferences, the CEDAW and its Optional protocol, and the Millennium Development Goals, in particular MDG 3 (to promote gender equality and women's empowerment), can a road be laid that will bring us to a world where men and women are equal? In the introduction to this book, we warned against the tendency to 'just add women and stir'. Women's perspectives must be fully integrated to reveal the differences, illustrate the power imbalances, and make women truly visible. This is not a simple recipe; it entails significant challenges not only for the actors but also to the status quo. The power differentials based on gender difference, affluence and poverty, and global North and South, that make up this status quo are quite intractable, and it may be that many of the proclamations and commitments emanating from the United Nations are still little more than adding women and stirring.

Stephen Lewis, then United Nations Special Envoy for AIDS in Africa, in an address to the International Panel on UN Reform, July 2, 2006, eloquently and passionately expresses the frustration that occurs when one is committed to working for women's This frustration is made all the more acute when we consider, as discussed previously, that one of the most effective ways to address the crises of poverty and HIV/AIDS is through the empowerment of women.

A Call For International Action

There is a crying need for an international agency for women. Every stitch of evidence we have, right across the entire spectrum of gender inequality, suggests the urgent need for a multilateral agency. The great dreams of the international conferences in Vienna, Cairo and Beijing have never come to pass. It matters not the issue: whether it's levels of sexual violence, or HIV/AIDS, or maternal mortality, or armed conflict, or economic empowerment, or parliamentary representation, women are in terrible trouble. And things are getting no better....

The suggestion has been made that UNIFEM alone should be transformed into a new, free-standing women's agency.... UNIFEM has at least made some impact despite being confined to subservient status as a department of UNDP (United Nations Development Programme). But it won't work.... UNIFEM, in its present form has never had extensive programming expertise, or operational experience in countries, or a range of government counterparts in Ministries, or financial and human resource autonomy, let alone sufficient breadth in its focus to represent half the world's population....

The suggestion has been made that we create some kind of coordinating Centre for Women's Empowerment and Gender Equality, in the fashion of UNAIDS.... But the UNAIDS analogy simply does not hold up to scrutiny. UNAIDS was designed to coordinate the separate agency responses to AIDS, using the cooperating partners' (including the World Bank) field-level capacity to provide resources and technical expertise to governments dealing with an unimaginably complex pandemic. But where gender is concerned, there's precious little at headquarters to coordinate, let alone at country level.... Advocacy without programme capacity is a recipe for the status quo. Sure, we'll have some heightened consciousness, but that's not genuine reform; that's intellectual dalliance. All the advocacy in the world (and UNAIDS has some limited country capacity as well), has not managed to stem the carnage of AIDS amongst women.

The proof is in the dying.

In fact, if I may digress for a moment, it's worth pointing out that if it were not for the unsung heroism of the women of Africa, including the grandmothers—impoverished, uneducated, disproportionately infected—the response of the international community would be branded a complete failure.

No, what we need is a full-fledged agency with real operational capacity on the ground to build partnerships with governments, to engage in public policy, to design and finance programmatic interventions for women, to give NGOs and community-based women's groups the support their voices and ideas have never had, to extract money from bilateral donors, to whip the UN family into shape, to bring substance and know-how to the business of gender mainstreaming, to involve women in every facet of life from development to trade to culture to peace and security, to lobby vociferously and indefatigably for every aspect of gender equality, to have sufficient staff and resources to make everyone sit up and take notice. That's exactly what UNICEF does for children. Why can't we have the same for more than half of humankind?

... First, how do you wed the human rights objectives of the Convention on the Elimination of all Forms of Discrimination against Women (CEDAW) with the operational capacity in the field? I submit that it's not so difficult. The provisions of CEDAW become the policy base for the women's agency. The Office of the High Commissioner for Human Rights (OHCHR) can then best service the CEDAW Committee while a new women's agency, as part of its mandate, funds the process. That's exactly what is now done by UNICEF and OHCHR in respect to the Convention on the Rights of the Child. It works and works well.

Second, how do you re-enforce and make more effective the concept of 'gender main-streaming'? ... Gender mainstreaming is not easy. When it's sloughed off on non-experts and made to stand on its own, rather than alongside targeted programmes to promote women's empowerment and human rights, it just doesn't work. The original idea was intended to use gender mainstreaming as a 'transformative' strategy ... that is to say, there would be a radical transformation in gender relationships. It has not happened, least of all within the United Nations itself. There is not a single assessment of gender mainstreaming that I have read—and there have been many assessments, commissioned by donors, compiled by the UN itself, done by NGOs—that is fundamentally positive. Every single one of them ranges from the negative to an unabashed indictment.

And the United Nations? The complexities of gender mainstreaming aside, it even flunks the test of gender parity, failing to reach its own target of 50/50 in staffing percentages in the vast majority of departments and agencies. For the UN Office in Geneva, the city in which we're meeting, the 50/50 target, at present rates, will be reached in 2072. The Department of Peacekeeping Operations at present rates, will reach the target by 2100. It makes gender mainstreaming the *reductio ad absurdum* of United Nations policy.

... Third, where will we get the money? Everyone argues that there's no money to be had and no patience for large additional sums. .... When it comes to women, western governments cry poverty whenever large sums are discussed. It's just unconscionable. As recently as one week ago, the Prime Minister of the United Kingdom asserted, in an op-ed for 'The Independent', co-authored by his Chancellor of the Exchequer (a member of this panel!) and his Minister of Development Cooperation, that world foreign aid jumped by 25% in 2005 over 2004, reaching over $100 billion annually, well on the way to $130 billion as promised for 2010.

So I ask: is more than half the world's population not entitled to one per cent of the total? What's happened to our sense of international values? How dare the leaders of the G8 crow about progress on aid and debt . . .while continuing to watch the economic, social, physical and psychological decimation of so many of the world's women? How in heaven's name can they be sanguine about the catastrophic loss of so much human potential?

. . . For me, everything I've ever known of gender inequality has been sharpened by witnessing the AIDS pandemic. And I can say, without fear of contradiction, that where the women of Africa are concerned, the UN has been a colossal failure. . . . For the young women in particular, there is a palpable sense of betrayal.

I want to change that view. I want the world to understand that if we had an international organization for women, with force and dollars and staff, we could save, liberate and enhance hundreds of millions of lives. I make that argument because this women's agency can be built on the foundation constructed over the years by the kaleidoscope of women's groups that have operated outside the UN, partly because there's been so little to affiliate with on the inside.

That's why a billion dollars is such a paltry sum. And let no one sow confusion: by an international organization for women, I don't mean a specialized agency like the WHO, or ILO, or FAO. I mean one of the powerful Funds or Programmes like UNICEF or UNDP or UNFPA or the World Food Programme.

Time and time again over the last two years Kofi Annan has called for a 'deep social revolution . . . to transform relationships between men and women at all levels of society'. He means, by that, women's empowerment and gender equality. Gender equality is not achieved in hesitant, tentative, disingenuous increments. It's achieved by bold and dramatic reform of the architecture of the United Nations. . . .

It is easy from the comforts of middle class, educated Canada to respond that women's empowerment and equality is 'not my issue, I have my equality and its guarantee in the Constitution'. This is not far-fetched, particularly given Canada's vocal support for CEDAW, the Beijing Platform, and the Millennium Development goals, as well as the Canadian government's claim that for most Canadian women equality has been achieved. Indeed, the point is driven home when media run obituaries for feminism as appeared with the proclamation on the front cover of *Time* magazine that 'feminism is dead' (n.a. 1998). However, we should not be complacent regarding the status of women either nationally or globally.

On 22 February 2010, the Feminist Alliance for International Action and the Canadian Labour Congress (CLC), along with the Canadian Teachers' Federation and the Public Service Alliance of Canada (PSAC), released a report intended for presentation at the Beijing +15 Meeting at the UN in March of the same year. The news was not good.

While the report praised as considerable Canada's achievements toward women's equality 'over the past decades', in the past six years the direction on equality has in fact been backwards.

[D]uring the period of 2004–2009, women's achievements in all twelve areas of critical concern outlined in the Beijing Platform for Action have slowed or been turned back. Canada no longer compares favourably against other nations in assessments of gender equality and the gender gap. For example, in the 2004 World Economic Forum Gender Gap Index, Canada was ranked 7th. In the 2009 Gender Gap Index, Canada ranked 25th. In 2009, Canada was ranked 73rd in the UN Gender Disparity Index. Canada has been strongly criticised by several UN human rights bodies on the issues of women's poverty and the endemic violence against Aboriginal women and girls. . . . [T]here has been a systematic erosion of the human rights of women and girls in Canada. The changes to gender architecture, the shifts in policy and programming within the Government, and the Government's response to the economic crisis have been felt by the most vulnerable women and girls in Canada. The organizations that provide those women and girls with an opportunity to bring their concerns forward have been eliminated, or gagged by new funding regulations. Women and girls in Canada call on the international community to condemn the policies that have resulted in the deaths of Aboriginal women, the abandonment of women living in poverty, and the curtailing of the democratic representation of women's needs and interests (Canadian Feminist Alliance for International Action & Canadian Labour Congress 2–3).

As we have discussed throughout this book, and as many Canadian political scientists have clearly shown (for example, see Dobrowolsky 2009, Brodie and Bakker 2007, Brodie 2008, and Bashevkin 2009), in the past decade, while promises and commitments may have been made by various governments, the practical efforts tell a story of cutbacks and retrenchment that have been harmful for women. Today we can characterize the political environment in which Canadian women must act as particularly chilly, if not frigid. It would appear that Sandra Burt's (2000) pessimistic prediction of women's influence in Canadian public policy development, discussed in chapter 6, has come true.

Indicative of the shift in the Canadian government's institutional and political support for women have been the changes to the Department of the Status of Women. Part of the process of cutting back the budget, closing 12 of the 16 regional offices, and moving to a results-based measure of programming, was a significant change in the Department's mandate, specifically the removal of the terms 'gender equality' and 'equality'. A comparison of the mandates and funding criteria of the Women's Program of the Status of Women Canada from May 2006 (web.archive.org) and March 2007 (Department of the Status of Women 2007), revealed that occurrences of the word 'equality' fell from 27 in May 2006 to just one in March 2007 (see also Newman 2008).

Compared to the first edition of this book, this is a much more pessimistic conclusion. Fifteen years after the Beijing World Conference on Women and at the close of the first decade of the twenty-first century it is very clear that there is an awful lot remaining to be done before women can approach equality with the world's men. However, we also have to remind ourselves that both in global politics and in the struggles of Canadian women, much has been accomplished and women's lives have been transformed for the better.

We must also remember that while the Women's Movement may be characterized as coming in waves, at no point in history were there no women active in the struggle for women's equality. As discussed in chapter 4, we may be at the beginning of a new wave of feminist or women's mobilization—a third wave. This new wave may not be as explicitly women-centred and cohesive as women's activism was in the first and second waves. It may also be undergoing a process of negotiating and constructing ways to make commitments to women's equality and autonomy relevant to the issues we face today. According to Shandi Miller (interviewed in AWID 2001), this feminism is still being developed, but it can be characterized by more awareness of and interest in international issues, as well as an understanding of how varied 'women' are. For Miller, the new generation of feminism is in a

> transition stage—between significant changes on a few levels, and not on others—in which it's difficult to define or make sense of where we are just yet. But I think it's really important to talk about feminism in terms of a third wave, and to start exploring what that can mean for all sorts of women and men, especially given all the media attention to the idea of 'post-feminism'. I know that there are people who are still passionate about feminism and that there are young women who are passionate and struggling with contradictions and all these new contexts we live in as Canadians. But not enough of them are talking and those who are, their voices are not being heard (ibid.).

The results of this transition may not end up looking like 'your mother's feminism' and other feminisms of the past. However, we can say that historically, when confronted by the injustice and inequality of their position, young women have always 'stepped up to the plate' and worked for a vision of equality and empowerment. But it has not been and never will be easy

Thus, expressions like 'the death of feminism' are obviously premature. Feminism continues to develop to meet the challenges that confront women globally. The future might not be 'feminist' according to the various theories and approaches we discussed in chapters 2 and 3, but it will certainly include women and their efforts to make a place for themselves in our world.

In advocating the construction of a 'big tent' for feminists and women political activists, we argue in favour of an inclusive view of what constitutes women's and feminist politics. We allow for a diversity of views and experiences, some of which might not always be identified as 'feminist', yet all of which envisage the goal of freedom from sexist role patterns and domination. Many young women share this goal, along with others associated with movements for globalization-from-below, anti-racism, sustainable development, environmentalism, and peace.

The fact that women's and feminist struggles continue in the twenty-first century indicates that they are far from irrelevant, even in a climate of 'I'm not a feminist but . . . '. These struggles revolve around building a better world for both women and men by securing greater reproductive rights, achieving equal pay and equal access to work, securing access to appropriate child care and adequate health care, achieving a more equitable division of domestic responsibility, ending violence against women and minorities, fighting racism, achieving greater assistance to the poor, combating environmental degradation, and securing peace. The list is endless.

What needs to be done? A great deal. As the Canadian experience shows, achieving change is a slow progression: two steps forward and one step back. It is telling, for example, that many of the recommendations of the Royal Commission on the Status of Women, tabled more than 30 years ago, are still to be fully met. Where there is movement, there may well be action, particularly if enough pressure can be brought to bear. There is also a need to keep up the pressure worldwide. As Sandi Cooper (2002, 24) points out, the tasks are great:

> Peace needs to be organized, economic justice needs to be insured, governments need to ensure the well-being of the least fortunate citizens, men and women must share the management of households because the socialization of children is the smallest pebble in the continuum toward world peace. The personal and private formulate the political; policy is not an abstraction based on universal norms and precepts. It is the expression of human agency.

Cooper's point brings us back to the concept of praxis. As we discussed in chapter 1, praxis speaks to the dynamic and contestatory nature of feminist thought and activity. Women's politics is about the continual creation and re-creation of the ideal of what a woman is, as well as what are the ideals of society. It is not about the failure or success of a form of politics or movement, nor is it about the success or failure of a particular public policy; rather, it is about the continual challenge and agenda presented by that movement. It is about making change, and it is in that context that feminist theory, the women's movement, women as political actors, and public policy all combine into women's politics.

Questions for Critical Thought

1. Is a 'deep social revolution' possible? Can the UN's Millennium Goal of promoting gender equality and women's empowerment be achieved without the significant inclusion of women in the running of all national governments and the structures of the United Nations? Does an international women's movement have enough 'revolutionary' potential to bring about the needed changes?
2. In an international system based on state sovereignty, how do we enforce and make effective the concept of gender mainstreaming?
3. Is 'thinking globally, acting locally' a meaningless slogan? If we cannot eradicate the power differentials based on gender, affluence, and poverty in our own country, how can we expect to make things more fair internationally?
4. How do we make connections and build a politics that is for and includes all the women of the world?

Recommended Websites

The Abortion Rights Coalition of Canada, http://www.arcc-cdac.ca/home.html, advocates for women's ability to exercise their right to this health service equitably and without barriers. Its website provides publications and news on all aspects of the abortion issue in Canada, breaking news, and guidelines for citizen action.

With a website that includes a repository of health information; education, public awareness, and research resources; and a map of local and provincial member organizations, the **Canadian Federation for Sexual Health** (Canadian member of Planned Parenthood), http://www.cfsh.ca, is a pro-choice, charitable organization dedicated to promoting sexual and reproductive health and rights in Canada and internationally.

The **Canadian Research Institute for the Advancement of Women**, http://criaw-icref.ca, documents the economic and social situation of women in Canada through research, making it available for public advocacy and education. The institute also provides tools to help organizations working to advance social justice and equality for women. Its website provides numerous resources on a host of issues that have an impact on women, including violence, poverty, diversity, history, health, economics, and more.

The **Canadian Women Voters Congress**, http://www.canadianwomenvoterscongress.org/, works to encourage Canadian women to develop strong and effective voices at all levels of government. Its website houses information about its events, campaigns, and monthly news updates.

Canadians for Choice, http://www.canadiansforchoice.ca, pursues education and research to advance the continuum of sexual and reproductive health choices for women and men in Canada and internationally. It regards sexual and reproductive rights as an integral part of the health and well-being of all persons. The organization's website provides information and links on sexual and reproductive rights and health, resources, and information on its scholarship program.

With its work, focus issues, initiatives, regional representation, and resources available on its website, the **Center for Reproductive Rights**, http://reproductiverights.org, operates on the premise that reproductive rights are at the very centre of human rights and advocates for women's right to choose whether and when to have a family, for access to the best reproductive healthcare available, and for freedom from coercion or discrimination when making choices.

Chronicling child care advocacy across the country and providing information on action, resources, press releases, and information about its members, the **Child Care Advocacy Association of Canada**, http://www.ccaac.ca/home.php, works to promote a publicly funded, inclusive, quality, not-for-profit child care system, an issue of importance to many Canadian women and their families.

DisAbled Women's Network (DAWN) **of Canada**, http://www.dawncanada.net/, is a national feminist organization composed of diverse women who self-identify as Women with disAbilities and are working to take control of their lives and bring an end to the stereotype that categorizes women with disabilities as dependent burdens on society. DAWN's website offers a history of the movement, member profiles, information on initiatives and 'dissonant' disabilities, news and viewpoints, community pages, and links.

Candidate rosters, historical election results, research on a variety of election-related topics, and newsroom releases can all be found at **Elections Canada**, http:www.elections.ca.

Equal Voice is an organization that advocates for women's equal representation in Canadian politics at all three levels of government, http://www.equalvoice.ca/mission. cfm. It has been working with the **Federation of Canadian Municipalities**, http://www.fcm.ca, and **Status of Women Canada**, http://www.swc-cfc.gc.ca/index-eng. html, through *The Women's Participation Project* to improve women's representation in municipal politics. Its extensive website offers research and reports, information on its provincial chapters as well as programs and events, and media resources and opportunities for action.

Feminist Alliance for International Action, http://www.fafia-afai.org/, is a comprehensive site for issues, news, action, and conferences and forums on a host of topics that affect women globally, including indigeneity, poverty, housing, child care, violence, employment, and pay equity.

For comparative cross-national data on women in national parliaments worldwide, see the website of the **Inter-Parliamentary Union**, http://www.ipu.org/wmn-e/classif. htm. Promoting Canadian women's equality through action, legal research, and education, the **National Association of Women and the Law**, http://www.nawl.ca/, provides information and a library of resources around issues such as Aboriginal women, pay equity, custody and access, sexual assault, violence, family law, immigration, and parental benefits.

The Native Women's Association of Canada, http://www.nwac.ca/, works collectively to enhance, promote, and foster the social, economic, cultural, and political well-being of First Nations and Métis women within First Nation, Métis, and Canadian societies. Its website houses research and data, a knowledge centre, a media centre, an activities map, and departments including environment, health, human rights, international affairs, labour market development, sisters in spirit, and youth.

Useful data on a myriad of topics of interest to women is compiled on the websites of the **Parliament of Canada**, http://www.parl.gc.ca. Also, visit the websites of the main political parties federally and provincially in order to track their efforts to involve more women in politics: **Bloc Québécois**, http://www.blocquebecois.org/accueil. aspx; **Conservative Party of Canada**, http://www.conservative.ca; **Green Party of Canada**, http://greenparty.ca; **Liberal Party of Canada**, http://www.liberal.ca; **New Democratic Party of Canada**, http://www.ndp.ca.

Subtitling itself 'Canada's Alternative Women's Movement', REAL **Women of Canada**, http://www.realwomenca.com/home.html, provides a public forum for women from all walks of life to express their views and work towards the goals of being Realistic, Equal, and Active for Life. The website outlines important issues; provides position papers, publications, and other resources; offers newsletters and alerts; makes available an archive of information and a comprehensive links listing; and details initiatives.

Bringing together researchers from around the world working in many different disciplines, the **Research Network on Gender Politics and the State**, http://libarts.wsu.edu/polisci/rngs/index.html, represents a long-term project on women's movements and the state as well as a series of future projects that focus on drawing connections between women's movements and states through women's policy agencies.

Status of Women Canada, http://www.swc-cfc.gc.ca, is a federal government organization that promotes the full participation of women in the economic, social, and democratic life of Canada. Its website offers comprehensive resources, including a media room, information about funding, gender-based analysis and strategic policy, a listing of commemorative dates, and a resource centre featuring publications, legal and statistical information, and an overview of the state of women in Canada.

Women's Legal Education and Action Fund, http://www.leaf.ca/, works towards ensuring the law guarantees substantive equality for all women in Canada. Its website offers in-depth information on legal cases, issues, and law reform; educational programs and resources; and a media room and events listings.

Annotated Bibliography

Compiled by Cheryl Auger

Chapter 1: Introduction

Burt, Sandra, and Lorraine Code (Eds). 1995. *Changing methods: Feminists transforming practice*. Peterborough, ON: Broadview Press.

A useful collection of essays that addresses questions such as what feminist methods are and how they are transforming the social sciences and humanities.

Gilligan, Carol. 1982. *In a different voice: Psychological theory and women's development*. Cambridge, MA: Harvard University Press.

Gilligan sets out to listen to the voices of women while challenging psychological theory that had not adequately recognized differences among men and women. She argues that women's moral reasoning tends to be more relational than that of men. This fascinating book has generated a great deal of subsequent debate on gender and difference and thus remains a classic in the field.

hooks, bell. 2000. *Feminism is for everybody*. Cambridge, MA: South End Press.

hooks describes what feminism is and why feminism is for women and men. It is a short, straightforward book that is easy to understand. It includes short chapters on major issues of concern to feminists, including education, bodies and beauty, feminist class struggle, women at work, violence, and marriage. Every student interested in feminism should read this book (or any of hooks's other work for that matter).

Phillips, Anne (Ed.). 1998. *Feminism and politics*. New York: Oxford University Press.

This insightful volume examines the scope and boundaries of politics as seen by leading political scientists, including Susan Moller Okin, Judith Butler, Kimberlè Crenshaw, Catharine MacKinnon, Jean Bethke Elshtain, and Iris Marion Young.

Vickers, Jill. 1997. *Reinventing political science*. Halifax: Fernwood Books.

Vickers explains and explores the resistance of the discipline of political science to feminist theory and insights while outlining a framework for feminist political science. She argues that four elements of the 'political science paradigm' have made it difficult to include women: the focus on the state; the acceptance of a public/private split; the unclear distinction between private and domestic; and the assumption that the structures and processes of the state are sex, gender, race, and class-neutral.

Chapter 2: Modern Feminist Theory

Arneil, Barbara. 1999. *Politics and feminism*. Oxford: Blackwell.

This book, along with Rosemarie Tong's *Feminist Thought*, provides a useful grounding in feminist theory. It examines dualities in Western political thought, such as culture versus nature and private versus public, that have emerged during the first, second, and third waves of feminist thought. An account of the history of feminism is also given to help readers understand the evolution and interconnection of the different waves of feminist thought.

Code, Lorraine (Ed.). 2000. *Encyclopedia of feminist theories*. London: Routledge.

Compiled by over 200 scholars from Canada, the United States, the UK, Australia, and the Netherlands, this volume is a great starting point for essays and assignments. It includes names, theories, concepts, and ideas associated with feminism. Each entry references other related terms and offers students a list of further readings.

Tong, Rosemarie Putnam. 1998. *Feminist thought: A more comprehensive introduction.* 2nd ed. Boulder, CO: Westview Press.
Tong's comprehensive introduction to feminist thought includes chapters on the major strains of feminist theory, including liberal feminism, radical feminism, Marxist and socialist feminism, postmodern feminism, and multicultural and global feminism. Each chapter seeks to explain the similarities, differences, and debates among feminists. The text introduces students to major thinkers within each tradition of feminism and can be used to supplement and clarify theoretical works.

Wollstonecraft, Mary. 1970. *A vindication of the rights of women.* Farnborough, UK: Gregg International.
Mary Wollstonecraft's *Vindication* is a fine example of liberal feminist thinking (though she never referred to it as such), written by a woman considered by many to be a mother of Western feminism (and the real life mother of Mary Shelley). She argues that women should have the right to opportunities in the public world because, contrary to popular opinion, women are rational creatures. Modern readers will likely find *Vindication* unsatisfying because of its reliance on classist and racist assumptions, but it is likely that readers in Wollstonecraft's era would have blushed at the suggestion that the family would not be destroyed if women entered the public domain.

Chapter 3: Contemporary Debates in Feminist Theory

Butler, Judith. 1999. *Gender trouble: Feminism and the subversion of identity.* New York: Routledge.
Though Butler intended it 'to criticize a pervasive heterosexual assumption in feminist literary theory' (vii), *Gender Trouble* has been heralded as the foundation of queer theory. Butler problematizes the way feminist theorists have conceptualized 'gender', challenges binary notions of masculine and feminine, and argues that gender is performative. The tenth anniversary edition is useful because it includes an updated preface in which Butler addresses comments and criticisms, including 'the difficulty of its style'.

Dossa, Parin. 2009. *Racialized bodies, disabling worlds: Storied lives of immigrant muslim women.* Toronto: University of Toronto Press.
Dossa responds to feminists' concerns that women who experience multiple forms of oppression are subject to social erasure in politics and research. By exploring personal narratives of racialized women with disabilities she sheds light on multiple and intersecting oppressions while revealing the relationship between experience-based knowledge, voice, and authority. She uses storytelling and narrative to generate opportunities for cross-cultural dialogue and conversations across political boundaries.

Emberley, Julia V. 1993. *Thresholds of difference: Feminist critique, Native women's writings, post-colonial theory.* Toronto: University of Toronto Press.
The writings of Native women are used to argue that the decolonization of feminism is required to ensure theory includes the voices of the oppressed. Emberley argues that the solution to the exclusive nature of theory can be found in the 'writings of subjects in resistance' (xvii). She relies on Marxism, critical theory, and postmodernism to advance her argument that Native women's writings offer an examination of ideological contradictions in dominant social relations and in modes of resistance.

Green, Joyce, ed. 2007. *Making space for Indigenous feminism*. Black Point, Nova Scotia: Fernwood Press.

> Green brings together Indigenous women from Canada, New Zealand and Scandinavia to discuss and debate the possibilities of Indigenous feminism. There is very little literature on Aboriginal women and even less on Aboriginal women claiming to be feminists or who write about Aboriginal feminism, making this volume all the more important. Green notes that the few Aboriginal women who do consider themselves feminists are cautious because it is a hotly debated subject. Yet she also suggests the power of Aboriginal feminism lies in its analysis of imperialism, colonialism, and racism and sexism from dominant societies as well as its ability to illuminate power abuses within Aboriginal communities.

Kristeva, Julia. 1986. *The Kristeva reader* (Toril Moi, Ed.) New York: Columbia University Press.

> Like much of the postmodern work discussed here, Kristeva's writing is dense, not easily accessible, and almost certainly requires a second or even third reading. This reader is helpful because it includes an introductory chapter outlining Kristeva's work and significance, as well as a diverse range of Kristeva's writing, with examples of her work on semiotics, psychoanalysis, and politics. Editor Toril Moi has thoughtfully ensured that each piece of Kristeva's writing is accompanied by an introduction explaining the significance of the work.

Namaste, Vivian. 2005. *Sex change, social change: Reflections on Iidentity, institutions and imperialism*. Toronto: Women's Press.

> *Sex Change, Social Change* is an accessible introduction to Namaste's research and advocacy for transsexual rights and recognition, including the right to appropriate and non-judgmental healthcare. The book is a series of interviews, short articles, and speeches that challenge the reader to rethink their ideas and assumptions about transsexual people. She critiques feminist theory for being overly abstract and failing to recognize the empirical realities and exclusions transsexual people face, such as poverty, lack of detox programs, funding for surgery, access to hormones in prison, and access to emergency shelter.

Nathani, Njoki, Katerina Deliovsky, and Erica Lawson (Eds). 2002. *Back to the drawing board: African-Canadian feminisms*. Toronto: Sumach Press.

> This volume is one of the few academic works in Canada on race and feminism. It attempts to build on work by black feminist scholars in Britain and the United States, such as Patricia Hill Collins, and includes essays on the need to rethink mainstream feminism to include black feminist thought, black women in graduate studies, and black women and the media.

Nicholson, Linda J. (Ed). 1990. *Feminism/postmodernism*. New York: Routledge.

> *Feminism/Postmodernism* helps to clarify some of the differences and similarities between feminism and postmodernism and illustrates why feminism and postmodernism have often had a contentious relationship. This nuanced and sophisticated edited volume represents some of the most important work on feminism and postmodernism, with essays by authors such as Donna Haraway, Judith Butler, Nancy Fraser, Sandra Harding, and Seyla Benhabib. Many students will find this a useful place to begin further research on postmodernism.

Chapter 4: The Women's Movement in Canada

Backhouse, Constance, and David H. Flaherty (Eds). 1992. *Challenging times: The women's movement in Canada and the United States*. Montreal and Kingston: McGill-Queen's University Press.

> This edited volume will be of interest to students in comparative politics or students interested in feminism in a comparative perspective because it includes chapters on Canadian and American

feminism. It also includes a number of chapters about Quebec feminism and the relationship between English-Canadian feminism and French-Canadian feminism, as well as relations with Aboriginal feminists.

Dobrowolsky, Alexandra. 2000. *The politics of pragmatism: Women, representation, and constitutionalism in Canada.* Don Mills, ON: Oxford University Press.
Dobrowolsky's study of women's constitutional struggles examines women's influence from the bottom up and attempts to overcome the 'dichotomous reasoning' that presents the women's movement as either within the state and political parties or outside of formal politics. It examines ideas, institutions, and the construction of collective identity and argues that the interest versus collective identity split in our understanding of social movements is theoretically useful but not always empirically accurate.

Harder, Lois. 2003. *State of struggle: Feminism and politics in Alberta.* Edmonton: The University of Alberta Press.
Harder provides an interesting and descriptive overview of feminism in the province of Alberta from the 1970s to the 1990s. She demonstrates that politics in Alberta has not been as consistently or monolithically conservative as some Canadians might believe. In addition, Harder explores the relationship between the forms of state, whether it be the welfare state or neo-liberal state, and the strategies of feminist claimsmakers.

Herizons Magazine
Herizons has a long history documenting Canadian feminist and women's movement activism. The magazine strives to 'deliver the inside scoop on the Canadian women's movement: health, activism, the environment, and legal cases affecting women' (website). Recent issues include articles on birth control for men, marketing and politics, pubic hair, and the history of women's activism. Past issues have focused on the ugly side of the beauty industry, women's human rights, and self-defence. *Herizons* provides a good alternative news source for students concerned about women's issues.

Miller, Michelle. 2008. *Branding Miss G: Third-wave feminists and the media.* Toronto: Sumach Press.
Branding Miss G uses the Miss G Project as a case study to illustrate some of the strengths and weaknesses of some third-wave feminist activism. The Miss G Project was originally created by a handful of female students at the University of Western Ontario in order to advocate for women's studies courses in the Ontario high school curriculum. Though Miller was an active member of Miss G, she worries that their recourse to 'girlie girl' images, strategies, and tactics could backfire by contributing to depoliticization and co-optation of the groups' original goals.

Pierson, Ruth Roach, Marjorie Griffin Cohen, Paula Bourne, and Philinda Masters. 1993. *Canadian women's issues: Twenty-five years of women's activism in English Canada.* Toronto: James Lorimer.
This book examines the Canadian women's movement, social policy, the justice system, and culture and communications. Each chapter is followed by a section of primary documents from the women's movement. How to begin a 'rap' or consciousness-raising group, CARAL's Abortion Caravan Demands, and NAC's memos on the Charter of Rights and Freedoms are just a few of the documents in this volume that demonstrate the language, tone, issues, and ideas that have characterized the feminist movement in Canada. These documents set the feminist scene for readers who may not have had personal experience with the second wave.

Rebick, Judy. 2005. *Ten thousand roses: The making of a feminist revolution.* **Toronto: Penguin Books.**

Rebick, one of Canada's best-known feminists, draws on her personal experience in the movement and over 100 interviews with feminist activists to create a concise history of feminist struggle in Canada. *Ten Thousand Roses* is a chronological account of Canadian feminist activism covering most of the major issues that galvanized women and representing every region in Canada. What's more, *Ten Thousand Roses* incorporates women's voices from a variety of organizations. The diversity of the movement is further captured in the free-standing interviews and statements by activists.

Vickers, Jill, Pauline Rankin, and Christine Appelle. 1993. *Politics as if women mattered: A political analysis of the National Action Committee on the Status of Women.* **Toronto: University of Toronto Press.**

This book reminds us of the important role NAC has played in the Canadian feminist movement. The authors argue that institutionalization of the women's movement was necessary for the generational success of the movement. While their analysis is insightful, recent events in the history of NAC documented in this volume might challenge their thesis. One hopes that the authors will soon provide an updated account of this organization.

Chapter 5: Women's Participation in Formal Politics

Andrew, Caroline, John Biles, Myer Siemiatyki, and Erin Tolley, eds. 2008. *Electing a diverse Canada: The representation of immigrants, minorities, and women.* **Vancouver: UBC Press.**

As the first book to offer a systemic examination of the electoral representation of immigrants, minorities, and women, this volume is long overdue. The book begins with a fairly basic question: '[t]o what extent do elected officials in Canada reflect the populations that elect them?' (4) The authors respond to that question with case studies of eleven Canadian cities and the House of Commons. The authors discover that there is an elected representative archetype and this archetype is male, white, middle class, middle aged, Christian, Canadian born, and majority language speaking. The over-representation of white middle-class males in Canadian politics is what they describe as the 'identity representation gap' (257). While they do not argue for perfect numerical representation, they are concerned about the exclusion of a number of groups and what it means for the health of Canada's democracy.

Bashevkin, Sylvia. 1993. *Toeing the lines: Women and party politics in English Canada.* **2nd ed. Toronto: University of Toronto Press.**

This book is a classic text on women and formal politics in Canada. Bashevkin's central thesis is: 'For the most part, women as a group are still "toeing the lines" in Canada and other party systems rather than participating in strategic, legislative and policy work that would transcend their conventional maintenance (including clerical) roles' (vi). She relies on interviews, party records, archives, and opinion surveys and includes a discussion of the suffrage movement, women's participation in major party organizations, and comparative perspectives on women and party politics. Although some Canadian political parties have become more accommodating of women over the years, this work remains an important study of women in Canadian politics.

Bashevkin, Sylvia, ed. 2009. *Opening doors wider: Women's political engagement in Canada.* **Vancouver: UBC Press.**

Bashevkin's edited volume emerged after a day-long conference focusing on two key questions: are doors to women's participation open wider and how can passageways be widened? It includes chapters by prominent Canadian political scientists, many of whom have been examining some form of these two questions for years. Elisabeth Gidengil, Joanna Everitt, and Susan Banducci ask if voters stereotype female party leaders; Manon Tremblay with Stephanie

Mullen explain why there are so many female politicians in the Quebec National Assembly compared with other provinces; and Mary Nadeau's chapter explores community and women's group participation with a look at race in the now defunct National Action Committee on the Status of Women.

Everitt, Joanna, and Brenda O'Neill (Eds). 2002. *Citizen politics: Research and theory in Canadian political behaviour.* Don Mills, ON: Oxford University Press.
Although this edited volume focuses on Canadian political behaviour in general, students of women and politics will find some of the chapters particularly useful, including those by the co-editors, as well as Yasmeen Abu-Laban and Jerome Black's chapters on immigrants and other ethnoracial minorities.

Tremblay, Manon, and Linda Trimble (Eds). 2003. *Women and electoral politics in Canada.* Don Mills, ON: Oxford University Press.
This comprehensive edited collection provides students with a broad and up-to-date survey of women and electoral politics, with sections on women and the electoral system, political parties, values and attitudes of the Canadian electorate, and political women and the media.

Trimble, Linda, and Jane Arscott. 2003. *Still counting: Women in politics across Canada.* Peterborough, ON: Broadview Press.
Still Counting was written because women are the most under-represented group in Canada: despite accounting for over 50 per cent of the population, women only make up approximately 20 per cent of elected officials in Canada. *Still Counting* is a short, accessible book with a wealth of facts and figures on women's participation in formal Canadian politics. The accompanying website, http://stillcounting.athabascau.ca, is an up-to-date source of information on women and formal politics.

Voyageur, Cora. 2008. *Firekeepers of the twenty-first century: First Nations women chiefs.* Montreal and Kingston: McGill-Queen's University Press.
Voyageur interviewed sixty-four First Nations women chiefs in order to find out how they became and stayed leaders, what they considered the cost and rewards involved in their positions, and whether or not they believed being a woman affected their experiences in First Nations politics. *Firekeepers* provides an overview of electoral politics among Canada's First Nations and it demonstrates that First Nations chiefs face some of the same challenges that other women politicians face in Canada; however, it also reveals some of the unique challenges faced by First Nations women in light of the Indian Act and the social and economic issues faced by a number of bands.

Chapter 6: The Practical Realities of Political Change

Andrew, Caroline, and Sanda Rodgers (Eds). 1997. *Women and the Canadian state/ Femmes et l'état canadien.* Montreal and Kingston: McGill-Queen's University Press.
This collection examines the impact of the Royal Commission on the Status of Women more than 20 years after its report. Contributors include activists, academics, and 'femocrats' writing on a variety of issues associated with the report, including pay equity, and violence against women, as well as Aboriginal women's struggle for sexual equality and the continued (in) visibility of immigrant and visible minority women vis-à-vis the Canadian state.

Bashevkin, Sylvia. 1998. *Women on the defensive: Living through conservative times.* Toronto: University of Toronto Press.
This book represents the first comparative analysis of the effect of conservative governments and policies on the women's movement in three countries: Canada, the UK, and the United

States. Examining judicial and legislative action across five areas (equal rights, family law, reproduction, violence, and employment), Bashevkin demonstrates the movements' strengths and setbacks.

Chappell, Louise. 2002. *Gendering government: Feminist engagement with the state in Australia and Canada.* Vancouver: University of British Columbia Press.
Following in the footsteps of Dorothy McBride Stetson and Amy Mazur's 1995 edited volume, *Comparative State Feminism*, Chappell examines how much of a role feminist activists play in political institutions and how state institutions in turn shape feminist activism in Australia and Canada.

Cohen, Marjorie Griffen and Jane Pulkingham, eds. 2009. *Public policy for women: The state, income security, and labour market.* Toronto: University of Toronto Press.
This excellent edited volume examines the ways neo-liberalism and the conservative shift in Canadian politics has affected public policy and how these policy changes, in turn, impact women. The chapters are written by activists and academics and they offer a range of perspectives on public policy and gender order changes. An important theme running through the volume 'is the importance of fashioning income, labour, and service supports in ways that recognize and value women's dual responsibilities as income earners and caregivers over the course of their lives and the lives for whom they provide care and financial support' (32–3). Another important theme in the volume is the importance of including the voices and experiences of marginalized women, like sex workers and poor women, in developing policy recommendations. There are chapters on Quebec's childcare program, the National Children's Agenda, gender mainstreaming, welfare reform, a guaranteed annual income, economic security and poverty.

Pal, Leslie. 1993. *Interests of state: The politics of language, multiculturalism, and feminism in Canada.* Montreal and Kingston: McGill-Queen's University Press.
Pal explores the relationship between the Department of the Secretary of State and the groups that it funds in the fields of official languages, multiculturalism, and feminism with a view to examining federal citizenship policy since the 1960s. The chapter on the Women's Program is of particular interest to students of women in politics. Pal's book is concerned with the ways in which the state shapes society and societal actors.

Royal Commission on the Status of Women. 1970. *Report of the Royal Commission on the Status of Women in Canada.* Ottawa: Information Canada.
The report is based on 468 briefs, over 1,000 letters of opinion, and the testimony of 890 witnesses who appeared before the Commission. It covers most facets of women's lives, including the economy, education, family, taxation, child care, poverty, immigration, and the law. Some of the Commission's recommendations enacted 30 years ago have become so commonplace that it is easy to forget women's fierce struggle to obtain the changes. Others, however, have not yet been achieved and are thus worth reflecting on.

Standing Committee on the Status of Women. 2007. *The impacts of funding and program changes at Status of Women Canada.* 39th Parliament, 1st Session Report (May). Ottawa: The Standing Committee on the Status of Women.
This government report provides a summary of the witness testimony and briefs presented to the Committee on the changes to Status of Women funding implemented under the Conservative government in 2006 and 2007. These changes included a decrease in the administrative budget and the introduction of new terms and conditions for the department's grants program, the Women's Programs. Groups consulted represented all of Canada's regions, rural and urban

communities, national and local organizations, groups that received funding from the Women's Programs and groups that did not. The majority of women's groups were concerned about the impacts of the closure of twelve of sixteen regional offices, the loss of the Policy Research Fund, changes to the mandate including the goal of seeking equality for women, and limitations on funding for research and advocacy activities.

Chapter 7: What is a Family?

Crittenden, Danielle. 1999. *What our mothers didn't tell us: Why happiness eludes the modern woman.* New York: Simon and Schuster.

Referred to 'as the most dangerous feminist in America' by Vanity Fair, Crittenden is a controversial figure. This book examines the issue of mother guilt—that guilty feeling working moms have in trying to 'have it all', which means leaving the kids in the care of others while they attempt to advance their careers. No matter how enlightened our public policy, Crittenden argues, mother guilt will not be eradicated; women—and public policies, one expects—should be more in tune with women's essential nature.

Eyer, Diane. 1996. *Motherguilt: How our culture blames mothers for what's wrong with society.* New York: Random House.

Like Eyer's first book, *Mother-infant Bonding*, *Motherguilt* illustrates how 'science is influenced by the prejudices, ineptitudes, and professional agendas of scientists' (ix). Eyer challenges North American society's tendency to blame individual mothers for a wide range of problems, arguing that many of these problems are actually collective matters.

Ladd-Taylor, Molly, and Lauri Umansky (Eds). 1998. *'Bad' mothers: The politics of blame in twentieth-century America.* New York: New York University Press.

While the authors in this collection recognize that there are legitimately bad mothers—for example, those who neglect their children or provide substandard care—the goal of these essays is to demonstrate how mother-blaming has changed over the last century while arguing that the definition of the bad mother has expanded. They explore the effects of mother-blaming on families and the greater implications for society.

Mandell, Nancy, and Ann Duffy (Eds). 2000. *Canadian families: Diversity, conflicts and change.* Toronto: Harcourt Brace.

The authors note that the Canadian family is currently in flux, yet there has not been a systematic effort to appraise this change. This book represents an effort to explore new avenues for understanding. It includes chapters on the history of the family in Canada, the families of native people, immigrants, and people of colour, and feminist contributions to legal reform, among others.

Minow, Martha, and Mary Lyndon Shanley. 1996. 'Relational rights and responsibilities: Revisioning the family in liberal political theory and law'. *Hypatia* 11 (1):4–29.

An excellent overview of the major theoretical perspectives on the family, this article explores the differences and similarities between the contract-based, community-based, and rights-based orientations in legal and political theory about the family.

Okin, Susan Moller. 1989. *Justice, gender and the family.* New York: Basic Books.

Beginning with the premise that women will not be able to gain equality in politics, at work, or in any sphere until there is justice within the family, Okin offers a compelling feminist critique of modern political theory. Okin's understanding of the family will prove thought-provoking and perhaps controversial among students.

Ranson, Gillian. 2010. *Against the grain: Couples, gender and the reframing of parenting.*
Toronto: University of Toronto Press.
   Against the Grain is the result of thirty-two interviews with couples who have unconventional
   ways of organizing their work-family lives. In other words, their families work against the grain
   of dominant understandings of mothering and fathering. For example, some of the couples
   engage in a role reversal where the father stays at home providing care and mom is the primary
   breadwinner while others split their domestic and work duties quite equally. Though most
   of the couples were heterosexual, three were gay and two were lesbian. Ranson looks at the
   unconventional families because 'they represent the change that gets missed when the focus is on
   the big picture of demographic patterns and dominant social trends' (6).

Ruddick, Sara. 1980. Maternal thinking. *Feminist Studies* 6 (2):342–67.
   Ruddick's classic and challenging article requires the reader to consider the nature of maternal
   thought and practice. Maternal practice consists of three demands: preservation, growth, and
   acceptability. Patriarchy and social hierarchies, as currently practised, have a damaging effect on
   maternal practice; however, maternal work can become 'a rewarding, disciplined expression of
   conscience' through feminist consciousness, which in turn can transform politics.

Chapter 8: The Family, Law, and Public Policy

Boyd, Susan B. (Ed). 1997. *Challenging the public/private divide: Feminism, law, and public
policy.* Toronto: University of Toronto Press.
   One of the few collections of essays on Canadian family law and policy, this volume explores
   how a dichotomous understanding of spheres of human activity (public/private, state/market,
   market/family, and state regulation/family relations) has contributed to women's oppression.
   Authors represent a range of fields from law to sociology. Topics covered include: regulating
   sexuality, violence and Aboriginal women, maternity benefits, perceptions of motherhood and
   custody decisions, and globalization.

Boyd, Susan. 2003. *Child custody, law, and women's work.* Don Mills, ON: Oxford University
Press.
   An outstanding synthesis of the work of a leading feminist family law scholar, Boyd's book
   examines how child custody law has evolved over time in Canada. It also well encapsulates
   current debates over child custody and women's and men's roles in the family. Boyd argues that
   a gender-neutral approach to family law and policy is 'deeply flawed and tragically wrong' (xi)
   because it does not take into account the gendered caregiving that still goes on in most families.

Lahey, Kathleen A., and Kevin Alderson. 2004. *Same-sex marriage: The personal and the
political.* Toronto: Insomniac Press.
   Lahey and Alderson offer an interesting account of the extension of civil marriage to same-sex
   couples in Europe and North America. It is one of the most up-to-date resources currently
   available on same-sex marriage, though it does not document the Canadian federal legislation
   adopted in 2005 making same-sex marriage legal throughout Canada. The first section of the
   book examines the legal and political struggles to bring about civil marriage. The second section,
   through a series of insightful interviews, explores the experiences of same-sex couples who have
   been among the first to marry.

Swift, Karen J. 1995. *Manufacturing 'bad mothers': A critical perspective on child neglect.*
Toronto: University of Toronto Press.
   This book is a provocative examination of child neglect in Canada. Swift examines how the
   concept of child neglect has changed over the last 100 years and argues that neglect is a socially

constructed category. The book is thus not just about child neglect but about the way social knowledge is generated and as such offers a critique of positivistic social science.

Rayside, David. 2008. *Queer inclusions, continental divisions: Public recognition of sexual diversity in Canada and the United States.* Toronto: University of Toronto Press.
Rayside's comparative study focuses on lesbian and gay relationship recognition, parenting, and schooling in Canada and the United States. The detail-rich book challenges the conventional notion that Canada is more progressive than the United States on LGBT issues. Rayside finds that there was a relatively uniform take off of relationship recognition and parental rights across Canada; however, Canada has a lamentable record on policy in its school systems. In the United States, the issue of relationship recognition is convoluted and sometimes confusing, but overall, Rayside finds a number of important gains. While there was an increase in the possibility of lesbians and gays having children, there was no take off in the United States; however, there were surprisingly high levels of activism and more real victories in US schools than in Canada.

Chapter 9: Pin Money, McJobs, and Glass Ceilings

Armstrong, Pat, and Hugh Armstrong. 2001. *The double ghetto: Canadian women and their segregated work.* 3rd ed. Don Mills, ON: Oxford University Press.
The authors' goal is to describe and explain the nature of women's work in the paid labour force in Canada. They argue that despite 100 years of feminist activism, there has not been 'a fundamental alteration in the division of labour by sex or in the nature of women's work in the labour force' (13). They use a variety of statistical evidence to demonstrate that women tend to do most of the household chores even if they work outside the home, women are concentrated in a limited number of occupations, and women continue to contend with lower wages.

Benoit, Cecilia M. 2000. *Women, work and social rights: Canada in historical and comparative perspective.* Scarborough, ON: Prentice Hall Allyn and Bacon Canada.
The book is a comparative look at women's work and social rights in Canada, the United States, and Sweden. It includes a historical analysis of women's work that reaches back to North American societies pre-European contact, a fascinating look at the impact of capitalism on women's work, and the role of the welfare state in the changing nature of women's work.

Luxton, Meg, Harriet Rosenberg, and Sedef Arat-Koc. 1990. *Through the kitchen window: The politics of home and family.* 2nd ed. Toronto: Garamond Press.
Through the Kitchen Window is a clever metaphor that links women's lives inside the home to the world outside. Beginning with the premise that there is a politics of home and family but the struggles that take place inside the home have been rendered invisible and 'mystified by the notion that the home is a protected refuge from the strife of the so-called "real" world' (9), the authors argue against the doctrine of separate spheres and help us discover the impact of economic insecurity on the family.

Standing Committee on the Status of Women. 2007. Report of the Standing Committee on the Status of Women: *Improving the economic security of women: Time to act.* Ottawa: Communication Canada, June 2007.
Improving the Economic Security of Women includes twenty-one recommendations ranging from a federal minimum wage set at $10 per hour to reforming the Live-in Caregiver Program to working with the provinces and territories to develop a national housing strategy. It 'identifies the common challenges faced by many women as well as the particular challenges faced by specific groups of women' (2). Groups identified as vulnerable include: immigrant women, rural women, Aboriginal women, women with disabilities, senior women, and single mothers. The report provides data to demonstrate why and how these groups are especially vulnerable to

economic insecurity. Though few of the recommendations have been implemented the report helps to show how and why women's economic equality is not secure.

Waring, Marilyn. 1996. *Three masquerades: Essays on equality, work and human rights*. Toronto: University of Toronto Press.
Academic, activist, farmer, and former parliamentarian, Marilyn Waring relies on her personal experience and the experiences of the world's women to illustrate how equality, work, and human rights are gendered male even when they refer to women. Waring takes issue with United Nations reports, particularly the UN System of National Accounts, which tend to ignore work done by women. The failure to recognize women's working lives means that policy has been misdirected and largely inappropriate.

Chapter 10: Challenging Market Rules and Balancing Work and Family Life

Bashevkin, Sylvia. 2002. *Welfare hot buttons: Women, work and social policy reform*. Toronto: University of Toronto Press.
This book explores the conservative policy legacy in Canada, the UK, and the United States, promises of leaders, and the consequences of social policy reform. It argues that politicians in all three countries set the tone of the welfare debate and, despite Third Way rhetoric about a middle path, introduced social assistance policy that was more punitive than the policy of their predecessors.

Brodie, Janine and Isabella Bakker. 2007. *Canada's social policy regime and women: An assessment of the last decade*. Ottawa Research Directorate Status of Women Canada, March 2007.
This study throws cold water in the face of anybody who thinks women have achieved gender equality in Canada. Brodie and Bakker provide an extensive overview of changes in Canada's social policy regime and they document how there has been an erasure of gender in policy development as market accountability and sound macroeconomics were given priority by politicians. They provide evidence to show how policy changes have resulted in the fragmentation and erosion of Canada's social assistance regime and consider how these changes have negatively affected women, especially single mothers, immigrant women, and visible minority women.

Dobrowolsky, Alexandra, ed. 2009. *Women and public policy in Canada: Neo-liberalism and after?* London: Oxford University Press.
Dobrowolsky's edited volume engages a number of well-respected authors in a discussion about how neo-liberalism has affected Canada's public policy, including Jane Jenson, Rianne Mahon, and Yasmeen Abu-Laban for example. While the authors tend to agree that neo-liberalism has been harder on women than men and harder on some women than others, even suggesting it has made women invisible, they disagree on the status and scope of neo-liberalism. Central questions in the text are: is neo-liberalism hegemonic or is it at an impasse; is post-neo-liberalism possible and what might come after; what or who is at risk; is the situation for women getting better, worse or is it static? Though this is not an introductory reader to feminist policy analysis, it does provide a number of tools to assist students. Each chapter contains a helpful bibliography, recommended reading, and questions for discussion.

Kainer, Jan. 2002. *Cashing in on pay equity? Supermarket restructuring and gender equality*. Toronto: Sumach Press.
This author is concerned with key questions of why the wage gap continues to exist and whether pay equity law is an effective tool for eliminating gender-wage inequality. Through a supermarket restructuring case study, Kainer argues that the struggle for pay equity is important, even if not

always successful, because of its potential to challenge the liberal view of the market, abstract individual, and premise of equal opportunity.

Little, Margaret Hillyard. 2005. *If I had a hammer: Retraining that really works*. Vancouver: University of British Columbia Press.
Little's engaging writing, coupled with her ability to generate trust among the participants in her study, make *If I had a Hammer* a fascinating, compassionate analysis. It explores the Women's Work Training Program in Saskatchewan, which is a long-term, intensive program that teaches women to become carpenters and helps them gain work experience in the Women's Construction Cooperative. Little establishes criteria for successful retraining programs for women and argues that the state should offer long-term retraining programs that lead to real opportunities rather than workfare and time-limited welfare.

McKeen, Wendy. 2004. *Money in their own name: The feminist voice in the poverty debate in Canada, 1970–1995*. Toronto: University of Toronto Press.
McKeen examines the mainstream poverty debate in Canada between the 1960s and 1990s, using published articles, reports, briefs, and submissions to legislative committees and commissions by non-governmental organizations and federal state actors as well as interviews. She argues that feminists felt compelled to change their discourse in order to maintain a significant voice in the debate. This has meant that feminists have unintentionally lent support to the neo-liberal model of social policy.

Timpson, Annis May. 2001. *Driven apart: Women's employment equality and child care in Canadian public policy*. Vancouver: University of British Columbia Press.
Timpson explores the history of employment equality policy and child care policy and contends that by the 1990s, questions about women's employment equality and child care in federal public policy had been driven apart, despite feminist concerns that women's productive and reproductive work be linked. Timpson's book examines why they were driven apart.

Chapter 11: Regulation and Control of Women's Bodies

Bordo, Susan. 1993. *Unbearable weight: Feminism, Western culture and the body*. Berkeley: University of California Press.
Unbearable Weight is a collection of essays that explore the cultural meanings ascribed to the female body. With essays on eating disorders, motherhood, the reproduction of femininity, and the postmodern body, Bordo challenges readers to move beyond the oppressor/oppressed model to recognize female agency and adequately address the contextuality of meaning associated with the body revealed through historical variations in our understanding of beauty.

Brownmiller, Susan. 1975. *Against our will: Men, women and rape*. New York: Simon and Schuster.
Against our Will is an extensive examination of male violence, from slavery to war to revolution. It asks poignant and controversial questions about power, sex, and strength and has become one of the most influential works on rape. Brownmiller relies on bold, gripping writing to make her case—and who could forget these famous words: rape is a 'conscious process of intimidation by which all men keep all women in a state of fear' (15)?

Cossman, Brenda, Shannon Bell, Lise Gotell, and Becki Ross. 1997. *Bad attitude/s on trial: Pornography, feminism, and the* Butler *decision*. Toronto: University of Toronto Press.
Bad Attitude/s on Trial is a critical analysis of pornography in Canada. It examines conflicts among feminists and the role of the state in the pornography debate. Cossman et al. argue that the Supreme Court's Butler decision has lent legitimacy to state censorship. The post-Butler era, they suggest, has been characterized by a proliferation of straight mainstream pornography while any

alternative representations of sexuality are the focus of state censorship. There are chapters on LEAF's position as intervener in *Butler*, an analysis of the decision itself, and the Canadian sex-related work produced by lesbians in the 1990s.

Doe, Jane. 2003. *The story of Jane Doe: A book about rape*. Toronto: Random House Canada.
Written by Canada's most famous rape survivor, Jane Doe's book describes her experiences as the fifth victim of Toronto's balcony rapist, his trial, and her successful lawsuit against the Toronto police force for negligence and a violation of Canada's Charter of Rights and Freedoms in the investigation of her rape. The story of Jane Doe is a feminist analysis of rape from a first-person perspective.

Dworkin, Andrea. 1981. *Pornography: Men possessing women*. New York: Perigee Books.
Dworkin's *Pornography* is not intended to be about what should or should not be sold or screened; rather, it is 'a book about the meaning of pornography and the system of power in which pornography exists. Its particular theme is the power of men in pornography' (10). It outlines seven elements of (male) power and demonstrates through concrete examples how each of the seven strains of power relates to pornography. For instance, Dworkin offers readers a captivating analysis of a photograph entitled 'Beaver hunters' that appeared in Hustler magazine, the legacy of the Marquis de Sade, and the relationship between pornography and force.

Jeffrey, Leslie Ann, and Gayle MacDonald. 2006. *Sex workers in the Maritimes talk back*. Vancouver: UBC Press.
Sex Workers in the Maritimes Talk Back features sex workers' own analyses of 'the powers that shape their lives and the world around them' (1). In it, Jeffrey and MacDonald interview sixty sex workers in New Brunswick and Nova Scotia about how they weighed choices between different forms of work; the positive aspects of their work, their concerns about violence and how to resist violence, stigma and dehumanization; their experiences with the laws that criminalize sex work and law enforcement; as well as health issues. Jeffrey and MacDonald rely on long quotations in order to show how sex workers understand their experiences in their own voices. *Talk Back* offers a frank discussion of a taboo and divisive issue that puts sex workers front and centre and as a result debunks some commonly held stereotypes about the lives and work of people in the sex industry.

McElroy, Wendy. 1995. *XXX: A women's right to pornography*. New York: St. Martin's Press.
McElroy adopts an individualist feminist perspective to argue that anti-pornography radical feminists have it all wrong. That is, pornography actually 'benefits women, both personally and politically' because it gives women the opportunity to pursue their sexuality without shame, guilt, or censure (ix). McElroy arrives at this conclusion after discussions with the real men and women who work in the business and reflecting on her own experience.

Chapter 12: Reproductive Rights and Technology

Brodie, Janine, Shelley A.M. Gavigan, and Jane Jenson. 1992. *The politics of abortion*. Don Mills, ON: Oxford University Press.
This book is the outcome of a conference of abortion policy experts at Harvard University in May 1988, just months after the Canadian Supreme Court handed down the Morgentaler decision. The book is organized into three main chapters. The first examines the prelude to the 1988 decision, the second examines the political struggle afterwards and the 1991 stalemate, and the third examines the legal face of abortion politics in Canada. It is a useful and detailed account of the Canadian abortion battle.

Childbirth by Choice Trust. 1998. *No choice: Canadian women tell their stories of illegal abortion.* Toronto: The Trust.
This book consists of 24 Canadian stories of illegal abortion, all first-hand accounts of women and doctors thwarting the law. Divided by era, the book includes stories from the turn of the century to the end of the Second World War, the 1940s, the 1950s, and the 1960s. Some of the accounts tell the story of dangerous self-induced abortion while others recount sleazy back-room abortions. In many cases, the woman involved kept her story a secret for years. *No Choice* breaks the silence and helps us understand the fear, shame, and humiliation that many women felt at the prospect of an unwanted pregnancy.

McLaren, Angus, and Arlene Tigar McLaren. 1997. *The bedroom and the state: The changing practices and politics of contraception and abortion in Canada, 1880–1997.* 2nd ed. Don Mills, ON: Oxford University Press.
During the first half of the twentieth century, the birth rate in Canada declined markedly even though the Criminal Code made it illegal to sell or advertise any device intended to prevent conception or cause abortion. McLaren and McLaren help to explain how and why Canada's laws lagged behind social practice by exploring forms of contraception used prior to the pill and how and why contraception gained legitimacy.

Richer, Karine. 2008. *Abortion in Canada: Twenty years After* R. v. Morgentaler. PRB 08-22E. Ottawa: Library of Parliament.
This government report provides readers with information on the Morgentaler decision, judicial decisions on abortion after Morgentaler, and the ongoing barriers women in Canada face in accessing their reproductive rights. It discusses the tensions involved in balancing the rights of the mother and the rights of the 'unborn child' and recent Private Members' Bill, C-484, introduced to target third parties 'who criminally attack a pregnant woman and in the process, harm or kill her unborn baby' (23). The report contains a number of helpful appendices, including the 1969 law that only allowed women to have abortions if they had the consent of a therapeutic board of doctors, the text of C-484, and latest statistics on abortion in Canada.

Royal Commission on New Reproductive Technologies. 1993. *Proceed with care: Final report of the Royal Commission on New Reproductive Technologies.* Ottawa: Supply and Services Canada.
The Royal Commission on New Reproductive Technologies (NRTs) (the Baird Commission) had a mandate to examine how NRTs should be handled in Canada. The commissioners sought advice from over 300 scholars/academics in over 70 disciplines, including social science, humanities, life science, medicine, genetics, ethics, and philosophy. By the time it had completed its hearings, over 40,000 Canadians had participated. The commission recommended legislation to prohibit, with criminal sanctions, several aspects of NRTs that they deemed harmful, both to the individuals involved as well as to society. The commission has been criticized, however, both in terms of the process and the outcome, particularly by feminists.

Shanley, Mary Lyndon. 1993. 'Surrogate mothering' and women's freedom: A critique of contracts for human reproduction. *Signs* 18 (3): 618–39.
Shanley examines the divisive debate among feminists and students of public policy over whether surrogate motherhood contracts are liberating or oppressive to women. Shanley carefully outlines arguments in favour of surrogate contracts in order to demonstrate their flaws. In a well-crafted argument, Shanley concludes that pregnancy contracts should not be enforceable, though she would not prohibit 'gift surrogacy' in which only payment of medical and living expenses would be permitted (624).

Shaw, Jessica. 2006. *Reality check: A close look at accessing abortion services in Canadian hospitals*. Ottawa: Canadians for Choice.
Canadians for Choice makes no apologies for their pro-choice position in *Reality Check*. Despite the fact that *Reality Check* was produced by a political organization, the report provides a comprehensive overview of the accessibility of abortion in Canada. The report is based on a year-long research project that involved a written survey from over seven hundred hospitals in Canada. In addition to the survey Canadians for Choice hired a researcher to call the hospitals as though she herself were pregnant and looking for an abortion. Their findings are shocking. Only 15.9% of Canadian hospitals provide accessible abortion services. In addition, these services are poorly dispersed across Canada with the majority within a 150 kilometer distance from the US border; wait-times, gestational limits and the availability of counseling vary from province to province; other barriers such as anti-choice healthcare professionals, unexpected costs and travel time as well as bad referrals.

Chapter 13: Global Women's Politics

Ackerly, Brooke A., Maria Stern and Jacqui True. 2006. *Feminist methodologies for International Relations*. Cambridge: Cambridge University Press.
Feminist Methodologies for International Relations is the first book that discusses how international relations (IR) feminist research is conducted. The chapters illustrate how IR methodologies build on feminist approaches from other disciplines and build on interdisciplinary work. The chapters 'emphasize that feminist IR is a collective, open, and ongoing project in which dialogue and diversity are seen as strengths' (15). *Feminist Methodologies for International Relations* includes chapters by well-known scholars such as J. Ann Tickner, Carol Cohn, and Christine Sylvester.

Enloe, Cynthia. 1990. *Bananas, beaches and bases: Making feminist sense of international politics*. Berkeley: University of California Press.
Enloe's ground-breaking study was one of the first to demonstrate the important role women play in international relations. *Bananas, Beaches and Bases* includes chapters on sexism and tourism, nationalism and masculinity, diplomatic wives, international politics of the banana, and domestic servants. It is immensely informative and readable. In fact, it is a must-read for all students interested in gender and international relations.

Haussman, Melissa, and Birgit Sauer. 2007. *Gendering the state in the age of globalizaiton: Women's movements and state feminism in postindustrial democracies*. Toronto: Rowman and Littlefield Publishers Inc.
The chapters in this edited volume draw on the research design used by the Research Network on Gender and Politics to examine whether women's movement actors and femocrats affected top priority policy issues in a number of western democracies. Chapters range from Indigenous rights in Australia to unemployment reform in Spain to reforming the House of Lords in the UK. Canadian students may be particularly interested in Melissa Haussman's chapter on Canadian health care. The volume offers an interesting comparative perspective on the impact of womens' movements as states restructure.

Keck, Margaret E., and Kathryn Sikkink. 1998. *Activists beyond borders: Advocacy networks in international politics*. Ithaca: Cornell University Press.
This book is an attempt to generate an understanding of international advocacy networks, more specifically their origins, strategies, limits, and effectiveness. It argues that international advocacy networks offer an alternative channel of communication to that of states and yet have tended to be ignored by political scientists.

Peterson, V. Spike, and Anne Sisson Runyan. 1999. *Global gender issues*. 2nd ed. Boulder, CO: Westview Press.
This highly readable text explores how world politics looks when viewed through a gender-sensitive lens. Organized around central themes in international relations, including security, economics, equity, and ecology, Peterson and Runyan argue that using a gendered lens allows us to recognize that the 'dilemma' of gender inequality is a central element of world politics.

Sjolander, Claire Turenne, Heather A. Smith, and Deborah Stienstra (Eds). 2003. *Feminist perspectives on Canadian foreign policy*. Don Mills, ON: Oxford University Press.
This recent Canadian addition to the literature on gender and foreign policy is first-rate. It focuses on issues facing women in international relations from a Canadian perspective and pays close attention to Canadian foreign policy-making. Starting with two pieces that argue for more serious integration of women and gender in both foreign policy and the study of international relations, the essays are divided into sections covering internationalism and globalization, human security, human rights, and women's organizing.

United Nations. 2001. *From Beijing to Beijing +5: Review and appraisal of the implementation of the Beijing Platform for Action*. New York: United Nations.
This volume is a synthesis of approximately 154 responses detailing participating countries' implementation of the Beijing Declaration and Platform for Action. The responses indicate that there has been some progress in generating gender equality but also make clear that the world's women are far from equal. Students interested in a specific country will find the report general and sometimes vague. Canada's report, Canada's national response to the UN questionnaire on implementation of the Beijing Platform for Action, is available in the publications section of the Status of Women website at http://www.swc-cfc.gc.ca.

Notes

Chapter 1

1   Code (1995, 15) defines androcentricity as 'the characteristic of being derived from, based upon, and relevant principally to the experiences of men'.

2   Nonetheless, some years ago a friend of one of the authors, while defending a dissertation in international relations that focused on attempts to establish an arms trade registry, was told by one of her examiners that peace studies is not international relations!

3   Most of the small number of men who have taken the course admit to having strong feminist sympathies. One male student, adamant that he was a feminist, set off a constructive and interesting debate as to whether men could be feminists. On the other hand, one rather honest man stated that he was taking the class to 'pick up chicks'. Whether he was successful or not was never established.

4   Michael Kimmel (1995), for example, categorizes men as anti-feminist, masculinist, or pro-feminist. He argues that anti-feminists rely on traditional religious ideas to demand that women return to the 'private' sphere of the home. Anti-feminist men 'yearn nostalgically for the traditional separation of spheres that kept women from explicitly challenging men's dominance in the public sphere' (561). Masculinists, in contrast, worry about women's dominance in the private sphere and the effects of gender socialization on men and boys. They fear that women have 'feminized' manhood and turned men and boys into wimps. Masculinists' goal, therefore, is to 'dislodge women's dominance in the home, and especially in the raising of young boys' (565). Kimmel argues that the masculinist movement ranges from Boy Scouts of America founder Ernest Thompson Seton, who reportedly argued in 1910 that women were turning 'robust, manly self-reliant boyhood into a lot of flat-chested cigarette smokers with shaky nerves and doubtful vitality' (565), to Robert Bly's Iron John movement, to various men's rights organizations.

   Pro-feminists, in contrast, are men who join with women to agitate 'for educational, labor, and political reforms' (562). They believe that feminism will bring about positive changes for men as well as women because 'current standards of masculinity are often pathological, locking men into behaviour that is destructive to women, children, and other men' (569).

5   Sexism can be defined as 'behavior, policy, language or other action of men or women which expresses the institutionalized, systematic, comprehensive or consistent view that women are inferior' (Kamen 1991, 27).

6   Schlafly's Eagle Forum (established in 1975 to fight passage of the Equal Rights Amendment in the US Constitution) is solidly pro-family (http://www.eagleforum.org). Schlafly herself contributes to public opinion-shaping in the US with radio commentary, the website, and her monthly *Phyllis Schlafly Report* (first published in 1967). Schlafly (1986) argues that the world is constructed around a divinely ordained hierarchy of authority based on the complementarity of male and female roles, with men as the natural governors of society. Yet Schlafly also argues that women can achieve anything they desire; that is, they are not held back by discrimination, although feminist legal scholar Catharine MacKinnon challenged her on that point in a debate at Stanford University on 26 January 1982. It had been widely reported that Schlafly wanted a post in the new Reagan presidential administration. MacKinnon challenged Schlafly on the grounds that because she was not appointed, she had been discriminated against: 'Mrs. Schlafly tells us that being a woman has not gotten in her way. I propose that any man who had a law degree and graduate work in political science; had given testimony on a wide range of important subjects for decades; had done effective and brilliant political, policy and organizational work within the party [the Republican Party]; had published widely, including nine books; and stopped a major

social initiative to amend the constitution just short of victory dead in its tracks [the Equal Rights Amendment]; and had a beautiful accomplished family—any man like that would have a place in the current administration . . . Phyllis Schlafly is a qualified woman.' Answered Schlafly: 'This has been an interesting debate. More interesting than I thought it was going to be . . . I think my opponent did have one good point—[audience laughter] Well, she had a couple of good points. . . . She did have a good point about the Reagan administration, but it is the Reagan administration's loss that they didn't ask me to [drowned out by audience applause] but it isn't my loss' (Dworkin 1983, 30).

7 Some might even claim that no female political figure or female-run organization in Canada is as decidedly anti-feminist as someone like Schlafly in the United States. REAL Women of Canada, for example, defends the concept of choice, in supporting the right of women to work as well as the right of women to stay home with their children if they choose. One could argue that any female politician is bound to become gender-sensitive when entering the very male world of politics. Deborah Grey, for example, declared in an interview on CBC Radio's *The Current* on 19 May 2005 dealing with reaction to Conservative MP Belinda Stronach joining the minority Liberal government just before a crucial Commons budget vote, 'I think these comments are a bit over the top' (referring to Conservative MPs and provincial politicians depicting Stronach as 'whoring herself' and as a 'dipstick'). Grey then added, in an albeit partisan jab: 'Frankly I get so tired of the self-righteousness of the other side. Let's go back to the spring I think it was in 1997 before the June election . . . and Doug Young [Liberal cabinet minister], when I got up and asked a question about pork barrelling in Question Period and he said, 'there's more than a slab of bacon talking there.' Where were the 'girls' then to get outraged and go and have a little press conference. . . . Where were they when it was their side of the House?' (http://www.cbc.ca/thecurrent/2005/200505/20050519.html).

8 Ironically, Schlafly is a lawyer as well as an author and lobbyist, positions that require abstract, rational, creative, and analytical thinking—characteristics she argues are the purview of men, not women (Schlafly 1986, 160–1). She herself, therefore, does not adhere to her own stereotypes and her own advice to women to focus on the home and on the practical and nurturing aspects of their personalities.

9 'Female' sports, in contrast, often emphasize sexuality and grace. Thus, strong women athletes may be seen as aberrations—as 'unfeminine'.

Chapter 2

1 Political commitment is also at stake. As Evans argues, 'the implication of a claim that all analysis must be understood by all, is that those committed to change must accept the given divisions within any society and not attempt to do anything to change those divisions except in terms of those existing divisions' (Evans 1997, 20). The separation of theory/academy and action/grassroots speaks to an unacceptable elitism and anti-intellectualism that goes against an inclusive vision of political struggle.

2 Hartmann and Mitchell have been labelled both Marxist and socialist feminists. For example, in Arneil (1999) they are classified as Marxist feminists, and in Andermahr, Lovell, and Wolkowitz (2000), Mitchell is listed under the entry for Marxist feminism. However, in Wilson (1991) the dual systems approach is classified as a socialist feminist approach. Tong (1998) makes little distinction between socialist and Marxist feminisms, arguing that there are merely 'differences in emphasis'; she thus covers them together. However, she does classify Mitchell and Hartmann as socialist feminists.

Chapter 3

1 The term subaltern is drawn from Gramsci's paper 'On the margins of history: History of the subaltern social group', (Sardar and Van Loon 1997) and refers to the variety of differently dominated and exploited groups that explicitly lack class consciousness.

2   Grey et al. (1995, 2–3) also remind us that cyborgs are not just manifestations in the fantasy world of science fiction: 'There are many actual cyborgs among us in society. Anyone with an artificial organ or supplement (like a pacemaker), anyone reprogrammed to resist disease (immunized) or drugged to think/behave/feel better (psychopharacology) is technically a cyborg. ... Even if many individuals in industrial and post industrial countries aren't full cyborgs, we certainly all live in a "cyborg society." Machines are intimately interfaced with humans on almost every level of existence not only in the West and Japan but among the elite in every country in the world.'

Chapter 4

1   The term 'wave' is explained in the next section.
2   Some male unionists supported suffrage for women for the same reason. However, their interest in having women on a more equal footing was based on the belief that it would force employers to pay women wages similar to men's, which would put an end to women undercutting men's wages and/or encourage employers to hire males over females (Prentice et al. 1988).
3   While public health reform often included campaigns against prostitution, which victimized lower-class and destitute women, the NCW mounted a campaign to establish a national department of health and urged the federal government to set up national health standards (Prentice et al. 1988).
4   World War I proved a blow to the movement. While the involvement of women in the war effort and the need for support in the referendum on conscription acted as incentives for the federal government to give women the vote, the war proved very divisive even among social feminists. The war pitted women who supported the righteousness of the war and the British Empire against those who saw the war as the epitome of the masculine public world they sought to change (Burt 1994).
5   Eligibility for Senate seats is determined by the Constitution Act, 1867. Section 24 states that 'qualified persons' are eligible for appointment to the Senate. Five Alberta women challenged the notion that women could not be appointed to the Senate because they were not 'persons'. The federal government insisted that women were not 'persons' because 'persons' had to be defined as it had been in 1867, when the Constitution was enacted, not according to what had developed subsequently, and at the time of Confederation, women did not hold any public offices. In 1928 the Canadian Supreme Court ruled in favour of the federal government, but in 1929 the Judicial Committee of the Privy Council, a British committee of law Lords that had ultimate authority over Canadian law, overturned that decision. It ruled that 'persons' included women, unless they were expressly excluded (rather than excluded women unless expressly included). The decision thus left open the possibility of excluding women from public office, but the government would have to be specific about it. However, the federal government capitulated, and the first woman appointed to the Senate in Canada was Cairine Wilson in 1930 (for more information, see Baines 1993).
6   Cairine Wilson was appointed to the Senate in 1930, Ina Fallis in 1935, Nancy Hodges in 1941, Mariana Godoin in 1953, Muriel McQueen Ferguson in 1953, Florence Elsie Inman in 1955, Olive Lilian Irvine in 1960, Josie Quart in 1960, and Mary Kinnear in 1967.
7   Ellen Louks Fairclough was the first female cabinet minister, named secretary of state in 1957, She also was acting prime minister for one day in February 1958 and served as minister of citizenship and immigration and postmaster general until the Progressive Conservative government's defeat in 1963. Other female cabinet ministers include Judy LaMarsh 1963–8, Jeanne Sauvé 1972–9, Iona Campagnola 1976–9, Monique Bégin 1976–9 and 1980–4, Flora MacDonald 1979–80 and 1984–8, Céline Hervieux-Payette 1983–4, Judy Erola 1980–4, Monique Vézina 1984–93, Barbara McDougall 1984–93, Shirley Martin 1988–93, Monique Landry 1986–93, Mary Collins 1989–93, Andrée Champagne 1984–6, Pat Carney 1984–8, Kim Campbell 1989–93, Pauline Browes 1991–3, Suzanne Blais-Grenier 1984–5, Barbara Sparrow 1993, Jane Stewart 1993–2003, Christine Stewart 1993–9, Lucienne Robillard 1995–2005, Maria Minna 1999–2002,

Anne McLellan 1993– , Diane Marleau 1993–9, Hedy Fry 1996–2002, Sheila Finestone 1993–6, Joyce Fairbairn 1993–7, Sheila Copps 1993–2003, Sharon Carstairs 2001–3, Susan Whelan 2002–3, Elinor Caplan 1999–2003, Claudette Bradshaw 1998– , Ethel Blondin-Andrew 1993–, Jean Augustine 2002–2004, Carolyn Bennett 2003– , Aileen Carroll 2003– , Hélène Scherrer 2003–4, Judy Sgro 2003–5, Liza Frulla 2003– , Albina Guarnieri 2003– , Belinda Stronach 2005– .

8 Thanks in great part to those women in the first wave who had fought for female university education in all disciplines and admission into the professions.

9 This is not to say that such activities were unique to feminism's second wave. Rowbotham (1992), in her history of women's social struggles, discusses numerous occasions when early feminists worked to create space to support women, such as cooperative houses, daycare centres and businesses. The anti-institutional focus also needs to be qualified since many of these services came to be funded by the state or, in the case of women's business initiatives, needed financial capital from banks and investors. However, as Roberta Hamilton (1996, 57–60) points out, this does not obviate the effect such endeavours had on influencing the way that mainstream structures thought about women.

10 An appeal to nationalism is not absent from the English Canadian movement either, as illustrated by the IODE's (Imperial Order of the Daughters of the Empire) and Women's Institute's conception of the Dominion of Canada within the British Empire and the Commonwealth (Prentice et al. 1988) and the more recent connection between some parts of the women's movement and anti-free trade campaigns.

11 This is not to say that NAC was the only women's organization active at the time. One can argue though, that it became the most visible within the political system. NAC continued its activity, as did organizations such as the Women's Institute, women's church groups, professional associations, labour associations, service organizations (for example, the IODE and women Rotarians), and a plethora of local ad hoc groups that emerged around specific issues. Not all of these of groups and organizations chose to affiliate with NAC; some undertook their activities independently of other women's groups and the state.

12 Bégin (1997, 17) lists the Human Rights Act 1977, child tax credit 1978, guaranteed income supplement for single women pensioners 1979 and 1984, the creation of women's studies chairs 1984, changes to the Indian Act regarding women's status 1985, amendments to the Criminal Code regarding sexual offences 1983 and 1988, and the Employment Equity Act 1986.

13 At the time of writing, at the end of 2010, a Conservative MP, Rod Bruinooge, had introduced a private member's bill C-501 that would make it a crime to coerce a woman into having an abortion. Prime Minister Stephen Harper was not supportive, encouraging government MPs to vote against the bill in Second Reading (CBC Radio. 2010. 'Abortion Coercion: Bill C-510.' (*The Current*. CBC Radio One, December 14, 2010).

14 This description has to be qualified as not unique to the Gen-Xers. The women's movement has historically used fun, sarcasm, irony, and playfulness as a form of transgression. In societies based on work, responsibility, and production, to engage in public play is to blur the boundaries of private and public and thumb one's nose at the powers that preach responsibility, duty, and rationality.

15 The Canadian Feminist Alliance for International Action (FAFIA), the Canadian Research Institute for the Advancement of Women, the DisAbled Women's Network of Canada, the Fédération des femmes du Québec, the National Association of Women and the Law, the National Council of Women of Canada, the Native Women's Association of Canada, the Provincial Advisory Council on the Status of Women for Newfoundland and Labrador, Manitoba's United Nation Platform for Action Committee, Canadian Labour Congress, Collectif Féminisme et Démocratie, Regroupement provincial des maisons d'hébergement et de transition pour femmes victimes de violence conjugale, Sexual Assault Centre London, YWCA Canada, the Antigonish Women's Resource Centre, the Métis National Council of Women, Réseau des table régionales des groups

de femmes du Quebec, Toronto Women's Call to Action (now the Toronto Women's City Alliance), the Women's Future Fund (shut down in 2008 after it became ineligible for SWC funding), the Canadian Federation of University Women, Canadian Women's Community Economic Development Council, Couseil d'intervention pour l'accès des femmes au travail, the Urban Core Support Network of St John, Winnipeg's Women's Health Clinic, and the Yukon Status of Women Council.

16 In April of 2010, MATCH International, which is Canada's only development organization to focus specifically on women in development, was informed by CIDA that funding would not be renewed for the next cycle of MATCH's projects. MATCH relies predominantly on CIDA for its continued funding.

Chapter 5

1   This survey covered both democratic and non-democratic countries, including countries such as Saudi Arabia and Oman that have no women in the lower house, making Canada's record look even less impressive.

2   The researchers coded all the studies they gathered on the basis of the empirical results reported regarding *stereotypical personality traits* (e.g., compassion, warmth, aggressiveness), *issue competency traits*, and *issue positions or partisan identification (beliefs)*. Based on these reports, they concluded that the literature as a whole revealed that 'female candidates are much more likely to be attributed stereotypically female traits than male candidates are to be attributed stereotypically male traits' (Banducci, Everitt, and Gidengil 2002, 8). However, 'female candidates are more likely to be seen as competent on stereotypical female issues and policy areas . . . and are significantly less likely to be seen as competent on stereotypical male issues/policies . . . but the advantage on stereotypical female policy competencies is much larger than the disadvantage for women candidates on male policy competencies' (Banducci, Everitt, and Gidengil 2002, 10). Furthermore, 'policy competencies appear to be the only category of stereotypes where women might suffer adverse effects.' In fact, 'women candidates are more likely to be ascribed both male and female personality traits' (ibid.).

3   The 2001 census figures reveal that about 21 per cent of women devoted 30 hours or more to unpaid household work in 2001, compared to 8 per cent of men, and about 16 per cent of women aged 15 and over devoted 30 hours or more to child care, compared to 7 per cent of men (Statistics Canada 2003a).

4   Norris and Inglehart (2001, 134) report that they found a relationship between a society's egalitarian attitudes toward women leaders and the proportion of women elected to the lower house of a national parliament, although they note significant outliers such as Australia, Spain, and the United States.

5   The time period of the study was from the early 1960s until the mid-1990s and included Anglo-American media.

6   A number of Conservative politicians reacted to Stronach's decision with vitriol. Ontario MPP Robert Runciman described her as a 'dipstick'—though an attractive one—and Alberta MLA Tony Abbott characterized her as a 'political harlot' and said she was 'basically whoring herself out to the Liberals' (Weber 2005).

7   Ian Brodie, executive director of the Conservative Party of Canada, reports that the Ellen Fairclough Fund had in fact been dormant for a few years before the merger of the Progressive Conservatives and Canadian Alliance in 2003, although there is some talk of reviving the foundation for the fall of 2005 (telephone interview with Jamie Beauregard, 5 July 2005).

8   The Legislative Democracy Commission in New Brunswick has also recently recommended an incentive scheme. See http://www.gnb.ca/0100/index-e.asp.

9   This committee was established in 1984 with the goal of electing women to half the seats in the House of Commons by 1994 (Bashevkin 1991, 74).

10 Political reforms discussed in the United States, such as term limits, would seem at first glance a good idea since they would reduce the incumbent phenomenon and allow for the contestation

of more open seats. Indeed, the so-called 'year of the woman' in 1992, when women increased their representation in the House of Representatives from 28 to 47 and in the Senate from two to seven, occurred in part because there were so many open seats. Fifty-four House members did not seek re-election, and 19 were defeated in primaries (McGlen and O'Connor 1998, 88). Thus, women were able to run in districts where there were no incumbents, which increased their chances of winning. However, term limits would prevent women and members of visible minorities from consolidating their hold on power once they succeeded in winning a seat.

11 For an excellent comparative overview of campaign finance laws in Canada and the United States, see Smith and Bakvis (2000).

12 See, for example, many of the essays in Milner (1999).

13 Prime Minister Chrétien also appointed Jean Augustine, the first black woman in a federal cabinet, as secretary of state for multiculturalism in June 2002 (Jones 2002, A23).

Chapter 6

1 For more details, see also Chappell (2002).

2 Dobrowolsky (2000a, 51), in a very good synopsis of the events around this conflict, points out that other executive members argued that CACSW had acted on their own accord. She quotes executive member Joanne Linzey: 'The executive requested that the minister meet with the full executive as we were no longer confident that Anderson would accurately represent the minister to us or us to the minister. The minister's parting sentence was "that it is your decision, it is your conference. I can live with it either way."'

Chapter 7

1 The following section relies heavily on Minow and Shanley's (1996) categorization and examination of these debates.

2 See, for example, Schultz (1982) and Shalev (1989).

3 *Hartshorne v. Hartshorne* [2002] B.C.C.A. 587.

4 Iris Marion Young (1997, 105) goes even further, stating that 'the institution of marriage is irreparably unjust. Its original and current meaning is to solidify male power in relation to women, and to draw an arbitrary line around legitimate relationships.'

5 The platform of the former Canadian Alliance displayed some affinity with communitarian thinking. Both the Canadian Alliance's *Declaration of Policy* (2002) and the Reform Party's *Blue Book* (1999) state that government legislation and programs should 'support and respect the role of the Canadian family' and that 'bills and regulations will be evaluated to ensure their effect on families is positive'. They declare the definition of the family to be 'individuals related by blood, adoption or marriage' and that marriage means the 'union of a man and a woman as recognized by the state'. These principles coincide with at least some communitarian principles. However, the party goes on to declare that it affirms 'the right and duty of parents to raise their children responsibly according to their own conscience and beliefs' and that 'no person, government or agency has the right to interfere in the exercise of that duty except through due process of law' (Canadian Alliance 2002). As will be seen, most communitarians would grant greater authority to the state to intervene in order to support families than the Alliance would have done, given its preference for the promotion of the private/market sphere over the public sphere. As Telford (2002, 126) argues, Preston Manning's, and indeed, the Reform Party/Canadian Alliance's 'neo-conservative republicanism is a communitarian philosophy but . . . it is a monistic communitarianism, as opposed to the pluralist communitarianism of Brian Mulroney or Joe Clark.' It is not yet clear which view dominates the merged Conservative Party of Canada, although it remains a communitarian party. One of its first acts in office after the federal election victory in January 2006 was to introduce the Universal Child Care Plan which grants all families $100 per month for each child under age six to be spent however families choose – in effect, a family allowance – but promoted as offering families 'choice in child care' (http://www.universalchildcare.ca/eng/choice/index.shtml).

6 Most notoriously, former US vice-president Dan Quayle, in an address to the Commonwealth Club of San Francisco on 19 May 1992, was quoted as saying, 'It doesn't help matters when prime time TV has Murphy Brown—a character who supposedly epitomizes today's intelligent, highly paid, professional woman—mocking the importance of fathers, by bearing a child alone, and calling it just another "lifestyle choice". I know it is not fashionable to talk about moral values, but we need to do it. Even though our cultural leaders in Hollywood, network TV, the national newspapers routinely jeer at them, I think that most of us in this room know that some things are good, and other things are wrong. Now it's time to make the discussion public' (http://www.xmission.com/~mwalker/DQ/quayle/qq/fam.values.html).

7 For example, in 2003, after the Ontario Court of Appeal declared unconstitutional the exclusion of same-sex marriages and the federal government proposed to amend federal marriage laws, public opinion polls revealed that nearly half of those surveyed were opposed to same-sex marriage, particularly older Canadians (32 per cent reported support for same-sex marriage) and faithful attendees of religious services (24 per cent reported support for same-sex marriage) (SES Canada Research Inc. 2003; NFO CFgroup 2003). Furthermore, a number of prominent academics, members of the clergy, and other public figures wrote a commentary in *The Globe and Mail* declaring a 'rational connection between marriage, gender complement, procreation and the rearing of children by their biological parents', (Allen et al. 2003, A19). However, an Angus Reid poll conducted in 2009—four years after the legalization of same-sex marriage—found that 61 per cent of those polled want same-sex marriage to remain legal. Not surprisingly, 81 per cent of those polled who were born after 1980 supported the continued legalization of same-sex marriage. More surprisingly, 46 per cent (nearly half) of those polled who were born before 1946 also supported the continued legalization of same-sex marriage (http://www.visioncritical.com/wp-content/uploads/2010/07/2010.07.26_SameSex.pdf).

8 Section 64 of Ontario's Family Law Act, for example, specifically declares that a 'married person has a legal personality that is independent, separate and distinct from that of his or her spouse'. That is, married and unmarried persons have the same legal capacities and the remaining vestiges of coverture have been abolished.

9 The overall number of divorces has greatly increased since the late 1960s as a result of revisions to divorce laws. In 1968, the year of the legislative changes, the number of divorces per 100,000 population was 54.8 (Statistics Canada 2000, 32, 42).

10 The Act applied to women aged 16 to 35 and allowed women to be placed in low-security correctional institutions for 'unmanageability and incorrigibility'. The Act was amended in 1919 to reduce the time a woman could be held in detention to two years. But it expanded judges' and magistrates' powers to incarcerate women for 'wayward social behavior'.

11 While the number of women who were actually convicted was small (Sangster 1996, 249), the Act gave tremendous power to police, social workers, and the Children's Aid Society to regulate women's behaviour, particularly their sexual behaviour. Almost half of the women were pregnant when they were sentenced to the reformatory, or they had a child outside of marriage (Sangster 1996, 248). Others were considered sexually promiscuous or had a venereal disease (which often led to painful and invasive medical 'treatments' in the reformatory). The Act gave tremendous power to parents as well: from about one-third to one-half of the actions were supported by parental complaints (ibid.).

12 *Egan v. Canada*, [1995] 2 S.C.R. 513; *Vriend v. Alberta*, [1998] 1 S.C.R. 493.

13 The monetary disincentive is true for employers, although the same is not true for governments (Rayside, 2008). For example, a major part of the impetus to amend the Ontario Family Law Reform Act in 1978 to give separating same-sex partners entitlement to support came from the government's desire to avoid social assistance claims by those who otherwise would have access to private sources of monetary support.

14 *M. v. H.*, [1999] 2 S.C.R. 3

15 *Re K and B et al.* (1995), 23 O.R. (3d) 679 (Prov. Div.); *Re A (Adoption)*, [1999] ABQB 879; and *M v. H*, [1999] 2 S.C.R. 3.

16   *Case v. Case* (1974), 18 R.F.L. 132; *Bernhardt v. Bernhardt* (1979), 10 R.F.L. (2d) 32.

17   *K v. K* (1976), 23 R.F.L. 58; *D. v. D.* (1978), 3 R.F.L. (2d) 327.

18   *Nova Scotia (Attorney General) v. Walsh*, [2002] 4 S.C.R. 325.

19   The federal Marriage (Prohibited Degrees) Act, 1990, did outline prohibitions against marriage between related persons (http://laws.justice.gc.ca/en/M-2.1/76156.html).

20   *Barbeau v. British Columbia (Attorney General)*, 2003 B.C.C.A 251.

21   *Halpern et al. v. Attorney General of Canada et al.* (2003), 65 O.R. (3d) 161.

22   The decision *Reference re same-sex marriage*, [2004] 3 S.C.R. 698 can be read at http://www. lexum.umontreal.ca/csc-scc/en/.

23   The text of the Bill can be located through the federal Department of Justice website at http://canada.justice.gc.ca/en/fs/ssm/.

Chapter 8

1   *Moge v. Moge*, [1992] 3 S.C.R. 627.

2   About half of divorcing couples have dependent children in Canada (Ambert 2002, 8), similar to the rates in most other OECD countries (OECD Family Database SF 3.2. http://www.oecd.org/doc ument/4/0,3343,en_2649_34819_37836996_1_1_1_1,00.html).

3   *Francis v. Baker*, [1999] 3 S.C.R. 250.

4   *R. v. R.* (2002) 58 O.R. (3d) 656 (Ont. C.A.).

5   *Thibaudeau v. Canada*, [1995] 2 S.C.R. 627.

6   For information on the Family Responsibility Office see its website: http://www.accesson.ca/en/ mcss/programs/familyResponsibility/.

7   *Contino v. Leonelli-Contino*, 2005 SCC 63.

8   For details on the federal child support guidelines under the Divorce Act, see the federal Department of Justice's website: http://www.justice.gc.ca/eng/pi/fcy-fea/lib-bib/pub/guide/index.html.

9   See, for example, section 24 of the BC Family Relations Act and section 24 of the Ontario Children's Law Reform Act.

10   However, as Boyd (2003a, 7) points out, these statistics 'include only cases decided by the divorce courts, or where custody agreements are affirmed by courts, and not those cases in which custody arrangements were decided completely outside of court or by courts dealing with non-divorce situations'. Also, the figures do not reveal that even in the case of joint legal custody, children are more likely to reside primarily with their mothers than with their fathers.

11   The number of fathers' rights groups has proliferated over the years. For a list of just some of the many groups, see Canadian Men's Rights Groups: http://www.fact.on.ca/director/director.htm.

12   See Canada (1998a; 1998b) for summaries of testimony from fathers' rights advocates to the 1998 Special Joint Committee on Custody and Access. Bala (1999) and Laing (1999) also provide useful summaries of the fathers' rights arguments.

13   For a good review of these perspectives, see Cohen and Gershbain (2001).

14   For critiques of the 1998 Special Joint Committee Final Report, see Boyd (2000a) and Cohen and Gershbain (2001).

15   Marcil-Gratton and Le Bourdais (1999, 36) found that 'fathers who made some payment, whether regularly or irregularly, were significantly more likely to see their children. Regular payments multiplied by 6.39 the chances that a father would see his children on a regular basis, compared to cases where no payment had been made in the last six months.' Of course, it is not clear whether these figures demonstrate that parents with access or joint custody are more likely to pay child support, or whether parents ordered to pay child support are more likely to demand access or joint custody.

16   For articles dealing with male spousal abuse see, for example, Pearson (1997) and Foss (2002).

17   The bill died when the parliamentary session ended and Paul Martin succeeded Jean Chrétien as prime minister in December 2003 (Schmitz 2005b, A8).

18 These groups assert, however, that flaws still exist in the proposed legislation. See, for example, Boyd (2003b) and Côté and Cross (2003).

19 *Tremblay v. Daigle*, [1989] 2 S.C.R. 530; *Planned Parenthood of Missouri v. Danforth*, 428 U.S. 52 (1976).

20 See, for example, the website of the National Center for Men and, in particular, information on its voluntary fatherhood project: http://www.nas.com/c4m/.

21 Kelly (2004–5, 165) points out the difficulties that non-biological parents have in asserting authority to complete tasks such as picking a child up from school or camp or taking a child to the doctor. Second parents can be treated as 'legal strangers' to the children they are raising, absent legal recognition of their parental rights.

22 See, for example, *S.G. v. L.C.*, [2004] Q.J. No. 6915 (Sup. Ct.); *M.A.C. v. M.K.*, [2009] O.N.C.J. 18; and *A. v. B., C and X*, [2007] R.D.F. 217. But see *A. v. B., X and C*, [2007] J.Q. No. 1895 and *L.O. v. S.J.*, [2006] J.Q. No. 450 (Sup. Ct.) where donor claims have been rejected.

23 *A.A. v. B.B.*, [2007] O.J. No. 2.

24 *R. v. Seaboyer; R. v. Gayme*, [1991] 2 S.C.R. 577.

25 *R. v. Daviault*, [1994] 3 S.C.R. 63.

26 *R. v. O'Connor*, [1995] 4 S.C.R. 411.

27 *R. v. Mills*, [1999] 3 S.C.R. 668.

28 *R. v. Lavallee*, [1990] 1 S.C.R. 852.

Chapter 9

1 Ann Crittenden (2001) provides an excellent history of how decision-makers at the US Census Bureau made a deliberate choice not to include many forms of labour, a choice then followed by other industrialized countries.

2 All of these numbers are for workers 25 and older. The youth unemployment rate for this period was 15.9 per cent and not broken down by gender.

3 Frederick and Fast's (2001, 10) report also reveals that women who were satisfied with life overall spent more time on paid work and fewer hours cleaning the house. In contrast, men were more content if they worked fewer hours for pay and spent more time on housework. As the adage says, 'the grass is always greener on the other side of the fence'.

4 It is not clear whether money exchanged in the grey and black markets is included, although according to Waring (1996, 47), the 'market activities' referred to as 'cash-generating activities' do include work of both legal and illegal status—for example, prostitution, the sale of children, deforestation, and the sale of armaments.

5 Average of quotes from Gibbons Park Montessori, $945 per month (not including $100 registration fee and The Little Red School House, Lambeth, $41.00 per day or $820 per month, September 22nd, 2009.

6 Based on estimates from Checker Limousine Service, London, Ontario, July 2010.

7 Based on hourly rate charged by Sparkles (not including taxes) in November 2009. The number of hours was downsized to 3 because, as a recent study by Bianchi seems to indicate, standards of cleanliness have decreased over the years.

8 Ontario Ministry of Labour. 'Minimum Wage Rates.' Minimum Wage: Your Guide to the Employment Standards Act. www.labour.gov.on.ca/english/es/guide/guide_4.html. Accessed September 22nd, 2009. There is also a 'Homeworkers Wage' which is set at 110 per cent of the general minimum wage. However, this refers to the following 'employees who do paid work in their own homes. For example, they may sew clothes for a clothing manufacturer, answer telephone calls for a call centre, or write software for a high-tech company' (ibid.). Therefore, it applies to traditional piecework employment and not to domestic service work.

9 A similar distinction can be seen in the prestige accorded to physicians in North America compared to that given to physicians in the former Soviet Union and Eastern Bloc. In North America, doctors are predominantly male, and it is considered an occupation with a great deal of prestige.

In the former Eastern Bloc, doctors did not appear to have a similar level of prestige, and interestingly, it was a profession in which women were highly represented.

10 One female colleague knew a male professor who referred to his Palm Pilot, a forerunner of the iPad, as 'his pocket wife'!

11 *Janzen v. Platy Enterprises Ltd.*, [1989] 1 s.c.r. 1252, 10 c.h.r.r. d/6205.

12 Unfortunately, the representation of men and women was not stated for the disciplines within each faculty.

13 This work load is slightly better for those with more education. 'Families in which neither partner graduated from university worked an average 16.3 hours per day compared with 15.2 hours for those in which both had a university degree. Most of the added time came from housework' (Marshall, 2006, 12–13).

14 Drolet's (2001) main focus is to show how measurement and methodological issues play important roles in studying the differences between men's and women's earnings. One argument she makes is in favour of using alternative competitive wage structures rather than considering the male wage structure the 'competitive or non-discriminatory wage structure'—that is, the norm.

15 Families or individuals fall below Statistics Canada's low income cutoffs if they spend, on average, at least 20 percentage points more of their pre-tax income on food, shelter, and clothing than the Canadian average.

Chapter 10

1 As a result, in the 1990s when responsibilities for social programs were downloaded to the provinces and social spending across the board was reduced, women were the hardest hit.

2 *Newfoundland (Treasury Board) v. N.A.P.E.*, [2004] 3 s.c.r. 381.

3 It should be noted that the author of the ILO report, Dr. Marie Thérèse Chicha is a Quebec-based professor.

4 See the federal Treasury Board Secretariat's summary of the federal contract compliance program http://www.tbs-sct.ca/pubs-pol/dcgpubs/Contracting/contractingpol_d_e.asp. Various provincial governments have similar contract compliance programs (Armstrong and Cornish, 1997, 72).

5 Marshall (2003, 11) reports that in 2000 approximately 46 per cent of mothers with newborns had no access to benefits.

6 Canada Child Care Act (Bill C-144), Second Session, Thirty-Third Parliament, 35-36-37 Elizabeth II, 1986-87-88.

7 Groups that mobilized against Bill C-144 included the Canadian Day Care Advocacy Association, trade unions (including the Canadian Labour Congress, the Public Service Alliance of Canada, the Canadian Union of Public Employees, and the National Union of Provincial Government Employees), the Canadian Teachers' Federation, the Federation of Nurses, women's groups (such as NAC and the Canadian Advisory Council on the Status of Women), anti-poverty groups (such as the National Anti-Poverty Organization and the National Council of Welfare), and other interest groups (such as the Canadian Jewish Congress and the Canadian Federation of students) (Phillips, 1989, 172).

8 For an excellent summary of these perspectives, see Bergmann (1998).

Chapter 11

1 The author, Sharon Lamb, was head of the American Psychological Association's Task Force on the Sexualization of Girls, APA, 2007.

2 Interestingly, the first case to challenge the idea that women were 'persons' under the law and therefore could hold official public office arose in 1917 before the 'famous five' challenged the federal government's refusal to appoint women to the Senate before the Canadian Supreme Court and the Judicial Committee of the Privy Council. Calgary lawyer John McKinley Cameron, frustrated that his client, an alleged prostitute, had been convicted and sentenced to six months of hard labour in 1917 challenged the authority of the sentencing judge, Alice Jamieson, to rule

on the case. He argued that Ms Jamieson as a woman was not competent to serve as a judge because she was not a person. Cameron lost at both the Alberta Supreme Court and the appeals levels, which meant that Lizzie Cyr, a poor, homeless, Aboriginal woman, had to serve her six months for having sex with a man in exchange for $10 and a place to stay. The man later went to the police and accused her of giving him gonorrhea, which led to a vagrancy charge (Burton 2004).

3 R. v. Hutt, [1978] 2 S.C.R. 476

4 Brock (2000) notes that when federal prostitution laws were challenged before the Supreme Court of Canada, LEAF did not intervene (Reference re ss. 193 and 195.1(1) (c) of the Criminal Code (Man.), [1990] 1 S.C.R. 1123 that dealt with the solicitation law and the bawdy-house law; and R. v. Downey, [1992] 2 S.C.R. 10 that dealt with the pimping law). Yet LEAF's support is crucial because when it does intervene on rights issues, it has often been successful (Manfredi, 2004). For example, as will be seen, LEAF successfully argued that pornography is a form of sexual exploitation that harms women.

5 For example, in January 2004 Joanne Webb, a salesperson for Passion Parties, which sells tools at home-based parties much like Tupperware, was arrested in Texas on a misdemeanour obscenity change (Navarro 2004, A12). Texas law, it turns out, still prohibits the sale of any items that are 'designed or marketed as useful primarily for the stimulation of human genital organs'. Her lawyer argued that under this law, even condoms could be seen as obscene.

6 Cossman and Bell (1997, 19) point out that the feminist anti-pornography movement, along with conservatives, had earlier proved persuasive in getting the 1985 Special Committee on Pornography and Prostitution to recommend the 'criminalization of violent and degrading sexually explicit material'. For an alternative perspective from the feminist anti-pornography arguments at the time see Burstyn (1985) and Lacombe (1994).

7 R. v. Butler, [1992] 1. S.C.R. 452.

8 The Court first had to tackle the question of what is meant by obscenity, what is covered under the obscenity provisions of the Criminal Code, then whether the Criminal Code provision violates the Charter, and then finally whether the provision can be upheld under section 1 of the Charter as a reasonable limit. (Section 1 of the Charter states that 'The Canadian Charter of Rights and Freedoms guarantees the rights and freedoms set out in it subject only to such reasonable limits prescribed by law as can be demonstrably justified in a free and democratic society.') Regarding the definition of obscenity, the longstanding definition derived from an 1868 decision from Britain, R. v. Hicklin, that ruled that the test of obscene material is 'whether the tendency of the matter charged as obscenity is to deprave and corrupt those whose minds are open to such immoral influences, and into whose hands a publication of this sort may fall'. In the late 1950s, the federal government adopted a statutory definition of obscenity in then-section 150(8): 'For the purposes of this Act, any publication a dominant characteristic of which is the undue exploitation of sex, or of sex and any one or more of the following subjects, namely, crime, horror, cruelty and violence, shall be deemed to be obscene'.

9 Justice Sopinka quoted from another ruling the kinds of material to which this would apply:

> Materials in which women are exploited, portrayed as desiring pleasure from pain, but being humiliated and treated only as an object of male domination sexually, or in cruel or violent bondage. Women are portrayed in these films as pining away their lives waiting for a huge male penis to come along, on the person of a so-called sex therapist, or window washer, supposedly to transport them into complete sexual ecstasy. Or even more false and degrading one is led to believe their raison d'être is to savour semen as a life elixir, or that they secretly desire to be forcefully taken by a male.

10 For a copy of the LEAF factum on Butler, see LEAF (1996). See Gotell (1997) for her argument that LEAF was not singularly influential if one sees the organization's arguments as similar to those of moral conservatives.

11   Sado-masochism, for example, is seen to play an emancipatory role in gay and lesbian culture (Benedet 2001, 197).

12   *Little Sisters Book and Art Emporium v. Canada (Minister of Justice)*, [2000] 2 S.C.R. 1120. See also Makin and Alphonso (2000, A1, A9).

13   For debate on the Little Sisters decision see Benedet (2001) and Ryder (2001). See also a summary of the *Little Sisters* decision and LEAF's position at http://www.leaf.ca/legal-status_00-01. html#customs. In May 1999, LEAF held consultation meetings and solicited opinions in advance from women across the country on how it should proceed. See Busby (1999).

14   *R. v. Sharpe*, [2001] 1 S.C.R. 45.

15   The definition of child pornography under section 163(1.1) of the federal Criminal Code includes: '(a) a photographic, film, video or other visual representation, whether or not it was made by electronic or mechanical means, (i) that shows a person who is or is depicted as being under the age of eighteen years and is engaged in or is depicted as engaged in explicit sexual activity, or (ii) the dominant characteristic of which is the depiction for a sexual purpose, of a sexual organ or the anal region of a person under the age of eighteen years; or (b) any written material or visual representation that advocates or counsels sexual activity with a person under the age of eighteen years that would be an offence under this Act.'

16   Justice L'Heureux-Dubé, with Justices Bastarache and Gonthier, went further and said that 'Expression that degrades or dehumanizes is harmful in and of itself, as all members of society suffer when harmful attitudes are reinforced.'

17   At the time of writing, Bill C-22 had been passed by the House of Commons and was under committee consideration in the Senate, Bill C-54 had passed Second Reading and was before the House of Commons Committee on Justice and Human Rights.

Chapter 12

1   McLaren and McLaren (1986, 132) note, however, that arrests and convictions were still occurring in the 1960s. The arrest of Harold Fine, a wholesale druggist in Toronto in 1960, galvanized Barbara and George Cadbury to form the Planned Parenthood Association of Toronto in 1961. That organization quickly opened chapters across Canada, eventually emerging as the Planned Parenthood Federation of Canada.

2   In order to perform a legal abortion, a doctor had to consult two or more medical practitioners and notify the head of the hospital in which the abortion was to be performed (McLaren 1993, 804). These practices were very similar to the ones codified in the Criminal Code in 1969.

3   The Childbirth by Choice Trust (1998, 159) notes that nearly 1,800 abortionists were charged criminally between 1900 and 1972, but only 1,155 were convicted. Because the authorities had difficulty making the case of criminal abortion, they proceeded with charges only in a small percentage of the cases that came to their attention.

4   Given the declining birth rate in the latter half of the nineteenth century and throughout the twentieth century, it is quite clear that contraception and abortion, though illegal, were being widely used to control birth (McLaren and McLaren 1986, ch. 2). McLaren (1993, 798) reports that the typical case in BC court records of women attempting to procure an abortion in the early twentieth century was that of a married woman in her mid-20s.

5   The Canadian Medical Association's proposal to change the Criminal Code did not involve recognizing abortion as a right but rather formalizing what was already existing practice in Canada: that is, abortions performed in hospitals under the scrutiny of abortion committees that determined whether an abortion was medically necessary (Haussman 2001, 66). Others joining in to push for liberalization included the Canadian Bar Association, the Canadian Labour Congress, and the Humanist Fellowship of Montreal, led by Dr Henry Morgentaler.

6   Interestingly, not even Justice Wilson dealt with the defence counsel's section 15 equality rights arguments or section 12 arguments regarding prohibitions against cruel and unusual treatment or punishment (Rodgers 2002, 335).

7   Justices McIntyre and LaForest disagreed with the majority because they felt that the Charter was silent on both the rights of women and the rights of the unborn, which meant that parliamentarians had decided that the Charter should have nothing to do with these issues. In other words, since the right was not explicitly articulated in the Charter, the Court should not read a right to abortion or to life into the Charter.

8   The Canadian Medical Association was also against the idea of recriminalization, arguing that abortion would be the only medical procedure labelled a crime, creating a major disincentive for doctors to perform abortions (Haussman 2001, 80).

9   In the United States, the reverse is true: 53 per cent of those surveyed in 2002 believed abortion is morally wrong, while 38 per cent believed abortion is morally acceptable. The Gallup public opinion survey has tracked opinion on abortion for a number of years. Since 1995, it has been polling on the question of whether Americans consider themselves 'pro-life' or 'pro-choice'. In 1995, 56 per cent of those polled described themselves as 'pro-choice' and 33 per cent 'pro-life'. Over time, those opinions have reversed. By May 2009, 51 per cent of those polled described themselves as 'pro-life' and 42 per cent 'pro-choice' (Gallup, 2009).

10 The PEI Court of Appeal ruled in *Morgentaler v. Prince Edward Island*, [1995] P.E.I.J. no. 20, 122 D.L.R. (4th) 728 that the province can refuse to pay for abortions performed in clinics (Richer 2008, 9). However, the Quebec Superior Court ruled in *Association pour l'accès à l'avortement c. Québec*, [2006] R.J.Q. 1938 that the Quebec government had to reimburse women who were charged extra fees in private clinics (because the Quebec government had lowered the reimbursement rate provided to physicians performing abortions in private clinics) (Richer 2008, 10).

11 Shaw (2006, 29) notes that a hospital in Iqaluit is now performing abortions.

12 Shaw (2006, 21) notes that as of July 2005, the province of Manitoba is now paying for abortion services in both hospitals and private clinics.

13 In *R. v. Morgentaler*, [1993] 3 S.C.R. 463 the Supreme Court of Canada ruled that provincial governments cannot legislatively prohibit abortion as that power falls under federal criminal law power (Richer 2008, 8).

14 Dr Morgentaler said that he decided to do so because women in the province had adequate access to abortion through Victoria General Hospital in Halifax (CP, 2003b).

15 *Borowski v. Canada (Attorney General)*, [1989] 1 S.C.R. 342. The details of the *Borowski* saga are covered in detail in Russell, Knopf, and Morton (1989, 547–56) from which the information in this section is extensively derived.

16 By this point, women's groups were increasingly applying for and being granted intervener status in Supreme Court cases. Intervener status means having the ability to participate in legal proceedings. In the *Borowski* case, the Court granted the Women's Legal Education and Action Fund (LEAF) intervener status, as well as the Interfaith Coalition on the Rights and Wellbeing of Women and Children, and REAL Women of Canada.

17 *Tremblay v. Daigle*, [1989] 2 S.C.R. 530.

18 The Canadian Charter of Rights did not apply because the matter involved a civil action between two private individuals.

19 These organizations included LEAF, the Canadian Abortion Rights Action League, and the Canadian Civil Liberties Union (to argue Daigle's case) and the Campaign Life Coalition, Canadian Physicians for Life, the Association des médicins du Québec pour le respect de la vie, and REAL Women of Canada (to argue Tremblay's case) (LEAF 1996, 103–4).

20 *R. v. Sullivan*, [1991] 1 S.C.R. 489.

21 Section 206 of the Criminal Code is quite specific about when that independent constitutional status is achieved: '(1) A child becomes a human being within the meaning of this Act when it has completely proceeded, in a living state, from the body of its mother whether or not (a) it has breathed, (b) it has an independent circulation, or (c) the navel string is severed; (2) a person commits homicide when he [sic] causes injury to a child before or during its birth as a result of which the child dies after becoming a human being.'

22 *R. v. Drummond*, [1996] 143 D.L.R. (4th) 368 (Ont. H.C.).
23 As Condit (1995, 38) argues, 'constructing the fetus as an independent person means recognizing the same distinct interests that all people have. In this framework, the needs and demands of the pregnant woman and her fetus may conflict': 'a woman's right to terminate a pregnancy is irreconcilable with the rights of a fetus to exist if the fetus is recognized as having such rights.'
24 Women have also been forced out of employment after becoming pregnant as well as banned from certain occupations because the workplace environment was deemed unsafe for women who might get pregnant (for example, Daniels 1993). Yet Field (1989) points out that even though exposure to some chemicals can harm men's reproductive capabilities, men are not banned from that type of employment.
25 *Dobson (Litigation Guardian of) v. Dobson*, [1997] 148 D.L.R. (4th) 332.
26 The circumstances behind this case are tragic. Cynthia Dobson was in a motor vehicle accident in 1993, 27 weeks pregnant when her car collided with a truck. The child was born by Caesarian section later that day, and the prenatal injuries caused permanent mental and physical impairment. Because the child's medical treatment was very expensive, and because Ms Dobson's insurance company was withholding money, the maternal grandfather, Gerald Price, the guardian of the child, launched a civil suit in 1995 alleging that the mother was negligent in not avoiding the accident. The question before the court was whether a mother should be liable in tort for damages to her child arising from a prenatal negligent act. A lower court judge ruled in the affirmative in 1997.
27 *Dobson (Litigation Guardian of) v. Dobson*, [1999] 2 S.C.R. 753.
28 *Winnipeg Child and Family Services (Northwest Area) v. G. (D.F.)*, [1997] 3 S.C.R. 925.
29 Mifepristone blocks the effects of progesterone, which is necessary for the fertilized egg to remain embedded in the uterus. Misoprostol induces labour.
30 In a case in Toronto in 1999, a man asked doctors to keep his pregnant but brain-dead wife connected to life support machines to let their 10-week-old fetus grow to the point of viability, a procedure the woman had not had time to consent to before she slipped into a coma (Foss 1999, A1, A8). The fetus died shortly afterwards, mooting the issue, but not before the husband and family's actions to keep the woman on life support prompted strong arguments on both sides of the debate.
31 *Reference re Assisted Human Reproduction Act*, 2010 SCC 61, reported at [2010] 3 S.C.R. 457.
32 See, for example, *Davis v. Davis*, 842 S.W.2d 588, 597 (Tenn. 1992). The ex-wife in this case wished to have the embryos transferred to herself in an effort to become pregnant. The ex-husband did not want the embryos to be used at all while he tried to decide whether he wanted to become a parent. After the initiation of the proceedings, both parties remarried, and the ex-wife decided that she no longer wanted to use the embryos herself but instead wanted to donate them to a childless couple. The ex-husband opposed that action as well. The couple had not signed a written agreement in advance of the fertilization procedure to set out clearly what to do with the embryos.

The Tennessee Supreme Court held that in a situation in which no prior agreement exists, one has to weigh and balance the interests of both parties. In this case, the court ruled that the interest of the person wishing to avoid procreation should prevail, as long as the other person had a 'reasonable possibility' of achieving parenthood by means other than use of the embryos. Given that Ms Davis wanted to donate the embryos and not use them herself, then the objecting party's interest in preventing the use of the embryos should prevail.
33 *In the Matter of Baby M.*, 109 N.J. 396 (1988).
34 Courts in Canada have also tended to rule that the woman who gives birth to a child is the legal mother, even if the egg comes from another woman (CP, 2003a, A12).
35 *Johnson v. Calvert*, 5 Cal. 4th 84 (1993).
36 Some researchers complain, for example, that Canada's ban against human cloning, contained in the final legislation, unduly limits the ability of researchers to clone human embryos in order to conduct stem-cell research and keep up with researchers around the world (Abraham 2005, A9).
37 *Doe v. Canada (Attorney General)*, 2007 ONCA 11.

Chapter 13

1 See also Peterson (1992), Tickner (1992), and Whitworth (1994).

2 For example, in 1907 the International Council of Women was one of only two NGOs invited to the Second Peace Conference at The Hague. Keck and Sikkink (1998, 55) argue 'This may be the earliest example of the now established practice of granting nongovernmental organizations a special role in international conferences.'

3 For women, however getting women on the agenda and into positions within the UN has not been without difficulty. As Enloe (1990, 121) comments, 'for an organization intended to change the world, the United Nations looked remarkably like the patriarchal status quo.' Women inside the United Nations have had to organize to make changes from within. For example, the Ad Hoc Group on Equal Rights for Women in the United Nations has lobbied the secretary general and the General Assembly since the 1980s to demand that women be appointed and promoted to more of the UN jobs that carry policy influence, technical responsibility and material rewards.

4 A growing critical literature on the global market for nannies and other immigrant workers includes Chang (2000), Hondagneu-Sotelo (2001), Parrenas (2001), Ehrenreich (2002), Tronto (2002), and Flanagan (2004).

5 The member organizations in the Joint Programme are UNHCR, UNICEF, WFP, UNDP, UNFPA, UNODC, ILO, UNESCO, WHO, and the World Bank.

References

Abortion Rights Coalition of Canada. 2010. *Anti-choice private member bills and motions introduced in Canada since 1987*. Online: http://www.arcc-cdac.ca/presentations/anti-bills.html.

Abraham, Carolyn. 2002. 'Woman with faulty gene gets embryo without it.' *The Globe and Mail* 27 February: A1, A9.

————. 2005. 'Embryo law outdated by advances, experts say.' *The Globe and Mail* 21 May: A9.

Achilles, Rona. 1993. 'Assisted reproduction: The social issues.' In Sandra Burt, Lorraine Code, and Lindsay Dorney (Eds), *Changing patterns: Women in Canada*, 488–516. Toronto: McClelland and Stewart.

Adams, Michael. 1998. *Sex in the snow: Canadian social values at the end of the millennium*. Toronto: Penguin Books.

Adamson, Nancy, Linda Briskin, and Margaret McPhail. 1988. *Feminist organizing for change: The contemporary women's movement in Canada*. Don Mills, ON: Oxford University Press.

Agnew, Vijay. 1996. *Resisting discrimination: Women from Asia, Africa and the Caribbean and the women's movement in Canada*. Toronto: University of Toronto Press.

Agocs, Carol and Bob Osborne. 2009. 'Comparing equity policies in Canada and Northern Ireland: Politic learning in two directions.' *Canadian Public Policy*, Vol. 35, No. 2, June 2009, pp. 237–262.

Akyeampong, Ernest B. 1994. 'Absenteeism at work.' *Canadian Social Trends* 2:279–81. Toronto: Thompson Educational Publishing with Statistics Canada.

————. 2004. 'Fact-sheet on work absences.' *Perspectives on Labour and Income* 5 (3) insert 2–10. Catalogue no. 75-001-XIE. Ottawa: Statistics Canada.

Alarcon, Cristina. 2009. 'The 'hijacking' of moral conscience from pharmacy practice: A Canadian perspective.' *The Annals of Pharmacotherapy* 43: 748–53.

Albanese, Patricia. 1996. 'Ethnic families.' In Maureen Baker (Ed.), *Families: Changing trends in Canada*, 3rd ed., 121–42. Toronto: McGraw-Hill Ryerson.

Alboim, Naomi. 1997. 'Institutional structure as change agent: An analysis of the Ontario Women's Directorate.' In Caroline Andrew and Sanda Rodgers (Eds), *Women and the Canadian state*, 220–7. Montreal and Kingston: McGill-Queen's University Press.

Alcoff, Linda. 1986. 'Cultural feminism versus post-structuralism: The identity crisis in feminist theory.' In Michelline Malson, Jean O'Barr, Sarah Westphal-Wihl and Mary Wyer (Eds), *Feminist theory in practice and process*, 295–326. Chicago: University of Chicago Press.

Allen, Douglas, et al. 2003. 'Don't kiss off marriage': Comment. *The Globe and Mail* 18 June: A19.

Allport, Jenny. 2004. 'Like oil and water.' *Bitch: Feminist Response to Pop Culture* 25: 53–4.

Almey, Marcia. 2006. *Women in Canada: Work chapter updates*. Cat. No. 89F0133XWE. Ottawa: Statistics Canada.

Alphonso, Caroline. 2005. '"Work within system", Morgentaler advises at 82'. *The Globe and Mail* 17 June: A3.

Ambert, Anne-Marie. 2002. *Divorce: Fact, causes, and consequences*. Ottawa: Vanier Institute of the Family.

American Psychological Association. 2007. 'Report of the task force on the sexualization of girls.' Available at: www.apa.org/pi/women/programs/girls/report.aspx

Andemahr, Sonya, Terry Lovell, and Carol Wolkowitz. 2000. *A glossary of feminist theory*. London: Arnold.

Anderssen, Erin. 2002a. 'Death in the nursery.' *The Globe and Mail* 16 March: F4.

————. 2002b. 'Paying for the sins of the father.' *The Globe and Mail* 11 May: F7.

Andrew, Caroline. 1984. 'Women and the welfare state.' *Canadian Journal of Political Science* 17: 667–83.

————, and Sandra Rodgers (Eds). 1997. *Women and the Canadian state/Les femmes et l'état canadien*. Montreal: McGill-Queen's University Press.

Angus Reid Group. 1999. 'Family matters: A look at issues concerning families and raising children in Canada today.' 27 September. http://www.ipsos-reid.com/search/pdf/media/pr990929_1.pdf.

Annan, Kofi. 2004. *Meeting global challenges: Healthy women, healthy world*. Address to the International Women's Health Coalition Third Annual Gala, 15 January.

Anzaldua, Gloria. 1990. 'La conciencia de la mestiza: Towards a new consciousness.' In Gloria Anzaldua (Ed.), *Making face, making soul: Haciendo caras creative and critical perspectives by feminists of color*, 377–89. San Francisco: aunt lute books.

AP. 1999. 'A birth spurs debate on using sperm after death.' *The New York Times* 27 March: A11.

AP. 2005. 'The unexpectant father.' *The Globe and Mail* 24 February, online ed.

Armstrong, Jane. 2002. 'B.C. court finds artistic merit in Sharpe's child-sex stories.' *The Globe and Mail* 27 March: A1, A4.

Armstrong, Pat. 1997. 'Pay equity: Not just a matter of money.' In Caroline Andrew and Sandra Rodgers (Eds), *Women and the Canadian state/Les femmes et l'état canadien*, 122–37. Montreal: McGill-Queen's University Press.

———. 2000. 'Restructuring public and private: Women's paid and unpaid work.' In Barbara Crow and Lise Gotell (Eds), *Open boundaries: A Canadian women's studies reader*, 184–93. Toronto: Prentice-Hall Canada.

———, and Mary Cornish. 1997. 'Restructuring pay equity for a restructured work force: Canadian perspectives.' *Gender, Work and Organization* 4:67–86.

Arneil, Barbara. 1999. *Politics and feminism*. Oxford: Blackwell.

———. 2006. *Diverse Communities: The Problem with Social Capital*. Cambridge UK: Cambridge University Press.

Arscott, Jane, and Linda Trimble. 1997. 'In the presence of women: Representation and political power.' In Jane Arscott and Linda Trimble (Eds), *In the presence of women: Representation in Canadian governments*, 1–17. Toronto: Harcourt Brace.

Ashford, Douglas. 1986. *The emergence of the welfare states*. Oxford and New York: Blackwell.

———, and E.W. Kelley (Eds). 1986. *Nationalizing social security in Europe and America*. Greenwich, CT: JAI Press.

Assembly of First Nations. 2010. '*AFN expresses concern over Pickton Inquiry mandate and chairperson*'. Online: http://www.newswire.ca/fr/releases/archive/September2010/30/c6859.html.

Astell, Mary. 1696/1970a. *A serious proposal to the ladies*. New York: Source Book Press.

———. 1697/1970b. *An essay in defence of the female sex*. New York: Source Book Press.

———. 1694 1970c. *Some reflections on marriage*. New York: Source Book Press.

Auger, Cheryl. 2010. 'Criminalized and licensed: Local politics and the regulation of sex work among consenting adults.' Paper presented to the Western Political Science Association, San Francisco, California, 3 April 2010.

AWID (Association for Women's Rights in Development). 2001. 'Is there a third wave of feminism emerging from young women? Interview with Shandi Miller on the state of feminism in young Canadian women.' http://www.awid.org/go.php?stid=89. Accessed 5 July 2004.

Bacchi, Carol Lee. 1999. *Women, policy and politics: The construction of policy problems*. London: Sage.

Backhouse, Constance, and David H. Flaherty (Eds). 1992. *Challenging times: The women's movement in Canada and the United States*, 21–38. Montreal and Kingston: McGill-Queen's University Press.

Bailey, Martha. 1999. *Marriage and marriage-like relationships*. Research report prepared for the Law Commission of Canada. http://www.lcc.gc.ca/en/themes/pr/cpra/bailey/bailey_main.asp.

Bailey, Sue. 2002. 'New child-porn bill unveiled.' *The Globe and Mail* 6 December: A12.

Baines, Beverley. 1993. 'Law, gender, equality.' In Sandra Burt, Lorraine Code, and Lindsay Dorney (Eds), *Changing patterns: Women in Canada*, 2nd ed., 243–78. Toronto: McClelland and Stewart.

Baines, Erin K. 2003. 'The contradictions of Canadian commitments to refugee women.' In Claire Tureene Sjolander, Heather A. Smith, and Deborah Stienstra (Eds). *Feminist perspectives on Canadian foreign policy*, 155–70. Don Mills, ON: Oxford University Press.

Bains, Camille. 2000. 'Doctors told to be more alert to heart disease among women: Signs differ from men and include jaw pain, nausea.' *The Toronto Star* 11 February: 33.

Baker, Michael, Jonathan Gruber, and Kevin Milligan. 2007. What we can learn From Quebec's Universal Child Care Program. E-brief. Toronto: C.D. Howe Institute.

Bakker, Isabella (Ed.). 1996. *Rethinking restructuring: Gender and change in Canada*. Toronto: University of Toronto Press.

Bala, Nicholas. 1999. 'A report from Canada's "gender war zone": Reforming the child-related provisions of the Divorce Act.' *Canadian Journal of Family Law* 16:163–227.

———. 2005. 'Equality and the family in historical and constitutional perspective.' Panel presentation, John and Mary A. Yaremko Programme on Multiculturalism and Human Rights Symposium and Companion Conference on Equality and the Family. 4 February, University of Toronto.

Banducci, Susan, Joanna Everitt, and Elisabeth Gidengil. 2002. 'Gender stereotypes of political candidates: A meta-analysis.' Paper prepared for the annual meeting of the International Society of Political Psychology, Berlin, Germany, 16–19 July.

Bannerji, Himani (Ed.). 1993. *Returning the gaze: Essays on racism, feminism and politics.* Toronto: Sister Vision Press.

Barakso, Maryann. 2004. *Governing now: Grassroots activism in the National Organization for Women.* Ithaca: Cornell University Press.

Barrette, Jacques. 2009. *Work/family balance: What do we really know? Contemporary family trends.* Ottawa: The Vanier Institute of the Family. Available at: www.vifamily.ca/sites/default/files/work_family_balance_1.pdf

Basden, Jane. 1993. 'Gales and gals: The Icelandic Women's Party.' *Herizons* 7, 3:13–14.

Bashevkin, Sylvia. 1985. *Toeing the lines: Women and party politics in English Canada.* Toronto: University of Toronto Press.

———. 1991. 'Women's participation in political parties.' In Kathy Megyery (Ed.), *Women in Canadian politics: Toward equity in representation*, 61–79. Vol. 6 of the research studies of the Royal Commission on Electoral Reform and Party Financing. Toronto: Dundurn Press: 61–79.

———. 1993. *Toeing the lines: Women and party politics in English Canada.* 2nd ed. Toronto: University of Toronto Press.

———. 1998. *Women on the defensive: Living through conservative times.* Toronto: University of Toronto Press.

———. 2002. *Welfare hot buttons: Women, work, and social policy reform.* Toronto: University of Toronto Press.

———. 2009. *Women, power, politics: The hidden story of Canada's unfinished democracy.* Don Mills, ON: Oxford University Press.

Baumgardner, Jennifer, and Amy Richards. 2000. *Manifesta: Young women, feminism and the future.* New York: Farrar, Straus and Giroux.

———. 2010. *Manifesta: Young women, feminism and the future. Tenth Anniversary Edition.* New York: Farrar, Straus and Giroux.

BCCLA (British Columbia Civil Liberties Association). 2000. '*R. v. Sharpe*: Intervenor factum.' Vancouver: BCCLA. http://www.bccla.org/othercontent/sharpescc.html.

Beaujot, Roderic. 2006. 'Gender models for family and work.' Horizons 8, no. 3 (April) pp. 24–6.

Beaupré, Pascale and Elizabeth Cloutier. 2006. Navigating family transitions: Evidence from the General Social Survey. Ottawa: Statistics Canada – Catalogue no. 89-625-XIE.

Beckwith, Karen. 1992. 'Comparative research and electoral systems: Lessons from France and Italy.' *Women and Politics* 12 (1):1–33.

Bedolla, Lisa García. 2007. 'Intersections of Inequality: Understanding Marginalization and Privilege in the Post-Civil Rights Era' *Politics and Gender* 3(2): 232–48.

Bégin, Monique. 1992. 'The Royal Commission on the Status of Women in Canada: Twenty years later.' In Constance Backhouse and David H. Flaherty (Eds), *Challenging times: The women's movement in Canada and the United States*, 21–38. Montreal and Kingston: McGill-Queen's University Press.

———. 1997. 'The Canadian government and the commission's report.' In Caroline Andrew and Sandra Rodgers (Eds), *Women and the Canadian state*, 13–26. Montreal: McGill-Queen's University Press.

Bellah, Robert N., Richard Madsen, William M. Sullivan, Ann Swidler, and Steven M. Tipton. 1985. *Habits of the heart: Individualism and commitment in American life.* New York: Harper and Row.

Belsey, Catherine. 1980. *Critical practice.* London: Methuen.

Benedet, Janine. 2001. '*Little Sisters Book and Art Emporium v. Minister of Justice*: Sex equality and the attack on *R. v. Butler*.' *Osgoode Hall Law Journal* 39:187–204.

Benhabib, Seyla. 1990. 'Epistemologies of postmodernism: A rejoinder to Jean-Francois Lyotard.' In Linda J. Nicholson (Ed.), *Feminism/postmodernism*, 107–30. New York: Routledge.

Benoit, Cecilia M. 2000. *Women, work and social rights: Canada in historical and comparative perspective.* Scarborough, ON: Prentice Hall.

Bergmann, Barbara R. 1998. 'The only ticket to equality: Total androgyny, male style.' *Journal of Contemporary Legal Issues* 9:75–86.

Berkovitch, N. 1999. 'The emergence and transformation of the international women's movement.' In J. Boli and G.M. Thomas (Eds), *Constructing world culture: International nongovernmental organizations since 1875*, 100–26. Stanford: Stanford University Press.

Bernhard, Judith, Patricia Landolt, and Luin Goldring. 2005. 'Transnational, multi-local motherhood: Separation and reunification among Latin American families in Canada.' CERIS working paper 40. http://ceris.metropolis.net/research-policy/wkpp_list.htm.

Black, Jerome H. 2002. 'Representation in the Parliament of Canada: The case of ethnoracial minorities.' In Joanna Everitt and Brenda O'Neill (Eds), *Citizen politics: Research and theory in Canadian political behaviour*, 355–72. Don Mills, ON: Oxford University Press.

———. 2003. 'Differences that matter: Minority women mps, 1993–2000.' In Manon Tremblay and Linda Trimble (Eds), *Women and electoral politics in Canada*, 59–74. Don Mills, ON: Oxford University Press.

———. 2008a. 'Ethnoracial minorities in the 38th Parliament: Patterns of change and continuity.' In Caroline Andrew (Ed.), *Electing a diverse Canada: The representation of immigrants, minorities, and women*. Vancouver: UBC Press: 229–53.

———. 2008b. 'The 2006 federal election and visible minority candidates: More of the same?' *Canadian Parliamentary Review* (Autumn): 30–36.

———, and Lynda Erickson. 2003. 'Women candidates and voter bias: Do women politicians need to be better?' *Electoral Studies* 22: 81–100.

Black, Naomi. 1988. 'The Canadian women's movement: The second wave.' In Sandra Burt, Lorraine Code, Lindsay Dorney (Eds), *Changing patterns: Women in Canada*, 80–102. Toronto: McClelland and Stewart.

Blais, André, Elisabeth Gidengil, Richard Nadeau, and Neil Nevitte. 2002. *Anatomy of a Liberal victory: Making sense of the vote in the 2000 Canadian election*. Peterborough, ON: Broadview Press.

Blank, Robert, and Janna C. Merrick. 1995. *Human reproduction, emerging technologies and conflicting rights*. Washington: Congressional Quarterly Press.

Bock, Gisela, and Pat Thane (Eds). 1991. *Maternity and gender policies: Women and the rise of the European welfare states, 1880s–1950s*. London and New York: Routledge.

Bookman, Ann, and Sandra Morgan (Eds). 1988. *Women and the politics of empowerment*. Philadelphia: Temple University Press.

Bordo, Susan. 1990. 'Feminism, postmodernism, and gender-scepticism.' In Linda J. Nicholson (Ed.), *Feminism/postmodernism*, 133–56. New York: Routledge.

———. 1993. *Unbearable weight: Feminism, Western culture, and the body*. Berkeley and Los Angeles: University of California Press.

Boyd, Susan B. (Ed.). 1997a. *Challenging the public/private divide: Feminism, law, and public policy*. Toronto: University of Toronto Press.

———. 1997b. 'Looking beyond Tyabji: Employed mothers: Lifestyles and child custody law.' In Susan Boyd (Ed.), *Challenging the public/private divide: Feminism, law and public policy*, 253–79. Toronto: University of Toronto Press.

———. 2000a. 'Can child custody law move beyond the politics of gender?' *University of New Brunswick Law Journal* 49:157–68.

———. 2000b. 'Custody, access, and relocation in a mobile society.' In Dorothy E. Chunn and Dany Lacombe (Eds), *Law as a gendering practice*, 158–80. Toronto: Oxford University Press.

———. 2001. 'Backlash and the construction of legal knowledge: The case of child custody law.' *Windsor Yearbook of Access to Justice* 20:141–65.

———. 2003a. *Child custody, law, and women's work*. Toronto: Oxford University Press.

———. 2003b. 'From custody and access to parental responsibilities? What does Bill C-22 offer to women and children?' *Jurisfemme: News from the National Association of Women and the Law* 22 (1) http://www.nawl.ca.

———. 2007. 'Gendering legal parenthood: Bio-genetic ties, intentionality and responsibility.' *Windsor Yearbook of Access to Justice* 25: 55–85.

———. 2010. 'Autonomy for mothers? Relational theory and parenting apart.' *Feminist Legal Studies* 18: 137–58.

Brean, Joseph. 2002. 'Joint custody on the rise in divorce settlements, Statistics Canada finds.'

National Post 3 December. http://www.fact.on.ca/news/news0212/np021203.htm

Brock, Deborah. 2000. 'Victim, nuisance, fallen woman, outlaw, worker? Making the identity "prostitute" in Canadian criminal law.' In Dorothy E. Chunn and Dany Lacombe (Eds), *Law as a gendering practice*, 79–99. Don Mills, ON: Oxford University Press.

Brockman, Joan. 2001. *Gender in the legal profession: Filling or breaking the mould?* Vancouver: University of British Columbia Press.

Brodie, Janine. 1995. *Politics on the margins: Restructuring and the Canadian women's movement.* Halifax: Fernwood Press.

——— (Ed.). 1996. *Women and Canadian public policy.* Toronto: Harcourt Brace.

———, and Isabella Bakker. 2007. *Canada's social policy regime and women: An assessment of the last decade.* Ottawa: Research Directorate Status of Women Canada, March 2007.

———, and Isabella Bakker. 2008. *Where are the women? Gender equity, budgets and Canadian public policy.* Ottawa: Canadian Centre for Policy Alternatives.

Brodie, Shelley, A.M. Gavigan, and Jane Jenson. 1992. *The politics of abortion.* Don Mills, ON: Oxford University Press.

Brooks, Abigail. 2004. 'Under the knife and proud of it: An analysis of the normalization of cosmetic surgery.' *Critical Sociology* 30:207–39.

Brooks, Stephen. 2000. *Canadian democracy: An introduction.* 2nd ed. Don Mills, ON: Oxford University Press.

Brown, Rita Mae. 2000. 'Roxanne Dunbar: How a female heterosexual serves the interests of male supremacy.' In Barbara Crow (Ed.), *Radical feminism: A documentary reader.* New York: New York University Press.

Brown, Wendy. 1983. 'Reproductive freedom and the right to privacy: A paradox for feminists.' In Irene Diamond (Ed.), *Families, politics, and public policy: A feminist dialogue on women and the state,* 322–38. New York: Longman.

Brownmiller, Susan. 1975. *Against our will: Men, women and rape.* New York: Simon and Schuster.

———. 1984. *Femininity.* New York: Fawcett Columbine.

Brunt, Rosalind. 1990. 'The politics of identity.' In Stuart Hall and Martin Jacques (Eds), *New times: The changing face of politics in the 1990s,* 150–9. London: Lawrence and Wishart.

Brush, Lisa D. 2002. 'Changing the subject: Gender and welfare regime studies.' *Social Politics.* Summer 2002, pp. 161–86.

Bunch, Charlotte. 1975. 'Lesbians in revolt.' In Nancy Myron and Charlotte Bunch (Eds), *Lesbianism and the women's movement,* 12–20. Baltimore: Diana Press.

———. 1990. 'Women's rights as human rights: Toward a re-vision of human rights.' *Human Rights Quarterly* 12:486–98.

Burrell, Barbara. 1994. *A woman's place is in the House: Campaigning for Congress in the feminist era.* Ann Arbor: University of Michigan Press.

———. 1998. 'Campaign finance: Women's experience in the modern era.' In Sue Thomas and Clyde Wilcox (Eds), *Women and elective office: Past, present, and future,* 26–37. New York: Oxford University Press.

———. 2000. 'Hillary Rodham Clinton as First lady: the people's perspective.' *The Social Science Journal* 37 (4): 529–46.

Burstyn, Varda (Ed.). 1985. *Women against censorship.* Vancouver: Douglas and McIntyre.

Burt, Sandra. 1990. 'Organized women's groups.' In William D. Coleman and Grace Skogstad (Eds), *Policy communities and public policy in Canada: A structural approach,* 191–211. Toronto: Copp Clark Pitman.

———. 1994. 'The women's movement: Working to transform public life.' In James P. Bickerton and Alain-G. Gagnon, *Canadian politics,* 2nd ed., 207–23. Peterborough, ON: Broadview Press.

———. 1995. 'Gender and public policy: Making some difference in Ottawa.' In François-Pierre Gingras (Ed), *Gender politics in contemporary Canada,* 86–105. Don Mills, ON: Oxford University Press.

———. 1997. 'The status of women: Learning to live without the state.' In Andrew F. Johnson and Andrew Stritch (Eds), *Canadian public policy: Globalization and political parties,* 251–74. Toronto: Copp Clark.

———. 2000. 'Looking backward and thinking ahead: Toward a gendered analysis of Canadian politics.' In Michael Whittington and Glen Williams (Eds), *Canadian politics in the 21st century,*

303–26. Scarborough, ON: Nelson Thomson Learning.

——, and Elizabeth Lorenzin. 1997. 'Taking the women's movement to Queen's Park: Women's interests and the New Democratic Government of Ontario.' In Jane Arscott and Linda Trimble (Eds), *In the presence of women: Representation in Canadian governments*, 202–27. Toronto: Harcourt Brace.

Burton, Sarah. 2004. 'The person behind the persons case.' *Beaver* 84:14–19.

Busby, Karen. 1994. 'LEAF and pornography: Litigating on equality and sexual representations.' *Canadian Journal of Law and Society* 9:165–92.

——. 1999. *LEAF and the Little Sisters case: Some issues to consider.* Issue paper commissioned by LEAF and available on the LEAF website in 1999–2000. On file with authors.

——. n.d. Little Sisters v. Canada: *What did the queer-sensitive intervenors argue?* Unpublished paper. http://www.umanitoba.ca/faculties/law/newsite/Courses/Busby/Const/littlesisters.pdf

Butler, Judith. 1990. *Gender trouble: Feminism and the subversion of identity.* New York: Routledge.

Byrne, Lesley Hyland. 1997. 'Feminists in power: Women cabinet ministers in the New Democratic Party (ndp) Government of Ontario', 1990–1995. *Policy Studies Journal* 25 (4):601–12.

Cameron, Angela. 2008. 'Regulating the queer family: The *Assisted Human Reproduction Act*.' *Canadian Journal of Family Law* 24: 101–22.

Cameron, Jamie. 1992. 'Abstract principle v. contextual conceptions of harm: A comment on R. v. Butler.' *McGill Law Journal* 37:1135–57.

Cameron, Stevie. 2010. *On the farm: Robert William Pickton and the tragic story of Vancouver's missing women.* Toronto: Knopf Canada.

Campbell, Angela. 2005. *How have policy approaches to polygamy responded to women's experiences and rights? An international, comparative analysis.* Final Report for Status of Women Canada. Online: http://papers.ssrn.com/sol3/papers.cfm?abstract_id=1360230

Campbell, Gail G. 1989. 'Disfranchised but not quiescent: Women petitioners in New Brunswick in the mid-19th century.' *Acadensis* 18 (2):22–54

——. 1990. 'The most restrictive franchise in British North America? A case study.' *Canadian Historical Review* 71 (2):158–88.

——. 2007. 'Conceiving parents through law.' *International Journal of Law, Policy and the Family* 21: 242–273.

Campion-Smith, Bruce, and Les Whittington. 2010. 'Long-gun registry survives tight Commons vote.' *Toronto Star.* Wed Sep 22 2010. http://www.thestar.com/news/canada/gunregistry/article/864804--long-gun-registry-survives-tight-commons-vote

Canada. Parliament. 2002. *The Canadian parliamentary guide.* Scarborough, ON: Thomson Gale.

Canada. Special Joint Committee on Custody and Access. 1998a. *For the sake of the children: Final report of the Special Joint Committee on Custody and Access.* Ottawa: Public Works and Government Services.

Canada. Special Joint Committee on Custody and Access. 1998b. *Proceedings of the Special Joint Committee on Child Custody and Access.* Ottawa: Public Works and Government Services.

Canadian Abortion Rights Action League. 2003. *Protecting abortion rights in Canada.* Ottawa: CARAL.

Canadian Alliance. 2002. *Declaration of Policy.* Calgary: The Party.

Canadian Centre for Justice. 2001. *Women in Canada.* Statistics Profile Series. Ottawa: Statistics Canada. Catalogue no. 85F0033MIE, June.

Canadian Feminist Alliance for International Action & Canadian Labour Congress. 2010. Reality check: Women in Canada and the Beijing Declaration and Platform for Action fifteen years on: A Canadian Civil Society response. February 22, 2010. Available online at http://www.fafia-afai.org/files/2010-02-22-Canada-Beijing+15-NGO-Report-EN.pdfs

Canadian Relocation Systems. 'Day Care and Child Care', 2004. http://relocatecanada.com/daycare.html. Accessed 12 August 2004.

Carbert, Louise. 2002. 'Historical influences on regional patterns of the election of women to provincial legislatures.' In William Cross (Ed.), *Political parties, representation, and electoral democracy in Canada*, 201–22. Don Mills, ON: Oxford University Press.

Carmichael, Amy. 2004. 'NAC seeks money to consult women.' *The Hamilton Spectator* 15 March: A10.

Carse, Alisa L. 1997. 'Pornography: An uncivil liberty?' In Patrice DiQuinzio and Iris Marion Young (Eds), *Feminist ethics and social policy*, 226–54. Bloomington and Indianapolis: Indiana University Press.

Carty, Linda (Ed.). 1993. *And still we rise: Feminist political mobilizing in contemporary Canada.* Toronto: Women's Press.

Cataldi, Sue. 1995. 'Reflections on "male bashing".' *NWSA Journal* 7 (2):76–85.

CAWP (Center for American Women in Politics). 2005. *Women of color in elective office* 2005. New Brunswick, NJ: cawp. http://www.rci.rutgers.edu/~cawp/Facts/Officeholders/color.pdf

CBC (Canadian Broadcasting Corporation). 2004. *Canada's child-care system languishing: oecd.* 25 October. www.cbc.ca/story/canada/national/2004/10/25/childcare_041025.html

CBC.ca. 2003. '"Nice boots" campaign draws unions' ire.' *cbc.ca News* 7 October. http://www.cbc.ca.

CBC Radio. 2010. Abortion coercion: Bill C-510. *The Current*. CBC Radio One. December 14, 2010.

Chang, Grace. 2000. *Disposable domestics: Immigrant women workers in the global economy.* Cambridge, MA: South End Press.

Chappell, Louise. 2002. *Gendering government: Feminist engagement with the state in Australia and Canada.* Vancouver: University of British Columbia Press.

Cheney, Peter. 2000. 'Is pornography out of control?' *The Globe and Mail* 2 December: F4, F5.

Chicha, Marie Thérèse. 2006. 'A comparative analysis of promoting pay equity: model and impacts.' Geneva: ILO, 2006.

Childbirth by Choice Trust. 1998. *No choice: Canadian women tell their stories of illegal abortion.* Toronto: The Trust.

———. 2005. *Abortion: The medical procedure.* http://www.cbctrust.com/medproc.html

Childcare Resource and Research Unit. 2007. 'Early childhood education and care in Canada.' www.childcarecanada.org/pubs/other/spaces/ccspacesstatistics07.pdf

———. 2009. 'Trends and analysis 2008: Quick facts.' www.childcarecanada.org. Accessed June 10, 2010.

Christian, Barbara. 1997. 'The race for theory.' In Sandra Kemp and Judith Squires (Eds), *Feminisms*, 69–78. Oxford: Oxford University Press.

Clark, Anne Marie, Elisabeth J. Friedman, and Kathryn Hochstetler. 1998. 'The sovereign limits of global civil society: A comparison of ngo participation in un World Conferences on the Environment, Human Rights, and Women.' *World Politics* 51 (1):1–35.

Clark, Campbell. 2002. 'PM scolds Liberal dissenter.' *The Globe and Mail* 28 January: A1, A4.

Clark, Warren. 2001. 'Economic gender equality indicators.' Insert in *Social Trends*, spring, no. 60 insert 1–8.

Clemens, Elizabeth S. 1999. 'Organizational repertoires and institutional change: Women's groups and transformation of American politics,' in Theda Skocpol and Morris P. Fiorina (Eds), *Civic engagement in American democracy.* Washington, D.C.: Brookings Institution.

Clemetson, Lynette. 2004. 'For abortion rights cause, a new diversity.' *New York Times* 24 April: A10.

CNN. 2004. 'Smart, savvy, strong-willed Rice charts her own course.' *People in the News Profile.* Online: www.cnn.com/cnn/Programs/People/shows/rice/profile.html

———. 2009. 'Sex trade, forced labour top UN human trafficking list.' February 16, 2009. http// edition.cnn.com/2009/WORLD/asiapcf/ow/16/un.trafficking. Accessed February 18, 2010.

Code, Lorraine. 1993. 'Feminist theory.' In Sandra Burt, Lorraine Code, and Lindsay Dorney (Eds), *Changing patterns: Women in Canada*, 2nd ed., 19–58. Toronto: McClelland and Stewart.

———. 1995. 'How do we know? Questions of method in feminist practice.' In Sandra Burt and Lorraine Code (Eds), *Changing methods: Feminists transforming practice*, 13–44. Peterborough, ON: Broadview Press.

——— (Ed). 2000. *Encyclopedia of feminist theories.* London: Routledge.

Cohen, Jonathan and Nikki Gershbain. 2001. 'For the sake of the fathers? Child custody reform and the perils of maximum contact.' *Canadian Family Law Quarterly* 19:121–83.

Cohen, Roberta. 1998. 'Protecting internally displaced women and children.' In Wendy Davies (Ed.), *Rights have no borders: Internal displacement world wide.* Norwegian Refugee Council/Global IDPSurvey. www.nrc.no/global_idp_survey/rights_have_no_borders/

Cohen, Yolande. 2000. 'Chronologie d'une émancipation. Questions féministes sur la citoyenneté des femmes.' *Globe: Revue internationale d'études québécoises* 3 (2):43–65.

Coleman, William D., and Grace Skogstad (Eds). 1990. *Policy communities and public policy in Canada: A structural approach.* Mississauga, ON: Copp Clark Pitman.

College of Physicians and Surgeons of Alberta. 2000. *Termination of Pregnancy: cpsa Policy.* June. http:// www.cpsa.ab.ca/publicationsresources/attachments_policies/Termination%20of%20Pregnancy.pdf

Colley, Susan. 1983. 'Free universal day care: The ofl takes a stand.' In Linda Briskin and Lynda Yanz (Eds), *Union sisters: Women in the labour movement*, 307–21. Toronto: The Women's Press.

Collier, Cheryl N. 2005. 'Do strong women's movements get results? Measuring the impact of child care and anti-violence movements in Ontario 1970–2000.' Paper presented at the annual meeting of the Canadian Political Science Association, 2–4 June, London, ON.

Collins, Daryl, Jonathan Morduch, Stuart Rutherford, and Orlanda Ruthven. 2009. *Portfolios of the Poor*. Princeton, NJ: Princeton University Press.

Collins, Gail. 2009. *When everything changed: The amazing journey of American women from 1960 to the present*. New York: Little, Brown and Company.

Collins, Patricia Hill. 1990. *Black feminist thought: Knowledge, consciousness, and the politics of empowerment*. Boston: Unwin Hyman.

Condit, Deidre Moira. 1995. 'Fetal personhood: Political identity under construction.' In Patricia Boling (Ed.), *Expecting trouble: Surrogacy, fetal abuse, and new reproductive technologies*, 25–54. Boulder, CO: Westview Press.

Conservative Party of Canada. 2006. *Stand up For Canada: Conservative Party of Canada federal election platform 2006._*

Cooke-Reynolds, Melissa, and Nancy Zukewich. 2004. 'The feminization of work.' *Canadian Social Trends* 72:24–9. Statistics Canada Catalogue no. 11-008.

Cool, Julie. 2004. 'Prostitution in Canada: An overview.' Ottawa: Library of Parliament, Political and Social Affairs Division. 1 September, 2004.

———. 2007. Child care in Canada: The federal role. Ottawa: Library of Parliament, PRB 04-20E

———. 2010. *Women in Parliament*. Background Paper No. 05-62-E. Ottawa: Library of Parliament.

Coontz, Stephanie. 1992. *The way we never were: American families and the nostalgia trap*. New York: Basic Books.

Cooper, Sandi E. 2002. 'Peace as a human right: The invasion of women into the world of high international politics.' *Journal of Women's History* 14 (2):9–27.

Copp, Terry. 1974. *The anatomy of poverty: The condition of the working class in Montreal, 1897–1929*. Toronto: McClelland and Stewart.

Cornish, Mary. 2008. 'Much work to be done on pay equity.' *Canadian HR Reporter*, February 25, 2008, p. 22.

——— and Fay Faraday. 2009. 'Pro-active employment equity obligations in Ontario and provincially regulated workplaces.' Cavalluzzo,Hayes, Shilton, McIntyre & Cornish, Barristers and Solicitors, Toronto, March 12, p. 12

Cossman, Brenda. 2002. 'Sexing citizenship, privatizing sex.' *Citizenship Studies* 6, 4: 483–506.

———. 2005. 'Contesting conservatisms, family feuds and the privatization of dependency.' *American University Journal of Gender, Social Policy and Law* 13: 415–509.

———. 2008. 'Betwixt and between recognition: Migrating same-sex marriages and the turn toward the private.' *Law and Contemporary Problems* 71: 153–168.

———, and Shannon Bell. 1997. 'Introduction.' In Brenda Cossman, Shannon Bell, Lise Gotell, and Becki L. Ross (Eds), *Bad attitude/s on trial: Pornography, feminism, and the Butler decision*, 3–47. Toronto: University of Toronto Press.

———, Shannon Bell, Lise Gotell, and Becki L. Ross (Eds). 1997. *Bad attitude/s on trial: Pornography, feminism, and the Butler decision*. Toronto: University of Toronto Press.

Côté, Andrée, and Julie Lassonde. 2007. 'Status report on pay equity in Canada.' National Association of Women and the Law Final Report of the Workshop on Pay Equity, 2–3 May, 2007 (Ottawa), pp. 1–14. Available online: http://www.nawl.ca/ns/en/documents/200709NAWLRepor tPayEquity.pdf

Côté, Andrée, and Pamela Cross. 2003. *Preliminary analysis of Bill C-22, an Act to Amend the Divorce Act*. Analysis prepared for the National Association of Women and the Law, the Ontario Women's Justice Network, and the Ontario Women's Network on Child Custody and Access. http://owjn. org/custody/c-22.htm

———, Carole Curtis, and Eileen Morrow. 2001. *Brief to the Federal-Provincial-Territorial Family Law Committee on Custody, Access and Child Support*. Brief prepared for the Ontario Women's Network on Custody and Access. http://www.owjn.org/custody/brief-e.htm

CP (Canadian Press). 1994. 'Morgentaler opens N.B. abortion clinic.' *The Globe and Mail* 29 June: A4.

———. 1997a. 'Fetus shot in suicide bid, court told.' *The Globe and Mail* 4 February: A6.

———. 1997b. 'Mother sued over prenatal injuries.' *The Globe and Mail* 4 February: A6.

———. 2000. 'Controversial same sex bill passes Commons.' *Virtual News Library* (Internet edition)

11 April.

———. 2002. 'Manitoba gay couples to get property rights.' *The Globe and Mail* 18 July: A6.

———. 2003a. 'Biological mother loses bid to be recognized.' *The Globe and Mail* 10 May: A12.

———. 2003b. 'Morgentaler closes Halifax abortion clinic.' *The Canadian Press Wire Service* 27 November.

———. 2003c. 'Women put the boots to sexist ad campaign.' *The Globe and Mail* 9 October: A9.

Cranswick, Kelly and Donna Dosman. 2008. 'Eldercare: What we know today.' *Canadian Social Trends*. Ottawa: Statistics Canada, October 21, 2008, Catalogue no. 11-008. pp. 48–54.

Crenshaw, Kimberlé Williams. 1991. 'Mapping the margins: Intersectionality, identity politics, and violence against women of color.' *Stanford Law Review* 43:1241–99.

———. 1997. 'Beyond racism and misogyny: Black feminism and 2 Live Crew.' In Cathy J. Cohen, Kathleen B. Jones, and Joan C. Tronto (Eds), *Women transforming politics: An alternative reader*, 549–68. New York: NYU Press.

Crittenden, Ann. 2001. *The price of motherhood: Why the most important job in the world is still the least valued*. New York: Henry Holt.

Crittenden, Danielle. 1996. 'The mother of all problems.' *Saturday Night* April: 44–54.

———. 1999. *What our mothers didn't tell us: Why happiness eludes the modern woman*. New York: Simon and Schuster.

Crosariol, Beppi. 2004. 'New spousal support rules welcomed by family lawyers.' *The Globe and Mail* 23 August: B11.

Crow, Barbara, and Lise Gotell. 2000. Chapter 2: 'Canadian women's movements.' In Barbara Crow and Lise Gotell (Eds), *Open boundaries: A Canadian women's studies reader*, 65–9. Toronto: Prentice-Hall Canada.

Cummings, Laura. 2003. 'The diet business: Banking on failure.' BBC *News Online Edition* 5 February. http://news.bbc.co.uk

Daalder, A.L. 2007. 'Prostitution in the Netherlands since the lifting of the brothel ban.' Amsterdam: WODC. www.wodc.nl www.wodc.nl/images/ob249a_fulltext_tcm44-83466.pdf. Accessed 15 January 2010.

Dabitch. 2003. 'Terra Boots terrorised by boot clad women.' *Adland* 9 October. http://ad-rag.com.

Daly, Mary. 1979. *Gyn/ecology: The metaethics of radical feminism*. London: Women's Press.

———. 1987. *Websters' First New Intergalactic Wickedary of the English Language*. Boston: Beacon Press.

Daniels, Cynthia. 1993. *At women's expense: State power and the politics of fetal rights*. Cambridge, MA: Harvard University Press.

———. 1997. 'Between fathers and fetuses: The social construction of male reproduction and the politics of fetal harm.' *Signs* 22:579–616.

Darcy, R., and Charles Hadley. 1988. 'Black women in politics: The puzzle of success.' *Social Science Quarterly* 69 (3): 629–45.

Davidson, Julia O'Connell. 2002. 'The rights and wrongs of prostitution.' *Hypatia* 17:84–98.

——— and Petter Gottschalk (Eds). 2011. *Internet child abuse: current research and policy*. New York: Routledge.

Davis, Angela. 1981. *Women, race and class*. New York: Random House.

———. 1989. *Women, culture, and politics*. New York: Random House.

Davis, Kathy. 1991. 'Remaking the she-devil: A critical look at feminist approaches to beauty.' *Hypatia* 6:21–43.

Day, Shelagh. 2003. 'Women's human rights: Canada at home and abroad.' In Claire Turenne Sjolander, Heather A. Smith, and Deborah Stienstra (Eds), *Feminist perspectives on Canadian foreign policy*, 126–35. Don Mills, ON: Oxford University Press.

de Beauvoir, Simone. 1952. *The second sex*. New York: Vintage Books.

de Gouges, Olympe. 1789/1989. *The rights of woman*. (Val Stevenson, trans.) London: Pythia Press.

Delany, Sheila. 1997. 'Mothers to think back through: Who are they? The ambiguous example of Christine de Pizan.' In Renate Blumenfeld-Kosinski (Ed.), *The selected writings of Christine de Pizan*, 312–28. New York: W.W. Norton.

de Lauretis, Teresa. 1991. 'Introduction: Queer theory: Lesbian and gay sexualities.' *differences* special issue, 3 (2):iii–xviii.

Della Porta, Donatella, and Mario Diani. 1999. *Social movements: An introduction*. Oxford: Blackwell

Press.

Delorey, A.M. 1989. 'Joint legal custody: A reversion to patriarchal power.' *Canadian Journal of Women and the Law* 3:33–44.

Demerson, Velma. 2004. *Incorrigible.* Waterloo, ON: Wilfrid Laurier University Press.

Department of Justice Canada. 2004a. *Canada Labour Code.* R.S. 1985, c. L-2. http://laws.justice. gc.ca/en/L-2/index.html

———. 2004b. *Canadian Human Rights Act.* R.S. 1985, c. H-6. http://laws.justice.gc.ca/en/H-6/index.html.

———. 2004c. *Support enforcement.* http://canada.justice.gc.ca/en/ps/sup/enforcement/index.html.

———. 2005a. *Pay equity review: Introduction: History of pay equity in Canada.* http://canada.justice. gc.ca/en/payeqsal/1100.html.

———. 2005b. *Spousal abuse: A fact sheet from the Department of Justice Canada.* Ottawa: Department of Justice Canada. Online: http://www.justice.gc.ca/en/ps/fm/spouseafs.html.

———. 2010a. 'Statement by Justice Minister Rob Nicholson following the Ontario Court of Appeal Stay Decision on the Bedford Prostitution Challenge.' December 2, 2010. http://www.justice. gc.ca/eng/news-nouv/nr-cp/2010/doc_32579.html. Accessed 10 February 2010.

———. 2010b. 'Government takes action to protect children from sexual predators.' November 4, 2010. http://www.justice.gc.ca/eng/news-nouv/nr-cp/2010/doc_32570.html. Accessed 11 February, 2011.

———. 2010c. 'Government of Canada introduces legislation protecting children from online sexual exploitation.' 6 May 2010. http://www.justice.gc.ca/eng/news-nouv/nr-cp/2010/doc_32509. html. Accessed 11 February 2011.

De Pizan, Christine. 1982. *The book of the city of ladies* (Earl Jeffrey Richards, trans.) New York: Quality Paperback Books.

———. 1997. *The selected writings of Christine de Pizan* (Renate Blumenfeld-Kosinski, Ed., Renate Blumenfeld-Kosinski and Kevin Brownlee, trans.). New York: W.W. Norton.

De Smet, Luke. 2010. 'Mad Men, season 4, episode 9, "The beautiful girls."' (21 September). Online: http://www.slantmagazine.com/house/2010/09/mad-men-season-4-episode-9-the-beautiful-girls/.

Dhillon, Sunny. 2011. 'Landmark ruling ends sperm and egg donor anonymity in B.C.' *The Globe and Mail* 19 May.

Dick, Caroline. 2006. 'The politics of intragroup difference: First Nations' women and the *Sawridge* dispute" *Canadian Journal of Political Science* 39 (1): 97-116.

Dietz, Mary G. 2003. 'Current Controversies in Feminist Theory.' *American Review of Political Science.* 6. 2003: 399–431.

DiManno, Rosie. 2010. 'Sexual anarchy does not await.' *Toronto Star.* Sunday 28 November 2010.

Doane, Mary Ann. 1987. 'Film and the masquerade.' *Screen* 23, pp. 3–4, 77–8.

Dobrowolsky, Alexandra. 2000a. *The politics of pragmatism: Women, representation, and constitutionalism in Canada.* Don Mills, ON: Oxford University Press.

———. 2000b. 'Intersecting identities and inclusive institutions: Women and a future transformative politics.' *Journal of Canadian Studies* 35 (4):240–59

———. 2009. 'Introduction: Neo-liberalism and after?' in Alexandra Dobrowolsky (ed.) *Women and public policy in Canada: Neo-liberalism and after?,* 1–24. Don Mills, ON: Oxford University Press.

———, and Jane Jenson. 2004. 'Shifting representations of citizenship: Canadian politics of "women" and "children".' *Social Politics: International Studies in Gender, State and Society* 11 (2):154–80.

———, and Ruth Lister. 2008. 'Social Investment: The Discourse and Dimensions of Change,' in Martin Powell, ed., *Modernising the Welfare State: The Blair Legacy.* Bristol: Policy Press, pp. 125–42.

Docherty, David C. 2002a. 'Citizens and legislators: Different views on representation.' In Neil Nevitte (Ed.), *Value change and governance in Canada,* 165–206. Toronto: University of Toronto Press.

———. 2002b. 'Political careers in Canada.' In Joanna Everitt and Brenda O'Neill (Eds), *Citizen politics: Research and theory in Canadian political behaviour,* 338–54. Don Mills, ON: Oxford University Press.

Dolan, Kathleen. 'Gender differences in support for women candidates: Is there a glass ceiling in American politics?' *Women and Politics* 17:27–41.

Dominus, Susan. 2004. 'What women want to watch.' *New York Times* 29 August: AR1, 6.

Dovi, Suzanne. 2002. 'Preferable descriptive representatives: Will just any woman, Black, or Latino do?' *American Political Science Review* 96 (4):729–43.

Dowling, Colette. 2000. 'Men: Meet your match.' *The Globe and Mail* 17 October: A19.

Drakich, Janice. 1989. 'In search of the better parent: The social construction of ideologies of fatherhood.' *Canadian Journal of Women and the Law* 3:69–87.

Drolet, Marie. 2001. 'The male-female wage gap.' *Perspectives on Labour and Income.* 2 (12):5–11. Statistics Canada Catalogue no. 75-001-XIE.

———. 2003. 'Motherhood and paycheques.' *Canadian Social Trends* 68:19–21. Statistics Canada Catalogue no. 11-008.

———. 2008. 'Not my mother's labour market: The evolution of gender pay differences.' Paper presented to the Pay Equity Commission Conference, Women and the Workforce: Opening doors, Closing the Gap. Toronto, ON. 5 November 2008. http://www.payequity.gov.on.ca/peo/english/pubs_conf/drolet.pdf. Accessed 8 December 2009.

Duffy, Ann, and Norene Pupo. 1992. *Part-time paradox: Connecting gender, work and family.* Toronto: McClelland and Stewart.

Duits, Linda and Liesbet van Zoonen. 2006. 'Headscarves and porno-chic: Disciplining girls bodies in the European multicultural society.' *European Journal of Women's Studies*, Vol. 13 No. 2: 103–7.

Dumont, Micheline. 1992. 'The origins of the women's movement in Quebec.' In Constance Backhouse and David H. Flaherty (Eds), *Challenging times: The women's movement in Canada and the United States*, 72–89. Montreal and Kingston: McGill-Queen's University Press.

Dworkin, Andrea. 1981. *Pornography: Men possessing women.* New York: Perigee Books.

———. 1983. *Right-wing women.* New York: Perigee Books.

Dylan, Arielle, Cheryl Regehr, and Ramona Alaggia. 2008. 'And justice for all? Aboriginal victims of sexual violence.' *Violence Against Women* 14, 6: 678–96.

Edut, Ophira. 2003. *Body outlaws: rewriting the rules of beauty and body image.* Emeryville, CA: Seal Press.

Ehrenreich, Barbara (Ed.). 2002. *Global woman: Nannies, maids, and sex workers in the new economy.* New York: Henry Holt.

Eisenstein, Zillah. 1979. *Capitalist patriarchy and the case for socialist feminism.* New York: Monthly Review.

EKOS Politics. 2010. 'Canadians decisively pro-choice on abortion.' Online: http://www.ekospolitics.com/wp-content/uploads/full_report_april_11.pdf.

Elder, Melissa. 2009. Healthcare: Cosmetic surgery markets: Products and services. Report HLC061A, BCC Research, June 2009. http://www.bccresearch.com/report/HLC061A.html. Accessed 18 January 2011

Eliasson, Mona, and Colleen Lundy. 1999. 'Organizing to stop violence against women in Canada and Sweden.' In Linda Briskin and Mona Eliasson (Eds), *Women's organizing and public policy in Canada and Sweden*, 280–309. Montreal and Kingston: McGill-Queen's University Press.

Elshtain, Jean Bethke. 1982. 'Feminism, family, and community.' *Dissent* Fall:442–9.

———. 1991. 'Against gay marriage—II.' *Commonweal* 118 (20):685–6.

———, Enola Aird, Amitai Etzioni, William Galston, Mary Ann Glendon, Martha Minow, and Alice Rossi. 1993. 'A communitarian position on the family.' *National Civic Review* 82 (1):25–35.

Engels, Friedrich. 1972. *The origin of family, private property and the state.* New York: Pathfinder Press.

Enloe, Cynthia. 1990. *Bananas, beaches and bases: Making feminist sense of international relations.* Berkeley: University of California Press.

———. 1993. *The morning after: Sexual politics at the end of the Cold War.* Berkeley: University of California Press.

Enos, Pualani. 1996. 'Prosecuting battered mothers: State laws' failure to protect battered women and abused children.' *Harvard Women's Law Journal* 19:229–68.

Equal Voice. 2011. 'With nominations now closed, incremental rise in female candidates.' Online: http://equalvoice.ca/speaks_article.cfm?id=449.

Erdman, Joanna N. 2004. *How the federal government learned to stop worrying and love the law: Challenging provincial failure to fund abortion clinics through the Canada Health Act.* Working Paper of the Health Systems Law and Policy Group, University of Toronto Faculty of Law. http://www.law.utoronto.ca/healthlaw/.

————, Amy Grenon, and Leigh Harrison-Wilson. 2008. 'Medication abortion in Canada: A right-to-health perspective.' *American Journal of Public Health* 98, 10: 1764–1769.

Erickson, Lynda. 1991. 'Women and candidacies for the House of Commons.' In Kathy Megyery (Ed.), *Women in Canadian politics: Toward equity in representation.* Vol. 6 of the research studies of the Royal Commission on Electoral Reform and Party Financing, 101–25. Toronto: Dundurn Press.

————. 1997. 'Might more women make a difference? Gender, party and ideology among Canada's parliamentary candidates.' *Canadian Journal of Political Science* 30 (4):663–88.

————. 1998. 'Entry to the Commons: Parties, recruitment, and the election of women in 1993.' In Manon Tremblay and Caroline Andrew (Eds), *Women and political representation in Canada,* 219–55. Ottawa: University of Ottawa Press.

Esping-Andersen, Gosta. 1990. *The three worlds of welfare capitalism.* Cambridge: Polity Press.

Etzioni, Amitai (Ed.). 1995. *Rights and the common good: The communitarian perspective.* New York: St. Martin's.

Evans, Jillian, and Allison Harell. 2005. *Gendered social capital and its political implications: The Canadian case in comparative perspective.* Paper presented at the Canadian Political Science Association Annual Meeting, University of Western Ontario, London, ON, June.

Evans, Mark. 2004. 'Porn goes wireless; profits seen.' *The National Post* 26 October: A3.

Evans, Mary. 1997. 'In praise of theory: The case for women's studies.' In Sandra Kemp and Judith Squires (Eds), *Feminisms,* 17–21. Oxford: Oxford University Press.

Evans, Patricia, and Gerda Wekerle (Eds). 1997. *Women and the Canadian welfare state: Challenges and change.* Toronto: University of Toronto Press.

Evans, Sara. 1979. *Personal politics: The roots of women's liberation in the civil rights movement and the New Left.* New York: Vintage Books.

Everitt, Joanna. 1998a. 'Public opinion and social movements: The women's movement and the gender gap in Canada.' *Canadian Journal of Political Science* 31 (4):743–65.

————. 1998b. 'The gender gap in Canada: Now you see it, now you don't.' *Canadian Review of Sociology and Anthropology* 35 (2):191–219.

————, and Elizabeth Gidengil. 2002. 'Damned if you do, damned if you don't: Television news coverage of female party leaders in the 1993 federal election.' In William Cross (Ed), *Political parties, representation, and electoral democracy in Canada,* 223–37. Don Mills, ON: Oxford University Press.

————. 2003. 'Tough talk: How television news covers male and female leaders of Canadian political parties.' In Manon Tremblay and Linda Trimble (Eds), *Women and electoral politics in Canada,* 194–210. Don Mills, ON: Oxford University Press.

Eyer, Diane. 1996. *Motherguilt: How our culture blames mothers for what's wrong with society.* New York: Random House.

Faludi, Susan. 1991. *Backlash: The undeclared war against American women.* New York: Crown.

Fast, Janet, and Moreno Da Pont. 2000. 'Changes in women's work continuity.' *Canadian Social Trends* 3:78–83. Toronto: Thompson Educational Publishing (with Statistics Canada).

————, and Judith Frederick. 2000. 'Working arrangements and time stress.' *Canadian Social Trends* 3:151–6. Toronto: Thompson Educational Publishing (with Statistics Canada).

————, Judith Frederick, Nancy Zukewich, and Sandra Franke. 2001. 'The time of our lives . . .' *Canadian Social Trends* winter: 20–3. Statistics Canada Catalogue no. 11-008.

Federal/Provincial/Territorial Working Group of Attorneys General Officials on Gender Equality in the Canadian Justice System. 1992. *Gender equality in the Canadian justice system.* Ottawa: Department of Justice.

Federation of Canadian Municipalities. 2002. 'Elected officials and city managers in Canada (By province and gender) FCM Databank.' *The Women's Participation Project.* Joint Venture by Status of Women Canada and the FCM. Online: www.equalvoice.ca/pdf/8_44a2566a47c52.doc.

————. 2004. *Increasing Women's Participation in Municipal Decision Making: Strategies for More Inclusive Canadian Communities.* Municipal Consultation Processes Project. Ottawa: FCM.

————. 2009. *Male-female gender statistics.* Ottawa: FCM. Online: http://www.fcm.ca/CMFiles/Female-Male%20Municipal%20Statistics-January%202020091OQD-2182009-3386.pdf.

Ferguson, Kathy E. 1984. *The feminist case against bureaucracy.* Philadelphia: Temple University Press.

————. 1987. 'Male-ordered politics: Feminism and political science.' In Terence Ball (Ed.), *Idioms of inquiry: Critique and renewal in political science,* 209–29. Albany: SUNY Press.

Field, Martha A. 1989. 'Controlling the woman to protect the fetus.' *Law, Medicine and Health Care* 17:114–29.

Findlay, Sue. 1987. 'Facing the state: The politics of the women's movement reconsidered.' In Heather Jon Maroney and Meg Luxton, *Feminism and political economy: Women's work, women's struggles,* 31–50. Toronto: Methuen.

Firestone, Shulamith. 1971. *The dialectic of sex: The case for feminist revolution.* Toronto: Bantam Books.

Flanagan, Caitlin. 2004. 'How serfdom saved the women's movement: Dispatches from the nanny wars.' *The Atlantic Monthly* March:109–28.

Flax, Jane. 1990. *Thinking fragments: Psychoanalysis, feminism and postmodernism in the contemporary west.* Berkeley: Univ. Calif. Press.

Flora, Peter, and Arnold J. Heidenheimer (Eds). 1981. *The development of welfare states in Europe and America.* New Brunswick, NJ, and London: Transaction Books.

Fong, Petti. 2011. 'Woman awaits landmark ruling on sperm-donor identities.' *The Toronto Star* (7 January).

Foot, David K. with Daniel Stoffman. 1998. *Boom, bust and echo 2000: Profiting from the demographic shift in the new millennium.* Toronto: Macfarlane, Walter and Ross.

Forbes Martin, Susan. 2004. *Women and migration: Consultative meeting on migration and mobility and how this movement affects women.* United Nations Division for the Advancement of Women, Malmo Sweden, 2-4 December 2003. Available at: http://www.un.org/womenwatch/daw/meetings/consult/CM-Dec03-WP1.pdf

Foss, Krista. 1999. 'Brain-dead woman loses fetus.' *The Globe and Mail* 4 December: A1, A8.

———. 2002. 'Men as likely to face abuse from partner, Statscan says.' *The Globe and Mail* 27 June: A8.

Fraser, Nancy. 1994. 'After the family wage: Gender equity and the welfare state.' *Political Theory* 22 (4):591–618.

Frederick, Judith A., and Janet E. Fast. 2001. 'Enjoying work: An effective strategy in the struggle to juggle?' *Canadian Social Trends* summer: 8–11. Statistics Canada Catalogue no. 11-008.

Friedan, Betty. 1963. *The feminine mystique.* New York: Dell.

———. 1981. *The second stage.* New York: Summit Books.

FRO (Family Relations Office, Ministry of Community and Social Services, Government of Ontario). 2004a. *Creating a tougher, fairer and more efficient family responsibility office.* News release 2 December. http://www.cfcs.gov.on.ca/CFCS/en/newsRoom/backgrounders/041202A.htm.

———. 2004b. *Family Responsibility Office by the numbers.* News release 2 December. http://www.cfcs.gov.on.ca/CFCS/en/newsRoom/backgrounders/041202.htm.

Frum, David. 1996. *What's right: The new conservatism and what it means for Canada.* Toronto: Random House.

Fudge, Judy. 1996. 'Fragmentation and feminization: The challenge of equity for labour-relations policy.' In Janine Brodie (Ed.), *Women and Canadian public policy,* 57–87. Toronto: Harcourt Brace.

Fuss, Diana. 1989. *Essentially speaking: Feminism, nature and difference.* New York: Routledge.

Future Group. 2006. *Falling short of the mark: An international study on the treatment of human trafficking victims.* www.thefuturegroup.org. Found at: http://www.oas.org/atip/canada/Fallingshortofthemark.pdf. Accessed 11 February 2011.

———. 2007. 'Report finds human trafficking risk at 2010 Olympics.' November 1, 2001. Available at: http://tfgwebmaster.site.aplus.net/wwwthefuturegrouporg/id50.html. Accessed 15 January 2011.

Galloway, Gloria. 2003. 'Aborted fetuses used in fertility treatment.' *The Globe and Mail* 2 July: A10.

Gallup. 2009. 'More Americans 'pro-life' than 'pro-choice' for first time.' Online: http://www.gallup.com/poll/118399/more-americans-pro-life-than-pro-choice-first-time.aspx

Galston, William A. 1995. 'A liberal-democratic case for the two-parent family.' In Amitai Etzioni (Ed.), *Rights and the common good: The communitarian perspective,* 139–49. New York: St. Martin's.

Gamble, Sarah (Ed.). 2001. *The Routledge companion to feminism and postfeminism.* New York: Routledge.

Gauthier, Anne Hélène. 1996. *The state and the family: A comparative analysis of family policies in industrialized countries.* Oxford: Clarendon Press.

Gelb, Joyce, and Maria Lief Palley. 1996. *Women and public policies: Reassessing gender politics.* Charlottesville, VA: University of Virginia Press.

Geller-Schwartz, Linda. 1995. 'An array of agencies: Feminism and state institutions in Canada.' In Dorothy McBride Stetson and Amy Mazur (Eds). *Comparative state feminism,* 40–8. Thousand Oaks, CA: Sage.

Gidengil, Elizabeth. 2007. 'Beyond the Gender Gap.' *Canadian Journal of Political Science* 40, 4: 815–831.

—— and Brenda O'Neill. 2006. *Gender and social capital.* New York: Routledge

—— and Brenda O'Neill (Eds). forthcoming. *Unequal returns: Gender, social capital and political engagement.* New York: Routledge.

——, Joanna Everitt, and Susan Banducci. 2009. 'Do voters stereotype female party leaders? Evidence from Canada and New Zealand.' In *Opening Doors Wider: Women's Political Engagement in Canada.* Ed. Sylvia Bashevkin. Vancouver: UBC Press: 167–193.

——, Joanna Everitt, André Blais, Patrick Fournier, and Neil Nevitte. 2006. *Gender and vote choice in the 2006 Canadian election.* Paper presented at the Annual Meeting of the American Political Science Association, Philadelphia, PA, 30 August–3 September.

——, Elizabeth Goodyear-Grant, Neil Nevitte, André Blais, and Richard Nadeau. 2003. *Gender, knowledge, and social capital.* Paper prepared for the Conference on Gender and Social Capital, University of Manitoba, May.

Gilligan, Carol. 1980. 'In a different voice: Women's conceptions of self and morality.' In Hester Eisenstein and Alice Jardine (Eds), *The future of difference,* 274–317. New Brunswick, NJ: Rutgers University Press.

——. 1982. *In a different voice: Psychological theory and women's development.* Cambridge, MA: Harvard University Press.

Glendon, Mary Ann. 1987. *Abortion and divorce in Western law.* Cambridge, MA: Harvard University Press.

Goldman, Emma. 1969. *Anarchism and other essays.* New York: Dover Publications.

Gorin, Tamara. 2000. *'Young' women controversy an unnecessary diversion tactic of patriarchy.* Vancouver Rape Relief and Women's Shelter web-site. http://www.rapereliefshelter.bc.ca/volunteer/discordes.html, originally published in *Discorder Magazine,* March 2000.

Grosz, Elizabeth. 1994. *Volatile bodies: Toward a corporeal feminism.* Bloomington: Indiana University Press.

Gotell, Lise. 1996. 'Policing desire: Obscenity law, pornography politics, and feminism in Canada.' In Janine Brodie (Ed.), *Women and Canadian public policy,* 279–317. Toronto: Harcourt Brace.

——. 1997. 'Shaping *Butler*: The new politics of anti-pornography.' In Brenda Cossman, Shannon Bell, Lise Gotell, and Becki L. Ross (Eds), *Bad attitude/s on trial: Pornography, feminism, and the Butler decision,* 48–106. Toronto: University of Toronto Press.

——. 1998. 'A critical look at state discourse on "violence against women": Some implications for feminist politics and women's citizenship.' In Manon Tremblay and Caroline Andrew (Eds), *Women and political representation in Canada,* 39–84. Ottawa: University of Ottawa Press.

——. 2002. 'The ideal victim, the hysterical complainant, and the disclosure of confidential records: The implications of the Charter for sexual assault law.' *Osgoode Hall Law Journal* 40, 3–4: 251–293.

——. 2010. 'Canadian sexual assault law: Neoliberalism and the erosion of feminist-inspired law reforms.' In *Rethinking rape law: International and comparative perspectives.* Clare McGlynn and Vanessa Munro (Eds). London: Routledge: 209–223.

——, and Janine Brodie. 1996. 'Women and parties in the 1990s: Less than ever an issue of numbers.' In Hugh Thorburn (Ed.), *Party politics in Canada,* 7th ed, 54–71. Scarborough, ON: Prentice Hall.

Gottlieb, Beatrice. 1997. 'The problem of feminism in the fifteenth century.' In Renate Blumenfeld-Kosinski (Ed.), *The selected writings of Christine de Pizan,* (Renate Blumenfeld-Kosinski and Kevin Brownlee, trans.), 274–96. New York: W.W. Norton.

Government of Canada. Women's Program of the Status of Women Canada, March 2006. http://www.swc.cfc.gc/funding/wp/wpguide_e.html. Accessed March 2007.

——. 2010. Canada's G8 priorities. News Release (26 January). Online: http://g8.gc.ca/3291/

canadas-g8-priorities/.

Graydon, Shari. 2005. 'Breast roulette.' *The Globe and Mail* 5 February: F7.

Greaves, Lorraine. 1993. 'What is the interrelationship between academic and activist feminism?' In Constance Backhouse and David H. Flaherty, *Challenging times: The women's movement in Canada and the United States*, 150–5. Montreal: McGill-Queen's University Press.

———, Colleen Varcoe, Nancy Poole, Marina Morrow, Joy Johnson, Ann Pederson, and Lori Irwin. 2002. *A motherhood issue: Discourses on mothering under duress*. Ottawa: Status of Women Canada.

Green, Joyce. 1993. 'Constitutionalizing the patriarchy: Aboriginal women and Aboriginal governance.' *Constitutional Forum* 4: 110–120

———. 2001. 'Canaries in the mines of citizenship: Indian women in Canada.' *Canadian Journal of Political Science* 34, no. 4: 715–38.

——— (ed.). 2007. *Making space for Indigenous feminism*. London: Zed Books. Greenhaus, Jeffrey H., and Nicholas J. Beutell. 1985. 'Sources of conflict between work and family roles.' *The Academy of Management Review* 10 (1):76–88.

Greer, Germaine. 1999. *The whole woman*. London: Transworld/Anchor.

Grey, Chris Hables (Ed.). 1995. *The cyborg handbook*. New York: Routledge.

———, Steven Mentor, and Heidi J. Figueroa-Sarriera. 1995. 'Introduction: Cyborgology: Constructing the knowledge of cybernetic organisms.' In Chris Hables Grey (Ed.), *The cyborg handbook*. New York: Routledge.

Griffen, Sandra. 2002. 11 September, 2000 to 11 December, 2001 *Interaction* 16 (1):6–7.

Grrrl Zine Network. n.d. http://grrrlzines.net. Accessed 21 May, 2004.

Guggenheim, Martin. 1994. 'The best interests of the child: Much ado about nothing?' In S. Randell Humm et al. (Eds), *Child, parent and state: Law and policy reader*, 27–35. Philadelphia: Temple University Press.

Guichon, Juliet. 2001. 'Stop the infant merchants.' *The Globe and Mail* 29 August: A13.

Gwyn, Richard. 1993. 'It's lonely at the top, especially for a single woman.' *The Toronto Star* 16 June: A19.

Gynuity Health Projects. 2010. 'Mifepristone approval.' Online: http://gynuity.org/resources/info/list-of-mifepristone-approval/

Ha, Tu Thanh. 2004. 'Pregnant woman called him "papa", sperm donor's court petition says.' *The Globe and Mail* 14 September: A11.

Hamilton, Roberta. 1996. *Gendering the vertical mosaic: Feminist perspectives on Canadian society*. Toronto: Copp Clark, Ltd.

Hancock, Ange-Marie. 2007. 'Intersectionality as a normative and empirical paradigm.' *Politics and Gender* 3(2): 248–54

Hankivsky, Olena. 2009. 'Gender mainstreaming in neoliberal times.' In *Public policy for women: The state, income security, and labour market issues*. Marjorie Griffin Cohen and Jane Pulkingham (Eds). Toronto: University of Toronto Press: 114–135.

Haraway, Donna. 1985. 'A manifesto for cyborgs: Science, technology, and socialist feminism in the 1980s.' *Socialist Review* 15 (80): 65–107.

———. 1990. 'A manifesto for cyborgs: Science, technology, and socialist feminism in the 1980s.' In Linda Nicholson (Ed.), *Feminism/postmodernism*, 190–233. New York: Routledge.

———. 1999. '"Gender" for a Marxist dictionary: The sexual politics of a word.' In Richard Parker and Peter Aggleton (eds), *Culture, society and sexuality: A reader*, 76-96. London: UCL Press.

Harding, Sandra. 1989. *Feminism and methodology*. Bloomington: Indiana University Press.

——— & Kathryn Norberg. 2005. 'New feminist approaches to social science methodologies: An introduction.' *Signs* 30 (4): 2009-2015.

Hargreaves, J.R, et. al. 2008. 'Systemic review exploring time trends in the association between educational attainment and risk of HIV infection in sub-Saharan Africa.' *AIDS* 22 (Supp 4): S5-S16.

Hartline, Sharon E. 1997. 'Intimate danger: The case for preemptive self-defense.' In Patrice DiQuinzio and Iris Marion Young (Eds), *Feminist ethics and social policy*, 159–72. Bloomington and Indianapolis: University of Indiana Press.

Hartmann, Heidi. 1981. 'The unhappy marriage of Marxism and feminism: Towards a more progressive union.' In Lydia Sargent (Ed.), *Women and revolution: A discussion of the unhappy marriage of marxism and feminism*, 1–41. Montreal: Black Rose Books.

———. 1982. 'Capitalism, patriarchy, and job segregation by sex.' In Anthony Giddens and David

Held (Eds), *Classes, power, and conflict*, 446–69. Berkeley: University of California Press.

Hartsock, Nancy. 1997. 'Comment on Hekman's "Truth and Method: Feminist Standpoint Theory Revisited": truth or justice?' *Signs* 22: 367–74.

Haussman, Melissa. 2001. 'Of rights and power: Canada's federal abortion policy 1969–1991.' In Dorothy McBride Stetson (Ed.), *Abortion politics, women's movements, and the democratic state*, 63–86. New York: Oxford University Press.

Hawkesworth, Mary E. 1989. 'Knower, knowing, known: Feminist theory and claims of truth.' In Micheline R. Malson, Jean F. O'Barr, Sarah Wesphal-Wihl and Mary Wyer (eds.), *Feminist theory in practice and process*. Chicago: Univ. of Chicago Press.

Health Canada. 2004. Assisted human reproduction. http://www.hc-sc.gc.ca/english/lifestyles/reproduction/index.htm.

Healy, Teresa. 2003. 'It's time for change: A feminist discussion of resistance and transformation in periods of liberal world order.' In Claire Turenne Sjolander, Heather A. Smith, and Deborah Stienstra (Eds), *Feminist perspectives on Canadian foreign policy*, 172–84. Don Mills, ON: Oxford University Press.

Henderson, Sarah L. & Alana S. Jeydel. 2010. *Women and politics in a global world*. New York: Oxford University Press.

Hennessy, Rosemary. 1993. 'Queer theory: A review of the *differences* special issue and Wittig's *The straight mind.' Signs* Summer: 964–73.

Herizons. 1999. 'New Feminist Alliance for Human Rights.' *Herizons*. 13 (2), Summer: 10

Hex, Celina. 2000. 'F-word, fierce, funny, feminists: An interview with Gloria Steinem and Kathleen Hanna.' *Bust* winter: 52–6.

Hirschmann, Nancy J. 1997. 'The theory and practice of freedom: The case of battered women.' In Mary Lyndon Shanley and Uma Narayan (Eds), *Reconstructing political theory*, 194–210. University Park, PA: University of Pennsylvania Press.

Hodgson, Dorothy L. 2002. 'Women's rights as human rights: Women in law and development in Africa (WiLDAF).' *Africa Today* 49 (2):3–26.

Hogg, Peter W. 1997. *Constitutional law of Canada*. Loose-leaf ed. Toronto: Carswell.

———. 2006. 'Canada: The Constitution and same-sex marriage.' *International Journal of Constitutional Law* 4, 3: 712–21.

Hondagneu-Sotelo, Pierrette. 2001. *Doméstica: Immigrant workers cleaning and caring in the shadows of affluence*. Berkeley: University of California Press.

hooks, bell. 1981. *Ain't I a woman: Black women and feminism*. Cambridge, MA: South End Press.

———. 1986. 'Sisterhood: Political solidarity between women.' *Feminist Review* 23:125–38.

———. 1988. *Talking back: Thinking black, thinking feminist*. Toronto: Between the Lines.

———. 1989. *Talking back: Thinking black, thinking feminist*. Cambridge, MA: South End Press.

———. 1994. *Teaching to transgress: Education as the practice of freedom*. New York, Routledge.

———. 2000. *Feminism is for everybody: Passionate politics*. Cambridge, MA: South End Press.

Huffman, Tracy. 2001. 'Contrite wife killer pleads guilty.' *The Toronto Star* 15 November: 4.

Hughes, Ed. 2000. 'Parents at a price.' *The Globe and Mail* 3 August: A15.

Human Resources and Skills Development Canada. 2001. Employment Equity Act review: A report to the Standing Committee on Human Status of Persons with Disabilities. http://www.rhdcc.gc.ca/eng/lp/lo/lswe/we/review/report/main.shtml. Accessed 9 June, 2010.

———. 2005. Addressing work-life balance in Canada. www.hrsdc.gc.ca/asp/gateway.asp?hr=/en/lp/spila/wlb/awlbc/01table_of_contents.shtml&hs=

Hurley, Mary C. 2005. *Sexual orientation and legal rights: Current issue review*. Ottawa: Parliamentary Information and Research Service, Library of Parliament.

Hynna, Martha. 1997. 'Women in the public service: A thirty-year perspective.' *Canadian Public Administration* 40 (4):618–25.

Ikemoto Lisa. 2009. 'Reproductive tourism: Equality concerns in the global market for fertility services.' *Law and Inequality* 27: 277–309.

IPU (Inter-Parliamentary Union). 2005. *Women in national parliaments*. www.ipu.org/wmn-e/world.htm 31 December. Women in National Parliaments. Available at: http://www.ipu.org/wmn-e/world.htm.

Irigaray, Luce. 1977. *Ce sexe qui n'est pas un*. Paris: Editions de Minuit.

———. 1985. *This sex which is not one*. (Catherine Porter, trans.) Ithaca: Cornell University Press.

———. 1993. *An ethic of sexual difference.* (Carolyn Burke and Gillian C. Gill, trans.) Ithaca: Cornell University Press.

Iyengar, Shanto, Nicholas A. Valentino, Stephen Ansolabeher, and Adam F. Simon. 1997. 'Running as a woman: Gender stereotyping in political campaigns.' In Pippa Norris (Ed.), *Women, media and politics,* 77–98. New York: Oxford University Press.

Jackson, Chris. 2000. 'Measuring and valuing households' unpaid work.' *Canadian Social Trends* 3:88–92. Toronto: Thompson Educational Publishing (with Statistics Canada).

Jackson, Robert J., and Jackson, Doreen. 2001. *Politics in Canada: Culture, institutions, behaviour and public policy.* 5th ed. Toronto: Prentice Hall.

Jaggar, Allison. 1983. *Feminist politics and human nature.* Brighton: Harvester Press.

Jaquette, Jane S. 1997. 'Women in power: From tokenism to critical mass.' *Foreign Policy* Fall.

Jeffrey, Leslie Ann. 2004. 'Prostitution as public nuisance: Prostitution policy in Canada.' In Joyce Outshoorn (Ed.), *The politics of prostitution: Women's movements, democratic states and the globalization of sex commerce,* 83–102. New York: Cambridge University Press.

Jenson, Jane. 1997. 'Competing representations: The politics of abortion in Canada.' In Caroline Andrew and Sandra Rodgers (Eds), *Women and the Canadian state,* 291–305. Montreal and Kingston: McGill-Queen's University Press.

Jervis, John. 1998. *Exploring the modern: Patterns of Western culture and civilization.* Oxford: Blackwell.

Jhappan, Radha. 1998. 'The equality pit or the rehabilitation of justice.' *Canadian Journal of Women and the Law* 60 (10):60–107.

———. 2002. *Women's legal strategies in Canada: A friendly assessment.* Toronto: University of Toronto Press.

Johnson-Steeves v. Lee [1997] 29 R.F.L. (4th) 126 (Alta. Q.B.).

Jones, Vernon Clement. 2002. 'Cabinet posting a benchmark.' *The Globe and Mail* 7 June: A23.

Kahn, Kimberly. 1996. *The political consequences of being a woman: How stereotypes influence the conduct and consequences of political campaigns.* New York: Columbia University Press.

Kamen, Paula. 1991. *Feminist fatale: Voices from the 'twentysomething' generation explore the future of the 'women's movement'.* New York: Donald I. Fine.

Kaminer, Wendy. 2000. 'Fathers in court.' *The American Prospect* 11 (21):62–3.

Kaplan, Robert D. 1994. 'The coming anarchy: How scarcity, crime, overpopulation, tribalism, and disease are rapidly destroying the social fabric of our planet.' *Atlantic Monthly* 271 (2).

Kaposy, Chris. 2010. 'Improving abortion access in Canada.' *Health Care Analysis* 18: 17–34.

Karpodinish v. Kantas 2006 BCCA 272, 27 R.F.L. (6th) 254.

Kay, Barry J., Ronald D. Lambert, Steven D. Brown, and James E. Curtis. 1988. 'Feminist consciousness and the Canadian electorate: A review of national election studies 1965–1984.' *Women and Politics* 8 (2):1–21.

Keck, Margaret, and Kathryn Sikkink. 1998. *Activists beyond borders: Advocacy networks in international politics.* Ithaca: Cornell University Press.

Keeble, Edna, and Meridith Ralston. 2003. 'Discourses and feminist dilemmas: Trafficking, prostitution, and the sex trade in the Philippines.' In Claire Turenne Sjolander, Heather A. Smith, and Deborah Stienstra (Eds), *Feminist perspectives on Canadian foreign policy,* 136–154. Don Mills, ON: Oxford University Press.

Keller, James. 2010. 'Abuse not unique to polygamy, professor says.' *The Globe and Mail* (15 December).

Kelly, Fiona. 2004–5. 'Nuclear norms or fluid families? Incorporating lesbian and gay parents and their children into Canadian family law.' *Canadian Journal of Family Law* 21: 133–78.

———. 2008–9. '(Re)forming parenthood: The assignment of legal parentage within planned lesbian families.' *Ottawa Law Review* 40: 185–223.

———. 2009. 'Producing paternity: The role of legal fatherhood in maintaining the traditional family.' *Canadian Journal of Women and the Law* 21: 315–351.

Kimmel, Michael S. 1995. 'Misogynists, masculinist mentors, and male supporters: Men's responses to feminism.' In Jo Freeman (Ed.), *Women: A feminist perspective,* 5th ed. Mountain View, CA: Mayfield Publishing.

Kirk, Gwyn, and Margo Okazawa-Rey. 2002. 'Women take on globalization and militarism.' In Mike Prokosch and Laura Raymond (Eds), *The global activist's manual: Local ways to change the world,* 42–4. New York: Thunder's Mouth Press/Nation Books.

Kitschelt, Herbert. 1986. 'Political opportunity structures and political protest: Anti-nuclear movements in four democracies.' *British Journal of Political Science* 16:57–85.

Knee, Jonathan. 2004. 'Is that really legal?' *New York Times* 2 May: WK 11.

Kolata, Gina. 1999. '$50,000 offered to tall, smart egg donor.' *The New York Times* 3 March: A10.

Kolder, Veronika E.B., Janet Gallagher, and Michael T. Parsons. 1987. 'Court-ordered obstetrical interventions.' *The New England Journal of Medicine* 316:1192–96.

Kolmar, Wendy, and Frances Bartkowski (Eds). 2000. *Feminist theory: A reader.* Mountain View, CA: Mayfield Publishing Company.

Kondro, Wayne. 2000. 'On the trail of sperm-donor dads.' *The Globe and Mail* 6 January: R3.

Kozhaya, Norma. 2007. Quebec's failed child care model. *National Post* 10 May, 2007. 14

Kristeva, Julia. 1977. *Des chinoises/About Chinese women.* (Anita Burrows, trans.) London: Boyars.

———. 1980. *Desire in language; A semiotic approach to literature and art.* (Thomas Gora, Alice Jardine, Leon S. Roudiez, trans.) New York: Columbia University Press.

———. 1984. *Revolution in poetic language.* (Margaret Walter, trans.) New York: Columbia University Press.

———. 1986. *The Kristeva reader.* (Toril Moi Ed.) New York: Columbia University Press.

Kronby, Malcolm C. 2001. *Canadian family law.* 8th ed. Toronto: Stoddard.

Kuczynski, Alex. 2004. 'A lovelier you, with off-the-shelf parts.' *The New York Times* 2 May: WK 1.

Kymlicka, Will. 1991. 'Rethinking the family.' *Philosophy and Public Affairs* 20 (1):77–97.

Lacombe, Dany. 1994. *Blue politics: Pornography and the law in the age of feminism.* Toronto: University of Toronto Press.

Ladd-Taylor, Molly, and Lauri Umansky (Eds). 1998. *'Bad' mothers: The politics of blame in twentieth century America.* New York: New York University Press.

Ladner, Kiera L. and Michael McCrossan. 2007. The Electoral Participation of Aboriginal People. *Working Paper on Electoral Participation and Outreach Practices.* Ottawa: Elections Canada.

Laghi, Brian. 2000. 'Ottawa introduces same-sex benefits.' *The Globe and Mail* 12 February: A4.

Lahey, Kathleen, A. 1999. *Are we persons yet? Law and sexuality in Canada.* Toronto: University of Toronto Press.

Laing, Marie. 1999. 'For the sake of the children: Preventing reckless new laws.' *Canadian Journal of Family Law* 16:229–82.

Lamb, Sharon. 2010. 'Feminist ideals for a healthy female adolescent sexuality: A critique.' *Sex Roles.* 62: 294–306.

———. 2010b. 'Porn as pathway to empowerment? A response to Peterson's commentary,' *Sex Roles.* 62: 314–17.

Landsberg, Michele. 2003. 'Children of divorce need our protection.' *The Toronto Star* 27 July: A2.

Lavigne, Marie, Yolande Pinard, and Jennifer Stoddart. 1979. 'The Fédération nationale Saint-Jean-Baptiste and the women's movement in Quebec.' In Linda Kealey (Ed.), *A not unreasonable claim: Women and reform in Canada, 1880s–1920s.* Toronto: The Women's Press.

Law, Sylvia A. 1999–2000. 'Commercial sex: Beyond decriminalization.' *Southern California Law Review* 73:523–610.

Lawlor, Allison. 2001. 'B.C. same-sex couples win parental rights.' *The Globe and Mail* 30 August: A8.

LEAF (Women's Legal Education and Action Fund). 1996. *Equality and the Charter: Ten years of feminist advocacy before the Supreme Court of Canada.* Toronto: Emond Montgomery Publications.

———. 1999. *Little Sisters Book and Art Emporium v. Minister of Justice (Canada):* LEAF factum. Toronto: leaf http://www.leaf.ca/facta/littlesisters.pdf.

———. n.d. *Commission of Inquiry into Certain Events at the Prison for Women in Kingston: Submission of Women's Legal Education and Action Fund on proposed cross-gender staffing at the new regional institutions for federally-sentenced women.* Toronto: LEAF.

Leblanc, Daniel. 1999. 'Plan rewards candidacies of women.' *The Globe and Mail* 27 October: A2.

Lefebvre, Pierre. 2004. 'Quebec's innovative early childhood education and child care policy and its weaknesses.' *Policy Options/Options Politiques.* March 2004, pp. 52–57.

Leibfried, Stephan (Ed.). 2001. *Welfare state futures.* Cambridge and New York: Cambridge University Press.

Levy, Ariel. 2005. *Female chauvinist pigs; women and the rise of raunch culture.* New York: Free Press.

Lewis, Jane (Ed.). 1993. *Women and social policies in Europe.* Aldershot, UK; Brookfield, VT: Edward Elgar.

Lewis, Stephen. 2001. 'Africa's capacity to deliver is huge. Interview with Stephen Lewis.' *Africa Recovery* 15 (1/2):12

———. 2005. 'Interview with Stephen Lewis.' CBC Radio 1 *Sounds like Canada* 18 October.

Li, Geoffrey. 2008. Homicide in Canada, 2007. Juristat Article, October 2008, Vol. 28 no. 9 Ottawa: Statistics Canada Catalogue no. 85-002-X,

Liberal Party of Canada. 2006. *Securing Canada's Success.*

Lorber, Judith. 1994. *Paradoxes of gender.* New Haven: Yale University Press.

Lorde, Audre. 1983. 'An open letter to Mary Daly.' In Cherrie Moraga and Gloria Anzaldua (Eds), *This bridge called my back: Writing by radical women of color*, 94–7. New York: Kitchen Table/ Women of Color Press.

———. 1984. 'Age, race, class, and sex: Women redefining difference.' In *Sister/Outsider*, 114–23. Freedom, CA: The Crossing Press.

Lovelace, Linda, with Mike McGrady. 1980. *Ordeal.* New York: Berkley Books.

Lowndes, Vivian. 2000. 'Women and social capital.' *British Journal of Political Science* 30 (3):533–7.

Luker, Kristin. 1984. *Abortion and the politics of motherhood.* Berkeley, CA: University of California Press.

Lunman, Kim. 2002. 'Ottawa targets child predators.' *The Globe and Mail* 2 December: A1, A5.

———. 2003. 'Ottawa backs gay marriage.' *The Globe and Mail* 18 June: A1, A8.

Luxton, Meg. 2001. 'Feminism as a class act: Working-class feminism and the women's movement in Canada.' *Labour/Le Travail* 48:63–88.

Lyotard, Jean-François. 1989. *The postmodern condition: A report on knowledge.* Geoff Bennington and Brian Massumi, trans. Minneapolis: University of Minnesota Press.

MacAfee, Michelle. 2005. 'Manitoba to appeal ruling on funding for private abortions.' *The Globe and Mail* 28 January: A5.

McCaskill, Norm. 2000. Telephone interview 7 December, Toronto.

McCormack, Thelma. 1996. 'Reproductive technologies: Rights, choice, and coercion.' In Janine Brodie (Ed.), *Women and Canadian public policy*, 199–221. Toronto: Harcourt Brace.

McCourt, K. Mark. 1991. 'Foetus status after R. v. Sullivan and Lemay.' *Alberta Law Review* 29:916–25.

McDermott, Patricia. 1996. 'Pay and employment equity: Why separate policies?' In Janine Brodie (Ed.), *Women and Canadian Public Policy*, 88–103. Toronto: Harcourt Brace.

Macdonald, Laura. 2003. 'Gender and Canadian trade policy: Women's strategies for access and transformation.' In Claire Turenne Sjolander, Heather A. Smith, and Deborah Stienstra (Eds), *Feminist perspectives on Canadian foreign policy*, 40–54. Don Mills, ON: Oxford University Press.

McElroy, Wendy. 1995. *XXX: A woman's right to pornography.* New York: St. Martin's Press.

McGhan, Meredith. 2000. 'Dancing toward redemption.' In Ophira Edut (Ed.), *Body outlaws: Young women write about body image and identity*, 165–75. Seattle, WA: Seal Press.

McGillivray, Anne, and Brenda Comaskey. 1999. *Black eyes all of the time: Intimate violence, aboriginal women, and the justice system.* Toronto: University of Toronto Press.

McGlen, Nancy E., and Karen O'Connor. 1998. *Women, politics, and American society.* 2nd ed. Upper Saddle River, NJ: Prentice Hall.

McInnes, Craig. 1994. 'Boyd backs off on gay spouses.' *The Globe and Mail* 9 June: A1, A10.

———. 1997. 'B.C. passes legislation redefining term "spouse".' *The Globe and Mail* 23 July: A3.

MacIvor, Heather. 1996. *Women and politics in Canada.* Peterborough, ON: Broadview Press.

———. 2003. 'Women and the Canadian electoral system.' In Manon Tremblay and Linda Trimble (Eds), *Women and electoral politics in Canada*, 22–36. Don Mills, ON: Oxford University Press.

McKeen, Wendy. 2004. *Money in their own name: The feminist voice in poverty debate in Canada, 1970–1995.* Toronto: University of Toronto Press.

MacKinnon, Catharine A. 1983. 'Feminism, Marxism, method and the state: An agenda for theory.' In . E. Abel and E.K. Abel (eds.), *The Signs Reader: Women, Gender and Scholarship*, 277–56. Chicago: Univ. Chicago Press.

———. 1987. *Feminism unmodified.* Cambridge, MA: Harvard University Press.

———. 1992. 'Feminist approaches to sexual assault in Canada and the United States: A brief retrospective.' In Constance Backhouse and David H. Flaherty (Eds), *Challenging times: The women's movement in Canada and the United States*, 186–92. Montreal and Kingston: McGill-Queen's University Press.

————. 1993. 'Prostitution and civil rights.' *Michigan Journal of Gender and Law* 1:13–31.

————, and Andrea Dworkin (Eds). 1997. *In harm's way: The pornography civil rights hearings.* Cambridge, MA: Harvard University Press.

McLaren, Angus. 1993. 'Illegal operations: Women, doctors, and abortion', 1886–1939. *Journal of Social History* 26:797–807.

————, and Arlene Tigar McLaren. 1986. *The bedroom and the state: The changing practices and politics of contraception and abortion in Canada,* 1880–1980. Toronto: McClelland and Stewart.

McLaren, Leah. 2000. 'Beauty spa or torture chamber? On being waxed, tweezed, threaded, burned, and steamed within an inch of my life.' *The Globe and Mail* 13 May: R3.

McLaughlin, Audrey. 1992. *A woman's place: My life and politics.* Toronto: MacFarlane Walker and Ross.

Macpherson, Kay. 1994. *When in doubt, do both: The times of my life.* Toronto: University of Toronto Press.

Macqueen, Ken. 1997. 'Four women appointed by PM in drive for 75: But Chrétien's action attacked as anti-democratic.' *The Hamilton Spectator* 12 March: B2.

Magid, Carolyn H. 1997. 'Does comparable worth have radical potential?' In Patrice DiQuinzio and Iris Marion Young (Eds), *Feminist ethics and social policy,* 125–42. Bloomington and Indianapolis: Indiana University Press.

Mahoney, Jill. 2004. 'Ontario plans to double jail terms for deadbeat parents.' *The Globe and Mail* 3 December: A7.

Makin, Kirk. 1999a. 'Ex-boyfriend ordered to pay prenatal costs'. *The Globe and Mail* 12 February: A1, A9.

————. 1999b. 'Supreme Court backs mother in epic child-support battle.' *The Globe and Mail* 17 September: A1, A6.

————. 2001. 'Top court rules 9–0: child porn law stays.' *The Globe and Mail* 27 January: A1, A5.

————. 2002a. 'Child-support case sets record.' *The Globe and Mail* 26 March: A1, A9.

————. 2002b. 'Common-law property rights denied.' *The Globe and Mail* 20 December: A1, A13.

————. 2005. 'Lesbians fighting sperm-donor law.' *The Globe and Mail* 15 February: A9.

————, and Caroline Alphonso. 2000. 'Gay-book sellers win Supreme Court case.' *The Globe and Mail* 16 December: A1, A9.

Makin, Kirk. 2010. 'Stay extension keeps prostitution laws in legal limbo'. Globe and Mail. 2 December 2010.

Victor Malarek. 2009. *The johns: Sex for sale and the men who buy it.* Toronto: Key Porter Books.

Mallan, Caroline. 2004. 'War on "deadbeats": Special team to trace delinquent parents, collect debts.' *The Toronto Star* 6 February: A1.

Mallick, Heather. 2002. 'Why did these children die?' *The Globe and Mail* 5 March: A15.

Malloy, Jonathan. 2003. *Between colliding worlds: The ambiguous existence of government agencies for aboriginal and women's policy.* Toronto: University of Toronto Press.

Mandel, Michael. 1992. *The Charter of Rights and the legalization of politics in Canada.* Toronto: Thompson Educational Publishing.

Manfredi, Christopher P. 2004. *Feminist activism in the Supreme Court.* Vancouver: University of British Columbia Press.

Mani, Lata. 1998. *Contentious traditions: The debate on Sati in colonial India.* Berkeley: University of California Press.

Mansbridge, Jane. 1999. 'Should blacks represent blacks and women represent women? A contingent "yes".' *The Journal of Politics* 61 (3): 628–57.

————, and Katherine Tate. 1992. 'Race trumps gender: The Thomas nomination in the black community.' *PS: Political Science and Politics* September: 488–92.

March, Kathryn S., and Rachelle Taqqu. 1986. *Women's informal associations in developing countries: Catalysts for change?* Boulder, CO: Westview Press.

Marchand, M.H., and Anne Sisson Runyan (Eds). 2000. *Gender and global restructuring: Sightings, sites and resistances.* London: Routledge.

Marcil-Gratton, Nicole, and Céline Le Bourdais. 1999. 'Custody, access and child support: Findings from the National Longitudinal Study of Children and Youth.' Paper presented to the Child Support Team, Department of Justice Canada. http://canada.justice.gc.ca/en/ps/pad/reports/anlsc.pdf.

Marsden, Lorna R. 1980. 'The role of the National Action Committee on the Status of Women in facilitating equal pay policy in Canada.' In Ronnie Steinberg Ratner (Ed.), *Equal employment policy for women*, 242–60. Philadelphia: Temple University Press.

Marshall, Katherine. 2003. 'Benefiting from extended parental leave.' *Perspectives* March. Statistics Canada Cat. No. 75-001-XIE: 5–11.

———. 2006. 'Converging gender roles.' *Perspectives* July 2006. Statistics Canda – Catalogue no. 75-001-XIE.

———. 2010. Employer top ups. *Perspectives on Labour and Income*. Statistics Canada. February 2010, pp.5-12. Catalogue no. 75-001-X

Mason, Mary Ann. 1988. *The equality trap*. New York: Simon and Schuster.

———, and Ann Quirk. 1997. 'Are mothers losing custody? Read my lips: Trends in judicial decision-making in custody disputes—1920, 1960, 1990, and 1995.' *Family Law Quarterly* 31 (2):215–36.

Matas, Robert. 2002. 'Immigration bureaucrats let man's three wives stay.' *The Globe and Mail* 7 October: A1, A4.

———. 2003. 'Hairdresser's tip led woman to huge child-support award.' *The Globe and Mail* 24 June: A1, A7.

Matland, Richard. 1998. 'Women's representation in national legislatures: Developed and developing countries.' *Legislative Studies Quarterly* 23 (1):109–25.

Mazzuca, Josephine. 2002. 'American and Canadian views on abortion.' *The Gallup Poll News Service* September 24. Toronto: The Gallup Organization.

Melucci, Alberto. 1989. *Nomads of the present: Social movements and individual needs in contemporary society*. Philadelphia: Temple University Press.

———. 1996. *Challenging codes: Collective action in the information age*. Cambridge: Cambridge University Press.

Merchant, Carolyn. 1992. *Radical ecology: The search for a livable world*. New York: Routledge.

Mies, Maria, and Vandana Shiva. 1997. 'Ecofeminism.' In Sandra Kemp and Judith Squires (Eds), *Feminisms*, 497–502. Oxford: Oxford University Press.

Mill, John Stuart, and Harriet Taylor. 1970. *Essays on sex equality*. Alice S. Rossi (Ed.). Chicago: University of Chicago Press.

Millar, Paul, and Sheldon Goldenberg. 1998. 'Explaining child custody determinations in Canada.' *Canadian Journal of Law and Society* 13 (Fall): 209–25.

Miller, Richard K. & Kelli Washington. 2009. *Health care business market research handbook*. Loganville, GA : Richard K. Miller & Associates.

Millett, Kate. 1970. *Sexual politics*. New York: Doubleday.

Milner, Henry (Ed.). 1999. *Making every vote count: Reassessing Canada's electoral system*. Peterborough, ON: Broadview Press.

Minow, Martha, and Mary Lyndon Shanley. 1996. 'Relational rights and responsibilities: Revisioning the family in liberal political theory and law.' *Hypatia* 11 (1): 4–29.

Miron v. Trudel [1995] 2 S.C.R. 418.

Mishler, William, and Harold D. Clarke. 1995. 'Political participation in Canada.' In Michael S. Whittington and Glen Williams (Eds), *Canadian politics in the 1990s*. 4th ed, 129–51. Toronto: Nelson Canada.

Mitchell, Alyson, Lisa Bryn Rundele, and Lara Karain (Eds). 2001. *Turbo chicks: Talking young feminisms*. Toronto: Sumach Press.

Mitchell, Juliet. 1974. *Psychoanalysis and feminism*. New York: Pantheon Books.

———. 1984. *Women: The longest revolution*. New York: Pantheon Books.

———. 1989. 'Selections from the position of women in women's estate.' In Roger S. Gottlieb (Ed.), *An anthology of Western Marxism: From Lukacs and Gramsci to socialist feminism*. New York: Oxford University Press.

Mitchell, Penni. 2005. 'The Revolution Continues.' *Herizons* Vol 18 (3), Winter 2005, p. 2.

Mitchinson, Wendy. 1979. 'The wctu: "For God, home and native land"; A study in nineteenth-century feminism.' In Linda Kealey (Ed.), *A not unreasonable claim: Women and reform in Canada 1880s–1990s*. Toronto: The Women's Educational Press.

Moffat, Gary. 1982. *A history of the peace movement in Canada*. Ottawa: Grapevine Press.

Molgat, Anne. n.d. 'Herstory: An action that will not be allowed to subside, NAC's first twenty-five years.' Additions by Joan Grant Cummings. http://www.nac-cca.ca/about/his_e.htm. Accessed 9 August 2004.

Moncrief, Gary F., and Donley T. Studlar. 1996. 'Women cabinet ministers in Canadian provinces 1976–1994.' *Canadian Parliamentary Review* autumn: 10–13.

Montpetit, Eric, Francesca Scala, and Isabelle Fortier. 2004. 'The paradox of deliberative democracy: The National Action Committee on the Status of Women and Canada's policy on reproductive technology.' *Policy Sciences* 37:137–57.

Moorcroft, Lois. 2005. 'Newfoundland women want pay equity too.' *Canadian Dimension* 39 (2):6–7.

Morgan, Robin. 1980. 'Theory and practice: Pornography and rape.' In Laura Lederer (Ed.), *Take back the night: Women on pornography*, 134–40. New York: William Morrow.

———. 1984. *Sisterhood is global: The international women's movement anthology*. Garden City, NJ: Anchor/Doubleday.

Morris, Aldon. 1984. *The origins of the civil rights movement: Black communities organizing for change.* New York: Free Press.

———. 2000. 'Charting futures for sociology: Social organization.' *Contemporary Sociology* May 2000, Vol. 29, No. 3. Pp. 445–54.

Morrison, Wayne (Ed.). 2001. *Blackstone's commentaries on the law of England.* v.1. London: Cavendish Publishing.

Morrow, Adrian and Caroline Alphonso. 2010. 'Women make the grade, but not the money.' *The Globe and Mail* 8 September: A1, A4.

Mouffe, Chantal. 1992. 'Feminism, citizenship and radical democratic politics.' In Judith Butler and Joan Scott (Eds), *Feminists theorize the political*, 369–84. New York: Routledge.

Mowani, Nurjehan. 1999. 'The reality of women's rights to refugee law.' Address to the International Law Society, Women and the Law, McGill University, Montreal. 17 February. Found at the Immigration and Refugee Board, Government of Canada website. www.irb-cisr.gc.ca/en/media/speeches/1999/ila_ehtm.

Mucalov, Janice. 2001. 'Whose best interests?' *National: The Official Magazine of the Canadian Bar Association* 10 (2):12–21.

Mulgrew, Ian. 2003. 'Dads and kids stand to lose under new law.' *The Vancouver Sun* 4 April: B4.

Mulvey, Laura. 1975. 'Visual pleasure and narrative cinema.' *Screen* 16, pp. 3–18.

Murrell, Audrey J. 2001. 'Career achievement: Opportunities and barriers.' In Judith Worell (Ed.), *Encyclopedia of women and gender.* San Diego: Academic Press.

Myles, John, and Quadagno, Jill. 2000. 'Envisioning a third way: The welfare state in the twenty-first century.' *Contemporary Sociology* 29 (1):156–67.

n.a. 1991. 'Polygamous spouses covered under B.C. family legislation, judge holds.' *The Lawyer's Weekly* 1 November: 4.

———. 1998. 'Is feminism dead?' *Time* 29 June.

———. 1999. 'You haven't come a long enough way, baby . . .' *The Cambridge Reporter* 8 December: 4A.

———. 2001. 'Court says woman can bar embryos' use.' *The New York Times on the Web* 15 August. http://www.nytimes.com.

———. 2003a. 'Beyond Botox: The cosmetic enhancement business.' *The Economist* 22 November. http://www.economist.com.

———. 2003b. 'Pots of promise.' *The Economist* 22 May. http://www.economist.com.

———. 2003c 'White couple wins black IVF twins.' *cnn.com* 26 February. http://edition.cnn.com/2003/WORLD/europe/02/26/britain.twins.reut/.

———. 2004. 'Sex is their business.' *The Economist* 2 September. http://www.economist.com.

———. 'Beauty and body image in the media.' Media Awareness Network. www.media-awareness.ca. Accessed January 21, 2010.

NAC (National Action Committee on the Status of Women). n.d. *About NAC.* http://nac-cca.ca/about_e.htm.

———. 2003. *Urgent message from the National Action Committee on the Status of Women.* 30 September. Email message circulated by Mariam Abou-Dib, Eastern Ontario regional representative.

NAC Young Womyn. n.d. *Canadian young womyn are a part of the Canadian women's movement.* http://nac-=cca/young/young_e.htm.

NAC. www.nac-cca.ca. Archived Results from Jan 01, 1996 – latest,' at Internet Archive: Way Back Machine. http://web.archive.org/web/*/http://www.nac-cca.ca. Accessed 14 December, 2010.

Nadeau, Mary-Jo. 2009. 'Rebuilding the house of Canadian feminism: NAC and the racial politics of participation.' In *Opening Doors Wider: Women's Political Engagement in Canada.* Ed. Sylvia Bashevkin. Vancouver: UBC Press: 33–50.

Naples, Nancy A. (Ed). 1998. *Community activism and feminist politics: Organizing across race, class, and gender.* New York: Routledge.

Navarro, Mireya. 2004. 'Arrest startles saleswoman of sex toys.' *New York Times* 20 January: A12.

NAWL (National Association of Women and the Law). 2006. *The Importance of Funding Women's Groups* (September). Online: http://www.nawl.ca/ns/en/Actions/act-swc.html.

NAWL (National Association of Women and the Law). 1998. *Custody and access: Brief to the Special Joint Committee on Child Custody and Access.* Ottawa: NAWL.

———. 2002. 'Lobby activities: Custody and access.' http://www.nawl.ca/lob-custody.htm.

Nelson, Lawrence J., and Nancy Milliken. 1988. 'Compelled medical treatment of pregnant women: Life, liberty, and law in conflict.' *Journal of the American Medical Association* 259:1060–7.

Nevitte, Neil, and Mebs Kanji. 2002. 'Canadian political culture and value change.' In Joanna Everitt and Brenda O'Neill (Eds), *Citizen politics: Research and theory in Canadian political behaviour,* 56–73. Don Mills, ON: Oxford University Press.

Newman, Jacquetta. 2008. 'Women in the 2005–2006 Canadian election: Keeping the volume down on women's political voices.' *British Journal of Canadian Studies* Vol. 21. No. 2, pp. 171–194.

———. 2009a. 'Small-p politics: Women working outside formal political structures,' in Mark Charlton and Paul Barker (Eds), *Crosscurrents Contemporary Political Issues,* 6th edition, Toronto: Nelson, pp. 265–75.

———. 2009b. 'Say it five times fast: The pitfalls of small-p politics and a plea for large-P politics.' In Mark Charlton and Paul Barker (Eds), *Crosscurrents Contemporary Political Issues,* 6th edition, Toronto: Nelson, pp. 276–288.

———, and A. Brian Tanguay. 2001. 'Crashing the party: The politics of interest groups and social movements.' In Joanna Everitt and Brenda O'Neill (Eds), *Citizen politics: Research and theory in Canadian political behaviour,* 387–412. Don Mills, ON: Oxford University Press.

NFO CFgroup. 2003. 'Public divided about definition of marriage.' 5 September. http://www.cbc.ca/stories/2003/09/04/samesexpoll030904.

Nicholson, Linda J. 1990. 'Introduction.' In Linda J. Nicholson (Ed.), *Feminism/postmodernism,* 1–16. New York: Routledge.

Norris, Pippa. 1997. 'Women leaders worldwide: A splash of color in the photo op.' In Pippa Norris (Ed.), *Women, media and politics,* 149–65. New York: Oxford University Press.

———, and Ronald Inglehart. 2001. 'Women and democracy: Cultural obstacles to equal representation.' *Journal of Democracy* 12 (3):126–40.

Nussbaum, Martha. 1999. 'Professor of parody.' *The New Republic* 220 (8): 37–45.

Oakley, Ann. 1997. 'A brief history of gender.' In Ann Oakley and Juliet Mitchell (Eds), *Who's afraid of feminism: Seeing through the backlash.* New York: The New Press.

O'Brien, Mary. 1989. 'State power and reproductive freedom.' In *Reproducing the world: Essays in feminist theory.* Boulder, CO: Westview Press.

OECD (Organisation for Economic Co-operation and Development). 2004. *Early childhood education and care policy: Canada country note.* Paris: OECD.

OED (*The Oxford English Dictionary*). 1985. Compact edition of the complete text. Oxford: Oxford University Press.

Office of the Auditor General of Ontario. 2010. *2010 Annual Report.* Toronto: Queen's Printer for Ontario.

Okin, Susan Moller. 1989. *Justice, gender, and the family.* New York: Basic Books.

———. 1996. 'Sexual orientation, gender, and families: Dichotomizing differences.' *Hypatia* 11: 30–48.

———. 1999. *Is Multiculturalism Bad for Women?* Princeton, NJ: Princeton Univ. Press.

O'Neill, Brenda. 1998. 'The relevance of leader gender to voting in the 1993 Canadian national election.' *International Journal of Canadian Studies* 17:105–30.

———. 2003. 'On the same wavelength? Feminist attitudes across generations of Canadian women.' In Manon Tremblay and Linda Trimble (Eds), *Women and electoral politics in Canada.* Don Mills, ON: Oxford University Press.

O'Neill, Brenda, Elisabeth Gidengil, and Lisa Young. 2008. 'Explaining feminist identification and gender related attitudes.' Paper presented at the annual meeting of the Canadian Political Science Association, University of British Columbia, Vancouver, BC, 4–6 June.

Ontario Coalition for Better Child Care. 2005. *Pay equity victory for women and unions—A fact sheet.* www.childcareontario.org. Accessed 6 July 2005.

Ontario Ministry of Labour. Minimum wage: Your guide to the Employment Standards Act. www. labour.gov.on.ca/english/es/guide/guide_4.html. Accessed 22 September 2009.

Orbach, Susie. 1978. *Fat is a feminist issue: The anti-diet guide to permanent weight loss.* New York: Paddington Press.

———. 1986. *Hunger strike: The anorectic's struggle as a metaphor for our age.* New York: W.W. Norton.

Osman, Mohamed and Sarah El Deeb. 2009. 'Pants pants revolution: Convicted woman leads charge to change Sudan's indecency laws.' *Globe and Mail* (8 September): A3.

Oulette, Grace. 2002. *The fourth world: An Indigenous perspective on feminism and Aboriginal women's activism.* Halifax: Fernwood Press.

Outshoorn, Joyce (Ed.). 2004. *The politics of prostitution: Women's movements, democratic states and the globalisation of sex commerce.* New York: Cambridge University Press.

Overall, Christine. 1992a. 'Feminist philosophical reflections on reproductive rights in Canada.' In Constance Backhouse and David H. Flaherty (Eds). *Challenging times: The women's movement in Canada and the United States,* 240–51. Montreal and Kingston: McGill-Queen's University Press.

———. 1992b. 'What's wrong with prostitution? Evaluating sex work.' *Signs* 17:705–24.

Owen, Dianne, and Jack Dennis. 1988. 'Gender differences in the politicization of American children.' *Women and Politics* 8:23–43.

Pal, Leslie A. 1993. *Interests of state: The politics of language, multiculturalism, and feminism in Canada.* Montreal and Kingston: McGill-Queen's University Press.

———. 1997. 'Beyond policy analysis: Public issue management in turbulent times.' Scarborough, ON: ITP Nelson.

Panetta, Alexandra. 2001. 'Poll reveals doubt on gay adoption.' *The Globe and Mail* 16 July: A4.

Parekh, Bikhu. 1996. 'Minority practices and principles of toleration.' *International Migration Review* 30 (1): 251–88.

Parrenas, Rhacel Salazar. 2001. *Servants of globalization.* Stanford: Stanford University Press.

Pateman, Carole. 1988. *The sexual contract.* Stanford: Stanford University Press.

Paul, Diane. 1997. 'From eugenics to medical genetics.' *Journal of Policy History* 9 (1):96–116.

Payne, Julien D., and Marilyn A. Payne. 2001. *Canadian Family Law.* Toronto: Irwin Law.

Pearson, Patricia. 1997. 'Women behaving badly.' *Saturday Night* September: 90–100.

Peterson, V. Spike. 1992. *Gendered states: Feminist (re)visions of international relations theory.* Boulder, CO: Lynne Reinner.

———, and Anne Sisson Runyan. 1993. *Global gender issues.* Boulder, CO: Westview Press.

Peterson, Zoë D. 2010. 'What is sexual empowerment? A multidimensional and process-oriented approach to adolescent girls' sexual empowerment.' *Sex Roles,* 2010 (62): pp. 307–13.

Phillips, Anne. 1998. 'Democracy and representation: or, Why should it matter who our representatives are?' In Anne Phillips (Ed.), *Feminism and politics,* 224–40. Oxford: Oxford University Press.

Philipps, Lisa. 2000. 'Taxing the market citizen: Fiscal policy and inequality in an age of privatization.' *Law and Contemporary Problems* Vol. 63, No. 4. Autumn 2000.

Phillips, Paul, and Erin Phillips. 1983. *Women and work: Inequality in the labour market.* Toronto: James Lorimer.

Phillips, Susan D. 1989. 'Rock-a-bye, Brian: The national strategy on child care.' In Katherine A. Graham (Ed.), *How Ottawa spends: The buck stops where?* 1989–90, 165–208. Ottawa: Carleton University Press.

———. 1991. 'How Ottawa blends: Shifting government relationships with interest groups.' In Frances Abele (Ed.), *How Ottawa spends: The politics of fragmentation* 1991–1992. Ottawa: Carleton University Press.

———. 1994. 'New social movements in Canadian politics: On fighting and starting fires.' In James P. Bickerton and Alain-G. Gagnon (Eds), *Canadian politics.* 2nd ed. Peterborough, ON: Broadview Press.

Philp, Margaret. 2000. 'Husbands also victims of spousal violence: Statscan.' *The Globe and Mail* 26 July: A3.

————. 2001. 'Gay adoption breaks new ground.' *The Globe and Mail* 9 July: A3.

Picard, André. 1999. 'Policy of testing for abnormal fetuses attacked.' *The Globe and Mail* 12 November: A9.

Pierson, Ruth Roach. 1995. 'Global issues.' In R.R. Pierson and M. Griffen (Eds), *Canadian women's issues volume II: Bold visions*. Toronto: James Lorimer.

Pitkin, Hannah. 1967. *The concept of representation*. Berkeley and Los Angeles: University of California Press.

Pitre, Sonia. 2003. 'Political parties and female candidates: Is there resistance in New Brunswick?' In Manon Tremblay and Linda Trimble (Eds), *Women and electoral politics in Canada*, 110–24. Don Mills, ON: Oxford University Press.

Place, Jeffrey. 1994. 'Gestational surrogacy and the meaning of "mother": *Johnson v. Calvert*', 8511 P.2d 776 (Cal. 1993). *Harvard Journal of Law and Public Policy* 17:907–18.

Posner, Richard. 2003. *Economic analysis of law*. 6th ed. New York: Aspen Publishers.

Praud, Jocelyne. 1998. 'Affirmative action and women's representation in the Ontario New Democratic Party.' In Manon Tremblay and Caroline Andrew (Eds), *Women and political representation in Canada*, 171–93. Ottawa: University of Ottawa Press.

————. 2003. 'The Parti Québécois, its Women's Committee, and the feminization of the Quebec electoral arena.' In Manon Tremblay and Linda Trimble (Eds), *Women and electoral politics in Canada*, 125–37. Don Mills, ON: Oxford University Press.

Prentice, Alison, Paula Bourne, Gail Cuthbert Brandt, Beth Light, Wendy Mitchinson, and Naomi Black. 1988. *Canadian women: A history*. Toronto: Harcourt Brace Jovanovich.

Priest, Lisa. 2001. 'New Brunswick occupies front line in fight for private-clinic abortions.' *The Globe and Mail* 5 March: A1, A5.

————. 2002a. 'Embryo-adoption program to offer infertile couples one last chance.' *The Globe and Mail* 4 March: A1, A4.

————. 2002b. 'Rules violations found at Canada's sperm banks.' *The Globe and Mail* 8 July: A1, A6.

Pross, Paul. 1990. 'Pressure groups: Talking chameleons.' In Michael S. Whittington and Glen Williams, *Canadian politics in the 1990s*. Scarborough, ON: Nelson Canada.

Quadrio, Carolyn. 2000. 'Psychiatry.' In Chris Kramarae and Dale Spender (Eds), *Routledge international encyclopedia of women: Global women's issues and knowledge*. New York: Routledge.

Ralston, Meredith. 1999. *Why women run*. Montreal: National Film Board.

Ramsey, Laura R., Megan E. Haines, Molly M. Hurt, Jaclyn A. Nelson, Dixie L. Turner, Miriam Liss, and Mindy J. Erchull. 2007. 'Thinking of others: Feminist identification and the perception of others' beliefs.' *Sex Roles* 56: 611–16.

Randall, Vicky. 1987. *Women and politics: An international perspective*. 2nd ed. Chicago: University of Chicago Press.

Rankin, L. Pauline, and Jill Vickers. 2001. *Women's movements and state feminism: Integrating diversity into public policy*. Ottawa: Status of Women Canada.

Roa, Jessica. 2010. 'It's the year of the value diet,' CNBC.com. at www.cnbc.com/id/37492840/ It_s_The_Year _of_The_Diet.html. Accessed January 18, 2011.

Rayside, David. 2008. *Queer inclusions, continental divisions: Public recognition of sexual diversity in Canada and the United States*. Toronto: University of Toronto Press.

Razack, Sherene. 2000. 'Gendered Racial Violence and Spatialized Justice: The Murder of Pamela George.' *Canadian Journal of Law and Society* 15: 91–130.

RCMP. 2010. 'Human trafficking in Canada: A threat assessment, executive summary.' Available at: http://www.rcmp-grc.gc.ca/pubs/ht-tp/htta-tpem-eng.htm. Accessed 5 February 2011.

RCSW (Royal Commission on the Status of Women in Canada). 1970. *Report of the Royal Commission on the Status of Women in Canada*. Ottawa: Information Canada.

Rebick, Judy. 2005. *Ten thousand roses: The making of a feminist revolution*. Toronto: Penguin Canada.

————. 2010. 'Happy IWD: Assessment of women's movement 40 years after Royal Commission the Status of Women.' *Rabble.ca News for the Rest of Us*. http://www.rabble.ca March 6, 2010. Accessed December 6, 2010.

Reform Party of Canada. 1999. *The blue book: Principles and policies of the Reform Party*. Calgary: The Party.

Rhoades, Helen. 2002. 'The rise and rise of shared parenting laws: A critical reflection.' *Canadian Journal of Family Law* 19:75–114.

Rhode, Deborah L. 2010. *The beauty bias: The injustice of appearance in life and law.* New York: Oxford University Press.

Rice, Carla. 1994. 'Out from under occupation: Transforming our relationships with our bodies.' *Canadian Woman Studies* 14:44–51.

Rich, Adrienne. 1976. *Of woman born: Motherhood as experience and institution.* New York: Norton.

———. 1997. 'Compulsory heterosexuality and lesbian existence.' In Sandra Kemp and Judith Squires (Eds), *Feminisms*, 320–5. Oxford: Oxford University Press.

Richer, Karine. 2008. *Abortion in Canada: Twenty years after R. v. Morgentaler.* PRB 08-22E. Ottawa: Library of Parliament.

Roa, Jessica. 2010. 'It's the year of the value diet.' CNBC.com. 18 January 2011. http://www.cnbc.com/id/37492840/It_s_The_Year_of_The_Diet.html. Accessed 18 January 2011.

Rodgers, Sandra. 2002. 'The legal regulation of women's reproductive capacity in Canada.' In Jocelyn Downie, Timothy Caufield and Colleen Flood (Eds), *Canadian health law and policy*, 331–65. Toronto: Butterworths.

Rosaldo, Michelle Z. 1974. 'Women, culture, and society: A theoretical overview.' In Michelle Z. Rosaldo and Louise Lamphere (Eds), *Women, culture and society*, 17–42. Stanford: Stanford University Press.

Rosin, Hanna. 2010. 'The end of men.' *The Atlantic* (July/August). Online: http://www.theatlantic.com/magazine/archive/2010/06/the-end-of-men/8135/.

Rosneil, Sasha. 1995. *Disarming patriarchy: Feminism and political action at Greenham.* Buckingham, UK: Open University Press.

Ross, Becki. 1988. 'Heterosexuals only need apply: The Secretary of State's regulation of lesbian existence.' *Resources for Feminist Research/Documentation sur la recherche féministe* 17 (3):35–8.

Rousseau, Jean-Jacques. 1762/1979. *Emile: Or on education.* (Allan Bloom trans. and notes) New York: Basic Books.

Rowbotham, Sheila. 1989. *The past is before us: Feminism in action since the 1960s.* London: Penguin Books.

———. 1992. *Women in movement: Feminism and social action.* New York: Routledge.

———. 1997. *A century of women: The history of women in Britain and the United States in the twentieth century.* Toronto: Penguin Books.

———. 1999. *Threads through time: Writing in history and autobiography.* Markham, ON: Penguin Books.

———, Lynn Segal, and Hilary Wainwright. 1979. *Beyond the fragments: Feminism and the making of socialism.* London: Merlin.

Royal Commission on New Reproductive Technologies. 1993. *Proceed with care: Final report of the Royal Commission on New Reproductive Technologies.* Ottawa: Minister of Supply and Services Canada.

Ruddick, Sara. 1980. 'Maternal thinking.' *Feminist Studies* 6 (2): 342–67.

Rupp, Leila J. 1997. *Worlds of women: The making of an international women's movement.* Princeton: Princeton University Press.

———. 2001. 'Is feminism the province of old (or middle-aged) women?' *Journal of Women's History* 12 (4):164–73.

Rusk, James. 1997. 'Ontario loses pay-equity fight.' *The Globe and Mail* 9 September: A1, A6.

Russell, Peter H., Rainer Knopff, and Ted Morton. 1989. *Federalism and the Charter: Leading constitutional decisions.* Ottawa: Carleton University Press.

Ryder, Bruce. 2001. 'The Little Sisters case, administrative censorship, and obscenity law.' *Osgoode Hall Law Journal* 39:207–27.

Sainsbury, Diane. 1994. *Gendering welfare states.* London: Sage.

———. 1999. *Gender and welfare state regimes.* Oxford, New York: Oxford University Press.

Sampert, Shannon, and Linda Trimble. 2003. ' "Wham, bam, no thank you, ma'am": Gender and the gender frame in national newspaper coverage of election 2000.' In Manon Tremblay and Linda Trimble (Eds), *Women and electoral politics in Canada*, 211–26. Don Mills, ON: Oxford University Press.

Sandel, Michael. 1989. 'Moral argument and liberal toleration: Abortion and homosexuality.' *California Law Review* 77 (3):521–38.

———. 2007. *The case against perfection: Ethics in the age of genetic engineering.* Cambridge, MA:

Harvard University Press.

Sangster, Joan. 1996. 'Incarcerating "bad girls": The regulation of sexuality through the Female Refuges Act in Ontario, 1920–1945.' *Journal of the History of Sexuality* 7:239–75.

———. 2001. *Regulating girls and women: Sexuality, family, and the law in Ontario, 1920–1960.* Toronto: University of Toronto Press.

Sapiro, Virginia. 1981. 'When are interests interesting? The problem of political representation of women.' *The American Political Science Review* 75 (3):701–21.

———. 1991. 'Gender politics, gendered politics: The state of the field.' In William Crofty (Ed.), *Political science: Looking to the future, volume one: The theory and practice of political science*, 165–87. Evanston, IL: Northwestern University Press.

Sardar, Ziauddin, and Borin Van Loon. 1997. *Cultural studies for beginners.* Cambridge, UK: Icon Books.

Saunders, Doug. 2002. 'Mom kills, Dad kills: Two takes on tragedy.' *The Globe and Mail* 2 March: A1, A2.

Scala, Francesca, Éric Montpetit, and Isabelle Fortier. 2005. 'The nac's Organizational practices and politics of assisted reproductive technologies in Canada.' *Canadian Journal of Political Science* 38(3): 581–604.

Schlafly, Phyllis. 1986. Phyllis Schlafly's alternative: 'The positive woman.' In James David Barber and Barbara Kellerman (Eds), *Women leaders in American politics*, 154–64. Englewood Cliffs, NJ: Prentice Hall.

Schlozman, Kay Lehman. 1990. 'Representing women in Washington: Sisterhood and pressure politics.' In Louise Tilly and Patricia Gurin (Eds), *Women, politics, and change*, 339–82. New York: Russell Sage.

———, Nancy Burns, Sidney Verba, and Jesse Donahue. 1995. 'Gender and citizen participation: Is there a different voice?' *American Journal of Political Science* 39:267–93.

Schmidt, Sarah. 2000. 'College girl to call girl.' *The Globe and Mail* 29 April: R7.

Schmitz, Cristin. 2005a. 'Woodbridge parents take fight to top court: Thousands affected.' *The National Post* 10 January: A7.

———. 2005b. 'Cotler hopes to reintroduce child-custody legislation.' *The National Post* 12 April: A8.

Scholz, Sally J. 2010. *Feminism: A beginner's guide.* Oxford: One World Publications/Oxford.

Schultz, Marjorie. 1982. 'Contractual ordering of marriage: A new model for state policy.' *California Law Review* 7 (2):204–334.

Sefton, Barbara Wylan. 1998. 'The value of mothering'. *Mothering Magazine* January/February: 28–9.

Séguin, Rhéal. 2005. 'Women fill most of PQ's leading jobs.' *The Globe and Mail* 8 June: A5.

SES Canada Research Inc. 2003. 'Political crossfire—Legalizing same-sex marriages; Generation and faith divide Canadians.' 7 September. http://www.sesresearch.com/news/press_releases/pr%20 September%207%202003.pdf.

Shaffer, Martha. 1991. 'R. v. Sullivan and Lemay: A case comment.' *McGill Law Journal* 36:1369–81.

Shakespeare, Tom. 1998. 'Choices and rights: Eugenics, genetics and disability equality.' *Disability and Society* 13:665–81.

Shalev, Carmel. 1989. *Birth power: The case for surrogacy.* New Haven: Yale University Press.

Shanley, Mary Lyndon. 1993. '"Surrogate mothering" and women's freedom: A critique of contracts for human reproduction.' *Signs* 18 (3): 618–39.

Sharpe, Sydney. 1994. *The gilded ghetto: Women and political power in Canada.* Toronto: HarperCollins.

Shaw, Jessica. 2006. *Reality check: A close look at accessing abortion services in Canadian hospitals.* Ottawa: Canadians for Choice.

Sheehan, Nancy A. 1984. 'The WCTU and education strategies on the Canadian prairie.' *History of Education Quarterly* 24 (1):101–19.

Shenon, Philip. 2000. 'Feminist coalition protests U.S. stance on sex trafficking treaty.' *The New York Times* 13 January: A5.

Siim, Birte. 1994. 'Engendering democracy: Social citizenship and political participation for women in Scandinavia.' *Social Politics*, 1, 1994, pp. 286–305.

Sinha, M., D. Guy, and A. Woollacott (Eds). 1999. *Feminisms and internationalism.* Oxford: Blackwell.

Skocpol, Theda. 1992. *Protecting soldiers and mothers: The political origins of social policy in the United States.* Cambridge, MA: Harvard University Press.

————. 1992. *Protecting soldiers and mothers: The politics of social provision in the United States 1870s to 1920s.* Cambridge MA: Harvard University Press.

Skrypnek, Berna J., and Janet E. Fast. 1996. 'Work and family policy in Canada: Family needs, collective solutions.' *Journal of Family Issues* 17 (6):793–812.

Slater, J., C. Green, G. Sevenhuysen, J. O'Neil, and B. Edginton. 2009. 'Socio-demographic and geographic analysis of overweight and obesity in Canadian adults using the Canadian Community Health Survey (2005).' *Chronic Diseases in Canada* 30, 1: 4–15.

Smith, Andrea. 2007. 'Native American feminism, sovereignty, and social change'. In Joyce Green (ed.), *Making space for Indigenous feminism.* London: Zed Books.

Smith, Dorothy. 1987. *The everyday world as problematic: A feminist sociology.* Boston: Northeastern Univ. Press.

Smith, Jennifer, and Herman Bakvis. 2000. 'Changing dynamics in election campaign finance: Critical issues in Canada and the United States.' *Policy Matters* 1 (4).

Smith, Joy. 2010. 'News release: Child trafficking bill overcomes final hurdle to become law.' Office of Joy Smith, M.P. Kildonan-St. Paul , June 17, 2010. http://www.joysmith.ca/speech. asp?newsID=528. Accessed February 10, 2011.

Smith, Miriam. 2000. 'Interest groups and social movements.' In Michael Whittington and Glen Williams (Eds), *Canadian politics in the 21st century,* 173–91. Scarborough, ON: Nelson Thomson Learning.

Solca, Luca, & Matt Wing. 2009. Black Book: LVMH King of the Luxury Jungle, 2009. P 139. http:// search.ebscohost.com/login.aspx?direct=true&db=bth&AN=45224793. Accessed January 10, 2011.

Solomon, Deborah. 2009. 'Questions for Jessica Valenti: Fourth-wave feminism.' *The New York Times Magazine* (13 November): 24.

Spivak, Gayatri Chakravorty. 1988. 'French feminisms in an international frame.' In *In other worlds: Essays in cultural politics.* New York: Routledge.

Stalker, Peter. 2001. *The no-nonsense guide to international migration.* Toronto: New Internationalist Publications and Between the Lines.

Standing Committee on the Status of Women. 2005. *Funding through the Women's Program: Women's groups speak out.* Ottawa: The Committee.

————. 2007. *The impacts of funding and program changes at Status of Women Canada.* 39th Parliament, 1st Session Report (May). Ottawa: The Committee.

————. 2007. *Report of the Standing Committee on the Status of Women: Improving the economic security of women: Time to act.* Ottawa: Communication Canada, June 2007.

————. 2007. Turning outrage into action to address trafficking for the purpose of sexual exploitation in Canada. Ottawa: Communication Canada, http://www.parl.gc.ca Available at: http://cmte. parl.gc.ca/content/hoc/committee/391/fewo/reports/rp2738918/feworp12/feworp12-e.pdf.

————. 2009. An analysis of the effects of the Public Sector Equitable Compensation Act: Report of the Standing Committee on the Status of Parliament. Ottawa: Public Works and Government Services Canada, June 2009.

Statistics Canada. 2000. *Women in Canada 2000: A gender-based statistical report.* Cat. no. 89-503-XPE. Ottawa: Minister of Industry.

————. 2001. 'Economic gender equality indicators 2000.' *Canadian Social Trends* special insert 60:1–8.

————. 2002a. 'Divorces.' *The Daily* 2 December. Ottawa: Minister of Industry. http://www.statcan. ca/Daily/English/021202/d021202f.htm.

————. 2002b. *Family history.* Cat. no. 89-575-XIE. Ottawa: Ministry of Industry. http://www. statcan.ca/english/freepub/89-575-XIE/89-575-XIE2001001.pdf.

————. 2003a. *The changing profile of Canada's labour force, 2001 Census.* Analysis Series. 11 February. Cat. no. 96F0030XIE2001009. Ottawa: Minister of Industry. http://www.statcan.ca.

————. 2003b. *Family violence in Canada: A statistical profile 2003.* Cat. no. 85-224-XIE. Ottawa: Minister of Industry. http://www.hc-sc.gc.ca/hppb/familyviolence/pdfs/2003famvioprofil_e.pdf.

————. 2003c. *Women in Canada: Work chapter updates.* Cat. no. 89F0133XIE. Ottawa: Ministry of Industry. http://www.statcan.ca/english/freepub/89F0133XIE/89F0133XIE02001.pdf.

————. 2005. *Child and spousal support: Maintenance enforcement survey statistics 2003–2004.* Ottawa: Statistics Canada.

————. 2005. 'Divorces.' *The Daily* 9 March. Online: http://www.statcan.gc.ca/daily-quotidi-en/050309/dq050309b-eng.htm.

————. 2005. 'Fact-sheet on work absences.' *Perspectives on Labour and Income.* April 2005. Statistics Canada – Catalogue no. 75-001-XIE.

————. 2006. 'Births.' *The Daily* 31 July. Online: http://www.statcan.gc.ca/daily-quotidien/060731/dq060731b-eng.htm.

————. 2006. *Women in Canada.* 5th edition. Ottawa: Statistics Canada Catalogue # 89-503-XIE

————. 2007. The Canadian labour market at a glance. Statistics Canada – Catalogue no. 71-222-X, p. 52.

————. 2007a. *Family portrait: Continuity and change in Canadian families and households in 2006, 2006 Census.* Cat. No. 97-553-XIE. Ottawa: Statistics Canada.

————. 2007b. 'Marriages.' *The Daily* 17 January. Online: http://www.statcan.gc.ca/daily-quotidi-en/070117/dq070117a-eng.htm.

————. 2008. 'Society and community.' *Canada Year Book 2008.* Statistics Canada – Catalogue no. 11-402-X, pp. 375–90.

————. 2009b. 'Canada's changing labour force, 2006 Census: The provinces and territories: Unpaid work.' www12.statcan.gc.ca/census-recensement/2006/as-sa/97-559/p3. Accessed 8 December 2009.

————. 2009. *Family violence in Canada: A statistical profile 2005.* Cat. No. 85-224-X. Ottawa: Statistics Canada Online: http://dsp-psd.pwgsc.gc.ca/collection_2009/statcan/85-224-X/85-224-x2009000-eng.pdf.

————. 2009a. 'Labour force characteristics by age and sex.' *Labour Force Survey November 2009.* 4 December 2009.

————. 2009a. 'Labour force survey November 2009–December 4, 2009.' www.statscan.gc.ca/subjects-sujets/labour-travail/lfs-epa/lfs-epa-eng.pdf. Accessed 7 December 2009.

————. 2010a. CANSIM Database Table 101-6512. *Number of dependents in divorces involving custody orders, by party to whom custody was granted, Canada, provinces and territories, annual(number).* Accessed 11 January 2011.

————. 2010b. *Child and spousal support: Maintenance enforcement survey statistics 2009–2010.* Ottawa: Statistics Canada. Online: http://www.statcan.gc.ca/pub/85-228-x/85-228-x2011000-eng.pdf.

Status of Women Canada. 1997. 'Women's Program funding to be more flexible and accountable.' 14 March. http://www.swc-cfc.gc.ca/news97/0314-e.html.

————. 2000a. *Descriptive list of approved grants and contributions provided through the Women's Program, Status of Women Canada, April 1, 1999, to March 31, 2000.* Ottawa: Status of Women Canada.

————. 2000b. *Women and men in Canada: A statistical glance.* Ottawa: Target Groups Project, Statistics Canada.

————. Women's Program. 2002. *Women's Program funding guidelines.* http://www.swc-cfc.gc.ca/wm-nprog/guidtxte.html.

——. 2007. *Who we are.* Available at www.swc-cfc.gc.ca/abu-ans/index-eng.html. Accessed March 2007.

Stepp, Laura Sessions. 2004. 'For abortion rights, a changing of the guard.' *The Washington Post* 24 April: C1, C4.

Stetson, Dorothy McBride. 1996. 'Feminist perspectives on abortion and reproductive technologies.' In Marianne Githens and Dorothy McBride Stetson (Eds), *Abortion politics: public policy in cross-cultural perspective,* 211–23. New York: Routledge.

————. 1997. *Women's rights in the USA: Policy debates and gender roles.* 2nd ed. New York: Garland.

———— (Ed). 2001. *Abortion politics, women's movements, and the democratic state: A comparative study of state feminism.* New York: Oxford University Press.

Stetson, Dorothy McBride, and Amy Mazur (Eds). 1995a. *Comparative state feminism.* Thousand Oaks, CA: Sage.

————. 1995b. 'Introduction.' In Dorothy McBride Stetson and Amy Mazur, *Comparative state feminism.* Thousand Oaks, CA: Sage.

Stewart, David K. 2002. 'Electing a premier: An examination of the 1992 Alberta pc universal ballot.' In Joanna Everitt and Brenda O'Neill (Eds), *Citizen politics: Research and theory in Canadian political behaviour,* 321–37. Don Mills, ON: Oxford University Press.

Stienstra, Deborah. 2000. 'Cutting to gender: Teaching gender in international relations.' *International Studies Perspectives* 1:233–44.

Stobert, Susan, and Kelly Cranswick. 2004. 'Looking after seniors: Who does what for whom.' *Canadian Social Trends* autumn: 2–6. Statistics Canada catalogue no. 11-008.

Strong-Boag, Veronica, Mona Gleason, and Adele Perry. 2002. Editors' introduction to Manon Tremblay, 'Quebec women in politics: A reappraisal.' In Veronica Strong-Boag, Mona Gleason, and Adele Perry (Eds), *Rethinking Canada: The promise of women's history*. 4th ed, 375–6. Don Mills, ON: Oxford University Press.

Struening, Karen. 1996. 'Feminist challenges to the new familialism: Lifestyle experimentation and the freedom of intimate association.' *Hypatia* 11 (1):135–54.

Stuart, Don, and Robert Delisle. 2001. *Learning Canadian criminal law*. Toronto: Carswell.

Studlar, Donley. 1999. 'Will Canada seriously consider electoral system reform? Women and aboriginals should.' In Henry Milner (Ed.), *Making every vote count: Reassessing Canada's electoral system*, 123–32. Peterborough, ON: Broadview Press.

———, and Richard E. Matland. 1996. 'The dynamics of women's representation in the Canadian provinces: 1975–1994.' *Canadian Journal of Political Science* 29 (2):269–93.

———, and Raymond Tatalovich. 1996. 'Abortion policy in the United States and Canada: Do institutions matter?' In Marianne Githens and Dorothy McBride Stetson (Eds), *Abortion politics: Public policy in cross-cultural perspective*, 75–95. New York: Routledge.

Stueck, Wendy. 2010. 'Canada would become magnet for polygamy if law struck down, court told.' *The Globe and Mail* (22 November).

Sussman, Deborah, and Martin Tabi. 2004. 'Minimum wage workers.' *Perspectives on Labour and Income*. 5 (3):5–8. Catalogue no. 75-001-XIE. Ottawa: Statistics Canada.

Swift, Karen J. 1995. *Manufacturing 'bad mothers': A critical perspective on child neglect*. Toronto: University of Toronto Press.

Talbot, Margaret. 1999. 'The little white bombshell.' *The New York Times Magazine* 11 July: 39–43, 48, 61–3.

Tarrow, Sidney. 1994. *Power in movement: Social movements, collective action and politics*. Cambridge, UK: Cambridge University Press.

Tatalovich, Raymond. 1997. *The politics of abortion in the United States and Canada: A comparative study*. New York: M.E. Sharpe.

Tate, Katherine. 2003. *Black faces in the mirror: African Americans and their representatives in the US Congress*. Princeton, NJ: Princeton University Press.

Taylor, Verta. 1989. 'Social movement continuity: The women's movement in abeyance.' *American Sociological Review*. 54 (5), 761–775.

Telford, Hamish. 2002. 'The Reform Party/Canadian Alliance and Canada's flirtation with republicanism.' In Hamish Telford and Harvey Lazar (Eds), *Canada: The state of the federation 2001: Canadian political culture(s) in transition*. Montreal and Kingston: McGill-Queen's University Press: 111–38.

Templin, Charlotte (1999). 'Hillary Clinton as threat to gender norms: Cartoon images of the First Lady.' *Journal of Communication Inquiry* 23 (1): 20–36.

Thomas, Sue. 1994. *How women legislate*. New York: Oxford University Press.

Thorbek, Susanne, and Bandana Pattanaik (Eds). 2002. *Transnational prostitution: Changing global patterns*. New York: Zed Books.

Tibbetts, Janice. 2002. 'Common law not equal to marriage.' *The National Post* 20 December online edition. http://fact.on.ca/news/news0212/np021220.htm.

———. 2003. 'Estranged parents don't have rights.' *The National Post* 28 March: A9.

Tickner, Ann. 1992. *Gender and international relations: Feminist perspectives on achieving global security*. New York: Columbia University Press.

Tiedge, Linda Beth, Camille B. Wortman, Geraldine Downey, Carol Emmons, Monica Biernat, and Eric Lang. 1990. 'Women with multiple roles: Role-compatibility perceptions, satisfaction, and mental health.' *Journal of Marriage and the Family* 2 (1):63–72.

Tiessen, Rebecca. 2003. 'Masculinities, femininities, and sustainable development: A gender analysis of DFAIT's sustainable development strategy.' In Claire Turenne Sjolander, Heather A. Smith, and Deborah Stienstra (Eds), *Feminist perspectives on Canadian foreign policy*, 108–23. Don Mills, ON: Oxford University Press.

Timpson, Annis May. 2001. *Driven apart: Women's employment equality and child care in Canadian public policy.* Vancouver: University of British Columbia Press.

———. 2002–3. 'Trudeau, women and the mystic North.' *London Journal of Canadian Studies* 18:41–61.

Tisdale, Sally. 1992. 'Talk dirty to me: A woman's taste for pornography.' *Harpers* 284 (1): 37–9, 42–6.

Tong, Rosemarie Putnam. 1998. *Feminist thought: A more comprehensive introduction.* 2nd ed. Boulder, CO: Westview Press.

Toughill, Kelly. 1993. 'Women slip in status, NAC says.' *Toronto Star* July 16, 1993. A14.

Touraine, Alain. 2000. *Revolution catalysts of change: Exploration, war, and revolution.* VHS Recording. Princeton, NJ: Films for the Humanities and Sciences.

Treasury Board of Canada Secretariat. 2009. 'Statement of the President of the Treasury Board Welcoming the Public Sector Equitable Compensation Act, February 9, 2009.' Available online http://www.tbs-sct.gc.ca/media/nr-cp/2009/0206b-eng#fspseca_.

———. 2010. Employment equity in the Public Service of Canada, annual report to Parliament 2008–2009. Ottawa: Her Majesty the Queen in Right of Canada, 2010. Catalogue no. BT1-9/2009 http://www.tbs-sct.gc.ca

Trebay, Guy. 2007. 'Fashion diary: Still too thin, and getting younger.' *The New York Times* September 27, 2007. www.nytimes.com/2007/09.27/fashion.html

Tremblay, Manon. 1998. 'Do female MPs substantively represent women? A study of legislative behaviour in Canada's 35th Parliament.' *Canadian Journal of Political Science* 31 (3):435–65.

———. 2002. 'Quebec women in politics: A reappraisal.' In Veronica Strong-Boag, Mona Gleason, and Adele Perry (Eds). *Rethinking Canada: The promise of women's history.* 4th ed. 375–93. Don Mills, ON: Oxford University Press.

———. 2003. 'The participation of Aboriginal women in Canadian electoral democracy.' *Electoral Insight* (November). Online: http://www.elections.ca/res/eim/article_search/article.asp?id=26&lang=e&frmPageSize=

———, and Caroline Andrew. 1998. *Women and political representation in Canada.* Ottawa: University of Ottawa Press.

———, and Réjean Pelletier. 2000. 'More feminists or more women? Descriptive or substantive representations of women in the 1997 Canadian federal elections.' *International Political Science Review* 21 (4):381–405.

———, and Réjean Pelletier. 2001. 'More women constituency party presidents: A strategy for increasing the number of women candidates in Canada?' *Party Politics* 7 (2):157–90.

———, and Linda Trimble. 2003. 'Women and electoral politics in Canada: A survey of the literature.' In Manon Tremblay and Linda Trimble. (Eds), *Women and electoral politics in Canada*, 1–20. Don Mills, ON: Oxford University Press.

———, with Stephanie Mullen. 2009. 'Women in the Quebec National Assembly: Why so many?' In Sylvia Bashevkin (Ed.) *Opening doors wider: Women's political engagement in Canada.* Vancouver: UBC Press, pp. 51–69.

Tremlett, Giles. 2005. 'Blow to machismo as Spain forces men to do housework.' *The Guardian* 8 April. http://www.guardian.co.uk/gender/story/0,11812,1454803,00.html.

Tribe, Laurence. 1990. *Abortion: The clash of absolutes.* New York: Norton.

Trimble, Linda. 1998. 'Who's represented? Gender and diversity in the Alberta legislature.' In Manon Tremblay and Caroline Andrew (Eds), *Women and political representation in Canada*, 257–89. Ottawa: University of Ottawa Press.

———. 2005. *Who framed Belinda Stronach? National newspaper coverage of the Conservative Party of Canada's 2004 leadership race.* Paper presented at the Canadian Political Science Association annual meeting, London, ON, 4 June.

———, and Jane Arscott. 2003. *Still counting: Women in politics across Canada.* Peterborough, ON: Broadview Press.

Trinh, T. Minh-ha. 1989. *Woman, native, other.* Bloomington, IN: Indiana University Press.

Tronto, Joan. 2002. 'The "nanny" question in feminism.' *Hypatia* 17 (2): 34–51.

Turpel, Mary Ellen. 1993. 'Patriarchy and paternalism: The legacy of the Canadian state for First Nations women.' *Canadian Journal of Women and the Law*, 6: 174–92.

Tyyska, Vappu. 1998. 'Insiders and outsiders: Women's movements and organizational effectiveness.'

The Canadian Review of Sociology and Anthropology 35:391–410.

United Nations. 1995. 'Beijing Declaration and Platform for Action.' At www.un.org/womenwatch/ daw/beijing/pdf/BDPfA%20E.pdf. Accessed November 4, 2010.

———. 2000a. *The world's women: Trends and statistics.* New York: United Nations.

———. 2000b. *Trafficking in women and girls: Report of the Secretary-General of the United Nations.* New York: United Nations.

———. 2001. *From Beijing to Beijing +5: Review and appraisal of the implementation of the Beijing Platform for Action.* New York: United Nations.

———. 2003. *Violence against women immigrant workers: Report of the Secretary-General of the United Nations.* July. New York: United Nations.

———. 2005. *The world's women 2005: Progress in statistics.* Available at: http://unstats.un.org/unsd/ demographic/products/indwm/wwpub.htm

United Nations Development Programme. 2000. *Women's political participation and good governance: Twenty-first century challenges.* New York: United Nations.

———. 2010. 'What is gender mainstreaming?' www.undp.org/women/mainstream/whais.html. Accessed February 16, 2010

UNAIDS. 2009. AIDS epidemic update: November 2009. Available at: www.unaids.org/en/media/ unaids/contentassets/dataimport/pub/report/2009/jc1700_epi_update_2009_en.pdf

UNIAP (United Nations Inter-Agency Project on Human Trafficking). 2009. 'Cambodia: Exodus to the sex trade? Effects of the global financial crisis on women's working conditions and opportunities.' SIREN Report. 20 July 2009. http://www.no-trafficking.org/reports_docs/siren/siren_cb-04.pdf. Accessed February 18, 2010.

UNIFEM. No date. 'Facts & figures on women, poverty and economics.' http://unifem.org/gender_is-sues/women_poverty_economics/facts_figures.php. Accessed 16 December, 2009.

———. 2008. Progress of the world's women 2008/2009: Who answers to women? Gender and accountability. Online: http://www.unifem.org/progress/2008

UNIFEM Canada. 2009. 'Violence against women.' 25 February 2009. http://www.unifemcanada.org/ index.php?view=article&id=49%3Aviolence-against –women.htm. Accessed February 4, 2010.

UNHCR (United Nations High Commissioner for Refugees). 2001. *Women, children and older refugees. The sex and age distribution of refugee populations with a special emphasis on UNHCR policy priorities.* Geneva: Population Data Unit, UNHCR. www.unhcr.ch.

United Nations Population Fund. 2004. *State of the world population 2004. The Cairo consensus at ten. Population reproductive health and the global effort to end poverty.* New York: United Nations.

University of Western Ontario. 2003. 'Full-time constituent enrolment 2002–2003.' In *Western Facts 2003.* www.uwo.ca/western/westernfacts/wf03/table_3d.html. Accessed 13 September 2004.

———. 2009a. 'Full-time constituent enrolment 2008–9 by faculty and gender.' In *Western Facts 2009.* www.ipb.uwo.ca/documents/2009_faculty_gender.pdf. Accessed 3 December 2009.

———. 2009b. 'Five-distribution of full-time faculty by faculty and gender.' In *Western Facts 2009.* www.ipb.uwo.ca/documents/2009_faculty_by_faculty_gender.pdf.

US State Department. 2009. 2009 Human rights reports: Canada. Available at: http://www.state. gov/g/drl/rls/hrrpt/2009/wha/136104.htm. Accessed February 2, 2011.

Valverde, Marianna. 1991. *The age of light soap and water: Moral reform in English Canada 1885–1925.* Toronto: McClelland and Stewart.

Vancouver Sun. 2007. 'Human trafficking a Games pitfall, researcher warns,.' *Vancouver Sun.* Canada.com November 2, 2007. Available at: http://www.canada.com/vancouversun/news/ business/story.html?id=c8b93773-4373-465c-92a3-4c5af740bec7. Accessed January 15, 2011.

Van Deven, Mandy. 2009. 'Just say yes: will a pro-sex philosophy be the next tool in the anti-rape arsenal?' *Herizons* 22 (4), Spring 2009, pp. 29–31.

Vanier Institute of the Family. 2010. *Families count: Profiling Canada's families.* Ottawa: Vanier Institute of the Family. Online: http://www.vifamily.ca/media/webfm-uploads/Publications/ FamiliesCount/Families_Count.pdf.

Verba, Sidney, Nancy Burns, and Kay Lehman Schlozman. 1997. 'Knowing and caring about politics: Gender and political engagement.' *The Journal of Politics* 59:1051–72.

Vickers, Jill. 1989. 'Feminist approaches to women in politics.' In Linda Kealey and Joan Sangster (Eds), *Beyond the vote: Canadian women and politics.* Toronto: University of Toronto Press: 16–36.

———. 1992. 'The intellectual origins of the women's movements in Canada.' In Constance

Backhouse and David H. Flaherty. (Eds), *Challenging times: The women's movement in Canada and the United States*, 39–60. Montreal and Kingston: McGill-Queen's University Press.

———. 1997a. *Reinventing political science: A feminist approach*. Halifax: Fernwood.

———. 1997b. 'Towards a feminist understanding of representation.' In Jane Arscott and Linda Trimble (Eds), *In the presence of women: Representation in Canadian governments*, 20–46. Toronto: Harcourt Brace.

———, Pauline Rankin, and Christine Appelle. 1993. *Politics as if women mattered: A political analysis of the National Action Committee on the Status of Women*. Toronto: University of Toronto Press.

Vosko, Leah F., Nancy Zukewich, and Cynthia Cranford. 2003. 'Precarious jobs: A new typology of employment.' *Perspectives on Labour and Income* 4 (10):16–26. Catalogue no. 75-001-XIE. Ottawa: Statistics Canada.

Wallace, Bruce, and Luke Fisher. 1999. 'Pay equity at last.' *Maclean's* 1 November: 28.

Walton, Dawn. 2002. 'Divorce rate up slightly, Statscan says.' *The Globe and Mail* 3 December: A4.

Wang, Youfa and May A. Beydoun. 2007. 'The obesity epidemic in the United States - Gender, age, socioeconomic, racial/ethnic, and geographic characteristics: A systematic review and meta-regression analysis.' *Epidemiologic Reviews* 29: 6–28.

Waring, Marilyn. 1996. *Three masquerades: Essays on equality, work and human rights*. Toronto: University of Toronto Press.

———. 1999. *Counting for nothing: What men value and what women are worth*. 2nd ed. Toronto: University of Toronto Press.

———. 2004. *Women and power*. Anniversary Lecture Series, Brescia College, London, ON, 24 June 2004.

Warner, Judith. 2009. 'Bo-tax backlash.' *The New York Times* (3 December). Online: http://opinionator.blogs.nytimes.com/2009/12/03/bo-tax-backlash/.

WCTU (Women's Christian Temperance Union, Canada). 1927. *Report of the Twenty-Fourth Convention of the Canadian Women's Christian Temperance Union*. London, ON: The Union and related miscellaneous material (microform), Weldon Library, University of Western Ontario.

Weber, Terry. 2005. 'Stronach deserves apology, mps say.' *The Globe and Mail* 18 May.

Weisbrod, Carol. 1994. 'The way we live now: A discussion of contracts and domestic arrangements.' *Utah Law Review* 2:777–815.

Weldon, S. Laurel. 2004. *Citizens, victims, deviants: Restructuring government response to violence against women in Canada*. Paper presented at the annual meeting of the American Political Science Association, Chicago.

———. 2006. 'Inclusion, solidarity, and social movements: The global movement against gender violence.' *Perspective on Politics* March 2006. Vol. 4. No. 1., pp. 55–74.

White, Julie. 1993. *Sisters and solidarity: Women and unions in Canada*. Toronto: Thompson.

White, Linda A. 2001a. 'The child care agenda and the social union.' In Grace Skogstad and Herman Bakvis (Eds), *Canadian federalism: Performance, effectiveness and legitimacy*, 105–23. Don Mills, ON: Oxford University Press.

———. 2001b. 'Child care, women's labour market participation, and labour market policy effectiveness in Canada.' *Canadian Public Policy* 27 (4):385–406.

———. 2001c. 'From ideal to pragmatic politics: Child care advocacy groups in the 1980s and 1990s.' In Susan Prentice (Ed.), *Changing child care: Five decades of child care advocacy and policy in Canada*, 97–116. Halifax: Fernwood.

———. 2004. 'Trends in child care/early childhood education/early childhood development policy in Canada and the United States.' *American Review of Canadian Studies* 34:665–87.

Whitehead, Barbara Dafoe. 1993. 'Dan Quayle was right.' *The Atlantic Monthly* April: 47–84.

———. 1997. *The divorce culture*. New York: Alfred Knopf.

Whitehead, Kalli & Tim Kurz. 2009. '"Empowerment" and the pole: A discursive investigation of the reinvention of pole dancing as a recreational activity.' *Feminism & Psychology*, 2009 (19): pp. 224–44.

Whittier, Nancy. 1995. *Feminist generations: The persistence of the radical women's movement*. Philadelphia: Temple University Press.

Whitworth, Sandra. 1994. *Feminism and international relations: Toward a political economy of gender in interstate and non-governmental institutions*. New York: St. Martin's Press.

Whitzman, Carolyn. 2002. 'The voice of women in Canadian local government.' In Caroline

Andrew, Katherine Graham, and Susan D. Phillips (Eds), *Urban affairs: Back on the policy agenda*, 93–118. Montreal and Kingston: McGill-Queen's University Press.

WEIGO (Women in Informal Employment Globalizing and Organizing). 2009. Informal workers in focus: Domestic workers. www.wiego.org/publications/FactSheets/WIEGO_Domestic_Workers. pdf. Accessed February 18, 2010.

WHO (World health Organization). 2009. *Women's health fact sheet.* November 2009. Available at: www.who.int/mediacentre/factsheets/fs334/en/index.html

Williams, Cara. 2005. 'The sandwich generation.' *Canadian Social Trends.* Summer 2005, 77. Statistics Canada Catalogue no, 11-008, pp. 16–21.

Williams, Melissa. 1998. *Voice, trust, and memory: Marginalized groups and the failings of liberal representation.* Princeton, NJ: Princeton University Press.

Williams, Patricia J. 1991. *The alchemy of race and rights: Diary of a law professor.* Cambridge, MA: Harvard University Press.

Wilson, Elizabeth. 1988. *Hallucinations: Life in the postmodern city.* London: Radius.

Wilson, Susannah, J. 1991. *Women, families, and work.* 3rd ed. Toronto: McGraw-Hill Ryerson.

Witt, Linda, Karen M. Paget, and Glenna Matthews. 1994. *Running as a woman: Gender and power in American politics.* New York: The Free Press.

Wolf, Naomi. 1990. *The beauty myth.* New York: Random House.

Wollstonecraft, Mary. 1787/1972. *Thoughts on the education of a daughter.* Clifton, NJ: A.M. Kelly.

———. 1792/1970. *A vindication of the rights of women.* Farnborough, UK: Gregg International.

Wylan Sefton, Barbara. 1998. 'The market value of the stay at home mother.' *The Art of Mothering* January/February: 28–9.

Wynn, L.L., Joanna N. Erdman, Angel M. Foster, and James Trussell. 2007. 'Harm reduction or women's rights? Debating access to emergency contraceptive pills in Canada and the United States.' *Studies in Family Planning* 38, 4: 253–267.

Yelaja, Prithi. 2002. 'Gender bias in cardiac care: study.' *The Toronto Star* 24 May: F1.

Young, Claire and Susan Boyd. 2006. 'Losing the feminist voice? Debates on the legal recognition of same sex partnerships in Canada.' *Feminist Legal Studies* 14: 213–240.

Young, Iris Marion. 1981. 'Beyond the unhappy marriage: A critique of dual systems theory.' In Lydia Sargent (Ed.), *Women and revolution: A discussion of the unhappy marriage of Marxism and feminism*, 43–69. Montreal: Black Rose Books.

———. 1990. 'Polity and group difference: A critique of the idea of universal citizenship.' In Iris Marion Young, *Throwing like a girl and other essays in feminist philosophy and social theory.* Bloomington, IN: Indiana University Press.

———. 1997. *Intersecting voices: Dilemmas of gender, political philosophy, and policy.* Princeton, NJ: Princeton University Press.

Young, Lisa. 1997. 'Fulfilling the mandate of difference: Women in the Canadian House of Commons.' In Jane Arscott and Linda Trimble (Eds), *In the presence of women: representation in Canadian governments*, 82–103. Toronto: Harcourt Brace.

———. 2002. 'Representation of women in the new Canadian party system.' In William Cross (Ed), *Political parties, representation, and electoral democracy in Canada*, 181–200. Don Mills, ON: Oxford University Press.

———. 2003. 'Can feminists transform party politics? The Canadian experience.' In Manon Tremblay and Linda Trimble (Eds), *Women and electoral politics in Canada*, 76–90. Don Mills, ON: Oxford University Press.

Young, Lisa, and William Cross. 2003. 'Women's involvement in Canadian political parties.' In Manon Tremblay and Linda Trimble (Eds), *Women and electoral politics in Canada*, 91–108. Don Mills, ON: Oxford University Press.

Yuval Davis, Nira. 1997. *Gender and nation.* London: Sage.

Zhang, Xuelin. 2009. 'Earnings of women with and without children.' *Perspectives.* March 2009. Statistics Canada Catalogue no. 75-001-X, pp. 5–13.

———. 2007. Gender differences in quits and absenteeism in Canada. Analytical Branch Research Paper Series. Ottawa: Statistics Canada. Catalogue no. 11F0019MIE-XIE.

Zukewich Ghalam, Nancy. 1994. 'Women in the workplace.' In *Canadian social trends: A Canadian studies reader*, 141–5. Toronto: Thompson Educational Publishing.

Credits

Grateful acknowledgement is made for permission to reproduce the following:

Page 16: Excerpt from Patricia Williams, *The Alchemy of Race and Rights*. Reprinted by permission of the publisher from *The Alchemy of Race and Rights: Diary of a Law Professor* by Patricia J. Williams, pp. 107–8, Cambridge, Mass.: Harvard University Press, Copyright © 1991 by the President and Fellows of Harvard College.

Page 91, Table 5.2: Reprinted with permission of the Publisher from *Electing a Diverse Canada: The Representation of Immigrants, Minorities, and Women* by Caroline Andrew, John Biles, Myer Siemiatycki, and Erin Tolley © University of British Columbia Press 2008. All rights reserved by the Publisher.

Page 100: Excerpt from *The New York Times*, May 17, 1999 © 1999 *The New York Times*. All Rights Reserved. Used by permission and protected by the Copyright Laws of the United States. The printing, copying, redistribution, or retransmission of this Content without express written permission is prohibited.

Page 103: Excerpt from *The New York Times*, May 17, 1999 © 1999 *The New York Times*. All Rights Reserved. Used by permission and protected by the Copyright Laws of the United States. The printing, copying, redistribution, or retransmission of this Content without express written permission is prohibited.

Page 238: Excerpt from Giles Tremlett, 'Blow to machismo as Spain forces men to do housework'. *The Guardian*, April 8, 2005. http://www.guardian.co.uk/gender/story/0,11812,1454803,00.html.

Page 311, box: Remarks to the High-Level Panel on UN Reform by Stephen Lewis, UN Special Envoy for AIDS in Africa, Geneva, Switzerland, July 2, 2006.

Page 314: Excerpt from Canadian Feminist Alliance for International Action & Canadian Labour Congress, 'Reality check: Women in Canada and the Beijing declaration and platform for action fifteen years on', 22 February 2010: http://www.canadianlabour.ca/sites/default/files/Canada-Beijing15-Reality-Check-2010-02-22-EN.pdf

Index

employment; labour *entries*; part-time work; work, women's
Johnson, Anna, 283
justice, fundamental, 55–6, 268

Kahn, Kimberly, 98, 104–5
Kamen, Paula, 7, 8
Kaplan, Robert, 290
Kay, Barry J., et al., 99–100
Keck, Margaret, and Kathryn Sikkink, 294, 295–6, 302, 350n2
Keeble, Edna, and Meredith Ralston, 306
Kelly, Fiona, 174, 175, 176, 344n21
Kolberg, Lawrence, 3
Kolmar, Wendy, and Frances Bartkowski, 51
Kristeva, Julia, 43–4, 45
Kronby, Malcolm C., 160
Kymlicka, Will, 139

labour: gendered division of, 102, 169, 208–10, 215, 216; Marxist view of, 28–31, 38, 42, 142, 197–8; *see also* breadwinners, male; employment; jobs
labour, women's: as domestic, 33, 66, 102, 140, 142–3, 169, 194–8; as invisible, 33, 187, 190, 196, 237, 292, 294; as productive, 62, 187–8, 196–8; as reproductive, 28, 30, 42, 142, 187; as unpaid, 194–8; value of, 196–8; *see also* caregivers, female; employment; jobs; work, women's
labour force, women in, 66, 72, 76, 117, 121, 186–7; gender convergence and, 208–10; high participation rate of, 194, 208; historic overview of, 186–94; increases of, 191–4; internationally, 307; as part-time, 205–6; as 'reserve' pool, 30, 31, 66, 189, 190; *see also* part-time work; work, women's
Lacan, Jacques, 43
Ladd-Taylor, Molly, and Lauri Umansky, 166
Lahey, Kathleen, 198
LaMarsh, Judy, 72, 109
Lamb, Sharon, 247, 345n1
Lamer, Antonio, 268, 275
latency, 60, 84–5
Lavallee, Lyn, 181, 182
Law, Sylvia, 247–8
LEAF: *see* Women's Legal Education and Action Fund
legislatures, women in, 4, 89, 298–300; barriers to, 97–117; mirror representation and, 92–7; proportional representation and, 115–16; *see also* politics, women in
Lemay, Gloria, 273
Leonelli-Contino, Joanne, 165
lesbian feminism, 7, 9, 35–6, 45–6, 49–50
Lesbian Mothers' Defence Fund, 157

lesbians: as barred from funding, 133; divorce and, 154–5, 158; family rights activism by, 157; 'fathers' for, 175–6; politics and, 33, 35–6; pornography and, 254, 259–61; sperm donation and, 279, 287–8
Lessing, Doris, 32
Levy, Ariel, 246
Lewis, Stephen, 311–13
LGBT Parenting Network, 157
L'Heureux-Dubé, Claire, 162, 258, 347n16
liberal feminism, 25–8, 29, 38, 59–60, 73, 302
liberalism, 17, 291
Liberal Party, 77, 79, 107–8, 115, 249, 262, 265; child care and, 230, 231, 232, 235; divorce and, 170–1; employment equity and, 223, 226; funding cuts by, 83, 95, 131; RCSW and, 72–3, 122; same-sex marriage and, 156; women in, 106, 107, 108–9, 111, 112, 117; women's movement and, 74, 123, 127, 136
Lill, Wendy, 103
'lipstick feminism', 245–7
Little Sisters Book and Art Emporium, 260–1
Lorber, Judith, 13, 14
Lorde, Audre, 38, 45–6
Lucas, Valerie, 170
Luxton, Meg, 61–2, 76

McCaskill, Norm, 108
Macdonald, Laura, 308
McDonough, Alexa, 95, 96–7, 106, 107
McGhan, Meredith, 245
McGillivray, Anne, and Brenda Comaskey, 183–4
MacInnis, Grace, 72
MacIvor, Heather, 98, 101–2, 111, 113, 134
'McJobs', 202–4, 205–6
MacKay, Peter, 106
McKeen, Wendy, 79, 193
MacKinnon, Catherine, 41–2, 248, 254–6, 258, 336–7n6
McLachlin, Beverley, 19
McLaren, Angus, 265; and Arlene Tigar McLaren, 347n1
McLaren, Leah, 242
McLaughlin, Audrey, 4, 107
magazines, online/blogs, 7, 259
Magid, Carolyn H., 223
Mansbridge, Jane, and Katherine Tate, 9
March, Kathryn S., and Rachelle Taqqu, 12
marriage: breakdown of, 140, 144, 146, 152, 160–2; common law principles of, 148–9, 155–6, 158, 177; contracts of, 139–42; interracial, 151; multiple, 151–2, 158; rape in, 4, 177, 178; same-sex, 152–8; women politicians and, 103–4; *see also* divorce;